Managing Investment Portfolios

A Dynamic Process

1985-1986 Update

Managing Investment Portfolios

A Dynamic Process

1985-1986 Update

Edited by

John L. Maginn, CFA
Donald L. Tuttle, CFA

Sponsored by

The Institute of Chartered Financial Analysts

 WARREN, GORHAM & LAMONT
BOSTON · NEW YORK

Foreword

The dynamics of the investment decision-making business and process, in its many forms and directions, have been and continue to be the prime catalyst in attracting a growing number of investment professionals, worldwide, to the programs and projects offered by the Institute of Chartered Financial Analysts. The ICFA's activities, designed by both practitioners and academics, provide candidates enrolled in the Chartered Financial Analyst study and examination program, those who already have earned and been awarded their CFA charter, and others in the investment profession, with "state-of-the art" educational and study materials that fully reflect the dynamics of the investment business and process. In fact, it is fair to state that educational and study materials developed by the ICFA, of which this *1985–1986 Update* is a prime example, have contributed to a higher level of understanding of investment theory and the application of that theory to practice by security analysts, portfolio managers, and others throughout the investment world.

In fulfilling its challenge to develop and keep current a body of knowledge, the ICFA identifies and assembles candidate curriculum and continuing educational materials from the available literature or, in its absence, creates the materials from sponsored research, seminars, and publications. The 1983 publication of *Managing Investment Portfolios: A Dynamic Process,* edited by Maginn and Tuttle, was the first major project of this type. In addition, over the past three years, the ICFA has held nine seminars covering specific subject areas, proceedings from which have been introduced into the candidate curriculum and the member continuing education programs. Among those seminars were *The Revolution in Techniques for Managing Bond Portfolios* in 1983, and *Options and Futures: New Route to Risk/Return Management* in 1984. The content of the proceedings of these two seminars, in updated and extended form, has been included in this *Update* as Chapters 9A, 16, 17 and 18.

The *Update* also reflects the work of the Fixed Income Analysis Review Committee, appointed by the ICFA in 1983 to review and make recommendations for revision of the fixed income curriculum of the CFA study program. Chapters 7A and 7B comprehensively cover the descriptive and analytical topics on fixed income securities recommended by that Review Committee.

The ICFA and its members are deeply indebted to those many CFAs and other investment professionals who devote an untold number of volunteer hours of time and effort to ICFA progress. Particular gratitude is directed to those accepting the challenge and responsibility of special projects, such as the authors and editors of this *Update,* whose contribution to the profession cannot be overestimated.

ALFRED C. MORLEY, CFA
President
The Institute of Chartered
Financial Analysts

June 1985

How To Use This Update

This *1985–1986 Update to Managing Investment Portfolios: A Dynamic Process* is intended to bring the main volume up to date and expand its coverage. The *Update* thus serves both as a means to keep the main volume current and, in its own right, as a reference to recent significant developments.

The chapter numbers and format of *Managing Investment Portfolios* are retained in the *Update* to facilitate its use. The following paragraphs indicate whether chapters in the *Update* are intended to replace or augment material in the main volume.

Chapter 5A updates and replaces Appendix D to Chapter 5 in the main volume, which deals with portfolio policies of individual investors. Chapter 5A covers changes in U.S. capital gains taxes, treatment of tax-exempt securities, and estate/gift taxes up through the tax provisions of the Deficit Reduction Act of 1984.

Chapters 7A and 7B are designed to augment Chapter 7 in the main volume on the micro factors involved in forming capital market expectations. Chapter 7A catalogs the types of fixed income securities, discusses their characteristics, and describes the workings of markets where they are traded. Chapter 7B discusses the return and risk tradeoffs of fixed income securities and reviews the techniques for analyzing them. Special emphasis is placed on the assessment of credit risk for corporate and municipal securities.

Chapter 9A is a replacement for Chapter 9 in the main volume on fixed income portfolio management. It focuses on four primary strategies—active, immunization, dedication, and combined active/passive—for managing fixed income portfolios.

Although Chapters 16, 17, and 18 contain essentially new material on futures and options, they have a direct bearing on Chapters 8, 9, and 10 in the main volume on asset allocation, fixed income portfolio management, and equity portfolio management decision making, respectively. Chapter 16 describes the various active contract types and how they are traded. Chapter 17 reviews the valuation process for these two "new" instruments, first for futures and then for option contracts. Chapter 18 covers the major portfolio management strategies employing futures and options, including how they apply at both macro and micro levels, and how they are both similar and different.

Part of this *Update* is a Cumulative Index with entries from both the main volume and this volume. The latter entries are preceded by the prefix

"U." The Cumulative Index should be used in place of the original index to the main volume. To look up a topic, the reader need only check the Cumulative Index for listings for the original main volume, the *Update,* or both.

The authors and editors of this *Update* are indebted to several individuals whose advice and suggestions materially improved the book's content. They include H. Gifford Fong, Gifford Fong Associates; Michael R. Granito, J.P. Morgan Investment Management Inc.; Elizabeth S. Hennigar, CFA, University of San Diego; Michael D. Joehnk, CFA, Arizona State University; Daryl R. Leehaug, CFA, Duff & Phelps, Inc.; Martin L. Leibowitz, Salomon Brothers, Inc.; Gary E. Mede, CFA, IAA Trust Company; Kenneth R. Meyer, Lincoln Income Group; Thomas S. Nadbielny, Travelers Investment Management Company; William L. Nemerever, CFA, Fidelity Management and Research Company; Eugene C. Rainis, CFA, Brown Brothers Harriman and Company; William K. Ryan, CLU, United of Omaha Life Insurance Company; Richard A. Witt, CFA, Mutual of Omaha Insurance Company and United of Omaha; and George H. Wood, CFA, Commerce Bank of Kansas City.

Donald L. Tuttle, CFA, *Editor-in-Chief*
John L. Maginn, CFA, *Associate Editor*

June 1985

Contents

7B   Fixed Income Analysis Process: Return and Risk Analysis [New]   7B-1

John L. Maginn, CFA
Marvin D. Andersen, CFA

Contributors

Marvin D. Andersen, CFA, is a Second Vice-President–Investments of Mutual of Omaha Insurance Company and United of Omaha Life Insurance Company. He received his B.A. degree in economics and finance from the University of Nebraska at Omaha. He began his investment career in 1968 as a security analyst for Mutual of Omaha. He is currently responsible for the analysis of government, municipal, and public utility bond holdings in the United States and Canada. He is a member of the Omaha-Lincoln Society of Financial Analysts and the Government Finance Officers Association.

David M. Dunford, CFA, is Vice-President–Portfolio Management and Public Bonds of Travelers Insurance Company where he is responsible for managing insurance company assets. He received an A.B. degree in economics from Princeton University and an M.B.A. in finance from New York University. Mr. Dunford joined Travelers in 1972 and was involved in pension fund asset management until 1984 with Travelers Investment Management Company, serving as director of the portfolio group from 1981 to 1984. Mr. Dunford's recent investment research has been devoted to defining the roles of futures and options in portfolio management. He is a member of the Hartford Society of Financial Analysts and the ICFA's Candidate Curriculum Committee. In 1985, he was appointed to the Financial Products Advisory Committee of the Commodity Futures Trading Commission.

Robert W. Kopprasch, CFA, is a Vice-President in the Bond Portfolio Analysis Group of Salomon Brothers Inc., where he is involved in solving a wide range of problems related to the hedging of fixed-income securities via the use of financial futures, fixed-income options and interest rate swaps. The author of a number of articles in leading journals and chapters in several books, Dr. Kopprasch previously was on the faculty of The American University of Washington, D.C. He received his B.S. and M.S. in Management and Ph.D. in Finance from Rensselaer Polytechnic Institute. He is a member of the Washington Society of Investment Analysts and the ICFA's Candidate Curriculum Committee.

Part II

Investor Objectives and Constraints

Determination of Portfolio Policies

CHAPTER **5A**

The Role of Taxes in the Investment Decision-Making Process

Jay Vawter, CFA

Over the past several decades, taxes have had an increasingly greater impact on Americans generally, and U.S. investors have certainly been no exception. Other than retirement funds and some endowment funds, investors must take account of the tax implications of their actions. Even portfolio managers who deal in tax-exempt funds should be aware of tax laws because of the effect of taxes on market liquidity, turnover, and security selection. The purpose of this chapter, an update of and replacement for Appendix D to Chapter 5 of the main volume, is to provide a basic understanding of the taxes that might have an impact on the investment decision-making process. Financial analysts should have a minimum working knowledge of taxation as it applies to investments and, at the very least, know when to refer problems to an attorney or an accountant.

CAPITAL GAINS TAXES

The rules on U.S. capital gains taxes for individuals are relatively simple. Any security sold in six months or less from the date of purchase is treated as a short-term transaction, whereas a security sold after six months is a long-term transaction. This represents a change in the law from the old rules and is a result of the Tax Reform Act of 1984. Specifically, all securities purchased after June 22, 1984 received a new treatment, that is, the six-month treatment, whereas any securities acquired on June 22, 1984 or earlier had been subject to the old one-year holding rule. Thus, starting June 23, 1985 all security transactions have been based on the new six-month rule. In addition, this modification of the law is valid only through 1987. Presumably Congress will review the rule by then to determine whether to extend it or go back to the one-year holding period.

To calculate the tax, an investor offsets short-term losses against short-term gains, then offsets long-term losses against long-term gains. Finally, the net results of those two calculations are offset against each other. If these calculations result in a long-term gain that exceeds long-term and short-term net losses, 40 percent of this net long-term gain is taxable at one's ordinary income tax rates. If they result in a short-term gain that exceeds short-term and net long-term losses, 100 percent of this net short-term gain is also taxed as ordinary income. The following is a straightforward capital gain and loss example.

Assume an investor's top income tax bracket is 40 percent with the following gains and losses: long-term capital gains of $10,000, long-term capital losses of $3,000, and short-term losses of $4,000.

Looking first at the short-term, there was a loss of $4,000 but no gain, leaving a net short-term loss of $4,000. Offsetting the long-term capital losses of $3,000 against long-term capital gains of $10,000 leaves a net long-term gain of $7,000. This gain is reduced by the net short-term loss. A taxable long-term gain of $3,000 remains, of which only 40 percent or $1,200 is taxable. When this investor's tax bracket of 40 percent is applied against the taxable gain, the tax is $480.

The above example results in a net gain. What if the investor has net losses for the year? Because only 50 percent of long-term gains were taxable under the previous capital gains tax laws, only 50 percent of net long-term losses can be used to reduce ordinary income for tax purposes. Furthermore, there is a limit on the amount of such losses that can be used to offset ordinary income. Up to $6,000 of *net* long-term losses can be used each year to generate a $3,000 reduction of ordinary income. This is the so-called 50 percent rule. A full 100 percent of *net* short-term losses can be so used to a limit of $3,000 each year. If an investor has both net long-term and short-term losses, the short-term losses must be used first; then, to the extent needed, (50 percent of) the long-term losses may be used. Interestingly, the Revenue Act of 1978 that reduced the taxable portion of capital gains from 50 to 40 percent did not modify the 50 percent rule with regard to net long-term losses. This means that a long-term loss standing on its own is worth somewhat more in tax savings to the investor than the same loss applied against long-term gains, which suggests a strategy of realizing $6,000 of net long-term losses each year, where it makes sense from an investment standpoint. Any amount of losses, either long-term or short-term, that exceeds these limits can be carried forward to future tax years indefinitely during the lifetime of the investor to offset any future capital gains, or ordinary income (up to the annual limit) if no gains exist. Any losses carried forward retain their character as to the holding period—a short-term loss is carried forward as a short-term loss, and a long-term loss is carried forward as a long-term loss. The following example illustrates the carry-forward principle.

Consider the same investor as in the previous problem, but with the following gains and losses: long-term capital gains of $4,000 and long-term capital losses of $11,000.

In this case, offsetting long-term gains and losses leaves a new long-term loss of $7,000. Only $6,000 of this, however, can be used in determining the amount by which ordinary income may be reduced before taxes. The remaining $1,000 may be used to offset any gains the following year, or to reduce ordinary income if there are no gains. As to the tax calculations, 50 percent of the $6,000 ($3,000) is used to reduce ordinary income before tax. The tax saving on a $3,000 reduction is $1,200 to the investor in a 40 percent tax bracket. Had this $7,000 loss been all short term, $3,000 could have been used to reduce ordinary income with the balance ($4,000) carried forward. The following example illustrates this point where the net loss is short term.

Again, take the same investor, with short-term capital gains of $2,000 and short-term capital losses of $4,000. In this case the investor has a net short-term capital loss of $2,000. Because this is less than the $3,000 limit, all if it may be used to offset ordinary income, resulting in an $800 tax saving to the investor in a 40 percent bracket.

As indicated, taxes often play an important role in investment decisions. However, all too often taxes take too important a role and, frequently, bad investment decisions are made because of tax considerations. Still, the decision on whether or not to realize a capital gain should take into account the tax cost of that decision and thus consider the future potential of the securities to be sold versus other opportunities. A simple calculation of the tax liability will give the portfolio manager a fairly good idea of how well the replacement stock must do to make up this tax cost and subsequently to provide a greater return over time. If it appears that the stock to be sold has increased in price to a point where it is fully priced or overpriced based on your own valuation criteria or if there are other, more attractively priced opportunities, it generally pays to take the gain, pay the tax, and switch to the other investment. Regrettably, many investors choose to hold an unattractive stock because they do not want to pay the capital gains tax and, therefore, they miss other, more attractive alternatives, or watch the profit disappear as the stock subsequently declines. The reduction of the maximum capital gain tax from nearly 50 percent (including the minimum tax on preference income) prior to the 1978 law to a maximum of 20 percent in the 1981 law certainly should have reduced the reluctance to sell stocks at gains.

There are times when gains or losses can be used successfully to improve the position of a portfolio. This is especially true now, in an era of discounted commissions, where the transaction costs need not significantly reduce the advantage of making tax-motivated switches. If a particular security has failed to live up to expectations and shows a loss, it may very well be desirable to sell it at a loss, either to offset other gains already realized or to reduce ordinary income to the limits mentioned earlier.

The timing of realization of tax losses is also important. Many investors wait until the end of the year. It may be assumed that if one investor has a loss in a stock, many others do also; stocks that have done unusually poorly in the last year or two will often be sold in heavy volume toward the end of the year, which depresses the price still further. This phenomenon is even more relevant for managers of tax-exempt funds who themselves have no tax-based motivation to sell at all. It is generally desirable, therefore, to complete tax loss selling well before the last month or two of the year. Failing this, one should keep in mind that a loss can be realized on a stock right up to the last day of the year, but a gain can be realized only if it will be settled by the end of the year. This means either selling the security at least five business days prior to the end of the year (remembering that Christmas is not counted as a business day), or delivering the stock for a cash settlement by the end of the year if the trade is made less than five business days before the end of the year.

Another technique is useful in tax selling. Under the present law, a security sold at a loss and repurchased in less than 31 days becomes a "wash sale" and the tax loss is negated. The investor has two ways to avoid this problem. The first involves purchasing a number of shares equal to those to be sold, thus "doubling up" the holding, and then selling the loss shares 31 days later. This establishes the desired tax loss and maintains the original position. The doubling up must be done at least 31 days before the year-end or the loss will be realized in the following year. The risk, of course, is that if the stock's price continues to fall during the 31-day period, the investor would have been better off selling the original shares outright without doubling up.

This suggests an alternative method—selling the stock, realizing the loss, then buying it back 31 days later. The risk of this is that if the stock increases in price in the interim, the investor must pay more to reestablish his position. The sale and buy-back technique may work best toward the end of the year when additional tax loss selling may push the stock's price lower and provide an opportunity to repurchase it at a cheaper price. Perhaps the safest way to deal with this problem is to sell the stock at a loss and buy a similar stock at the same time. Wash sale rules do not apply to gains—a stock can be sold with a gain and be bought back at once, thereby taking the capital gain and reestablishing a cost basis based on the repurchase price.

TAX-EXEMPT SECURITIES

Certain types of securities produce income that is exempt from federal and, in some cases, state income taxes. The most prevalent are tax-exempt bonds issued by states, counties, and municipalities. For individuals in high tax brackets who need fixed income, tax-exempt bonds offer a useful and valuable alternative to taxable securities such as federal government obligations and corporate issues. In order to determine whether it is advantageous to use tax-exempt bonds, a simple calculation can be made. Simply *multiply* one minus the investor's highest or marginal tax bracket by a taxable yield, such as that available on AAA telephone bonds. If the net yield produced by this calculation is below the tax-free yield of municipal bonds of comparable quality, it will pay to use municipals. An alternate way of making this comparison is to see if the taxable equivalent yield of a tax-free obligation exceeds the yield available on similar risk taxable bonds. The formula is exactly the reverse of the one just used: the tax-exempt yield is *divided* by one minus the investor's marginal tax bracket. For example, if taxable yields are 12 percent, tax-exempt yields are 9 percent, and the investor's tax bracket is 40 percent, the calculation is:

$$9\% \div (1 - 0.4) =$$
$$9\% \div 0.6 = 15\%$$

Because this 15 percent figure is higher than the actual taxable yield of 12 percent, it is clearly advantageous to buy tax-exempt bonds.

Making the decision to buy taxable bonds or tax-exempts is not quite so simple, however. Tax-exempt bonds tend to be considerably less marketable in most cases than corporate or government bonds. Thus, the yield differentials that one might expect may or may not prove to be the case in the actual marketplace due to the differential in marketability.

In addition, while it might pay to buy a certain amount of tax-exempt bonds, too much tax-exempt interest could pull the taxpayer into such a low bracket that further purchases would be disadvantageous relative to taxable bonds. One must also keep in mind potential changes in the investor's tax bracket due to retirement, change of job, or other reasons. The purchase of tax-exempt securities must also take into account state taxes that may be payable. While it is desirable to own issues in one's own state to get the benefit of further tax exemption (most states tax the interest of other states' tax-free issues), the principle of geographical diversification that suggests spreading risk among issues from other states will usually be an overriding consideration.

Finally, with the maximum tax on unearned income reduced from 70 percent to 50 percent on January 1, 1982 (as a result of the 1981 Tax Act), the tax benefit of municipal bonds became less for high bracket investors. The effects of income tax indexing starting in 1985 should also be monitored carefully in determining the desirability of tax-exempt bonds.

Another form of tax-exempt income applies only to corporations. Under the corporate dividend exclusion, 85 percent of all dividend income is tax-exempt for corporate holders. As a result, preferred stocks, high yielding common stocks, and convertible preferreds are particularly useful to casualty insurance companies, personal holding companies, and other corporations. Because preferred stocks are a relatively scarce security relative to the demand for them by corporations, it is not unusual for preferred stock yields to be as low as, or in some cases lower than, the bonds or debentures of the same issuer, despite their junior status. Corporations also are frequent purchasers of utility common stocks, which provide relatively high dividends that are 85 percent tax-exempt. As of mid-1985, the maximum effective tax rate on dividends received by corporations was 6.9 percent (100 percent minus 85 percent times a 46 percent effective corporate tax rate).

U.S. ESTATE TAXES

The Economic Recovery Tax Act of 1981 (ERTA) has had a sweeping effect on estate tax rules and regulations and, therefore, on estate planning. The net effect of this law is the elimination of most estates from any estate taxation whatsoever over the next few years. A discussion of the broad principles follows. Individual circumstances may well dictate different approaches, and legal counsel in these matters is essential.

There are several aspects to estate tax law that may have a direct effect on the investment decision-making process. These have to do with lifetime gifts, the stepped-up cost basis on assets at death, the Unified Tax Credit, and, finally, the marital deduction. The lifetime-gifts option has been changed significantly by ERTA. Under the old law, gifts of up to $3,000 per donor could be made to an unlimited number of donees each year. In addition, there was a lifetime exemption of $30,000 per donor. Thus, with the consent of a spouse, gifts of up to $6,000 annually and $60,000 more (the two lifetime maximums) could be made by a couple to their children, grandchildren, and others.

ERTA increased the amount of these gifts from $3,000 to $10,000 annually and eliminated the $30,000 lifetime exemption. Thus, under the new rules, a couple can give up to $20,000 to each child, grandchild, or other person each year. Furthermore, gifts made for school tuitions or medical expenses are no longer subject to gift tax rules as they were previously.

Note that these limits do not apply to charitable donations. Deductible charitable donations are determined by federal income tax laws, rather than estate and gift tax laws, and may be well in excess of these limits, depending on the donor's income level.

Certain strategies can be applied to making nontaxed gifts of $10,000 to individuals or making income tax-deductible charitable gifts (limited to a percentage of income) to colleges, foundations, and so on. For gifts to one's family, it might be desirable to give away stocks having a very low cost basis to members in low tax brackets who could sell these securities with little or no capital gains tax effect, especially given the low effective capital gains tax rates applicable. On the other hand, if the donee is in a high tax bracket, this approach would clearly reduce the value of the gift, so cash or higher cost securities might be more appropriate. In the case of charitable gifts, it is by far best to give away securities with a low cost basis rather than selling the securities, paying capital gains tax, and then making the gift in cash. The recipient can sell the securities and pay no capital gains tax. In making large charitable gifts, however, one must be mindful that the deduction limits under federal income tax law are lower for gifts of appreciated property than for gifts of cash.

Another change concerning gifts has to do with the old contemplation of death rule. Under this rule, all gifts made within three years of death were regarded as having been made in contemplation of death and were added back into the estate for tax purposes. Recent law eliminates this rule. All gifts, no matter when made, are excluded from the taxable estate to the extent that they meet the annual exclusion rules just discussed. Gifts exceeding the $10,000 annual exclusion rules ($20,000 for couples) are treated under the Unified Tax Credit rules discussed elsewhere.

An aspect of estate taxation that has an extremely important effect on investing is the provision that the cost basis of all property—securities, real estate, or other assets—will be stepped up, either to the value on the date of death or six months later at the option of the executors. Before the unlimited marital deduction rules became law in 1981, there was a definite incentive to take the lower of these two valuations in order to reduce estate taxes. However, with the unlimited marital deduction allowed by the 1981 legislation, assets left to a surviving spouse would have no estate tax, thereby creating an incentive to take the higher of the two valuations to establish a higher cost basis for securities inherited to reduce the future potential capital gains liability. The Tax Reform Act of 1984 changed this rule and eliminated this benefit. The new law states that the alternative valuation date can be used only to reduce estate taxes and cannot be used solely to raise the cost basis of securities inherited. Thus, an estate left to someone other than a surviving spouse would normally opt for the lower valuation in order to reduce estate taxes, and an estate left to a surviving spouse could not take the alternative valuation if its only favorable effect was a higher cost basis.

The stepped-up basis rule allows some insight into the interplay between capital gains taxes and estate planning. Frequently, older investors own stocks purchased many years earlier that are on the books at extremely low cost. Because the cost basis will be stepped up at death to the date-of-death valuation, a real deterrent exists to taking these gains and paying a sizeable capital gains tax. The problem discussed previously of imposing a tax judgment in addition to an investment judgment is even more acutely felt in the case of older investors, simply because the potential time horizon for recovering the tax in other, more attractive investments is potentially much shorter than for younger persons. In many cases, however, investors have lived beyond normal expectations and judicious sales for investment reasons might well have been made had it not been for the tax constraint. This surely has had some effect on the overall liquidity of our financial markets, since a considerable amount of securities no doubt are frozen because of it. The recent trend toward lower capital gains tax rates may significantly mitigate this problem.

The Tax Reform Act of 1976 introduced a new concept to estate and gift taxation, the Unified Tax Credit. Prior to this legislation, estates enjoyed a $60,000 exemption from estate tax, with the balance being taxed according to estate tax tables. Gifts could be made during one's lifetime in excess of the then $3,000 annual exclusion and the $30,000 lifetime exemption and were subject to a tax equal to 75 percent of the estate tax rates. The 1976 Act eliminated the $60,000 estate exclusion, the $30,000 lifetime gift exemp-

TABLE 5A-1. U.S. Estate and Gift Tax Rate Schedule

From	To	Amount in This Column	+ Percentage	In Excess Over
$ 0	$ 10,000	$ 0	18	$ 0
10,000	20,000	1,800	20	10,000
20,000	40,000	3,800	22	20,000
40,000	60,000	8,200	24	40,000
60,000	80,000	13,000	26	60,000
80,000	100,000	18,200	28	80,000
100,000	150,000	23,800	30	100,000
150,000	250,000	38,000	32	150,000
250,000	500,000	70,800	34	250,000
500,000	750,000	155,800	37	500,000
750,000	1,000,000	248,000	39	750,000
1,000,000	1,250,000	345,800	41	1,000,000
1,250,000	1,500,000	448,300	43	1,250,000
1,500,000	2,000,000	555,800	45	1,500,000
2,000,000	2,500,000	780,800	49	2,000,000
2,500,000	3,000,000	1,025,800	53	2,500,000
3,000,000	and over	1,290,800	55	3,000,000

SOURCE: U.S. Internal Revenue Service.

tion and the 75 percent gift tax rule, combining estates and gifts and making available to them a Unified Tax Credit. Under this rule, the value of an estate is calculated at the time of death, including any gifts made over and above the annual exclusion. The tax table shown in Table 5A-1 is then applied. From the resulting tax a credit is taken, which under the 1976 law rose to $47,000 in 1981. The practical effect of this credit was to eliminate all tax on estates up to $175,625, the amount of an estate which would have generated a tax of $47,000. ERTA merely extends the principle of the Unified Tax Credit by increasing the credit as follows:

Year	Unified Tax Credit	Amount of Estate Exempted from Tax
1985	$121,800	$400,000
1986	155,800	500,000
1987	192,800	600,000

Thus, by 1987, all estates of $600,000 or less will be exempt from any estate tax whatsoever. In addition, the 1981 Act reduced the maximum tax rate from 70 percent on estates of $2,500,000 and over to (as amended by the 1984 Act) 55 percent on estates of $3,000,000 and over during 1985 through 1987 and 50 percent on estates of $2,500,000 and over starting in 1988.

Perhaps the most significant change of ERTA was the major revision in the marital deduction rules. Prior to the Tax Reform Act of 1976, one-half of any estate could be left outright to a surviving spouse free of estate tax. The portion left as a marital deduction passed to the surviving spouse either outright, without restriction, or in trust, with the surviving spouse having a general power of appointment (meaning that this spouse could leave the assets to anyone he or she chose). The Tax Reform Act of 1976 changed these rules slightly. Under that act one-half of an estate or $250,000, whichever was larger, could be left to a surviving spouse under the marital deduction. Again, the surviving spouse was required to have at least a general power of appointment over the assets.

The 1981 legislation permits a marital deduction of up to 100 percent of the estate, meaning that an entire estate can be left outright to a surviving spouse without any estate tax. Also, under the 1981 legislation, the decedent's estate can be left in such a way that the surviving spouse did not necessarily have a general power of appointment over the assets received under the marital deduction. This is known as a qualified terminable interest property trust, or a Q-TIP trust. Under a Q-TIP trust, the decedent can assure that assets left to a surviving spouse pass, upon that spouse's death, to whomever the original decedent chose, perhaps his or her own children. Under the old rules, where the surviving spouse had a general power of appointment, the surviving spouse might well have remarried and could have left the entire estate to the children or spouse of the second marriage, totally disinheriting the children of the first spouse.

There is a potential flaw in the 1981 legislation: If one's spouse became terminally ill, the other, possessing low cost basis stocks, might well make a gift of those stocks to the dying spouse. The gift would have no estate or gift tax implications since unlimited gifts can be made between spouses. Upon the death of the spouse receiving the gift, the cost of the assets would be stepped up to date-of-death valuation and passed back to the donor spouse. However, anticipating this possibility, ERTA prohibits the stepped-up basis on such assets (between spouses) within one year of the time such gifts are made. Thus, if the terminally ill spouse did, in fact, die in less than one year, the assets would be left to the surviving spouse at their original, low cost basis.

Simply because the current law allows an entire estate to be left to a surviving spouse without tax does not necessarily mean that it should be. If the estate is of sufficient size, the entire estate could be subject to considerable taxation upon the death of the surviving spouse.

The primary objective of estate planning is usually to minimize the estate tax of both the first person to die and the surviving spouse upon his or her eventual death. However, the need of the surviving spouse for flexibility must be balanced against this objective. Often a compromise is required.

There are three levels of estate value that must be considered in determining the best overall estate planning strategy. In this discussion, the amount that would be exempt from tax in 1987, or $600,000, is used but one should be careful to substitute the appropriate amount actually exempt for each of the years before 1987. Thus, if the date of death were 1985, a figure of $400,000 would be substituted.

The first of these levels are estates up to $600,000. For these estates, the surviving spouse could inherit the entire amount of the estate tax free. Upon the spouse's death, the whole estate would be passed on to the heirs tax free under the Unified Tax Credit rules. This, of course, assumes that no growth occurs in the estate and, thus, suggests that perhaps even in this case the entire amount should not be left outright to the surviving spouse, particularly if there were a significant age difference between the two spouses. For example, if the first spouse to die were 70 and the surviving spouse were only 55, it could be assumed that an estate of, say, $500,000 could well exceed $600,000 by the time the surviving spouse dies. It might therefore be desirable to leave at least part of this estate outside of the marital deduction, in trust for the couple's children with the surviving spouse retaining a life income interest in the trust. Such a trust is usually referred to as an exemption equivalent trust and the assets escape taxes in the estates of both spouses.

The second level includes estates ranging from $600,000 up to $1.2 million. It is possible by careful planning to take advantage of two Unified Tax Credit exemptions. Consider, for example, an estate of $1 million. It would be possible to leave $600,000 outright to the surviving spouse, recognizing that he or she in turn could leave this estate at death, taking advantage of yet another $600,000 exemption. The remaining $400,000 could be put in trust for their children, with the surviving spouse receiving income from the trust for life. However, as in the examples cited for estates up to $600,000, it can be assumed that the value of the marital portion of the estate would grow over time. If there were a significant age difference between the decedent and the surviving spouse, it might well pay to reverse the amount of these bequests, leaving $400,000 to the surviving spouse and putting $600,000 into a trust with the spouse as life income beneficiary and their children as remaindermen.

Finally, the last level of estates to be considered includes those of $1.2 million or more. Where the life expectancy of the surviving spouse is relatively short or health is poor, suggesting the probability of death soon after the first spouse, it would be advisable to split this estate into two equal portions. The first $600,000 in each would be tax free upon the death of each respective spouse, and the balance, given the progressive nature of the tax tables, would be taxed at the lower brackets. Thus, the combined tax paid on these two estates would be less than if only $600,000 were left outright to the surviving spouse, with the balance going into trust. However, if the life expectancy of the surviving spouse is relatively long, it would probably be advisable to leave the tax-exempt portion of the first estate, $600,000, in trust outside of the marital deduction to take advantage of the Unified Tax Credit, with the balance of the estate left to the surviving spouse outright. Although this would result in a higher tax when the surviving spouse passes on, the time value of money accruals on funds invested rather than paid in taxes would probably more than offset the additional tax if the surviving spouse, in fact, lived for many years following the death of the first spouse.

Consistent with our previous comment on estate taxes suggesting that individual circumstances may dictate a different outcome than that covered by broad principles, it is useful to give the executor of an estate discretion to choose the *best* approach after the death of an individual, adjusting to conditions that may be different than at the time when a will is drawn.

Let us illustrate these principles with the following examples:

(1) *A widower dies in 1986, leaving his entire estate of $450,000 to his son.*

Using the tax amounts and rates in Table 5A-1, the tax from an estate of this size is $138,800. However, the Unified Tax Credit for 1986 is $155,800, an amount exceeding the tax due. Thus, this estate has no tax.

(2) *A widower dies in 1985, leaving his estate of $500,000 to his sister. Two years earlier he had made a gift to her of $60,000, the only gift he has ever made to anyone.*

Under the Unified Tax Credit rule we must add back part of the gift to the estate of $500,000. Of the gift made two years earlier, $10,000 would have been exempt from any taxation under the annual exclusion rules. Thus, $50,000 of that gift must be added into the estate for tax purposes, leaving a taxable estate of $550,000. Using Table 5A-1, the tax is $174,300. In 1985 the Unified Tax Credit is $121,800, leaving a total tax due to the federal government of $52,500.

(3) *In 1987 a man dies, leaving an estate of $1.1 million. His wife is 35 years old and they have three children.*

Although there are several possibilities here, the conditions of the situation suggest that $600,000, equal to the amount of estate exempt from all tax, be left outside the marital deduction in an exemption equivalent trust. The widow would receive income from this trust for her life, with the corpus passing on to her children upon her death. The remaining $500,000 might well be left in a second trust under the marital deduction, also with the children as remaindermen, but with the widow receiving income for life (a Q-TIP trust). The smaller amount is left to her because she is quite young, and it can be expected that the growth of her portion over time will put the value of her estate well above her $600,000 exemption.

In addition, because of her age, it is not unlikely that she will remarry and even have additional children from the new marriage. If her first husband had set up the marital portion in a trust for the benefit of the couple's children, she would be prohibited from leaving her share of the estate to the children or spouse of a new marriage. Even if she were older, such that she would not be expected to have children of her own from a second marriage, this approach might still be appropriate in order to ensure that upon her death the estate would go to the children of the first marriage. Prior to the 1981 legislation, this would not have been possible; she would have been required to have a general power of appointment over the marital portion.

(4) *A woman dies in 1989, leaving an estate of $3 million. Her husband is 87 years old and suffers from chronic heart problems.*

Given the advanced age and poor health of the surviving spouse in this case, it would be appropriate to split the estate into two equal portions, one marital and one nonmarital. The nonmarital portion would go into a trust, with the couple's children, if any, as remaindermen. Of this portion of the estate, $600,000 would pass without estate tax under the Unified Tax Credit rules. The estate tax on $1,500,000 would be $363,-000 ($555,800 from the tax tables minus the Unified Tax Credit of $192,800). Assuming the husband passed away fairly soon, his estate would have a $600,000 exemption and an additional tax of $363,000, making a total tax on the two estates of $726,000. Had only $600,000 been put into a trust for the children, with the balance of $2.4 million passing to the husband under the marital reduction, if he died soon after, the total tax would have been $784,000 ($976,800 on $2,400,000, less a Unified Tax Credit of $192,800).

Had the surviving husband been much healthier and younger, it probably would have been desirable to leave only $600,000 outside the marital deduction, with the balance outright to the surviving spouse. Given a long life expectancy, additional earnings on the amount of tax saved at the time ($363,000) would more than offset the reduced amount of tax paid by splitting the estate as described in our example. It seems likely that in most instances, leaving the estate, after the $600,000 nonmarital portion, outright to the survivors will be preferred.

Another way to save estate tax is through the use of *flower bonds*. Certain U.S. Treasury obligations issued many years ago carry a right to pay estate taxes using the bond at par value rather than at cost or current market value. Issued when interest rates were significantly lower than now, these low coupon bonds sell at substantial discounts. Thus, for example, one can buy an issue at 75 cents on the dollar and use it to pay estate taxes at 100 cents on the dollar, with the 25 cents differential accruing to the estate. Estate planning for an elderly investor might well include flower bonds. One drawback, however, is that yields on these bonds tend to be well below comparable yields on nonflower issues of the U.S. Treasury or corporations, thus reducing the income flow during the investor's remaining lifetime. Under certain circumstances, when the cost of borrowing is not too high relative to the interest earned on flower bonds, it may well pay to borrow, using the flower bonds as collateral. (Because of the high cost of borrowing and the low yields on flower bonds, this has not been practical for many years, except on a near deathbed basis.) Thus, it is not necessary to liquidate other assets, perhaps with substantial capital gains, in order to buy flower bonds. The bonds must have been purchased and provision made for payment prior to death by someone legally competent to do so, either the investor (or his conservator) personally or if done by an agent, they must be confirmed by the investor.

In many states deathbed purchases of flower bonds may not be valid if the dying individual is not competent at the time of purchase. In these states the law automatically revokes powers of attorney when the grantor becomes incompetent. Thus, if the grantor of a power of attorney is in a coma or otherwise insufficiently competent to legally ratify a purchase, it is important to check state law before making the purchase.

TAX SHELTER CHANGES

In an effort to curtail tax shelter abuses, the 1984 tax act includes a number of new provisions. By and large, the changes are directed towards increased penalties, additional recordkeeping, and registration requirements. A primer on tax shelters in the post-1984 tax legislation environment is included at the end of this chapter.

Shelters sold on or after September 1, 1984 must be registered with the Internal Revenue Service (IRS) if either of two conditions exist: the tax shelter offering is subject to federal or state securities registration, or five or more investors make a total investment of $250,000 or more. A tax shelter is defined as an investment whose ratio of tax benefits to actual investment, calculated *before* taking into account the tax effects of rental income from the property, is larger than 2:1 in *any* of the first five years.

The 1984 law provides an incentive for investors to scrutinize a tax shelter before they buy in. On any underpayment of over $1,000 attributable to any "tax motivated transaction," interest is charged at 120 percent of the normal interest rate applied to deficiencies. Tax motivated transactions include those involving valuation overstatements over 150 percent, losses or investment tax credits disallowed by reason of the IRS' at-risk rules, certain tax straddles, and accounting methods that result in substantial distortions of income in *any* period.

REAL ESTATE TAX CHANGES

In general, the 1984 Act extends to 18 years the accelerated cost recovery system (ACRS) recovery period for property previously treated as 15-year real property. As a result, annual depreciation deductions dropped from 6.7 to 5.6 percent under the straight-line method and from 11.67 to 9.72 percent under the ACRS method.

ALTERNATIVE MINIMUM TAX

One of the more vexing provisions of the U.S. tax code for individuals who invest in tax shelters in general and real estate shelters in particular is the alternative minimum tax (AMT), a tax that is calculated under separate rules and must be paid if it is greater than an individual's regular tax.

In certain circumstances, the AMT can thwart even the most carefully devised tax strategy. Among other things, the special AMT rules do not allow one to reduce the AMT by claiming most tax credits, such as those common to real estate shelters. Nor do they allow certain itemized deductions such as state and local taxes.

Calculating the AMT is not a simple proposition. The basic departure point on one's tax return is adjusted gross income. From this figure, certain deductions are allowed such as charitable deductions, medical expenses in excess of 10 percent of adjustable gross income, casualty losses, and interest expense on a personal residence. But state and local income taxes are not. Added back to this figure are certain tax preference items, such as the 60 percent portion of long-term capital gains omitted when calculating the regular tax, the bargain element of any incentive stock options that were exercised, and the excess of accelerated depreciation over straight-line depreciation on property that is a shelter.

This calculation produces the AMT income from which a specific exemption is deducted: $40,000 for married taxpayers filing jointly, $30,000 for single taxpayers, and $20,000 for married taxpayers filing separately. To this AMT taxable income figure a flat tax rate of 20 percent is applied. If the resulting tax is larger than the regular tax, the larger AMT must be paid. Nonrefundable tax credits, other than the foreign tax credit, cannot be claimed against the AMT liability, although some credits can be carried over or back to reduce taxes in other tax years.

One of the unusual effects of being subject to the AMT is the reversal of normal year-end tax strategies to postpone income and accelerate expenses. Because of the flat 20 percent AMT rate, income subject to high regular tax rates may be accelerated while deductions worth up to 50 percent on the dollar under regular tax rates may be deferred.

FOUNDATION TAX CHANGES

The change in the tax status of foundations is relatively small. The principal change is a provision for the elimination or reduction of the two percent excise tax that private foundations pay on investment income. If a foundation meets four fairly formidable qualifications, it qualifies as an *exempt operating foundation* not subject to the tax. If a foundation meets a five percent payout percentage (relative to its assets) for five years plus other qualifications, the tax is reduced to one percent.

INSURANCE TAX CHANGES

The tax statutes applying to life insurance had changed very little in the 25-year period between the Life Insurance Company Tax Act of 1959 and the Deficit Reduction Act of 1984. In fact, one of the characteristics of the life insurance industry was the stability of its tax laws. Another characteristic was the extreme complexity of the 1959 law. The effective tax rates for life insurance companies could vary widely on the basis of the size, operating characteristics, and corporate form (mutual or stock) of the company. As noted in the main volume, the industry's effective tax rate in the early 1980s was 25 to 30 percent; however, for some major companies the effective rate was at or near 46 percent. This variability was exacerbated by the high interest rates that prevailed in the late 1970s and early 1980s and produced "excess earnings."

The 1984 Act made sweeping changes in the taxation of life insurance companies. The most significant change in the provisions of the 1984 tax law was the standardization of the treatment of all life insurance companies. Under the new law, the basis for taxation is essentially a life insurance company's statutory gain from operations, in contrast to the old law where a company could be taxed on its investment income or its gain from operations or some combination of both. For mutual companies, a tax on their "equity base" is calculated and added to the basic income tax.

Under the 1984 law, all companies are permitted to take a special deduction of 20 percent of their tentative life insurance company taxable income (LICTI). As a result of this special life insurance company deduction, the maximum tax rate is 36.8 percent (46 percent × .80 = 36.8 percent) instead of the corporate rate of 46 percent. It should be noted that this special deduction is subject to change by Congress and is expected to be used as a means of adjusting (upward or downward) the total federal income tax revenue collected from the industry.

The new law continued the requirement, but modified the formula, that the investment income of a life insurance company be allocated between (1) the policyholders' share, the portion relating to dividends and the actuarially assumed interest rate necessary to fund reserves, and (2) the company's share, the portion available to be used for general corporate purposes or to be transferred to surplus. It is an anomaly of the tax code that life insurance companies pay tax on interest from tax-exempt bonds and they pay a higher tax on dividends from preferred and common stocks relative to other corporate owners of these securities, and thus do not realize the full corporate dividend exclusion of 85 percent. As a result, investments in tax-exempt bonds and dividend-producing stocks are less attractive to a life insurance company than they are to a casualty insurance company or other taxable investors.

Another important change was a new federally prescribed minimum reserve method for computing reserves for tax purposes. Rather than delve into the complexities of this issue, it is sufficient to point out that the recalculation of these reserves generally has produced lower reserve figures for tax purposes. Thus, to the extent that the industry's deductions for reserves in the future are lower under the new formula, the amount of income subject to tax will be increased.

In summary, the 1984 Act simplified the tax code for the life insurance industry but increased the uncertainty regarding future tax rates and tax treatment. For an industry that must make long-term projections in conjunction with its liabilities, current and future tax rates are an important investment policy consideration.

There were no meaningful changes in the tax treatment of nonlife insurance companies as a result of the Deficit Reduction Act of 1984.

CONCLUSION

Only a few of the more typical tax implications of investment management have been reviewed in this supplement. Many other aspects must be considered in estate planning, and this should be done only with the advice of competent legal counsel. The investment manager should at least have a basic understanding of these principles in order to direct clients to legal counsel where called for and to understand the investment implications of the advice received from legal counsel. Each situation is different and offers the investment manager considerable opportunity to enhance the value of his or her services in working with the client.

A Primer on Tax Shelters in the Post-1984 Tax Legislation Environment

The following is a checklist of items that the novice considering a tax shelter investment should look for.

1. *Know the species of the shelter under consideration.* Publicly offered partnerships are registered with the Securities and Exchange Commission (SEC), and the offering document is called a prospectus. Private programs are not SEC registered and are offered through memoranda. There is no ceiling on the number of limited partners in a public program. Private deals are limited to 35 sophisticated outside investors who meet specific criteria set forth by the SEC. These programs generally require a much higher initial investment.

   The front page of the offering document states the nature of the program and its *unit size* (the amount of its minimum investment). Prominently displayed are warnings and caveats about the extraordinary risks and long-term nature of the shelter investment program. Investors should be prepared to lose every dollar invested.

2. *Check the broad outline of the program.* Every memorandum and prospectus carries a summary of the offerings in its first few pages. This should be reviewed closely; it touches on all the major points of concern for an investor, such as whether the investor meets the program's suitability standards, the proposed activities of the partnership, use of proceeds, fees, and the allocation of losses and revenues.

   The investor suitability standards set forth the minimum net worth and income required for participation. An investor should meet these minimums comfortably.

3. *Read both the short sketch in the summary and the full-blown description of the "proposed activities."* Make sure it is specific on exactly what the investor's money will be used for, whether it be residential or commercial real estate, exploratory drilling in oil and gas, or motion picture production. Avoid programs whose description is vague or where invested funds go into a "blind pool," requiring blind faith.

4. *Pay close attention to how the show will be run.* The "use of proceeds" section tells how much of the invested capital will go for fees and commissions and how much will actually end up in the business at hand. This is usually more clearly outlined in the text than in the summary, and should be stated in both percentage and dollar amounts.

   Commissions in general should not run more than 8 percent. A one-time organizational fee of 3 percent and an annual management fee of .25 percent are considered reasonable. This means approximately 88 cents of each dollar invested goes into the partnership's actual business. In addition, look for telltale evidence elsewhere in the offering document, often in the footnotes, that might detail additional promotion charges or built-in profits for the sponsor. This can add up to 25 percent of invested capital.

5. *Consider whether the deal makes economic sense.* The "allocation of losses and revenues" is the basis for the investment value of a tax shelter. There are many ways to divide partnership profits and losses. The key is to figure out exactly what the partnership defines as profits and losses. In oil programs, the sponsor could take a royalty before the revenues ever get to the partnership's profit-and-loss statement. In real estate, the general partner could collect large management fees and payments on a land lease, before turning over the remainder of the revenues to the partnership. In either case, the program has a lot less economic appeal.

6. *Read the "limited partnership agreement."* It is usually found in the exhibit section of the prospectus and is the document's single most important (although usually the most unintelligible) part. It is the legal contract encompassing the rest of the memorandum or prospectus. This is what an investor signs to become a limited partner, and because its terms are legally binding, it should be read with care. Professional legal assistance should be considered.

7. *Take a good look at the financial strength, reputation, and experience of the general partner.* Since this is the person who will be investing and managing the money, a summary of past deals—including financial statements—should be included with the offering documents. An investor should, at a minimum, investigate the general partner's background to ascertain whether the general partner is reputable, whether prior offerings were profitable before taxes were considered, whether the price paid for the property is not exorbitant, and what the results were of previous tax examinations of offerings by the IRS. Be wary of general partners with little experience in the field or who aren't investing much of their own money in the partnership.

8. *Carefully study the "tax opinion" section of the prospectus.* As difficult as it may be, this is an extremely critical section to understand. Recent and proposed tax law changes make it especially important for an investor to verify that the structure of the deal is legally sound and that the losses are deductible. Avoid programs where the deductions depend on a novel or disputed interpretation of tax law.

9. *Before committing, an investor should reevaluate his tax strategy in risk-reward terms.* Assuming that at this point the investor—with or without the assistance of an unbiased tax shelter professional—has assessed the risk-reward ratio for the proposed shelter. The alternatives should be considered the same way. That is, risk-adjusted after-tax return expectations of real estate, oil, personal property leasing, or research and development projects should be compared with the same expectations for conventional investments such as tax-exempt bonds, taxable bonds, stocks and deferred annuities, and for special tax deferred provisions such as IRAs, Keogh plans, and employee salary reduction plans. Only after making such a final, comprehensive comparison, can a truly rational decision be made.

Part III

Expectational Factors [New]

CHAPTER **7A**

The Fixed Income Analysis Process: Types and Characteristics of Fixed Income Securities and Markets

John L. Maginn, CFA
Marvin D. Andersen, CFA

INTRODUCTION

In the fourth edition of their classic work, *Security Analysis* [1962], Ben Graham and David Dodd devoted an entire section to the selection of fixed income securities. Graham and Dodd described bonds as being less attractive than equities because bonds are a security with a limited return. In their opinion, the selection of bonds must emphasize the avoidance of loss. Thus, they viewed the analysis of bonds as a negative art—a process of exclusion and rejection rather than a process of search and acceptance, which more aptly typifies equity analysis.

The purpose of Chapters 7A and 7B is to outline and describe the analytical process for fixed income investments, namely bonds, mortgages, and preferred stocks. The term *fixed income,* as used by investment professionals, indicates that the income return on these securities is limited. However, this nomenclature is somewhat outdated in this day of floating rate, adjustable rate, and other forms of variable income returns. However, even these innovations result in limitations on the expected income return, albeit within a range of potential returns.

Chapter 7A outlines the research process and describes the characteristics of various fixed income securities and the markets for such securities. The approach taken in Chapter 7B is to define, describe, and discuss the analysis process in terms of the expectational factors—expected return (both income and changes in principal value) and expected risk—that are the micro-inputs to the portfolio management process and the building of efficient portfolios. While these two chapters treat all aspects in a summary form, the subject justifies a volume of its own. It is hoped that this effort will stimulate such an enterprise.

RESEARCH FUNCTION

Fixed income analysis can be described in several different dimensions although, as noted above, the emphasis is on risk analysis. The analyst is concerned with initial credit analysis, rating changes, and the monitoring of financial trends of companies whose securities are owned in the portfolio or considered as a potential investment. Like the equity analyst, the fixed income analyst is involved in absolute evaluations of the security itself as well as relative comparisons, relative to similar companies by industry or quality rating and/or relative to the portfolio specifications—objectives and constraints.

The research functions that are performed by a fixed income analyst can be outlined as follows:

1. Maintain and update knowledge of the characteristics of fixed income securities and markets, especially new forms of such securities.
2. Apply appropriate valuation model(s) for the type of fixed income securities involved to determine the expected return from probabilistic range of possible returns.
3. Determine the systematic (interest rate) risk exposure for alternate fixed income investments.
4. Determine the unsystematic (specific) risk based on these considerations:
   a. Credit or default risk
   b. Indenture provisions risk
5. Provide the portfolio manager with the expected return and risk factors to be considered for each fixed income investment analyzed.
6. Select or participate with the portfolio manager in the selection of securities for inclusion in portfolios based on the matching of portfolio objectives and constraints with the expected return/risk characteristics of the fixed income securities analyzed.

Initial Credit Analysis

The initial analysis of the credit of the issuer (borrower) of fixed income securities and/or ultimate guarantor is conducted at the time the investment is made, either prior to the initial offering or prior to purchase in the secondary market.

The primary objective of fixed income analysis is to determine the certainty of the payments. A fixed income investment is a loan and fixed income investors are lenders of money. If held to maturity, the return on such an investment is determined by the amount and timing of interest payments and principal repayments. The quality of such investments is determined by the probability of receiving those payments as they are due.

For most fixed income investors, the *sine qua non* is the expectation of payments on a certain or specified schedule as well as on a contractual basis. The attraction of fixed income investments is the certainty of these payments, as contrasted with the variability of payments on equity investments, e.g., dividends on common stock or rents from real estate property. To determine the certainty of payments, the analyst must determine the creditworthiness of the issuer and/or the guarantor in much the same way that a banker evaluates the credit status of a potential borrower.

Much of the literature and tradition of fixed income analysis has focused on the determination of default risk. Historically, this focus was appropriate and reflected the economic environment and character of the bond markets up until the late 1960s. The depression of the 1930s dramatized the dimensions of default risk and traumatized investors in general for many years thereafter. During the 1940s, 1950s, and much of the 1960s interest rates were relatively stable. Furthermore, adverse changes in the credit quality of an issue, while monitored and noted by rating agencies, did not elicit much of a reaction by investors because of the prevailing attitude that bonds were purchased to be held to maturity.

Since the late 1960s, the character of the bond market, the volatility of interest rates, and the prevailing attitude of fixed income investors has changed dramatically. Investors still are attracted to bonds for their security or risk-minimization characteristics in a portfolio context, and they are willing to forego the higher, long-term expected returns associated with investments such as common stocks. Nevertheless, a growing segment of the fixed income investor population has broadened its approach to encompass active trading. The motivation for such trading is the potential for price appreciation resulting from changes in interest rates, changes in spreads between sectors of the market, or changes in absolute or relative credit quality.

The anticipation of interest rate changes and spread changes, not caused by credit risk shifts, is a responsibility more typically assigned to portfolio managers, strategists, and/or economists. It would follow quite logically that the anticipation of credit rating changes is a responsibility typically assigned to fixed income analysts. In the absence of a sufficient analytical staff, portfolio managers may attempt to handle both of these responsibilities.

Ratings—Evaluation and Anticipation

Fixed income analysis is aided by the availability of rating services that establish credit quality ratings for most of the issuers of publicly traded bonds and preferred stocks. Services such as Moody's, Standard & Poor's, Duff &

Phelps, Fitch's, and in Canada, the Canadian Bond Rating and Dominion Bond Rating services, are used by investors to determine the creditworthiness of an issuer. While such ratings have proved to be valid, they are not fool-proof indicators of risk.

Some portfolio managers or investors depend on these rating agencies for all or most of the credit analysis. They use the ratings as the sole or primary measure of expected risk. Their rationale is threefold: (1) the historic validity of the ratings, (2) the acceptance of the ratings in the marketplace, and (3) the time and cost associated with doing one's own analysis. Also, there is a feeling among fixed income investors that controlling interest rate risk (systematic risk) is a far more important determinant of performance than credit risk (unsystematic risk).

Many fixed income investors do not rely exclusively on the rating agencies. They supplement the work of the rating agencies with their own credit analysis. As discussed by Gifford Fong, in Chapter 9A of this Supplement, there are two reasons for this activity, both of which are based on the assumption that yields in the marketplace are closely correlated to agency ratings, *ceteris paribus*.

1. The analyst's assessment of credit quality may be more accurate and/or timely than those of the rating agencies. In this case, the portfolio manager can achieve added yield at relatively small cost in terms of credit risk exposure, or can avoid paying, in terms of reduced yield, for nonexistent incremental quality.
2. Agency ratings for bonds are revised upward or downward only as it is clear that the issuer's financial circumstances have changed. With astute credit analysis, it may be possible to anticipate such upgrades or downgrades and profit from the yield and price changes that ensue.

Monitoring Credits

The directives of Graham and Dodd and other students of fixed income securities focus on the susceptibility of companies to change in their creditworthiness. As noted by Peter Bernstein in Chapter 6 of the main volume, the owner of any security that has a maturity date beyond the next five minutes cannot escape making a bet on the future. Thus, the fixed income analyst has a responsibility to monitor the financial trends and position of the borrowers (issuers). This responsibility is well accepted by the managers of actively traded fixed income portfolios.

For more passive or buy-and-hold portfolios, these cautions are well recognized. However, it seems that—particularly in the 1950s and 1960s and even today—too little time and attention have been given to the monitoring of credits, despite the fact that such buy-and-hold portfolios have been typically heavily concentrated in long-dated bonds with maturities of up to 30 years. However, the increased volatility of the U.S. economy and capital markets in the 1970s and (to date) 1980s has heightened the erosion of credit

TABLE 7A-1. Largest U.S. Bankruptcies (1970–82)[a]

	Total Liabilities ($ millions)	Bankruptcy Petition Date	Filed Under
1. Penn Central Transportation Co.	3,300	June 1970	Chapter VII, Section 77
2. Wickes	2,000	Apr. 1982	Chapter II
3. Itel	1,700	Jan. 1981	Chapter II
4. Manville Corp.	1,116	Aug. 1982	Chapter II
5. Braniff Airlines	1,100	May 1982	Chapter II
6. W. T. Grant Co.	1,000	Oct. 1975	Chapter XI
7. Seatrain Lines	785	Feb. 1981	Chapter II
8. Continental Mortgage Investors	607	Mar. 1976	Chapter XI–X
9. United Merchants & Manufacturing	552	July 1977	Chapter XI
10. AM International	510	Apr. 1982	Chapter II
11. Saxon Industries	461	Apr. 1982	Chapter II
12. Commonwealth Oil Refining Co.	421	Mar. 1978	Chapter XI
13. W. Judd Kassuba	420	Dec. 1973	Chapter XI
14. Erie Lackawanna Railroad	404	June 1972	Chapter VIII, Section 77
15. White Motor Corp.	399	Sept. 1980	Chapter II
16. Investors Funding Corp.	379	Oct. 1974	Chapter X
17. Sambo's Restaurants	370	June 1980	Chapter II
18. Food Fair Corp.	347	Oct. 1978	Chapter XI
19. Great American Mortgage & Trust	326	Mar. 1977	Chapter XI
20. McLouth Steel	323	Dec. 1981	Chapter II
21. U.S. Financial Services	300	July 1973	Chapter XI
22. Chase Manhattan Mortgage & Realty Trust	290	Feb. 1979	Chapter XI
23. Daylin, Inc.	250	Feb. 1975	Chapter XI
24. Guardian Mortgage Investors	247	Mar. 1978	Chapter XI
25. Revere Cooper & Brass	237	Oct. 1982	Chapter II
26. Chicago, Rock Island & Pacific	221	Mar. 1975	Chapter VIII, Section 77
27. Equity Funding Corp. of America	200	Apr. 1973	Chapter X
28. Interstate Stores, Inc.	190	May 1974	Chapter XI
29. Fidelity Mortgage Investors	187	Jan. 1975	Chapter XI
30. Omega, Alpha Corp.	175	Sept. 1974	Chapter X
31. Lionel Corp.	165	Feb. 1982	Chapter II
32. Reading Railroad	158	Nov. 1971	Chapter VIII, Section 77
33. Boston & Maine Railroad	148	Dec. 1975	Chapter VIII, Section 77
34. Westgate-California	144	Feb. 1974	Chapter X
35. Colwell Mortgage & Trust	142	Feb. 1978	Chapter XI
36. Pacific Far East Lines	132	Jan. 1978	Chapter XI
37. Allied Supermarkets	124	June 1977	Chapter XI
38. Penn Dixie Co.	122	Apr. 1980	Chapter II

SOURCE: Altman [1983].
[a] Does not include commercial banking entities.

quality and the risk of default—or more specifically, the specter of bankruptcy. According to Edward Altman, a noted authority on bankruptcy, corporate failure is no longer the exclusive province of the small, under-capitalized business but occurs increasingly among the large industrial and financial corporations.

Altman [1983] describes the decade of the 1970s as a watershed period for major business failures. The $3 billion Penn Central bankruptcy in 1970 heralded the new wave of larger firm failures. He compiled a listing (see Table 7A-1) of the largest U.S. bankruptcies in terms of dollar liabilities for the period 1970–1982. His list does not include financial organizations such as commercial banks and savings and loan associations but does include real estate investment trusts (REITs).

While the subject of bankruptcy analysis is treated in more detail in Chapter 7B, the foregoing discussion is a dramatic indication of the need for monitoring fixed income credits. Macroeconomic, social, and political conditions change, as do micro conditions that are unique to an industry or firm. These changes affect the expected risk for a fixed income security.

Relationship to Portfolio Management

As was mentioned previously, some fixed income investors rely exclusively on the rating agencies for the analysis of issues and the quantification of expected risk, while others rely on their own staff's analysis. No matter how it is done or by whom, credit analysis is an important part of the portfolio management process. It provides the portfolio manager with a basis for the measurement of expected risk, that is, the probability of realizing an expected, albeit limited, income return from bonds.

That is the traditional description of the role of fixed income analysis in the portfolio management process. It is still an appropriate description in the context of a passive or buy-and-hold fixed income portfolio strategy. By holding securities to maturity, any capital changes resulting from interest rate changes are neutralized or ignored (by holding to maturity, the par amount of the bond will be received). Therefore, portfolio return is controlled by coupon payments and the reinvestment of proceeds. Since interest rate forecasting is largely ignored, analysis is important to minimize the risk of default on the securities held.

ALTERNATIVE PORTFOLIO STRATEGIES

In the 1970s and 1980s, there has been a trend toward more active forms of fixed income portfolio management. There are at least two primary reasons for this trend:

1. Potential for capital gains (losses) from fixed income securities has increased as a result of the volatility of interest rates over this period. This amplitude, as well as the increased frequency of interest rate

changes, has resulted in a sharp change in the riskiness (changes in market value) of fixed income securities. This is reflected in Table 9-6 of the main volume.

2. Potential for default or change in quality (an increase or reduction in quality rating by a rating agency or as perceived either by independent analysts or market participants) has increased for the reasons stated previously. Default risk has both systematic and unsystematic elements, as noted by Fong. Either the act or threat of default or changes in general business conditions affect the market value of fixed income securities.

It is the opportunity for significant changes in interest rates or credit quality and the resulting effect on the market value of the securities that has fostered semi-active and active portfolio strategies. The ability to analyze and anticipate changes in the credit quality of the issuer is a key element of certain of these strategies. For others, the ability to identify properly and thus control credit risk is a key element.

Security Selection

The long-standing role of the equity analyst is the responsibility for individual security recommendations and/or selection. Fixed income portfolio management styles and practices vary considerably. Many fixed income portfolio managers function in a "triad" role of manager, trader, and analyst, with very little of their time spent on the lattermost function. These are the managers referred to previously who depend almost exclusively on the published quality ratings (from the rating agencies) to provide risk analysis. This multifunctional approach is most often associated with small investment organizations with limited staff resources to devote to analysis. It is also associated with active management where unsystematic risk factors are often deemed to be of lesser concern because of the relatively short time horizon associated with these strategies.

The role of the fixed income analyst as the risk quantifier and security selector or recommender is perhaps best defined in larger investment organizations and/or those firms, such as life insurance companies, that are active participants in the private placement market. The securities issued in this market are typically not rated, although the issuer or guarantor may have public issue securities that are rated. For the most part, the private placement market requires a substantial degree of credit analysis; thus, the analyst plays a key and often dominant role in the area of security selection.

By definition, the "junk" bond or speculative grade sectors of the bond market are characterized as having a high degree of unsystematic risk. This is yet another segment of the market in which credit analysis plays an important role. Both the private placement market and the so-called junk or speculative sector of the bond market are discussed in more detail in this chapter and in Chapter 7B.

TYPES AND CHARACTERISTICS OF FIXED INCOME SECURITIES

To effectively analyze securities, the fixed income analyst must understand the characteristics of many different types of securities that are issued and traded in the bond and preferred stock markets.

In 1983, the market value of publicly traded common stocks in the United States was estimated at approximately $2.1 trillion. But, the fixed income portion of the investment markets in the United States was estimated at over $5.3 trillion at book value. More important, in terms of new securities being issued, the fixed income market far overshadows the stock market. For 1984, Salomon Brothers estimated that the net issuance of mortgages, bonds, and loans in the United States exceeded $762 billion (see Table 7A-2). The new issuance of preferred stock raised the estimate to $767 billion.

With the increased volume of fixed income financing, the variety and variation of issues or alternative forms of investments has exploded. This has increased the challenge and complexity of the analyst's task with regard to the terms and indenture provisions of an issue that must be analyzed. The analyst's primary responsibility is the determination of the unsystematic risk factors involved that might disrupt or impair the issuer's generation of cash flow to service the debt. In many cases, the fixed income analyst is expected to be able to forecast the expected cash flow (income and principal repayment) from a security as well as estimate the probability of call or redemption features prematurely shortening the average life of the investment.

SECTORS OF THE MARKET

As might be expected of such a voluminous market, the range of types of investments is also large. This chapter identifies and describes briefly the major sectors or types of securities within this vast market. The comments concentrate on the main features of importance to an analyst. For more detailed treatment of some of the types and characteristics of fixed income securities, see any of the standard investment texts cited in the Further Reading section at the end of this chapter.

The fixed income market can be subdivided in many ways. For purposes of this chapter, the market is discussed within the context of four major areas, or sectors: bonds, mortgages, combinations (principally fixed income securities with a conversion or exchange option), and preferred stock. The sequence of the discussion of the sectors within each of these four areas of the market is based on the importance of analysis in the management of a portfolio of securities drawn from the sector rather than the size of the sector as measured by the par amount or number of issues outstanding.

TABLE 7A-2. Supply and Demand for Credit in the United States (Annual Net Increases in Amounts Outstanding) (dollars in billions)

	1979	1980	1981	1982	1983	1984E	1985P	Amount Outstanding 12-31-84E
Net Demand								
Privately Held Mortgages	$113.1	$ 84.2	$ 73.7	$ 15.9	$ 83.7	$148.5	$136.4	$1,485.5
Corporate and Foreign Bonds	35.7	40.2	34.9	39.1	37.9	50.5	45.3	656.9
Total Long-Term Private	148.8	124.3	108.6	54.9	121.7	199.0	181.7	2,142.4
Short-Term Business Borrowing	98.0	67.1	117.3	47.5	60.1	141.6	153.2	1,006.7
Short-Term Household Borrowing	49.3	11.2	37.7	27.7	60.5	97.9	120.7	695.5
Total Short-Term Private	147.2	78.3	155.0	75.2	120.6	239.5	273.9	1,702.2
Privately Held Federal Debt	76.2	118.7	123.0	214.1	241.0	257.3	277.9	1,728.1
Tax-Exempt Notes and Bonds	27.8	31.9	29.5	63.9	54.3	66.5	63.2	542.8
Total Government Debt	104.0	150.6	152.4	278.0	295.3	323.8	341.1	2,270.9
Total Net Demand for Credit	$400.0	$353.3	$416.0	$408.1	$537.6	$762.4	$796.7	$6,115.6
Net Supply*								
Thrift Institutions	$ 56.5	$ 54.5	$ 27.8	$ 31.3	$136.8	$155.8	$171.7	$1,117.1
Insurance, Pensions, Endowments	77.9	88.2	89.2	107.1	96.1	105.3	105.4	1,190.2
Investment Companies	29.3	15.9	72.4	52.4	6.0	49.9	58.0	261.3
Other Nonbank Finance	27.8	13.1	28.8	4.9	12.0	50.6	41.3	307.8
Total Nonbank Finance	191.4	171.7	218.1	195.6	250.9	361.5	376.5	2,876.3
Commercial Banks	122.2	101.4	107.6	107.2	140.2	169.0	164.8	1,761.6
Nonfinancial Corporations	7.0	1.8	18.4	13.6	22.8	12.6	23.1	160.6
State and Local Governments	7.1	0.6	2.0	10.3	17.2	11.0	9.7	93.6
Foreign Investors	–4.6	23.2	16.3	18.1	28.5	30.7	30.8	283.2
Residual: Households Direct	76.9	54.6	53.7	63.3	78.1	177.8	191.9	940.4
Total Net Supply or Credit	$400.0	$353.3	$416.0	$408.1	$537.6	$762.4	$796.7	$6,115.6

* Excludes funds for equities and other demands not tabulated above. E = estimated. P = preliminary.

SOURCE: Salomon Brothers [1985].

Corporate Bonds

The "corporate" segment of the U.S. bond market includes the bonds issued by public (stockholder-owned) and private (closely held) companies that are incorporated in the United States. This includes the U.S. incorporated subsidiaries of foreign corporations. It should be noted that some foreign corporations also sell bonds in the U.S. market denominated and payable in U.S. dollars. As shown in Table 7A-3, Salomon Brothers' estimate of total domestic corporate bonds outstanding was $594 billion as of December 31, 1984.

Public Issues or Private Placements

In the case of corporate bonds, new issues can be further classified as public offerings or private placements. The former are registered with the Securities and Exchange Commission (SEC) and are sold to both individual and institutional investors. Private placements are sold almost exclusively to institutional investors, particularly life insurance companies and pension funds. Private issues are not registered and are placed either by the issuing company directly or via an investment banker to a limited number of investors. The advantage to the issuer is the lack of registration and the reduced administrative cost because of the limited number of investors. The advantage for the investor is the ability to negotiate terms and rates that are more attractive than those available in the public market. The relative size of these two sectors of the corporate new issue market is illustrated in Table 7A-3.

There is a key distinction, from an analytical viewpoint, between the analysis of the debt securities of a corporation and those of a municipal or federal agency issue. That distinction is based on the competitive forces that affect businesses operating in the private sector rather than the public sector of the economy. Thus, an analysis of the business plan or corporate strategy of the corporation issuing fixed income securities is an important part of the analysis of corporate bonds. Industry position, relative operating efficiency, and industry risk are all factors to be identified and evaluated by the analyst. The analytical tools and techniques are discussed further on in this chapter.

Generally, corporate bonds are subdivided into four sectors: (1) industrial, (2) utility, (3) transportation, and (4) financial. The organizational structure of the Corporate Finance Department of Standard & Poor's (S&P) is cited below to provide examples of the subclassifications that exist within the major corporate sectors listed above.

Industrial. S&P monitors over 1,000 U.S. industrial corporations, both parent companies and their subsidiaries, which can include captive finance companies and special-purpose or dummy corporations. The latter are often established by one or more (joint venture) corporations for special-purpose financing. The 51 industries followed by the industrial staff of S&P are outlined below.

Aerospace and Defense
Agricultural Commodities
Agricultural Cooperatives
Apparel
Appliances
Auto, Auto Related, Trucks
Beverages
Broadcasting
Building Materials
Cable Television
Cement
Chemicals
Computer and Office Equipment
Construction and Engineering
Contract Drillers
Electrical Equipment
Food Products
Forest Products
Glass Products
Hand and Power Tools
Health Care
Homebuilders
Hospital Chains
Hotels/Gaming
Household Products
Integrated Steel Producers

Leisure Time
Machinery
Major Integrated Oils
Metal Cans
Motion Picture Companies
Natural Gas
Newspapers
Nonfood Consumer Products
Oil Service
Other Oils
Packaging
Paper and Forest Products
Primary Metals and Minerals
Project Financing
Publishing
Restaurants
Retailing
Semiconductors
Specialty Steel Producers
Sweetener Industry
Telecommunications Manufacturing
Textiles
Tire and Rubber
Tobacco
Transportation

Utility. At S&P, the utility and transportation industries are grouped together in one organizational unit. However, for purposes of this chapter, the commentary is divided.

S&P monitors over 300 U.S. utilities, which are divided into the following four industry groups: (1) electric utilities, (2) natural gas utilities, (3) telecommunications, and (4) water utilities.

Competitive factors play a key role in the analysis of industrial companies. For utilities, regulatory factors, or what is often described as the quality of regulation, is a key variable in the analysis. This is a result of the monopoly, or near monopoly, position of most utilities. The recent deregulation of the telephone industry is changing the way analysts view telephone utilities, with regulatory factors now being overshadowed by competitive considerations.

Transportation. Deregulation has also changed the way analysts view the transportation industries in the United States. These changes, which occurred

TABLE 7A-3. Domestic Corporate and Foreign Bonds Sold in the U.S. (Annual Issuance, Retirements and Net Increases in Amounts Outstanding) (dollars in billions)

	1979	1980	1981	1982	1983	1984E	1985P	Amount Outstanding 12-31-84E
Domestic Corporate								
Public Straight Bonds	$ 16.4	$ 19.1	$ 12.5	$ 12.7	$ 16.8	$ 12.3	$ 14.2	
Public Straight Notes	6.8	15.5	16.7	21.0	17.2	29.2	36.4	
Private Straight Issues	18.4	13.9	15.1	17.1	20.5	14.2	9.5	
Convertible Issues	0.6	4.0	4.4	3.0	6.5	4.2	7.3	
Exchanges for Stock	3.0	1.7	2.2	6.7	4.9	16.9	10.4	
Retirements	13.3	14.8	21.5	28.1	31.8	28.0	34.8	
Net Domestic Issuance	31.8	39.3	29.4	32.4	34.2	48.7	43.0	594.1
Foreign Sold in the U.S.								
Public Issues	$ 3.5	$ 2.5	$ 6.8	$ 5.7	$ 4.9	$ 3.9	$ 4.5	
Private Issues	1.1	1.2	0.4	0.8	0.6	0.1	0.5	
Retirements*	0.8	2.8	1.7	−0.2	1.8	2.3	2.7	
Net Foreign Issuance	3.9	0.8	5.4	6.7	3.8	1.8	2.3	62.8
Combined Net Issuance	$ 35.7	$ 40.2	$ 34.9	$ 39.1	$ 37.9	$ 50.5	$ 45.3	$ 656.9

Ownership

Mutual Savings Banks	$ −1.1	$ 0.7	$ −1.0	$ −1.1	$ 3.0	$ −0.7	$ 0.7	$ 21.2
Life Insurance Companies	11.6	8.7	7.3	16.2	16.7	21.5	21.7	240.6
Property Liability Companies	2.0	0.0	2.8	−0.5	−4.2	−1.6	−1.6	20.0
Priv. Noninsured Pension Funds	12.8	10.7	3.4	1.1	5.8	1.7	4.6	94.0
State and Local Retirement Funds	3.2	9.5	9.1	5.2	2.7	1.1	4.5	112.6
Endowments	0.2	0.3	0.2	0.9	0.9	1.1	1.2	16.7
Stock Mutual Funds	0.8	1.3	1.6	0.2	2.7	1.4	2.9	14.4
Security Brokers and Dealers	−1.5	0.7	2.7	−0.5	−0.2	1.6	0.7	8.3
Total Nonbank Finance	28.0	31.9	26.2	21.5	27.5	25.9	34.5	527.6
Commercial Banks	−0.1	0.6	0.0	1.9	3.9	2.6	0.4	15.7
Foreign*	2.6	8.2	8.4	10.6	4.9	7.0	5.4	52.8
Residual: Households Direct	5.1	−0.5	0.3	5.1	1.6	15.0	4.9	60.8
Total Ownership	$ 35.7	$ 40.2	$ 34.9	$ 39.1	$ 37.9	$ 50.5	$ 45.3	$ 656.9

* Foreign purchases of new foreign offerings are included in retirements and, thus, are not in ownership calculation.

SOURCE: Salomon Brothers [1985].

TABLE 7A-4. Corporate Bonds by Type of Issue (Annual Issuance,* Retirements* and Net Increases in Amounts Outstanding*) (dollars in billions)

	1979	1980	1981	1982	1983	1984E	1985P	Amount Outstanding 12-31-84E
Straight Public Debt								
Public Utility	$ 5.3	$ 6.9	$ 7.8	$ 8.9	$ 6.3	$ 4.8	$ 4.9	
Communications	3.7	5.9	3.9	1.1	3.1	0.5	0.9	
Transportation	0.8	1.4	0.7	0.7	0.7	1.2	1.4	
Industrial	5.9	10.3	9.2	9.2	5.3	8.9	17.4	
Sales Finance	1.6	3.7	2.5	4.8	4.1	9.1	9.9	
Other Finance and Real Estate	3.0	2.0	2.1	2.9	4.2	2.8	2.7	
Commercial Banks	2.2	2.2	1.8	3.9	6.6	8.3	8.3	
Commercial and Miscellaneous	0.7	2.1	1.2	2.3	3.8	5.8	5.1	
Total Public Straight Issues	23.2	34.6	29.3	33.7	34.0	41.4	50.6	
Merger Exchange Bonds for Stock	1.6	0.9	1.1	3.6	4.9	16.9	10.4	
Maturing Public Straights	5.5	4.4	6.1	7.6	6.8	6.4	13.9	
Calls	0.0	0.2	0.4	2.7	2.0	1.5	3.4	
Sinking Fund Retirements	2.5	4.8	5.8	4.5	6.8	8.4	5.6	
Debt/Equity Swaps	0.0	0.0	0.7	5.9	2.0	0.9	0.2	
Net Increase in Public Straights	16.8	26.1	17.4	16.7	21.3	41.2	38.0	391.7

Straight Private Debt**

Public Utility	$ 3.8	$ 1.7	$ 3.6	$ 1.8	$ 1.5	$ 1.7	$ 2.0	
Communications	0.5	0.5	0.3	0.4	0.0	0.0	0.0	
Transportation	4.3	3.0	2.4	1.9	1.0	0.7	0.1	
Industrial	6.0	4.9	5.9	7.8	6.5	4.5	3.4	
Sales Finance	1.4	1.2	1.3	2.0	7.6	2.5	0.4	
Other Finance and Real Estate	0.0	0.0	0.0	0.0	0.1	0.9	0.1	
Commercial Banks	0.8	0.7	0.8	2.5	1.4	0.9	0.4	
Commercial and Miscellaneous	1.5	1.8	0.8	0.7	2.4	3.1	3.1	
Total Private Straight Issues	18.4	13.9	15.1	17.1	20.5	14.2	9.5	
Maturing Private Straights	4.7	4.8	5.2	5.6	6.9	5.8	5.7	
Net Increase in Private Straights	13.7	9.1	9.9	11.5	13.6	8.4	3.8	180.9
Net Increase in Straight Bonds***	$ 30.5	$ 35.2	$ 27.3	$ 28.2	$ 34.9	$ 49.6	$ 41.8	$ 572.6
Net Increase in Convertible Bonds	1.4	4.2	2.2	4.2	-0.8	-0.8	1.2	21.6
Net Increase in Corporate Bonds	$ 31.8	$ 39.3	$ 29.4	$ 32.4	$ 34.2	$ 48.7	$ 43.0	$ 594.1

* Salomon Brothers estimates.
** Many private placements have equity features.
*** Excludes convertible bonds.

SOURCE: Salomon Brothers [1985].

in the late 1970s and early 1980s, have shifted the analyst's focus from regulatory to competitive factors. S&P divides the approximately 100 transportation companies that are monitored into five industry groups: (1) airlines, (2) ocean shipping, (3) railroads, (4) transportation leasing, and (5) trucking. Another industry classification that is notable from a fixed income standpoint, but not covered by S&P, is barge lines or domestic water transportation.

Financial. At S&P, the financial sector is divided into two broad areas: (1) financial and mortgage-related and (2) bank and international. For purposes of this chapter, mortgage-related and international securities are discussed as separate and distinct types of fixed income securities. The strictly financial industries followed by S&P are divided into the following groups:

Banks and bank holding companies
Brokerage (securities brokers and investment bankers)
Finance
Homebuilders
Insurance
Leasing
Letters of credit (issues for which the primary security (guarantee) is a
    letter of credit issued by a bank)
Mortgage bankers
Real estate investment trusts (REITs)
Structured financings [a broad term, in this context representing (1) issues
    for which the primary security (guarantee) is a surety bond issued by an
    insurance company and (2) project financing for which the primary
    security is the cash flow from the project (nonrecourse financing) or
    support agreements (recourse financing) with the project sponsors or
    participants]
Thrift institutions (savings banks or S&Ls)

To reflect the relative importance of industry groups within the corporate sector, Salomon Brothers' tabulation of corporate bonds by type of issue is shown in Table 7A-4. It should be noted that the S&P and Salomon Brothers classifications vary somewhat. Nevertheless, the tabulation is informative.

It is also worth noting that corporations have reacted to the volatile interest rate conditions of the 1970s and early 1980s by shortening the maturity of bond financings. As illustrated in Table 7A-5, the volume of new publicly offered corporate bonds with a maturity of greater than 20 years has trended irregularly downward. Over the same time period, floating rate bonds and intermediate term (3–10 years) maturity issues have increased. (Due to classification differences, Table 7A-5 does not reconcile with other tables in this chapter.)

Municipals

Municipal bonds are issued by governmental entities, usually for the purpose of financing capital projects. In the United States, these securities are exempt

TABLE 7A-5. Volume of New Publicly Offered Corporate Bonds, 1972 and 1976-84 (dollars in billions)

	1972	1976	1977	1978	1979	1980	1981	1982	1983	1984[a]
Conventional										
Greater Than 20 Years	$11.1	$16.6	$17.0	$12.2	$14.3	$17.9	$ 8.2	$ 8.6	$11.0	$ 2.2
3–10 Years	3.7	7.0	3.9	4.6	5.5	14.5	15.4	13.8	9.1	10.2
10–20 Years	1.0	0.3	0.8	0.8	0.7	0.8	0.7	1.9	1.3	1.0
Floating Rate, 1–3 Years	—	0.3	0.1	0.4	2.5	0.7	0.3	3.9	5.8	9.8
Convertibles	2.3	0.8	0.4	0.3	0.6	4.0	4.4	2.7	5.9	0.6
Extendables	—	—	—	—	—	—	—	2.0	1.5	3.6
All Other	—	0.2	0.1	0.1	0.2	0.5	4.6	3.5	3.9	1.4
Total	$18.0	$25.2	$22.3	$18.4	$23.8	$38.4	$33.6	$36.4	$38.5	$28.8

SOURCE: Salomon Brothers [1984].
[a] Through August.

from federal taxes on their coupon interest, and are frequently referred to as tax-exempts. In Canada, municipal securities are taxable, but in virtually all other aspects share the same general characteristics of their U.S. counterparts.

Municipal debt outstanding in the United States totaled over $543 billion at year-end 1984, compared to domestic corporate debt of $594 billion, according to Salomon Brothers estimates. The relative sizes of the new issue corporate and municipal markets in the United States were closely correlated from 1978 to 1981 as shown in Table 7A-6. The sharp increase in new municipal financings since 1982 reflects the large number of mortgage revenue and private purpose industrial revenue bonds that were sold in those years.

TABLE 7A-6. Net Increase of New Issue Municipal and Domestic Corporate Debt Sold in the U.S. ($ Billions)

Net New Issuance	1979	1980	1981	1982	1983	1984E	1985P
Municipals	$27.8	$31.9	$29.5	$63.9	$54.3	$66.5	$63.2
Corporates	31.8	39.3	29.4	32.4	34.2	48.7	43.0

SOURCE: Salomon Brothers [1985].

In Canada, the net annual increase in debt outstanding of provincial and municipal issuers is substantially larger than that of corporate issuers, as seen in Table 7A-7. Provincial debt issuance includes guaranteed debt, such as the province-owned electric utilities, as well as the large amounts of provincial debt issued in recent years to promote economic stability.

TABLE 7A-7. Net Increase of New Issue Municipal and Domestic Corporate Debt Sold in Canada and Abroad * ($C Millions)

Net New Issuance	1979	1980	1981	1982	1983	1984
Municipals	$ 587	$ 439	$ 361	$ 977	$ 765	$ 1,037
Provincials (Direct & Gtd.)	6,468	8,639	12,525	14,914	12,631	9,408
Total	7,055	9,078	12,886	15,891	13,396	10,445
Corporates	2,772	3,695	6,064	4,422	2,671	2,956

* C—Canadian Dollars.

SOURCE: Bank of Canada [1985].

Municipal vs. Corporate Analysis. There were approximately 82,341 governmental units in the United States in 1982, according to that year's

Census of Governments. Comparable figures are not available for Canada, but the numbers would be far less because of the relative size of the country and the use of consolidated and regional forms of government involving fewer governmental entities. These U.S. governmental units include states, cities, counties, school districts, and water, sanitary and other special districts, as well as numerous authorities. It is estimated that about 53,000 have debt outstanding or have sold bonds at one time or another. There are a multitude of different borrowers for a variety of purposes.

In contrast, as noted by Moody's [1982], there are approximately 3,000 stocks and 3,000 corporate bonds listed on the New York and American Stock Exchanges. The SEC requires the publication of detailed information on publicly distributed stocks and corporate bonds. The SEC has no jurisdiction over municipal issuers, although it does have control over brokers and dealers in municipal securities if they engage in fraudulent practices.

The Municipal Securities Rulemaking Board, which was created by Congress in 1975, deals primarily with setting industry standards, but these regulations are far less stringent than those of the SEC. Since municipal securities are authorized and issued by states and their political subdivisions, federal attempts at regulation tread on state rights. Thus, to determine creditworthiness, the municipal analyst must sort through a whole range of unique factors that are not encountered in the analysis of corporate bonds. These include a lack of standardized accounting practices, along with legal restrictions and political factors.

The Canadian Experience. In Canada, the provincial governments exercise far greater control over their political subdivisions than do the states in the United States. This includes fiscal oversight, and tends to prevent serious financial problems from developing. These governments play a greater role in economic stabilization, health care, and welfare. As a result, Canadian municipal debt levels tend to be lower and their finances overall appear to be less strained than those of cities of comparable size in the United States.

Types of Municipal Bonds. There are several types of municipal bonds, but mainly these are variations or hybrids of three basic types: general obligation, special tax, and revenue bonds. General obligation bonds are secured by the full faith and credit and, usually, the unlimited taxing power of the issuer. In cases where the issuer does not pledge all of its taxing power, such as those issued by some cities in Texas and Ohio, the bonds are called limited tax bonds. The bonds may be supported by tax rates that are limited to a specific percentage of assessed value of taxable property, such as 2.5 percent in Ohio.

Special tax bonds are not secured by the full faith and credit of a state or municipality, but are payable from a specifically pledged source of revenue, such as a single tax or series of taxes. Many state highway bonds fall into this category and may be secured by gasoline taxes or registration fees.

Revenue bonds, which are the last major category, continue to increase in importance. As the name implies, such bonds are secured by the revenues of an enterprise or special authority created to operate a project, which is designed to be self-supporting from user fees or charges, such as a water department. In addition, an issue may be a dual or "double-barrelled" obligation, meaning that it has two sources of payments. An example of such an issue is a sewer bond with both user charges and a general obligation pledge.

In Canada, most municipal bond issues are in the general obligation category. While debt may be issued for self-supporting enterprises, such as water and sewer, it is nonetheless issued as general obligation debt.

The Decline of General Obligation Bonds. General obligation bonds have traditionally implied strong security. The near-default of New York City in 1975, the default of Cleveland, Ohio on its general obligation notes in 1978, as well as property tax limitation measures, such as Proposition 13 in California, placed doubts in the minds of investors as to the credit superiority of general obligation bonds over revenue bonds. Since 1970, general obligation bonds have declined from 66 percent of new municipal security issues to 25 percent in 1983. Part of the explanation for this shift in recent years is due to the large amount of mortgage revenue, pollution control, and private purpose industrial development financing.

General obligation bonds will continue to be a major factor in the market but will probably continue to decline in relative importance. General obligation bonds generally require voter approval, while revenue bonds do not. In those cases where voter approval would be difficult to obtain, it is likely revenue bond financing would be used.

Municipal Defaults. The default of the Washington Public Power Supply System[1] Project 4 and 5 bonds in August 1983, representing $2.25 billion

---

[1] The Washington Public Power Supply System (WPPSS) sought to build five nuclear power plants in the State of Washington in the early 1970s. Projects 1, 2, and 3 were backed indirectly by the Bonneville Power Administration (BPA), an agency of the Federal Government, through "net billing agreements" with the 88 participants. The participants were largely public utility districts in Washington, Oregon and Idaho. Projects 4 and 5 did not involve the BPA and were backed by the 88 participants directly. Plagued by massive cost overruns, revised power forecasts which indicated all of the power would not be needed, as well as financing difficulties, WPPSS sought to cancel Projects 4 and 5 in 1982. At the time of the termination, some $2,250,000,000 of Project 4 and 5 bonds were outstanding, while $6,125,000,00 of Project 1, 2 and 3 bonds were outstanding. Faced with the prospect of having to pay off $2.25 billion of bonds for which no power would ever be generated, some of the participants went to court in an attempt to invalidate their contracts. On June 15, 1983, the Washington State Supreme Court declared the participants' agreements for Project 4 and 5 bonds were invalid as the participants lacked the authority to enter into the contracts. The agreements for Project 1, 2 and 3 bonds were not affected by this decision. This set the stage for the largest municipal bond default in history. (For a complete discussion of WPPSS see "WPPSS: From Dream to Default" by Howard Gleckman, a special reprint by *The Bond Buyer* of a series of 4 articles that appeared in *Credit Markets* during January, 1984.)

of bonds, is the largest municipal default to date. It is exceeded only on the corporate side by the Penn Central Bankruptcy of 1970, which involved about $3 billion.

While defaults in municipal finance are relatively few and far between, municipal bonds are not risk-free. An important difference between the default of municipal securities and those of corporate issuers is that state and municipal issuers tend to have perpetual existence, which serves to insure that some form of debt remedy is usually accomplished. The market demands repayment. If the entity is going to continue in existence, chances are it will require debt financing at some point in the future, so it cannot escape repayment.

Default by municipal issuers in Canada has been almost nonexistent since the depression years of the 1930s. Many provinces have established municipal authorities, which issue debt for the various municipal entities, such as the Municipal Finance Authority of British Columbia. Others have fiscal oversight boards, which must approve the issuance of debt. The Ontario Municipal Board is an example of such a board. Generally these authorities and boards require five-year capital-debt plans and exercise a degree of fiscal control that is not present in the U.S. municipal market.

Governments and Agencies

In the United States, government securities are those bills, notes, and bonds issued by the U.S. Treasury that represent the marketable segment of the Treasury market. The balance of the privately held U.S. Treasury debt is classified as nonmarketable, that is, it is sold to other governments, agencies, and, as special series, to foreign governments. Table 7A-8 is a summary of the outstanding U.S. Treasury debt and its ownership. Based on the size, strength, and stability of the U.S. government, these bonds are assumed to be free of default risk and are therefore accorded the highest credit standing.

The same immunity from default is not associated with the securities of many other governments outside of the United States because of the political, economic, and foreign-exchange risks involved. In the early 1980s, awareness of the credit risk associated with sovereign governments has been heightened by the concerns regarding the ability of countries such as Poland, Mexico, Argentina, and Brazil to meet the interest and principal payments on their foreign debt.

Investors divide the securities issued by agencies of the U.S. federal government into two categories: (1) those agencies whose securities (principal and interest payments) are guaranteed directly by the federal government; and (2) those agencies that are established by the federal government but whose securities are not guaranteed directly by the federal government. The distinction between guaranteed and nonguaranteed agencies is recognized by professional investors, but is often misunderstood by the casual investor.

TABLE 7A-8. Treasury Debt (Annual Net Increases in Amounts Outstanding) (dollars in billions)

	1979	1980	1981	1982	1983	1984E	1985P	Amount Outstanding 12-31-84E
Outstanding								
Marketables								
Bills	$ 10.9	$ 43.5	$ 28.9	$ 66.8	$ 32.0	$ 30.9	$ 36.2	$ 374.7
Notes	17.6	38.3	53.7	89.7	108.3	116.6	117.5	690.0
Bonds	14.7	10.7	14.5	4.7	29.1	33.4	45.1	167.1
Total Marketable	43.2	92.5	97.1	161.2	169.4	180.9	198.8	1,231.8
Nonmarketables								
Government Account Series	19.9	5.4	11.6	8.8	26.5	30.3	50.3	262.2
State and Local Series	0.3	−0.8	−0.9	2.7	11.1	6.9	5.0	43.6
Foreign Government Series (US$)	−3.8	−6.0	−2.7	−2.0	−2.5	−1.6	−2.5	8.8
Foreign Public Series (Non-US$)	3.1	1.2	−2.4	−2.3	−1.7	0.0	0.0	0.0
Savings Bonds	−1.1	−7.3	−4.4	−0.1	2.7	3.1	3.2	74.0
Guar. and Noninterest-Bearing	−5.7	0.1	0.1	0.0	8.1	−0.1	0.0	9.9
Total Nonmarketable	12.7	−7.4	1.3	7.1	43.2	38.6	56.0	398.5
Total Public and Guar. Debt	55.9	85.0	98.5	168.2	213.5	219.5	254.7	1,630.4
Less Trust Fund Holdings	17.3	5.2	10.8	6.1	26.9	30.3	50.3	266.6
Less Agency Holdings	−0.2	0.4	0.2	1.5	−0.8	1.7	0.0	4.3
Less Federal Reserve Holdings	6.9	3.9	9.6	8.4	12.6	1.7	10.0	153.6
Privately Held Treasury Debt	$ 31.9	$ 75.5	$ 77.8	$152.3	$174.8	$185.9	$194.4	$1,206.0

Ownership

Mutual Savings Banks	$ −0.2	$ 0.8	$ −0.2	$ 0.7	$ 3.8	$ 0.3	$ 2.1	$ 10.2
Savings and Loan Associations	−2.9	5.7	−3.5	7.5	16.8	6.9	1.6	37.2
Credit Unions	0.1	3.2	0.7	8.4	10.0	0.3	2.4	23.7
Life Insurance Companies	0.1	1.0	2.3	8.4	12.1	7.8	8.0	36.4
Property Liability Companies	0.2	1.6	1.4	0.6	3.3	2.7	4.0	20.1
Priv. Noninsured Pension Funds	6.6	13.0	15.9	25.4	10.2	7.9	6.9	109.0
State and Local Retirement Funds	5.3	6.2	6.6	9.3	13.3	17.4	9.0	67.6
Endowments	−0.1	0.2	0.2	0.1	0.2	1.1	0.7	2.1
Money Market Funds	4.2	−2.2	18.0	21.1	−19.8	−8.9	0.1	13.9
Stock Mutual Funds	0.0	0.3	0.9	2.3	0.6	2.6	2.7	8.3
Security Brokers and Dealers	1.9	−1.4	−0.6	0.4	−12.4	17.5	−1.0	9.8
Total Nonbank Finance	15.1	28.5	41.8	84.2	38.0	55.6	36.3	338.3
Commercial Banks	0.3	15.7	2.0	20.0	44.8	7.4	−4.0	186.5
Nonfinancial Corporations	2.8	2.9	3.0	3.1	4.5	−0.1	−0.5	25.2
State and Local Governments	0.3	−0.8	−0.9	2.7	11.1	6.1	5.0	42.9
Foreign Investors	−14.1	10.6	7.0	8.0	16.9	20.2	18.0	186.5
Residual: Households Direct	27.4	18.6	24.8	34.2	59.9	96.6	139.7	426.5
Total Ownership	$ 31.9	$ 75.4	$ 77.8	$152.3	$174.8	$185.9	$194.4	$1,206.0

SOURCE: Salomon Brothers [1985].

Table 7A-9 lists the agencies that are the most active issuers of fixed income securities and provides a brief summary of their purpose and the investment characteristics of their securities (including whether the agencies' bonds are guaranteed by the federal government).

International

Using S&P as an example, the analysis and rating of international securities is divided into two subgroups: private sector and public sector. Private sector international issuers can be defined as banks, utilities, transportation, and industrial companies that are incorporated or domiciled in countries other than the United States. Since many countries have state-owned corporations, the public sector international issuers include corporate issuers and banks that are owned by a sovereign government, the sovereign government itself, non-U.S. municipalities, export credit institutions, and supranational organizations. Typically, the latter are joint ventures in which more than one sovereign government participates, such as the International Bank for Reconstruction and Development (World Bank), the Inter-American Development Bank, and others.

The analysis of international securities requires an assessment of the economic and political risks inherent in the issuer's country of incorporation or domicile. Both the portfolio manager and the analyst must assess the country risks involved. A comprehensive discussion of the analysis of international securities is beyond the scope of this chapter. However, given the increased interest in foreign securities in general and emerging interest in foreign bonds in particular, this subject may well be addressed in future Updates or by other authors.

Money Market Instruments

Money market instruments is a term that is applied to a virtual smorgasboard of short-term or short-maturity securities, that is, securities maturing in one year or less.

Commercial Paper. Commercial paper is the largest and best recognized type of money market instrument, with the exception of U.S. Treasury bills. At the end of 1984, the amount of commercial paper outstanding was $237 billion, while U.S. Treasury bills outstanding totaled $375 billion. Maturities of commercial paper tend to be concentrated within 5 to 90 days. From an analytical standpoint, commercial paper is evaluated in much the same way as any corporate fixed income security. Greater emphasis may be placed on liquidity and financial flexibility because of the short time horizon involved. Commercial paper ratings are provided by Moody's, S&P, Fitch, and Duff and Phelps. This is yet another aspect of commercial paper that is comparable to corporate fixed income securities.

Bankers Acceptances. Bankers acceptances (BAs) are similar in form to commercial paper. They are money market instruments with typical maturity of 270 days or less, and are sold on a discount yield basis. BAs are actually drafts drawn by the customer on its bank, which the bank accepts or agrees to pay at a particular date in the future. Such securities bear the double guarantee of the issuer and the accepting bank; thus BAs are considered a low-risk investment. Nevertheless, the analyst would be well advised to evaluate the creditworthiness of both the issuer and the accepting bank. Salomon Brothers estimated that $75.7 billion of bankers acceptances were outstanding at year-end 1984.

Certificates of Deposit. Certificates of deposit (CDs) are essentially receipts issued by a bank or savings and loan institution for funds deposited at the bank or savings and loan for a specified period at a specified rate of return. Amounts up to $100,000 per account are insured by the Federal Deposit Insurance Corporation (FDIC) or Federal Savings and Loan Insurance Corporation (FSLIC). CDs issued in amounts of $100,000 or more are considered negotiable and trade in the secondary market. From an analytical standpoint, the creditworthiness of the issuing bank or savings and loan should be evaluated since there is no insurance protection beyond the first $100,000 issued by a single issuer to a single account. It should be noted that CDs are also issued with maturities beyond one year and, in those cases, are not considered money market instruments.

For additional information on the broad array of money market instruments, a standard investment text or Stigum [1983] should be consulted.

Other Bonds or Bond Equivalents

Other bonds, or bond equivalents, are terms applied to some of the newer bond forms. This chapter will not attempt to cover all the established and emerging new bond types or forms. Rather, the comments below will be directed at the analyst's considerations regarding a selected few of these other bonds, specifically guaranteed investment contracts, variable rate bonds, and zero coupon bonds.

Guaranteed Investment Contracts. Guaranteed investment contracts (GICs) are annuity-type insurance contracts that are sold to qualified pension plans. The U.S. and Canadian insurance companies issuing the contract may guarantee the interest rate that they will pay on both the original principal and interest (a compound contract) or may limit the guarantee rate to principal only and agree to pay out interest annually (an interest payout or simple interest contract). GICs typically have a term of 2 to 10 years. Like bonds, GICs must be analyzed to assure that the insurance company issuing the contract is capable of paying the interest and principal when due.

TABLE 7A-9. Selected Federal Agency Obligations as of December 31, 1983 [a]

Issuing Agency	Types of Securities	Debt Outstanding ($ billion)	Guarantee	Ownership	Supply Credit To (For)
Banks for Cooperatives[b]	Debentures	$ 6.5	No	Cooperative Associations	Agricultural cooperatives owned and controlled by farmers
Export-Import Bank	Debentures Participations Discount notes	10.0	Yes	U.S. Government	Foreign buyers of American exports
Farmers Home Administration	Insurance contract notes	3.5	Yes	U.S. Government	Small or low-income farmers for real estate, housing, or equipment needs
Federal Home Loan Banks	Bonds Discount notes	54.8	No	Member Thrift Institutions	Member thrift institutions
Federal Housing Administration	Debentures	0.3	Yes	U.S. Government	Home financing sector by insuring loans made by qualified lending institutions
Federal Intermediate Credit Bank[b]	Debentures	20.0	No	Credit Associations	Institutions which in turn make agriculture and livestock loans
Federal Land Banks[b]	Bonds	45.0	No	Federal Land Bank Associations	Federal Land Banks that in turn make long-term first mortgage loans of farm properties

Issuer	Type of Security	Amount	Taxable	Guaranteed by	Purpose
Federal National Mortgage Corporation	Debentures, Discount notes	74.9	No	Thrift Institutions and Private Investors	Home mortgage financing by operating in the secondary mortgage market
Government National Mortgage Corporation	Participations, Pass-throughs	8.3	Yes	U.S. Government	Selected types of home mortgages particularly for low-income housing
Inter-American Development Bank	Bonds	3.5	No	U.S. Government and Foreign Governments	To further economic and social development of its regionally developing member countries
Maritime Administration (Title XI)	Bonds	6.0	Yes	U.S. Government	Loans for the construction of maritime vessels
Small Business Administration	Debentures	10.0	Yes	U.S. Government	Small business loans
Student Loan Marketing Association	Notes	8.0	Yes	U.S. Government	Student loans
Tennesee Valley Authority	Bonds, Discount notes	14.3	No	U.S. Government	The development and utilization of the resources of the Tennessee River Basin
U.S. Postal Service	Bonds	1.5	No	U.S. Government	Operation of U.S. Postal Service
Washington Metro Transit	Transit bonds	1.2	Yes	Federal and State Government	Construction of rail transit system in Washington, D.C. area

SOURCE: Mutual of Omaha Investment Division [1984].

a There are some 200 government guarantee loan programs, of which only a few are of major significance and are listed in this table.

b Since 1977, the debt of these agencies has been consolidated under a single issuer, The Farm Credit Banks.

TABLE 7A-10. Floating Rate Note Issuance (1978–84) (dollars in millions)

Year	AMOUNT BY SECTOR			AMOUNT BY INDEX		
	Domestic	European	Total	T-Bill	LIBOR	Other
1978	$ 200	$ 1,535	$ 1,735	$ 200	$ 1,535	$ —
1979	2,691	3,275	5,966	2,441	3.275	250
1980	300	5,552	5,852	250	5,602	—
1981	85	3,400	3,485	0	3,400	85
1982	1,140	7,165	8,305	1,100	7,165	40
1983	4,485	10,600	15,085	3,985	11,000	100
Jan.–April 1984	1,425	8,000	9,425	800	8,625	0
Total	$10,326	$39,527	$49,853	$8,776	$40,602	$475

SOURCE: The First Boston Corporation [1984].

Floating or Variable Rate Notes. Floating rate notes are referred to often as variable rate or adjustable rate notes, with the distinction being the frequency at which the coupon rate may be changed. Floating rate notes may be changed every six months or less while adjustable rate issues change over time periods longer than six months. Floating rate issues are popular both in the United States and Europe. European issues float with changes in the London Interbank Offered Rate (LIBOR), and U.S. issues float with changes in the U.S. Treasury bill rates. Table 7A-10 illustrates the volume of floating rate notes issued from 1978 through April 1984.

Zero Coupon or Mini-Coupon Bonds. The high interest rates that prevailed in the early 1980s prompted some corporations to offer zero or mini-coupon rates on new issues of bonds. Such securities offered investors above average call protection and reduced reinvestment risk in the event that interest rates declined. The increased corporate issuance resulted from the low coupon or current interest cost to the issuer, and the increased investor acceptance resulted because little or none of the return depended on interest-on-interest. The corporation was thus able to borrow at yield levels below the going market.

In the United States, original issue discount bonds are not eligible for capital gains treatment of the discount. Thus, their appeal has been limited to nontaxable investors, such as pension funds, endowment funds, Keogh Retirement Plans, and Individual Retirement Accounts (IRAs).

Junk Bonds. The term *junk bonds* covers a wide spectrum of primarily corporate bonds and includes all bonds rated Ba or lower. Although the term is applied broadly, it is becoming popular to differentiate between "true" junk bonds and high yield bonds. "True" junk bonds are issued by companies whose quality ratings have fallen because of financial troubles. For example, International Harvester's bond rating has declined from A in 1980 to Ccc as of mid-1985. High yield bonds are issued by companies that the common stock analyst would describe as emerging companies, that is, relatively new companies that have not yet achieved "investment grade" (Baa or above) quality status for their bonds by the rating agencies, but are considered by analysts to offer the potential for upgrading as the companies' prospects for above average growth and profitability are achieved. Analysts approach these high yield bonds in much the same way that they analyze stocks, spending more time on the fundamentals than they would spend on investment grade bonds or bonds with higher quality ratings.

Interest in junk and/or high yield bonds is increasing because investors consider this sector of the market to be relatively "inefficient" and to offer the opportunity for above average returns relative to higher rated issues. Dean Witter estimated the value of all low grade bonds at $10 billion as of the end of 1983. New issues of high yield bonds are gaining increasing acceptance among bond investors who are willing to accept the higher risks associated with such bonds. In addition, a growing number of junk bond portfolios are being established on the premise that the high unsystematic risk of such bonds can be mitigated within a broadly diversified portfolio. Unlike common stock portfolios, broad diversification of a bond portfolio generally requires a substantial investment since a "round lot" for bonds is at least $100,000. It should be noted that Altman [1985] has calculated that the average annual default rate in low-rated, nonconvertible bonds was 1.60 percent between 1974 and 1984. This contrasts with a much lower rate of 0.08 percent for the total corporate debt universe over the same time period.

The latest and perhaps the most controversial development is the use of junk bonds to finance the takeover of corporations through a leveraged buyout (LBO). Most of the purchase price paid for the takeover company is borrowed from lenders such as banks, insurance companies, and pension funds, largely via private placement issues, through the issuance of notes, debentures and (in some cases) preferred stocks. As a result of such borrowings, the capitalization and coverage ratios of the company being bought out often falls into the category of Ba or lower rated bonds. The assumption of LBOs is that the interest, dividends, and principal payments are expected to be paid out of a more efficient operation and from the sale of certain of the assets of the acquired company. In mid-1985, several major takeovers were unfolding and junk bond financing was being considered or arranged.

Mortgages

The mortgage markets in the United States are receiving increased attention from traditional bond investors, especially pension funds. At year-end 1984, Salomon Brothers estimated that privately held mortgages totaled approximately $1.5 trillion (see Table 7A-11). On this basis, mortgages represent the second largest segment of the fixed income markets behind privately held U.S. Treasury and federal agency debt, which Salomon Brothers estimated at $1.7 trillion. If privately held mortgage securities are included, the total mortgage market rivals the federal debt market in size.

TABLE 7A-11. Private Participation in Mortgage Market ($ Billions)

	1979	1980	1981	1982	1983	1984E	1985P	Amount Outstanding 12-31-84E
Privately held mortgages	$113.1	$ 84.2	$ 73.7	$ 15.9	$ 83.7	$148.5	$136.4	$1,485.5
Privately held mortgage securities	23.1	19.2	15.0	49.5	66.4	37.7	55.8	283.7
Total	$136.2	$103.4	$ 88.7	$ 65.4	$150.1	$186.2	$192.2	$1,769.2

SOURCE: Salomon Brothers [1985].

The analysis of mortgages requires the use of analytical techniques that are similar in concept to bond analysis but unique in their application to the mortgage market. The major originators or direct purchasers of mortgages typically have a specialized staff of mortgage loan analysts or, as they are sometimes described, underwriters. A comprehensive treatment of the subject of mortgage analysis is beyond the scope of this summary.

Mortgage Securities. A mortgage security is a relatively new fixed income instrument that is gaining wide acceptance. In effect, these bonds, in three forms, represent the security of the traditional mortgage markets. Packaging mortgages in the form of a bond security represents a major breakthrough and innovation in the fixed income markets. The historical mortgage market limitations on marketability, regionalization, liquidity, and so on are reduced greatly, if not eliminated, through mortgage securities.

Table 7A-12 reflects the current size and growth of mortgage securities (mortgage pool holdings) from the late 1970s. As of year-end 1984, the total amount oustanding of mortgage pool holdings exceeded $283 billion. The net increase in outstanding mortgage pool holdings indicates the rapid growth through 1984. Salomon's estimate of a net increase of $55.8 billion in 1985 reflects a sharp increase from the 1984 estimate of $37.7 billion.

In mid-1985, the three most popular forms of mortgage securities were: (1) mortgage backed or mortgage collateralized bonds, (2) mortgage pass-through certificates, and (3) mortgage pay-through bonds.

One characteristic of mortgage securities is that in most cases the final maturity is uncertain because the underlying mortgages permit the borrower to prepay principal. Thus, the expected return on such securities can only be estimated. While certain conventional guidelines have been established, experience with mortgage securities has shown that historical repayment experience must be correlated to the current interest rate environment. Mortgagees will accelerate prepayment of, or refinance, high interest rate mortgages when interest rates decline. Conversely, prepayments of lower interest rate mortgages will moderate when interest rates are rising. To a certain extent, the resale or turnover of real estate, especially residential property, is related to the level of interest rates, with the turnover rate slowing at higher interest rate levels.

Mortgage Backed or Mortgage Collateralized Bonds. As the name implies, mortgages are used as collateral for these bonds. The issuer owns the collateral and receives the cash flow from these mortgages unless there should be a default on the bonds. In that case, the trustee for the bondholders can enforce the bondholders' interest in the mortgages and sell the collateral to redeem the outstanding bonds and pay all interest that is due. For the analyst, the key considerations, as spelled out by S&P, are: (1) the quality of the collateral, (2) the quantity of the collateral, and (3) the general creditworthiness of the issuer.

TABLE 7A-12. Real Estate Mortgages and Factors in the Housing Market, 1979–1985 (Annual Net Increase in Amounts Outstanding) (dollars in billions)

	1979	1980	1981	1982	1983	1984E	1985P	Amount Outstanding 12-31-84E
Outstanding Mortgages								
1–4 Family	$120.0	$ 96.7	$ 76.0	$ 52.5	$108.7	$136.8	$146.9	$1,351.2
Multifamily	7.7	8.7	4.0	5.4	8.3	18.3	18.7	167.2
Commercial	24.0	20.1	24.2	23.7	47.4	50.3	48.4	399.7
Farm	11.8	9.3	9.7	5.0	2.9	2.9	2.8	112.5
Total Mortgages	163.5	134.9	113.9	86.5	167.2	208.3	216.7	2,030.6
Less:								
Mortgage Pool Holdings	23.1	19.2	15.0	49.5	66.4	37.7	55.8	283.7
Federal Agency Holdings	21.0	21.6	17.5	16.2	11.3	13.0	14.4	200.5
State and Local Housing Agencies	6.3	9.9	7.6	4.9	5.9	9.1	10.0	60.9
Privately Held Mortgages	$113.1	$ 84.2	$ 73.7	$ 15.9	$ 83.7	$148.5	$136.4	$1,485.5

Private Ownership

Mutual Savings Banks	$ 3.6	$ 0.6	$ −0.4	$ −2.6	$ 3.3	$ 13.8	$ 10.7	$ 111.2
Savings and Loan Associations	44.0	28.3	18.0	−23.6	45.8	76.3	77.6	604.3
Credit Unions	0.6	0.5	0.5	0.5	0.5	0.5	0.5	6.5
Life Insurance Companies	12.6	12.3	6.7	4.2	9.6	9.4	9.6	161.0
Private Noninsured Pension Funds	0.3	0.6	0.1	0.4	1.1	0.6	0.8	5.8
State and Local Retirement Funds	1.0	1.3	1.8	1.3	0.8	1.0	1.0	15.8
Endowments	0.2	0.0	0.1	0.1	0.1	0.1	0.1	1.7
Real Estate Investment Trusts	0.0	−0.1	−0.5	0.1	0.0	0.1	0.2	2.1
Mortgage Corporations	0.8	0.6	2.9	1.1	1.4	1.2	1.4	19.0
Total Nonbank Finance	63.2	44.0	29.2	−18.5	62.6	102.8	101.7	927.2
Commercial Banks	30.7	18.1	21.4	15.0	29.4	40.7	38.7	370.9
Residual: Households Direct	19.2	22.1	23.1	19.4	−8.2	5.0	−4.0	187.4
Total Private Ownership	$113.1	$ 84.2	$ 73.7	$ 15.9	$ 83.7	$148.5	$136.4	$1,485.5

SOURCE: Salomon Brothers [1985].

Mortgage Pass-Through Certificates. These certificates represent an ownership interest in a pool of mortgages. The cash flow resulting from these mortgages passes through from the mortgagees to the certificate holders in amounts sufficient to repay principal and interest on the certificates. The issuer's only responsibility is to service the mortgages as an intermediary. The certificates are not the obligation of the issuer and thus, there is generally some form of mortgage insurance or federal agency guarantee. In fact, agencies of the federal government are the major issuers of pass-through securities.

Again using S&P as a guide, the analyst should focus on:

1. The quality of the loan pool and the amount of loss coverage (insurance against default).
2. The quality of the mortgage insurer or entity providing the coverage.
3. The cash advance capability of the servicing agent issuing the certificates.

Mortgage Pay-Through Bonds. Created in the early 1980s, pay-throughs represent a new financing instrument that is gaining acceptance rapidly. With a pay-through bond, the cash flow generated from the mortgage pool being used as collateral is dedicated to bond repayment. Pay-throughs depend on the cash flow of the collateral rather than the market value of the collateral, whereas mortgage-backed securities are protected by the marketability (ability to sell and realize the market value) of the collateral. Unlike pass-throughs, the collateral for pay-throughs is older, more mature pools of lower yielding mortgages which are owned by thrift institutions, homebuilders, or mortgage bankers. By dedicating a pool of these lower yielding mortgage holdings, the issuer is in effect raising cash without having to sell the underlying mortgage collateral and realize a loss. The book loss is a result of the rise in interest rates. Because lower yielding mortgages are used, pay-through pools are over-collateralized in terms of the par or maturing value of the mortgages. In effect, the amount of bonds that can be supported by a collateral pool is equal to the present value of the collateral pool when discounted at the effective yield on the pay-through bonds being issued.

The mortgage collateral pool can be designed and structured to accommodate any desired bond repayment schedule as long as the collateral cash flow is sufficient to fund the bond payment. Thus, some of these securities are described as collateralized mortgage obligations (CMOs) because the pay-through financings are structured so as to provide investors with the opportunity to participate in the short-term, intermediate-term or longer-term segments of the underlying cash flow stream.

For the analyst, S&P identifies four key factors in analyzing these mortgage pay-through securities:

1. The credit risk inherent in the mortgage collateral, which may be offset in whole or in part by cash reserves, letter of credit, mortgage insurance, or overcollateralization on a present value basis.
2. The reinvestment rate risk on mortgage prepayments and foreclosure recoveries.

3. The collateral cash flow coverage of scheduled bond payments.
4. The issuer and the effect of its insolvency on the bonds (the issuer must be bankruptcy proof).

The fourth factor is important but protection can be provided if the corporation issuing the securities establishes a single-purpose corporation to hold the collateral and issue the bonds. The bondholder is thus protected from the potential bankruptcy of the builder/developer that owned the mortgages.

Combination Securities

The term combination fixed income securities is used in this chapter to describe some old and new securities that have traditional fixed income security characteristics but also provide the investor an option that has a value. The nature and variety of these options attached to fixed income securities is increasing so rapidly that this chapter will cite only one brief example rather than attempt to provide an exhaustive inventory.

Convertible Securities. The oldest and most widely recognized combination securities are those bonds or preferred stocks issued by corporations (publicly traded or privately held) that provide the holder with the option of converting into a specific number of shares of common stock during a specified period at a specified price. Generally, the common stock into which the fixed income securities are convertible is that of the issuer. In those cases, the analysis of these convertible securities has a single focus, the issuer. However, while still an exception, it is becoming more common for the conversion privilege to apply not to the issuer's stock but rather the stock of another (related or nonrelated) company that the issuer holds as an investment. In those cases, the analysis must focus on both the issuer of the fixed income securities and also the corporation whose stock actually would be received upon conversion.

From an analytical standpoint, convertible securities are generally considered as deferred common stock, making them essentially common stock equivalents. Thus, the equity analyst typically is responsible for the analysis of convertible securities. The fixed income analyst may be consulted with regard to the terms of the bonds. In large investment organizations, an analyst or group of analysts may specialize in convertible securities.

The discussion of exchangeable securities and other combination securities is beyond the scope of this Update. Such subjects are covered in Atchison-DeMong-Kling [1985], Fabozzi and Pollack [1983], and some of the newer investment texts.

Preferred Stocks

Preferred stock is often considered a hybrid security. It is a form of equity and is classified as such on the balance sheet of a corporation. Because the return from preferred stocks is a contractually specified fixed rate dividend payment, it is analyzed and rated like a bond. Thus, creditworthiness is the primary analytical consideration.

Most of the outstanding preferred stocks have been issued by utilities as a substitute for debt in order to retain some balance between debt and equity in their capital structure. The first adjustable rate preferreds (ARPs) were issued in 1982. ARPs have become a popular financing option for some non-utility corporations, especially bank holding companies. At the end of 1984, there were 114 issues of ARPs with a total book value of over $10.5 billion according to Merrill Lynch [1985]. Like the floating rate bonds discussed earlier, the dividend rate on ARPs can change, with each quarterly dividend payment based on changes in some predetermined index, such as the Treasury bill rate.

In the United States, one of the attractions of preferred stocks is the fact that preferred dividends qualify for the 85 percent dividend exclusion for corporate investors (that is, only 15 percent of the amount of the dividend received is taxed). At the current corporate tax rate of 46 percent, the effective maximum tax rate by a corporate investor on dividends received is 6.9 percent. Preferred stocks can and often do trade at a premium (lower yield) than do the bonds of the same issuer. This occurs when the tax preference feature of the preferred essentially offsets its subordinated position in the capital structure.

The premium paid for preferreds by corporate investors also explains why they are an attractive form of financing for corporations with low marginal tax rates. For those corporations, the penalty of using preferred stock (whose dividends are paid out of after-tax income) rather than bonds (whose interest payments are paid out of before-tax income) is minimized. Low marginal tax rates may result from tax credits, depreciation tax benefits, loss carry forwards, and so on. One of the reasons that bank holding companies issued preferred stock in the early 1980s was to take advantage of their low marginal tax position and maintain a conservative or acceptable debt to equity ratio.

In 1984, several companies issued convertible exchangeable preferred stock which provides the issuer the option to exchange the convertible preferred for convertible subordinated debentures after some specified time period. Such exchangeable issues provide the issuer tax planning and capital structure flexibility.

TYPES AND CHARACTERISTICS OF FIXED INCOME MARKETS

The analyst must also have a thorough understanding of fixed income markets. Even though some larger institutions have a trading department, the analyst should be familiar with the sources of investment alternatives within the context of new issue and secondary markets.

The New York Stock Exchange (NYSE) and the Dow Jones Industrial Average symbolize the stock market in America. Television and radio news broadcasts as well as newspapers and periodicals feature the movements in the stock market, with pictures of floor trading on the NYSE and reference to the Dow Jones Industrial Average, S&P's 400 Stock Index, NYSE Index, or some other indicator of the trend of the equities market.

The bond market, despite its size and importance, does not have similar symbols that are recognized by the public. In fact, the fixed income markets, because of their size and diversity, remain a bit of a mystery to many investors as well as to the public at large. Institutional investors use as indexes of bond market performance the indexes compiled by Salomon Brothers, Inc. and Shearson Lehman Brothers, Inc. The Shearson Lehman indexes are referenced in Chapter 9A of this Update.

The bond markets can be classified and compared in several different ways: primary or new issue markets versus secondary markets, public issue markets versus private placement markets, and domestic fixed income securities versus foreign fixed income securities markets. The following comments are intended to provide an overview of the fixed income markets.

New Issue Market

The size and diversity of the public market for net new issues of fixed income securities, including mortgages and preferred stock, issued in the United States is awesome as indicated previously in Table 7A-2. The net increase in total credit projected by Salomon Brothers [1985] for 1985 was $796.7 billion, including $274 billion of short-term borrowings (loans) by business and households combined, which were to be provided by the banking and finance industry.

New issues are typically underwritten by investment bankers, or primary dealers in the case of U.S. Treasury and Federal Agency issues who acquire the total issue from the issuer. The underwriters, on their own or through a selling group of participating investment brokerage firms, sell the issue to interested investors.

Secondary Market

At the end of 1984, the amount of fixed income securities outstanding (excluding short-term bank loans) was estimated by Salomon Brothers at $4.4 trillion. Although this could be considered the size of the secondary market, a substantial percentage of outstanding fixed income securities were purchased with the intention to hold to maturity. It is estimated that a very large percentage of the activity in the secondary market results from the trading in U.S. Treasury, federal agency, and approximately 100 of the largest corporate issues that are outstanding. Thus, it is difficult to estimate the size of the total secondary market for fixed income securities.

The secondary market for bonds has three segments: (1) the exchange (auction) market, (2) the over-the-counter (dealer) market, and (3) direct (investor to investor) markets. Of the three, the dealer market accounts for almost all of the total secondary market volume in bonds. Although the NYSE has over 3,000 bonds listed, typical trading daily volume averaged only about $25 million in 1980. The American Stock Exchange also has listed bond trading but daily volume averages about $2 million. Both exchanges do serve a role in handling small trades of 1 to 100 bonds. Investor-to-investor trading is possible and does occur. From a practical standpoint, a dealer will typically be asked to serve as a middleman in these trades to authenticate them, that is, lend assurance that the value agreed upon is representative of the market at that time and that the transaction is being consummated on an arm's-length basis.

Since the late 1960s, a secondary market in private placement securities has developed and is now growing rapidly. This is largely an over-the-counter market with a small but growing number of dealers servicing this specialized segment. The development of this secondary market has added a liquidity dimension to the private placement market.

Unlike bonds, preferred stocks are traded actively on both the exchange (especially the NYSE) and in dealer markets. However, most preferreds trade relatively infrequently on low volume, many on less than a daily basis. Again, certain dealers specialize in trading preferreds.

Foreign Fixed Income Securities Markets

The market for foreign bonds can be divided into U.S. pay (dollar denominated) and foreign currency denominated issues. The analyst should be aware of such markets but the subject is beyond the scope of this Supplement. The reader is directed to Fabozzi and Pollack [1983] for a comprehensive discussion of these markets.

SUMMARY

The research process for fixed income securities is similar to that for equities. However, the objective of controlling risk dominates the analysis of fixed income securities, and thus can be described as a negative art. Rating agencies provide a source of credit analysis for fixed income investors. In fact, some individual investors and portfolio managers substitute these ratings for their own analysis. Larger institutional investors, in general, and insurance companies, in particular, tend to do their own analysis and some even have their own internal ratings.

The increased volatility of interest rates and general business conditions has generated substantial changes in both the bond and mortgage markets. Investors require and demand a greater variety of fixed income alternatives in an attempt to (1) retain the benefits of the certainty of payment, (2) diversify more broadly by coupon and maturity (duration) to offset the higher level of systematic risk caused by high and volatile interest rates that in turn have resulted from the inflation prone character of the United States economy, and (3) be assured that portfolio unsystematic risk has been eliminated or severely minimized.

FURTHER READING

The authors and the Institute of Chartered Financial Analysts gratefully acknowledge the work of Dr. Richard W. Stolz of Arizona State University in assembling and annotating much of the bibliography for this chapter.

Most textbooks on the general subject of investments devote at least a chapter to the types and characteristics of fixed income securities and fixed income markets, including Fischer and Jordan [1983], Francis [1980], Garbade [1982], Gitman and Joehnk [1984], Graham, Dodd and Cottle [1962], Jacob and Pettit [1984], Jensen and Smith [1984], Jones [1985], Khoury [1983], Phillips and Ritchie [1983], Radcliffe [1982], Reilly [1985], and Sharpe [1985].

For corporate securities, Standard and Poor's *Credit Overview* [1982] is especially useful for defining the types and characteristics of fixed income securities including mortgage backed securities.

For municipal securities, Standard and Poor's *Credit Overview-Municipal Ratings* [1983] and Zabozzi, Feldstein, Pollack, and Zarb [1983] offer the most definitive background information.

For money market instruments, Stigum's books [1982 and 1983] are the most useful and comprehensive source of background information.

Because mortgage-type securities have become a significant part of the fixed income market in the 1970s and early 1980s, much of the reference material is in the form of journal articles, seminar proceedings and the research material of investment banking firms such as Salomon Brothers and First Boston Corporation.

In the area of foreign securities, much has been written about foreign common stocks but the material regarding foreign bonds is limited. Again journal articles and especially the work of Hanna at Salomon Brothers represent important sources of background information.

BIBLIOGRAPHY

Altman, Edward I., *Corporate Financial Distress,* New York: John Wiley & Sons, 1983.

————, **and Scott Nammacher,** "The Default Rate Experienced on High Yield Corporate Debt," Morgan Stanley & Co., Incorporated, 1985.

Atchison, Michael D., Richard F. DeMong and John L. Kling, "New Financial Instruments: A Descriptive Guide," Financial Analysts Research Foundation, 1985.

Ayers, Herbert F. and John Y. Barry, "The Equilibrium Yield Curve for Government Securities," *Financial Analysts Journal,* May/June 1979.

Bank of Canada, *Bank of Canada Review,* 1985.

Berlin, Howard, *The Dow Jones-Irwin Guide to Buying and Selling Treasury Securities,* Homewood, Il.: Dow Jones-Irwin, 1982.

Bierman, Harold, Jr., "Convertible Bonds as Investments," *Financial Analysis Journal,* March/April 1980.

Braswell, R. C., W. J. Reinhart, and J. R. Hasselback, "The Tax Treatment of Municipal Discount Bonds: Correction of a Fallacy," *Financial Management,* Spring 1982.

Cohen, J., E. Zinbarg, and A. Ziekel, *Investment Analysis and Portfolio Management,* 4th Ed., Homewood, Il.: Richard D. Irwin, 1982.

Controller General of the U.S., "Trends and Changes in the Municipal Bond Market as They Relate to Financing State and Local Infrastructure," GAO/PAD-83-46, September 12, 1983.

Darst, David, *The Handbook of Bond and Money Markets,* New York: McGraw-Hill Book Co., 1983.

Fabozzi, Frank, J., ed., *Readings in Investment Management,* Homewood, Il.: Dow Jones-Irwin, 1983.

Fabozzi, Frank, J., Sylvan G. Feldstein, Irwin M. Pollack and Frank G. Zarb, eds., *The Municipal Bond Handbook I,* Homewood, Il.: Dow Jones-Irwin, 1983.

———, ———, ———, and ———, eds. *The Municipal Bond Handbook II,* Homewood, Il.: Dow Jones-Irwin, 1983.

———, **and Irwin M. Pollack, eds.** *The Handbook of Fixed Income Securities,* Homewood, Il.: Dow Jones-Irwin, 1983.

Feldstein, Sylvan G., *The Dow Jones-Irwin Guide to Municipal Bonds,* Homewood, Il.: Dow Jones-Irwin, 1985.

First Boston Corporation, "Bond Market Year-End Review," 1983.

———, "Floating Rate Notes: A Review of Product Development," April 1984.

Fischer, Donald E. and Ronald J. Jordan, *Security Analysis and Portfolio Management,* 3rd Ed., Englewood Cliffs, N.J.: Prentice-Hall, 1983.

Francis, Jack Clark, *Investments,* 3rd Ed., New York: McGraw-Hill, 1980.

Fred, F. and G. Brown, "Medium-Term Note Programs—An Introduction to GMAC Shelf Paper," Salomon Brothers, January 1984.

Francis, Jack Clark, D. E. Farrar, and C. Lee, eds., *Readings in Investments,* New York: McGraw-Hill, 1980.

Garbade, Kenneth D., *Securities Markets,* New York: McGraw-Hill, 1982.

Gitman, Lawrence J. and Michael D. Joehnk, *Fundamentals of Investing,* 2nd Ed., New York: Harper & Row, 1984.

Gleckman, Howard, "WPPSS: From Dream to Default," *The Bond Buyer,* January, 1984.

Graham, Benjamin C., David Dodd and Sidney Cottle, *Security Analysis,* 4th Ed., New York: McGraw-Hill, 1962.

Gross, William H., "Coupon Valuation and Interest Rate Cycles," *Financial Analysts Journal,* July/August 1979.

Hanna, J., "Eurodollar Floating-Rate Notes: Determinants of Price Behavior," Salomon Brothers, September 1981.

———, **B. Brittain, and T. Hung,** "Values in International Currency and Fixed-Income Markets—May, 1983," Salomon Brothers, May 1983.

———, ———, **and G. Parente,** "The Case for Currency-Hedged Bonds," Salomon Brothers, November 1983.

———, **and V. Gadkari,** "International Investment Ideas—Eurodollar FRNs Plus Options: One Solution to the Portfolio Manager's Dilemma?" Salomon Brothers, October 1983.

——— and ———, "International Investment Ideas—Seven Ways to Play a Weak Dollar Scenario," Salomon Brothers, March 1984.

———, and **T. Hung,** "New Issue Activity in International Bond Markets: 1983–84 Review and Outlook," Salomon Brothers, January 1984.

———, ———, and **G. Parente,** "Eurodollar Zero-Coupon Bonds: Valuation and Trading Techniques," Salomon Brothers, May 1983.

———, ———, and **R. Segal,** "International Investment Ideas—Playing the Euro-dollar-U.S. Treasury Yield Differential," Salomon Brothers, August 1983.

———, and **R. Segal,** "How Big is the World Bond Market?—1983 Update," Salomon Brothers, August 1983.

——— and ———, "International Investment Ideas—New Dimensions in the Eurodollar and CATS Zero-Coupon Bond Markets," Salomon Brothers, September 1983.

———, and **C. Staley,** "International Bond Manual—U.S. Dollar," Salomon Brothers, May 1983.

Hemphil, George H., *The Postwar Quality of State and Local Debt,* National Bureau of Economic Research, 1971.

Inman, Robert P., "Anatomy of a Fiscal Crisis," *Business Review,* Federal Reserve Bank of Philadelphia, September/October, 1983.

Institute of Chartered Financial Analysts, "New Developments in Mortgage-Backed Securities," Homewood, Il.: Dow Jones-Irwin, 1985.

———, *CFA Readings in Fixed Income Securities Analysis,* Charlottesville, Va.: The Institute of Chartered Financial Analysts, 1985.

Jacob, Nancy L. and R. Richardson Pettit, *Investments,* Homewood, Il.: Richard D. Irwin, 1984.

Jensen, Michael and Clifford Smith, eds., *The Modern Theory of Corporate Finance,* New York: McGraw-Hill, 1984.

Johnson, R. Stafford and David Loy, "A Note on the Implications of Corporate Bond Diversifications," unpublished paper, Xavier University, Cincinnati, 1984.

Jones, Charles P., *Investments: Analysis and Management,* New York: John Wiley & Sons, 1985.

Khoury, Sarkis, J., *Investment Management,* New York: Macmillan, 1983.

Kinney, James and R. T. Garigan, ed., *The Handbook of Mortgage Banking,* Homewood, Il.: Dow Jones-Irwin, 1984.

Kolb, Robert W., *Interest Rate Futures: A Comprehensive Introduction,* Dame, 1982.

Lamb, Robert and Stephen P. Rappaport, *Municipal Bonds: The Comprehensive Review of Tax Exempt and Public Finance,* New York: McGraw-Hill, 1980.

Levy, Haim, "The Yield Curve and Expected Inflation," *Financial Analysts Journal,* November/December 1982.

Loosingian, Allan M., *Interest Rate Futures,* Homewood, Il.: Dow Jones, 1980.

Merrill Lynch, Pierce, Fenner, Smith, Inc., "A Review of Adjustable Rate Preferred Stocks," Jan. 1985.

Moody's Investors Service, *Pitfalls in Issuing Municipal Securities,* 1982.

Mysak, Joe, "Insured Bonds Make Up 23% of First Half's Tax-Free Issues," *The Bond Buyer,* July 19, 1984.

Parente, G., "An Anatomy of the Eurodollar Floating-Rate Note Market," Salomon Brothers, March 1984.

Phillips, Herbert E., and John C. Ritchie, *Investment Analysis and Portfolio Selection,* South-Western, 1983.

Post, Lawrence A., "Yield to Early Maturity," *Financial Analysts Journal,* November/December 1973.

Radcliffe, Robert C., *Investment: Concepts, Analysis, and Strategy,* Glenview, Il.: Scott, Foresman and Company, 1982.

Reilly, Frank K., *Investment Analysis and Portfolio Management,* 2nd Ed., Hinsdale, Il.: Dryden Press, 1985.

Rowland, Mary, "The Analyst as a Sleuth," *Institutional Investor,* February 1984.

Salomon Brothers Inc., "Prospects for Financial Markets," 1984 and 1985.

Sharpe, William F., *Investments,* 3rd Ed., Englewood Cliffs, N.J.: Prentice-Hall, 1985.

Sherwood, Hugh, *How to Invest in Bonds,* Rev. Ed., New York: McGraw-Hill, 1983.

Soldofsky, Robert, "The Risk-Return Performance of Convertibles," *Journal of Portfolio Management,* Winter 1981.

Sorensen, Eric, and James Wert, "A New Tool for Estimating New Issue Bond Yields," *Journal of Portfolio Management,* Spring 1981.

Standard and Poor's Corporation, *Credit Overview,* 1982.

————, *Credit Overview—Municipal Ratings,* 1983.

Standard and Poor's Ratings Guide, New York: McGraw-Hill, 1979.

Stigum, Marcia, *The Money Market,* Rev. Ed., Homewood, Il.: Dow Jones-Irwin, 1983.

————, *Money Market Calculations: Yields, Break-Evens and Arbitrage,* Homewood, Il.: Dow Jones-Irwin, 1982.

Tinic, Seha M. and Richard R. West, *Investing in Securities,* Addison-Wesley, 1979.

Van Horne, James C., *Financial Market Rates and Flows,* 2nd Ed., Englewood Cliffs, N.J.: Prentice-Hall, 1984.

Waldman, M., "The FHLMC Discount CMO," Salomon Brothers, January 1984.

————, "High-Coupon Mortgage Securities as Short-Term Investments," Salomon Brothers, April 1983.

Williams, Arthur, III, "The Bond Market Line: Measuring Risk and Reward," *Journal of Portfolio Management,* Summer 1980.

CHAPTER **7B**

The Fixed Income Analysis Process: Return and Risk Analysis

John L. Maginn, CFA
Marvin D. Andersen, CFA

INTRODUCTION

With the background information provided in Chapter 7A, the analyst has an understanding of fixed income securities and their markets. To evaluate the appropriateness and relative valuation of these fixed income securities, a framework for the analysis of return and risk is provided in this chapter.

The subject of return analysis is treated in two perspectives: the mathematical properties of fixed income securities and the terms of the individual issue or issues being considered by the analyst. Risk analysis is discussed in the classic dimensions of systematic and unsystematic risk. The chapter outlines a step-by-step process for the analysis of two types of fixed income securities: corporate bonds and municipal bonds. It is explained that the process logic is adaptable to all types of fixed income securities. Again, this chapter treats return and risk analysis in a summary form.

VALUATION MODEL FOR FIXED INCOME SECURITIES/MATHEMATICS OF BOND PRICING

The three principal sources of return from fixed income securities are:

1. Coupon or interest payments, either fixed or variable, or dividend payments in the case of preferred stocks.

2. Capital changes, that is, changes in market value resulting from changes in interest rates, or to a much lesser extent, changes in credit quality.
3. Reinvestment returns, that is, over time horizons of greater than two or three years, the interest earned on coupons that are reinvested at some assumed (or experienced) reinvestment rate. The reinvestment return is the key determinant of whether the total realized compound return actually received, over several holding periods for portfolios that reinvest all coupons and interest, will be higher or lower than the yield calculated at the time of the purchase of each security.

As stated previously, the expected return to the investor in money market instruments, bonds, mortgages or preferred stocks can be measured on a total return basis, that is, on income earned plus the change in the price of the investment during the holding period, all relative to price at the beginning of the period. However, there is a third dimension of return for fixed income securities: the reinvestment returns for those portfolios where the coupons (or preferred dividends) received are rolled over or invested in other fixed income instruments. Depending on the time horizon and/or strategy specified for the portfolio, the dominant source of return actually realized over time will vary.

For the passive or buy-and-hold portfolio, the analyst must focus on the safety of principal and continuity of income over a relatively long holding period to the maturity of that investment (nonsinking fund preferred stocks have no stated term or maturity). The passive investor's return can be comprised of both income earned and the difference, if any, between cost and par value. For the passive investor, par value is the ultimate market value. Typically, the income return is the most important aspect for a passive investor since they tend to be income maximizers rather than total return maximizers.

For the typical semiactive portfolio, income will also be the primary determinant of return although such strategies as immunization are based on the timing and amount of both income and principal payments and their present value. These strategies recognize the opportunity for changes in market value and the potential for the realization of capital gains or losses within the investor's holding period. Thus, the change in market value aspect of total return is of significance to the semiactive investor.

Finally, for the actively managed fixed income portfolio, capital, appreciation or depreciation will be a primary determinant of return. The active investor's motivation is to seek a higher total return by trading in an effort to realize capital appreciation, which, for taxable investors, has special added attractiveness. The income component of return is not ignored by such investors. As Fong indicates in Chapter 9A of this Supplement, their objective is to maximize total return, whether it be from capital changes, income, or a combination thereof.

MATHEMATICAL PROPERTIES OF FIXED INCOME RETURNS

To be able to identify or evaluate expected returns, the analyst must understand the mathematics of returns from fixed income securities. In fact, it is not uncommon for a fixed income analyst, especially within a smaller firm, to negotiate and/or trade fixed income securities. Thus, knowledge of the mathematical concepts involved, as well as the formulation and application of yield formulas, is important.

The most widely read discourse on the mathematical properties of fixed income securities is *Inside the Yield Book* that was co-authored by the late Sidney Homer and Martin Leibowitz [1972]. This book was written in the early 1970s coincident with the increasing volatility of interest rates and the emergence of semiactive and active bond portfolio strategies. For a complete treatment of the subject of the mathematics of bonds the reader should refer to *Inside the Yield Book*. The following discussion will provide only an overview of this important subject.

Compound Interest

The concept of interest-on-interest is familiar to most savers and investors. The importance and, more particularly, the potency of earning interest on the reinvested coupon has received increased attention in the high interest rate environment that has characterized the past 15 years from the early 1970s to the mid-1980s. Homer and Leibowitz [1972] describe interest compounding at high rates as one of the most potent growth forces in our investment markets. As indicated previously, it is one of the most, if not the most, important determinant of return for longer term investors in bonds and preferred stocks.

The bond investor is at the mercy of future interest rates for both the market value of his holdings and the rate at which his investment will compound. The uncertainty of future interest rates complicates the analyst's task and suggests that Bernstein's multiscenario approach to forecasting expected returns should be employed (see Chapter 6 of the main volume).

Since the returns, whether income or capital, from any investment will be realized in the future, the concept of the time value of money is central to any evaluation. In fact, the effect of time on both the future value and the present value of expected payments must be considered. One dollar received today is worth more than one dollar received in the future measured on either a future or present value basis, since the dollar received today can be invested and begin earning a return immediately.

Space limitations do not permit a discussion of future value and present value computations. Again, the reader is directed to Homer and Leibowitz [1972] or any mathematics of finance text.

Yield Measures

There are several measures of yield that the analyst could use to determine the income component of the expected return from a fixed income investment. Each of the yield measures will be described briefly. For a more comprehensive discussion of these yield measures, the reader is directed to Homer and Leibowitz [1972].

Current Yield. The current yield relates the annual coupon interest payment to the market price. It does not take into account explicitly the two other sources of return—reinvestment of interest and capital changes. The latter is an important factor when the market price or purchase price is at a premium to par or a discount to par.

Preferred stock yields are calculated on a current yield basis since most preferred stocks do not have a fixed maturity. The exceptions are preferred issues with mandatory sinking funds that, in effect, create an average maturity for the issue.

Yield to Maturity. In addition to coupon, capital appreciation and depreciation is taken into consideration via accretion of discount and amortization of premium, respectively, in the yield to maturity calculation. Reinvestment of interest is also considered, although the calculation implicitly assumes that coupon payments are all reinvested when received at a rate equal to the yield to maturity at the purchase date. Yield to maturity can be thought of as the discount rate that equates the present value of the future cash flow (periodic, usually semiannual, coupon payments plus the redemption value at maturity) to the current market price.

Yield to Discounted Cash Flow. This yield measure is used when there is a mandatory pro rata sinking fund. The yield to discounted cash flow (DCF) is the discount rate that equates the present value of all the future cash flows, periodic coupon payments, and periodic principal (sinking fund) payments to the current market price. The calculation discounts each interest payment and each principal payment. It is the accepted yield measure for secondary market activity in private placements because most private issues have a mandatory pro rata sinking fund that periodically retires each holder's proportionate share of the bonds outstanding. Thus, both interest and principal cash flow streams are predictable and can be accurately discounted back to a present value.

Yield to Call. If a bond can be called prior to maturity, investors will calculate yield in two ways: (1) yield to maturity, assuming all principal is paid at maturity and (2) yield to call, assuming the bond is called at the earliest date and at the call price specified in the indenture. Most investors will use the lower of the two yields in evaluating the attractiveness of an investment because the lower yield represents the minimum potential return.

The yield to call is the discount rate that equates the present value of the cash flows (periodic coupon payments plus the call price that will result if the bond is called) to the market price. The analyst must be aware that yield to call, like yield to maturity, assumes that all coupon payments will be reinvested at a rate equal to the yield to maturity at the purchase date. Furthermore, the yield to call does not reflect how the proceeds will be reinvested after the bond is called. Thus, direct comparison with the yield to maturity is misleading since the time periods are different. Since most bonds are called during periods when interest rates have declined significantly, the reinvestment risk for the investor after the bonds are called is substantial and may adversely affect expected return or total realized return projections.

Total Realized Compound Yield. Since the rate at which coupon payments will be reinvested is uncertain, especially over long holding periods, the analyst can only develop a range of potential returns. The range will be determined by varying the reinvestment rate assumptions. The analyst is thus able to estimate the underlying fully compounded growth or accumulation rate of an investment under varying reinvestment rates. Homer and Leibowitz [1972] describe this measure as the total realized compound yield or return.

Price Volatility

The market value of a bond is influenced by many factors which the analyst must consider to estimate the expected return on a fixed income investment. Premium and discount bonds will change in value due to the passage of time even if market yields do not change. However, the price volatility described below is that associated with changes in market yields. The reader is directed to Homer and Leibowitz [1972] for a more comprehensive discussion.

Relative to Coupon Rate. The volatility of a bond's market price or value increases as the coupon rate decreases, assuming a given maturity and initial yield. This relationship is illustrated in Table 7B-1, which covers coupon rates ranging between 5 and 12 percent and price increases and decreases of 200 basis points (where one basis point equals .01 percent), respectively.

Relative to Maturity. The volatility of a bond's market price increases the longer the period of time until maturity, assuming all other factors are constant. This relationship is illustrated in Table 7B-2, which covers a range of maturities from 1 to 30 years and price increases and decreases of 200 basis points, respectively.

Relative to the Level of the Initial Yield. The volatility of a bond's market price increases the higher the initial yield level, assuming all other factors

TABLE 7B-1. Bond Price Volatility for Bonds Yielding 9 Percent and 20 Years to Maturity

	COUPON RATE							
	5 Percent	6 Percent	7 Percent	8 Percent	9 Percent	10 Percent	11 Percent	12 Percent
Initial price	$63.20	$72.40	$ 81.60	$ 90.80	$100.00	$109.20	$118.40	$127.60
Price if yield changes by:								
−200 bp	78.64	89.32	100.00	110.68	121.36	132.03	142.71	153.39
−100	70.31	80.21	90.10	100.00	109.90	119.79	129.69	139.59
−50	66.61	76.15	85.69	95.23	104.77	114.31	123.85	133.39
−10	63.86	73.13	82.39	91.66	100.93	110.19	119.46	128.73
+10	62.54	71.68	80.82	89.95	99.09	108.22	117.36	126.49
+50	60.03	68.91	77.80	86.68	95.56	104.44	113.32	122.20
+100	57.10	65.68	74.26	82.84	91.42	100.00	108.58	117.16
+200	51.86	59.88	67.91	75.93	83.95	91.98	100.00	108.02
Percentage change in price if yield changes by:								
−200 bp	+34.43%	+23.37%	+22.55%	+21.89%	+21.36%	+20.91%	+20.53%	+20.21%
−100	+11.25	+10.79	+10.42	+10.13	+9.90	+9.70	+9.54	+9.40
−50	+5.40	+5.18	+5.01	+4.88	+4.77	+4.68	+4.60	+4.54
−10	+1.04	+1.01	+0.97	+0.95	+0.93	+0.91	+0.90	+0.89
+10	−1.04	−0.99	−0.96	−0.94	−0.91	−0.90	−0.88	−0.87
+50	−5.02	−4.82	−4.66	−4.54	−4.44	−4.36	−4.29	−4.23
+100	−9.65	−9.28	−9.00	−8.77	−8.58	−8.42	−8.29	−8.18
+200	−17.94	−17.29	−16.78	−16.38	−16.05	−15.77	−15.54	−15.34

SOURCE: Fabozzi and Pollack [1983].

TABLE 7B-2. Bond Price Volatility for 9 Percent Coupon Bonds Selling at Par

			YEARS TO MATURITY				
	1	5	10	15	20	25	30
Initial price	$100.00	$100.00	$100.00	$100.00	$100.00	$100.00	$100.00
Price if yield changes by:							
−200 bp	101.90	108.32	114.21	118.39	121.36	123.46	124.94
−100	100.94	104.06	106.80	108.65	109.90	110.74	111.31
−50	100.47	102.00	103.32	104.19	104.77	105.15	105.40
−10	100.09	100.40	100.65	100.82	100.93	101.00	101.04
+10	99.91	99.61	99.35	99.19	99.09	99.02	98.98
+50	99.53	98.05	96.82	96.04	95.56	95.25	95.06
+100	99.07	96.14	93.77	92.31	91.42	90.87	90.54
+200	98.15	92.46	88.05	85.47	83.95	83.07	82.55
Percentage change if yield changes by:							
−200 bp	+1.90%	+8.32%	+14.21%	+18.39%	+21.36%	+23.46%	+24.94%
−100	+0.94	+4.06	+6.80	+8.65	+9.90	+10.74	+11.31
−50	+0.47	+2.00	+3.32	+4.19	+4.77	+5.15	+5.40
−10	+0.09	+0.40	+0.65	+0.82	+0.93	+1.00	+1.04
+10	−0.09	−0.39	−0.65	−0.81	−0.91	−0.98	−1.02
+50	−0.47	−1.95	−3.18	−3.96	−4.44	−4.75	−4.94
+100	−0.93	−3.86	−6.23	−7.69	−8.58	−9.13	−9.46
+200	−1.85	−7.54	−11.95	−14.53	−16.05	−16.93	−17.45

SOURCE: Fabozzi and Pollack [1983].

TABLE 7B-3. Bond Price Volatility for a 9 Percent Coupon, 20-Year Bond for 25 Percent Increase in Market Yield

Initial Yield	New Yield After 25 Percent Increase	Change in Basis Points	Initial Price	New Price	Percentage Change in Price
4.00%	5.00%	100 bp	168.39	150.21	−10.80%
6.00	7.50	150	134.67	115.41	−14.30
8.00	10.00	200	109.90	91.42	−16.82
10.00	12.50	250	91.42	74.48	−18.53
14.00	17.50	350	66.67	53.12	−20.32

SOURCE: Fabozzi and Pollack [1983].

are constant. This relationship is illustrated in Table 7B-3, which shows the volatility of a bond with a 9 percent coupon and a maturity of 20 years, assuming a 25 percent increase in market yield.

Relative to the Duration of a Bond. Duration is a much better measure of price volatility than is maturity. Maturity only takes into consideration the final payment and not the size and timing of all interest payments in present value terms. Duration is a measure of the weighted average term to maturity and is calculated by stating all cash flows, both interest and principal, in terms of their present value. The duration (or modified duration) of a bond is a measure of the sensitivity of a bond's market price to a change in market yields. For example, the market price of a bond with a duration of 4.62 can be expected to change by approximately 4.62 percent if market yields change by 100 basis points. Because of its sensitivity properties, duration has been used as one measure of the systematic risk of a bond. See the Appendix to Chapter 9A of this Supplement for more on duration and its properties.

Pricing Off a Benchmark. It should be noted that the yield basis upon which a bond is sold or traded is often measured as a spread off of or differential relative to some indicator of the market or benchmark. For example, most U.S. corporate bonds and Federal agency issues are priced off of some average yield spread relationship relative to a U.S. Treasury of comparable coupon, and maturity and/or duration. Federal agency bonds in June 1985 were trading at approximately a 10 to 15 basis point yield spread over the comparable U.S. Treasury bonds, and Aa rated industrial bonds were trading at approximately a 20 to 30 basis points spread. These are exceptionally narrow yield spreads on a historical basis.

Traditionally, private placements have been priced in relationship to comparable public issues. The spread between privates and publics has varied widely. For short periods of time, privates have sold through publics, that is, privates provided less yield than publics, although a positive spread of 25 basis points or more has existed generally. In the 1980s, even the private placement market uses the U.S. Treasury market as a benchmark. In June

1985, A rated or equivalent private placements were trading at approximately a 50 to 70 basis point spread over the comparable U.S. Treasury. Again, these are relatively narrow spreads on a historical basis.

Terms of the Issue

Fixed income securities are a loan, and as such, carry with them a legal obligation to make payments in the future. The terms of this obligation are spelled out in the agreement or indenture that is the actual contract between the issuer and the fixed income security holder. This contract specifies the legal conditions that must be met by the issuer. At this point, the terms of the indenture that relate to the expected return on the securities will be discussed. The risk dimension of the indenture is discussed further on in this chapter.

Timing of Interest and Principal Payments. The frequency or timing of payments of interest and principal by the issuer affects the return because of the time value of money concepts previously discussed. Thus, the analyst must examine the indenture to determine the schedule of interest and principal payments. One of the attractions of mortgages is the fact that typically they require monthly payment of interest and principal. Bonds typically pay interest semiannually and principal payments may be made on a semiannual or annual basis (if there is a sinking fund) or at maturity. Investors prefer payments to be more frequent or to begin sooner since this gives them more time to reinvest the payments and earn interest-on-interest. Obviously, in periods of declining interest rates, less frequent principal payments would be desirable since under those conditions reinvestment rates would be lower than the yield of purchase.

Sinking Funds. The principal payments for bonds can vary. Most U.S. government, agency, and public corporate bonds have a single payment of principal at maturity and are called *bullets* or *term bonds.* Other bonds may have sinking funds to which periodic payments are made for the ultimate repayment of bond principal; they are often called *sinkers.* Private placements of corporate bonds typically have mandatory pro rata sinking funds, although many are also issued as bullets. Moreover, the sinking funds on private placements tend to be much larger and are often *full sinkers,* that is, most or all entire issue is retired on a proportional basis prior to maturity. Public corporate bonds with maturities greater than ten years may also have a sinking fund, but typically such sinkers are not pro rata and do not retire a significant portion of the outstanding issue prior to maturity except by random call or market purchase by the fund trustee.

Municipal bonds are issued as either term (bullet) bonds or serial bonds, with consecutive chronological maturities typically from one to ten or one to twenty years or longer. Serials and sinkers accomplish a similar objective for the issuer—periodic retirement of a portion of the issue. For the lender or investor, they are quite different. Serials allow the investor to pick and purchase specific maturities. The investor who purchases a pro rata sinking fund issue, in effect, purchases a series of maturities, and must consider the weighted average life in evaluating the time period of his investment. With non-pro rata sinkers, it is not possible to determine the average life since it is uncertain when each of the outstanding bonds will be called.

The principal payments on mortgages can also vary. Residential mortgages and some nonresidential (for example, commercial and industrial) mortgages pay both interest and principal on a monthly basis. The proportions will vary under a schedule of level (equal) payments with interest comprising the major portion of the payment in the early years and principal accounting for a steadily greater portion of the payment over the life of the mortgage. In recent years, bullet maturities for nonresidential mortgages have become more common, especially for loans with a maturity of five to ten years. Also, commercial and industrial mortgage loans are being made with payments based on a 20 to 30 year amortization schedule but with a balloon or large final payment of all outstanding principal at the end of some shorter period, such as 5 years or 10 years. This is a well established method of shortening the maturity of a mortgage.

Finally, the analyst must determine from the indenture provisions or mortgage agreement what rights the issuer of a bond or mortgage has to accelerate or make unscheduled sinking fund payments. Such payments further increase the uncertainty as to the average life and/or final maturity of the issue and, as a result, prepayment penalties are often made a part of the indenture.

Preferred stocks issued prior to the mid-1970s typically did not have sinking funds. Since that time, it has become common for preferred stock issues to provide for periodic sinking fund payments designed to retire the entire issue over periods of time ranging from as short as five years to as long as 40 years.

Refunding or Call Provisions. The analyst should be aware of call and refunding provisions that provide the issuer the opportunity to retire all or any part of the issue prior to maturity or prior to all or any part of the schedule of sinking fund payments. There are three types of call provisions:

1. The bonds can be callable at any time, meaning that the issuer can give notice of 30 to 60 days and retire any or all of the issue, thus providing the investor no protection.
2. The bonds can be noncallable for life, meaning that the issuer cannot call the issue before maturity under any circumstances.
3. The bonds can be noncallable for a specified period (also known as a deferred call) after which the issuer is free to call the issue.

In the third case, the analyst should be aware that an issuer is typically required to pay a call premium. The premium over par may vary but can be as high as the amount of the coupon at the beginning of the call period. Typically, the premium declines to zero one or two years prior to or at the final maturity date of the issue.

The call provision and refunding provision are often confused by inexperienced analysts or investors. A noncallable bond provides more protection to the investor than does a bond with a nonrefundable provision. The refunding provision only controls one means of retiring an outstanding issue, which is the retirement of an issue from the proceeds of a new issue of bonds at a lower coupon. In recent years, uninformed or unsuspecting investors experienced the refunding of high coupon bonds from the proceeds of new issues of preferred stock or common stock or even proceeds from the sale of individual assets or whole divisions of the issuer's business. Some electric utilities even have provisions in their indentures that allow deficiencies in the maintenance and replacement fund to be satisfied with property, cash, or bonds. Under just such a provision, Florida Power & Light Company refunded over $63 million of relatively high coupon bonds in 1977 at a special redemption price of $101.65. The bondholders sued the company unsuccessfully.

Why are these provisions important? In simplest terms, because the issuer wants the lowest cost of capital, while the investor wants the highest return on his or her investment. Although circumstances and market conditions may require an issuer to sell bonds when interest rates are relatively high, most issuers are anxious to reduce their cost of capital by paying off high coupon debt as soon as their resources and the indenture provisions of the outstanding issue permit. Conversely, the investor wants to retain the high coupon bonds and protect this attractive return until maturity or for as long as the indenture provisions permit, to forestall reinvesting the proceeds in a lower rate environment thus reducing the return on the amount of funds invested.

Indexed or Adjustable Payments. Another form of indenture provision that has gained popularity over the past decade is a provision for indexed or adjustable payments rather than a fixed coupon amount. Such securities are broadly classified as *floating rate* or *floaters.*

Floating rate issues are obligations with coupon payments that are dependent on future interest rate levels. As was explained in Chapter 7A, most floaters have provisions in their indentures that specify periodic rate adjustments called *resets* that fix the coupon rate at a given spread over the yield to maturity on a predetermined base index. The revised coupon rate remains in effect until the next reset date. Most U.S. floating rate notes have coupons that are adjusted semiannually at a spread above either the three-month (91-day) or six-month (180-day) Treasury bill. Floaters have also been popular in the Eurodollar market where the coupons are adjusted periodically at a spread above the London Interbank Offering Rate (LIBOR).

The basic attraction of floaters to the investor or portfolio manager is the control of principal risk due to interest rate fluctuations. For fixed rate securities, bond prices must adjust to changes in interest rate levels in the marketplace to provide a competitive yield. With a floater, the coupon rate periodically responds to the shift in interest rates thus reducing, but not eliminating, price volatility. The frequency of the resets influences the extent to which a floater reduces price volatility. It should also be noted that changes in quality ratings can affect the spread on floaters or the market's perception of the appropriate spread.

Extendible and Retractable Issues. In Canada, bond investors have been able to invest periodically in issues that are described as extendible or retractable. Extendible issues provide the purchaser of the bond with an option to extend the original maturity, typically by an increment of 5 to 10 years with no change in coupon, thus providing the investor with a hedge against changes in interest rates at the time of the original maturity of the bond. If rates have risen, the holder does not have to extend, while if rates have declined, the holder probably will extend. Retractables, on the other hand, provide the purchasers of the bond with the option to reduce or retract the original maturity of the bond to an earlier date, thus providing the investor with a hedge against rising interest rates. In return for these very attractive options, the issuer is typically able to borrow at below market rates, with the differential reflecting the value that investors impute to such options. In the United States, issuers and underwriters have been reluctant to provide bond investors with comparable options. Certain U.S. issues have been described as extendible, but in almost all cases, the coupon rate is subject to change if the maturity is extended, resulting in what is essentially a floating rate issue.

TAX CONSIDERATIONS

The analyst needs to consider the tax position of the investor and the after tax return on any investment. For a detailed discussion of tax considerations for individual investors see Chapter 5 in the main volume and Chapter 5A in this Supplement.

Nontaxable accounts, such as pension and endowment funds, should avoid municipal bonds in the United States and preferred stocks in the United States and Canada because the returns on these securities are usually only attractive to taxable individual and corporate investors, and even then, only to those investors that have a marginal tax rate in the upper range of the tax brackets. Even the return on discount bonds in the United States historically has reflected the differential between ordinary income tax rates assessed against the interest income and the capital gains tax rate assessed against the difference between cost and par. However, as a result of the 1984 Tax Act, accretion of original issue and secondary market discounts on bonds issued after July 18, 1984 will be taxed as ordinary income.

Tax Characteristics of Fixed Income Securities

As just noted, certain securities are afforded special income tax treatment. The following list is not intended to be complete but rather to identify a few examples of U.S. tax preferenced securities with which most analysts should be familiar.

U.S. Treasury Issues. Interest is taxable by the federal government but not by state or local governments.

Federal Agencies. Interest is taxable by the federal government, but for certain federal agencies is exempt from state and local government income taxes. Examples of the latter include Federal Home Loan Bank and Federal Farm Credit Bank issues.

U.S. Corporate Bonds. Interest is taxable by federal, state and local governments.

U.S. Municipal Bonds. Interest is not taxable by the federal government. Most states exempt interest on municipals domiciled within that state. Most, but not all states tax interest paid on municipal issues that are domiciled outside the state (see Table 7B-4).

TABLE 7B-4. State Income Tax Treatment of Municipal Bond Interest

State	INDIVIDUALS		CORPORATIONS	
	Own State	Other States	Own State	Other States
Alabama	NT	T	NT	T
Alaska	NT	NT	NT	NT
Arizona	NT	T	NT	T
Arkansas	NT	T	NT	T
California				
Franchise Tax	—	—	T	T
Income Tax	NT	T	NT	T
Colorado	NT	T	NT	T
Connecticut	NT	T	T	T
Delaware	NT	T	NT	T
Dist. of Col.	NT	T(1)	NT	T
Florida	NT	NT	T	T
Georgia	NT	T	NT	T
Hawaii	NT	T	NT	T
Idaho	NT	T	NT	T
Illinois	T	T	T	T
Indiana	NT	NT	NT	NT
Iowa	T	T	T	T
Kansas	T	T	T	T
Kentucky	NT	T	NT	T
Louisiana	NT	T	NT	T
Maine	NT	T	NT	NT
Maryland	NT	T	NT	T
Massachusetts	NT	T	T	T
Michigan	NT	T	NT	T

(continued)

TABLE 7B-4. (continued)

	INDIVIDUALS		CORPORATIONS	
State	Own State	Other States	Own State	Other States
Minnesota	NT	T	T	T
Mississippi	NT	T	NT	T
Missouri	NT	T	NT	T
Montana	NT	T	T	T
Nebraska	NT	NT	NT	NT
Nevada	NT	NT	NT	NT
New Hampshire	NT	T	NT	NT
New Jersey	NT	T	T	T
New Mexico	NT	NT	NT	NT
New York	NT	T	T	T
North Carolina	NT	T	NT	T
North Dakota	NT	T	NT	T
Ohio	NT	T	NT	NT
Oklahoma	T	T	T	T
Oregon	NT	T	T	T
Pennsylvania	NT	T	NT	NT
Rhode Island	NT	T	NT	T
South Carolina	NT	T	NT	T
South Dakota	NT	NT	NT	NT
Tennessee	NT	T	T	T
Texas	NT	NT	NT	NT
Utah	NT	NT	T	T
Vermont	NT	NT	NT	NT
Virginia	NT	T	NT	T
Washington	NT	NT	NT	NT
West Virginia	NT	T	NT	T
Wisconsin	T	T	T	T
Wyoming	NT	NT	NT	NT

NT = Not Taxable   (1) = Taxable if purchased after 1991
T = Taxable

This chart was prepared from data supplied by Arthur Andersen & Co. and by Commerce Clearing House. It is based on laws, regulations and rulings in effect as of June, 1984. Since the various laws and administrative interpretations are subject to change, consult your tax adviser for further information.

SOURCE: Mutual of Omaha Insurance Company.

U.S. Preferred Stocks. Dividends are taxable by federal, state and local governments. Corporations that own preferred stocks are allowed to exclude 85 percent of the dividend and must pay tax on only 15 percent of the dividends received. This is known as the *corporate dividend exclusion.* Common stocks receive the same tax treatment for corporate owners.

ANALYSIS OF INTEREST RATE OR SYSTEMATIC RISK

Returns cannot be discussed without also discussing the risk associated with such returns. The investment literature has tended to divide the risk associated with a particular investment into at least two parts:

1. Systematic or market risk
2. Unsystematic risk

For fixed income securities, systematic risk arises from the influence of overall changes on interest rates. Such changes have a twofold effect: (1) capital or market value of principal changes and (2) reinvestment rate changes. Because a change in interest rates can affect returns on all fixed income securities, systematic risk is a pervasive characteristic and the most significant aspect of risk in bond investing. Bonds, mortgages, and preferred stocks tend to be homogeneous, that is, they have far more similarities than differences. Thus, the effects of overall market conditions have a much greater impact on returns. This is in sharp contrast to common stocks or other types of equity investments such as real estate, which tend to be more heterogeneous. Such investments have much more risk specific to the individual security or investment, and the effects of overall market conditions, while important, have a much smaller impact on returns.

This distinction between the relative importance of these two risk factors for fixed income and equity securities is important. It explains the amount of time and effort devoted to common stock analysis. It also explains why so many fixed income investors tend to rely on the rating agencies for all or a major part of the analysis of individual securities.

As explained in Chapter 7A of this Supplement, U.S. Treasury securities are the only ones considered to be default free. Thus, a portfolio of U.S. Treasury securities can be thought of as having only systematic risk, that is, bonds with price and return variation due only to changes in interest rates.

The major problem facing the fixed income analyst in evaluating systematic risk is threefold: (1) estimating changes in the level of interest rates (that is, the *level* of the yield curve); (2) estimating changes in maturity yield spreads (that is, the *shape* of the yield curve); and (3) estimating sector and/or credit quality yield spreads, a difficult task as the following comments will indicate.

Efficiency of the Fixed Income Market

The efficient market hypothesis argues that capital market prices fully reflect all information so that consistently superior performance in return-risk terms on the part of investors is difficult if not largely unattainable. The hypothesis assumes that knowledgeable investors have almost simultaneous access to information and that they react accordingly. Since the bond market is dominated, to an even greater extent than the stock market, by knowledgeable and well-informed investors, it can be described as relatively efficient. It should be noted that the relative efficiency of the bond market varies by sector. Because of a lack of credit and liquidity risk, it is generally accepted that the government market is the most efficient sector. This subject is discussed in more detail in Reilly [1985] and most other standard investment texts. The following comments are necessarily brief.

Covariance of Bond Returns. As already noted, because changes in interest rates have a pervasive effect on the returns on all bonds, the covariance or correlation of individual returns on investment grade bonds of similar coupon and maturity is large and positive.

Security Market Line. The relationship of return and risk is relatively well defined in the bond markets. As might be expected, bond prices are bunched closely along the security market line in those parts or sectors of the market that are characterized by active markets with frequent and sizeable transaction activity in terms of either new issues or secondary market trading or both. Like stocks, undervalued bonds are identified as those falling above the security market line based on expected return and estimated interest rate or systematic risk considerations. Conversely, overvalued bonds are identified as those falling below the line. As just noted, the markets are considered relatively efficient for U.S. Treasury bonds that are actively traded. Thus most active Treasury issues would be expected to be located on or in very close proximity to the security market line.

Determinants of Interest Rates

Typically, although the fixed income analyst may not necessarily be required to forecast interest rates, he should be expected to understand the determinants of interest rates and the basic concepts involved. As mentioned previously, expected returns for fixed income securities are largely a function of the expected trend of interest rates and yield spreads. This subject can only be discussed briefly in the context of this Supplement.

Term Structure of Interest Rates

The *term structure of interest rates,* or more popularly termed, the *yield curve,* reflects the relationship between yield to maturity and term to maturity. According to McEnally [1980], the yield curve can serve the analyst as a basis for: (1) analyzing the returns for different types of bonds and different terms, (2) assessing the consensus expectation of future interest rates, (3) pricing fixed income securities, and (4) swaps between sectors or maturities.

Forecasts of Interest Rates

In determining expected returns, the analyst must make some explicit or implicit judgment about the future trend of interest rates. At least two problems are associated with such forecasts: (1) the forecast error is notoriously high, even among the most respected students of interest rates, and (2) the time period of most forecasts is limited to a few months or a few years. The short length of the forecast period is particularly troublesome because the analyst is dealing with securities that quite often have a duration and maturity that extend well beyond the forecast period. Thus, such forecasts tend to better serve the interests of active portfolio strategies primarily because of their shorter time horizon.

Interest Rate Scenario Analysis

Faced with the prospect of attempting to identify and evaluate expected returns, the fixed income analyst may select a multiscenario approach for interest rates. As mentioned previously, this methodology is explained by Bernstein in Chapter 6 of the main volume. The advantage of the multiscenario approach is that a range of possibilities are posted and evaluated. Probabilities can be applied and adjusted so that the analyst can measure the effect of different interest rate environments on the expected return for a bond or group of alternative bond investments.

ANALYSIS OF FINANCIAL OR UNSYSTEMATIC RISK

Spread Risk and Credit Risk

In Chapter 9 of the main volume, Appendix A provides a series of historical illustrations of the volatility of both interest rates and yield spreads. The analyst must bear in mind that not only the level of rates might change but the intersector relationship (spread) might also change as these graphs illustrate.

If interest rates do not change and the security is held to maturity, the only source of expected risk in nominal terms is default. As mentioned previously, in this sense unsystematic risk is of much less importance for fixed income securities than for stocks. Nevertheless, the analyst must be aware of spread risk, especially yield spreads based on credit risk.

As Fong indicated in Chapter 9 of the main volume, credit analysis is concerned with the assessment of default risk—the probability that the issuer will be unable to meet all contractual obligations fully and in a timely manner. Default risk is important for two reasons: (1) because of the chance of loss of principal and income due to the actual act of default by an issuer of a fixed income security and (2) because of the likelihood of declines in market value on an absolute or relative basis that are precipitated by the increased probability of default. The accepted measure of default risk is typically the issuer's quality rating by one or more of the rating agencies. For publicly issued bonds and preferred stocks, adverse changes in the evaluation of an issuer's creditworthiness are reflected typically via a downgrading of the issuer's quality rating by one or more of the rating agencies. These downgrades can affect the value of the security even though no act of default actually takes place. This is the aspect of unsystematic risk that justifies the role of the credit analyst outside the rating agencies.

A Tale of Two Credits

"News that Caterpillar Tractor Co. (Grant's, July 2, 1984), one of the Street's premier inflation plays, lost 31% more in the third quarter than it had in the year-ago period and that, as the Journal reported, 'further massive cuts are likely to be necessary if (the company) is to post a profit next year,' raises some interesting questions about the nature of risk and the efficiency of markets. As the table shows, the rise of the dollar and the slump of the earth-moving business have taken their toll on Cat's balance sheet. As recently as 1981 (the year of its last profit), the company was covering its interest charges four times over; in the 12 months ended June, it failed to cover them once."

"Not every major American industrial corporation has suffered the Caterpillar disease, as the table shows. Goodyear Tire & Rubber Co., for one, is making money and enhancing its balance sheet, the strength of the dollar notwithstanding. In 1981, it covered its interest expense by less than three times; at midyear 1984, it covered it by more than six times."

Caterpillar Tractor Co.

	1984*	1983	1982	1981	1980	1979
Cash flow/total debt (%)	18.6	8.8	13.9	60.4	69.9	51.5
Total debt/capital (%)	41.2	40.2	42.8	31.9	28.6	31.6
Pretax interest coverage (x)	0.44	(0.62)	(0.45)	4.57	5.60	6.22

Goodyear Tire & Rubber Co.

	1984*	1983	1982	1981	1980	1979
Cash flow/total debt (%)	18.6	8.8	13.9	60.4	69.9	51.5
Total debt/capital (%)	41.2	40.2	42.8	31.9	28.6	31.6
Pretax interest coverage (x)	0.44	(0.62)	(0.45)	4.57	5.60	6.22

* 12 months ended June 30
SOURCES: Moody's, Standard & Poor's, June 10-Q Reports of Caterpillar and Goodyear.

"If for no other reason than Cat is hemorrhaging while Goodyear is profitable, one might expect that the rating agencies and the bond market would have drawn some hard distinctions between the two credits. The distinctions are these. In July, Moody's downgraded the senior debt of Cat from A1 to A2, while reaffirming its confidence in Cat's ability to remain 'a major competitor in world markets.' In September, Moody's upgraded the senior debt of Goodyear from A3 to A1. Thus, the net difference between the companies amounts to one-third of one grade."

"Last week, a corporate bond trader, asked to venture a yield quote for the infrequently traded Caterpillar Tractor 8.60s of 1999, said: 12.45%. Asked for a quote on the equally scarce Goodyear Tire 8.60s of 1995, he said: 12.40%. Net difference: five basis points."

"Is everybody awake out there?"

SOURCE: Grant's Interest Rate Observer [10/22/84].

Spread risk may be considered in at least three dimensions: maturity risk, sector risk, and credit risk. Maturity risk spreads are systematic because they are a part of the yield curve, specifically the steepness or flatness of the curve across the spectrum of maturity dates. Sector risk spreads and credit risk spreads within sectors are unsystematic and can be diversified away within a bond portfolio. Mispricing of spreads can and does occur, less frequently in the more efficient sectors of the market, such as governments and agencies and more frequently in the less efficient sectors of the market, such as lower rated (Ba or BB or below) corporates.

Such analysis can maximize extra market return or minimize unsystematic risk for fixed income investors, since yields in the marketplace are closely correlated to agency ratings. The rationale, as stated by Fong in Chapter 9 of the main volume is as follows:

1. The analyst's assessment of credit quality may be more "accurate" than those of the rating agencies. In this case, the portfolio manager can achieve added yield at relatively small cost in terms of credit risk exposure or can avoid paying in terms of reduced yield for nonexistent incremental quality.

2. Quality ratings for bonds and preferred stocks are revised upward or downward by the agencies only as it is clear that the issuer's financial circumstances have changed. Even the *credit alerts* or *credit watch lists* of the rating agencies tend to lag behind some adverse circumstances. Thus, with astute credit analysis, it may be possible to anticipate such upgrades or downgrades and profit from the yield and price changes that ensue by more "timely" assessments of credit quality.

The box on page 7B-18 graphically illustrates the opportunity for astute analysis. As noted, the deterioration in the credit quality of Caterpillar Tractor and improvements in the credit quality of Goodyear had not been fully recognized by the rating agencies or the market.

No such agencies exist for the rating of mortgage investments, although mortgage backed securities are rated. Thus, in the mortgage field, credit analysis and the evaluation of unsystematic risk is the sole responsibility of the investor. However, if the borrower (owner) or the major tenants for a commercial or industrial property is a publicly owned corporation, it is possible that bond and/or preferred stock quality ratings can be utilized as a partial surrogate for mortgage credit analysis.

CREDIT ANALYSIS—CORPORATE SECURITIES

The task of the analyst as a risk quantifier is aided by the quality ratings that are an integral part of the U.S. and Canadian bond markets. Almost all publicly issued bonds and preferred stocks and even some private placement bonds are regularly evaluated and rated by one or more of the rating agencies. Some issues are not rated because their small size does not justify the costs to the

TABLE 7B-5. Corporate Bond Credit Quality Ratings

Moody's	Standard and Poor's	Duff and Phelps	Fitch	Canadian Bond Rating Service	Definition
Investment Grade					
Aaa	AAA	1	AAA	A++	Highest credit quality. Risk factors are only slightly more than for U.S. Treasury debt.
Aa1	AA+	2	AA+	A+	High credit quality. Risk is modest but may vary slightly due to changes in economic conditions.
Aa2	AA	3	AA		
Aa3	AA–	4	AA–		
A1	A+	5	A+	A	Good credit quality. Risk factors are more variable and greater in periods of economic stress.
A2	A	6	A		
A3	A–	7	A–		
Baa1	BBB+	8	BBB+	B++	Adequate credit quality. Risk factors are subject to considerable variability through economic cycles.
Baa2	BBB	9	BBB		
Baa3	BBB–	10	BBB–		

Below Investment Grade

Moody's	S&P			Duff and Phelps	Description
Ba1	BB+		BB+	11	Speculative credit quality. Risk factors are highly variable but obligations are likely to be met when due.
Ba2	BB		BB	12	
Ba3	BB−		BB−	13	
B1	B+	B+	B+	14	Moderate default risk exists.
B2	B	B	B	15	
B3	B−		B−	16	
Caa	CCC	C	CCC	17	High default risk exists.
Ca	CC		CC	a	
Ca	CC		CC		
C	C	C	C		Income bonds in which interest is not being paid.
D	D	D	DDD		In default.
			DD		
			D		

SOURCES: Moody's Investor Services; Standard and Poor's Corporation; Duff and Phelps, Inc.; Fitch Investors Service, Inc.; Canadian Bond Rating Service.

a Duff and Phelps ratings 18–20 are reserved for later use.

issuer. There are also certain major industries, such as the financial services industry, that are not rated by Moody's as a matter of policy.

Ratings by Rating Agencies

A tabulation of the corporate bond rating classifications used by each of the rating agencies is provided in Table 7B-5. The tabulation reflects an attempt to cross classify and generally define the ratings. Experienced analysts understand that although each rating agency evaluates the same information for each issue, the weighting of the different factors and the conclusions drawn can vary from one rating agency to another. If there is a difference between the ratings that Moody's and Standard and Poor's assign on issue the issue is described as having a *split rating*. It is rare that such split ratings are more than one rating grade apart.

Since the rating is assigned to the issue, issuers can have more than one rating if they have both senior and subordinated securities outstanding. It should also be noted that issues are initially rated at the time they are issued. These initial ratings influence both the effective interest rate and the marketability of the new issue. During the years the issue is outstanding, the agencies continue to review the issue. When justified, ratings may be revised either upward or downward; such revisions are commonly done in increments of one rating grade or one step within a grade. These revisions affect holders in so far as they influence the marketability of the issue in the secondary market. Additionally, credit ratings and anticipated changes (up or down) in ratings affect the yield spread at which a bond trades relative to the market. The issuer is affected by such revisions to the extent that the revision influences the future cost of capital when the issuer borrows additional funds or issues additional debt.

As noted by Cohen, Zinbarg and Ziekel [1982], a major reason for the wide-spread use of the bond quality ratings of reputable agencies is their record of correlation with actual default and financial deterioration experience. A number of studies have been done covering periods from 1900 to the early 1980s that substantiate the efficacy of bond ratings both for corporate and municipal bonds. While not perfect, the rating agencies have a credible record. Several of the studies are noted in the bibliography at the end of this chapter.

Ratings Not a Recommendation to Buy or Sell

The rating services warn the investor that a rating is not a recommendation to buy, sell, or hold a security. The rating agency cannot possibly determine the suitability of a particular security for any one portfolio. In addition, the rating agencies have not performed an audit nor can they attest to the authenticity of the information given to the rating service by the issuer.

Internal Rating Systems

While public ratings serve in general as a measure of the quality of an issue, to the analyst they should be viewed as a bench-mark. The bond analyst should be able to give each security a rating as a result of analyzing the credit and then determine its suitability for purchase or sale in the portfolio. The fact that there is often a difference of opinion among the rating agencies makes this imperative. Since there is no general agreement among the rating agencies as to the weighting of the factors of analysis, there is an opportunity for the keen analyst to capitalize on certain situations and to anticipate some upgrades and downgrades before they happen and before they are recognized by the market.

An internal rating system can be as formal as that of the rating agencies, with the analyst's own weightings given to the various factors that can then be further broken down into their component parts. As an example, population trends would be a sector of economic analysis for municipal bonds. Numerical values could be given to each of the components, and the total value would establish the possible rating, which could be compared with ratings of similar types of securities.

In the process of analyzing a security, the analyst will tend to rate the security, whether it is done formally as just described, or informally by subjective reasoning. Regardless of which system is employed, the internal rating should be recorded to properly reflect the analyst's or portfolio manager's assessment of the security each time the issue is reviewed.

CREDIT ANALYSIS PROCESS

The analysis of the creditworthiness of borrowers is as old as the practice of lending money. *Webster's* defines analysis as an examination of anything to distinguish its component parts or elements separately or in their relation to the whole. Such an examination implies an integrated set of activities that combine in a logical, orderly manner to produce a desired product (in this case, a qualification and, in most cases, quantification of the borrower's or issuer's willingness and ability to repay the principal and pay interest for the use of lenders' funds and all other borrowed funds over a finite period of time). There are no ironclad rules but rather a process logic that permits the analyst to be as quantitative or judgemental and as simple or complex as is deemed appropriate for the investor and/or the assignment.

The credit analysis functions that are performed by a fixed income analyst can be outlined as follows:

1. Determining the issuer's financial record and past history of payment of all contractual obligations.
2. Determining the issuer's current financial position and the microeconomic, political, and social trends that influence the operations and

profitability of the issuer's business, with particular emphasis on the effect of adverse changes in business conditions (inflation, deflation, recession, decline in industry demand, and the like) on the issuer's financial position.

3. Determining the *pro forma* effect of this proposed fixed income securities offering on the financial position (for example, based on the current income statement and balance sheet), of the issuer.
4. Quantifying and documenting to the degree possible, projections of the issuer's financial record and prospects, preferably on a multi-scenario forecast basis.
5. Making a comparative analysis of the proposed new issue relative to the credit analysis standards and guidelines of the investor and to other similar fixed income investment alternatives available at the time.

Because of the limits of this chapter, the credit analysis process will be described fairly succinctly. However, the reader should be aware that this process can be modified to fit the characteristics of all four corporate sectors (and the subindustry categories contained therein) mentioned previously in this chapter: industrial, utility, transportation, and financial. Further on in this chapter, the process has been modified to analyze municipal bonds and could be further modified to apply to mortgages and preferred stocks.

One of the most comprehensive discussions of corporate credit analysis is contained in the *Credit Overview* published by Standard & Poor's in 1982. Appendix A is an excerpt from the *Overview*, that presents in outline form the rating profiles for each of the following types of companies: industrial, retail, bank holding company; thrift institution; finance; insurance; and public utility. The rating profile for a sovereign government is also included. Much of the discussion that follows is drawn from the *Overview*.

Analysis of the Issuer's Business

The credit analysis process begins with an analysis of the business of the issuer. Competitive forces are a fact of life in the industrial sector of the corporate world. The influence of these forces is a source of risk within the context of the industry in which the company competes and for the company itself. With the current trend toward deregulation in the United States, competitive factors are taking on more significance within the utility, transportation, and financial sectors. Fixed income analysts as well as equity analysts can gain valuable insights from Michael Porter's important books, *Competitive Strategy* [1980] and *Competitive Advantage* [1985], which can be applied to the analysis of an issuer's business.

Industry Risk. The characteristics and expectations for the industry in which the issuer is classified should be identified by the analyst. It is especially helpful to measure the expected risk that may be associated with or inferred from the character of the industry or industries within which the issuer's company competes. A study of the industry can serve as a major filter to determine whether the analyst wants to proceed with further credit analysis. An industry characterized by stable or growing demand for its products, and only average competition provides a more healthy environment for all companies within the industry and compliments the internal strengths of the company. Conversely, an industry with weak demand for its product or a fiercely competitive industry adds to the expected risk of the company.

Economic Trends. The position or strength of the industry within the economy is an initial and key factor for the analyst to consider. Standard business cycle analysis can be applied. In fact, the analyst may find it helpful to classify the industry within broad economic sectors such as:

- Consumer goods and services
- Interest rate-sensitive
- Intermediate goods and services
- Cyclical

Such a classification helps identify the company with the industry and/or profit cycle of the economy. It also helps the analyst answer such questions as: Is the industry in a growth, stable, or declining phase? Is the business cyclical? Are changes within the industry more or less volatile than the economy as a whole? What has been the experience of the industry in periods of general economic deterioration characterized by recession, hyperinflation, high interest rates, and the like?

Fixed income analysts, like equity analysts, review industry trends and use regression analysis techniques. However, the purpose of the two types of analysis is different. The fixed income analyst is trying to determine the stability of revenues and earnings. For the equity analyst, these tools and techniques are used to determine the growth characteristics and growth potential of an industry. In addition, the fixed income analyst is attempting to anticipate the worst set of circumstances or expectations, namely recession or depression, and to judge debt servicing ability under those circumstances. Conversely, the equity analyst is attempting to anticipate the most likely or best set of expectations, usually involving positive growth and positive earning power.

Domestic and Foreign Competition. A second factor to consider is the degree of competition within the industry. In today's global economy, both domestic and foreign competition must be considered. What is the ease of entry? Are substitute products or services readily available? To what extent does cost efficiency or location determine a comparative advantage? As mentioned previously, Porter's work in the area of competitive strategies is a good guide to the factors to be considered.

Technological Factors. The threat of obsolescence has long been identified with high technology industries such as electronics and computers. But technological change has had a profound effect on such basic industries as rubber (radial tires) and steel (electric furnaces, continuous casting, and mini mills). These changes came from within an industry while others originated outside the industry (such as linotypes replaced by computers). Given the growth in technology and the forecasts of even more rapid technological progress, fixed income analysts may be forced to shorten the time horizon over which they are willing or able to determine expectations that involve significant risk. The potential for technological change to radically modify, in a short period of time, the risk profile of industries and companies, may have a profound and limiting effect on long-term (that is, 20 to 40 years) financing.

Regulatory Factors. The role of regulation in the U.S. economy is changing. The deregulation of the airline industry in the late 1970s has profoundly and adversely affected the credit standing of the airline industry and is considered by many to have led to the bankruptcy of Braniff Airlines and the near or temporary failure of other airlines.

However, it is dangerous to generalize about deregulation. In 1984, several electric utilities, namely Public Service of New Hampshire, Consumers Power, and Long Island Lighting, publicly announced the potential for their respective bankruptcies. In each case, regulatory intransigence regarding the escalating costs, shoddy workmanship, and delays associated with nuclear plants has been cited as one of the factors contributing to these companies' perilous financial position. In Canada, the National Energy Policy, passed by the federal government in the early 1980s, left companies such as Dome Petroleum and Hudson's Bay Oil and Gas in a very vulnerable financial position. Both existing regulation and the potential for future regulation or deregulation must be considered carefully by the fixed income analyst.

Capital Requirements. Certain industries can be characterized as capital intensive. This is certainly a characteristic of the heavy manufacturing industries (such as steel and machinery), certain of the intermediate goods industries (such as chemicals and petroleum), and regulated industries such as utilities and transportation. The analyst must consider future capital requirements of a business relative to cash flow projections for the firm. The repayment or refunding of outstanding debt as well as the issuance of new bonds must be taken into consideration in evaluating the company's capital requirements relative to its ability to service such debt.

Industry Sensitivity. Moody's Investors Service recently completed a study for a client which identified the sensitivity of selected sectors and industries to changes in certain political, social, and economic factors. Each sector or industry was scored on a scale of 1 to 5, with 1 representing no sensitivity and 5 representing the highest degree of sensitivity. See Table 7B-6 for a recent set of rankings for 47 sectors and industries.

Issuer's Industry Position

In addition to understanding the industry risks, the analyst should evaluate the issuer's relative position within the industry or industries in which that company is operating.

Market Position. The business segment disclosures contained in annual reports and 10K filings can be particularly helpful in this regard. Trade publications may also provide market share statistics or relative rankings of competing companies by product or product line. The risk of default should vary inversely with the strength of the issuer's industry position. The following caveat is worth repeating: Strong companies in weak industries (for example, industries declining due to obsolescence or intense competition) may be almost as risky as weak companies in strong industries.

Operating Efficiency. The analyst should evaluate the company's margins relative to those of the industry. Is the issuer's margin at or above the industry average? Is the issuer the low cost producer? Is the industry or the issuer unionized?

Does the issuer control unique or low cost sources of supply? To what extent does vertical or horizontal integration play a role in the issuer's efficiency? What is the pricing policy of the industry and the issuer? All of these factors and others can influence operating efficiency.

Comparative Advantage. Finally, it is important to determine if the issuer has some combination of technology, operating efficiency, brand loyalty, patents, and so on that provides a comparative advantage that is likely to last for a number of years. This advantage should be measured within the domestic market and within the international market, if one exists, for the issuer's products.

Management Evaluation

The analysis of an issuer's business would not be complete without evaluating management. Personal interviews and/or a review of the issuer's financial performance will provide necessary information. Particular attention should be paid to the evolution of the issuer's financial structure and controls.

Continuity. The longevity of management can be viewed as a potential source of stability. It can also increase the probability that the past record of the firm may be projected into the future on the assumption that the business plan has not and will not be changed radically. New management does not necessarily indicate risk. In fact, new management can provide the opportunity for rejuvenation and redirection with the result being greater stabil-

TABLE 7B-6. Industry Sensitivity (1 = No Sensitivity, 3 = Average, 5 = Highest)

SECTOR Subgroup	General Economic Cycles	LDC Economies in Particular	Interest Rates	Inflation	Oil & Gas Prices	Other Commodity Prices	Protectionist Legislation	Other Legislation	Technological Change
TECHNOLOGY									
Electronics	3	1	2	2	1	1	4	2	5
Office Equipment	3	2	2	2	1	1	4	2	5
Telecommunications	3	1	3	2	1	1	4	2	5
Aerospace	4	2	2	1	3	3	4	2	4
FINANCE									
Finance & Insurance Cos.	3	4	5	2	2	2	2	5	3
Banks-Money Center	4	1	5	3	2	2	1	5	3
Banks-Regional	3	5	5	2	3	2	2	5	3
Banks-Foreign	2	3	5	2	3	2	1	5	3
Fin. Services & Brokerage	4	1	3	3	1	2	2	5	3
BASIC INDUSTRY									
Chemicals	5	4	3	3	3	3	3	3	3
Machinery & Equip.	4	4	4	3	5	3	2	4	4
Forest Products	4	3	4	3	2	4	3	2	3
Steel	5	5	3	3	2	3	4	3	2
Metals & Mining	5	5	4	3	2	5	5	3	3
Textiles & Apparel	4	4	4	3	3	4	4	3	2
Cement	5	1	4	4	2	2	5	2	3
Containers	3	2	4	3	4	2	3	3	2
Transport-Air	5	3	3	4	3	2	1	4	3
-Ground	4	1	3	2	5	3	3	5	3
-Sea	5	2	3	3	4	3	5	5	2

ENERGY	4	3	3	3	5	2	3	4	2
Oil & Gas Integrated	4	4	4	3	5	3	3	4	2
Oil & Gas Producers	4	2	3	4	5	2	2	4	2
Oil Service	5	2	3	3	5	2	2	4	4
Coal Producers	5	2	3	3	5	3	4	3	2
UTILITIES	3	1	4	4	3	1	2	4	3
Electric	3	1	4	5	3	1	1	4	2
Gas Pipelines & Distributors	4	1	3	3	5	2	3	4	2
Telecommunications	2	1	3	4	1	1	1	4	5
Telephones/Telecommunications	2	1	4	4	1	1	2	4	4
CONSUMER CYCLICAL	4	1	4	4	3	3	3	3	3
Autos, Trucks, Parts	4	2	4	3	4	2	5	4	4
Rubber & Tires	4	1	4	3	4	3	2	3	3
Building Related	5	1	5	4	2	4	2	3	2
Retail	4	1	4	4	2	2	3	2	3
Household Equipment	4	1	3	3	2	2	4	3	4
CONSUMER STABLE & GROWTH	2	1	2	1	1	2	1	3	3
Food/Food Processing	1	1	1	1	1	1	2	2	1
Leisure & Ent.	3	1	2	2	1	1	1	3	3
Drugs & Medical Supplies	1	1	1	1	1	1	2	4	4
Hospital Management	1	1	2	1	1	1	1	5	2
Beverages	2	2	1	1	1	2	1	3	2
Supermarkets	3	1	1	3	2	3	1	2	3
Commun. & Publishing	2	1	2	2	1	2	1	3	4

SOURCE: Moody's Investor's Service [1984].

ity. However, frequent or turbulent changes in management are a cautionary signal for the analyst since they may indicate instability and increase the risk that the past record cannot be assumed to be an indicator of the company's future ability to service its debt.

Proprietary Interest. Lenders and stockholders prefer to have management share the risks to some extent through significant ownership of the common stock. The significance of management's ownership position cannot be measured only on a relative basis in terms of the percentage of the company's outstanding shares, particularly in very large corporations. Rather, management's proprietary interest must also be measured in terms of absolute dollars of current market value. It is assumed that management's motivation and prudence will be enhanced the greater the personal financial risk or reward that their decisions entail.

Relative Standing Within the Industry. Often the analyst can gain a valuable perspective on the management of a company by interviewing suppliers, customers, competitors, and industry consultants. Typically, the senior management of a company or the management organization will have an established reputation in the industry. Such insights assist the analyst in the evaluation of how the company got to where it is today and the efficacy of its plans for the future.

Analysis of the Issuer's Financial Position

The next step in the analytical process is a thorough (initial or follow-up) review of the financial characteristics and strengths or weaknesses of the issuer. Several chapters could be devoted to this subject with a comprehensive explanation of the tools and techniques used by the analyst to evaluate the issuer's financial position. The following discussion should be viewed as an outline and brief summary of this important area.

Accounting Quality. The first step in the analysis of the issuer's financial position is a determination of the quality of the accounting methods used in the issuer's statements. It is done primarily by a thorough study of the footnotes to the financial statements and auditor's opinions. Is the accounting liberal or conservative? That is, do the accounting methods used by the issuer predominantly maximize revenues and minimize costs, producing the largest earnings figure possible (liberal) or do they tend to do just the opposite (conservative)? Is the auditor's opinion unqualified or "clean" (in that all matters are handled in conformity with generally accepted accounting principles) or is it qualified (in that departures from generally accepted accounting principles or significant uncertainties affecting the financial statements are noted by the auditors)?

The accounting considerations to be reviewed include:
- Determination of consolidated and unconsolidated subsidiaries and the basis for consolidation
- Off balance sheet financing
- Method of recognizing income
- Funding of current and future pension fund liabilities
- Depreciation method
- Inventory valuation method
- Amortization of intangibles
- Treatment of investment tax credits

The analyst must evaluate the issuer's accounting policies on an absolute basis as well as a basis relative to industry standards or norms in an effort to determine the quality of the balance sheet, income statements, and sources-and-uses statements provided. Table 7B-7 is an example of a comparison of certain accounting practices of a selected sample of companies representing the retailing industry.

It should also be recognized that credit analysis and ratings are not audits. The analyst can and should adjust published financial statements as necessary to seek credible and comparable data. The quality of the analysis is related to the quality of the accounting data.

Furthermore, the analyst should evaluate and compare accounting policy as well as accounting statements over a sufficient recent period of time such as 5 to 10 years or over a period that encompasses a complete business cycle. Changes in accounting practices, if any, should be noted and adjustments made in historical data before any trend analysis is performed.

Earnings Protection. After determining the accounting quality of the issuer's statements and making the appropriate adjustments, the analyst then considers the *earnings protection* or the extent to which the company's profitability supports or covers the actual and *pro forma* interest payments and principal repayments. As Graham and Dodd [1962] noted, safety is measured by the ability of the issuer to generate sufficient earnings to meet all of its obligations. To measure the degree of safety (or lack thereof) reflected in a particular issuer's financial position, the analyst uses a series of ratios. The reader should be aware that most but not all of these ratios are uniform. Some adjustments can and are made to the financial data to meet the individual rating agency's or analyst's own preference.

It should be noted that where possible the sufficiency of cash flows as well as earnings should be evaluated. Unfortunately, net income or earnings is subject to management's desire to reflect the most favorable picture. The substitution of cash flow data would be helpful to the analyst. However, without explicit disclosure of this data by companies, the analyst is forced to develop a sources-and-uses statement using net (after-tax) earnings as the starting point.

TABLE 7B-7. Comparison of Principal Accounting Practices, 1984

	Inventories	Depreciation	Interest on Property Under Construction	Service Charge Income	Investment Tax Credit	New Store Costs	Finance Subsidiary	Real Estate Subsidiary
General Merchandise								
Montgomery Ward	LIFO since 1976	Straight line	Capitalized since 1980	Deducted from SG&A	Flow through	Expensed as incurred	Nonconsolidated	None
J. C. Penney	LIFO since 1974	Straight line	Capitalized	Deducted from SG&A	Flow through	Expensed in year of opening	Nonconsolidated	Nonconsolidated
Sears Roebuck	LIFO since 1975	Straight line	Capitalized	Included in revenues	Flow through	Expensed	Consolidated	Consolidated
Department Stores								
Allied Stores	LIFO	Straight line	Capitalized since 1980	Deducted from SG&A	Flow through	Expensed as incurred	Consolidated	Consolidated
Associated Dry Goods	LIFO since 1974	Straight line	Capitalized since 1980	Included in sales	Flow through	Expensed in month of opening	Nonconsolidated	None
Carter Hawley Hale	LIFO Department Stores —1974 Other—1981	Straight line	Capitalized	Included in sales	Flow through	Expensed in year of opening	Nonconsolidated	Consolidated
Dayton Hudson	LIFO	Straight line	Capitalized since 1980	Included in sales	Flow through	Expensed	None	None
Federated	LIFO	Straight line	Capitalized	Included in sales	Flow through	Expensed	Nonconsolidated	Nonconsolidated
May	LIFO—83% FIFO—17%	Straight line	Capitalized	Included in sales	Deferred	Expensed in year of opening	Consolidated	Consolidated
Discount—Variety								
K Mart	LIFO—87% FIFO—13%	Straight line	Capitalized	—	Flow through	Expensed in year of opening	None	None
Woolworth	LIFO—47% FIFO—53%	Straight line	Capitalized since 1981	—	Flow through	Expensed as incurred	None	Consolidated

SOURCE: McCarthy, Crisanti & Maffei, Inc. [1984].

Quantitative measures can be used to identify the characteristics and the profile of the earnings protection that an issuer provides a current or prospective lender. These ratios include profitability and coverage factors.

Profitability Factors. The ratios that can be calculated to measure profitability include: the pretax margin or margin of safety, income tax rate, return on assets, return on total capital, and return on equity. The formulation of these ratios can be described as follows:

$$\text{Pretax profit margin (or margin of safety)} = \frac{\begin{array}{c}\text{net income + income taxes + minority interest} - \\ \text{net earnings of unconsolidated subsidiaries} + \\ \text{extraordinary losses - extraordinary income}\end{array}}{\text{revenue - returns - excise taxes (if any)}}$$

$$= \frac{\text{pretax earnings}}{\text{net revenue}}$$

The higher the pretax margin figure, the more profitable the business is considered to be on an absolute basis. The pretax margin is also known as the margin of safety because it represents the percentage of sales remaining after all expenses including interest have been paid. In other words, it is an indicator of the degree to which sales relative to expenses could decline before the issuer's ability to meet interest expenses would be impaired. Implicit in the margin of safety concept is the assumption that the relationship of expenses to sales will remain the same.

The analyst should also use other ratios to help quantify the tax position of the issuer's business. The income tax rate formula is:

$$\text{Effective income tax rate} = \frac{\text{current and deferred income taxes}}{\text{pretax earnings}}$$

where current and deferred income taxes include federal, foreign, state (provincial), and local taxes.

This measure indicates the tax burden of the company on an absolute basis. When comparing the profitability of two companies, it is important to evaluate the tax environment in which each company operates. In general, low tax environments are preferred to high. The relative tax position of a company may affect its ability to compete and maintain its margin of safety in the long run.

Other measures of profitability are well-known to the equity analyst and are also used by fixed income analysts on either a pretax or after tax (net income) basis. The formulas are indicated below and explanations of these ratios can be found in most investment texts.

$$\text{Net income margin} = \frac{\text{net income}}{\text{revenues}}$$

$$\text{Return on assets} = \frac{\text{net income}}{\text{total assets}}$$

$$\text{Return on common equity} = \frac{\text{net income}}{\text{common equity}}$$

$$\text{Return on capital} = \frac{\text{net income}}{\text{total capital}}$$

where total capital is the sum of debt and equity.

Coverage Factors. The coverage ratio is the key indicator of earnings protection for the fixed income analyst. It measures the number of times earnings or income available for the payment of interest exceeds actual or *pro forma* interest expense. The higher the coverage ratio, the greater the degree of earnings protection provided to the investor.

In addition to the coverage of interest expense, the analyst can also calculate the coverage of total fixed charges, both interest and principal payments. For preferred stocks the coverage of fixed charges plus preferred dividends can be calculated. The formulation of each of the coverage ratios, typically calculated on a pretax basis because interest is a tax deductible expense, is described as follows:

$$\text{Interest coverage} = \frac{\text{pretax earnings} + \text{interest expense} + \frac{1}{3} \text{ of lease rental expense} + \text{capitalized interest}}{\text{interest expense} + \frac{1}{3} \text{ of lease rental expense} + \text{capitalized interest}}$$

where $\frac{1}{3}$ of lease rental expense is considered by most analysts to be an equivalent interest factor for lease obligations.

$$\text{Fixed charges coverage} = \frac{\text{pretax earnings} + \text{interest expense} + \frac{1}{3} \text{ of lease rental expense} + \text{amortization of debt discount}}{\text{fixed charges}}$$

where fixed charges include interest expense, $\frac{1}{3}$ of lease rental expense, and amortization of debt discount.

If the issue being analyzed is preferred stock, then the dividends on preferred stock should be added to the fixed charge figure. This formula is known as the tax adjusted comprehensive measure of fixed charge and preferred dividend coverage.

$$\text{Coverage of fixed charges and preferred dividends} = \frac{\text{income available for interest or charges}}{\text{fixed charges} + \dfrac{\text{preferred dividend}}{(1 - \text{effective tax rate})}}$$

It should be noted that sometimes preferred dividend coverage is calculated on a residual basis, that is, net income is divided by preferred dividends. Since this formulation ignores the prior leverage inherent in interest expense, the ratio is of little value and can be misleading to the unsuspecting investor.

One other coverage ratio that should be noted involves total debt service, which includes both interest expense (and tax-adjusted preferred dividends) and principal payments due on long-term debt. Principal payments can represent payments at maturity or periodic sinking fund payments on outstanding issues. Sinces some preferred stock issues have sinking funds, this measure also should include fund payments for such issues. It is also applicable to mortgages or mortgage related financings where payments include both interest and principal. The formula is:

Coverage of total debt service

$$= \frac{\text{available for interest or charges}}{\text{fixed charges} + \dfrac{\text{preferred dividends}}{1 - \text{effective tax rate}} + \text{principal payments due}}$$

To the extent that the analysts could determine a company's actual cash flow, such figures could be substituted for income available to calculate coverage. Unfortunately, as Hawkins [1977] and other accounting texts have noted, a company's "true" cash flow cannot be determined from published financial statements. Nevertheless, as noted in the section on cash flow adequacy, the analyst must be aware of cash flow trends as indicated by a sources-and-uses analysis and make the best estimates possible within the limits described above.

Leverage and Asset Protection. Long-term debt as a percent of total capitalization is the traditional measure of the degree to which a corporation is using financial leverage. However, corporations have increased the usage of short-term debt for other than seasonal purposes. For many such companies, short-term borrowings must be considered as part of the permanent capital. Another trend that has diluted the significance of the debt to total capital ratio is the popularity of off-balance sheet financing techniques, such as certain forms of leasing.

The formulation of the leverage ratio can be described as follows:

$$\text{Leverage ratio} = \frac{\begin{array}{l}\text{short-term debt} + \text{current maturities of long-term debt} - \\ \text{long-term debt (less current maturities)} + \text{capitalized} \\ \text{lease obligations} + \text{production payments (for extractive} \\ \text{industries)}\end{array}}{\begin{array}{l}\text{short-term debt} + \text{long-term debt} + \text{leases} + \text{production} \\ \text{payments} + \text{minority interest} + \text{preferred stock} + \\ \text{common equity}\end{array}}$$

$$= \frac{\text{fixed obligations}}{\text{total capitalization}}$$

Asset values have become distorted over the past two decades of increased inflation, technological change, and international competition. For some companies, historical asset values are understated relative to current market or replacement values and thus the equity is also understated. Other companies may have obsolete plants, such as most of the steel industry, and thus asset values and equity may be overstated.

While the analyst cannot be expected to appraise the assets of each and every corporation being studied, it is important to be mindful of such factors as the age of plants, usable plant capacity, and the like. Adjustments should also be made to intangible assets and to current assets to reflect obsolete inventory and uncollectible receivables. The keen analyst will also adjust for differences in inventory and depreciation accounting methods when comparing companies.

Another ratio used by analysts, and often used as a covenant or restriction in bond indentures, is the ratio of net tangible assets to long-term debt. Admittedly, this ratio becomes more important in a liquidation situation, but it does provide an indication of the asset protection provided to the bondholders.

The formulation for this ratio is:

$$\text{Tangible asset ratio} = \frac{\begin{array}{l}\text{total assets} - \text{intangible assets} - \text{current liabilities} - \\ \text{deferred taxes} - \text{other liabilities} - \text{minority interest}\end{array}}{\begin{array}{l}\text{long-term debt} + \text{capitalized leases} + \\ \text{production payments}\end{array}}$$

$$= \frac{\text{net tangible assets}}{\text{long-term debt}}$$

The ratio is expressed as a percentage. For example, 250 percent means that for every dollar of long-term debt outstanding there are $2.50 of tangible assets. Of course, these calculations are based on the book value rather than the market value of the assets. Thus, the analyst must be cautious in the application of this ratio even under conditions of default. It should be remembered that asset protection is not the primary determinant of safety. That is the function of earning power and cash flow adequacy.

Cash Flow Adequacy. Three alternatives are available for the repayment of fixed obligations. First, external funds can be provided by issuing new debt or equity to extend or pay off outstanding obligations. The utility industry and other capital intensive industries provide examples of companies that are frequently refinancing debt obligations.

A second alternative is the sale of assets to raise cash to pay down (partially reduce) or pay off fixed obligations. These sales can involve certain assets such as a specific plant or equipment. It can also, and more typically does, involve the sale of a subsidiary or division of a company. In the early 1980s, such sales were commonplace following almost two decades of acquisitions, largely through the use of debt, by conglomerates and other large corporations.

Finally, debt can be repaid with cash or funds generated in the normal course of business. The ability of a corporation to refinance or sell assets is not considered a measure of creditworthiness by most long-term lenders. Cash flow adequacy is the ability to generate sufficient funds internally to pay expenses and meet the cash outflows associated with interest and principal payments. After the trend of coverage, the trend and level of cash flow is the next most important indicator of the creditworthiness of the borrower.

Analysts prepare an analysis of internal and external cash generation to assess the borrower's ability to prudently finance capital expenses. An example of a cash flow analysis is shown in Table 7B-8. Note the distinction between internal and external cash generation and the relationship of "free" cash flow to capital expenditures.

TABLE 7B-8. UAL, Incorporated Cash Flow Analysis (dollars in thousands)

	1981	1982	1983
Internally Generated (Used) Cash:			
Net Income	($ 70,530)	$ 10,950	$142,045
Depreciation and Amortization	315,509	368,124	411,324
Deferred Income Taxes	(84,326)	(25,927)	98,644
Other	21,940	30,055	40,336
Cash Generated by Operations:	$182,593	$383,202	$692,349
Cash Generated (Used) By:			
Accounts Receivable	14,553	(6,186)	(167,392)
Inventories	34,653	1,685	(14,407)
Other Current Assets	0	0	0
Accounts Payable and Other Accruals	59,753	117,755	208,730
Advanced Ticket Sales	(37,949)	(6,550)	101,051
Cash Generated by Change in Working Capital	$ 71,010	$106,704	$127,982
Total Internally Generated (Used) Cash:	253,603	489,906	820,331
Less: Dividends	(368)	(348)	(16,604)
Free Cash Flow (FCF):	$253,235	$489,558	$803,727
Cash (Applications):			
Capital Expenditures	(450,514)	(834,477)	(861,973)
Acquisitions	0	0	0
Other	36,430	16,450	29,975
Total Applications	($414,084)	($818,027)	($831,998)
Net Internal Cash Flow:	($160,849)	($328,469)	($ 28,271)
External Cash Sources (Uses):			
Short-Term Debt-Net	26,512	(102,719)	111,955
Long-Term Debt-Net	(77,392)	643,039	(440,246)
Equity:			
Preferred Stock	0	0	0
Common Stock	0	0	343,128
Sale of Assets	0	0	0
Capital Lease Obligations	87,427	(47,939)	(43,667)
Other	0	(49,732)	40,446
Total External Cash Flow:	$ 36,547	$442,649	$ 11,616
Total Cash Generated	($124,302)	$114,180	($ 16,655)
Beginning Cash:	318,923	194,621	308,801
Ending Cash:	194,621	308,801	292,146
Net Increase (Decrease) In Cash:	($124,302)	$114,180	($ 16,655)
FCF/Capital Expenditures (%):	56.2%	58.7%	93.2%

SOURCE: Mutual of Omaha Insurance Company [1984].

The primary measure of cash flow adequacy is the ratio of long-term debt (including capitalized leases) or total debt (including short-term debt) to total funds from operations. The first two terms—long-term debt and total debt—have already been described.

Funds from operations consist of net earnings plus depreciation and amortization plus increases in deferred income taxes and deferred investment tax credits and other noncash charges that are added back.

Some analysts will also use the sources-and-uses statement figures for net cash flow from operations to compare with long-term debt in an effort to measure cash flow adequacy.

The formula is:

$$\text{Cash flow adequacy } (\times) = \frac{\text{long-term debt}}{\text{funds from operations}}$$

or, alternatively,

$$= \frac{\text{total debt}}{\text{funds from operations}}$$

The ratio can be used to estimate the number of years required to retire debt solely from the internal cash flow of the company. Of course, it is not practical to assume that for several years all internal cash flow could be dedicated to the retirement of debt. Such a practice would limit the future growth of the business. It suggests a liquidation condition. Nevertheless, the significance of the ratio is that the lower the number of years to pay off debt, the stronger the credit position or financial flexibility of the company.

It should also be noted that some analysts reverse the ratio to reflect funds from operation as a percentage of one or both of the debt figures. This formulation is:

$$\text{Cash flow adequacy } (\%) = \frac{\text{funds from operations}}{\text{long-term debt}}$$

or, alternatively,

$$= \frac{\text{funds from operations}}{\text{total debt}}$$

In this form, the measure of protection is just the reverse—the higher the ratio, the better it is for the bondholder.

Financial Flexibility. One of the characteristics of a well-managed company in capital intensive industries is the flexibility to adjust financing programs even during periods of economic stress. It is particularly important to be able to make such adjustments without seriously impairing credit quality.

Leveraged buy-outs have become popular over the past three years since mid-1982. John Shad, chairman of the U.S. Securities and Exchange Commission (SEC), noted recently that these buy-outs are being financed through large loans. He warned that the net effect is that debt is being used to retire equity in a leveraging-up of a company's capitalization (the greater the leverage, the greater the risk to the company's shareholders and creditors). An example of what Mr. Shad was describing was the leveraged buy-out of Blue Bell, Inc., the second largest manufacturer of branded (Wrangler, Blue Bell, and Jantzen) apparel. Approximately $500 million of debt and $55 million of preferred stock were issued to effect the leveraged buy-out. As a result, Blue Bell's debt ratio (debt as a percentage of total capital) increased from 35 percent to 88 percent. Of equal concern is the fact that the five-year projections of debt repayment made no allowance for a slowdown in business or a recession. Baldwin-United, Charter Corp., Lionel, Saxon Industries, and Wickes Corp. are all recent examples of major bankruptcies that resulted from heavy debt incurred by companies in aggressive acquisition programs.

It is important for an analyst to be aware of indenture restrictions that would limit a company's financing options. For example, Commonwealth Edison was required to make use of debenture and preferred stock financing in the early 1980s because their first mortgage debt outstanding was at or near the maximum permitted by the indenture. Commonwealth's extraordinary financing needs arose from cost overruns and delays associated with the company's multi-plant nuclear construction programs.

It is also important that the analyst review the footnotes to the financial statements to determine any encumbrances. In the late 1960s and early 1970s the W.T. Grant Company expanded rapidly into discount merchandising. This expansion program created a substantial financing burden that ultimately resulted in bankruptcy for the corporation in 1975. Two years earlier a careful reading of the company's financial statement indicated that essentially all of the company's assets were encumbered (pledged as collateral to secure the company's short-term and long-term borrowings), which represented 83 percent of total capital in mid-1973. Appendix B is a review of the W.T. Grant situation based on excerpts from a report prepared for an investment committee by the author in late 1973. It is a classic example of a company's loss of financial flexibility during a period of economic stress. For a more comprehensive discussion of the W.T. Grant situation the reader is directed to the Largay and Steckney [1980] article.

Other Ratios. A number of other ratios can be applied by analysts to determine liquidity (such as the current ratio and quick ratio) and other factors reflecting the financial characteristics of the issuer. Cohen, Zinbarg, and Ziekel [1982] provide an excellent summary of widely used financial ratios.

Comparative Analysis

The fixed income analyst has many alternatives from which to select investments that are appropriate for a particular employer or client. The investment policy statements of the employer or client should indicate the degree of risk willing to be assumed. In the bond market, such risk is typically denoted by identifying a range of acceptable quality ratings. For example, the investor may be willing to purchase only those securities rated A or better. Thus, the analyst will compare available investment opportunities with established port-folio specifications.

The analyst also compares issues within an industry and within a rating category. Appendix C is a series of tabulations prepared by a fixed income research firm, McCarthy, Crisanti and Maffei, Inc., for the comparative analy-sis of 11 companies operating within specified sectors of the U.S. retail industry.

Appendix D is a summary prepared by Merrill Lynch of 33 ratios and other variables that serve as a basis for making comparisons between four bond quality rating categories. The data covers the period from 1973 to 1984. company's financial ratios with an average for that rating class for each of 12 prior years.

major rating categories also prepared by Merrill Lynch. For each statistic, a 12-year average, standard deviation, range, and ratio of standard deviation to 12-year average is provided for each of the four quality ratings for the period 1973—1984. These appendixes give the reader some insight into the compara-tive analysis techniques that are used by fixed income analysts.

Actual and Pro Forma Analysis

For the analyst, historical or actual data is generally available. This past record may or may not be an adequate indicator of the future. As noted previously, it is important that the historic period covered does span a business cycle so that the performance of the company during a period of economic stress can be evaluated on a quasi-worst case basis.

Pro forma analysis is used to reformat or reflect the data under some change in conditions. In the case of fixed income securities, the analyst may adjust the actual data for the prior few years to determine coverage, leverage, and other measures, if the securities about to be issued (or newly issued) had been outstanding during those prior years. Admittedly, this format does not reflect the increased earnings and cash flows that would be expected to result from the increase in the capital invested in the company that such a bond issue would have produced.

Projections and Probabilities

Because interest or preferred dividends will be paid out of future earnings, the fixed income analyst, like the equity analyst, must make future projections of the borrower's operating and financial position. Multiscenario forecasting and regression analysis techniques assist the analyst in this difficult task. The relatively long holding periods and maturities of fixed income securities only increase the difficulty of the analyst's task and increase the chance for error. For example, 20 years ago utility bonds were cited as examples of safety and stability for investors. However, during the decade of the 1970s and early 1980s, the number of utilities rated below A quality increased from 4 percent of the total in 1970 to 33 percent of the total in 1981.

Because of the possibility of default on future payments of interest (or preferred dividends) and principal, the analyst should either explicitly or, more often, implicitly calculate a probability distribution of future cash flows payable to the bondholders at specified future dates. For U.S. Treasury bonds and some other sovereign issues, the probability of payment can be considered to be 1.0. Jacob and Pettit [1984] cover this subject in a comprehensive manner and the reader is directed to that text for additional information and examples. Space does not permit a detailed discussion of this important subject within the context of this Update.

Application of Bankruptcy Tests

As noted previously, macroeconomic conditions have heightened default risk and the potential for companies both small and large to fail. However, as Edward Altman [1983] has noted, in almost all cases the fundamental business failure problems lie within the firm itself. Thus, he argues that certain financial ratios are effective indicators and predictors of corporate bankruptcy. The extensive bankruptcy studies of Altman and his defense of the analytical and practical value of financial ratios have been well-received in the financial community.

Although ratio analysis has long been used for assessing creditworthiness, the approach has been univariate, that is, focused on one variable at a time. Ratios were interpreted individually with no common agreement as to the order of importance for forecasting impending problems.

Predictive Models. Altman recognized that the predictive value of these ratios might be better captured by combining several measures into a multivariate predictive model. His goal was to determine which ratios are the most important in detecting bankruptcy potential and what weightings should be attached to those ratios. The latter required Altman to determine empirically how the weightings should be established.

His approach was based on linear multiple discriminant analysis, a statistical technique widely used in the biological and behavioral sciences. Simply stated, multiple discriminant analysis attempts to derive a linear combination of the characteristics which "best" discriminate between various groups. Such analysis is described as multivariate because it provides the ability to consider an entire profile or array of properties (represented by the variables) that are common to a particular group or subsample, as well as the interaction of these properties. For a complete description of Altman's research, which led to the development of his "Z-score" and later models, the reader is encouraged to review the appropriate bibliographical references at the end of this chapter.

TABLE 7B-9. Corporate Bankruptcies: Scores and Auditor Opinions (1978–1982)

Company	Auditor	Bankruptcy Filing Date	Modified Z-Scores		Auditor Opinions	
			One Year Prior	Two Years Prior	One Year Prior	Two Years Prior
Advent Corp.	Arthur Andersen	3/81	−0.49	−0.78	E	E
Allied Artists	Price Waterhouse	4/79	−0.82	−1.26	OK	OK
Allied Supermarkets	Deloitte Haskins & Sells	11/78	−0.83	−0.74	OK	OK
Arctic Enterprises	Arthur Andersen	2/81	−0.83	−0.05	OK	OK
Barclay Enterprises	Touche Ross	6/81	−0.99	−0.21	E	OK
Bobbie Brooks	Peat Marwick Mitchell & Co.	1/82	−0.29	−0.05	OK	E
Capehart	Laventhol & Horwath	2/79	−0.56	−0.98	OK	OK
City Stores	Touche Ross/Ernst & Ernst	7/79	−0.31	−0.35	OK	OK
Commonwealth Oil Refining	Deloitte Haskins & Sells	7/79	−1.20	−0.83	E	E
Cooper-Jarrett, Inc.	Peat Marwick Mitchell & Co.	12/81	−1.22	−0.97	E	E
E.C. Ernst	Richard Eisner	12/78	−0.81	0.44	OK	OK
Garcia Corp.	Ernst & Ernst	8/78	−1.02	−0.58	E	OK
General Recreation	Arthur Andersen	12/78	−2.41	−1.25	E	OK
Goldblatt Bros.	Arthur Andersen	6/81	−0.54	0.21	OK	OK
GRT Corp.	Price Waterhouse/Ernst & Ernst	7/79	−0.66	−0.25	OK	OK
Inforex, Inc.	Arthur Andersen	10/79	0.24	−0.06	OK	OK
Interlee (FDI)	Arthur Young & Co.	12/78	−0.32	−0.31	OK	OK
Lafayette Radio Electronics	Touche Ross	1/80	−0.77	−0.44	E	OK
Lionel Corp.	Price Waterhouse	2/82	−0.19	0.28	OK	OK
Lynnwear Corp.	Brout & Co.	2/81	−0.59	−0.06	OK	OK
Mansfield Tire and Rubber	Arthur Young & Co.	10/79	−0.90	−0.24	E	E
Mays Department Stores	Arthur Andersen	1/82	1.18	1.07	OK	OK
McLouth Steel	Ernst & Whinney	12/81	−0.49	0.06	OK	OK
Metropolitan Greeting Cards	Touche Ross/J.K. Lasser	1/79	−0.95	−0.30	E	OK

Murphy Pacific Marine Salvage

Company	Audit Firm	Date				
Company	Timothy Kip Firm	5/79	-0.49	0.21	OK	OK
National Shoes	Peat, Marwick, Mitchell & Co.	12/80	-0.16	-0.15	OK	OK
North American Development Corp.	Arthur Young & Co.	N.A.	-2.58	-2.30	OK	OK
Orange Blossom Products	Levine, Cohn et al./Haskins & Sells	6/79	-2.46	-2.19	E	OK
Pantry Pride	Laventhol & Horwath	10/78	-0.12	-0.15	OK	OK
Pathcom Inc.	Ernst & Ernst	1/78	-0.98	-0.70	E	OK
Penn Dixie Industries	Coopers & Lybrand	4/80	-0.70	0.19	E	OK
Piedmont Industries	Ernst & Ernst/S.P. Leidesdorf	2/79	-0.29	-0.22	OK	OK
Reinell Industries	Price Waterhouse	1/79	-1.43	-1.18	E	OK
Richton International	Arthur Andersen	3/80	-0.08	0.62	E	E
Sambo's Restaurants Inc.	Touche Ross	6/81	0.11	-0.35	E	E
Sam Solomon	Arthur Young & Co.	5/81	-0.27	-0.20	E	OK
Shulman Transport Enterprises	Touche Ross	8/78	-1.11	-0.97	N.A.	N.A.
Stevecoknit, Inc.	Arthur Andersen	11/81	-0.36	0.10	OK	OK
Swift Industries	Coopers & Lybrand	N.A.	-1.86	-1.08	OK	E
Tenna	Ernst & Whinney	12/79	-0.27	-0.67	OK	E
The Upson Co.	Price Waterhouse	6/80	-0.44	-0.27	OK	OK
West Chemical Products	Ernst & Ernst	1/79	-0.12	1.05	E	OK
White Motors	Ernst & Whinney	9/80	-0.24	-0.35	OK	OK
Wilson Freight	Ernst & Whinney	7/80	-0.92	-0.55	OK	OK

Summary of Results

Number of Correct Bankruptcy Indications		41	34	17	9
Number of Observations		44	44	43	43
Percentage Accuracy		93%	76%	40%	21%

SOURCE: Altman [1983].

KEY:

E = Qualified opinion
OK = Unqualified opinion

Z-Score. Altman's Z-score model is a linear analysis that uses five objectively weighted measures to arrive at an overall score. That score then becomes the basis for classifying firms into groupings. Some 22 variables were researched and eventually five were selected as being the most reliable predictors of bankruptcy. The five ratios are:

(X_1) Working Capital/Total Assets. A measure of net liquid assets to total capitalization that Altman found to be the best liquidity measure for his work.

(X_2) Retained Earnings/Total Assets. A measure of cumulative profitability over time, the size of which implicitly and typically gives consideration to the age of the firm (an especially important variable since in 1980 approximately 54 percent of the firms that failed had been in business only five years or less).

(X_3) Earnings Before Interest and Taxes/Total Assets. A measure of the productivity or the earning power of the firm's assets, which is the ultimate test of the firm's ability to continue in business.

(X_4) Market Value of Equity/Book Value of Total Liabilities. A measure of how far a firm's net assets can decline in terms of market value before the liabilities exceed the assets and the firm becomes insolvent. This ratio adds a market value dimension which Altman indicates had not been considered in other studies of business failures. (Altman has an alternate model for private firms that substitutes the book value of equity and has different coefficients for each of the five variables.)

(X_5) Sales/Total Assets. A measure of the sales generating ability of the firm's assets, which reflects the management's ability to deal with competitive conditions. (According to Altman, this ratio is the least significant on an individual basis, but because of its unique relationship to his other variables, this ratio ranks second in its contribution to the overall discriminating ability of the model.)

The formula for Altman's Z-score model empirically derived from a sample of 66 companies over the period 1946–1965 is:

$$Z = 1.2X_1 + 1.4X_2 + 3.3X_3 + 0.6X_4 + 1.0X_5$$

Altman's research established that firms with a Z-score (standardized statistic) of 2.99 clearly fall into the nonbankrupt prone sector while firms with a score below 1.81 are all bankrupt. The area between 2.99 and 1.81 is considered a gray area. It should be noted that the factor coefficients that Altman used may change as the sample changes or because of changes in the time period covered.

According to Altman, a bankruptcy classification model and the auditor's report have a different but analogous function. Auditors do not attempt to predict bankruptcy and an unqualified opinion is not a guarantee that a company will not fail. For example, it is possible that historical cost does not fairly represent the realizable value of assets but because it meets the auditor's guidelines for accounting statement presentation, no qualification is entered. Some audit teams are using prediction techniques such as a Z-score approach to assist them in their work. Table 7B-9 assesses 44 bankruptcies in the period from 1978 to 1982 comparing auditor opinion and a modified Z-score measure.

Zeta Model and A-Score. Based on further proprietary research, Altman developed his Zeta model and more recently an A-score model. Table 7B-10 illustrates the predictive ability of the Zeta model. It lists 64 companies which filed for bankruptcy since the date the Zeta model was developed through 1982. Note that even five years prior to the final annual statement date (prior to bankruptcy), the Zeta model was 63 percent accurate. That percentage increased each year, reaching 95 percent at the final statement date. It should also be noted that the average Zeta score decreases as bankruptcy approaches. The last column lists the number of consecutive months that the Zeta score was negative. The average for the 64 firms in Altman's table was 57 months.

Based on Altman's impressive results, his predictive techniques have received increased attention and recognition. The applications in monitoring extreme credit risk are numerous. Altman's work has caught the attention of bankers, auditors, fixed income analysts, and managers of "junk" bond portfolios, to name a few.

Other Bankruptcy Models. Christine V. Zavgren [1984] has developed a series of five bankruptcy models, one for each year in advance, which predicts with 70 percent accuracy, a bankruptcy five years in advance and with 90 percent accuracy, a bankruptcy one year in advance. Her model is based on the following key factors: debt-to-equity ratio, quick or acid-test ratio, inventory turnover, receivables turnover, current ratio, return on capital, and net operating asset turnover.

CREDIT ANALYSIS—MUNICIPAL SECURITIES

The analysis of municipal securities introduces the analyst to some unique factors not considered in corporate analysis. The following section describes the process used for analyzing municipal securities.

Credit Ratings and the Rating Process

Municipal finance has been in a period of transformation during the past decade. Much of the change was shaped by events not only from within, but also by society's changing perception of the role of government. The near default of New York City in 1975 led to a need for increased disclosure. This was particularly true in the case of general obligation bonds. Also, there was

TABLE 7B-10. Companies Which Have Failed Since ZETA Was Developed (1977–1982)

Company Name	Date Bankrupt	Final Statement Date	ZETA SCORES					Number of Months With Negative Score Prior to Failure
			Final Statement Date	Final Statement Date −1	Final Statement Date −2	Final Statement Date −3	Final Statement Date −4	
AM International	4/14/82	7/81	−4.60	−0.18	0.35	1.01	0.32	20
Acme Hamilton Mfg.	2/28/78	10/76	−5.54	−4.40	−4.25	−4.00	−4.12	124
Advent	3/17/81	3/80	−6.10	−4.22	−1.41			36
Alan Wood Steel	6/10/77	12/76	−4.92	−3.18	−0.31	−0.84	−1.33	89
Allied Artists	4/5/79	3/78	−7.07	−8.18	−7.14	−2.29	−1.40	120
Allied Supermarkets	11/6/78	6/78	−6.11	−5.28	−4.59	−2.92	−2.41	88
Apeco Corp.	10/19/77	11/76	−8.29	−1.53	−2.16	0.94	4.67	35
Arctic Enterprises	2/17/81	3/80	−4.12	−2.06	−0.78	0.26	0.54	35
Auto Train Corp.	9/80	12/79	−9.30	−8.42	−5.76			33
Barclay Inds. Inc.	6/81	7/80	−10.47	−4.80	−3.78	−2.83	−0.17	59
Bobbie Brooks	1/17/82	4/81	−1.98	−1.69	−0.29	−0.97	−3.03	103
Braniff Airlines	5/13/82	12/80	−3.40	−2.18	1.21	1.02	0.63	28
B. Brody Seating	2/4/80	8/79	−4.87	−3.02	−1.15	−0.41	−1.32	53
Capehart Corp.	2/16/79	3/78	−11.34	−6.54				24
Commonwealth Oil	3/3/78	12/76	−2.57	−1.72	0.26	0.63	1.12	26
Cooper Jarrett	12/28/81	12/80	−8.56	−6.93	−5.18	−4.04	−3.98	120
Eagle Clothes	11/1/77	12/75	−2.89	−2.38	−2.30	−1.83	−1.18	70
Ernst, E. C.	12/4/78	3/78	−4.49	0.78	2.00	1.81	2.04	8
FDI Inc.	12/1/78	4/77	−5.75	−5.93	−5.06	−0.58	−0.45	79
Filigree Foods	4/2/76	7/74	−3.89	−3.97	−3.80	−4.87	−5.62	68
First Hartford	2/23/81	4/79	−10.00	−7.30	−7.67	−5.45	−5.42	123
Food Fair Inc.	10/3/78	7/77	−0.61	−0.68	−1.01	0.52	0.62	38
Frigitemps	3/24/78	12/76	−1.65	−1.08				27

Company								
GRT Corp.	7/14/79	3/78	-3.46	-1.62	-2.92			39
Garcia Corp.	8/8/78	7/77	-4.69	-2.49	0.61			24
Garland Corp.	4/29/80	10/79	-1.85	-0.61	-0.04	2.54	0.70	30
General Recreation	12/21/78	12/77	-14.41	-6.79	-4.39	-0.67		48
Goldblatt Bros.	6/16/81	1/80	-2.35	-1.71	-0.59	0.36	0.46	41
Good, L. S. & Co.	5/27/80	1/79	-2.75	-2.17	-1.63	-1.37	-1.31	64
Inforex	10/79	12/78	-3.69	-4.22	-3.66	-4.43		46
Itel	1/19/81	12/79	-6.62	-1.79	-1.88	-1.15	-1.68	85
Keydata Corp.	11/31/80	7/80	-15.79	-9.55	-8.44	-7.25	-7.17	64
Lionel	2/82	12/80	-1.61	-1.91	-2.19	-1.23	-1.70	121
Lynnwear Corp.	2/81	11/79	-5.46	-2.05	-2.10	-1.80	-0.94	98
Mansfield Tire	10/79	12/78	-8.20	-1.09	1.31	0.90	0.84	22
Mays, J. W. Inc.	1/26/82	7/81	-2.03	-1.04	-0.44	-0.40	-0.74	78
McLouth Steel	12/8/81	12/80	-2.17	0.32	0.34	-0.45	2.29	11
Metropolitan Greetings	1/18/79	12/77	-5.94	-3.89	-3.63	-2.45		49
Morton Shoe Cos.	1/1/82	6/81	-5.05	-2.72	-1.32	2.05	-2.26	137
National Shoes	12/12/80	1/79	-2.56	-1.05				46
Neisner Bros. Inc.	12/77	1/77	-2.84	-3.02	-0.41	-0.98	-1.07	58
Nelly Don Inc.	11/29/78	11/77	-16.73	-7.11	-1.81	-3.40	-1.70	72
Novo Corp.	9/78	12/76	-5.03	-4.66	-4.28	-3.07	-3.23	128
Pacific Far East	1/2/78	12/76	-3.52	-3.95	-3.36	-4.74	-2.41	72
Pathcom	11/30/81	12/80	-29.56					11
Penn Dixie Inds.	4/7/80	12/78	-2.88	-3.54	-4.28	-1.28	0.15	51
Piedmont Inds.	2/22/79	5/78	-1.90	-1.38				21
Red Ball Express	4/26/82	12/80	-2.75	-0.58	-1.71	-0.78	-2.46	94
Richton International	3/18/80	4/79	0.15	1.08	-0.62	0.25	-0.59	0
Sambo's Restaurants	11/82	12/80	-3.51	-4.28	0.49	1.10	1.32	35
Saxon Inds.	4/15/82	12/80	0.27	-0.06	-0.54	-0.34	-0.50	0
Seatrain Lines	2/11/81	6/80	-2.41	-2.69	0.14	-2.77	-3.27	115
Shulman Trans. Ent.	8/21/78	12/77	-7.31	-4.29	-2.58			32
Sitkin Smlt & Ref.	3/13/78	6/77	-4.07	-3.12	-2.58	-1.52	-0.17	68
Solomon, Sam Inc.	8/29/80	1/79	-2.03	-2.09	-1.24			31

(continued)

TABLE 7B-10 (continued)

Company Name	Date Bankrupt	Final Statement Date	ZETA SCORES Final Statement Date	Final Statement Date -1	Final Statement Date -2	Final Statement Date -3	Final Statement Date -4	Number of Months With Negative Score Prior to Failure
Stelber Industries	3/10/76	6/73	-5.97	-2.40	-2.21	-2.93	-3.94	80
Stevcoknit Inc.	11/81	1/81	-2.47	-2.45	-0.07	0.01	0.70	34
Tenna Corp.	6/25/81	1/79	-0.70	-1.52	1.87	2.21	3.36	41
United Merch. & Mfg.	7/12/77	6/76	-0.38	0.24	1.72	3.23	3.04	12
Universal Cont'r	3/22/78	11/76	-5.03	-5.32	-4.02	-2.96	-2.26	111
West Chem Prods.	2/29/79	11/78	-0.31	0.35	5.70	5.98	5.44	3
White Motor Corp.	9/4/80	12/79	-1.41	-1.95	-1.80	-1.85	-2.39	116
Wickes Cos.	4/25/82	1/81	-0.92	0.39	0.48	0.77	0.91	15
Wilson Freight Co.	7/80	12/79	-3.87					7
Average Score			-5.04	-2.93	-1.81	-1.10	-0.84	
Number of firms correctly classified			61	56	45	35	31	
Number of firms incorrectly classified			3	6	13	17	18	
Total number of firms			64	62	58	52	49	
Percent correct			95	90	78	67	63	
Percent incorrect			5	10	22	33	37	
Average number of months of lead time								57

SOURCE: Altman [1983].

TABLE 7B-11. Moody's Investors Service, Inc. Municipal Bond Rating Revisions (1979–1984)

	1979	1980	1981	1982	1983	1984	Total
Downgradings	220	112	171	263	261	214	1,241
Upgradings	125	103	91	136	104	98	657

SOURCE: *Moody's Bond Survey* [February 11, 1985].

a need for governmental entities to conform to generally accepted accounting principles. A growing distrust of government has in part been responsible for the imposition of spending lids by the voters in sections of the country. The default of the Washington Public Power Supply System (WPPSS) has led to a closer scrutiny of the economic feasibility of enterprise projects, and the need to question not only the ability to pay, but also the willingness to pay.

These emerging factors have placed greater pressures on the rating agencies to anticipate the effects of these changes and to further fine tune the rating process. In the five-year period from 1979 to 1984, the number of ratings lowered by Moody's Investor Services exceeded upgradings by almost two-to-one, as seen in Table 7B-11.

Ratings by Rating Agencies

Presently there are four major municipal bond rating services. They are Moody's Investors Service, Standard & Poor's Corporation, Fitch Investors Service, Inc., and White's Tax Exempt Bond Market Ratings. While Moody's, Standard & Poor's, and Fitch tend to use traditional credit rating methods, White's rating is based primarily on how the issue will trade in the market. Fitch tends to concentrate on certain specialized areas of the municipal market while Moody's and Standard & Poor's rate the full gamut of municipal bond issues. While they do not rate a broad spectrum of municipals, Duff and Phelps does rate industrial revenue and pollution control bonds. Moody's has been rating municipal credits since 1918, while Standard & Poor's began in 1940. Table 7B-12 illustrates the Moody's and Standard & Poor's ratings for municipal bonds.

Both Moody's and Standard & Poor's also rate a number of Canadian municipal issuers as well. The Canadian Bond Rating Service, which is the major credit rating service in Canada, has only in recent years begun to rate municipal issues.

All of the rating services are independent of any outside influence and they guard this independent objectivity carefully. Each rating service reviews municipal securities on application by the issuer for a fee. They continue to review the issue until the bonds mature. If additional bonds are sold, and no application for a rating is received, the rating may be withdrawn. A rating may also be withdrawn if the issuer fails to provide timely information on an ongoing basis. The rating services must be able to support their ratings with

TABLE 7B-12. Municipal Debt Rating Definitions

Moody's	Standard & Poor's	Definition
Investment Grade		
Aaa	AAA	Highest quality.
Aa	AA	Still high quality, but margin of protection may not be as large as first category.
A	A	Strong capacity to pay principal and interest, but may be somewhat more susceptible to changing conditions.
Baa	BBB	Adequate capacity to pay principal and interest, but certain protective elements may be lacking that make them vulnerable during adverse economic conditions.
Below Investment Grade		
Ba, B	BB, B, CCC, CC	Predominantly speculative. No assurance of the ability to pay interest and principal over time.
Caa, Ca, C	C, D	In poor standing or in default.
Within the ratings of Aa, A, Baa, Ba and B Moody's further designates those that possess the strongest investment attributes by the numerical modifier of 1, 2, or 3. For example, bonds may be rated Aa1, Aa2, or Aa3.	The ratings of "AA" to "B" may be modified by the addition of a plus or minus sign to show relative standing within the major rating categories.	

adequate information. Since May 1980, Standard & Poor's has required that all financial statements submitted to them conform with Generally Accepted Accounting Principles (GAAP). They also require that those statements be certified by an outside independent accounting firm or by appropriate state or local auditing agencies.

Factors Used in the Rating Analysis

Both Moody's and Standard & Poor's tend to concentrate on four main factors in their analysis of general obligation bonds.

Debt Factors. This includes a complete analysis of the entity's debt structure, its history of debt issuance and repayment, as well as its overall debt burden, which includes other entities (overlapping debt) having the same claim on property in the area for taxation purposes. The debt burden will be measured against the ability of the entity to repay based on the income of its households and other budget resources. Debt limits imposed by law, as well as future plans for debt issuance, must be considered.

Financial or Fiscal Factors. This involves a complete examination of the entity's financial operation and records, including the budget document, which in municipal finance is the legal authorization for all spending. The history of the entity's financial operations as well as the entity's pension liabilities are also considered.

Government or Administrative Factors. This entails an examination of the type of government entity involved, such as city, county, school district, and so on, and the services provided. This analysis will take into consideration intergovernmental factors as well as the success of management and elected officials to govern effectively within the legal and political constraints that are present.

Economic Analysis. This includes an analysis of the economy of the entity, including population growth, wealth indicators and diversity of the economy and the performance of the economy of the entity in the past, and its prospects for the future.

While Moody's and Standard & Poor's generally use the same four factors in their analysis, it is in the *weighting* of those factors that often leads to a split rating on an issue. Moody's tends to place more weight on the debt and financial factors, while Standard & Poor's tends to place heavier emphasis on economic analysis.

An Example of Rating Disagreement

A recent example of a wide divergence of opinion between the two rating agencies was that of Allegheny County, Pennsylvania. Standard & Poor's gave Allegheny County an AA rating. Moody's rated the bonds Baa1 (almost two full grades lower than Standard & Poor's) from 1978 until 1983 when the bonds were upgraded to an A rating. Moody's, in supporting the lower credit rating for five years, was concerned with the county's above average overall debt, unfunded pension liabilities, budgetary practices of shifting funds from the county tax levy to the county institution district levy, and the real estate property assessment system. Standard & Poor's higher credit rating was based upon the affluence and diversity of the economy of the area, and accounting procedures which were being adapted to GAAP. The two services were reviewing the same information, but used significantly different weightings to indicate their respective assessments of the relative quality of debt of this issuer, Allegheny County.

The Power to Influence

Not only do the rating agencies possess considerable power to influence the market, they can also use that power to force municipal officials to act responsibly. In May 1984, the Snohomish Public Utility District Commissioners in Everett, Washington voted to withhold payments that were due the Washington Public Power Supply System. This was to protest the Supply System's refusal to repay loans the District had extended to the System in 1982. The loans were for the purpose of shutting down Nuclear Projects 4 and 5, which had been cancelled. (The bonds issued for these projects themselves later went into default, after the Washington Supreme Court ruled that the participants including Snohomish Public Utility District lacked authority to enter into the agreements.) The rating agencies, sensing an unwillingness on the part of Snohomish to honor its contractual obligations, reacted promptly. Moody's suspended the ratings of the Snohomish Public Utility District, while Standard & Poor's placed the District on their "Creditwatch," which meant further action would be forthcoming. The District's Commissioners rescinded their action and the ratings were restored. This averted a potential chain of events, which could have had serious implications for both Snohomish and WPPSS.

CREDIT ANALYSIS PROCESS FOR GENERAL OBLIGATIONS

There are no ironclad rules for municipal analysis as we have observed in our discussion of the rating agencies. The basic objectives of municipal analysis are to determine the creditworthiness of an issuer presently, and to attempt to project or anticipate the most adverse set of circumstances or scenario that could confront the issuer, and cause credit deterioration or default, such as a recession or depression. As indicated previously, the major factors of municipal analysis are economic, debt, financial, and governmental. Each of these factors must be carefully weighed, recognizing that there may be acceptable trade-offs between the factors, which can lead to differences in opinion as to the credit quality of an issuer. The analyst must develop through experience an insight as to the political, social, and economic factors, which may not always be readily apparent in the statistics. In the final analysis, the real creditworthiness of a municipal entity is dependent upon the willingness of the residents or customers to bear tax and/or rate increases necessary to repay the debt.

The major factors of municipal analysis for U.S. municipal tax-exempt credits apply equally to Canadian municipal taxable credits. The fact that one is taxable and the other is tax-exempt has no bearing on the analytical process. The same factors apply whether the entity being analyzed is a state, province, county, city, regional district, school district, or any other type of general obligation issuer.

The Analysis of the Economic Base

The credit analysis process begins with an analysis of the economic base of the issuer. This includes a study of the current economy, economic history, and future prospects. A study of the economy can serve as a major filter to determine whether to proceed with further credit analysis. A growing, vibrant economy will be in a better position to withstand economic shocks than one that is stagnant or declining.

Population Trends. Population comparisons should be made of the last three or four decades measuring both absolute and percentage changes. For a state or province, comparisons should be made with the growth rates of other states or provinces in the same region as well as the national growth rate. A city should have its growth rate compared with the county and metro area, as well as the state or province and the national growth rate. These comparisons will provide a basis for evaluating the overall growth trends.

A consistent pattern of growth is usually the most desirable, since this indicates economic vitality. On the other hand, if the population is growing very rapidly, new services must be provided, which could put a strain on the community's debt burden and budget. There may also be debt limits that would prevent additional financing and that could cause further stress on the community's finances if additional services have to be met from current tax revenues. However, rapid population growth may be accompanied by strong growth in assessed valuation and thus the ability to financially handle the growth may pose no real problems.

A declining population poses a warning signal that may indicate a lack of economic stability. Whatever the cause for the decline, it needs to be investigated. A situation where a city has lost population, but the surrounding county has gained population may indicate that the city is prevented from annexing suburban areas. Theoretically, the demand for and cost of municipal services should decline with population. Experience shows that such declines in service do not always occur, because of the high fixed cost nature of such services. The result is an increase in the cost burden per capita when a decline in population occurs.

Wealth and Income Trends. In analyzing the economy of an area, the analyst needs to examine per capita income figures as well as estimated per household income. This information may be obtained from the Bureau of Census publications or *The Annual Survey of Buying Power* published by Sales Marketing Management. This publication, which is published in July each year, includes the most current estimates of demographic and socioeconomic factors of regions, states, provinces, metropolitan markets, counties, and cities. The figures obtained for the entity under study should be compared with similar figures for the state or province, region and nation to evaluate the community's relative ranking. If the growth rate for the entity is less than that for the state, province, or nation, it may be an indication of economic maturity or stagnation. In addition, retail sales per capita, which are also contained in *The Annual Survey of Buying Power,* when compared with the same entities just mentioned, are a good indication of a community's importance as a retail trade center.

Employment Sources and Trends. A diversified economy is obviously more desirable than one largely dependent on a single industry or a few major employers. As an example, the state of Michigan has long been dependent on the auto industry, accounting for 34 percent of manufacturing employment in 1983, down from more than 50 percent in the 1960s and 1970s. In recent years, the state has suffered from high unemployment while the auto industry adjusted to the oil crisis of the early 1970s, recessions, and high interest rates that severely affected the industry. The state has since embarked on a program of economic redevelopment to lessen its dependence on the auto industry.

A state or community is affected on both the revenue and the expenditure side if its major industry is in a severe recession or, worse still, secular decline. First, there is a loss of tax revenues as a result of high unemployment, declining retail sales, and property values. Second, the demand for welfare and unemployment benefits increases expenditures, placing a further strain on the entity's finances.

The analyst should make a list of the largest employers, the number of employees for each, and their products and services to determine the extent of employee-weighted industry diversification. The trend of unemployment over at least the past five years should also be analyzed, and if possible, the period should include the last economic recession. In reviewing the distribution of employment, it is preferable to have the broadest possible distribution of employment among services, government, education, and trade, as well as manufacturing. While there is no hard and fast rule, if manufacturing employment is above 40 percent of total employment, manufacturing employment should be carefully reviewed to determine if it is well distributed among several employers and industries. The closing of a major plant, strikes, or bankruptcy of a major company can deliver a severe blow to the local economy if it is not broadly based.

State capitals and university-dominated communities are usually less susceptible to the effects of a recession, due to the large number of permanent governmental employees. Communities that have large military bases require special scrutiny in order to determine the permanence of the base. The closing of a military base can be devastating to the local economy.

The importance of the economic vitality of the community cannot be overemphasized. Obviously, few entities can avoid financial difficulty over the long run if their economy is deteriorating. A strong economy not only can support its government and debt obligations, but it should also provide an environment which will attract new industry and residents, and thus induce solid growth.

Analysis of Financial Trends

Once the determination has been made that the economy of an issuer is satisfactory, attention can be given to the debt, financial, and governmental factors.

Debt Load. Debt incurred by a community must be related to its present assets and its potential to repay that debt in the future. In analyzing the debt of a governmental entity, the total amount of general obligation debt outstanding should be determined. The issuer's debt history (its uses, purposes, and types of debt instruments) should be reviewed. How much short-term debt is outstanding? Has the trend been to repay such debt by year-end, or is it steadily increasing to form a permanent base of debt that realistically is long-term in nature? Has the entity ever defaulted and, if so, how was the default handled? Is there a debt limit and, if so, is the entity approaching the limit?

Debt figures for the past five years or longer should be obtained to determine if debt has been rising or declining. A growing community will be issuing debt to meet capital needs. A declining area may be issuing debt to fund budget shortfalls. In reviewing the debt history, it is also necessary to determine what plans have been made for the retirement of the debt. Are specific property levies or other funds pledged for the retirement of the debt? What are the future plans for debt issuance?

One of the more important ratios relates the total general obligation debt of the issuer to the market value of the real property in the tax base. Since other entities also have a claim on the tax base, the ratio of overall applicable debt to the market value of the real property should also be calculated. Any self-supported debt such as water revenue bonds should be excluded from these ratios. Overall debt includes the proportionate share of any other overlapping entity whose debt is paid out of the same real estate tax base. This would include school districts, special districts such as sewer, and junior college districts to name a few. The higher the debt ratio, the greater the chance of credit deterioration. There is no prescribed ratio of debt to market value or estimated full value where a community could be considered marginal, but a generally accepted rule of thumb suggests that anything in excess of 8 to 9 percent should raise warning flags. A ratio of less than 5 percent would be considered excellent. Moody's publishes an annual survey, shown in Table 7B-13, which provides a handy guide for the range of net debt per capital and the ratio of net debt to estimated full value (EFV). Table 7B-14 ranks the states on the basis of the ratio of net debt to estimated full value.

$$\text{Net debt ratio} = \frac{\text{total general obligation debt}}{\text{estimated market value of real property}}$$

$$\text{Overall debt ratio} = \frac{\text{total general obligation debt} + \text{proportionate share of all overlapping entities}}{\text{estimated market value of real property}}$$

TABLE 7B-13. City and County Debt Medians, 1985

Cities

Population Range	Net Debt Per Capita				Ratio of Net Debt to E.F.V. (%)			
	DIRECT NET DEBT	OVERALL NET DEBT			DIRECT NET DEBT	OVERALL NET DEBT		
	Median	Low	Median	High	Median	Low	Median	High
500,000 and over	$559	$271	$ 857	$ 2,004	1.6	0.9	4.2	8.9
300,000 to 499,999	406	215	718	1,659	2.3	1.1	3.1	10.4
200,000 to 299,999	539	291	706	1,206	2.2	1.6	2.6	9.0
100,000 to 199,999	362	85	554	5,211	1.6	0.3	2.5	9.3
50,000 to 99,999	369	59	658	3,199	1.7	1.0	2.8	16.1
25,000 to 49,999	384	10	689	4,135	1.8	0.1	2.9	15.0
10,000 to 24,999	533	134	713	5,843	2.1	0.2	3.3	24.5
Under 10,000	792	151	1,064	15,907	2.4	0.1	3.6	20.0

Counties

Population Range	Net Debt Per Capita				Ratio of Net Debt to E.F.V. (%)			
	DIRECT NET DEBT	OVERALL NET DEBT			DIRECT NET DEBT	OVERALL NET DEBT		
	Median	Low	Median	High	Median	Low	Median	High
1,000,000 and over	$139	$168	$1,049	$ 1,981	0.4	0.03	4.2	4.1
250,000 to 999,999	158	275	607	2,071	0.6	0.7	2.5	5.2
100,000 to 249,999	96	150	580	1,379	0.4	0.6	2.5	5.5
Under 100,000	196	96	488	156,271	0.7	0.4	2.1	12.2

SOURCE: Moody's Investors Service [1985].

It is also helpful for comparison purposes to determine debt per capita. This ratio should be calculated for both net debt and overall applicable debt. Guideline figures for cities and counties of various sizes are also shown in Table 7B-13, while Table 7B-15 ranks the states on the basis of net tax-supported debt per capita. The formulas are:

$$\text{Net debt per capita} = \frac{\text{net debt}}{\text{population of issuing entity}}$$

$$\text{Overall debt per capita} = \frac{\text{overall debt}}{\text{population of issuing entity}}$$

TABLE 7B-14. State Rankings of Net Tax-Supported Debt as a Percent of Estimated Full Valuation

Rank	State	Percent of Estimated Full Valuation
1	Delaware	4.9
2	Hawaii	4.7
3	New York	4.2
4	Massachusetts	3.6
5	Pennsylvania	3.4
6	Connecticut	3.1
7	Maryland	2.7
8	Louisiana	2.7
9	Alaska	2.5
10	Alabama	2.5
11	West Virginia	2.0
12	Mississippi	1.8
13	New Mexico	1.7
14	Washington	1.7
15	Vermont	1.6
16	Illinois	1.5
17	New Jersey	1.5
18	Rhode Island	1.5
19	Montana	1.5
20	Maine	1.3
21	Wisconsin	1.3
22	New Hampshire	1.2
23	Ohio	1.2
24	Kentucky	1.1
25	Florida	1.1
26	Minnesota	1.0
27	South Carolina	1.0
28	Utah	0.9
29	Tennessee	0.9
30	Georgia	0.8
31	Kansas	0.7
32	Michigan	0.6
33	North Carolina	0.6
34	Missouri	0.6
35	Oregon	0.6
36	Arizona	0.5
37	California	0.4
38	Virginia	0.3
39	Nevada	0.3
40	North Dakota	0.2
41	Oklahoma	0.2
42	South Dakota	0.2

TABLE 7B-14 (continued)

Rank	State	Percent of Estimated Full Valuation
43	Texas	0.1
44	Nebraska	0.1
45	Colorado	0.1
46	Idaho	0.1
47	Arkansas	0.1
48	Wyoming	0.1
49	Indiana	0.01
50	Iowa	0.003
	Median	**1.1**

SOURCE: Moody's Investors Service [1985].

TABLE 7B-15. State Rankings of Net Tax-Supported Debt Per Capita

Rank	State	Debt Per Capita
1	Alaska	$1,992
2	Hawaii	1,600
3	Delaware	1,101
4	Massachusetts	773
5	Connecticut	725
6	Louisiana	671
7	Maryland	670
8	New York	607
9	Washington	579
10	Vermont	499
11	Kentucky	458
12	Alabama	441
13	West Virginia	435
14	Pennsylvania	394
15	New Jersey	388
16	New Hampshire	342
17	Rhode Island	327
18	Wisconsin	316
19	Illinois	309
20	New Mexico	307
21	Minnesota	293
22	Ohio	291
23	Maine	283
24	Montana	283
25	Mississippi	259
26	Florida	256
27	Georgia	238
28	Utah	199
29	Oregon	190

Rank	State	Debt Per Capita
30	South Carolina	185
31	Michigan	143
32	North Carolina	143
33	California	129
34	Tennessee	128
35	Nevada	105
36	Kansas	90
37	North Dakota	89
38	Virginia	82
39	Missouri	75
40	Arizona	71
41	Texas	52
42	Oklahoma	44
43	Wyoming	33
44	South Dakota	30
45	Nebraska	25
46	Idaho	19
47	Colorado	16
48	Arkansas	8
49	Iowa	1
50	Indiana	0.4
	Median	**258**

SOURCE: Moody's Investors Service [1985].

Another important ratio is net general obligation debt to personal income. This ratio will measure to some degree the amount of underlying wealth that supports the debt. It is particularly helpful when reviewing a state or province and then comparing it with other states and provinces, as shown in Table 7B-16. It can also be used with other general obligation issuers. A good source to use for personal income is the "Estimated Buying Income" figures from the *Survey of Buying Power by Sales Marketing Management*. The formula is:

$$\text{Debt as a percent of personal income} = \frac{\text{net debt}}{\text{personal income for the entity}}$$

TABLE 7B-16. State Rankings of Net Tax-Supported Debt as a Percent of 1983 Personal Income

Rank	State	Percent of Personal Income
1	Hawaii	13.4
2	Alaska	12.1
3	Delaware	8.8
4	Louisiana	6.6
5	Massachusetts	5.9

TABLE 7B-16 (continued)

Rank	State	Percent of Personal Income
6	Maryland	5.2
7	Vermont	5.0
8	Connecticut	4.9
9	Kentucky	4.9
10	Alabama	4.8
11	Washington	4.8
12	West Virginia	4.7
13	New York	4.7
14	Pennsylvania	3.4
15	New Mexico	3.2
16	Mississippi	3.2
17	New Hampshire	2.9
18	Maine	2.9
19	Montana	2.9
20	Rhode Island	2.8
21	Wisconsin	2.8
22	New Jersey	2.8
23	Ohio	2.6
24	Illinois	2.5
25	Minnesota	2.5
26	Georgia	2.3
27	Florida	2.3
28	Utah	2.3
29	South Carolina	2.0
30	Oregon	1.8
31	North Carolina	1.5
32	Tennessee	1.3
33	Michigan	1.2
34	California	1.0
35	Nevada	0.9
36	North Dakota	0.8
37	Kansas	0.7
38	Missouri	0.7
39	Arizona	0.7
40	Virginia	0.7
41	Texas	0.4
42	Oklahoma	0.4
43	South Dakota	0.3
44	Wyoming	0.3
45	Nebraska	0.2
46	Idaho	0.2
47	Colorado	0.1
48	Arkansas	0.1
49	Iowa	0.01
50	Indiana	0.004
	Median	**2.4**

SOURCE: Moody's Investors Service [1985].

Trend of Assessed Valuation. Property taxes in recent years have become less important for many governmental entities. Voters imposed lid measures, such as Proposition 13 in California and Proposition 2½ in Massachusetts, which have complicated the revenue picture and caused local governments to diversify their revenue sources. Nevertheless, the entity's history of assessed market valuations, and more importantly, estimated full or market value for the past ten years, serve as important measures of the tax base. A declining trend may indicate that assessment procedures are outmoded, or that industry is departing. Large tracts of land may have been removed from the tax rolls, pending redevelopment, such as a downtown redevelopment plan. On the other hand, large tracts of land being converted to nontaxable status could be an especially troubling sign.

Ideally, assessed valuation and full or market value should have a history of moderate or steady growth. Assessed valuation showing a steady decline usually means a loss of industry. Population losses and credit deterioration will tend to follow.

Tax Collections. While the importance of property taxes may be declining as a source of revenue for some entities, it is still important that a community strives to collect 100 percent of the taxes due. Often a community will collect at least 95 percent of the taxes due and will ultimately reach about 100 percent as delinquent taxes are collected. If tax collections fall below 90 percent without achieving close to 100 percent as delinquent taxes are collected, it is cause for some concern and explanation. It is necessary to study the history of tax collections for a period of at least ten years. Increasing delinquencies are not only a sign of credit deterioration but also a signal that financial management is not as strong as it should be.

Cash Flow Analysis. Municipal accounting involves the use of a number of fund accounts of which the general fund is usually the major operating account. In some cases debt service may be paid from the general fund. If there is a separate debt service fund it should be combined with the general fund to measure cash flow. The analyst should be aware of any restricted funds that may be included in the general fund such as government grants, which could not be used to pay debt service.

It is necessary to review the trend of the general fund over a period of perhaps five years and determine if there has been a positive balance or if the balance has been declining. It is also important to determine if the entity resorted to the use of tax anticipation notes on a regular basis, or funding of year-end deficits with long-term bonds. The analyst needs to be aware of any unusual transfers in or out of the general fund to make it appear in better financial condition than it really is. When reviewing a state or province, it is usually necessary to combine all of the various funds to obtain a true picture of the financial condition. It is also desirable to compare current expenditures with current revenues over a period of at least five years to determine if the entity is operating within its means. If an entity has a deficit for two years in a row, it could well be a sign of major problems and could ultimately lead to serious credit deterioration. If the general fund is running deficits in periods of economic prosperity, what will it do in a recession or depression?

Sources of General Fund Revenues. General fund revenues for local governments depend to a large extent on property taxes. School districts may receive some form of state aid as well as revenues from property taxes. State governments tend to have the widest choice of revenue sources.

The analyst will want to determine the major revenue sources over the past five years and perhaps calculate each as a percentage of the total. Any decline in the importance of a key revenue source should be further investigated to determine the cause. The adoption of property tax limitation measures by some states has caused many entities to look for new sources of revenue such as user fees to replace declining property revenues.

The dependence on intergovernmental aid such as federal revenue sharing needs to be studied carefully. Entities that become dependent upon such sources may be hardpressed to find alternative sources, especially in times of economic recession, if the federal or state government cuts back such funds, to balance their own budgets, for example.

Unfunded Pension Liabilities. The financial distress encountered by New York City in 1975 led to further concern with off balance sheet obligations such as pension funds. This in turn produced a heightened awareness of growing liabilities for present and future payments to beneficiaries of public retirement systems.

Disclosure of pension liabilities tends to be relatively poor in official statements and documents. Many issuers do not use proper methods of funding their pension liabilities such as the state of Massachusetts, which utilizes a pay-as-you-go basis.

Among the warning signs that an analyst should look for in the public pension area are:

1. Inadequate disclosure of current pension liabilities;
2. Infrequent actuarial evaluations;
3. Lack of advance funding of future pension benefits;
4. Frequent shifts from one actuarial firm to another; and
5. Inappropriate or unrealistic actuarial assumptions such as a high actuarial rate of return or a low salary progression rate or both.

The analyst should attempt to determine the amount of unfunded pension liability and whether the pension system is based on sound actuarial funding. By determining the total per capita obligations (both bond and unfunded pension liabilities), the analyst has a benchmark to use in comparing with similar credits of the same size and rating.

Municipal Accounting. Audits prepared by a firm of independent CPAs are still fairly infrequent for issuers of general obligation bonds. Financial data is usually prepared by the issuer's own auditors, or those of an overlapping political entity such as a county or state. Many governmental bodies still use cash accounting, which records revenues when received and expenses when paid, that can mask serious problems. GAAP require the use of modified accrual accounting, which records revenue when earned and expenses when incurred.

Some characteristics set governmental accounting apart from corporate accounting. First, governmental accounting is not profit oriented. The primary purpose of governmental accounting is the allocation of resources. Second, the dominance of the budget document and the legal compliance with that document is paramount in governmental reporting. Finally, there is no single regulatory body to enforce compliance with GAAP for municipalities, such as the SEC has done for U.S. corporations since 1933.

The Governmental Accounting Standards Board (GASB), an independent standard-setting body, was formed in 1984. GASB replaces the National Council on Governmental Accounting, which was formed in 1934 under the auspices of the Municipal Finance Officers Association. While GASB lacks the power to force compliance with GAAP, it is expected that the market will demand it in due time. One of the first areas that this new board will address is pension accounting. There has been considerable disagreement in this area between the governmental and private sectors. With the GASB, both the quality and detail of financial information should improve.

Analysis of Legal and Governmental Factors

General obligation bonds are backed by the full faith and credit of the issuer. In order to assure repayment of the debt, the issuing entity pledges to use its powers to tax to the fullest if the bonds are unlimited tax bonds.

Since general obligation bonds generally require voter approval, the analyst will want to verify that an election was held, to be certain that the bonds were voter approved. This has been particularly necessary in those states that have passed property tax lids. Most of the lid measures specifically exclude voter-approved bonds. If the bonds were not voter approved in these states, debt service for the bonds could be under the spending lid.

The legal opinion is perhaps one of the most important documents that the analyst will review. It must be issued by recognized attorneys who specialize in public finance. For tax-exempt securities in the United States, the analyst will want to verify that the bonds are in fact tax-exempt and that the ordinance or authorization for the bonds was duly adopted and is enforceable. The legal opinion is a comment as to an issue's legality only and has no bearing on any other aspects of quality.

Governmental or political factors are the most difficult to analyze. Unlike the rating services, the analyst seldom has the opportunity to visit with governmental officials personally. There are some signs, however, to look for in appraising the governmental or political factors. These could include a history of labor problems, friction, and disagreement on the governing board or council, and frequent changes of appointed administrators, to name a few.

The default of Cleveland in 1978 was due in part to a bitter political struggle between the then Mayor Dennis Kucinich and the Cleveland business community over the sale of the city's electric power system. The banks refused to renew the city's notes when they came due. Thus it is possible for a political struggle to exacerbate a financial crisis and cause a default.

Some judgments as to the managerial capabilities of government can also be drawn from analyzing available data. Are budget projections close to the actual figures? Are pension plans adequately funded? Are revenues chronically overestimated while expenditures are consistently underestimated? Are financial records in good order? What is the record with regard to tax collections? These are a few of the questions that will allow the analyst to form some type of opinion as to the quality of management.

The municipal market is, to a large degree, a self-regulated industry. More complete and timely disclosure, which has been demanded by investors in recent years, has provided the analyst with more information to facilitate a credit decision. Nonetheless, the analyst must be on the alert for unusual situations. No two bond issues or issuers are alike.

CREDIT ANALYSIS PROCESS FOR REVENUE BONDS

In recent years there has been a proliferation of new and different types of municipal revenue bond financing. The analytical process for revenue bonds varies depending on the type of bond involved. Each revenue bond category such as electric, water, sewer, hospital, housing, or resource recovery, and so on, has its own unique characteristics that are a part of the analytical process. In this brief overview, only a basic framework involving general characteristics of revenue bond analysis applicable to all revenue bonds can be addressed.

Analysis of the Economic Viability of the Project Being Financed

The municipal utility industry today is in an era in which projects are of immense size utilizing sophisticated technology. The tremendous cost of these projects, whether it be an electric generating plant, a water or sewer treatment plant, or a resource recovery plant pose even greater potential risks for the bondholder. The default of the $2.25 billion Washington Public Power Supply System Project 4 and 5 bonds in August 1983 has heightened the awareness by analysts that the economics of any project must be carefully scrutinized.

Characteristics of the Service Territory. The process should begin with an analysis of the economy of the area or the service territory using the same techniques as were discussed in the analysis of general obligation bonds. Population growth, indicators of wealth, and the diversification of the area's economy will play a major role in determining the economic feasibility of a project. Lack of industry diversification may cause problems if one of the major employers or customers of the system leaves the area or ceases operation. The analysis of the area economy should provide valuable clues as to the ability of the entity to afford the project under consideration. If the issuing entity provides a utility service, the specific service territory should be clearly defined, as well as the ability to expand that territory. In addition, the major customers or users of the service should be identified.

Economic Need for the Project. It is axiomatic in revenue bond analysis that the more economic justification a project provides, the less likely it is that there will be serious problems through the life of the bonds. To help arrive at a decision on the project's justification, there are some questions that need to be answered in the course of the analysis. Is there a real need for the project? Could the community do without the project? Does the project provide the potential for future savings for the participants or owners? Are there environmental or legal reasons that the project must be built, such as a city being forced to build a sewage treatment plant to clean up a stream or river? Is there evidence of broad support for the project, or has it already passed through a series of closely decided political and legal hurdles that indicate further opposition? Is there a demonstrated willingness on the part of the community or customers to pay the price of the project?

Most utilities have a monopoly on their service territory, but an important question to be raised is whether there are competing facilities nearby that could provide the service cheaper, thus creating an environment that would make it difficult to raise rates?

A good example of this is the Seabrook Nuclear plant, which in 1984 was being built by Public Service of New Hampshire and other participants, including Massachusetts Municipal Wholesale Electric Company, a non-profit group of municipal power companies. The plant has been plagued by enormous cost overruns and the cost of power will be expensive, if it is ever completed. Quebec Hydro to the north is willing to sell cheap hydro power at prices far below the projected cost of power from the Seabrook Nuclear Project. This has not escaped the attention of the Massachusetts Municipal Wholesale Electric Company customers, who have put enormous pressure on the company making it more difficult to raise rates to fund their share of construction costs. High rates can also cause industries to leave the area or prevent new ones from moving in, thereby affecting the economic growth of an area and directly or indirectly affecting the viability of public revenue bonds.

Feasibility Study. Most revenue bond financings will involve a feasibility study prepared by a reputable engineering or consulting firm. Such studies can be voluminous. A study will be made of the physical soundness of the system and its ability to produce a service that can be provided at a price consumers are willing and/or able to pay. It will determine the adequacy of supply for a water system, the sufficiency of fuel for an electric plant, or the demand for beds in the case of a hospital. It should be prepared by a well known firm with experience in projects of a similar nature.

In reviewing the feasibility study, the first question to be determined is how realistic are the demand assumptions for the product or service? If conservative assumptions are substituted, does the project continue to stand on its own merits? How do the growth rates used in the study compare with the industry average or with similar credits?

Another important consideration is the technology involved in the project. Has it proven successful or is it entirely new? Does the issuing entity possess the management capability to run the plant or project successfully? Are there similar plants operating at the present time? Is the engineering and construction firm involved in the project experienced in this technology? Since interest costs are usually capitalized during construction in a municipal utility project, the construction timetable must be realistic or the debt load (principal plus capitalized interest) may be increased to levels in excess of those that were projected or are reasonable.

Often, a municipal electric utility or resource recovery unit will be built with ample capacity for future growth. In those instances it is necessary to verify that a market for the excess capacity exists and that the timetable estimated is totally realistic, particularly if the sale of that excess capacity is important to the financial feasibility of the project. While the feasibility study is another important tool in the analytical process, the analyst needs to test its assumptions and if necessary, question its conclusions.

Analysis of the Bond Indenture or Ordinance

The bond indenture or bond ordinance in municipal finance is the legal document in which the governing body issuing the bonds spells out the legal protection measures for the bondholder. The indenture remains in effect for the life of the bonds or until the bonds are called or refunded. Municipal bonds are presently registered but in previous years were usually issued in bearer form and the owners were essentially unknown, making it almost impossible to obtain approval from bondholders for changes in the indenture.

Bond indentures in recent years have effectively become more complex. At the same time many of the provisions designed to protect bondholders have been weakened. Since municipal enterprises are not intended to generate large profits to provide cushions in the event of economic downturns or system problems, the margin for error on the part of the issuing entity has narrowed considerably. This means that the analyst's task in assessing expected risk is even more critical. A detailed analysis of the indenture or ordinance is necessary to determine that the bondholder's interests have been protected.

Specific Pledge of Revenue. The project being financed is usually secured by user charges for a service or product. These enterprise revenues are specifically pledged for the payment of debt service on the bonds. Usually the pledge is one of net revenues, that is, the revenues remaining after the payment of operating expenses of the system. Occasionally the pledge may be that of gross revenues, which would be available before operating expenses. Since there may be more than one lien position, the analyst will want to be certain that there is no prior lien. If one exists, the analyst will want to determine if the prior lien is closed, preventing the issuance of additional prior lien bonds under the indenture.

Flow of Funds. Next to the revenue pledge, the analysis of the flow of funds is one of the most important areas that must be reviewed in the bond indenture. The indenture will set forth the manner in which revenues are to be applied to the cost of operation and maintenance, debt service and contingencies. To protect the bondholders' interest and assure the prompt payment of interest and principal, a *revenue fund* is usually set up to receive all income from the operation of the enterprise. As an example, revenue fund receipts are usually distributed monthly in the following manner:

- *Operation and Maintenance Fund.* This fund meets all operating expenses.
- *Debt Service Fund.* This fund is sufficient to pay principal and interest. For serial bonds, typically a monthly amount is usually deposited, which is equal to approximately one-sixth of the next maturing semi-annual interest payment, plus one-twelfth of the next annual principal payment. Interest earned on the fund, as well as the other funds, belongs to the issuing entity and may be withdrawn for deposit into the general fund or retained in the debt service fund.
- *Reserve Fund.* This fund is usually set up to pay interest and principal in case there is a deficiency in the debt service fund. The fund is usually equal to the maximum principal and interest payable in any one year. It may be funded at the time of the bond sale, or within a reasonable period of time, such as five years after the sale of the bonds.
- *Revenue and Replacement Fund.* This fund is usually established to provide funds for future service extensions or to meet emergency repairs or operating costs. The size of this fund may be an arbitrary amount depending on the type of project—water facilities, electric generating plant, or hospital.

Ideally, surplus funds are either retained in the system for further improvements or to retire debt. In some cases surplus funds may be transferred to the general fund of the issuing entity, particularly if the entity is a city.

Establishment of a Debt Service Reserve. The establishment of a debt service reserve is somewhat unique to municipal finance. The principal purpose behind a debt service reserve is to provide funding so as to give an entity that is experiencing financial difficulty the equivalent of a period of time such as one year to take corrective action. The indenture may require a debt service reserve equal to either the maximum or the average principal and interest requirements in any one year, or some other, perhaps arbitrary amount. The fund is usually established from bond proceeds or it may be accumulated within a reasonable period of time such as 60 months after the sale of the bonds. If at any time funds are withdrawn to pay principal and interest, the fund must soon thereafter be restored to its proper level. Preferably, the debt service reserve should be held by a trustee. As indentures are weakened, debt service reserves are not necessarily equal to maximum principal and interest in any one year, but may be maximum interest only or some other arbitrarily determined amount.

Additional Bonds Test. The additional bonds test is an important covenant to ensure that the system's finances are not unduly strained by issuing too much debt. Usually the indenture will require that revenues in the preceding year of the proposed debt issuance be sufficient to cover present or prospective debt service by some stated coverage figure such as 1.35× or 1.50×. It also forces the issuing entity to raise fees or rates charged in advance of the additional debt issuance.

Call or Refunding Provisions. The indenture will spell out the call or refunding provisions of an issue. Revenue and general obligation bonds may be noncallable or provide a call feature only after five to ten years of the date of the issue. In Canada, many long-term municipal bonds have a fifteen-year period before the bonds may be called.

The bond indenture will usually provide for a call price at a premium over face or par value that is reduced for every annual call date past the original first date that the bonds are callable.

Retractable or Extendible Options. Canadian municipal issues sometimes provide retractable or extendible options. A retractable bond allows the bondholder to return the bond at a specified date before the stated maturity for full payment. By the same token, an extendible option would allow a bondholder to extend the maturity at some specified date. In the U.S. municipal market, some bonds have been issued with various put provisions, which allow the holder an early redemption option.

Other Covenants. The indenture will also contain other covenants such as a pledge to maintain the system in a proper manner. There will usually be a rate covenant, which promises to charge rates sufficient to cover all operating expense and to meet debt service payments on time. There should be a provision for an annual audit by a certified public accountant, plus the furnishing of copies of the audit to all bondholders in a timely manner. The enterprise generally will pledge to maintain proper insurance, and to provide no free service. In addition, the indenture will define the events of default, including the failure to observe any of the covenants of the indenture, and the appropriate remedies. Finally, the indenture will specify the eligible investments that may be used for the reserve funds. The usual requirement is in U.S. government securities, but it may vary according to state law.

Analysis of Financial Trends

The financial position and trends of municipalities are viewed in a somewhat different perspective than are corporates, because corporates are vulnerable to competitive forces. Nevertheless, careful analysis of financial trends is an essential aspect of the evaluation of risk for revenue bonds.

Debt Load. In reviewing the debt load of a revenue bond issuer, more emphasis is placed on future debt issuance than historical debt issuance. This is in contrast to the analysis of the general obligation debt load. It is necessary to learn as much as possible concerning the issuing entity's plans or needs for future debt, its ability to support that debt, and its ability to issue the debt in accordance with the bond ordinance's additional bonds test.

For a municipal electric utility, for example, the growth trends for long-term power demands on both a historical and projected basis should be obtained. Capacity and peak loads should be compared with on-line resources and projects under construction to determine the need for additional facilities.

One ratio that is used in municipal utility revenue bond analysis is the total amount of debt divided by the number of customers or utility connections. When compared with other entities of the same size and rating, the debt per customer or per connection statistics can give some clue as to the relative debt burden. The formula is:

$$\text{Debt per customer} = \frac{\text{total debt}}{\text{number of customers}}$$

The debt ratio, which is the net funded debt divided by the sum of fixed assets plus net working capital is sometimes used. Municipal projects such as electric power joint action projects often are supported entirely by debt, so the ratio does not have as much validity as in corporate analysis.

$$\text{Debt ratio} = \frac{\text{net funded debt}}{\text{fixed assets} + \text{net working capital}}$$

Joint action agencies, which are common in municipal finance, usually consist of two or more entities that join together to form a common system. Often a joint action agency may involve a power plant, but it could be any type of enterprise function in which the participants are seeking economies of scale, a consolidated management of staff, and/or a reduction of the financial burden by allocating the cost among its members.

The analyst should also be aware of off-balance sheet financing. This is particularly true of municipal electric corporations, who are participating in joint action agencies to build power plants. To determine an entity's true financial position, the analyst should include the ownership interest in all joint action projects. The participant's share of the joint action project debt should be added to the participant's own debt.

Coverage of Debt Service. If an analyst were able to select only one ratio for revenue bond analysis, it would probably be debt service coverage. Debt service coverage is calculated as the net revenue available for debt service divided by maximum annual principal and interest requirements. This is an indication of the flexibility that an entity has with regard to its cash requirements. The formula is:

$$\text{Debt service coverage} = \frac{\text{net amount available for debt service}}{\text{maximum annual principal and interest}}$$

For debt service coverage, a historical review of at least five years of coverage is necessary to determine the ability and willingness of an issuer to maintain sound financial operations. If there are wide swings in coverage from one year to the next, further investigation is necessary.

Municipal entities often have the authority to set their own utility rates. An analysis of the historical debt service coverage should indicate the ability and willingness of the entity to raise rates quickly, to eliminate financial shortfalls, rather than waiting until the increase is imperative to avoid disaster. This analysis may also give some indication as to the political climate in the rate setting environment.

Rate Comparisons. Rates have already been touched on. Rate comparisons with other entities in the same area and around the country are helpful to determine how much rate flexibility the issuer may have. If rates are already too high by comparison, it will be extremely difficult to raise them further.

One term that is heard often in the electric utility industry is "rate shock," which is caused by a sudden increase in rates as a project is completed and brought on-line. Potential rate shock is essentially what caused several of the participants in the Washington Public Power Supply System Project 4 and 5 bonds to seek to nullify their contractual responsibilities. To ease the problem, there should be less reliance on *capitalized interest,* which often requires that funds be borrowed to pay interest during construction. This would force the issuing entity to raise rates and pay interest costs *during* the construction period from internally generated funds. Rates would thus be raised gradually during the construction and start-up phase of a project. This is not to imply that the analyst will be able to structure the financing, but only to suggest some of the future problems that can result from too much reliance on capitalized interest by the issuer.

Legal and Regulatory Factors

The importance of the review and analysis of the legal basis for an authority's issuance of bonds cannot be understated. The powers granted to municipal entities vary, especially between states. Thus, the analyst must research both legal and regulatory factors.

Legal Opinion. There was a time in municipal analysis when the legal opinion received little notice in the analytical process other than checking to make certain that the law firm writing the opinion was listed in *The Bond Buyer's Directory of Municipal Bond Dealers.* This is no longer the case. As indicated previously with general obligation bonds, the legal opinion is one of the most important documents that the analyst will review. This is especially true of revenue bonds. Since revenue bonds do not as a rule require voter approval, it is important that the issuer's authority to issue revenue bonds be carefully validated.

One very key question to be resolved is whether the legislation that created the financing vehicle has been court tested and found to be duly legal. Unless it has been specifically court tested, or a highly similar issue has been ruled upon by the courts, one has only a legal opinion to rely on, which may turn out to be of little value if not specifically upheld by the courts.

Legal or Regulatory Limitations. Many municipal bond financings, such as joint action agencies formed to build an electric generating plant, involve a number of participants. These legal arrangements can become quite complex. Again, the history of the default on $2.25 billion Washington Public Power Supply System Project 4 and 5 bonds has taught municipal analysts to question the authority of participants to enter into the contracts. The initial legal opinion for the Washington Public Power Supply System Project 4 and 5 bonds indicates that the contracts were proper and enforceable, in other words, ironclad. Nevertheless, in 1983 the Washington State Supreme Court found several points in which the contracts failed to conform to the state's statutes resulting in their being declared unenforceable. Interestingly, the Oregon State Supreme Court upheld the legality of similar contracts in early 1984.

One common element in joint action agencies involving a power plant is the long-term power sales contract. These contracts are of two types. A *take-and-pay* contract requires the participant to pay only for the power taken or purchased. The agency usually agrees to supply all or a share of the energy to the participants at a price sufficient to cover all costs including debt service. By contrast, a *take-or-pay* contract requires the participant to pay for a predetermined purchase of the capacity of the project. The contract usually requires the participant to pay whether or not the project is completed or operating and whether or not the participant ultimately needs or uses its proportionate share of the capacity. In addition, there is usually a step-up provision that requires the other participants to make the payments of a participant who has defaulted.

Analysts should recognize that while corporations use such contracts extensively, they may or may not be actually authorized for a governmental entity. Some states have expressed explicit statutory authority for municipalities to enter into these types of contracts. Other states lack this language in their statutes. Since joint action agencies have become so popular in municipal finance, it is incumbent upon the analyst to determine if statutory authority for these contracts exist in the state(s) that is under consideration.

One last caveat: legal protection should not be placed above economic protection in the rank ordering of priorities in municipal revenue bond analysis. The economics of a project and the willingness as well as the ability of the municipality to pay should be the analyst's primary concern. If a project is needed and can be completed within reasonable financial limits, legal problems are far less likely. It is, however, of absolute necessity that the analyst be assured that the statutory authority exists and the particular statutes have been court tested.

Substitution of Credit

The municipal market has used third party guarantees of payment of interest and principal on its revenue bonds for a number of years. Often these were in the form of a state/provincial or federal backing of local or public authority financing such as the federal guarantee of local public housing authority bonds. In recent years in the United States, newer forms of payment guarantees have come about in the form of guarantees issued by commercial banks and municipal bond insurance firms.

Letters of Credit

A letter of credit issued by a commercial bank guarantees the payment of interest and principal on the guaranteed credit if the issuer is unable to do so. Usually the letter of credit is issued by the guaranteeing bank to the bond trustee, but it may also be issued directly to the bondholder. Typically, letters of credit are issued for short-term securities although some have been written for as long as ten years.

The analyst needs to be aware that because of certain quirks in the municipal bankruptcy law, it is necessary that specific safeguards be included in the letter of credit agreement. One of these involves the fact that if a municipal entity were to declare bankruptcy within 90 days after making a principal and interest payment, it is possible that the bankruptcy judge could order the return of the principal and interest that was received. As a result, the letter of credit may not be applicable or enforceable when the bondholder needs it the most. To satisfy this problem, many letter of credit agreements are drawn so that the issuer is required to make payment to the trustee 91 days prior to the due date. In this case, the letter of credit would be enforceable. The analyst needs to make certain that the bond counsel who works for the issuer has taken into account the protection available in the event of bankruptcy.[1]

[1] In 1976, the Municipal Bankruptcy Law Amendment to Chapter IX of the Federal Bankruptcy Law was passed. The bill was originally designed as an aid to larger cities facing default and contained a number of controversial sections such as the one just mentioned. Some bankruptcy experts question the constitutionality of the law and indicate there would surely be a court test if and when the law is ever used. The Congress in 1984 was considering changes in the law.

The financial strength of the bank issuing the letter of credit needs to be analyzed carefully. However, the creditworthiness of the issuer should always be paramount in all analyses. While a letter of credit should be considered as a further enhancement of the credit, it is not a substitute for a weak credit.

Insurance Guarantees. Private municipal bond insurance has become increasingly popular for both general obligation and revenue bond issues in recent years. According to a recent report by the Public Securities Association, insured issues made up 23 percent of new long-term tax-exempt volume in the first half of 1984. The par value of new insured issues was $7.4 billion out of the $32 billion in long-term issues sold. This compares with 15 percent of the new issue market in 1983 and 9 percent in 1982. One of the reasons for the increased popularity of insured bonds is the ever-increasing importance of the individual investor in the municipal market.

In 1985, there were four major insurers of municipal bonds. They include the Municipal Bond Insurance Association, American Municipal Bond Assurance Corporation, Health Industry Bond Insurance by American Health Capital, and Financial Guaranty Insurance Company. The insurance companies issue policies to the bond issuer that provide that any deficiencies in principal and interest payments will be made up by the insurer. In 1984, Moody's began rating issues with insurance guarantees, thereby joining Standard & Poor's and Fitch in rating such issues.

The benefit to the issuer is that if the issue is insured, its rating is upgraded to a triple A by Standard & Poor's. While this does not mean the issuer will be able to sell bonds on a triple A basis, there will be some interest savings over what the bonds would sell at based on the issuer's own (uninsured) rating. The obvious benefit to the investor is the freedom from credit risk. In addition, insured securities tend to be more marketable and thus become a more liquid investment.

Defeasance/Pre-Refunding

State and local governments have in recent years made heavy use of refunding issues. Sometimes it has been to achieve more favorable borrowing terms. Often it is used by a revenue bond issuer, who needs to issue a large amount of debt, but is hindered by the overly restrictive terms of a bond covenant such as the additional bonds test. One way to essentially eliminate this restriction is a process called *defeasance* or the *effective advance refunding* of the bond in question.

Defeasance or effective advance refunding is the process of issuing refunding bonds to provide for the retirement of the outstanding bonds that are not immediately callable. The funds are usually set aside, in escrow, for retirement of the refunded bonds at the earliest call date or as the bonds mature. The Internal Revenue Service has strict arbitrage rules that prevent a municipal entity from profiting on the interest differentials. Thus, an entity with 6 percent tax-free bonds cannot use market rate 12 percent U.S. Treasuries and pocket the 6 percent coupon difference. The U.S. Treasury issues a special series of state and local U.S. Treasury bonds that provide the coupon necessary to pay the debt service and premium on the outstanding bonds.

Since the outstanding bonds are backed by U.S. Treasury securities, the rating services normally assign them a triple A rating. The defeased bonds relinquish their claims on the original security pledged to their payment. This enables the issuer to pledge the original security to a new issue of refunding bonds. Finally, defeasance does not result in increased debt in any statutory sense since the funds for the advance refunding are held in escrow in default-free bonds. The defeased bonds will no longer appear on the balance sheet of the issuer as debt, but there usually is a footnote explaining the refunding. Figure 7B-1 is an illustration of the steps involved in the defeasance or effective advance refunding of an issue.

BOND INDENTURE ANALYSIS

As mentioned previously, the bond indenture is the contract or agreement between the borrower and the lender that spells out, generally in lengthy detail, the rights and obligations of both parties. The obligations are spelled out in terms of covenants or agreements between the borrower and the lender. The typical corporation issues bonds of the same class under a common indenture. Thus, it is possible to find first mortgage bond indentures of major corporations that date back to the early 1940s and 1950s but are the basis for issuing bonds today. Preferred stocks are issued under contracts but different terms can be associated with different series of stock.

The risk dimensions of the indenture do not always receive the same attention as the return characteristics. Some authors and many investors consider these provisions of the indenture of little interest because it is assumed that the trustee (typically a bank or trust company) is being paid to safeguard the interests of the owners of the securities. Although that assumption is correct, it fails to recognize that the trustee is not responsible for anticipating problems or determining the sufficiency and appropriateness of the covenants that protect the investor against erosion of credit. There are many examples of investors being unpleasantly surprised by some aspect of the indenture, because they did not bother to analyze the terms.

Caveat emptor prevails in the bond market! Thus, a thorough analysis of the specific risk characteristics of an issue must include an analysis of the terms of the indenture. This is particularly the case for private placements because the terms are negotiable between the borrower and the lender. Indenture analysis should also be an integral part of the evaluation of public bonds, especially lower rated issues.

The following discussion will be limited to only three of the risk-limiting characteristics of indentures, although there are a larger number of potential protective covenants that attempt to minimize the potential for credit risk.

Figure 7B-1. Example of Defeasance or Effective Advance Refunding.

City has $30 million original bonds outstanding with 6 percent coupon . . .

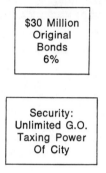

Moody's Rating "A"

City sells $30 million 5 percent advance refunding bonds, and uses proceeds to purchase $30 million in U.S. Treasury securities.

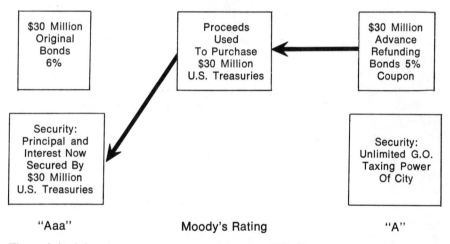

"Aaa"   Moody's Rating   "A"

The original bonds are now secured by the U.S. Treasury securities as to principal and interest and are thus defeased. The advance refunded bonds are secured by the same security which secured the original bonds.

The three aspects of indenture analysis covered here are security, lien positions, and protection against changes in ownership. (A separate section was provided earlier for the discussion of municipal revenue bond indentures.)

Security

It is important to determine what the collateral or security for the bond issue is. Corporate mortgage bonds provide the lender the first claim on specified corporate assets, such as property, plant and/or equipment. Collateral trust bonds also designate specific collateral, usually marketable securities or equipment, as security. Debentures are unsecured obligations of a corporation, somewhat like a long-term account payable.

In some indentures, the borrower agrees to maintain some minimum value of pledged assets. If the market value declines, the borrower would be expected to pledge additional collateral in the amount necessary to meet or exceed the minimum.

Collateral provisions of bonds were extremely important prior to the Great Depression. However, the experience of that era proved how quickly asset values can deteriorate and how difficult it is to reach agreement on valuation, especially for assets such as real estate that are not traded in continuously transacted marketplaces. Court proceedings can take years to establish valuations and the priority of claims on assets.

Lien Positions

Provisions of the indenture can specify the priority of claims. An *equal-and-ratable-security* or *pari passu clause* specifies that if a prior lien is subsequently placed on the corporate assets that have been designated as specific collateral, the bonds covered by this indenture will be provided an equal and *pro rata* share in the lien. *After-acquired-property clauses* specify that property acquired after the issuance of a first mortgage bond will fall under the lien of that mortgage unless the bondholders agree to waive this provision.

Preferred stock is classified as equity from a legal standpoint and has a junior lien position to all debt. Even the omission of dividends is not an act of default for a preferred.

Protection Against Changes in Ownership

Over the past twenty-five years, there have been numerous mergers and acquisitions. In some cases, the acquiring company was a weaker credit, that is, it had a lower bond quality rating than the company being acquired. For example, U.S. Steel was rated A in 1981 when it acquired Marathon Oil that was rated AA by Standard & Poor's. After the merger, Standard & Poor's lowered the rating of Marathon's bonds, essentially on the premise that a subsidiary cannot be stronger from a credit worthiness standpoint than its parent. Bond investors are afforded little or no protection against the dilution of the quality of their holdings as the result of an acquisition. Private placement bond investors have some ability to negotiate protective provisions, such as a *put option* guaranteeing a specified selling price, in the event of a change in ownership that is not acceptable to the bondholders.

LIQUIDITY RISK ANALYSIS

Despite its overall size, the liquidity of the bond market is somewhat limited. As noted in the discussion of the U.S. secondary markets, the only actively traded bonds are those issued by the U.S. Treasury and, to a lesser extent, certain federal agencies. In the corporate and municipal markets, only the securities of the top 100 or so issuers (as ranked by the dollar amount of bonds outstanding) trade with any frequency.

Marketability Factors

There are several factors that can affect the marketability of municipal and corporate bonds. One such factor is the size of the original issue. With such a wide diversity of issuers, many municipal and private placement issues are of relatively small size. This is especially true for municipal issues. Some are less than $5 million par value. With issues of that size there will be little opportunity for more than a regional interest in the bonds. On the other hand, the bonds of a major issuer, who is in the market often or sells large issues of bonds ($100 million or more), may enjoy a relatively active secondary market.

Various types of bonds can be out of favor in the market place at certain times. Since the default of the Washington Public Power Supply System Project 4 and 5 bonds in August 1983, any project involving nuclear construction has suffered in the municipal market place, as well as any joint action project. Joint action projects in general have come under increased scrutiny as suspicion over the validity and enforcement of take-or-pay contracts has increased. This was also true in the mid- and late seventies as large central core cities suffered because of New York City's and Cleveland's financial problems. The market can and often does assume a "guilt by association" posture, at least in the initial period following public awareness of the problem. Electric utilities attempting to complete nuclear construction projects have experienced a guilt by association reception in the new issue and secondary corporate markets.

In the municipal market, municipal bond insurance tends to enhance the liquidity of issues that are insured. More buying and selling activity occurs for these issues because the insurance has removed the factor of credit risk that once may have been a stumbling block to a liquid market.

Stability of Rating

There is no guarantee of the stability of a rating with the possible exception of insured municipal securities. The rating services emphasize that their ratings reflect the status of the issuer at one point in time. Obviously there are many factors that can affect the status of a credit rating. Changing economic conditions and changing industry or political situations are but a few of the possibilities.

It should be noted that a municipal entity that does not perceive the need to enter the marketplace in the foreseeable future may tend to be more careless with their bond rating. If they are operating a water enterprise, they may not desire to keep rates high enough, so that coverage ratios will justify a double A rating. While this may be shortsighted, it must be remembered that municipalities set their own rates. These decisions can and often do become involved in political decisions, in which the bondholders are the last ones to be considered.

TIME HORIZON—MULTIPLE PERSPECTIVE

The question of time horizon for a fixed income investor involves multiple perspectives. In so far as the fixed income analyst is involved in the selection of securities, these holding period factors should be considered: holding period of the investor, holding period/duration of securities, and maturity period of the securities. The importance of these three factors is a function of the portfolio strategy—active, semiactive, or passive.

Holding Period of the Investor

Active management strategies normally entail time horizons that are relatively short, such as one year, over which returns and risk are measured. For such investors, short-term performance measurement is a fact of life. To achieve total return objectives, such active investors will often utilize long duration and long-term maturity issues in an effort to maximize capital gain opportunities provided by a decline in interest rates over a relatively short holding period.

Holding Period/Duration of the Fixed Income Securities

Semiactive management strategies, such as immunization and dedication, are based on the duration of the assets. This is typically a time period which is determined by or related to the duration characteristics of the liabilities and/or to established portfolio objectives and constraints.

Maturity Period of Fixed Income Securities

As noted previously, the maturities of fixed income securities cover a broad range from very short to very long periods of time. The final maturity of the security is the date of the last payment of principal and interest. Buy-and-hold or passive portfolio managers focus heavily on the maturity of obligations.

For a more complete treatment of the subject of time horizons and portfolio strategies, the reader should consult Chapter 9A of this Update.

SUMMARY

The analysis of fixed income securities is a systematic process that can add value to a portfolio. While some investors depend on the rating agencies and indenture trustees, others realize the limitations of such an approach and devote the necessary resources to their own analysis or secure the research of the few firms specializing in this field.

It is important that the investor fully understand that the expected return on a fixed income security involves more than the coupon rate. A knowledge of bond mathematics, an appreciation of the history and complexity of interest rate forecasts, and an understanding of the specific payment terms of the issue is essential. In the bond market, *caveat emptor* prevails.

The analysis of risk, both systematic and unsystematic, is the primary objective of bond analysis. Through analysis, an estimate of the certainty of payment can be determined as well as the potential for changes in the quality rating of a bond. The latter provides some unique opportunities for the keen analyst and is becoming an increasingly important aspect of the fixed income analyst's responsibilities.

The analysis process outlined in this chapter is applicable to all fixed income securities and need only be supplemented by consideration of those return and risk factors that may be unique to an industry group or sector of the market. The role of analysis is to determine the expected return and the expected risk for a particular fixed income security or class of securities.

It is important that analysts evaluate a company's or entity's ability to finance its continued operations and growth. Thus, the basic tools of fixed income analysis must be understood and applied even by the equity analyst. Indeed, fixed income analysis and its interface with bond portfolio management is receiving increased recognition on its own as volatile business conditions have increased the specter of default or deterioration in credit quality for bond issuers. At the same time, some investors are seeking higher expected returns by accepting the risk associated with lower quality bonds and using analysis and portfolio diversification to screen and control these risks.

These two chapters have highlighted the complexity of the fixed income markets and the contributions from fixed income analysis. As noted at the outset, this subject is worthy of more comprehensive exposition.

FURTHER READING

The authors and the Institute of Chartered Financial Analyst gratefully acknowledge the work of Dr. Richard W. Stolz of Arizona State University in assembling and annotating much of the bibliography for this chapter.

In terms of a comprehensive treatment of the subject of the analysis of fixed income securities, the authors found a dearth of information on the subject. Some textbooks and a number of journal articles cover parts of the overall subject extremely well. Graham, Dodd and Cottle's [1962] detailed approach to the subject has not been updated by more recent authors. The same is true of Sauvain's [1973] approach to ratio analysis. Most of the textbooks noted as Further Reading for Chapter 7A of this supplement provides some coverage of the analysis of fixed income securities.

As fixed income securities have attracted more attention in the high and volatile interest rate environment from the 1970s to date, Fong [1983] and various articles authored or co-authored by Leibowitz have made major contributions to the literature regarding valuation of fixed income securities.

The classic primer on the mathematical properties of fixed income securities is Homer and Leibowitz [1972].

Interest rate risk and the pricing of bonds has received considerable attention in journal articles such as Brennan and Schwartz [1982], Williams [1980], McEnally [1980] and Diller [1981].

As one might imagine, credit analysis or the analysis of specific risk has been covered in the most comprehensive manner by Standard and Poor's [1982]. For information of the comparative analysis of issuers of corporate bonds, Appendexes C, D, and E provide a meaningful format.

For a discussion of the characteristics of a company's financial statements that might indicate the potential for bankruptcy, the work of Altman [1983] is valuable.

The subject of the analysis of municipal bonds is covered in a very comprehensive manner by Fabozzi, Feldstein, Pollack, and Zarb [1983].

Included in the bibliography are a number of citations that deal with some aspect of the analytical process. The reader is encouraged to examine these references for suggested further reading on a specific subject.

BIBLIOGRAPHY 7B

Alexander, Gordon J. and Roger D. Stover, "Pricing in the New Issue Convertible Debt Market," *Financial Management,* Fall 1977.

Altman, Edward I., *Corporate Financial Distress,* New York: John Wiley & Sons, 1983.

Ascher, Leonard W., "Selecting Bonds for Capital Gains," *Financial Analysts Journal,* March/April, 1971.

Bierwag, G. O., G. G. Kaufman, R. Schweitzer, and A. Toevs, "The Art of Risk Management in Bond Portfolios," *Journal of Portfolio Management,* Spring 1981.

———, ———, **and A. Toevs,** "Duration: Its Development and Use in Bond Portfolio Management," *Financial Analysts Journal,* July/August 1984.

Bilingham, Carol J., "Strategies for Enhancing Bond Portfolio Returns," *Financial Analysts Journal,* May/June 1983.

Brennan, Michael J. and Eduardo S. Schwartz, "Bond Pricing and Market Efficiency," *Financial Analysts Journal,* September/October 1982.

Cheney, John M., "Rating Classification and Bond Yield Volatility," *Journal of Portfolio Management,* Spring 1983.

Cohen, J. B., E. D. Zinbarg and A. Ziekel, Investment Analysis and Portfolio Management, Fourth Edition, Homewood, Il.: Richard D. Irwin, Inc., 1982.

Dietz, P., H. R. Fogler, and A. Rivers, "Duration, Nonlinearity, and Bond Portfolio Performance," *Journal of Portfolio Management,* Spring 1981.

Diller, Stanley, "Analyzing the Yield Curve: A New Approach," *Financial Analysts Journal,* March/April 1981.

Drexel Burnham Lambert, Inc., "The Case for High Yield Bonds," 1984.

Duff and Phelps, Inc., "The Duff and Phelps Approach to Utility Credit Analysis," 1983.

Duff and Phelps, Inc., *The Duff and Phelps Fixed Income Summary Book,* 1983.

Edelman, Richard B., "A New Approach to Ratings on Utility Bonds," *Journal of Portfolio Management,* Spring 1979.

Ehrhardt, Michael C., James V. Jordan and Richard McEnally, "An Evaluation of Alternative Measures of Bond Risk," Working Paper for Presentation at the Financial Management Association Annual Meeting, Toronto, October 12, 1984.

Fabozzi, Frank J. and Irving M. Pollack (eds.), The Handbook of Fixed Income Securities, Homewood, Il.: Dow Jones-Irwin, 1983.

———, **Sylvan G. Feldstein, Irving M. Pollack, and Frank G. Zarb,** *The Municipal Bond Handbook I,* Homewood, Il.: Dow Jones-Irwin, 1983.

———, ———, ———, **and** ———, *The Municipal Bond Handbook II,* Homewood, Il.: Dow Jones-Irwin, 1983.

Farrell, James L. *Guide to Portfolio Management,* New York: McGraw-Hill, 1983.

Feldstein, Sylvan G., *The Dow Jones-Irwin Guide to Municipal Bonds,* Homewood, Il.: Dow Jones-Irwin, 1985.

Ferri, Michael G., "How Do Call Provisions Influence Bond Yields?" *Journal of Portfolio Management,* Winter 1979.

——— **and Charles Martin,** "The Cyclical Pattern in Corporate Bond Quality," *Journal of Portfolio Management,* Winter 1980.

Finnerty, John D., "Preferred Stock Refunding Analysis: Synthesis and Extension," *Financial Management,* Autumn 1984.

Fischer, Donald E. and Ronald J. Jordan, *Security Analysis and Portfolio Management,* 3rd Ed., Prentice-Hall, 1983.

Fogler, H. Russell and Michael Joehnk, "Deep Discount Bonds: How Well Do They Perform?" *Journal of Portfolio Management,* Spring 1979.

Fong, Gifford and Frank Fabozzi, *Fixed Income Portfolio Management,* Homewood, Il.: Dow Jones-Irwin, 1984.

———, **C. Pearson, and O. Vasicek,** "Bond Performance: Analyzing Sources of Return," *Journal of Portfolio Management,* Spring 1983..

Francis, Jack Clark, Investments, 3rd Ed., New York: McGraw-Hill, 1980.

———, *Management of Investments,* New York: McGraw-Hill, 1983.

Gay, Gerald D. and Robert W. Kolb, (eds.) *Interest Rate Futures: Concepts and Issues,* Richmond, Va.: Robert F. Dame, 1982.

——— **and** ———, "The Management of Interest Rate Risk," *Journal of Portfolio Management,* Winter 1983.

Gleckman, Howard, *WPPSS: From Dream to Default,* The Bond Buyer, 1984.

Gombola, Michael J. and J. Edward Ketz, "A Caveat on Measuring Cash Flow and Solvency," *Financial Analysts Journal,* September/October 1983.

Graham, Benjamin C., David Dodd and Sydney Cottle, *Security Analysis,* Fourth Edition, New York: McGraw-Hill, 1962.

Grant's Interest Rate Observer, "Bleeding Cat," October 22, 1984.

Gurwitz, Aaron S., "Twelve Improvements in the Municipal Credit System," *Quarterly Review,* Federal Reserve Bank of New York, Winter 1983–84.

Hawkins, David F., *Corporate Financial Reporting,* Revised Edition, Homewood, Il.: Richard D. Irwin, Inc., 1977.

Hemphil, George H., *The Postwar Quality of State and Local Debt,* National Bureau of Economic Reasearch, 1971.

Hoffland, David L., "The Price-Rating Structure of the Municipal Bond Market," *Financial Analysts Journal,* March/April 1972.

Homer, Sidney and Martin L. Leibowitz, *Inside the Yield Book: New Tools for Bond Market Strategy,* Englewood Cliffs, N.J.: Prentice-Hall, 1972.

Inman, Robert P., "Anatomy of a Fiscal Crisis," *Business Review,* Federal Reserve Bank of Philadelphia, September/October 1983.

Jacob, Nancy L. and R. Richardson Pettit, *Investments,* Homewood, Il.: Richard D. Irwin, 1984.

Johnson, James M., "When are Zero Coupon Bonds the Better Buy?" *Journal of Portfolio Management,* Spring 1984.

Kalotay, Andrew J., "Refunding Considerations for High-Coupon Debt," Salomon Brothers, June 1983.

———— **and A. Janson,** "Refinancing Prospects for Public Utility Debt," Salomon Brothers, October 1983.

————, "The After-Tax Duration of Original Issue Discount Bonds," Salomon Brothers, August 1983.

————, "An Analysis of Original Issue Discount Bond," *Financial Management,* Autumn 1984.

————, "The Effect of Sinking Funds on the Cost of Debt," Salomon Brothers, September 1981.

Kidwell, David S. and Timothy W. Koch, "Why Does the Revenue Bond/GO Yield Spread Vary?" *Journal of Portfolio Management,* Summer 1982.

Klaffky, T., "A New Approach to Evaluating the Treasury Yield Curve," Salomon Brothers, August 1983.

————, "The CATS Market at the Beginning of 1984," Salomon Brothers, January 1984.

———— **and R. Kopprasch,** "Understanding the Volatility of CATS and other Zero-Coupon Bonds," Salomon Brothers, May 1983.

Kopprasch, R., "Callable CATS vs. Similar Products—A Comparison of Yield Calculations," Salomon Brothers, June 1983.

Lamb, Robert and Stephen P. Rappaport, *Municipal Bonds: The Comprehensive Review of Tax Exempt and Public Finance,* New York: McGraw-Hill, 1980.

Largay, James A., III and Clyde P. Stickney, "Cash Flows, Ratio Analysis and the W. T. Grant Company Bankruptcy," *Financial Analysts Journal,* July/August 1980.

Leibowitz, Martin L., "New Vistas for Innovation: The Many Dimensions for Change in the Fixed Income Markets," Salomon Brothers, November, 1981.

————, "Total Return Management," Salomon Brothers, 1979.

————, "Volatility Characteristics of Tax-Exempt Bonds," Salomon Brothers, May 1981.

McAdams, Lloyd, "How to Anticipate Utility Bond Rating Changes," *Journal of Portfolio Management,* Fall 1980.

McCarthy, Crisanti & Maffai, Inc., "Retail Industry Comparative Statistics Report," 1984.

McEnally, Richard W., "How to Neutralize Reinvestment Rate Risk," *Journal of Portfolio Management,* 1980.

McGuire, Thomas J., "The Problem of the One and the Many," Speech at the Conference Board 1984 made available by Moody's Investors Service, 1984.

McKeon, J. "The Anatomy of the Secondary Market in Corporate Bonds," Salomon Brothers, September 1981.

Merrill Lynch, Pierce, Fenner & Smith Inc., "U.S. Industrial Corporations: Financial Ratios 1973–1984," June 1985.

Moody's Investors Service, *1985 Medians and Selected Indicators of Municipal Performance,* 1985.

Moody's Bond Survey, Moody's Investors Service, February 11, 1985.

Morris, Robert B, III, "Fundamental Factors Affecting Electric Utility Bond Ratings: A Quantitative Approach," *Financial Analysts Journal,* September/October 1982.

Mysak, Joe, "Insured Bonds Make Up 23% of First Half's Tax-Free Issues," *The Bond Buyer,* July 19, 1984.

Osteryoung, Jerome S. and Dallas R. Blevins, "A New Approach to Ratings on State GO's," *Journal of Portfolio Management,* Spring 1979.

Peavy, John W., III, "Forecasting Industrial Bond Rating Changes: A Multivariate Model," *Review of Business and Economic Research,* Spring 1984.

———— **and Jonathan A. Scott,** "Rating a New Industry and Its Effect on Bond Returns: The Case of the AT&T Divestiture, Unpublished Paper, Southern Methodist University, Dallas, 1984.

Perry, Larry G., Glen V. Henderson, Jr. and Timothy P. Cronan, "Multivariate Analysis of Corporate Bond Ratings and Industry Classifications," *Journal of Financial Research,* Spring 1984.

Pitts, M., "Options on Futures on Fixed-Income Securities," Salomon Brothers, December 1983.

————, "The Valuation of Options on Fixed-Income Securities," Salomon Brothers, October 1982.

Porter, Michael, *Competitive Strategy,* New York: Macmillan, 1980.

————, *Competitive Advantage,* New York: Macmillan, 1985.

Rebell, Arthur, and Gail Gordon, *Financial Futures and Investment Strategy,* Dow Jones-Irwin, 1984.

Reilly, Frank K., *Investments,* Hinsdale, Il.: Dryden Press, 1982.

————, *Investment Analysis and Portfolio Management,* Second Edition, Homewood, Il.: Dryden Press, 1985.

———— **and Rupinder S. Sidhu,** "The Many Uses of Bond Duration," *Financial Analysts Journal,* July/August 1980.

Sales Marketing Management, *Annual Survey of Buying Power,* July 1984.

Sauvain, Harry C., *Investment Management,* Fourth Edition, Englewood Cliffs, N.J.: Prentice-Hall, 1973.

Singleton, J. C. and P. L. Gronewoller and H. W. Hennessey, "The Time Invariance Properties of Important Bond Rating Standards," *Review of Business and Economic Research,* Fall 1983.

Smith, Wade S., *The Appraisal of Municipal Risk,* Chicago: The Lakeside Press, 1979.

Sorensen, Eric H., "Bond Market Ratings versus Market Risk Premiums, *Journal of Portfolio Management,* Spring 1980 .

————, "Who Puts the Slope in the Municipal Yield Curve?" *Journal of Portfolio Management,* Summer 1983.

Standard and Poor's Corporation, *Credit Overview,* 1982.

Standard & Poor's, *Credit Overview—Municipal Ratings,* 1983.

Standard and Poor's Ratings Guide, New York: McGraw-Hill, 1979.

Van Horne, James C., "Called Bonds: How Does the Investor Fare?" *Journal of Portfolio Management,* Summer 1980.

Waldman, M. and T. Lupo, "Risk-Controlled Arbitrage for Thrift Institutions," Salomon Brothers, October 1983.

Yawitz, J., K. Maloney, and W. Marshall, "The Term Structure and Callable Bond Yield Spreads," *Journal of Portfolio Management,* Winter 1983.

Zavgren, Christine B., "Assessing the Vulnerability to Failure of American Industrial Firms: A Logistic Analysis," Unpublished Paper, Purdue University, Lafayette, In., 1984.

APPENDIX A

Rating

Profile Outlines

Industrial company rating methodology profile

I. **Industry risk:** Defined as the strength of the industry within the economy and relative to economic trends. This also includes the ease or difficulty of entering this industry, the importance of any diversity of the earnings base and the role of regulation and legislation.
   A. Importance in the economic cycle.
   B. Business cyclicality; earnings volatility, lead-lag and duration, diversity of earnings base, predictability and stability of revenues and earnings.
   C. Economic forces impacts; high inflation, energy costs and availability, international competitive position, social-political forces.
   D. Demand factors; real growth projections relative to GNP and basis for projections, maturity of markets.
   E. Basic financial characteristics of the business: fixed or working capital intensive; importance of credit as a sales tool.
   F. Supply factors: raw materials, labor, over/under utilized plant capacity.
   G. Federal, state, foreign regulation.
   H. Potential legislation.
   I. Fragmented or concentrated business.
   J. Barriers to entry/ease of entry.

II. **Issuer's industry position—market position:** The company's sales position in its major fields and its historical protection of its position and projected ability for the future.
   A. Ability to generate sales.
   B. Dominant and stable market shares.
   C. Marketing/distributing requirements of business—strengths, weaknesses, national, international, regional.
   D. R&D—degree of importance—degree of obsolescence—short or long product life.
   E. Support/service organization.
   F. Dependence on major customers/diversity of major customers.
   G. Long-term sales contracts/visibility of revenues/backlogs/prepayments (e.g., subscriptions).
   H. Product diversity.

III. **Issuer's industry position—operating efficiency:** This covers the issuer's historical operating margins and assesses its ability to maintain or improve them based upon pricing or cost advantages.
   A. Ability to maintain or improve margins.
   B. Pricing leadership.
   C. Integration of manufacturing operations.
   D. Plant and equipment: modern and efficient or old and obsolete. Low or high cost producer.
   E. Supply of raw material.
   F. Level of capital and employee productivity.
   G. Labor; availability, cost, union relations.
   H. Pollution control requirements and impact on operating costs.
   I. Energy costs.

IV. **Management evaluation:**
   A. The record of achievement in operations and financial results.
   B. Planning—extent, integration and relationship to accomplishments. Both strategic and financial. Plan for growth—both internal and external.
   C. Controls—management, financial and internal auditing.
   D. Financing policies and practices.
   E. Commitment, consistency and credibility.
   F. Overall quality of management; line of succession—strength of middle management.
   G. Merger and acquisition considerations.
   H. Performance vs. peers.

V. **Accounting quality:** Overall accounting evaluation of the methods employed and the extent to which they overstate or understate financial performance and position.
   A. Auditor's qualifications.
   B. LIFO vs. FIFO inventory method.
   C. Goodwill and intangible assets.
   D. Recording of revenues.
   E. Depreciation policies.
   F. Nonconsolidated subsidiaries.
   G. Method of accounting and funding for pension liabilities. Basic posture of the pension plan assumptions.
   H. Undervalued assets such as LIFO reserve.

VI. **Earnings protection:** Key measurements indicating the basic long-term earnings power of the company including:
   A. Returns on capital.
   B. Pretax coverage ratios.
   C. Profit margins.
   D. Earnings on asset/business segments.
   E. Sources of future earnings growth.
   F. Pension service coverage.
   G. Ability to finance growth internally.
   H. Inflation-adjusted earning capacity.

VII. **Financial leverage and asset protection:** Relative usage of debt, with due allowance for differences in debt usage appropriate to different types of businesses.
   A. Long-term debt and total debt to capital.
   B. Total liabilities to net tangible stockholders' equity.
   C. Preferred stock/capitalization.
   D. Leverage implicit in off-balance sheet financing arrangements, production payments, operating rentals of property, plant and equipment, nonconsolidated subsidiaries, unfunded pension liabilities, etc.
   E. Nature of assets.
   F. Working capital management—accounts receivable, inventory, and accounts payable turnover.
   G. Level, nature and value of intangible assets.
   H. Off-balance sheet assets such as undervalued natural resources or LIFO reserve.

VIII. **Cash flow adequacy:** Relationship of cash flow to leverage and ability to internally meet all business cash needs.
   A. Evaluation of size and scope of total capital requirements and capital spending flexibility.
   B. Evaluation of variability of future cash flow.
   C. Cash flow to fixed and working capital requirements.
   D. Cash flow to debt.
   E. Free cash flow to short-term debt and total debt.

IX. **Financial flexibility:** Evaluation of the company's financing needs, plans, and alternatives and its flexibility to accomplish its financing program under stress without damaging creditworthiness.
   A. Relative financing needs.
   B. Projected financing plan.
   C. Financing alternatives under stress—ability to attract capital.
   D. Capital spending flexibility.
   E. Asset redeployment potentials—nature of assets and undervalued liabilities.
   F. Nature and level of off-balance sheet assets or liabilities. This would include vested pension benefits and LIFO reserves.
   G. High level of short-term debt/high level of floating rate debt.
   H. Heavy or unwieldy debt service schedule (bullet maturities in future)—either of debt or sinking fund preferred stock.
   I. Heavy percentage of preferred stock as a percentage of total capital.
   J. Overall assessment of near-term sources of funds as compared to requirements for funds/internal financial self-sufficiency/need for external financing.
   K. Ownership/affiliation.

Retail company rating methodology profile

I. **Industry risk:** Defined as the strength of the industry or segment within the economy and relative to economic trends. This also includes the ease or difficulty of entering this industry, the importance of any diversity of the earnings base and the role of regulation and legislation.
   A. Industry overview and economic environment
      1. Necessity of a particular segment of the trade
      2. Character of goods sold (luxuries or necessities, durables or consumables, big ticket or small ticket, staple or fashion, level of volume, unit profitability, relative breadth and depth of lines, lead times)
   B. Short- and long-term outlook
   C. Relative sensitivity of this segment to changes in:
      1. Inventories
      2. Receivables
      3. Leases vs. owned property

   D. Population factors:
      1. Rate of growth: absolute, by region
      2. Trend in real DPI per capita
      3. Savings rates
      4. Effect of demographics on
         a. Age brackets
         b. Household formations
   E. Effect of economy on performance:
      1. Sensitivity to recession
      2. Lags or leads other segments
   F. Impact of:
      1. Legislation
      2. Regulation
      3. Controls
   G. Ease of entry
   H. Susceptibility to changes in the state of the art and to new formats

II. **Trade position—revenues:** The company's historical, current, and anticipated sales position in its major fields.
  A. Relative position in market; price leadership
  B. Attractiveness of geographical territory and site selections therein
  C. Customer franchise:
    1. Customer recognition
    2. Image
    3. Customer loyalty
  D. Diversity of mix: breakdown of sales
  E. Merchandising skills
  F. Promotional and advertising effectiveness

III. **Trade position—operating efficiency:** An assessment of the firm's historical operating margins and its ability to maintain or improve them based upon pricing or cost advantages.
  A. Condition of physical plant:
    1. Degree of modernity of stores, distribution centers, manufacturing facilities
    2. Productivity of physical plant
    3. Degree of computerization and automation
  B. Economies of scale:
    1. Extent of vertical integration
    2. Bulk buying
    3. Optimal use of facilities
    4. Clustering of stores (advertising, distribution, supervision)
  C. Gross profit margin factors:
    1. Markdown experience and policy
    2. Shrinkage rates
    3. Branded vs. private label products
    4. Imports vs. domestic goods.
  D. Relative exposure to energy costs and availability
  E. Relative vulnerability to contingent rents
  F. Labor—labor intensiveness of operations, cost, availability, productivity, turnover, and stoppage experience
  G. Margins:
    1. Ability to maintain or improve margins
    2. Relative to peers
    3. Track record and stability
  H. Size of administrative overhead
  I. Capital efficiency trends

IV. **Management evaluation:**
  A. The record of achievement in operations and financial results
  B. Planning—extent, integration and relationship to accomplishments. Both strategic and financial
  C. Controls—management, financial and internal auditing
  D. Financing policies and practices
  E. Commitment to stated plans and credibility
  F. Overall quality of management; line of succession—strength of middle management
  G. Merger and acquisition considerations
  H. Peformance vs. peers
  I. Other

V. **Accounting quality:** Overall accounting evaluation of the methods employed and the extent to which they overstate or understate financial performance and position.
  A. Auditor's qualifications
  B. LIFO vs. FIFO inventory method
  C. Goodwill and intangible assets
  D. Depreciation policies
  E. Nonconsolidated subsidiaries
  F. Method of accounting and funding for pension liabilities. Basic posture of the pension plan assumptions
  G. Undervalued assets such as LIFO reserve and owned properties
  H. Reserving policy
  I. Contingent rentals, sub-lease income

VI. **Earnings protection:** Key measurements indicating the basic long-term earnings power of the company including:
  A. Returns on assets
  B. Pretax fixed charge coverage with rent expense
  C. Profit margins
  D. Earnings stability and growth
  E. Return and earnings assessed on an inflation-adjusted basis

VII. **Financial leverage and asset protection:** Relative usage of debt, with due allowance for differences in debt usage appropriate to different types of businesses.
  A. Total debt/total equity
  B. Total liabilities/total equity
  C. Total debt/total capitalization plus capitalized rents
  D. Total equity/total capitalization plus capitalized rents
  E. Preferred stock/total capitalization
  F. Salability of assets
  G. High level of short-term or floating rate debt
  H. Off-balance sheet assets and contingent liabilities
  I. Level and pattern of store closing reserves.
  J. Leverage implicit in off-balance sheet financing arrangements, operating rentals of property, plant and equipment, nonconsolidated subsidiaries, unfunded pension liabilities, etc.
  K. Nature of assets.
  L. Working capital management—accounts receivable, inventory, and accounts payable turnover. Seasonal borrowing patterns.
  M. Level, nature and value of intangible assets

VIII. **Cash flow adequacy:** Relationship of cash flow to leverage and ability to meet all business cash needs.
  A. Measured against total debt and annual debt servicing requirements
  B. Consistency and predictability of cash flow; level of depreciation component
  C. Cash flow to cash requirements
  D. Cash flow measurements as adjusted to reflect working capital requirements and inflation-adjusted fixed capital requirements

IX. **Financial flexibility:** Evaluation of the company's financing needs, plans, and alternatives and its flexibility to accomplish its financing program under stress without damaging creditworthiness.
   A. Relative financing needs
   B. Projected financing plan
   C. Financing alternatives—ability to attract capital
   D. Capital spending flexibility
   E. Asset redeployment potentials—nature of assets and undervalued liabilities
   F. Nature and level of off-balance sheet assets or liabilities. This would include unfunded vested pension benefits and LIFO reserve
   G. Bank lines:
      1. Magnitude
      2. Strength and diversity of lenders
      3. Terms: compensating balances or fees; price of lines
   H. Comparative liquidity: availability of receivables for sale; short-term investments
   I. High level of short-term debt or high level of floating rate debt
   J. Heavy or unwieldy debt service schedule (bullet maturities in future)—either of debt or sinking fund preferred stock
   K. Heavy percentage of preferred stock as a percentage of total capital
   L. Overall assessment of near-term sources of funds as compared to requirements for funds/internal financial self-sufficiency/need for external financing
   M. Ownership/affiliation
   N. Restrictive loan covenants; capacity for sales/leasebacks; debt capacity

Bank holding company rating methodology profile

I. **Company characteristics:** Definition of the type of holding company, description of the operating subs, and evaluation of scope of operations, importance in markets and competition.
   A. Holding company type, bank only or bank and non-banks, multi-bank vs. unit bank
   B. Operating entities description, areas of location of business, international vs. domestic, commercial banking vs. consumer banking
   C. Regulated by whom, subject to what state laws, usury ceilings, unusual tax situations
   D. Primary competition, critical mass for market leadership, unusual areas of expertise or strength
   E. Company diversification by lines and types of business
   F. Diversification of funding sources, stability and strength of local funding sources, access to national market sources
   G. Concentrations of lending risk, by industry, by country and type of borrower (public vs. private), by product line

II. **Asset quality:** Determination of the credit quality of funds uses.
   A. Comparison of historical charge-off record to industry and peer norms
   B. Historical non-performing assets to industry peers
   C. Conservatism of management, reserving policy, recovery rate, recent gross charge-offs
   D. Analysis of non-performers and charge-offs by type, indication of reasons for problems, geographic, industry concentration, lending aggressiveness, lack of controls
   E. Analysis of current loan portfolio condition, non-performer breakout, appraisal of current condition
   F. Assessment of potential areas of problems
   G. Investment portfolio credit quality
   H. Earnings coverage of potential problems

III. **Asset/liability management:** To what degree is management able to measure and react to interest rate environment changes.
   A. General evaluation of company's measurement abilities
   B. Ability to measure short-term position taking and strategic positions
   C. Analysis of shifts in position over the past few years, rationale behind changes
   D. Ability of the company to shift positions, how flexible is the balance sheet
   E. Management's expressed philosophy regarding position taking
   F. Susceptibility to structural changes in the banking industry

IV. **Liquidity:** Potential liability loss and diversity of funding sources.
   A. Individual bank characteristics that promote liquidity, upstream and/or downstream correspondents, government underwriting bank
   B. Asset sources of liquidity, net liability sensitivity
   C. Diversification of funding sources, access to funding sources, stability, importance in individual liability markets
   D. Use of the discount window, access to the Federal Reserve

V. **Capital adequacy:** Equity cushion available to support operating deficiencies.
   A. Capital ratio comparison with peers
   B. Off-balance sheet risk assessment
   C. Relationship of asset quality to capital
   D. Investment portfolio depreciation to capital
   E. Dividend payout ratio/internal growth rate of equity
   F. Ability to tap outside sources of equity, market to book of equity
   G. Capital composition analysis, preferred stock, convertibles, common

VI. **Profitability:** Earnings protection and ability to form capital to promote growth.
  A. Margin trends, net interest income trends, ability to maintain volume
  B. Other income analysis, breakdown, variability or consistency of other income categories, ability to grow non-interest income
  C. Operating expense ratios, composition of overhead, ability to cover overhead growth, level and trend of overhead ratios
  D. Impact of loss provisions, current level, past volatility, relationship of provisions to maintenance of adequate reserves
  E. Tax payment position and cushion, lines of business and strategies that impact on tax cushion, consequences of asset decisions and interest rate levels on cushion
  F. Net operating income analysis, peer relationships
  G. Impact of securities gains or losses and other unusual gains or extraordinary losses
  H. General opinion of quality and consistency of earnings and profitability

VII. **Capitalization breakdown/holding company vs. operating subs:** Analysis of liability structure and cash flow at the parent level.
  A. Debt capital composition, maturity breakdown
  B. Non-restricted sources of funds, dividend capacity of nonbank subs
  C. Net asset liquidity at the parent level
  D. Double leverage ratios, composition of double leverage
  E. Present subsidiary payout policy, extra or reserve bank dividend ability
  F. Financing philosophies, acquisition and expansion plans
  G. Projected cash flow adequacy of the parent

VIII. **Recent earnings and future developments:** Near-term operating results and known future developments impacting operating results.
  A. Impact of interest environment on recent results
  B. Near-term earnings prospects based on interest rate scenario and economic environment
  C. Recent unusual income or cost streams
  D. Impact of branch, building, or acquisition expansion on projections
  E. Management's competence at forward planning, how realistic

Summary:

The ability of the company to sustain or improve upon the key characteristics outlined above including both quantitative and subjective appraisals.

Thrift institution rating methodology profile

I. **Market position and area:**
  A. Absolute size
  B. Relative size and competitive position
  C. Geographical scope and penetration
  D. Economic base
  E. Political and regulatory environment

II. **Profitability:**
  A. Level and trend of historical earnings
  B. Quality of earnings
  C. Overhead control
  D. Interest spread analysis
  E. Earnings outlook

III. **Asset liability management:**
  A. Exposure to interest rate risk
  B. Lending and investment strategy
  C. Liability management

IV. **Liquidity:**
  A. Level of liquid assets
  B. Historical deposit flows
  C. Liability breakdown
  D. Commitment position
  E. Borrowing flexibility
  F. Liquidity outlook

V. **Asset quality:**
  A. Level and trend of non-performing assets
  B. Current asset mix—risk evaluation
  C. Construction loan exposure and risk
  D. Loan underwriting standards
  E. Asset quality outlook

VI. **Financial leverage:**
  A. Level and trend of capital ratio
  B. Dividend policy (if applicable)
  C. Capital outlook

VII. **Management**

Finance company rating methodology profile

I. **Industry risk:** The relationship of the industry to the economy and the possible impact of various economic scenarios. This section also covers the ramifications of legislation.
   A. Importance of the industry within the economy
   B. Influence of inflation
   C. Need for capital
   D. Legislation and regulation

II. **Asset portfolio evaluation—qualitative analysis:** An analysis of the composition of the portfolio with respect to type, mix, and diversity of receivables and evaluation of growth prospects.
   A. Basic characteristics
      1. Consumer vs. commercial
      2. Secured vs. unsecured
      3. Size: absolute and relative
   B. Diversity
      1. Geographic
      2. Customer
      3. Type of product, manufacturer, supplier
      4. Internal guidelines limiting concentrations
   C. Lending criteria
   D. Growth
      1. Relative to peer group
      2. Fundamental portfolio characteristics during periods of either rapid growth or decline

III. **Asset portfolio evaluation—quantitative analysis:** Performance of the portfolio with respect to a quantitative assessment of the credit quality.
   A. Credit quality
      1. Delinquencies
      2. Charge-offs
      3. Recoveries
      4. Policies with respect to payment definition, charge-offs, extensions and business rewritten
   B. Reserve adequacy
      1. Coverage levels, trends relative to peers and portfolio characteristics
      2. Methodology for establishing reserves
      3. Adjustments reflecting changes in the portfolio and the economic environment
   C. Liquidity
      1. Salability of receivables: time frame, market size, discounting
      2. Realizable value of owned equipment and property

IV. **Non-finance activities:** An evaluation of non-finance related businesses
   A. Characteristics of activity
      1. Risk vs. return
      2. Management involvement
      3. Prospects
   B. Does it provide dividends or require capital?
   C. Is the activity appropriately capitalized? Is there double leverage?
   D. Plans for future diversification
      1. Acquisitions or start-up?
      2. Divestitures?

V. **Capitalization:** Analysis of capital leverage, debt maturity, financing requirements.
   A. Appropriateness of total leverage in relation to peer group
   B. Mix of fund sources
   C. Debt servicing capacity
   D. Use of "bullet" debt or preferred stock; preferred stock/capitalization
   E. Equity quality
      1. Goodwill and intangibles
      2. Equity investments
      3. Excess or inadequate loss reserves
      4. Understated assets and off-balance sheet liabilities.
   F. Financing needs and plans
      1. Short- and long-term financing requirements
      2. Growth flexibility
      3. Projected changes in leverage

VI. **Asset and liability management:** An examination of the company's funding of its assets. This section examines the company's management of assets and liabilities with regard to maturity and interest rate sensitivity. What is the company's philosophy toward matching interest sensitive liabilities with interest sensitive assets and what has been the performance?
   A. Interest rate sensitivity: assets vs. liabilities
      1. Percentage of floating rate assets and liabilities; management philosophy toward interest sensitive assets and liabilities on the balance sheet
      2. Percentage of assets where the interest rate can be fixed at specific levels
   B. Company policy regarding the matching of interest sensitive assets and liabilities; what is the degree of tolerance for mismatching between its assets and liabilities?
   C. Maturity structure: assets and liabilities
      1. Nominal and average life
      2. Actual experience

VII. **Earnings protection:** Review of the company's performance, based on profitability measures.
   A. Trend of key profitability measures—growth, yields, spreads, returns, both absolute and relative to peers
   B. Level and volatility of interest coverage
   C. Expectations regarding future operating results
      1. In relation to past performance
      2. In relation to peers

VIII. **Ownership/affiliation:** Discussion of the degree of strength derived from parental support.
   A. Nature of relationship
      1. Legal
      2. Financial
      3. Management
   B. Past support and ability and willingness of owner/affiliate to provide added protection in the future
   C. Does the ownership/affiliation either strengthen or weaken the owner's creditworthiness?

IX. **Management:** Evaluation of management's performance, policies, controls, planning, and depth.
   A. Planning and controls
   B. Response of management to changing conditions
   C. Depth and capability of middle management
   D. Management credibility
   E. Management philosophy towards acquisitions, diversification, portfolio risk and leverage

X. **Accounting:** Analysis of accounting methods and comparison with industry practices.
   A. Auditors' report
   B. Conservative vs. liberal accounting practices
   C. Treatment of investment tax credit
   D. Write off method and reserves for losses
   E. Treatment of intangible assets
   F. Accounting practices of non-finance activities
   G. Off-balance sheet liabilities and understated assets

Insurance company rating profile

I. **Industry risk:** A determination of the inherent risk in the type of insurance business being underwritten.
   A. Relative pricing stability and the nature of competition from within and outside the industry.
   B. Nature of tail in claims reporting or settlement.
   C. Real or potential regulatory or legislative strengths or problems.
   D. Sensitivity to inflation and changing economic scenarios.
   E. Relative growth potential of the market.

II. **Company characteristics:** An assessment of the structure of the company, its market position and its diversification.
   A. Mix of insurance business: life vs. health vs. property-casualty, etc.
   B. If property-casualty, nature of tail: long or short.
   C. Risk diversification: geographically and by product line.
   D. Market factors: niches, competition, distribution system, major sources of business (either broker or customer).
   E. Organizational factors: holding vs. operating company, ownership of non-insurance activities, cash generators/users, level and use of debt.
   F. Size and age of company: on an absolute and relative basis.

III. **Underwriting performance:** Evaluation of the company's ability to grow the underwriting business and maintain profitability, as well as the quality of those earnings.
   A. Growth of business: past and prospective for types of policies being written, assets and earnings—on an absolute and relative basis.
   B. Sources, stability and quality of underwriting earnings: profits by underwriting segments, effect of reinsurance and reserve changes, inflation and cyclical sensitivity.
   C. Return on assets, profit margins: on an absolute and relative basis.
   D. Adequacy of reserves: development of reserves on prior years' books of business, Schedule P analysis, etc.

IV. **Investment activities:** An assessment of the performance and risk characteristics of the investment portfolio.
   A. Portfolio composition: breakdown by type of investment and policy regarding new investments.
   B. Portfolio quality: average ratings for bonds, nature of common stock investments, investments in parents, subsidiaries and affiliates, and policy regarding quality of new investments.
   C. Concentrations: by issuer, industry and geographically (for mortgage and real estate investments).
   D. Maturity structure and liquidity considerations: average maturity of bond portfolio, amount of investments maturing within one year, publicly traded bonds versus private placements, total cash flow expected from portfolio in next year, percentage of overall cash flow (including from operations) committed, and policy regarding lending and investment commitments.
   E. Performance: current yield and trend in yield relative to peer group, delinquency and default rates on bond and mortgage portfolio—currently and in the past, performance and quality of equity investments.

V. **Non-insurance activities:** An analysis of investments in non-insurance related subsidiaries that the issuer currently owns, as well as the track record of past ventures.
   A. Appropriateness of activity: tie-in to insurance, risk, return and/or prospects.
   B. Is activity appropriately capitalized currently and will outside capital be required in the future?
   C. Acquisitions, divestitures and future diversification.

VI. **Earnings protection:**
   A. Fixed charge coverage, debt servicing capability.
   B. Profit margins.
   C. Return on assets for consolidated entity.
   D. Earnings mix, stability and growth.

VII. **Leverage:** An evaluation of the adequacy of the surplus to cover the risks inherent in the underwriting business and the investment portfolio, internal growth, and the quality of any excess surplus. The appropriateness of the current and projected levels of debt.
   A. Historical and projected operating leverage: primarily, the premiums written to statutory surplus for a property-casualty insurer and the liabilities to statutory surplus plus mandatory security valuation reserves for a life insurance company.
   B. Sufficiency of capital for future growth.
   C. Surplus quality: vulnerability to downturn in equity markets (common stocks to statutory surplus), adequacy of reserves, intangible assets, double leverage and investments in parents, subsidiaries and affiliates.
   D. Debt leverage: current and forecasted level, usage of short-term debt.
   E. Shareholder dividend policy.

VIII. **Financial flexibility:** An assessment of the ability to raise funds and/or increase liquidity quickly.
   A. Position and visibility of the company within its own and other markets.
   B. Restrictions on cash flows and/or dividends by regulations, indentures, etc.
   C. Diversification of cash flows and/or dividend streams.
   D. Ability of the company and industry to attract equity capital.

IX. **Management evaluation:**
   A. Extent of planning and forecasting and quality of previous projections.
   B. Record of achievement.
   C. Philosophy regarding acquisitions or expansion, operating and financial leverage.
   D. Responsiveness to changing market, economic, regulatory and/or legislative conditions.
   E. Depth and experience of middle management.
   F. Controls: internal auditing, investment committee practices.

Addendum

I. **Industry risk:**
   A. Life companies are viewed as having lower business risk than health and property-casualty insurers as the revenue and earnings streams usually are more predictable, less volatile, and show year to year growth. Also, life insurance loss reserving is much more a science than health and property-casualty reserving. Health insurers are next in line in terms of earnings stability and reserving methods, but closer to the volatile property-casualty insurers than the stable life companies. Of course a health or property-casualty company can structure its business or carve out a good niche that will offset initial concerns.
   B. The tail of a property-casualty business refers to the length of time between putting a policy on the books and paying on the last claim. Long-tail business is viewed as less desirable for three reasons: inflation plays havoc with reserves; the adequacy of reserves remains questionable longer; and since reserves/surplus is much higher for a long-tail company, reserve adequacy is much more important.

II. **Underwriting performance:**
   A. In assessing reserve adequacy for a property-casualty insurer, emphasis is placed on reserve development, which shows how much a company has added to reserves one year and then two years after the original reserve had been established on past years' books of business. Also used are prospective methods, which project ultimate losses on a book of business based on trends of paid losses on past years' books. The results of reserve adequacy tests cannot be heavily weighted as there are flaws in each approach.

Public utility rating methodology profile

Non-financial criteria

I. **Market or service territory**
   A. General:
      1. Size & growth rate of market
      2. Economic trends
      3. Diversity of customer base
      4. Demand components
      5. Dependencies
      6. Per capita income
      7. Area ratings
      8. Customer growth
      9. Other
   B. For telephone utilities:
      1. Toll growth and the intercity common carriers

II. **Fuel-power supply**
   A. For electric utilities:
      1. Fuel mix
      2. Fuel contracts
      3. Reserve margin
      4. Reliability
      5. Environmental factors
      6. Transmission capability
      7. Power purchases/power sales
      8. Other
   B. For gas pipelines and distributors:
      1. Long-term supply adequacy
      2. Non-traditional sources such as LNG
      3. Reserve life indices
      4. Gas supply diversification

III. **Operating efficiency**
   A. For electric utilities:
      1. Peak load and capacity factors
      2. Environmental problems
      3. Generating plant availability
      4. Plant outages
      5. KWH pricing
   B. For gas pipelines and distributors:
      1. Plant utilization
      2. Storage adequacy
      3. Lost and unaccounted gas
      4. Non-gas operating costs
   C. For telephone utilities:
      1. Central office modernization
      2. Maintenance costs
      3. Trouble reports
      4. Public service commission complaints
      5. Held orders and service levels

IV. **Regulatory treatment**
   A. Earnable returns on equity
   B. Regulatory quality
      1. Quality of earnings
      2. Aids to cash flow
   C. Regulatory timing
      1. Earnings stabilization techniques
      2. 'Make-whole' processes
      3. Forecasted test years and rate bases

V. **Management**
   A. Results and commitments, including to credit quality
   B. Strategic & financial planning
   C. Public and private priorities
   D. Effective communication with the public, regulatory bodies, and the financial community
   E. Financial policies and controls
   F. Business philosophy
   G. Other

VI. **Competition/monopoly balance**
   A. Relative exposure to competition
   B. Gas utilities and alternate fuel costs
   C. Telephone utilities and other common carriers and equipment suppliers
   D. Electric utilities and competitive energy sources
   E. Move to diversify
   F. Diversification risks and compensatory financial policies

Financial criteria

I. **Construction/asset concentration risk**
   A. Nature and breakdown of projected expenditures
   B. Projected cancellations
   C. Post completion risks
   D. Construction expenditures to capitalization
   E. Construction work in progress to capitalization and common equity

II. **Earnings protection**
   A. Pretax coverages including and excluding AFDC for debt and senior equities
   B. Returns on equity
   C. Overall returns on capital
   D. Risk-adjusted benchmarks

III. **Debt leverage**
   A. Capital ratios
   B. Funding ratios
   C. Short-term debt/capitalization
   D. Off-balance sheet commitments and liabilities
   E. Inflated or undervalued assets
   F. Risk-adjusted benchmarks

IV. **Cash flow adequacy**
   A. Capital spending needs
   B. Net (of common dividends) cash flow ex AFDC/capital outlays
   C. Net cash flow/capitalization
   D. Refunding requirements
   E. Gross cash flow service of gas company debt

V. **Financial flexibility/capital attraction**
   A. Cash flow—capital requirement deficiencies
   B. Need and ability to sell common equity
   C. Market/book value
   D. Indenture and charter tests
   E. Preferred stock ratio
   F. Short-term debt usage
   G. Non-traditional financing resources

VI. **Accounting quality**
   A. Overlaps other criteria areas
   B. Regulatory treatment
      1. 'Flow thru' vs. normalization
      2. Depreciation rates
      3. Balancing accounts
   C. Management treatment
      1. Unbilled revenues
      2. Off-balance sheet financings
   D. Current costs vs. historic costs

Sovereign government rating methodology profile

Political risk

I. **Characteristics of political system**
   A. Type of government
   B. Process and frequency of political succession
   C. Degree of public participation
   D. Degree of centralization in decision-making process

II. **Executive leadership**
   A. Relationship with supporting government institutions
   B. Relationship with supporting political coalitions

III. **Government institutions**
   A. Responsiveness and access to executive leadership
   B. Effectiveness and efficiency
   C. Policy responsibilities

IV. **Social coalitions**
   A. Major socio-economic and cultural groups (*i.e.*, church, military, landowners, management, labor, ethnic groups, etc.)
   B. Political parties and their constituencies

V. **Social indicators**
   A. Level and growth of per capita income, and other measures of the standard of living
   B. Distribution of wealth and income
   C. Regional disparities
   D. Homogeneity of the populace

VI. **External relations**
   A. Relationship with major trading partners
   B. Relationship with neighboring countries
   C. Participation in international organizations

Economic risk

I. **Demographic characteristics**
   A. Level and growth of population
   B. Age distribution
   C. Urbanization trends

II. **Structure of the economy**
   A. Extent and quality of infrastructure
      1. Transportaion and communications
      2. Utilities
      3. Housing
      4. Education
      5. Health services
   B. Natural resource endowment
      1. Agriculture, forestry, fishing
      2. Non-energy minerals
      3. Energy resources
   C. Distribution of productive activities
      1. Agriculture and livestock
         a. Land tenure system
         b. Degree of mechanization
         c. Principal crops
         d. Markets

2. Forestry and fishing
3. Mining
4. Construction
   a. Residential
   b. Non-residential
5. Manufacturing
   a. Concentration and size of manufacturers
   b. Product types (*i.e.*, consumer, intermediate and capital goods)
   c. Markets
6. Services—financial/non-financial, public/private
   D. Public sector participation in productive activities

III. **Recent economic trends**
   A. Composition and growth of aggregate demand (nominal and real terms)
      1. Consumption
         a. Private sector
         b. Public sector
      2. Investment
         a. Private sector
         b. Public sector
      3. External savings (*i.e.*, exports—imports)
   B. Domestic economy
      1. Total production (*i.e.*, GDP)
      2. Production by sector
         a. Agriculture, forestry and fishing
         b. Mining
         c. Construction
         d. Manufacturing
         e. Utilities
         f. Services
      3. Prime movements and major determinants
         a. External factors
         b. Wages
         c. Public sector deficit financing
         d. Private sector credit expansion
         e. Supply bottlenecks
      4. Employment trends
         a. Level of growth of employment and labor force
         b. Labor participation rates
         c. Unemployment rate and structure
         d. Sectoral trends
         e. Regional trends
         f. Composition of employment: public vs. private
   C. External sector
      1. Current account balance
         a. Export growth and composition
            i. Agricultural commodities
            ii. Minerals
            iii. Manufactured goods
         b. Destination of exports (*i.e.*, markets)
         c. Price and income elasticity of exports
         d. Import growth and composition
            i. Food
            ii. Other consumer goods
            iii. Energy
            iv. Other intermediate goods
            v. Capital goods

e. Price and income elasticity of imports
f. Geographic origin of imports
g. Terms of trade
h. Services account
  i. Interest payments and receipts
  ii. Transportation
  iii. Other
i. Transfers
2. Capital account balance
  a. Direct investment
  b. Long-term capital flows
    i. Private sector
    ii. Public sector
  c. Short-term capital flows
  d. Access to capital markets
    i. Types of instruments used
    ii. Types of borrowers & lenders
3. International reserves
  a. Level
  b. Composition (*i.e.,* gold, foreign exchange)
  c. Secondary reserves
4. External debt
  a. Amount outstanding
  b. Composition by borrower
    i. Central government
    ii. Other public sector
    iii. Publicly guaranteed
    iv. Private
  c. Composition by lender
    i. Bilateral
    ii. Multilateral
    iii. Private financial institutions
    iv. Suppliers credits
  d. Maturity structure
  e. Currency composition
  f. Growth rate
  g. Comparison with export earnings and GDP
  h. Debt service payments
    i. Amortization
    ii. Interest
    iii. Comparison to export earnings
    iv. Future debt service schedule

IV. **Economic policy**
A. Price and wage policies
  1. Wage settlement process
    a. Trade union activity
    b. Management groups
    c. Role and influence of government
  2. Degree of wage indexation
  3. Productivity trends
  4. Non-wage benefits and unemployment insurance
  5. Direct price controls
    a. Public sector tariffs
    b. Private sector pricing
  6. Price subsidies (agricultural, industrial, etc.)
B. Monetary policy
  1. Level of development of financial system
    a. Types of financial institutions
    b. Types of financial instruments
    c. Role of government in credit allocation
    d. Foreign participation
  2. Trends for monetary aggregates
    a. Money supply growth targets and actual experience

b. Domestic credit expansion
  i. Public sector
  ii. Private sector
c. Velocity (national income/money supply)
d. Changes in international reserves
3. Monetary policy instruments
  a. Reserve requirements
  b. Open market operations
  c. Credit controls
  d. Interest rate regulations
  e. Ability to sterilize international reserve flows
  f. Controls on foreign borrowing and lending
  g. Rediscount facilities
C. Fiscal policy
  1. Structure of the public sector
    a. Central government
    b. Social security system
    c. State agencies and enterprises
    d. Regional and local governments
  2. Budgetary process
    a. Executive branch
    b. Legislative branch
    c. Major constituencies (business, labor, etc.)
  3. Revenues
    a. Composition
      i. Direct taxes—personal income, corporate income, property, others
      ii. Indirect taxes—valued added, sales, export & import duties, others
      iii. Service charges and public sector tariffs
    b. Income elasticity of revenues
    c. Distribution of tax burden by income groups
    d. Overall tax burden (% of GDP)
    e. Tax collection and evasion
    f. Tax incentives (*i.e.,* investment, export, employment)
  4. Expenditures
    a. Current expenditures
      i. Distribution by expenditure category
      ii. Transfers to households
      iii. Transfers to other levels of government
    b. Capital expenditures
  5. Current operating balance (absolute level and relative to GDP)
  6. Gross financing requirements (*i.e.,* operating balance plus net capital expenditures)
    a. Trend relative to GDP
    b. Means of financing
      i. Domestic money creation
      ii. Domestic borrowing
      iii. External borrowing
  7. Public sector debt: domestic and external
    a. Size (direct and guaranteed)
    b. Debt service requirement
    c. Debt management
D. External policies
  1. Exchange rate policy
  2. International reserve management
  3. Export promotion measures
  4. Import substitution/trade protectionist measures
E. Long-term planning and special programs
  1. Energy
  2. Industrial development/restructuring
  3. Employment creation
  4. Others

APPENDIX B

Memo Written in Early 1974 on W.T. Grant Company's Credit Problems

In the mid 1960s, W. T. Grant, one of the oldest national retailers in the United States, embarked on a major program to enter the field of discount merchandising. This shift in the company's emphasis from the traditional variety stores largely reflected the growing acceptance of discount retailing and a reaction to the success of one of their major competitors, Kresge and their K marts. Many other old line retailers such as Woolworth, Daytons, and Federated Department Stores, also entered the field during the 1970s. However, within the past two years, the increased competition, coupled with less stable economic conditions, has resulted in declining profits. Some discounters have been forced to retrench and others, such as Arland, Unishops, and Interstate Stores, have become financial fatalities.

Grant's finances have been long considered secure: Dividends have been paid continuously since 1907; outstanding debentures are rated "A" by Moody's; and the common stock is ranked "A" by Standard & Poor's. However, we have been concerned about the operations of Grant for over a year and have monitored its financial and monthly sales reports closely. The company's discount operations now dominate, with almost one-half of Grant's stores and almost three-fourths of total store space opened in the past ten years, while the old downtown stores are being phased out. The financing burden created by this expansion has necessitated substantial debt and lease financing. If the Company's substantial short-term debt position is included, total debt would account for 83 percent of total capitalization.

Capitalization
(Millions)
7/31/73

	BOOK		PRO FORMA TO INCLUDE LEASES	
	$	%	$	%
Short-term Debt	413	43	413	22
Long-term Debt	223	23	223	12
Capitalized Leases			900	49
Stockholders' Equity	322	34	322	17
Total	958	100	1,858	100

The cash flow to service this debt is the Achilles' heel for Grant. Relative to its size, Grant's expansion has severely strained its internal cash generation ability and left it vulnerable to declining profit margins. Within the past four months, Grant's position has deteriorated further and volume growth slowed to 3.7 percent in the retailers most important month—December.

Thus, the contraction in volume jeopardizes the company's dividend paying ability, weakens its credit rating, and increases the need for capital, for both short-term (working capital) and long-term purposes. Earnings estimates have been drastically reduced for the fiscal year ending January 31, 1974, to $1.25 versus the

Monthly Retail Sales
(% Change Same Month One Year Ago)

1973	Kresge	Woolworth	Grant
February	19.9%	14.0%	22.7%
March	16.7	5.1	13.9
April	30.7	35.0	22.3
May	18.0	18.0	16.0
June	24.3	23.0	30.5
July	22.0	19.0	15.1
August	17.5	16.2	12.9
September	25.0	18.0	8.6
October	19.0	18.7	8.7
November	21.8	17.3	9.3
December	20.1	19.3	3.7

$2.70 reported last year. Thus, earnings will not be sufficient to cover the current dividend of $1.50 and the prospects for 1974 reflect even less favorable industry conditions.

The directors are scheduled to have their next dividend meeting at the end of February. A new president has recently been elected and other management changes are likely as the company attempts to cut back store expansion and dispose of marginal stores and take other defensive action. Needless to say, the current economic uncertainties make Grant's weakened position even more questionable.

To make matters even worse, Grant has pledged its receivables and inventories as security for bank lines. Literally, the equity will be wiped out by the encumberances in the event of default. Furthermore, the company has no financing flexibility since no security is available for a potential lender. This is not obvious yet, but a careful reading of the company's financial statements and footnotes reflects these encumbrances.

For additional background information, the following data is provided.

Current Data

Year Ending 1/31 of Following Year	Net Sales (Mil.)	Pretax Margin	Net Income (Mil.)	Return on Equity	PER SHARE Earnings	PER SHARE Dividend	Price Range
1963	$ 699	3.18%	$10.7	14.4%	$ .91	$ .60	$13-10
1964	770	5.36	22.0	17.8	1.84	.60	20-12
1965	840	6.70	30.7	19.2	2.54	.80	31-18
1966	921	5.82	30.7	16.8	2.50	1.10	35-21
1967	980	5.64	32.0	15.7	2.58	1.10	37-21
1968	1,096	6.52	37.7	15.3	2.71	1.30	45-30
1969	1,211	6.32	41.4	14.3	2.99	1.40	59-39
1970	1,254	5.44	39.2	12.8	2.87	1.50	52-27
1971	1.375	4.20	34.9	10.7	2.51	1.50	71-42
1972	1,645	3.55	37.5	10.8	2.70	1.50	49-35
1973E	1,850	1.10	17.4	N.A.	1.25	1.50	44-11

Other Financial Data
(Millions)

	Net Cash Flow (Net Inc. + Depr. − Div.)	Total Capital Expenditures	Long-Term Debt	Min. Annual Lease Rentals	Shareholders' Equity
1968	$27.1	$10.5	$ 43.3	$37.2	$280.1
1969	29.0	13.6	35.4	41.3	290.6
1970	25.9	16.1	32.3	46.6	302.0
1971	22.9	25.9	128.4	56.3	325.7
1972	27.0	26.3	126.6	69.6	334.3
1973E	4.3	25.0	223.0	89.2	N.A.

SOURCE: Mutual of Omaha Insurance Company.

APPENDIX C
Retail Industry Comparative Statistics

TABLE 1. 1983 Summary of Significant Ratios

	General Merchandise			Department Stores						Discount—Variety	
	Montgomery Ward	J.C. Penney	Sears Roebuck	Allied Stores	Associated Dry Goods	Carter Hawley	Dayton-Hudson	Federated	May	K mart	Woolworth
Ratings (as of 5/24/85):											
M C M	BB	A	AA—	A—	A—	BBB	A+	AA	A	A	BBB—
Moody's/S&P	Baa3/BBB—	A1/A+	Aa2/AA	A2/A	A2/A+	Baa2/BBB	Aa2/AA	Aaa/AA	A1/AA	A2/A+	Baa1/BBB
Combined Fixed Charge Coverage[a]											
Interest											
1983	1.27	3.39	2.02	3.72	4.18	1.72	5.74	6.57	6.39	3.94	3.40
1982	0.47	3.06	1.58	2.63	2.80	1.35	5.80	4.85	5.10	2.53	2.39
Interest + ⅓ Rents											
1983	1.24	2.74	1.94	3.15	3.45	1.57	4.50	5.48	5.06	3.22	2.19
1982	0.51	2.51	1.55	2.33	2.50	1.29	4.53	4.11	4.21	2.19	1.77
Debt % Capitalization											
Long-Term Debt	26.7	32.4	43.1	43.9	32.6	40.0	32.8	21.3	32.6	46.3	29.7
Total Debt	28.4	32.4	55.1	48.0	33.6	40.4	33.0	29.0	33.3	47.0	33.0
Total Combined Debt[a] + Present Value of Non-Capitalized Leases (PVNCL)[a]	65.2	46.5	66.5	48.0	39.6	53.4	33.0	29.0	33.3	47.0	33.0
Cash Flow % Long-Term Debt[a]	67.5	52.2	67.8	55.1	48.9	63.1	42.4	33.9	41.2	59.8	57.4
Combined Cash Flow[a]											
% Combined Total Debt	20.0	39.6	—	29.8	48.0	27.5	53.1	85.7	53.2	30.1	60.2
% Comb. Total Debt + PVNCL	4.4	23.4	25.0	25.4	36.0	17.5	52.5	56.7	51.5	29.2	51.7
% Comb. Current Liabilities	4.0	18.6	22.8	19.0	24.6	11.7	35.2	45.2	36.7	17.4	18.8
Current Ratio	4.4	28.9	—	30.4	31.0	26.7	32.9	32.3	36.4	30.2	36.6
Quick Ratio	1.17	2.20	2.13[b]	2.04	1.67	1.66	1.72	1.58	2.11	1.90	1.83
Combined Quick Ratio[a]	0.55	1.03	—	1.28	0.58	0.31	0.89	0.89	1.38	0.46	0.23
	1.30	1.56	—	1.28	0.76	1.23	0.89	0.90	1.38	0.46	0.23
Sales ($MM)	6,003	12,078	35,883	3,676	3,718	3,633	6,963	8,690	4,229	18,598	5,456
Net Income ($MM)	56.0	467	1,342	128.5	115.5	59.3	243.2	311.7	186.6	492.3	118.0
Return on Sales (%)	0.9	3.9	3.7	3.5	3.1	1.6	3.5	3.6	4.4	2.6	2.2
Return on Average Equity (%)	3.4	13.8	14.4	14.0	16.7	7.9	16.8	14.0	17.0	17.8	11.6

[a] Company + non-consolidated finance subsidiary.
[b] Data are for domestic merchandising, credit and international merchandising.

SOURCE: McCarthy, Crisanti & Maffei, Inc.

TABLE 2. Principal Accounting Practices

	Inventories	Depreciation	Interest on Property Under Construction	Service Charge Income	Investment Tax Credit	New Store Costs	Finance Subsidiary	Real Estate Subsidiary
General Merchandise								
Montgomery Ward	LIFO since 1976	Straight line	Capitalized since 1980	Deducted from SG&A	Flow through	Expensed as incurred	Nonconsolidated	None
J. C. Penney	LIFO since 1974	Straight line	Capitalized	Deducted from SG&A	Flow through	Expensed in year of opening	Nonconsolidated	Nonconsolidated
Sears Roebuck	LIFO since 1975	Straight line	Capitalized	Included in revenues	Flow through	Expensed	Consolidated	Consolidated
Department Stores								
Allied Stores	LIFO	Straight line	Capitalized since 1980	Deducted from SG&A	Flow through	Expensed as incurred	Consolidated	Consolidated
Associated Dry Goods	LIFO since 1974	Straight line	Capitalized since 1980	Included in sales	Flow through	Expensed in month of opening	Nonconsolidated	None
Carter Hawley Hale	LIFO Department Stores —1974 Other—1981	Straight line	Capitalized	Included in sales	Flow through	Expensed in year of opening	Nonconsolidated	Consolidated
Dayton Hudson	LIFO	Straight line	Capitalized since 1980	Included in sales	Flow through	Expensed	None	None
Federated	LIFO	Straight line	Capitalized	Included in sales	Flow through	Expensed	Nonconsolidated	Nonconsolidated
May	LIFO—83% FIFO—17%	Straight line	Capitalized	Included in sales	Deferred	Expensed in year of opening	Consolidated	Consolidated
Discount—Variety								
K mart	LIFO—87% FIFO—13%	Straight line	Capitalized	—	Flow through	Expensed in year of opening	None	None
Woolworth	LIFO—47% FIFO—53%	Straight line	Capitalized since 1981	—	Flow through	Expensed as incurred	None	Consolidated

SOURCE: McCarthy, Crisanti & Maffei, Inc. [1984].

TABLE 3. Fixed Charge Coverage

	GENERAL MERCHANDISE			DEPARTMENT STORES						DISCOUNT—VARIETY	
	Montgomery Ward	J.C. Penney[b]	Sears Roebuck	Allied Stores	Associated Dry Goods	Carter Hawley	Dayton-Hudson	Federated	May	K mart	Woolworth[c]
Combined Interest[a]											
1983	1.27	3.39	2.02	3.72	4.18	1.72	5.74	6.57	6.39	3.94	3.40
1982	0.47	3.06	1.58	2.63	2.80	1.35	5.80	4.85	5.10	2.53	2.39
1981	0.40	3.05	1.27	3.28	2.77	1.33	6.07	6.91	5.58	2.01	2.44
1980	0.40	2.49	1.79	4.84	4.17	1.82	9.14	6.67	4.95	2.76	3.48
1979	1.26	2.44	2.41	5.61	4.29	2.56	16.39	6.86	5.28	4.44	3.12
1978	1.81	3.07	2.65	5.56	4.16	2.96	14.68	8.37	5.54	5.31	3.57
Combined Interest + ⅓ Rents[a]											
1983	1.24	2.74	1.94	3.15	3.45	1.57	4.50	5.48	5.06	3.22	2.19
1982	0.51	2.51	1.55	2.33	2.50	1.29	4.53	4.11	4.21	2.19	1.77
1981	0.44	2.52	1.26	2.86	2.48	1.26	4.53	5.70	4.58	1.75	1.83
1980	0.44	2.08	1.73	3.94	3.32	1.66	5.88	5.56	4.19	2.29	2.39
1979	1.24	2.05	2.28	4.54	3.32	2.23	8.39	5.76	4.55	3.42	2.29
1978	1.73	2.45	2.51	4.49	3.15	2.53	8.17	6.78	4.88	3.96	2.51

a Company + non-consolidated finance subsidiary.
b Excludes discontinued automotive operations, 1981 and 1980 restated.
c Results for 1981 and 1980 restated to reflect discontinuance of U.S. Woolco operations and sale of interest in British subsidiary.

TABLE 4. Capitalization

	GENERAL MERCHANDISE			DEPARTMENT STORES						DISCOUNT—VARIETY	
	Montgomery Ward	J.C. Penney	Sears Roebuck	Allied Stores	Associated Dry Goods	Carter Hawley	Dayton-Hudson	Federated	May	K mart	Woolworth
PERCENTAGE OF CAPITALIZATION											
Short-Term Debt											
1983	2.4	0.0	21.1	7.2	1.5	0.8	0.4	9.8	1.1	1.3	4.7
1982	3.0	2.2	16.2	3.1	1.7	0.9	0.5	13.0	1.8	1.4	2.1
1981	4.1	0.3	19.2	15.8	1.5	2.3	6.3	14.4	1.2	4.8	6.1
1980	4.2	0.5	29.4	2.3	1.2	1.3	3.0	5.9	1.3	1.3	10.0
1979	4.6	0.6	29.2	1.6	1.7	1.6	1.1	15.5	1.7	5.9	3.6
1978	1.4	0.5	—	1.9	1.1	2.2	1.2	14.0	3.1	1.4	1.8
Long-Term Debt											
1983	26.7	32.4	43.1	43.9	32.6	40.0	32.8	21.3	32.6	46.3	29.7
1982	27.2	30.0	39.8	47.7	36.8	45.8	31.9	24.9	36.2	48.2	34.1
1981	27.9	32.3	39.2	43.1	34.7	47.5	26.4	21.8	35.8	46.9	35.4
1980	44.5	33.5	27.9	37.8	22.2	48.8	22.9	23.2	37.9	46.5	34.0
1979	30.5	24.1	28.5	35.2	24.3	46.1	16.5	18.1	42.2	42.7	36.8
1978	31.2	26.3	—	38.2	25.4	49.0	17.5	19.2	41.6	44.0	39.4
Total Debt											
1983	28.4	32.4	55.1	48.0	33.6	40.4	33.0	29.0	33.3	47.0	33.0
1982	29.4	31.5	49.5	49.3	37.8	46.9	32.2	34.7	37.3	48.9	35.4
1981	30.8	32.5	50.9	52.1	35.7	48.7	31.1	33.1	36.6	49.4	39.4
1980	46.8	33.8	49.1	39.3	23.2	49.3	25.2	27.8	38.7	47.2	40.6
1979	33.7	24.6	49.4	36.2	25.6	46.8	17.4	30.8	43.2	46.1	39.1
1978	32.1	26.6	—	39.4	26.2	50.2	18.4	30.5	43.4	44.7	40.4
Total Combined Debt (TD Comb.)[a]											
1983	65.2	46.5	55.1	48.0	39.6	53.4	33.0	29.0	33.3	47.0	33.0
1982	65.7	47.6	49.5	49.3	43.5	58.9	32.2	34.7	37.3	48.9	35.4
1981	67.6	48.2	50.9	52.1	46.0	59.6	31.1	33.1	36.6	49.4	39.4
1980	77.0	50.9	49.1	39.3	35.9	59.8	25.2	27.8	38.7	47.2	40.6
1979	73.7	51.8	49.4	36.2	36.2	58.1	17.4	30.8	43.2	46.1	39.1
1978	70.9	54.0	—	39.4	33.9	57.8	18.4	30.5	—	44.7	40.4
TD Comb. + Est. Pres. Value Non-Capitalized Leases[a]											
1983	67.5	52.2	57.3	55.1	48.9	63.1	42.4	33.9	41.2	59.8	57.4
1982	67.9	54.3	51.8	57.1	52.7	66.9	41.7	38.6	44.5	61.1	58.1
1981	69.5	55.3	52.8	59.3	54.4	67.5	39.3	36.0	43.5	61.3	55.2
1980	78.4	58.0	50.8	46.5	47.5	69.3	35.1	31.1	45.1	58.8	54.0
1979	75.4	58.9	50.9	44.2	48.2	68.5	28.9	33.7	48.7	57.6	59.5
1978	72.7	60.8	—	46.4	46.7	67.0	30.5	33.7	47.9	56.4	60.4

[a] Company + non-consolidated finance subsidiary.

TABLE 5. Liquidity and Working Capital Statistics

	GENERAL MERCHANDISE			DEPARTMENT STORES						DISCOUNT—VARIETY	
	Montgomery Ward	J.C. Penney[c]	Sears Roebuck	Allied Stores	Associated Dry Goods	Carter Hawley	Dayton-Hudson	Federated	May	K mart	Woolworth[d]
Working Capital ($MM)											
1983	279.0	2161.0	8350.0[b]	770.1	375.3	374.6	868.6	979.2	908.0	2267.7	594.0
1982	143.0	1789.0	6964.0[b]	717.9	336.0	345.4	718.3	760.7	795.1	1827.2	647.0
1981	149.0	1707.0	—	475.5	258.8	341.8	508.9	728.6	686.0	1472.8	1023.0
1980	59.0	1387.0	—	581.8	226.4	377.6	381.3	793.8	683.7	1526.5	1065.0
1979	133.5	948.0	—	514.9	228.8	347.2	438.8	553.2	589.0	1387.8	756.0
1978	362.7	1136.0	—	531.6	222.9	357.4	427.6	590.9	511.7	1307.5	728.8
Current Ratio											
1983	1.17	2.20	2.13[b]	2.04	1.67	1.66	1.72	1.58	2.11	1.90	1.83
1982	1.09	1.99	2.37[b]	2.26	1.75	1.71	1.75	1.49	2.10	1.84	1.88
1981	1.09	2.01	—	1.65	1.64	1.85	1.57	1.53	2.05	1.77	2.47
1980	1.08	1.80	—	2.52	1.83	2.07	1.50	1.77	2.14	1.91	2.47
1979	1.09	1.58	—	2.40	1.88	2.04	1.70	1.48	2.05	1.78	1.95
1978	1.26	1.73	—	2.51	2.05	2.15	1.70	1.62	2.06	1.94	2.04
Quick Ratio											
1983	0.55	1.03	—	1.28	0.58	0.31	0.89	0.89	1.38	0.46	0.23
1982	0.51	1.05	—	1.41	0.67	0.33	0.92	0.86	1.36	0.31	0.35
1981	0.48	1.03	—	1.01	0.50	0.40	0.77	0.90	1.28	0.11	0.02
1980	0.41	0.84	—	1.73	0.81	0.64	0.77	1.04	1.39	0.18	0.03
1979	0.36	0.47	—	1.59	0.91	0.68	0.98	0.89	1.28	0.21	0.04
1978	0.44	0.35	—	1.68	0.96	0.85	0.87	0.99	1.26	0.20	0.10
Combined Quick Ratio[a]											
1983	1.30	1.56	—	1.28	0.76	1.23	0.89	0.90	1.38	0.46	0.23
1982	1.28	1.59	—	1.41	0.94	1.20	0.92	0.87	1.36	0.31	0.35
1981	1.33	1.61	—	1.01	0.83	1.14	0.77	0.92	1.28	0.11	0.02
1980	1.40	1.46	—	1.73	1.13	1.24	0.77	1.06	1.39	0.18	0.03
1979	1.40	1.17	—	1.59	1.23	1.30	0.98	0.91	1.28	0.21	0.04
1978	1.41	1.07	—	1.68	1.41	1.27	0.87	1.02	1.26	0.20	0.10
Combined Short-Term Debt Percentage Combined Current Assets[a]											
1983	29.9	10.8	—	8.8	13.8	2.6	0.4	12.0	1.1	1.5	5.5
1982	29.6	10.6	—	4.1	9.4	7.2	0.6	18.0	2.0	1.8	2.3
1981	29.2	8.9	—	21.8	18.9	14.5	7.8	20.5	1.3	6.8	7.3
1980	28.4	11.2	—	3.0	8.4	16.2	3.7	8.1	1.4	1.9	12.8
1979	27.8	21.1	—	2.0	11.8	15.4	1.1	21.4	2.1	7.5	4.9
1978	25.1	22.1	—	2.3	6.3	12.2	1.1	19.5	4.0	1.8	2.5

a Company + non-consolidated finance subsidiary.
b Data represents Merchandise Group only.
c Excludes discontinued automotive operations, 1981 and 1980 restated.
d Results for 1981 and 1980 restated to reflect discontinuance of U.S. Woolco operations and sale of interest in British subsidiary.

TABLE 6. Liquidity, Working Capital and Property Statistics

	GENERAL MERCHANDISE			DEPARTMENT STORES						DISCOUNT—VARIETY	
	Montgomery Ward	J.C. Penney	Sears Roebuck	Allied Stores	Associated Dry Goods	Carter Hawley	Dayton-Hudson	Federated	May	K mart	Woolworth
LIQUIDITY & WORKING CAPITAL STATISTICS											
Receivables Turnover (days)[a]											
1983	307	174	—	114	109	129	153	131	159	—	—
1982	327	183	—	116	113	155	155	135	168	—	—
1981	358	183	—	115	110	150	146	131	160	—	—
1980	385	183	—	127	114	151	151	135	159	—	—
1979	395	183	—	125	108	139	120	132	155	—	—
1978	380	117	—	125	105	—	120	129	148	—	—
Inventory Turnover (days)[b]											
1983	56	54	—	49	50	68	57	49	52	67	69
1982	60	50	—	53	52	71	56	47	56	70	72
1981	61	49	—	48	54	65	58	45	57	66	72
1980	67	52	—	46	47	61	55	45	57	72	72
1979	76	61	—	47	47	60	44	43	55	72	70
1978	75	63	—	48	50	—	45	43	—	70	69
PROPERTY STATISTICS											
No. of Retail Stores Operated	375	1597[i]	813[c]	570	318	1085	1075	424[e]	195[h]	2361[g]	4486[j]
MM Sq. Ft. Retail Space	31.1	62.8[i]	112.5[d]	37.1[d]	34.2[d]	29.2[d]	42.0	54.2[e]	36.1[h]	127.0[g]	45.9
% Owned	—	—	53	—	45	—	—	44[f]	66	—	—

a Company + non-consolidated finance subsidiary.
b Based on sales.
c Data represents Domestic Merchandise Group only.
d Gross space.
e Excluding supermarkets.
f Based on number of stores.
g K mart and Jupiter stores only.
h Excluding Volume shoe stores.
i Excludes catalog sales centers, drug stores and Belgian stores.
j Excluding leased departments.

TABLE 7. Receivables Statistics

	GENERAL MERCHANDISE			DEPARTMENT STORES						DISCOUNT—VARIETY	
	Montgomery Ward	J.C. Penney	Sears Roebuck[a]	Allied Stores	Associated Dry Goods	Carter Hawley	Dayton-Hudson	Federated	May	K mart	Woolworth
No. of Accounts (MM)											
1983	7.9	15.9	25.6	N.A.	N.A.	4.8	N.A.	N.A.	4.3	—	—
1982	7.9	15.4	24.8	N.A.	N.A.	4.4	N.A.	N.A.	4.0	—	—
1981	8.6	15.0	24.5	N.A.	N.A.	4.3	N.A.	N.A.	3.7	—	—
1980	8.8	13.0	24.5	N.A.	N.A.	3.9	N.A.	N.A.	3.6	—	—
1979	8.8	14.3	25.9	N.A.	N.A.	3.5	N.A.	N.A.	3.8	—	—
Average Account Balance ($)											
1983	485	218	423	N.A.	N.A.	162	N.A.	N.A.	206	—	—
1982	481	224	376	N.A.	N.A.	172	N.A.	N.A.	205	—	—
1981	464	213	352	N.A.	N.A.	169	N.A.	N.A.	201	—	—
1980	459	202	328	N.A.	N.A.	162	N.A.	N.A.	185	—	—
1979	452	201	309[b]	N.A.	N.A.	155	N.A.	N.A.	158	—	—
Write-Offs Percentage Credit Sales											
1983	2.4	1.6	0.7	0.7	1.0	1.7	1.9	0.9	0.8	—	—
1982	2.9	1.8	0.9	0.9	1.3	1.8	1.8	1.1	1.5	—	—
1981	3.0	1.7	1.1	0.5	1.0	1.7	1.7	0.9	0.9	—	—
1980	3.1	1.9	1.1	1.0	1.2	1.8	2.0	1.2	1.0	—	—
1979	1.9	1.5	0.7	0.9	0.9	1.1	1.6	1.0	0.8	—	—
Loss Reserve Percentage Receivables											
1983	3.5	2.0	—	1.7	3.1	1.5	2.7	2.1	2.4	—	—
1982	3.8	2.0	—	1.7	3.3	1.5	3.1	2.1	2.7	—	—
1981	3.8	2.0	—	2.0	3.3	1.5	3.3	2.0	2.7	—	—
1980	3.3	2.0	—	1.9	3.4	1.5	4.6	2.2	2.9	—	—
1979	2.9	2.0	—	1.9	3.3	1.4	4.0	2.3	2.7	—	—

TABLE 7. Receivables Statistics (continued)

	GENERAL MERCHANDISE			DEPARTMENT STORES						DISCOUNT—VARIETY	
	Montgomery Ward	J.C. Penney	Sears Roebuck[a]	Allied Stores	Associated Dry Goods	Carter Hawley	Dayton-Hudson	Federated	May	K mart	Woolworth
Finance Charges ($MM)											
1983	654	569	1404	109.1	58.3	N.A.	124.3	176.2	115.2	—	—
1982	646	528	1158	93.8	52.7	93.8	102.2	153.9	99.4	—	—
1981	634	411	1040	70.9	46.0	76.8	79.2	125.0	85.3	—	—
1980	623	360	967	62.1	40.1	65.4	64.6	109.5	72.7	—	—
1979	572	370	951	60.7	33.6	57.4	56.8	100.4	69.2	—	—
Finance Charges Percentage of Sales											
1983	10.9	4.7	6.4	3.0	1.6	N.A.	1.8	2.0	2.7	—	—
1982	11.6	4.6	5.8	2.9	1.7	3.1	1.8	2.0	2.7	—	—
1981	11.0	3.6	5.4	2.6	1.7	2.7	1.6	1.8	2.5	—	—
1980	11.3	3.3	5.4	2.7	2.1	2.5	1.6	1.7	2.3	—	—
1979	10.9	3.4	5.4	2.8	1.9	2.4	1.7	1.7	2.3	—	—
Finance Charges Percentage of Avg. Outstandings											
1983	17.4	16.4	17.2	14.4	12.9	N.A.	15.5	14.1	14.7	—	—
1982	17.6	15.9	16.2	14.3	12.1	13.9	15.1	13.4	13.8	—	—
1981	16.0	14.2	15.1	13.3	11.4	12.4	14.4	12.1	13.1	—	—
1980	16.0	13.1	14.5	13.5	10.9	12.4	13.5	11.9	12.6	—	—
1979	15.9	13.4	14.2	13.4	10.4	12.6	13.1	11.8	12.8	—	—

[a] Data represents Domestic Merchandise Group only.
[b] Revolving charge accounts only.
N.A.—Not Available.

TABLE 8. Sales Statistics

	GENERAL MERCHANDISE			DEPARTMENT STORES						DISCOUNT—VARIETY	
	Montgomery Ward	J.C. Penney[a]	Sears Roebuck[b]	Allied Stores	Associated Dry Goods	Carter Hawley	Dayton-Hudson	Federated	May	K mart	Woolworth[d]
Total Sales ($MM)											
1983	6003	12078	20439	3676	3718	3633	6963	8690	4212	18598	5456
1982	5584	11414	18779	3216	3189	3055	5661	7699	3654	16772	5124
1981	5742	11369	18229	2733	2751	2871	4943	7068	3401	16527	5075
1980	5497*	10824*	16831	2268	1952	2633	4034	6301	3150	14204	5102
1979	5251	10856	16813	2210	1783	2408	3385	5806	2957	12731	6785
1978	5014	10845	—	2083*	1606*	2117*	2962*	5405*	2716*	11696	6103
Percentage Change From Prior Year											
1983	7.5	5.8	8.8	14.3	16.6	18.9	23.0	12.9	15.3	10.9	6.5
1982	(2.8)	0.4	3.0	17.7	15.9	6.4	14.5	8.9	7.4	1.5	1.0
1981	4.5	5.0	8.3	20.5	40.9	9.0	22.6	12.2	8.0	16.4	(0.5)
1980	4.7	4.6	0.1	2.6	9.5	9.3	19.2	8.5	6.5	11.6	5.8
1979	4.7	4.0	(2.6)	6.1	11.1	13.8	14.3	7.4	8.8	14.0c	11.2
1978	10.2	15.8	—	9.1	9.4	12.8	18.7	9.8	14.4	16.2c	10.3
Percentage Change— Comparable Stores											
1983	N.A.	5.3	N.A.	11.4	N.A.	15.1	11.0	6.7	10.4	9.2	N.A.
1982	N.A.	(0.4)	N.A.	3.1	N.A.	3.4	7.0	1.7	5.0	(1.4)	N.A.
1981	N.A.	2.4	N.A.	5.8	N.A.	6.3	9.0	7.0	4.8	10.4	N.A.
1980	N.A.	1.1	N.A.	0.0	N.A.	6.1	5.0	5.5	3.3	3.8	N.A.
1979	N.A.	1.1	N.A.	1.1	N.A.	6.9	7.9	5.1	3.3	5.5	N.A.
1978	N.A.	15.1	N.A.	6.9	N.A.	7.4	8.9	6.8	6.1	8.1	N.A.
Sales/Sq. Ft. Selling Area ($)	h	h	g	g						f	
1983	159	176	180	99	—	—	—	—	—	155e	86
1982	143	166	164	88	—	—	—	—	—	142e	79
1981	147	165	160	83	—	—	—	—	—	146	76
1980	146	160	150	76	—	—	—	—	—	139	73
1979	145	161	153	74	—	—	—	—	—	138	69
1978	144	157	127	71	—	—	—	—	—	135	63

* Fifty-three weeks.
a Excludes discontinued automotive operations, 1981 and 1980 restated.
b Data represents Domestic Merchandise Group only.
c Excluding Australian operations.
d Results for 1981 and 1980 restated to reflect discontinuance of U.S. Woolco operations and sale of interest in British subsidiary.
e K mart stores only.
f Woolworth domestic stores only.
g Gross square feet.
h Full line stores only.
N.A.—Not Available

TABLE 9. Sales Statistics

	GENERAL MERCHANDISE			DEPARTMENT STORES						DISCOUNT—VARIETY	
	Montgomery Ward	J.C. Penney[c]	Sears Roebuck[a]	Allied Stores	Associated Dry Goods	Carter Hawley	Dayton-Hudson	Federated	May	K mart	Woolworth[d]
PERCENTAGE OF SALES											
Credit Sales											
1983	56.8	49.9	58.9	65.6	62.6	60.4[b]	39.0	56.5[b]	60.3[b]	—	—
1982	55.1	47.8	56.0	63.8	62.1	59.9[b]	38.0	55.4[b]	59.0[b]	—	—
1981	54.1	45.2	53.6	61.9	62.2	59.1[b]	36.4	55.8[b]	57.8[b]	—	—
1980	53.5	42.2	52.4	58.3	59.9	56.5[b]	35.9	55.0[b]	55.9[b]	—	—
1979	56.8	43.0	54.2	59.9	61.4	57.4[b]	40.0	57.2[b]	56.7[b]	—	—
1978	56.4	42.2	55.6	58.4	60.2	56.0[b]	40.4	57.5[b]	56.4[b]	—	—
Leased Dept. Sales											
1983	—	—	—	7.5	—	—	—	2.3	4.6	—	4.4
1982	—	—	—	7.4	—	10.0	—	2.1	4.5	—	4.6
1981	—	—	—	6.9	—	6.0	—	2.1	4.4	—	5.3
1980	—	—	—	6.1	—	5.4	—	2.2	4.3	—	5.2
1979	—	—	—	7.4	—	5.7	—	2.3	4.0	—	7.3
1978	—	—	—	6.7	—	5.8	—	2.3	4.1	—	8.2
Catalog Sales											
1983	19.9	15.2	18.1	—	—	—	—	—	—	—	—
1982	20.5	14.9	18.7	—	—	—	—	—	—	—	—
1981	20.5	14.8	19.9	—	—	—	—	—	—	—	—
1980	20.4	14.2	20.4	—	—	—	—	—	—	—	—
1979	22.1	13.4	20.4	—	—	—	—	—	—	—	—
1978	21.8	11.2	20.3	—	—	—	—	—	—	—	—

a Data represents Domestic Merchandise Group only.
b Based on department store sales only.
c Excludes discontinued automotive operations, 1981 and 1980 restated.
d Results for 1981 and 1980 restated to reflect discontinuance of U.S. Woolco operations and sale of interest in British subsidiary.

TABLE 10. Expense Ratios

	GENERAL MERCHANDISE			DEPARTMENT STORES						DISCOUNT—VARIETY	
	Montgomery Ward	J.C. Penney[b]	Sears Roebuck	Allied Stores	Associated Dry Goods	Carter Hawley	Dayton-Hudson	Federated	May	K mart	Woolworth[c]
PERCENTAGE OF REVENUES											
Operating Ratio (Incl. Deprec.)											
1983	92.6	91.3	91.3[d]	91.1	92.4	94.8	92.3	92.1	90.9	94.5	95.1
1982	96.9	91.7	92.3	92.4	93.2	94.6	92.3	93.3	91.7	96.2	96.1
1981	96.8	92.1	93.5	92.2	93.1	94.6	93.2	92.4	91.9	97.0	95.4
1980	96.9	93.8	—	92.0	94.0	93.9	93.5	92.7	92.0	95.8	94.6
1979	91.9	93.9	—	91.1	94.3	92.4	92.7	92.6	91.4	94.3	95.2
1978	91.8	93.8	—	91.0	94.9	92.0	92.1	92.2	91.0	93.7	94.9
Selling, Gen'l & Admin.											
1983	19.2	24.6	28.7[d]	24.0	17.3	24.4	16.7	19.5	20.7	22.9	25.9
1982	19.5	24.2	29.9	24.4	17.7	25.1[a]	17.4	19.8	21.0	23.6	26.5
1981	19.8	23.9	29.5	24.8	18.1	25.5[a]	17.9	20.0	20.9	22.8	26.2
1980	19.8	23.3	—	24.6	19.0	30.4	18.2	19.9	20.5	23.2	25.6
1979	18.1	23.3	—	24.0	19.4	29.1	18.5	19.7	20.2	22.1	24.2
1978	18.7	23.3	—	24.1	20.2	28.2	18.2	19.4	19.7	21.2	24.3
Depreciation											
1983	1.6	1.3	1.0	2.2	2.3	2.1	1.9	2.4	2.3	1.4	1.8
1982	1.7	1.3	1.1	2.3	2.3	2.2	1.9	2.4	2.4	1.5	1.9
1981	1.8	1.3	1.1	1.9	2.0	2.3	1.7	2.2	2.4	1.4	1.8
1980	1.6	1.3	1.1	1.8	2.1	2.2	1.7	2.4	2.4	1.4	1.7
1979	1.4	1.2	1.1	1.7	2.1	2.2	1.5	2.2	2.4	1.3	1.6
1978	1.4	1.1	1.2	1.7	2.2	2.1	1.4	2.2	2.3	1.2	1.7
Advertising											
1983	5.0	3.2	2.5	3.5	3.6	1.8	2.3	2.8	3.1	2.3	1.9
1982	5.2	2.8	2.4	3.5	3.6	1.6	2.4	2.6	3.1	2.4	2.0
1981	4.9	2.6	2.5	3.1	3.5	1.5	2.4	2.4	3.1	2.3	1.9
1980	4.6	2.4	2.3	3.6	3.8	2.1	2.3	2.4	3.1	2.4	1.8
1979	4.2	2.4	2.2	3.5	3.6	1.9	2.2	2.1	2.9	2.3	2.5
1978	4.0	2.6	—	3.5	3.6	1.9	2.2	2.0	2.9	2.3	2.5

a Restated to include occupancy and buying costs in cost of goods sold.
b Excludes discontinued automotive operations, 1981 and 1980 restated.
c Results for 1981 and 1980 restated to reflect discontinuance of U.S. Woolco operations and sale of interest in British subsidiary.
d Data represents Domestic Merchandise Group only.

TABLE 11. Expense Ratios

	GENERAL MERCHANDISE				DEPARTMENT STORES					DISCOUNT—VARIETY	
	Montgomery Ward	J.C. Penney	Sears Roebuck	Allied Stores	Associated Dry Goods	Carter Hawley	Dayton-Hudson	Federated	May	K mart	Woolworth[a]
PERCENTAGE OF SALES											
Interest & Discount Paid to Outsiders											
1983	1.7	1.4	4.8	2.3	1.5	1.8	1.3	1.2	1.5	1.5	1.6
1982	1.0	1.3	5.5	2.8	1.9	2.4	1.3	1.4	1.7	1.6	2.0
1981	1.5	1.2	5.7	2.5	1.5	2.2	1.1	1.1	1.5	1.7	2.0
1980	1.2	0.9	4.6	1.7	0.7	1.9	0.7	1.1	1.7	1.6	1.7
1979	0.9	0.6	3.8	1.6	0.8	1.8	0.5	1.1	1.7	1.3	1.7
1978	0.8	0.6	2.9	1.6	0.7	1.9	0.5	0.9	1.7	1.2	1.6
Paid to Non-Consolidated Finance Subsidiaries											
1983	6.2	2.0	0	0	0.5	2.0	0	0	0	0	0
1982	8.4	2.0	0	0	0.9	2.6	0	0	0	0	0
1981	10.6	2.1	0	0	1.4	3.1	0	0	0	0	0
1980	10.1	2.4	0	0	1.2	2.5	0	0	0	0	0
1979	8.4	2.8	0	0	0.8	1.7	0	0	0	0	0
1978	5.8	2.2	0	0	0.8	1.2	0	0	0	0	0
Rents											
1983	2.0	3.2	—	1.9	1.7	2.4	1.4	0.9	1.5	1.4	4.8
1982	1.8	3.2	—	2.0	1.5	2.4	1.5	1.0	1.4	1.4	4.7
1981	1.6	3.0	—	1.7	1.5	2.3	1.4	0.9	1.3	1.7	4.6
1980	1.6	3.0	—	1.6	1.7	2.6	1.5	0.8	1.2	1.7	4.1
1979	1.5	2.9	—	1.5	1.7	2.4	1.5	0.8	1.0	1.7	3.3
1978	1.5	2.6	—	1.5	1.8	2.3	1.5	0.8	0.8	1.6	3.3

[a] Results for 1981 and 1980 restated to reflect discontinuance of U.S. Woolco operations and sale of interest in British subsidiary.

TABLE 12. Income Statistics

	GENERAL MERCHANDISE			DEPARTMENT STORES						DISCOUNT—VARIETY	
	Montgomery Ward	J.C. Penney[a]	Sears Roebuck	Allied Stores	Associated Dry Goods	Carter Hawley	Dayton-Hudson	Federated	May	K mart	Woolworth[b]
Net Income ($MM)											
1983	56.0	467.0	1342.0	128.5	115.5	59.3	243.2	311.7	186.6	492.3	118.0
1982	(79.0)	415.0	861.2	87.1	78.4	38.9	198.4	232.8	141.7	285.8	82.0
1981	(131.0)	388.0	650.1	88.3	69.8	36.4	159.5	258.3	130.0	220.3	82.0
1980	(107.0)	276.0	610.0	83.9	52.2	55.2	138.2	219.6	115.2	260.5	120.0
1979	73.4	261.0	830.0	90.1	43.9	69.7	126.5	203.2	113.2	358.0	152.0
1978	119.4	276.0	921.5	82.3	34.5	63.8	97.6	197.9	104.6	343.7	130.3
Percentage Change From Prior Year											
1983	—	12.5	55.9	47.5	47.3	52.4	22.6	33.9	31.7	72.3	43.9
1982	—	7.0	32.5	(1.4)	12.4	4.3	24.4	(9.9)	9.0	29.7	0
1981	—	40.6	6.6	5.9	34.8	(32.4)	15.4	17.6	12.9	(15.5)	(31.7)
1980	—	5.7	(26.5)	(6.9)	18.9	(20.8)	9.3	8.1	1.7	(27.2)	(4.8)
1979	(38.5)	(8.1)	(8.7)	9.5	27.2	9.2	29.6	2.7	8.9	4.2	17.9
1978	6.9	(4.8)	10.0	11.6	(18.4)	14.6	6.5	0.9	13.6	15.4	52.4
Payout Ratio—Percentage											
1983	5.4	34.3	40.0	30.1	40.0	72.7	24.8	34.3	30.3	26.9	49.2
1982	—	35.2	55.3	42.5	50.7	101.6	27.9	43.8	36.8	47.0	69.5
1981	—	33.2	66.0	40.1	48.6	97.2	31.7	35.7	37.5	54.0	68.3
1980	—	46.4	65.8	41.4	40.8	55.3	32.9	39.7	38.2	43.5	46.7
1979	69.2	46.7	50.4	35.3	46.2	41.4	32.1	40.4	31.6	28.8	32.9
1978	40.6	42.8	44.4	32.1	58.8	39.0	39.6	39.6	29.4	25.6	34.5

a Excludes discontinued automotive operations, 1981 and 1980 restated.
b Results for 1981 and 1980 restated to reflect discontinuance of U.S. Woolco operations and sale of interest in British subsidiary.

TABLE 13. Profitability Statistics

	GENERAL MERCHANDISE			DEPARTMENT STORES						DISCOUNT—VARIETY	
	Montgomery Ward	J.C. Penney[c]	Sears Roebuck	Allied Stores	Associated Dry Goods	Carter Hawley	Dayton-Hudson	Federated	May	K mart	Woolworth[d]
Gross Profit Margin (Percentage)											
1983	26.6	33.3	37.4[e]	32.3	24.9	29.5	29.3	27.9	29.8	27.7	32.6
1982	22.6	32.5	37.6[e]	31.3	24.5	30.4[b]	30.1	27.0	29.2	26.7	32.3
1981	23.3	31.8	36.0[e]	31.9	25.0	30.9[b]	29.6	27.7	29.0	25.2	32.6
1980	22.9	29.5	—	31.7	25.0	43.4	29.5	27.2	28.5	26.7	32.7
1979	26.4	29.5	—	32.0	25.1	43.5	30.5	27.2	28.8	27.1	30.6
1978	27.5	29.5	—	32.3	25.3	43.2	30.6	27.2	28.3	26.8	31.1
Pretax Margin (Percentage)											
1983	—	6.5	—	6.5	6.0	2.8	6.4	6.8	8.1	4.6	3.8
1982	(6.3)	6.0	—	4.9	4.6	2.2	6.7	5.5	7.1	2.5	2.6
1981	(8.5)	5.9	—	5.7	4.6	2.2	5.8	6.7	7.2	1.7	3.6
1980	(7.8)	4.0	—	6.6	5.0	2.5	6.2	6.4	6.8	2.8	4.2
1979	(1.6)	4.1	—	7.4	4.2	4.3	7.1	6.5	7.3	4.6	3.3
1978	1.6	3.5	—	7.5	3.6	5.1	6.7	7.0	7.5	5.2	3.7
Net Income/Sales (Percentage)											
1983	0.9	3.9	3.7	3.5	3.1	1.6	3.5	3.6	4.4	2.6	2.2
1982	(1.4)	3.6	2.9	2.7	2.5	1.3	3.5	3.0	3.9	1.7	1.6
1981	(2.3)	3.4	2.4	3.2	2.5	1.3	3.2	3.7	3.8	1.3	1.5
1980	(1.9)	2.5	2.4	3.6	2.7	2.2	3.4	3.5	3.6	1.8	2.2
1979	1.4	2.2	3.4	4.0	2.5	2.9	3.7	3.5	3.8	2.8	1.8
1978	2.4	2.5	—	3.9	2.1	3.0	3.3	3.7	3.8	2.9	1.7

Return on Average Equity (Percentage)

1983	3.4	13.8	14.4	14.0	16.7	7.9	16.8	14.0	17.0	17.8	11.6
1982	(4.9)	13.5	10.1	10.5	11.0	5.6	15.6	11.4	14.2	11.3	6.9
1981	(9.2)	13.9	8.2	11.5	10.6	6.0	14.1	13.6	14.1	9.2	5.8
1980	(8.4)	10.7	8.1	11.4	9.8	9.6	13.6	12.7	13.6	11.5	8.5
1979	5.5	10.7	11.4	13.2	8.7	12.5	14.3	12.9	14.7	17.5	12.3
1978	9.3	12.3	13.5	13.3	7.1	12.6	16.5	13.6	—	19.3	11.5
Book Value Per Share											
—1983 Year End	a	43.94	27.60	46.00	50.74	21.27	15.91	48.03	40.17	23.35	31.93
Earnings Per Share											
—1983 Year End	a	6.25	3.80	5.61	5.95	1.90	2.52	6.41	6.48	3.80	3.67
Market Price Per Share											
—5/23/84	a	50.75	31.13	41.75	46.75	21.63	26.25	44.00	52.00	28.00	33.88
—52 Week Price											
—High	—	66.75	45.13	56.50	71.50	32.25	41.00	69.00	63.00	39.25	39.38
—Low	—	47.75	29.50	38.50	46.13	18.25	26.13	43.25	45.50	26.75	29.88

a Subsidiary of Mobil Corp.
b Restated to include occupancy and buying costs in cost of goods sold.
c Excludes discontinued automotive operations, 1981 and 1980 restated.
d Results for 1981 and 1980 restated to reflect discontinuance of U.S. Woolco operations and sale of interest in British subsidiary.
e Data represents Domestic Merchandise Group only.

TABLE 14. Cash Flow Statistics

	GENERAL MERCHANDISE			DEPARTMENT STORES						DISCOUNT—VARIETY	
	Montgomery Ward	J.C. Penney[a]	Sears Roebuck	Allied Stores	Associated Dry Goods	Carter Hawley	Dayton-Hudson	Federated	May	K mart	Woolworth[b]
Cash Flow ($MM)											
1983	120.0	677.0	2999.0	225.5	212.5	143.6	398.7	541.0	299.2	762.3	262.0
1982	23.0	614.0	2114.0	175.9	163.3	115.9	328.7	457.1	248.9	555.5	212.0
1981	(41.0)	509.0	1791.0	155.0	127.2	110.3	266.1	456.1	223.3	450.6	168.0
1980	(123.0)	374.0	—	130.0	94.2	129.3	214.8	383.4	207.0	442.4	211.0
1979	82.0	334.0	—	130.8	83.1	141.3	178.4	361.3	196.3	522.8	254.0
1978	189.3	402.0	—	120.2	70.0	122.4	144.3	333.7	174.2	487.9	234.0
Cash Flow Percentage of L.T. Debt											
1983	20.0	39.6	40.4	29.8	48.0	27.5	53.1	85.7	53.2	30.1	60.2
1982	3.8	44.4	36.3	22.2	37.4	19.8	52.1	65.4	42.2	23.0	41.1
1981	—	36.2	33.6	25.6	33.3	18.9	62.2	82.5	41.5	20.8	30.5
1980	—	27.4	—	28.4	60.4	21.9	67.7	69.4	38.0	21.7	39.9
1979	13.9	41.7	—	33.8	50.4	28.3	93.6	100.0	33.0	32.0	33.6
1978	31.6	47.8	—	29.7	41.9	24.0	84.3	92.8	31.0	32.5	30.7
Retained Cash Flow ($MM)											
1983	117.0	517.0	—	186.8	166.3	100.1	338.3	434.1	242.6	630.1	204.0
1982	19.0	468.0	—	138.8	123.5	76.4	273.3	355.1	196.4	432.5	155.0
1981	(46.0)	380.0	—	119.6	93.3	74.0	215.7	364.0	174.4	333.1	112.0
1980	(128.0)	246.0	—	95.3	72.9	95.7	169.3	296.3	162.9	331.6	155.0
1979	31.2	212.0	—	98.9	62.9	110.2	137.9	279.3	161.9	419.8	204.0
1978	140.8	284.0	—	93.7	49.8	95.1	105.6	255.4	143.4	400.0	189.0

Retained Cash Flow Percentage of Cap. Exp. + Long-Term Invest.

Year										
1983	96.7	116.7	181.2	90.9	94.8	101.1	144.3	135.7	143.1	155.7
1982	27.5	163.1	141.9	156.7	53.2	96.3	75.4	123.7	109.4	133.6
1981	—	185.4	38.7	22.1	47.7	85.0	87.8	114.7	54.8	76.2
1980	—	85.1	98.2	105.4	56.4	48.4	86.5	121.2	54.6	91.7
1979	12.5	59.7	79.3	105.4	60.8	63.2	109.1	107.4	87.5	107.9
1978	78.8	85.0	120.0	60.7	62.4	67.6	104.7	82.7	82.6	106.8

Retained Cash Flow Percentage of Cap. Exp. + L. T. Invest. + Inc. (Dec.) in Rec. & Inv.

Year										
1983	44.0	55.9	57.3	57.0	45.8	50.3	67.1	77.6	84.5	138.8
1982	17.1	110.1	74.5	64.7	34.2	48.0	52.8	80.9	74.5	108.4
1981	—	44.3	18.7	16.1	44.2	44.8	54.4	58.2	36.7	79.4
1980	—	49.2	94.6	81.7	38.7	38.7	64.2	78.2	46.6	93.9
1979	46.8	78.5	56.1	54.6	63.7	45.6	54.1	65.3	47.6	61.6
1978	51.1	54.9	80.3	47.7	33.3	37.9	60.5	48.8	57.5	54.9

Note: Cash flow is net income plus depreciation and/or depletion plus deferred taxes and an adjustment for capitalized interest. Retained cash flow is cash flow minus dividends.

[a] Excludes discontinued automotive operations, 1981 and 1980 restated.
[b] Results for 1981 and 1980 restated to reflect discontinuance of U.S. Woolco operations and sale of interest in British subsidiary.

TABLE 15. Combined Cash Flow Statistics

	GENERAL MERCHANDISE			DEPARTMENT STORES						DISCOUNT—VARIETY	
	Montgomery Ward[a]	J.C. Penney[b]	Sears Roebuck	Allied Stores	Associated Dry Goods	Carter Hawley	Dayton-Hudson	Federated	May	K mart	Woolworth[c]
Combined Cash Flow ($MM)[a]											
1983	137.0	725.0	1578.0	225.5	216.1	158.9	398.7	541.0	299.2	762.3	262.0
1982	25.0	664.0	2114.0	175.9	168.4	134.4	328.7	457.1	248.8	555.5	212.0
1981	(31.0)	562.0	1791.0	155.0	134.2	115.2	266.1	456.1	223.3	450.6	167.0
1980	(22.0)	429.0	—	130.0	98.3	142.1	214.8	383.4	207.0	442.4	230.0
1979	163.8	394.0	—	130.8	85.7	149.3	178.4	361.4	196.3	522.8	254.0
1978	240.6	445.0	—	120.2	72.2	126.6	144.3	334.2	174.2	487.9	234.0
Percentage of Combined Total Debt[a]											
1983	4.4	23.4	25.0	25.4	36.0	17.5	52.5	56.7	51.5	29.2	51.7
1982	0.8	22.6	24.5	20.8	29.1	13.8	51.3	40.9	40.1	22.3	38.7
1981	—	20.6	20.9	17.8	21.9	12.0	49.5	46.5	40.2	18.8	24.9
1980	—	15.3	—	26.7	32.2	15.3	59.8	54.5	36.8	21.1	27.8
1979	4.3	14.5	—	32.4	29.4	18.4	87.9	49.6	31.7	28.0	30.5
1978	7.5	16.1	—	28.3	28.6	17.6	78.9	50.3	30.9	31.5	29.3
Percentage of Combined Total Debt + Est. Present Value of Non-Capitalized Leases[a]											
1983	4.0	18.6	22.8	19.0	24.6	11.7	35.2	45.2	36.7	17.4	18.8
1982	0.7	17.3	22.3	15.2	20.1	9.6	34.1	34.5	29.8	13.6	13.3
1981	—	15.5	19.4	13.3	15.6	8.6	34.4	40.9	30.2	12.0	8.4
1980	—	11.5	—	19.9	19.9	10.2	37.2	46.4	28.2	13.2	10.9
1979	4.0	10.9	—	23.1	17.9	11.8	45.7	43.5	25.4	17.6	13.3
1978	6.8	12.1	—	21.2	16.7	11.9	40.7	43.5	25.8	19.7	13.0
Percentage of Combined Current Liab.[a]											
1983	4.4	28.9	8.7	30.4	31.0	26.7	32.9	32.3	36.4	30.2	36.6
1982	0.8	25.9	8.1	30.8	32.3	23.5	34.5	29.7	34.4	25.5	28.8
1981	—	24.5	—	21.1	23.6	20.5	29.6	33.4	34.2	22.7	24.2
1980	—	18.0	—	33.9	26.7	26.7	28.3	37.2	34.4	26.5	29.1
1979	5.4	14.8	—	35.7	26.2	30.3	27.2	31.6	33.9	29.3	31.8
1978	9.0	16.7	—	34.2	31.1	30.7	23.5	35.2	36.2	35.1	33.4

[a] Company + non-consolidated finance subsidiary.
[b] Excludes discontinued automotive operations, 1981 and 1980 restated.
[c] Results for 1981 and 1980 restated to reflect discontinuance of U.S. Woolco operations and sale of interest in British subsidiary.

TABLE 16. Seasonal Statistics

	GENERAL MERCHANDISE			DEPARTMENT STORES						DISCOUNT—VARIETY	
	Montgomery Ward	J.C. Penney[a]	Sears Roebuck	Allied Stores	Associated Dry Goods	Carter Hawley	Dayton-Hudson	Federated	May	K mart	Woolworth[b]
Percentage Change in Sales From Prior Year											
April Quarter—											
1983	4.5	1.7	16.3	13.7	8.0	13.1	22.2	13.7	15.3	9.3	4.7
1982	(10.9)	(2.0)	10.3	27.9	41.2	6.5	15.0	7.0	3.7	8.0	0.9
1981	9.8	11.7	—	11.1	14.6	11.2	29.1	14.5	9.5	11.7	—
1980	0.5	(4.7)	—	2.1	8.6	11.0	15.2	9.0	6.7	14.0	9.6
July Quarter—											
1983	4.5	3.1	20.0	16.5	17.4	18.7	24.4	16.9	15.8	12.6	4.6
1982	(3.2)	1.6	8.1	28.2	20.2	5.0	13.2	5.4	4.6	3.2	2.3
1981	13.8	9.2	—	12.7	14.2	13.1	28.3	14.6	11.6	15.9	—
1980	(1.9)	(3.9)	—	1.9	8.3	7.9	15.1	6.9	5.0	14.0	6.5
October Quarter—											
1983	9.7	5.4	19.0	13.2	21.6	20.3	21.8	11.7	14.9	11.6	8.4
1982	(4.0)	(1.4)	10.0	15.7	4.8	3.2	14.0	8.5	6.7	(3.1)	(0.7)
1981	3.2	6.4	—	22.0	12.0	8.4	20.3	11.3	6.7	19.0	—
1980	3.5	(1.2)	—	2.2	7.7	8.0	20.8	8.4	7.9	10.0	6.9
January Quarter—											
1983	9.9	10.5	21.9	14.1	17.6	21.6	23.5	10.7	15.2	10.2	7.6
1982	4.5	2.5	10.4	8.0	9.7	9.5	15.4	12.9	12.1	(0.2)	1.4
1981	(3.7)	(2.2)	—	30.0	9.7	5.8	17.2	9.8	5.6	17.6	—
1980	13.2	(5.5)	—	3.7	12.1	10.2	22.9	9.4	6.5	8.8	3.8

TABLE 16. Seasonal Statistics (continued)

	GENERAL MERCHANDISE			DEPARTMENT STORES						DISCOUNT—VARIETY	
	Montgomery Ward	J.C. Penney[a]	Sears Roebuck	Allied Stores	Associated Dry Goods	Carter Hawley	Dayton-Hudson	Federated	May	K mart	Woolworth[b]
Profit Margin (Percentage)											
April Quarter—											
1983	1.4	2.4	2.1	1.7	0.5	0.9	1.6	2.3	2.4	1.1	0.1
1982	(5.1)	2.4	1.1	0.4	0.1	0.4	1.5	1.8	1.6	0.1	—
1981	(4.2)	2.1	0.9	2.4	1.0	1.0	1.4	2.7	2.3	1.0	0.6
1980	(3.8)	1.0	—	1.6	0.7	1.0	1.7	2.0	1.9	1.3	0.1
July Quarter—											
1983	0.7	2.1	3.6	2.0	2.1	0.6	2.3	2.1	3.4	2.5	1.3
1982	(1.6)	1.9	2.3	0.7	0.7	(0.1)	2.1	1.3	2.6	1.4	0.2
1981	(2.0)	1.7	2.0	1.4	0.6	0.9	1.6	2.4	2.6	1.4	0.3
1980	(2.5)	0.7	—	1.0	0.7	1.4	1.7	1.8	2.2	1.7	0.2
October Quarter—											
1983	0.5	3.2	3.2	2.2	1.6	0.6	2.7	2.7	3.5	1.8	1.5
1982	(2.6)	2.9	2.2	1.6	1.1	0.7	2.8	2.1	3.0	0.7	1.1
1981	(3.9)	3.1	1.9	1.5	1.4	0.6	2.7	3.0	2.8	0.3	1.4
1980	(2.8)	2.4	—	2.9	2.2	1.6	3.0	3.1	2.9	0.9	1.1
January Quarter—											
1983	3.8	6.2	5.4	6.5	6.2	3.3	5.9	6.0	7.0	4.3	4.8
1982	1.6	6.2	5.2	6.5	5.9	3.2	6.1	5.5	6.7	3.1	4.4
1981	(0.1)	5.7	4.1	5.9	5.2	2.1	5.7	5.6	6.4	2.2	3.5
1980	0.1	4.7	—	7.2	5.4	3.5	5.7	5.8	6.4	2.9	2.6

a Excludes discontinued automotive operations, 1981 and 1980 restated.

b Results for 1981 and 1980 restated to reflect discontinuance of U.S. Woolco operations and sale of interest in British subsidiary.

APPENDIX D
Selected Financial Ratios and Statistics for U.S. Industrial Corporations Grouped by Bond Credit Rating, 1973–84

LEVERAGE & CAPITALIZATION	1984	1983	1982	1981	1980	1979	1978	1977	1976	1975	1974	1973
Coverage (x)												
Aaa/AAA	15.06	11.62	10.86	12.15	13.71	14.74	13.21	14.31	13.15	11.47	15.77	16.30
Aa2/AA	7.50	5.99	4.85	6.11	8.76	10.20	8.80	7.57	8.09	8.66	10.87	9.19
A2/A	3.09	3.18	2.63	3.55	4.12	5.11	5.59	4.69	5.12	4.45	5.23	5.70
Baa2/BBB	2.18	1.03	−1.02	3.42	2.91	4.35	4.39	3.62	4.04	2.37	2.65	3.97
S.T. Debt/Total Cap. (%)												
Aaa/AAA	4.68	3.66	4.99	5.67	4.75	6.72	7.14	7.08	6.57	6.99	9.01	7.09
Aa2/AA	4.89	5.51	5.70	6.34	5.74	5.86	3.90	4.49	4.27	4.74	4.55	4.13
A2/A	5.59	5.52	4.53	5.82	5.78	6.24	4.97	4.95	5.94	6.99	11.58	10.27
Baa2/BBB	4.72	3.78	2.69	6.03	7.55	7.74	6.75	5.67	5.06	9.44	14.60	10.30
L.T. Debt/Total Cap. (%)												
Aaa/AAA	12.27	13.42	14.35	13.97	13.41	14.52	14.64	15.14	15.99	16.57	14.88	14.30
Aa2/AA	21.51	23.70	24.71	23.55	24.28	23.34	25.91	26.44	26.43	25.70	22.85	22.63
A2/A	30.51	30.49	34.82	30.57	30.61	30.68	31.35	30.42	29.98	30.90	28.04	27.32
Baa2/BBB	44.22	37.00	37.26	30.72	32.77	32.47	36.72	35.14	33.70	34.34	32.79	32.71
Total Debt/Total Cap. (%)												
Aaa/AAA	16.95	17.08	19.34	19.64	18.16	21.24	21.78	22.22	22.56	23.56	23.89	21.39
Aa2/AA	26.40	29.21	30.41	29.89	30.02	29.20	29.81	30.93	30.70	30.44	27.40	26.76
A2/A	36.10	36.01	39.35	36.39	36.39	36.92	36.32	35.37	35.92	37.89	39.62	37.59
Baa2/BBB	48.94	40.78	39.95	36.76	40.32	40.21	43.47	40.81	38.76	43.78	47.39	43.01
Preferred/Total Cap. (%)												
Aaa/AAA	0.00	0.01	0.18	0.19	0.48	0.44	0.55	0.40	0.41	0.42	0.47	0.30
Aa2/AA	0.88	0.35	0.31	1.38	1.61	1.46	0.94	0.20	0.21	0.39	0.55	0.47
A2/A	2.28	2.86	1.89	2.24	2.60	1.68	2.41	2.07	1.97	1.99	2.00	1.92
Baa2/BBB	6.67	2.39	0.30	0.91	1.00	0.98	0.60	0.63	1.29	1.24	2.01	2.07

	1973	1974	1975	1976	1977	1978	1979	1980	1981	1982	1983	1984
Minority Interest/Total Cap. (%)												
Aaa/AAA	1.24	1.29	1.23	1.33	1.29	1.28	1.14	1.54	1.71	1.47	0.98	1.42
Aa2/AA	0.28	0.46	0.32	0.15	0.57	1.08	1.36	1.29	1.02	0.76	0.51	0.44
A2/A	1.00	0.94	1.34	1.02	0.84	0.91	0.96	1.20	1.24	1.33	1.42	1.37
Baa2/BBB	1.15	1.12	1.84	1.26	1.26	0.75	0.57	0.89	1.05	0.18	0.07	0.53
Common Equity/Total Cap. (%)												
Aaa/AAA	77.07	74.35	74.79	75.70	76.09	76.39	77.18	79.82	78.46	79.01	81.93	81.63
Aa2/AA	72.48	71.49	68.85	68.94	68.31	68.17	67.98	67.08	67.71	68.52	69.93	72.28
A2/A	59.50	57.45	58.76	61.09	61.73	60.36	60.44	59.81	60.13	54.43	59.71	60.25
Baa2/BBB	53.76	49.48	53.13	58.69	57.29	55.18	58.24	57.79	61.28	59.27	56.76	43.86
S.T. Debt/Total Debt (%)												
Aaa/AAA	33.14	37.70	29.67	29.10	30.53	32.78	31.63	26.13	28.85	25.81	21.41	27.59
Aa2/AA	15.45	16.61	15.57	13.91	14.50	13.08	20.07	19.12	21.20	18.74	18.87	18.54
A2/A	27.32	29.21	18.46	16.54	14.00	13.70	16.91	15.89	16.00	11.52	15.32	15.49
Baa2/BBB	23.96	30.82	21.56	13.06	13.91	15.54	19.25	18.73	16.39	6.72	9.25	9.63
S.T. Debt/Cur. Liabilities (%)												
Aaa/AAA	18.16	19.48	16.03	14.93	15.26	15.34	14.26	10.09	12.78	12.31	9.06	11.77
Aa2/AA	16.83	15.08	17.06	15.82	17.27	13.26	14.48	13.51	15.65	13.55	12.92	12.23
A2/A	29.25	31.83	22.55	18.09	14.10	13.69	15.44	15.96	15.59	14.69	16.53	17.43
Baa2/BBB	31.31	37.08	24.58	12.47	14.27	20.31	20.92	21.44	18.03	8.17	10.30	16.42
S.T. Debt/Cur. Assets (%)												
Aaa/AAA	11.42	12.88	10.35	9.36	9.46	9.84	9.50	6.92	9.46	9.09	6.41	7.97
Aa2/AA	8.09	8.14	8.90	8.20	8.96	6.97	9.35	9.01	9.87	9.34	8.83	7.73
A2/A	16.00	17.87	11.01	9.09	7.46	7.35	9.03	9.15	9.56	8.42	10.44	10.71
Baa2/BBB	15.53	20.19	13.93	6.95	7.78	9.99	10.64	11.39	9.51	4.73	5.90	11.44
Total Liabilities/Equity (%)												
Aaa/AAA	80.71	94.11	92.76	91.89	92.01	95.34	95.17	93.45	94.85	92.28	89.94	89.52
Aa2/AA	74.01	82.30	89.00	90.23	92.02	96.22	109.83	113.58	103.38	117.90	116.21	103.40
A2/A	114.13	122.04	117.56	115.00	118.49	124.75	133.26	124.09	126.01	130.18	122.98	122.23
Baa2/BBB	130.89	154.41	151.61	139.67	146.97	141.70	131.33	129.00	115.68	145.05	153.58	184.81

Working Capital/Term Debt (%)												
Aaa/AAA	154.28	124.06	100.05	111.46	160.49	162.85	177.52	176.62	163.79	144.61	159.08	161.17
Aa2/AA	108.24	83.39	76.57	100.54	87.57	95.17	102.49	91.13	95.02	99.12	112.63	117.28
A2/A	65.99	63.77	65.99	77.13	88.16	93.43	100.12	102.65	108.44	105.14	101.27	106.37
Baa2/BBB	28.21	73.95	64.25	97.38	94.82	110.00	93.56	94.36	95.65	85.42	100.50	102.22
Long Term Debt/Net Plant (%)												
Aaa/AAA	14.83	15.64	16.71	16.81	17.67	21.20	22.69	24.82	25.51	26.05	23.60	22.36
Aa2/AA	29.01	30.50	31.18	34.70	33.53	32.20	37.56	37.59	38.92	38.30	35.28	35.16
A2/A	45.37	45.30	52.12	46.51	50.79	51.77	53.54	52.61	54.93	57.39	54.07	53.66
Baa2/BBB	49.71	51.36	48.54	55.76	67.27	65.40	69.69	69.60	67.96	70.18	78.36	71.10
Net Tangible Assets/L.T. Debt (%)												
Aaa/AAA	765.10	703.16	649.14	656.16	691.15	628.18	618.98	591.25	572.67	550.52	599.69	637.99
Aa2/AA	422.02	387.61	372.27	386.64	378.24	400.85	362.13	356.47	359.59	366.12	411.34	414.93
A2/A	298.98	296.80	267.92	317.31	299.88	299.86	289.26	301.27	301.19	288.03	302.44	314.60
Baa2/BBB	211.43	255.28	257.52	297.27	272.57	274.46	246.98	260.63	271.26	249.80	249.70	263.42
Cash Flow/L.T. Debt (%)												
Aaa/AAA	248.08	206.77	185.23	188.95	198.59	163.30	145.88	131.62	121.97	96.23	130.95	145.40
Aa2/AA	103.56	83.25	75.57	84.21	91.11	95.50	77.56	66.91	65.76	68.62	83.47	68.30
A2/A	53.11	45.62	40.01	49.25	49.03	53.92	51.44	45.56	48.95	42.60	53.30	52.73
Baa2/BBB	29.34	21.47	29.24	50.41	34.09	45.07	37.55	33.92	43.13	25.87	35.25	34.25
LIQUIDITY												
Current Ratio (x)												
Aaa/AAA	1.48	1.41	1.35	1.35	1.46	1.50	1.56	1.61	1.60	1.55	1.51	1.59
Aa2/AA	1.58	1.46	1.45	1.58	1.50	1.55	1.90	1.93	1.93	1.92	1.85	2.08
A2/A	1.63	1.58	1.74	1.63	1.74	1.71	1.86	1.89	1.99	2.05	1.78	1.83
Baa2/BBB	1.43	1.75	1.73	1.90	1.88	1.97	2.03	1.83	1.79	1.76	1.84	2.02
Quick Ratio (x)												
Aaa/AAA	0.92	0.94	0.86	0.84	0.91	0.94	0.97	0.99	1.00	0.96	0.89	0.99
Aa2/AA	0.88	0.83	0.80	0.79	0.77	0.87	1.07	1.07	1.17	1.14	1.09	1.23
A2/A	0.78	0.79	0.79	0.79	0.84	0.80	0.96	0.91	0.91	0.91	0.79	0.86
Baa2/BBB	0.65	0.67	0.78	0.95	0.96	1.03	1.09	0.80	0.82	0.80	0.87	1.02

	1973	1974	1975	1976	1977	1978	1979	1980	1981	1982	1983	1984
Cash/Current Assets (%)												
Aaa/AAA	20.21	16.49	20.45	22.96	21.83	22.15	20.00	20.57	17.27	20.71	25.11	21.00
Aa2/AA	20.06	16.49	17.32	20.73	16.06	15.84	15.27	11.20	10.87	15.27	16.27	15.09
A2/A	10.90	8.73	9.88	11.97	12.42	12.21	10.13	10.16	12.99	7.91	9.47	8.76
Baa2/BBB	10.51	7.61	9.00	13.35	10.06	13.15	11.38	10.58	11.40	12.11	7.53	8.45
Cur. Liabs./Tot. Liabs. (%)												
Aaa/AAA	62.53	65.66	62.50	62.83	63.12	63.47	63.74	62.71	59.42	55.48	54.77	54.37
Aa2/AA	45.49	50.91	45.10	43.29	41.20	44.20	53.07	54.44	54.06	51.83	52.21	52.90
A2/A	50.09	50.10	43.44	45.28	46.45	46.44	49.42	46.79	46.62	39.95	43.39	41.96
Baa2/BBB	45.02	49.54	46.58	48.45	46.74	42.07	47.56	46.44	46.45	38.05	40.32	30.75
Acts. Rec./Cur. Assets (%)												
Aaa/AAA	42.05	42.23	41.27	39.55	39.73	40.41	42.26	41.57	44.53	42.45	41.69	41.53
Aa2/AA	39.10	42.22	42.38	39.66	39.65	40.60	40.62	40.14	38.76	39.77	40.24	40.81
A2/A	36.07	35.89	34.81	33.69	35.86	39.05	36.90	37.87	35.61	37.42	40.24	39.24
Baa2/BBB	40.51	39.62	36.26	32.16	33.47	40.67	41.08	40.69	38.83	33.00	30.82	37.18
Inventory/Current Assets (%)												
Aaa/AAA	34.39	38.17	36.11	35.25	35.52	34.36	34.11	32.94	32.09	30.36	28.11	30.79
Aa2/AA	38.40	39.55	38.66	37.76	41.93	40.12	40.94	45.15	46.45	41.36	40.00	39.69
A2/A	50.22	52.91	52.62	51.76	49.21	45.62	49.30	47.97	47.48	50.15	46.74	47.48
Baa2/BBB	46.59	50.17	51.60	51.76	53.39	43.50	43.92	43.79	46.91	50.92	53.94	49.63
PROFITABILITY												
Pretax Margin (%)												
Aaa/AAA	14.82	13.60	11.48	11.22	11.56	10.97	11.53	10.66	11.30	10.96	13.19	15.21
Aa2/AA	10.88	11.74	11.40	11.21	10.72	12.33	12.82	11.08	9.15	7.40	8.79	9.83
A2/A	7.99	8.90	6.70	7.27	6.29	7.62	7.38	6.44	5.89	5.76	7.24	7.51
Baa2/BBB	6.08	4.33	2.96	5.38	4.82	7.62	6.94	5.83	7.11	−5.58	0.04	5.22
Available Income as % of Sales												
Aaa/AAA	15.62	14.71	11.76	11.95	12.21	11.70	12.57	11.74	12.30	12.11	14.38	16.20
Aa2/AA	12.03	12.79	12.76	12.71	12.30	13.86	14.13	12.61	10.75	9.35	10.44	11.37
A2/A	9.36	10.68	8.52	8.82	7.77	9.00	8.92	8.27	7.94	8.99	10.16	10.90
Baa2/BBB	7.81	6.68	5.03	8.86	6.30	9.24	8.27	7.86	9.72	−0.03	2.24	9.88

Available Income as % of Assets

Aaa/AAA	19.97	18.25	16.51	18.26	18.09	18.65	17.60	18.34	17.30	16.37	20.50	19.03
Aa2/AA	16.65	15.28	13.61	15.52	18.85	19.36	16.93	14.09	14.00	14.76	16.18	13.09
A2/A	11.34	11.03	10.71	10.94	11.88	13.14	12.31	10.59	11.92	11.28	13.36	11.62
Baa2/BBB	10.63	3.17	−0.03	12.34	10.08	12.82	12.56	9.70	10.54	7.07	8.34	9.53

R.O.R. Common-after tax (%)

Aaa/AAA	20.91	17.31	16.01	17.87	17.12	17.83	16.42	16.40	15.43	11.96	15.14	16.85
Aa2/AA	15.65	13.07	11.94	16.86	18.93	19.35	16.61	13.87	13.79	13.55	15.58	12.09
A2/A	10.43	10.96	10.86	11.47	13.97	15.83	14.02	10.93	12.62	11.04	14.66	12.74
Baa2/BBB	7.10	−2.80	−16.30	12.26	11.08	16.81	15.15	10.26	12.45	5.16	7.99	10.23

R.O.R. Total Capital—pretax (%)

Aaa/AAA	32.27	29.23	25.86	30.09	29.19	26.68	27.94	28.65	26.75	25.79	31.28	27.93
Aa2/AA	25.40	23.63	20.91	24.95	29.70	30.85	24.43	19.62	19.58	20.74	22.99	17.80
A2/A	16.27	16.18	15.19	16.80	18.08	20.23	18.81	15.64	16.95	15.45	19.03	16.54
Baa2/BBB	14.91	4.63	−4.81	17.87	15.60	20.03	16.81	15.13	15.86	9.80	11.64	13.22

MISCELLANEOUS Cash Flow/Cap. Expenditures (%)

Aaa/AAA	160.72	164.97	127.87	113.03	118.11	128.95	143.19	144.93	153.64	119.55	130.61	165.06
Aa2/AA	131.96	138.02	108.25	123.83	121.39	127.52	140.17	116.93	108.38	93.11	107.22	150.54
A2/A	145.82	144.99	106.68	107.11	110.76	122.42	132.41	117.11	132.30	115.41	119.71	137.03
Baa2/BBB	177.73	107.09	76.52	124.80	97.48	134.40	119.63	133.52	192.07	107.24	115.55	122.12

Retained Cash Flow/Cap. Expenditures (%)

Aaa/AAA	122.50	126.06	97.17	85.63	90.77	99.30	107.71	106.25	114.52	86.75	99.24	122.86
Aa2/AA	106.83	109.21	85.41	99.44	100.07	106.06	114.69	95.73	86.60	73.35	87.69	115.74
A2/A	122.27	108.10	81.57	85.91	87.56	99.52	108.40	92.11	106.86	91.53	97.53	111.44
Baa2/BBB	149.90	75.15	59.39	106.20	81.37	114.26	101.00	110.36	168.85	89.30	98.27	103.49

	1984	1983	1982	1981	1980	1979	1978	1977	1976	1975	1974	1973
Tax Rate (%)												
Aaa/AAA	43.15	47.61	46.24	42.82	49.09	49.64	50.88	52.59	52.18	61.36	59.92	49.80
Aa2/AA	48.76	54.01	50.80	44.26	51.00	51.95	46.06	42.89	43.05	46.41	44.50	41.11
A2/A	41.18	40.02	33.27	41.12	37.34	40.21	42.58	42.32	41.93	42.77	42.81	41.19
Baa2/BBB	53.74	N.M.	−6.86	40.15	37.62	37.00	41.05	44.34	39.76	45.93	37.91	40.92
Number of Companies												
Aaa/AAA	10	14	17	17	21	22	20	20	19	20	14	12
Aa2/AA	15	18	22	40	40	38	37	26	23	20	18	12
A2/A	28	29	30	68	83	74	60	47	44	48	40	44
Baa2/BBB	7	11	11	17	23	26	29	22	20	22	24	28
Total Companies	60	72	80	142	167	160	146	115	106	110	96	96
Moody's Average Yields of Industrial Bonds (%)												
Aaa	12.61	11.56	13.35	13.70	11.57	9.39	8.58	7.86	8.23	8.61	8.42	7.28
Aa	12.95	12.00	14.03	14.19	11.99	9.65	8.74	8.04	8.59	8.90	8.64	7.40
A	13.43	12.53	15.00	14.62	12.44	9.91	8.94	8.36	8.88	9.21	8.90	7.63
Baa	13.84	12.90	15.77	15.48	13.39	10.42	9.35	8.87	9.67	10.26	9.14	8.07
Spreads in Basis Points Between												
Aaa & Aa	34	44	68	49	42	26	16	18	36	29	22	12
Aa & A	48	53	97	43	45	26	20	32	29	31	26	23
A & Baa	41	37	77	86	95	51	41	51	79	105	24	44
% Difference Between												
Aaa & Aa	102.70%	103.81%	105.09%	103.58%	103.63%	102.77%	101.86%	102.29%	104.37%	103.37%	102.61%	101.65%
Aa & A	103.71%	104.42%	106.91%	103.03%	103.75%	102.69%	102.29%	103.98%	103.38%	103.48%	103.01%	103.11%
A & Baa	103.50%	102.95%	105.13%	105.88%	107.64%	105.15%	104.59%	106.10%	108.90%	111.40%	102.70%	105.77%

SOURCE: Merrill Lynch [1985].

APPENDIX E
Summary Statistics for Selected Financial Variables for U.S. Industrial Corporations Grouped by Bond Credit Rating, 1973–84

	12-Year Average	Standard Deviation	RANGE High	RANGE Low	Standard Deviation/ Average
LEVERAGE & CAPITALIZATION					
Coverage (x)					
Aaa/AAA	13.53	1.69	16.30	10.86	12.50%
Aa2/AA	8.05	1.69	10.87	4.85	20.94%
A2/A	4.37	1.00	5.70	2.63	22.91%
Baa2/BBB	2.83	1.51	4.39	−1.02	53.29%
S.T. Debt/Total Cap. (%)					
Aaa/AAA	6.20	1.41	9.01	3.66	22.82%
Aa2/AA	5.01	0.76	6.34	3.90	15.11%
A2/A	6.52	2.08	11.58	4.53	31.96%
Baa2/BBB	7.03	3.11	14.60	2.69	44.27%
L.T. Debt/Total Cap. (%)					
Aaa/AAA	14.46	1.11	16.57	12.27	7.66%
Aa2/AA	24.25	1.54	26.44	21.51	6.34%
A2/A	30.47	1.73	34.82	27.32	5.69%
Baa2/BBB	34.99	3.40	44.22	30.72	9.73%
Total Debt/Total Cap. (%)					
Aaa/AAA	20.65	2.28	23.89	16.95	11.06%
Aa2/AA	29.26	1.49	30.93	26.40	5.10%
A2/A	36.99	1.30	39.62	35.37	3.52%
Baa2/BBB	42.02	3.35	48.94	36.76	7.97%
Preferred/Total Cap. (%)					
Aaa/AAA	0.32	0.18	0.55	0.00	55.12%
Aa2/AA	0.73	0.49	1.61	0.20	67.23%
A2/A	2.16	0.32	2.86	1.68	14.81%
Baa2/BBB	1.67	1.63	6.67	0.30	97.13%
Minority Interest/Total Cap. (%)					
Aaa/AAA	1.33	0.18	1.71	0.98	13.74%
Aa2/AA	0.69	0.39	1.36	0.15	56.92%
A2/A	1.13	0.20	1.42	0.84	17.49%
Baa2/BBB	0.89	0.48	1.84	0.07	53.84%
Common Equity/Total Cap. (%)					
Aaa/AAA	77.70	2.39	81.93	74.35	3.08%
Aa2/AA	69.31	1.75	72.48	67.08	2.52%
A2/A	59.47	1.84	61.73	54.43	3.10%
Baa2/BBB	55.39	4.62	61.28	43.86	8.33%
S.T. Debt/Total Debt (%)					
Aaa/AAA	29.53	3.99	37.70	21.41	13.53%
Aa2/AA	17.14	2.52	21.20	13.08	14.68%
A2/A	17.53	5.10	29.21	11.52	29.08%
Baa2/BBB	16.57	6.54	30.82	6.72	39.49%

	12-Year Average	Standard Deviation	RANGE		Standard Deviation/ Average
			High	Low	
S.T. Debt/Cur. Liabilities (%)					
Aaa/AAA	14.12	2.95	19.48	9.06	20.91%
Aa2/AA	14.81	1.66	17.27	12.23	11.20%
A2/A	18.76	5.74	31.83	13.69	30.59%
Baa2/BBB	19.61	8.07	37.08	8.17	41.17%
S.T. Debt/Cur. Assets (%)					
Aaa/AAA	9.39	1.70	12.88	6.41	18.07%
Aa2/AA	8.62	0.77	9.87	6.97	8.99%
A2/A	10.51	3.10	17.87	7.35	29.49%
Baa2/BBB	10.67	4.16	20.19	4.73	39.04%
Total Liabilities/Equity (%)					
Aaa/AAA	91.84	3.81	95.34	80.71	4.15%
Aa2/AA	99.01	13.41	117.90	74.01	13.55%
A2/A	122.56	5.49	133.26	114.13	4.48%
Baa2/BBB	143.73	16.62	184.81	115.68	11.57%
Working Capital/Term Debt (%)					
Aaa/AAA	149.67	23.87	177.52	100.05	15.95%
Aa2/AA	97.43	11.40	117.28	76.57	11.70%
A2/A	89.87	16.45	108.44	63.77	18.31%
Baa2/BBB	86.69	21.27	110.00	28.21	24.54%
Long Term Debt/Net Plant (%)					
Aaa/AAA	20.66	3.92	26.05	14.83	18.98%
Aa2/AA	34.49	3.13	38.92	29.01	9.07%
A2/A	51.51	3.71	57.39	45.30	7.20%
Baa2/BBB	63.74	9.39	78.36	48.54	14.72%
Net Tangible Assets/L.T. Debt (%)					
Aaa/AAA	638.67	57.52	765.10	550.52	9.01%
Aa2/AA	384.86	21.93	422.02	356.47	5.70%
A2/A	298.13	12.18	317.31	267.92	4.08%
Baa2/BBB	259.19	19.69	297.27	211.43	7.60%
Cash Flow/L.T. Debt (%)					
Aaa/AAA	163.58	41.17	248.08	96.23	25.17%
Aa2/AA	80.32	11.63	103.56	65.76	14.48%
A2/A	48.79	4.32	53.92	40.01	8.86%
Baa2/BBB	34.97	7.88	50.41	21.47	22.54%
LIQUIDITY Current Ratio (x)					
Aaa/AAA	1.50	0.09	1.61	1.35	5.83%
Aa2/AA	1.73	2.22	2.08	1.45	12.54%
A2/A	1.79	0.14	2.05	1.58	7.76%
Baa2/BBB	1.83	0.15	2.03	1.43	8.45%

	12-Year Average	Standard Deviation	RANGE High	Low	Standard Deviation/ Average
Quick Ratio (x)					
Aaa/AAA	0.93	0.05	1.00	0.84	5.32%
Aa2/AA	0.98	0.16	1.23	0.77	16.46%
A2/A	0.84	0.06	0.96	0.78	7.21%
Baa2/BBB	0.87	0.14	1.09	0.65	15.56%
Cash/Current Assets (%)					
Aaa/AAA	20.73	2.20	25.11	16.49	10.63%
Aa2/AA	15.87	2.77	20.73	10.87	17.44%
A2/A	10.46	1.57	12.99	7.91	15.03%
Baa2/BBB	10.43	1.89	13.35	7.53	18.17%
Cur. Liabs./Tot. Liabs. (%)					
Aaa/AAA	60.88	3.72	65.66	54.37	6.11%
Aa2/AA	49.06	4.59	54.44	41.20	9.36%
A2/A	45.83	3.07	50.10	39.95	6.70%
Baa2/BBB	44.00	5.15	49.54	30.75	11.71%
Acts. Rec./Cur. Assets (%)					
Aaa/AAA	41.61	1.28	44.53	39.55	3.07%
Aa2/AA	40.33	1.06	42.38	38.76	2.62%
A2/A	36.89	1.86	40.24	33.69	5.05%
Baa2/BBB	37.02	3.62	41.08	30.82	9.77%
Inventory/Current Assets (%)					
Aaa/AAA	33.52	2.68	38.17	28.11	8.00%
Aa2/AA	40.83	2.52	46.45	37.76	6.16%
A2/A	49.29	2.24	52.91	45.62	4.54%
Baa2/BBB	48.84	3.61	53.94	43.50	7.40%
PROFITABILITY					
Pretax Margin (%)					
Aaa/AAA	12.21	1.51	15.21	10.66	12.38%
Aa2/AA	10.61	1.49	12.82	7.40	14.07%
A2/A	7.08	0.87	8.90	5.76	12.30%
Baa2/BBB	4.23	3.55	7.62	−5.58	83.93%
Available Income as % of Sales					
Aaa/AAA	13.10	1.58	16.20	11.70	12.03%
Aa2/AA	12.09	1.34	14.13	9.35	11.06%
A2/A	9.11	0.97	10.90	7.77	10.60%
Baa2/BBB	6.82	2.93	9.88	− 0.03	43.02%
Available Income as % Assets					
Aaa/AAA	18.24	1.18	20.50	16.37	6.47%
Aa2/AA	15.69	1.91	19.36	13.09	12.16%
A2/A	11.68	0.86	13.36	10.59	7.34%
Baa2/BBB	8.90	3.71	12.82	−0.03	41.68%

	12-Year Average	Standard Deviation	RANGE		Standard Deviation/ Average
			High	Low	
R.O.R. Common—after tax (%)					
Aaa/AAA	16.69	2.07	20.91	11.96	12.41%
Aa2/AA	15.11	2.37	19.35	11.94	15.69%
A2/A	12.46	1.71	15.83	10.43	13.76%
Baa2/BBB	7.45	8.65	16.81	−16.30	116.17%
R.O.R. Total Capital— pretax (%)					
Aaa/AAA	28.47	1.98	32.27	25.79	6.94%
Aa2/AA	23.38	3.83	30.85	17.80	16.40%
A2/A	17.10	1.52	20.23	15.19	8.91%
Baa2/BBB	12.56	6.51	20.03	−4.81	51.80%
MISCELLANEOUS Cash Flow/Cap. Expenditures (%)					
Aaa/AAA	139.22	17.97	165.06	113.03	12.91%
Aa2/AA	122.28	15.78	150.54	93.11	12.90%
A2/A	124.31	13.32	145.82	106.68	10.71%
Baa2/BBB	125.68	30.69	192.07	76.52	24.42%
Retained Cash Flow/Cap. Expenditures (%)					
Aaa/AAA	104.90	13.56	126.06	85.63	12.93%
Aa2/AA	98.40	12.50	115.74	73.35	12.70%
A2/A	99.40	11.69	122.27	81.57	11.76%
Baa2/BBB	104.80	28.94	168.85	59.39	27.61%
Tax Rate (%)					
Aaa/AAA	50.44	5.45	61.36	42.82	10.81%
Aa2/AA	47.07	3.97	54.01	41.11	8.44%
A2/A	40.56	2.65	42.81	33.27	6.52%
Baa2/BBB	37.41	14.73	53.74	−6.86	39.37%

SOURCE: Merrill Lynch [1985].

APPENDIX F
Municipal Bond Worksheet
ISSUER: Portland, Oregon

Investment Service Rating
Moody's: Aaa
Standard & Poor's: Not rated

POPULATION

	1950[a]	1940–50 Percentage Change	1960[a]	1950–60 Percentage Change	1970[a]	1960–70 Percentage Change	1980[a]	1970–80 Percentage Change
City of Portland	373.6	22.3%	372.7	−0.3%	379.9	1.9%	366.4	−3.5%
Multnomah County	471.5	32.8	522.8	10.9	554.7	6.1	562.6	1.4
State of Oregon	1,521.3	39.6	1,768.7	16.3	2,091.4	18.2	2,663.1	25.9
U.S.A.	150,697.4	14.5	179,323.2	18.5	203,212.9	13.3	226,545.8	11.4

[a] In thousands

RETAIL SALES AND INCOME STATISTICS
(1982 SALES & MARKETING MANAGEMENT)

	Retail Sales Per Capita	EFFECTIVE BUYING INCOME		
		Per Capita	Per Household	Median
City of Portland	$6,582	$9,753	$21,959	$18,611
Multnomah County	6,428	9,768	23,020	20,125
State of Oregon	5,328	8,569	22,193	19,571
U.S.A.	4,718	9,300	25,507	22,000

DISTRIBUTION OF EMPLOYMENT FOR 1980
PORTLAND METRO AREA

	No.	%
Wholesale and Retail	136,965	23.5%
Manufacturing	120,301	20.6
(Durable)	(87,499)	(15.0)
(Non-Durable)	(32,802)	(5.6)
Services	117,482	20.2
Transportation & Utilities	49,623	8.5
Finance, Insurance, & Real Estate	43,888	7.5
Education	43,559	7.5
Construction	36,373	6.2
Government	22,449	3.9
Agriculture, Forestry & Fisheries	10,822	1.9
Miscellaneous (Mining)	902	.2
Total Employment	582,364	100.0%

MAJOR EMPLOYERS

Name of Firm	Product	Number of Employees
Tektronix, Inc.	Electronic instruments	16,000
Crown Zellerbach Corp.	Pulp and paper mills packaging	4,973
Intel Corp.	Semiconductor integrated circuits	3,000
Freightliner Corp.	Heavy-duty trucks	1,900
Publishers Paper Company	Lumber and wood products	1,800
Boeing of Portland	Aircraft frame structures	1,600
Pendleton Woolen Mills	Apparel	1,500
Omark Industries, Inc.	Sawchains and power tools	1,428
Precision Castparts	Steel castings	1,400
Jantzen, Inc.	Sportswear and swimwear	1,383

AGRICULTURAL PRODUCTION

	Multnomah County	State of Oregon
Value of Agricultural Production ($Mil.)	$ 24.4	$1,267.3
% Crops	84.7%	54.6%
% Livestock	15.3	45.4
Average Production		
Per Acre	$ 567	$ 69
Per Farm	46,923	36,583
Per Square Mile	363,095	44,046

Financial Data

TREND OF ASSESSED VALUES
($000)

Year	Multnomah County Assessed Valuation*	Percentage Change	City of Portland Assessed Valuation*	Percentage Change	Current Tax Collections
1979–80	$12,869,356	24.0%†	$ 8,713,348	22.1%†	98.04%
1980–81	13,924,532	8.2	9,504,166	9.1	95.06
1981–82	14,887,331	6.9	10,228,514	7.6	96.74
1982–83	15,864,822	6.6	10,910,700	6.7	96.61
1983–84	17,186,890	8.3	11,866,835	8.8	In Process

* Equilization rate changes annually—1984 equalization rate is 88.1%, which means the estimated market value for the City of Portland was $13,475,225,000.
† Large percentage change in 1979–80 was due to a property revaluation.

DEBT STATEMENT
September 30, 1984
($000)

Bonded Debt Outstanding		$238,810
Unfunded Debt:		
Lease/Rental Obligations	$59,484	
Improvement warrants	2,442	
Certificate of participation notes	13,500	
TANS (commercial paper)	30,000	105,426
Gross direct debt		$344,236
Less:		
Revenue bonds	$94,460	
Self supporting water G.O.	98,590	
TANS	30,000	
Certificate of participation notes	13,500	
(previously funded)		236,500
Direct net debt		$107,686
Overlapping debt		191,822
Overall net debt		$299,508

DEBT RATIOS

Net Debt	Per Capita	Moody's[1] Median	Per Cent Full Value	Moody's[1] Median
Direct	$295	$474	0.9%	2.2%
Overall	817	609	2.5	3.3

[1] Moody's Median for cities 300,000 to 499,999 population.

CURRENT ACCOUNT AND GENERAL FUND ANALYSIS
(INCLUDING DEBT SERVICE FUND)
($000)

	1978–79	1979–80	1980–81	1981–82	1982–83
Revenues	$119,333	$119,683	$131,566	$142,360	$149,177
Expenditures	114,939	117,853	129,198	140,783	144,424
Cash Surplus/Deficit	4,394	1,830	2,368	1,577	4,753
General Fund Balance	9,964	10,138	9,604	5,261	5,099

Revenue Analysis		Expenditure Analysis	
Percentage of Total Revenues (All Funds)		Percentage of Total Expenditures (All Funds)	
	1983		1983
Property Taxes	34.7%	Public Safety	33.6%
Intergovernmental Revenues	30.0	General Government	25.5
Licenses and Permits	13.2	Highways and Streets	16.9
Charges for Services	12.5	Capital Outlay	7.8
Special Assignments	3.0	Debt Service	5.3
Miscellaneous Revenues	6.6	Other	10.9
	100.0%		100.0%

Part IV

Integration of Portfolio Policies and Expectational Factors [New]

Fixed Income Portfolio Management Strategies

_____ **Donald L. Tuttle, CFA**

With the exceptionally high and volatile interest rate environment of the 1970s and early 1980s came an explosion of interest in fixed income instruments and a revolution in the techniques of managing bond portfolios. The stodgy world of buy-and-hold, income-maximizing bond investment stereotypes began to give way to modern fixed income portfolio management with coincidental changes in the bond market environment and the publication of landmark early literature. Present day active bond management essentially dates from the 1972 publication of Sidney Homer and Martin Leibowitz's _Inside the Yield Book_ on bond price volatility, reinvestment rate risk, and swapping/trading strategies. The current breed of bond immunization/ dedication decision models, on the other hand, largely stems from Laurence Fisher and Roman Weil's rediscovery of Macaulay's duration measure and its usefulness in building guaranteed return, reinvestment rate risk-insulated portfolio, as discussed in their 1971 _Journal of Business_ article. As the content of this chapter attests, both the theory and the practice of bond investing have come a long way in the last dozen or so years.

This chapter draws heavily on two sources. The first is Gifford Fong's Chapter 9, "Portfolio Construction: Fixed Income," in the main volume, especially pages 308–342. It serves to update, amplify, and effectively replace those pages. The second source is the proceedings of an Institute of Chartered Financial Analysts (ICFA) continuing education seminar entitled _The Revolution in Techniques for Managing Bond Portfolios_ published by the ICFA in 1983.

Specifically, presentations on the four principal active or semiactive approaches to fixed income portfolio management have been edited for inclusion here: H. Gifford Fong of Gifford Fong Associates on active portfolio management, William L. Nemerever, CFA of Fidelity Management and Research Company on classical immunization techniques, Michael R. Granito of J. P. Morgan Investment Management on the management of dedicated bond portfolios, and Kenneth R. Meyer of Lincoln Income Group on combination active/passive portfolio strategies. To them should go the credit for the content of each of the discussions of active and semiactive strategies that follows.

PASSIVE OR BUY-AND-HOLD STRATEGY

A buy-and-hold strategy essentially means purchasing and holding a security to maturity or redemption (e.g., by the issuer via a call provision) and then reinvesting cash proceeds in similar securities. Ongoing cash inflows, as well as outflows, are generally present via coupon income being received and reinvested. The emphasis is on minimizing the expectational inputs, that is, the assumptions about the future level and direction of interest rates. By holding securities to maturity, any capital change resulting from interest rate change is neutralized or ignored (by holding to maturity, the par amount of the bond will be received). Portfolio return, therefore, is controlled by coupon payments and reinvestment proceeds. While interest rate forecasting is largely ignored, analysis is important to minimize the risk of default on the securities held.

Income-Maximizing Investors

The passive, or buy-and-hold, strategy is used primarily by income-maximizing investors who are interested in the largest coupon income over a desired horizon. These types of investors include endowment funds, bond mutual funds, insurance companies that are seeking the maximum yield over an extended period of time, or other large pools of money where the size of the fund and large cash inflow make portfolio turnover difficult because of possible market impact. The buy-and-hold strategy was justifiable for many investors because fixed income securities were traditionally characterized as safe assets with predictable cash flows and low price volatility. By assuming a long-term perspective, a return in excess of inflation with interest rate risk minimized is the objective. This is a classic example of seeking less than maximum return to avoid the inherent risk associated with the highest return strategy, and, in turn, is dictated by the investment objectives, constraints, and attendant policies as discussed in Chapters 4 and 5 of the main volume.

Techniques and Vehicles

One technique for a passive strategy is an index fund. Index funds basically provide diversification along with minimum transaction costs. This is certainly a tractable notion for equities as exemplified by Standard & Poor's (S&P) 500-type and other funds as discussed in Chapter 10 of the main volume. For bonds, index funds take on new meaning.

The fixed income market is much larger than the equity market in terms of both the dollar amount and number of issues outstanding. Because of this fragmentation, replication of a significant percentage of the total market capitalization can be considered a problem. However, indexes can be selected on the basis of maturity, coupon, issuing sector, quality, or combination thereof. Table 9A-1 lists 60 bond market sectors, each of which is a potential ingredient for indexing. From the variation in return for various market cycles, it can be seen that the correct selection of the sector to index for a particular time period can make a sizable difference. However, broad replication of the market is not difficult. While more diverse than the stock market in types and number of issues, the dominance of the systematic risk component for institutional-grade fixed income securities provides a fairly homogeneous universe from a return/risk standpoint.

Once the desired index or *bogey* is chosen, the next task is forming a representative portfolio. One of the key considerations in forming such a portfolio is the number of bonds necessary to obtain adequate diversification. McEnally and Boardman [1979] have shown how diversification of bonds varies with portfolio size. It appears that the effect of portfolio size parallels closely the relationship found in common stock portfolios. This suggests that once an index is selected, it can be replicated with a manageable number of securities, probably fewer than 40. Table 9A-2 provides the relationship between portfolio size and the mean and standard deviation of returns, both empirically observed as well as theoretically expected.

ACTIVE STRATEGIES

Total Return-Maximizing Investors

For those seeking the highest return for a given level of risk, active strategies offer the greatest opportunity. These are used primarily by total return-maximizing investors, either in single or multiple holding period frameworks. The objective is to maximize return, whether it be from capital changes or income or a combination thereof.

Most pension funds and some closed-end mutual funds embrace this approach. Since it requires making assumptions about the future, the greater the accuracy of those assumptions, the greater the return for a given level of risk. Active strategies, which are dominated by interest rate anticipation and sector/security strategies, actually span a fairly wide range of possibilities. Indeed, the increased volatility of the bond market has stimulated the development of active management techniques.

TABLE 9A-1. Sector Trend—Absolute Total Return

Sector Name	Bear Cycle (12/72–8/74)	Rank	Bull Cycle (8/74–12/76)	Rank	Full Cycle (12/72–12/76)	Rank	Bear Cycle (12/76–9/30/81)	Rank	Bull Cycle (9/30/81–10/31/84)	Rank
Government/Agency Index	1.75%	3	31.47%	58	33.77%	32	15.78%	8	66.80%	56
Government/Corporate Index	−4.80	20	39.68	56	32.98	46	6.85	22	74.06	49
GNMA Index	−4.64	19	44.75	35	38.07	4	−8.57	39	96.19	15
Yankee Index	N/A		N/A		N/A		14.97	10	78.58	41
Intermediate Government/Agency Index	2.82	1	30.24	59	33.91	28	21.73	3	63.48	59
Intermediate Government/Corporate Index	1.78	2	32.20	57	34.55	22	20.51	4	65.41	58
Intermediate Yankee Index	N/A		N/A		N/A		23.09	1	69.91	52
Long-Term Government/Agency Index	−6.31	22	42.58	41	33.58	35	−14.73	50	84.77	36
Long-Term Government/Corporate Index	−12.14	46	51.23	16	32.87	48	−14.64	49	94.88	18
Long-Term Yankee Index	N/A		N/A		N/A		−0.21	26	95.48	17
Long-Term Eurobond Index	N/A		N/A		N/A					
Industrials	−7.90	25	44.88	34	33.43	38	−6.42	34	87.93	30
Utilities	−12.69	48	52.62	14	33.25	42	−9.51	41	94.74	19
Finance	−8.23	28	45.83	31	33.83	31	0.49	24	91.47	26
AAA Rated	−8.91	31	46.94	27	33.85	30	11.80	18	68.47	55
AA Rated	−10.24	39	47.15	26	32.08	51	−7.07	36	87.15	33
A Rated	−11.39	44	48.30	24	31.41	54	−5.46	32	92.55	24
BAA Rated	−17.42	57	64.24	3	35.63	17	−2.64	30	103.07	8
AAA Industrials	−6.54	23	42.70	40	33.37	39	−9.52	42	80.78	38
AA Industrials	−7.11	24	43.66	39	33.45	37	−6.51	35	82.77	37
A Industrials	−8.28	29	45.14	33	33.12	43	−5.82	33	87.21	31
BAA Industrials	−9.83	35	53.03	12	37.99	5	−1.81	29	109.78	5
AAA Utilities	−9.98	36	49.26	22	34.36	24	−15.23	52	92.18	25
AA Utilities	−11.72	45	49.46	20	31.94	52	−10.76	43	93.02	23
A Utilities	−13.54	51	51.05	18	30.60	56	−7.25	37	93.92	21

BAA Utilities	-23.65	58	70.57	2	30.23	58	-3.10	31	99.05	13
AAA Finance	-5.92	21	42.17	42	33.75	33	-0.30	27	78.20	43
AA Finance	-8.11	27	46.15	30	34.30	26	-0.58	28	84.91	35
A Finance	-10.04	37	47.70	25	32.87	49	2.37	23	100.02	11
BAA Finance	-11.29	42	55.64	7	38.07	03	-0.01	25	103.41	7
Intermediate Industrials	-0.83	5	38.17	51	37.02	10	13.75	13	73.22	51
Intermediate Utilities	-3.22	16	41.81	43	37.24	7	16.75	6	76.55	45
Intermediate Finance	-2.82	14	39.16	48	35.24	20	12.79	16	78.31	42
Intermediate AAA Industrials	-0.83	6	36.63	56	35.50	19	14.04	12	66.10	57
Intermediate AA Industrials	-0.10	4	36.76	55	36.62	13	13.12	15	69.22	54
Intermediate A Industrials	-1.28	11	38.94	50	37.16	9	14.08	11	74.00	50
Intermediate BAA Industrials	-0.92	7	44.67	36	43.34	1	16.51	7	86.08	32
Intermediate AAA Utilities	-1.38	10	38.10	52	36.19	15	11.18	20	69.42	53
Intermediate AA Utilities	-1.88	12	39.25	47	36.63	12	13.56	14	74.33	47
Intermediate A Utilities	-3.38	17	39.73	49	35.01	21	17.27	5	76.84	44
Intermediate BAA Utilities	-9.72	34	50.31	19	37.20	8	22.71	2	79.00	40
Intermediate AAA Finance	-3.20	15	37.72	53	33.31	41	12.52	17	74.16	48
Intermediate AA Finance	-1.18	9	37.53	54	35.91	16	11.30	19	74.99	46
Intermediate A Finance	-4.02	18	41.19	44	35.51	18	15.22	9	79.32	39
Intermediate BAA Finance	-1.05	8	44.00	38	42.49	2	7.90	21	89.28	29
Long-Term Industrials	-9.08	32	46.80	29	33.47	36	-13.61	46	95.79	16
Long-Term Utilities	-14.43	53	55.43	8	33.00	45	-15.41	54	100.82	10
Long-Term Finance	-13.12	50	53.88	6	33.69	34	-15.28	53	115.60	4
Long-Term AAA Industrials	-8.42	30	44.66	37	32.48	50	-16.52	57	85.75	34
Long-Term AA Industrials	-8.02	26	45.73	32	34.04	27	-15.04	51	89.71	28
Long-Term A Industrials	-9.19	33	46.81	28	33.32	40	-12.27	44	93.52	22
Long-Term BAA Industrials	-11.33	43	55.31	9	37.71	6	-8.84	40	126.85	3
Long-Term AAA Utilities	-11.17	41	51.22	17	34.33	25	-18.27	59	94.08	20
Long-Term AA Utilities	-13.73	52	51.98	15	31.11	55	-15.70	55	98.42	14
Long-Term A Utilities	-15.34	55	54.19	10	30.54	57	-13.86	47	101.35	9
Long-Term BAA Utilities	-28.19	59	80.03	1	29.28	59	-12.69	45	109.30	6
Long-Term AAA Finance	-10.17	38	49.05	23	33.89	29	-16.17	56	90.03	27
Long-Term AA Finance	-12.24	47	53.20	11	34.45	23	-16.90	58	99.52	12
Long-Term A Finance	-16.72	56	58.31	5	31.84	53	-14.25	48	136.01	2
Long-Term BAA Finance	-15.32	54	61.49	4	36.75	11	-7.57	38	139.07	1

SOURCE: Shearson Lehman/American Express, Inc., Corporate Bond Research Department, November 13, 1984.

TABLE 9A-2. Return Variance of Randomly Generated Portfolios of Corporate Bonds of All Quality Classes, January 1973 to June 1976 ($\times$ 10')

Number of Bonds in Portfolio	Mean[a] (Standard Deviation) of V_{Pn}	Theoretical[a] V_{Pn}
1	9.367 (7.471)	9.257
2	7.469 (3.972)	7.148
4	6.004 (2.102)	6.094
6	5.782 (1.701)	5.742
8	5.591 (1.469)	5.566
10	5.376 (1.327)	5.461
12	5.401 (1.220)	5.391
14	5.341 (1.098)	5.340
16	5.299 (1.035)	5.303
18	5.266 (0.973)	5.273
20	5.274 (0.902)	5.250
40	5.155 (0.633)	5.144

SOURCE: McEnally and Boardman [1979].
[a] Variable V_{Pn} is the expected value of the variance of returns of portfolios constructed by investing $1/n$ of the portfolio in each of n randomly selected securities.

Techniques and Vehicles

The following discussion gives the reader a brief overview of several techniques commonly used in active fixed income techniques. Following a discussion of the return simulation process and portfolio optimization, each of these techniques will be examined in detail.

Interest Rate Anticipation Strategies. From the standpoint of having the greatest effect on marginal return for fixed income portfolios, interest rate anticipation strategies offer the greatest potential. These are essentially strategies that seek to forecast the future change in interest rates and involve varying the maturity or, more precisely, varying the duration of the portfolio. (See the Appendix and discussion further on in this chapter for more on the concept of duration.) If the expectation is for rates to rise, the duration of the portfolio should be reduced to minimize the effect on portfolio value. If rates are expected to decline, then the duration of the portfolio should be lengthened.

This sounds relatively easy, but in fact it is, at best, extremely difficult to forecast the future direction of rates, much less their magnitude. Many assert that it is impossible. The important point is that regardless of one's conviction, rate anticipation must be dealt with, if for no other reason than that it is usually the dominant source of incremental return and incremental risk.

Relative Return Value Analysis. The second item, relative return analysis, is a framework for comparing the returns of alternative securities. This recognizes that choosing the highest expected return security may be inappropriate, since either it may not be the security with the highest *realized* return, or the level of associated risk may be undesirable. The objective is to identify the highest expected return security for a given level of risk.

Strategic Frontier Analysis. Strategic frontier analysis is a method of evaluating both the upside as well as the downside return characteristics of a security. It is a procedure for analyzing the return behavior of securities under alternative interest rate scenarios.

Timing. Timing is a consideration integral to all of these techniques. That is, one of the necessary conditions for any successful strategy is not only knowing what to do, but also *when* it should be done. To draw upon an analogy from stock valuation analysis, it is necessary not only to know which stock is undervalued, but also when it will become fairly valued. Therefore, whenever one pursues active management and adopts a particular technique, the element of timing cannot be overlooked.

Sector/Security Strategies. Sector/security strategies may be further classified into the three categories.

CREDIT ANALYSIS. Credit analysis stresses the expected changes in the default risk of securities. This default risk has both macro as well as micro implications. From a macro standpoint, general business conditions may have an effect on the ability of issuers to fulfill their credit obligations. This can be contrasted to the micro orientation of evaluating individual issuers. Quality ratings are available for many issuers from rating agencies—Duff and Phelps, Fitch, Moody's, Standard & Poor's—that seek to quantify the risk of default. While they are not foolproof, they do provide a respected benchmark from which an analyst's own research can anticipate changes, resulting in potential security valuation enhancement.

SPREAD ANALYSIS. Spread analysis is based on sectoral relationships and an assumption that subclasses of fixed income securities tend to have similar price behavior. Relative price change is monitored, and, whenever abnormal relationships emerge, sector swaps can be identified. This can result in a relative price advantage as sector yields return to what is perceived as a more normal relationship.

Spread relationships, which involve the difference in yield between two sectors, can be tracked, and their historical average can be used as a guide for their normal value in this type of analysis.

VALUATION ANALYSIS. The last example of a sector/security strategy, valuation analysis, is one of the more recent developments in bond management. Valuation analysis is an approach that, in effect, identifies the intrinsic value of a security based upon the characteristics of that security. The normal value of each characteristic is in turn estimated from the average value for that characteristic in the marketplace. Comparing the intrinsic value to the actual price provides a measure of the over- or undervaluation of the bonds.

Finally, there is an "other" category. Although several specific strategies for active bond management have just been identified, in reality there is a continuum of strategies, of which only a few have been mentioned. Considered together, these strategies could very well be termed *expectations management*. They include the use of the total realized yield concept, pure yield pickup or substitution or intermarket spread trades or exchanges, and various maturity-spacing strategies.

PORTFOLIO OPTIMIZATION

The final section in the process concerns itself with portfolio optimization. This can be thought of as a strategy for quantifying the optimal integration of return and risk expectations with desired portfolio objectives and policy.

Portfolio optimization starts with a basic set of expectations in the form of expected rates of return and proceeds to structure a portfolio, taking into account the needs of the client in the form of desired portfolio parameters. These parameters are a direct result of identifying the preferences and requirements of the client, as well as the style and emphasis of the manager. Examples of these considerations include a minimum yield objective, minimum and/or maximum concentration constraints, desired duration range or level, and minimum portfolio return requirement.

The objective of portfolio optimization may be expressed as maximizing the return of the portfolio for a given level of acceptable risk. The expected returns come directly from the expectations that are provided. The estimate of risk is not so straightforward. Two alternative portfolio optimization approaches are identified, and they differ primarily in their treatment of risk.

Variance/Covariance Approach

The first approach is akin to the traditional Markowitz formulation, which suggests that risk can be represented by the variance of portfolio returns.

This, in turn, can be derived from the estimated covariance matrix of security returns. The problem with this alternative is the difficulty in estimating the covariance matrix, especially because of its nonintuitive nature. Even if bonds did not have a constantly shortening term to maturity, changes in the level and shape of the yield curve—the underlying cause of bond systematic risk—could produce senseless or even perverse covariance relationships.

Worst Case Approach

Using the worst case approach, the second category of portfolio optimization, the estimated returns—specifically the interest rate scenario with the lowest returns—serve as the measure of risk. The portfolio is then structured by the optimization process to achieve at least the worst case scenario return while simultaneously maximizing the return of another scenario. In other words, if one were to do a scenario projection of expected rates of return of the portfolio, the worst case return of the scenarios being used would be the measure of risk, and the optimization process would try to enhance return over and above this identified risk level.

Specifically, the objective of this approach becomes maximizing bond portfolio expected return with risk, defined as the level of return under the worst case interest rate scenario, constrained to some minimum level. Risk is specified in terms of minimally acceptable return levels that in turn are a direct result of the interest rate scenarios. However, the heavy reliance on the particular scenario used can create some problems with this approach. The analytical procedure is linear, allowing the use of a computationally efficient linear programming optimization algorithm. A detailed example is illustrated in Appendix B to Chapter 9 of the main volume.

THE PORTFOLIO MANAGEMENT PROCESS IN DETAIL

Now that the principal techniques of active bond portfolio management, including the final step of optimization, have been described briefly, they will be examined in greater detail. In reviewing the specific techniques, it is important to keep in mind the underlying conceptual framework of return and risk generation that makes them rational tools of analysis. In other words, while it is important to understand *how* a technique is used, it is more important to understand *why* it is useful. Once this is established, the user can pick and choose among techniques as appropriate to fit his or her needs.

The active bond portfolio management process, in a global sense, is depicted in Figure 9A-1. The process typically begins at the upper left with an existing portfolio and a potential purchase list.

The key to this overall process resides in the step identified next: return simulation. Return simulation is the process by which a set of expectations are transformed into expected rates of return. These expected rates of return

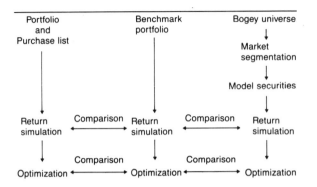

Figure 9A-1. Active Management Framework. (SOURCE: Gifford Fong Associates)

capture all the expectations that go into the process, whether they are expecta-tions about interest rate changes, credit risk changes, or spread relationship changes. Mutually consistent sets of expectations are formed into scenarios along with probability estimates to produce a bottom-line number, an ex-pected rate of return for each individual security and for the portfolio as a whole.

The results from return simulation lead directly to portfolio optimization, which can actually suggest specific changes to the portfolio by taking the ex-pected rates of return that have been defined from the return simulation pro-cess and integrating other appropriate portfolio policy considerations. Thus, a manager's specific client preferences, or the particular managerial style that has been adopted, can then be incorporated in the optimization process.

Comparison With a Benchmark Portfolio

Along with the analysis of the manager's own portfolio, a second step is identi-fied by the center vertical track of Figure 9A-1. This is the identification of some benchmark portfolio, some representative portfolio with which the man-ager's portfolio will be compared. This can be whatever portfolio the manager and his client, for example, decide is the appropriate comparison portfolio.

By going through the same process of subjecting the benchmark portfolio to the return simulation process, expectations are transformed into expected rates of return. Those expected rates of return can then be subjected to the same type of policy considerations in coming up with a portfolio optimization analysis. With an actual portfolio and an identified benchmark or comparison portfolio, one can evaluate the ability of the manager's portfolio to outper-form the benchmark that has been identified in connection with this active management process.

Comparison With Bogey Universe Portfolios

There is also a third alternative that starts with a bogey universe, the right-hand column of Figure 9A-1. The basic difference between this third track and the second track is that the bogey universe usually contains a much broader universe of securities relative to those in a typical benchmark portfolio. For example, consider an index such as the Shearson/Lehman Corporate Bond Index, which is made up of approximately 3,000 to 4,000 securities. That type of bogey may be appropriate; however, in order to subject it to the same kind of expectations transformation and optimization analysis that was done in the first track, there are interim steps that need to be taken to reduce that large universe to a manageable sample of securities.

What has been identified is a two-step process. Starting with the 3,000 or 4,000 securities, an analysis called *market segmentation,* which essentially separates the universe into sectors, can be accomplished. These sectors are tranformed into *model securities* that can, in effect, replicate the return behavior of the larger universe that was initially identified. The model securities are then subjected to the *return simulation process,* which provides the transformation of expectations into expected rates of return. The resulting set of expected rates of return can be subjected to an *optimization process.*

At the optimization level, cross comparisons can be made to determine how the portfolio—before and after portfolio changes are made—compares with a benchmark portfolio or, alternatively, the bogey universe that was identified.

This is a rather simplified schematic and it should be noted that much of the essence of the technique is really captured in the return simulation process. Thus, regardless of which techniques are chosen, the important step is subjecting the technique to this return simulation step.

INTEREST RATE ANTICIPATION

The most important specific technique, from the standpoint of potential incremental impact on return and risk, has been identified as interest rate anticipation. As it turns out, interest rate anticipation can be evaluated very effectively through the return simulation process. The following discussions examine this process and identify the inputs, analysis, and resulting output in more detail.

Inputs

Multi-Scenario Projections. The inputs include a multiscenario projection of interest rate change. The use of a multiscenario input is very important. It is well known that interest rate anticipation, or the prediction of what interest rates will do, is a very risky process. In fact, it may be so risky that it cannot be done. Still, the active bond manager must be able to evaluate the portfolio and buy/hold/sell decisions in terms of the potential impact of various alternatives. If the manager does not have high convictions, then a very wide scenario projection of interest rates is appropriate. If the manager has high convictions, then attention should certainly be paid to the outcome of the most likely scenario, but at the same time, the results of a relatively unexpected scenario should not be overlooked.

Another reason why a multiscenario projection of interest rate change is important is that it reflects not only the uncertainty associated with the process, but it allows one to do sensitivity analysis to evaluate the outcomes of other scenarios.

An example of a table that summarizes inputs for simulating the effect of interest rate change in a three-scenario format is shown in Table 9A-3. A time frame of one year has been chosen, but this could vary depending on one's own expectations and desires. The three scenarios are derived from interest rate change experience over the preceding 32 years. There is a bullish scenario, a market-implicit forecast, and a bearish scenario, each assigned an equal probability of occurrence. Figures in Table 9A-3 reflect the forecast yield for each scenario, as well as the present yield to maturity for each maturity period shown.

TABLE 9A-3. Return Simulation Example of Bond Portfolio Analysis

PORTFOLIO: Model Portfolio—U.S. Treasury

INTEREST RATE PROJECTION: 10-5-84 to 10-5-85

SCENARIO 1 (33.33% Probability): Falling Rates, 32-Year Historical Volatility Basis (5-52 to 10-84); Reinvestment Rate is Calculated for Each Bond.

SCENARIO 2 (33.33% Probability): Market Implicit Forecast; Reinvestment Rate is Calculated for Each Bond.

SCENARIO 3 (33.33% Probability): Rising Rates, 32-Year Historical Volatility Basis (5-52 to 10-84); Reinvestment Rate is Calculated for Each Bond.

Interest Rate Projection

| | | FORECAST YIELD (PERCENT) | | |
Maturity (Yrs.)	Present YTM (%)	Scenario 1	2	3
0.250	10.880	7.460	12.490	16.360
0.500	11.120	8.420	12.570	16.410
1.000	11.460	8.190	12.530	16.710
2.000	11.960	8.960	12.530	16.270
3.000	12.130	9.480	12.600	15.610
4.000	12.260	9.910	12.640	15.300
5.000	12.350	10.170	12.640	15.100
10.000	12.360	10.770	12.510	14.260
20.000	12.290	11.010	12.400	13.980
30.000	12.280	11.040	12.390	14.000

SOURCE: Gifford Fong Associates.

These scenarios of interest rate change are expressed in terms of yield curve changes, but they can also include spread relationship changes. That is, credit analysis or other types of spread relationship analysis can also be incorporated in the basic framework.

Importance of Time Horizon. Previously, it was noted that timing is very important. By specifying a time horizon in this process, the portfolio manager is able to test the implications of various timing horizons for the overall process. Thus, for example, if it seems that rates are going to change to a particular level, how quickly or slowly that change takes place can have a material effect on whether one should take a particular action and when.

The last two inputs are, first, the current portfolio and second, the potential purchases that are being considered. Given that there is an existing portfolio, and given that there are potential additions to that portfolio, the manager will want to subject them both to the interest rate changes and other expected return dynamics associated with the inputs described previously.

Analysis: Converting Rate Changes to Returns

The basic analysis lies in the conversion of interest rate change to expected rates of return. Much time and effort goes into this analysis, especially the formulation of expectations. But the bottom-line expression of these expectations has to be in terms of expected rates of return. The process of converting to expected rates of return incorporates a framework which allows the evaluation of the risk inherent in that formulation process. If it is done in terms of interest rate changes and the resulting expected rates of return, a framework emerges for the systematic evaluation of the riskiness associated with each potential outcome.

Table 9A-4 exemplifies the result of translating interest rate change into expected rates of return for individual securities. In this example a hypothetical Treasury bond portfolio is analyzed. The columns are largely self-explanatory, but those of particular importance are described below:

Yield curve = return due to changes in the nominal yield curve.
Time = return assuming the initial yield curve remains constant over the projected horizon.
Spread change = return attributable to spread change and volatility effects that are assumed to be zero for Treasury issues.
Earned interest = interest accrued over the projection period.
Maturity/call = change in principal value for securities projected to be called or to mature.
Reinvestment = interest-on-interest earned over the projection period.
Total return = the sum of all components of return.
Duration = first figure in the column is current duration; remaining figures are the durations at the *end* of the assumed holding period for the particular scenario.

TABLE 9A-4. Bond Portfolio Analysis of Model U.S. Treasury Bond Portfolio: Three Scenario Interest Rate Forecast (Current Date: 10-5-84)

Face Value ($000)	Bond Description		Price ($0)	Yield to Effective Maturity (%)	Yield Curve	Time	Spread Change	Earned Interest	Call	Maturity	Reinv.	Total Return (%)	Effective Maturity Date	Duration (yrs.)	Note
					COMPONENTS OF RETURN (%)										
$0	Cash Equivalents 0.0% 1 888888AA 11-23-84 TR AAA	Curr:	98.636	10.50 MAT									11-23-84	0.13	
		Scen 1:	100.000	0.0 MAT	0.0	0.0	0.0	0.0		1.4	7.6	9.0	11-23-84	0.0	Matured
		Scen 2:	100.000	0.0 MAT	0.0	0.0	0.0	0.0		1.4	10.2	11.6	11-23-84	0.0	Matured
		Scen 3:	100.000	0.0 MAT	0.0	0.0	0.0	0.0		1.4	12.2	13.6	11-23-84	0.0	Matured
		Comp:	100.000	0.0	0.0	0.0	0.0	0.0		1.4	10.0	11.4	11-23-84	0.0	
$176267	1.0–2.0 Yr 11.3270% 2 888888AB U.S. Treasury 4-14-86 TR AAA	Curr:	99.341	11.81 MAT									4-14-86	1.44	
		Scen 1:	101.707	7.93 MAT	1.7	0.7	0.0	11.4	0.0		0.3	14.1	4-14-86	0.52	
		Scen 2:	99.373	12.60 MAT	−0.7	0.7	0.0	11.4	0.0		0.3	11.8	4-14-86	0.52	
		Scen 3:	97.441	16.63 MAT	−2.6	0.7	0.0	11.4	0.0		0.4	9.9	4-14-86	0.52	
		Comp:	99.507	12.39	−0.5	0.7	0.0	11.4	0.0		0.3	11.9	4-14-86	0.52	
$85055	2.0–3.0 Yr 11.5460% 3 888888AC U.S. Treasury 4-4-87 TR AAA	Curr:	98.922	12.06 MAT									4- 4-87	2.24	
		Scen 1:	104.073	8.59 MAT	4.4	0.9	0.0	11.7	0.0		0.3	17.2	4- 4-87	1.42	
		Scen 2:	98.675	12.54 MAT	−1.1	0.9	0.0	11.7	0.0		0.4	11.8	4- 4-87	1.42	
		Scen 3:	93.653	16.51 MAT	−6.2	0.9	0.0	11.7	0.0		0.4	6.8	4- 4-87	1.41	
		Comp:	98.800	12.55	−1.0	0.9	0.0	11.7	0.0		0.4	11.9	4- 4-87	1.42	
$57868	3.0–4.0 Yr 11.3810% 4 888888AD U.S. Treasury 4-1-88 TR AAA	Curr:	97.669	12.22 MAT									4- 1-88	2.97	
		Scen 1:	104.662	9.24 MAT	6.3	0.9	0.0	11.7	0.0		0.3	19.1	4- 1-88	2.24	
		Scen 2:	97.478	12.59 MAT	−1.1	0.9	0.0	11.7	0.0		0.4	11.8	4- 1-88	2.23	
		Scen 3:	90.857	15.97 MAT	−7.9	0.9	0.0	11.7	0.0		0.4	5.1	4- 1-88	2.22	
		Comp:	97.666	12.60	−0.9	0.9	0.0	11.7	0.0		0.4	12.0	4- 1-88	2.23	
$45716	4.0–5.0 Yr 12.5920% 5 888888AE U.S. Treasury 3-16-89 TR AAA	Curr:	100.858	12.34 MAT									3-16-89	3.54	
		Scen 1:	108.282	9.71 MAT	7.2	0.2	0.0	12.5	0.0		0.3	20.2	3-16-89	2.92	
		Scen 2:	99.833	12.65 MAT	−1.2	0.2	0.0	12.5	0.0		0.4	11.9	3-16-89	2.90	
		Scen 3:	92.437	15.51 MAT	−8.5	0.2	0.0	12.5	0.0		0.4	4.6	3-16-89	2.87	
		Comp:	100.184	12.62	−0.8	0.2	0.0	12.5	0.0		0.4	12.2	3-16-89	2.90	

SOURCE: Gifford Fong Associates.

The foregoing analysis can be extremely helpful in executing an effective active management strategy. Analytical insights are achieved by partitioning a set of expected interest rate changes into implied rates of return. This provides an important dimension for evaluating rate anticipation strategies.

Return Simulation Output

Total Return and Its Components. The output, which is the product of the analysis of the inputs by the return simulation process, includes the total portfolio return and the components of that portfolio return. This portfolio return and its components can be expressed, not only in terms of the total returns for the individual securities, but also in terms of their identifiable sources. For example, a return partitioning can be done that identifies which parts of the total return are due to actual yield curve changes, to spread relationship changes, and to other factors such as the assumed reinvestment rate. The latter, of course, would be a function of the length of the time horizon.

Thus, an analysis of the components of portfolio return would provide the manager with some additional insights about where those returns come from, and with a better basis for understanding the nature of the returns generated.

Analytical Extensions. The final output is labeled *analytical extensions.* This brings attention to the fact that this whole return simulation process is really an integration process. It is a process that can take many different sets of expectations and transform them into a single set of universally appealing bottom line numbers, namely, expected rates of return. Once those bottom line expected returns are known, other types of analysis that can provide further insight into the available managerial decisions can be initiated.

Types of Interest Rate Changes

In a diagrammatic framework, the return simulation process is described in Figure 9A-2. This figure is drawn from Fong's chapter in the main volume and is repeated here because of the key importance of the analysis in the return simulation process. The bottom yield curve is labeled "Yield Curve 1." This is the existing yield curve. In an interest rate anticipation framework, there is likely to be some change in the existing yield curve, and that is represented by a shift to "Yield Curve 2."

The starting point is position A_1. The return simulation process essentially defines the rates of return as the existing portfolio or security moves from the current position, represented by position A_1, to one of the alternative positions identified by points B_1 through B_4. One of the ways of evaluating a portfolio is to assume that interest rates will not change. That has been popularly labeled "rolling along" or "riding the yield curve." Even if the security or

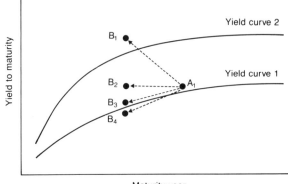

Figure 9A-2. Bondsens Yield Curve Analytical Framework. (SOURCE: Gifford Fong Associates)

portfolio, starting at position A_1, rolls along the yield curve, a number of things could happen. If it rolls to position B_3, the bond (or portfolio) essentially rolls along the yield curve with the passage of time, keeping the small positive spread of the bond relative to the yield curve constant. That is probably the most passive assumption that one might make.

Alternatively, the security might move to position B_2, in which case there would actually be a widening of the positive spread relative to the yield curve at the end of the holding period, but with no change in the yield curve itself. Alternatively, the security might move to position B_4, which would result in a negative spread relative to the yield curve at the end of the period, again with no shift of the curve. Thus, as the security or portfolio moves to these various positions, there are certain return implications.

The bond could also move up to position B_1, which represents a more dynamic return interaction, because at B_1 the bond would be moving to a new, higher yield curve *as well as* widening the positive spread that existed relative to the yield curve at position A_1. The point is that once the decision is made to enter and make use of this return simulation process, the manager is able to evaluate alternatives and the implications of those alternatives.

Relative Return Analysis

Figure 9A-3, depicting *Relative Return Analysis,* is a representation of the kind of return analysis that allows one to compare alternative securities systematically. Whether a return simulation process to define expected rates of return or some alternative mechanism is used, one can lay out the results in this type of two-dimensional framework with total return on the vertical axis and duration on the horizontal axis. Figure 9A-3 is based on data from Tables 9A-3 and 9A-4.

Within the diagram there are a number of securities labeled numerically. The total portfolio, represented by the letter T, is also shown. A least-squares

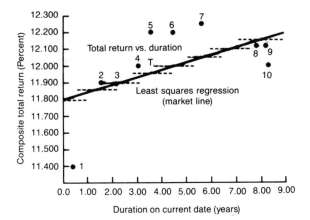

Figure 9A-3. Relative Return Analysis for a Three-Scenario Interest Rate Forecast for a Model Portfolio of U.S. Treasury bonds From October 5, 1984 to October 5, 1985. (SOURCE: Gifford Fong Associates)

regression line is drawn through these dots and represents the fair value or equilibrium projected return-risk tradeoff of the universe of securities being evaluated.

Using the regression line as fair value, it can be assumed that those securities below the line are overvalued, and those securities above the line are undervalued. Given this kind of two-dimensional framework, the manager has the ability—at least a first cut—to differentiate the return characteristics of the securities in this portfolio. This form of analysis is very similar to the Security Market Line approach used fairly widely in the analysis of equity securities.

Duration as a Risk Proxy. In the fixed income market, there is not a measure of risk comparable to the equity risk measure of beta. What has been used in this figure is duration. Duration is not necessarily the optimal risk measure. It is a measure of volatility. Although volatility is not necessarily the best measure of risk, duration does quantify risk to the extent that volatility is a risk surrogate. Also, duration is a measure of the longness of the security, a better measure, in many situations, than maturity. Thus, it is an approach that can be used for differentiating securities.

If there is not a better bond summary risk measure than duration that is akin to beta on the equity side, and if the horizontal axis can be considered a normalization for volatility, judgments about any two securities that lie along the same vertical line projecting upward from any given duration level can be made. For example, if security number 4 is compared with the total portfolio, it can be concluded that the total portfolio has the same volatility as security 4, but that security 4 has a higher payoff. Therefore, if a higher payoff for the same volatility is desired, an increase in the concentration in security 4 would certainly be recommended.

Strategic Frontier Analysis

The next series of exhibits provides a framework leading up to what is called *Strategic Frontier Analysis*. Figure 9A-4 measures total expected return on the vertical axis. This most likely would be the total expected return of the most likely scenario of interest rate change, although the return of the most optimistic scenario of interest rate change could be used.

The return of the worst case scenario is on the horizontal axis. Again, these scenarios are used in the return simulation process.

In Figure 9A-4, there are a number of dots representing the individual security holdings in the portfolio being analyzed and the securities on the potential purchase list. The letter "T" in the middle of this diagram is the portfolio average return, and we can see that this represents a particular position within this framework. Any particular position (dot) is defined by the return under the most likely scenario (or the optimistic scenario) along one axis, and the return from the worst case scenario along the other axis.

Partitioning into Quadrants. Once this basic type of framework is established the diagram can actually be partitioned into quadrants as displayed in Figure 9A-5. The expected returns are on both axes. The individual securities are represented by the dots. The portfolio average is represented by the plot at the intersection of the axes.

Implications of Quadrant Selection. Partitioning this diagram into the four quadrants allows one to draw conclusions about the return behavior of the securities that fall into each of these quadrants.

Securities within quadrant I might be considered *aggressive* securities. They are aggressive from the standpoint that, if the most likely scenario prevails, the manager would do extremely well. If the worst case scenario pre-

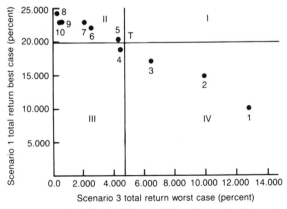

Figure 9A-4. Upside/Downside Tradeoff for a Three-Scenario Interest Rate Forecast for a Model Portfolio of U.S. Treasury bonds from October 5, 1984 to October 5, 1985. (SOURCE: Gifford Fong Associates)

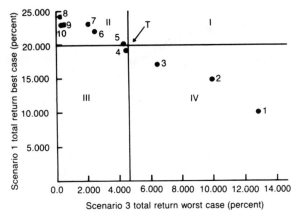

Figure 9A-5. Strategic Frontier Analysis for a Three-Scenario Interest Rate Forecast for a Model Portfolio of U.S. Treasury bonds from October 5, 1984 to October 5, 1985. (SOURCE: Gifford Fong Associates)

vails, the manager would do relatively badly. Thus, if there were very high convictions about the most optimistic scenario, the manager would tend to choose securities from this quadrant.

Securities within quadrant IV, might be considered *defensive* securities. They are defensive in that, if the worst case scenario prevails, the manager does relatively well. However, if the most likely scenario occurs, the manager does relatively poorly. Thus, if it is desirable to posture the portfolio defensively, the manager concentrates it in securities that fall within quadrant IV.

Quadrant III contains securities that might be considered *inferior*. They are inferior because, regardless of scenario outcome—either the most likely or worst case—these securities perform relatively worse than the portfolio average. Securities falling into quadrant III are the potential sales from the existing portfolio since, by definition, they are no win situations.

That leaves the securities falling in quadrant II. These might be considered *superior* securities because, regardless of scenario outcome, these securities would always outperform the portfolio. They are no lose situations. Assuming they can be identified, an increase in holdings of bonds of this type would tend to move the portfolio results to the upper right quadrant, quadrant II, thereby enhancing the overall portfolio results, regardless of the scenarios being evaluated.

The Strategic Frontier. Figure 9A-6 is another characterization of this type of analysis, where the curved line traced out is called a *strategic frontier.* This frontier essentially maps out the upper right region, from which securities that would do the best job, given our convictions, would be chosen. For example, if maximum offense or maximum aggressiveness was desired, and there was a willingness to give up the defensive nature of some of the other securities under consideration, the manager would choose securities along the strategic frontier mapped in or near the upper left quadrant. If a maxi-

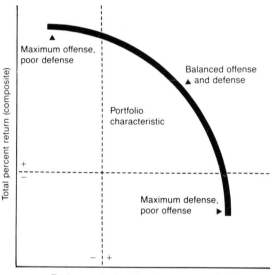

Figure 9A-6. Strategic Frontier Analysis. (SOURCE: Gifford Fong Associates)

mum defensive posture was desired, and there was a willingness to live with the relatively poor returns should the most likely scenario prevail, the manager would choose securities along the frontier that were located in or near the lower right quadrant.

The ultimate objective, especially in the face of high uncertainty and in unsteady conviction about either scenario, would be to drive the portfolio results into the upper right quadrant as far as possible.

Timing Implications of Active Strategies

The two diagrams in Figure 9A-7 provide some perspective on the implications of the timing of the strategy. The top diagram depicts an upward-sloping yield curve. Typically, when this type of yield curve shape occurs in the interest rate cycle, interest rates are anticipated to rise in the future. If interest rates rise, the manager will want to shorten maturity in order to minimize the price impact of that rise in yield. However, once maturity is shortened, the portfolio will experience the lower returns implied by that upward sloping yield curve. Therefore, unless a manager can systematically evaluate what the timing impact might be, that is, how soon and how fast those yields are going to go up, the manager will be under the gun in terms of lower rates of return, by having a short portfolio.

Alternatively, if a negatively sloping yield curve exists, rates are expected to decline. The manager wants to lengthen portfolio maturity to get the price impact of declining rates, but as can be seen by the downward sloping yield curve, if this is done the portfolio will suffer from lower yields and returns with those types of securities until rates do in fact decline.

Usefulness of a Bond Valuation Strategy

The last active strategy involves a bond valuation process and the recommended purchase or sale of under or over valued bonds, respectively.

Estimating Yield Premium. The essence of the active technique of bond valuation is the ability to evaluate the difference between the actual yield and default-free yield that constitutes the yield premium. For example, in evaluating a corporate bond, a manager wants to determine what the yield premium on that bond is, ascertain what the components of that yield premium are, define what the normal values for that yield premium are, and then compare the normal or normalized value of that bond's yield with its actual yield. The difference is either the bond's over or under valuation, depending on whether it is a positive or negative difference.

The yield premium is basically a compensation to the investor for a number of things, such as default risk, issuer options, and tax effects. The problem in bond valuation is to attribute a value to each of these factors and any others that are significant.

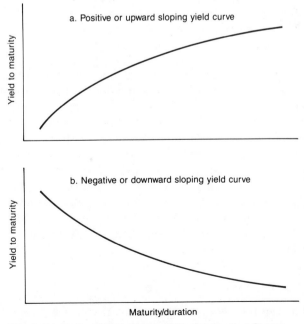

Figure 9A-7. Two Yield Curves With Contrasting Slopes.

Use of Regression Analysis. The basic methodology used in this strategy is multiple regression analysis characterized by the following equation.

$$Y = B_1X_1 + B_2X_2 + \ldots + B_NX_N + E$$

The explained or analyzed variable is represented by Y, the yield premium that is being predicted. That yield premium is in turn a function of a number of explanatory factors, the X variables. These factors represent the basic components of that yield premium. Once the coefficients, represented by the Bs, are estimated by running the regression analysis, the basis has been established by which the manager can assign values for each component of the particular corporate bond being evaluated. The manager can then add up the relevant components for that particular security. This becomes the intrinsic value of the yield premium that, when added to a risk-free nominal yield, produces an intrinsic value for the bond, which can then be compared with the actual quote on that security. The difference is either the under-valuedness or overvaluedness of the bond.

For an example of the type of output that can be generated by bond valuation analysis, see Table 9A-5.

OTHER ACTIVE STRATEGIES OR TACTICS

In addition to the active strategies already discussed, a number of other approaches may be identified. While their potential effect on total portfolio return may not be as great, they still may make a significant contribution and, for many managers, represent a chosen expertise.

Total Realized Yield

As intimated in the discussion of immunization, implicit in the yield to maturity of a fixed income security is an assumption about the ability to reinvest coupon payments at the same rate. If the reinvestment rate is different, the actual realized return will diverge considerably from promised yield. In maximizing the total return, the management of cash flow is therefore important, and increasingly so the longer the time horizon. Part of the problem is the ability to reinvest what may be relatively small amounts of funds, since transaction costs and available investment alternatives may be unfavorable. Return simulation analysis, discussed previously, can be a useful tool for determining the optimal strategy for reinvesting bond portfolio cash flow; it requires expectations of the direction, shape, and timing of interest rate (yield curve) changes.

Pure Yield Pickup Trade or Exchange

Switching to a security having a higher yield is called a pure yield trade or exchange (sometimes referred to by other writers as a swap). The transac-

TABLE 9A-5. Bond Valuation Computer Program Output (Valuation Date: 3-1-84)

Bond Description		Default-Free	Issuing Sector	Quality	Current Yield	Call Effect	Fitted Value	Actual Value	Residual	T-Stat
1 010235AA										
Alabama Bancorporation	Price ($)	88.980	-2.196	0.312	-1.150	-0.123	85.823	99.875	14.052	
10.250% 9- 1-99 F2 T	Yield (%)	11.816	0.348	-0.050	-0.187	0.020	12.322	10.266	-2.055	-4.35
2 010392BU										
Alabama Power Co.	Price ($)	126.915	-5.598	0.370	-1.476	-5.288	114.923	110.500	-4.423	
18.250% 10- 1-89 E3 V	Yield (%)	11.563	1.219	-0.083	0.333	1.239	14.271	15.368	1.097	2.32
3 023771AF										
American Airlines Inc.	Price ($)	93.821	-0.375	-3.434	-0.637	0.0	89.374	97.500	8.126	
10.000% 6- 1-89 I4 X	Yield (%)	11.595	0.102	0.955	0.182	0.0	12.834	10.625	-2.209	-4.67
4 030177AL										
American Tel & Teleg Co.	Price ($)	77.952	0.0	-1.444	-0.117	0.0	76.390	81.922	5.532	
2.875% 6- 1-87 T2 P	Yield (%)	11.146	0.0	0.637	0.052	0.0	11.836	9.466	-2.370	-5.01
5 039483AC										
Archer Daniels Midland Co.	Price ($)	39.006	-0.304	-1.474	0.290	0.0	37.518	37.263	-0.255	
0.0 % 5- 1-92 I3 C	Yield (%)	11.870	0.102	0.505	-0.101	0.0	12.375	12.463	0.089	0.19
6 046753BT										
Atchison Topeka & Santa Fe	Price ($)	98.679	-0.217	0.0	-0.151	0.0	98.311	95.000	-3.311	
8.750% 3-15-85 R1 A	Yield (%)	10.118	0.228	0.0	0.160	0.0	10.505	14.096	3.590	7.59
7 066050AF										
Bankamerica Corp.	Price ($)	72.350	-2.027	0.287	-0.861	-0.004	69.744	65.615	-4.129	
8.350% 5-15-87 F2 T	Yield (%)	11.871	0.348	-0.050	0.152	0.001	12.322	13.100	0.778	1.65
8 134429AA										
Campbell Soup Co.	Price ($)	92.061	-0.420	0.0	-0.738	0.0	90.904	90.152	-0.752	
9.875% 6-15-90 I1 A	Yield (%)	11.685	0.102	0.0	0.180	0.0	11.967	12.152	0.185	0.39

TABLE 9A-5. Bond Valuation Computer Program Output (Valuation Date: 3-1-84)

Bond Description		Default-Free	Issuing Sector	Quality	Current Yield	Call Effect	Fitted Value	Actual Value	Resid-ual	T-Stat
9 177342AD Citizens Utils. Co. Del. 8.300% 3- 1-85 G2 P	Price ($)	98.341	-1.070	0.390	-0.137	0.0	97.524	95.915	-1.609	3.81
	Yield (%)	10.090	1.180	-0.433	0.151	0.0	10.988	12.792	1.803	
10 252741AG Diamond Shamrock Corp. 10.625% 5- 1-93 I3 U	Price ($)	93.815	-0.535	-2.599	-0.971	0.0	89.709	89.896	0.187	-0.08
	Yield (%)	11.739	0.102	0.505	0.194	0.0	12.539	12.501	-0.038	
11 283695AU El Paso Nat. Gas Co. 16.700% 5- 1- 2 G4 W	Price ($)	136.175	-10.596	-2.717	-2.424	-6.625	113.812	108.000	-5.812	1.81
	Yield (%)	11.813	1.180	0.330	0.304	0.888	14.514	15.370	0.855	
12 313311HD Federal Farm Cr. Bns. 12.850% 10-22-84 AG A	Price ($)	101.717	-0.088	0.0	-0.144	0.0	101.485	101.563	0.078	-0.27
	Yield (%)	9.959	0.143	0.0	0.234	0.0	10.336	10.209	-0.127	
13 313388LP Federal Home Loan Bns. 12.150% 12-27-93 AG A	Price ($)	102.337	-0.831	0.0	-1.267	0.0	100.238	99.313	-0.925	0.35
	Yield (%)	11.736	0.143	0.0	0.222	0.0	12.101	12.265	0.164	
14 313400BN Federal Home Loan G. Corp. 12.500% 9-30-93 AG A	Price ($)	105.117	-1.209	0.0	-1.872	0.0	102.036	98.062	-3.974	1.08
	Yield (%)	11.869	0.143	0.0	0.228	0.0	12.240	12.750	0.510	
15 371046AL General Tel. Co. Calif. 5.750% 3- 1-92 T4 W	Price ($)	69.321	0.0	-4.491	-0.387	-0.000	64.442	66.837	2.395	-1.34
	Yield (%)	11.776	0.0	1.161	0.105	0.000	13.042	12.406	-0.636	
16 373334BW Georgia Power Co. 17.500% 10- 1-91 E1 E	Price ($)	128.773	6.919	-2.239	-1.681	0.0	117.935	111.000	-6.935	2.93
	Yield (%)	11.671	1.219	0.415	0.319	0.0	13.624	15.012	1.387	

SOURCE: Gifford Fong Associates.

tion may be made to achieve either a higher coupon yield or a larger yield to maturity. It would appear that such transactions would always be made as long as there is no significant shift in risk level (or liquidity). However, accounting rules or regulatory mandates constrain some investors from yield pickup trades that create a loss, unless offset by a gain elsewhere in the portfolio, even though a portfolio benefit would result.

Substitution Trade or Exchange

This transaction involves substituting one security for another that has a higher yield to maturity but is otherwise identical in terms of maturity, coupon, and quality. This type of trade depends on a capital market imperfection. As such, the portfolio manager expects the yields to maturity on the two securities to reestablish a normal yield spread relationship, usually resulting in a price increase and hence capital appreciation for the holder of the higher yielding issue. The workout period (time for the expected realignment in yields to occur) can be critical, since the sooner it occurs, the greater the return on an annualized basis; if the security must be held to maturity, the marginal contribution to realized annual return may be small.

Intermarket or Sector Spread Trade or Exchange

Based on the expected normal yield relationship between two different sectors of the bond market, trades may be made when there is a perceived misalignment. This may involve switching to the higher yielding security when the yield spread is too wide and is expected to narrow, and to the lower yielding security when the spread is too narrow and is expected to widen. The risk, especially of the latter switch, is that the anticipated adjustment will not be made, resulting in a reduced portfolio yield.

Maturity-Spacing Strategies

Alternative portfolio maturity structures may be used. These include a balanced maturity schedule with equal spacing of maturities held; an all-short or all-long maturity strategy; or a *barbell* structure, where bond holdings are concentrated in short maturities and long maturities, with the intermediates of lesser or no importance. The rationale for an equal-maturity portfolio is to provide some reinvestment risk protection, spreading out reinvestment over the full interest rate cycle. That is, there will be a relatively continuous cash flow over time from maturity *laddering,* and these funds can be reinvested at the then current rates. The effects of overall interest rate change will tend to be averaged and the extremes of return and risk will be truncated. An all-short or all-long maturity portfolio strategy is frequently a temporary strategy adopted as a result of rate (change) anticipation, but it is a strategy of potentially large reinvestment rate risk. For those who stay with an all-short portfolio there is usually either a preference for high liquidity or an extreme aversion to principal risk. A barbell approach anticipates that the best return/risk reward is achieved by balancing the defensive qualities of short-term securities with the aggressive qualities of long-term securities and avoiding the intermediates.

There is no assurance, from empirical testing of these various strategies, that any one has been consistently superior over time (see, for example, Fogler, Groves, and Richardson [1976] and Fogler and Groves [1976]).

Consistency of Style

As a general observation, consistency of management style is important. Given the range of strategies and expertise required, it is important to identify the style that is compatible with the investment policy established for the portfolio or is most effective for the portfolio management organization. Pursuing this style with emphasis should provide the best results. This is not to say that other strategies should be neglected. In some cases there should be attempts at insulating the portfolio from the effects of interest rate change or quality effects; in other cases there might be some attempts at, for example, substitution trading. The point is that consistency of management style, assuming the rationale for that style has been carefully thought, should provide superior results over time and therefore should be stressed.

Measuring Bond Performance

To provide a standard by which both short- and long-term performance of active strategies may be evaluated, the concept of a *baseline portfolio* has been suggested by Leibowitz [1979]. This is a normative portfolio that is structured to reflect the minimum portfolio risk that will also fulfill the investment return objectives of the client over the long term. The performance of the actual portfolio can be compared to the baseline portfolio results over time, with the latter portfolio serving as a benchmark standard of comparison.

The manager then has an objective standard by which he can be evaluated and that can serve to guide his future management activity. Structural deviations from the benchmark may be evaluated in terms of their return/risk experience compared to the baseline portfolio. Since there is a high covariability of most fixed income returns, this can be a useful approach. The primary problem with using a baseline evaluative approach arises in properly defining the objectives of the client and translating these objectives into a representative portfolio structure.

One further comment about these state-of-the-art methods that constitute the active management process. The most difficult task is still the formation of expectations. However, once conceived, these expectations can be nurtured to maturity through the methods just discussed. A framework for better investment decision making under conditions of uncertainty is thus provided, contributing to better returns and consistency of return achievement. This kind of investment result, if accompanied by effective communication, should make for greater investment management success.

ANALYSTS' QUESTIONS AND ANSWERS

Question: Explain the difference between volatility and risk, as well as the concept of duration, duration as it began, and duration as it now looks. Where is that concept going?

Answer: Duration, as originally formulated, had three basic applications. One application is a measure of longness. The maturity of a security is one measure of longness; duration is another measure, one that not only takes into account the maturity of the instrument, but also the interim cash flows and when they occur. For example, if a security has high coupons and the same maturity as another security with low coupons, the security with the higher coupon payment stream will have a smaller duration.

Duration can be thought of as a measure of the time it takes to receive one half of the present value of the payments of that security. It is a present-value, weighted cash-flow measure for a security.

Duration is considered a much better measure of longness than maturity, because it takes into account the size and timing of the interim cash flows. It was also used as a measure of volatility. For instance, assume that the only kind of yield curve changes are parallel shifts, characterized by yield curves that shift by an equal number of basis points all along the yield curve. A security with a duration of two would then have twice the price volatility of a security with a duration of one. The duration numbers are expressed in years. It would be a two-year duration security versus a one-year duration security. The one with the two-year duration would have twice the price volatility of the one-year duration security.

The problem with the use of duration, in a volatility sense, is that, if there are nonparallel shifts in the yield curve in which short rates move more than long rates—which frequently occurs—then there is no longer a one-to-one or proportionate type of volatility relationship. The security with the duration of one will no longer have half the volatility of the security with the duration of two. At best, some type of partial relationship is achieved, although not necessarily a linear relationship, depending on the nature of the yield curve shift.

Duration is a measure of volatility, but not necessarily of risk. Even in the volatility sense, duration is not an ideal measure because of this non-parallel yield curve change effect. A very high-duration security (a very long bond with a duration of 8) when compared with a very short-duration security (a security with a duration of 1) depending on the yield curve change, is not necessarily the more risky security. For example, consider a 1,000-basis-point shift in short rates and a 500-basis-point shift in long rates. If a long-duration security is compared with a short-duration security under this kind of a yield curve shift, which is the riskier security? Duration may not necessarily capture what a manager would like to see captured by a risk measure in that kind of situation.

Duration vs. Standard Deviation. The measure of standard deviation of expected returns is a reasonable, rational measure of riskiness in the fixed income area, just as it is in the equity area. Fixed income researchers have tried to draw a parallel between beta and duration. Under capital market theory, there is a linear relationship between return and beta. The higher the risk, specifically the beta risk, the higher the return. It is a linear type of relationship. An equity portfolio with a beta of 1 could be compared with an equity portfolio with a beta of 2, and the one with the beta of 2 would be twice as volatile.

That type of relationship holds in the linear fashion in the fixed income area *only* if yield curve changes are parallel changes. If nonparallel rate changes occur, then that one-to-one, or linear type of relationship, no longer holds.

Question: If duration can be used as a fixed income risk proxy only under very limited circumstances, what should be used as the universally satisfactory measure of risk in the fixed income area instead?

Answer: There is no universally accepted or universally applicable measure of risk that is comparable to the beta measure used with equities. Many researchers look at it from the standpoint of risk being *scenario dependent.* That is, risk is defined as certain rates of returns achieved under a given scenario of interest rate expectation, specifically under a worst case scenario. From there, investment strategy is formulated; it is based on trying to enhance returns, given a bogey defined by the worst case expectation. It is very much a moving target. One simply cannot say a particular risk measure exists, evaluate the portfolio relative to that particular measure, and get a standard by which to proceed.

One of the more recent attempts at trying to come up with a unifying number, such as a beta, is to take the *relative duration* of the portfolio, with the duration of some bogey as the reference point. Assume that the bogey is the Shearson Lehman Government/Corporate Bond Index. If the duration of that index is divided into the duration of the portfolio, it produces a measure of relative riskiness. However, the bond portfolio is still subject to the same problem of nonparallel yield curve changes and the inherent distortion involved with that type of comparison.

Question: How does a manager deal with the problem of creating a portfolio for a given client that, in risk terms, is appropriate for that client's risk posture?

Answer: The manager should take a portfolio, subject it to the return simulation process, and evaluate what types of returns actually result, given the worse case scenario.

This accomplishes much. First, the manager actually subjects the portfolio to some explicit expression of his expectations. Second, the results of the return simulation process provide the manager with a tool with which he can communicate his expectations and the possible implications of those expectations for a very real portfolio. Of course, in using the portfolio optimization process, the manager also incorporates individual client objectives and constraints in formulating the final optimum portfolio.

Question: In Figure 9A-1, in the discussion of portfolio simulation, there were three portfolios: the investor's portfolio, the benchmark portfolio, and the bogey universe. If the benchmark portfolio is not a market average type of portfolio, what is it?

Answer: The benchmark portfolio could be any portfolio agreed upon as the relevant comparison portfolio. Marty Leibowitz came up with this formulation, which he calls the *baseline portfolio*. The baseline portfolio is supposed to be a portfolio that represents the base case. It is the portfolio with which active management is compared.

There is a problem in how one actually builds a baseline portfolio, but once it is defined, that baseline portfolio would be the benchmark. In the return simulation process, the manager is actually comparing the impact of his expectations, as personified by the actively managed portfolio, to this baseline portfolio. Therefore, he has a basis of comparison to see whether, in fact, his expectations are being translated into a portfolio that will outperform that baseline portfolio.

Question: Essentially, are the baseline and the bogey universe portfolios very similar, or almost the same thing?

Answer: The baseline portfolio is not the same as the bogey universe portfolio. The latter is a portfolio that is very broadly based, such as the universe that is used in the Shearson Lehman Government/Corporate Bond Index. However, those two are, in turn, different from the actual portfolio being managed.

Question: Using the portfolio optimization technique with an actively managed portfolio almost requires instantaneous data access, evaluation, and optimization. What kinds of tools would the manager really need to use this technique on a day-to-day basis?

Answer: The question is that, logistically, what are the necessary requirements for actually making use of tools like the return simulation process? Time-sharing computers and microcomputers, for example, are certainly available, and these types of analyses lend themselves to that kind of computational framework.

One of the other key inputs is, of course, pricing, and that is more difficult to achieve. All the analyses used in active management are very sensitive to pricing. One must have good executable prices, which, in some cases, can be difficult to obtain. However, if the manager works closely with a number of dealers, good price data can be achieved on a timely basis.

Question: In the bond valuation process, some of the elements that had to be evaluated were the call and sinking fund features of the instrument. What type of work has to be done?

Answer: There are basically two ways of approaching that problem. One way is to do a form of Monte Carlo simulation in which the manager, in effect, evaluates the value of the security under various interest rate scenarios, and estimates what the effect under each scenario would be from that call or sinking fund feature. That becomes a fairly complicated and computationally bound type of analysis.

An alternative way of approaching this is to actually do a form of option pricing analysis, which is a much more direct analytical approach. The option pricing formulation shows that the value of a call feature really varies across time.

For example, when there are mostly discount securities in the marketplace, call and sinking fund features are not operative, so they have very low value. As an environment of decreasing rates is approached, the call feature starts to have some effect; then, of course, its value increases.

This overall process requiries analysis on a periodic basis so that the manager can, in effect, at any time, do a cross-section analysis across a fairly broad universe. One can then capture the emergence of the value of the call.

CLASSICAL IMMUNIZATION

The simplest and most straightforward of the hybrid strategies having both active and passive elements, the so-called semiactive bond portfolio management strategies, is *classical immunization*. It is not a recently developed technique; it was originally formulated a number of years ago by Macaulay [1938] and Redington [1952]. Only with the high yields of the 1970s and early 1980s and the desire to convert those yields to high multiyear bond returns was interest in exploring and using classical immunization stirred.

Accumulation-Maximizing Investors

Accumulation-maximizing investors, who require a high degree of assurance of a specific compound return over a particular time horizon, use this semiactive bond management approach. By accepting a more modest return than the highest that can be expected (via optional active management), they achieve a greater likelihood of realizing the desired return. This is another example of the classic tradeoff between return and risk. More recent work has extended the concept of immunization to explicit risk measures and multiperiod analysis, making the use of this technique neither simple nor straightforward.

This section of the chapter will deal with several subtopics: the concept of duration and the duration and yield curve dynamics essential to the use of this strategy, the principles and mechanics of immunization, selected uses of classical immunization, and some practical problems associated with this strategy.

Definition of Immunization

As a starting point, immunization can be defined as: *any investment strategy designed to minimize the risk of reinvestment over a specific time horizon.* This is perhaps the most straightforward definition of immunization, but there are a number of other definitions. The various definitions do not differ very much but the details are important, especially in relation to a client's particular preferences. Differences in expectations are related to the key differences in the various definitions.

Another definition of immunization is: assuring that the assets at the end of the horizon period are greater than, or equal to, some minimum level or some minimum target that might have been established. Instead of minimizing the reinvestment risk, the investor maximizes the probability that asset values will be greater than or equal to a specific dollar amount.

Immunization has also been defined as: achieving the maximum return possible with minimum reinvestment risk—a maxi-min strategy.

Finally, the definition that originated with F. M. Redington, a British actuary who coined the term immunization and used it in the context of investing the assets of a life insurance company, is to invest the company's assets in such a way that its "book of business" would be unaffected by changes in the general level of interest rates.

It is apparent that all of these are basically ways of achieving the same end, but the primary focus will be on the first definition. This is the approach used by many semiactive managers. That is, the clients who use immunization strategies are primarily interested in minimizing their reinvestment risks, and most of the definitions now seem to focus on that.

Unfortunately, most of the exciting work done on immunization was completed prior to the advent of the zero coupon bond, an instrument that, in and of itself, minimizes the risk of reinvestment. Although zeros will be discussed, immunization with coupon-bearing instruments is an important technique and a formidable challenge to the semiactive manager. Specifically, if a guaranteed return is locked in with a riskless zero coupon bond strategy, can the semiactive manager earn a superior return with a limited-risk coupon-paying bond strategy?

Historical Interest in Immunization

The initial interest in immunization strategies was not connected with separately managed bond portfolios but instead with insurance company guaranteed investment contracts (GICs). This began in the early 1970s when the insurance industry, in a very innovative fashion, actively started creating GIC contracts with guaranteed long-term rates of 8, 9, and even 9.5 percent. They were attractive because of the high yields—relative to historical yield levels—and the guarantees provided. The guarantee is extremely important to the client and thus is a competitive tool and is an issue that non-insurance company managers constantly have to deal with. The fact that GIC contract holders are allowed to value GIC portfolios at cost is also important.

The past nine years have seen a lot of interest in both GICs and separately managed immunized portfolios. Figure 9A-8 shows estimates of what immunized portfolio assets were through 1982. The plot begins in 1975 at about $15 million. By 1978 it had grown to about $50 million, and in 1982 was about $6.8 billion. These are stand-alone, single-period immunized portfolios. By the end of 1984, the total amount in immunized and dedicated portfolios was estimated to be in the $20 to $30 billion range or even higher. The figure shows that there has been a large amount of money, especially in the last several years, invested via immunization techniques.

Before getting into the mechanics of immunization, it should be pointed out that the real issues surrounding immunization have nothing to do with duration matching or security selection. That is, the important considerations are asset allocation and market timing. Clearly, as pointed out in Chapter 8 of the main volume, asset allocation decision making is an important determinant of portfolio performance. Similarly, the time at which one decides to pursue

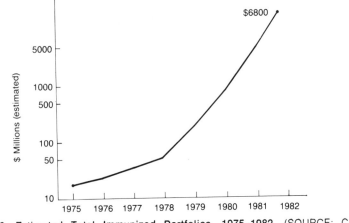

Figure 9A-8. Estimated Total Immunized Portfolios, 1975–1982. (SOURCE: Capital Management Sciences)

an immunization strategy is key. Those decisions are first and foremost, along with the time horizon that is selected, but they tend to get overlooked much of the time.

One of the real values of immunization is that clients are required to provide a very specific set of objectives. As a result, the immunized manager has a very good idea of what he is expected to do, a highly desirable situation from the manager's perspective.

DURATION AND YIELD CURVE DYNAMICS

Duration is the keystone of immunization theory. It is not something that a semiactive manager can be for or against. It is simply a measure that describes certain key analytical characteristics of a bond or portfolio of bonds. What is important is the *extent* to which the manager uses it to draw conclusions.

Although many researchers have made contributions in this field, Frederick R. Macaulay is credited with starting this incredible rush to certainty in 1938. The approach that he took, without having immunization in mind, was to weight the cash flows received on a fixed income instrument.

The standard concept of maturity for a bond is concerned with just the final maturity and has nothing to do with cash flow weightings. However, Macaulay believed that such a concept did not make any sense because the influence of the cash flows on a bond's price depends a lot on *when* they are received *as well as* their *present value*.

The basic formula for the most straightforward measure of duration, Macaulay's duration, is the sum of the present values of each of the cash flows over the life of a bond multiplied by the time they are received divided by the bond's price. An example of a calculation of Macaulay's duration can be found in the Appendix to this chapter. Technically speaking, the denominator should be price plus accrued interest. In any event, this fairly simplistic and straightforward measure is the foundation for the immunization of bond portfolios. However, it was not until much later that researchers explored its uses.

In the mid-1940s, Paul J. Samuelson and J. R. Hicks independently hit on similar ways of looking at weighted cash flows. Samuelson, in his studies of the banking industry, and Hicks, in other economic investigations, developed duration measures very similar or equivalent to Macaulay's.

In 1952, however, someone finally did something with duration. It was the English actuary, F. M. Redington, the father of immunization, who coined the word and used it in connection with life insurance company investment strategies.

This began much research into the area. In a capsulized history of duration and immunization, the key participants and dates are Macaulay in 1938, Samuelson and Hicks in the mid-1940s, F. M. Redington in 1952, and Lawrence Fisher and Roman Weil at the University of Chicago, who did some interesting work in the 1960s simulating the results one might achieve by following immunization strategies. More recently, a number of other researchers have made important contributions.

USES OF DURATION

There are a number of definitions of and mathematical formulas for duration and the one that is selected should depend on how the manager plans to use it. The most simple and universal is Macaulay's duration.

Measuring Price Volatility

A variant of Macaulay's duration is a measure called modified duration. It is the specific link between a bond's duration and its bond price volatility for small changes in interest rates. The formula, as demonstrated by Michael Hopewell and George Kaufman [1973], is

$$\text{Modified duration} = \frac{\text{Macaulay's duration}}{1 + \dfrac{\text{Yield to maturity}}{\text{Number of coupon payments per year}}}$$

where the number of coupon payments per year usually is two. That is, in using duration to measure the volatility of a bond for a specific change in yield to maturity, modified duration is the measure that should be used. The relationship is given by the formula

Percentage change in bond's price =

$$-(\text{Modified duration}) \times \frac{\text{Change in market yield in basis points}}{100}$$

For example, the duration of the 12 percent coupon bond with eight years to maturity and selling to yield 9 percent, illustrated in this chapter's Appendix, is 5.57 years. The modified duration for this bond would be

$$\text{Modified duration} = \frac{5.57}{1 + \dfrac{.09}{2}}$$
$$= 5.33$$

The percentage decline in the bond's price if the yield rises 50 basis points would be

$$\text{Percentage change in the bond's price} = -(5.33) \times \frac{50}{100}$$
$$= -2.665\%$$

Tied in with this use of modified duration is the notion of using duration as a measure of risk. While duration is not an exhaustive measure of risk, clearly it is a factor in the risk of owning a bond that cannot be ignored. Regardless of how yields change, it captures much of the effect of that change. Exactly how the effect is phrased may be a subject for discussion but it is definitely some component of the risk of a bond. Certainly duration is a better measure than average maturity.

Duration Mechanics

It is important to develop an intuitive feel for the properties of duration because it is constantly used in managing immunized portfolios. One principal reason for this is the volatile bond markets seen in recent years. These volatile markets cause changes in immunized portfolios necessitating constant monitoring and adjustment of the portfolio. In truth, *there is absolutely nothing passive about an immunized portfolio.* Specifically, an important part of managing the portfolio is understanding how and why the duration of a portfolio changes over time. Figure 9A-9 is an interesting, though not exhaustive, illustration. Generally, duration varies a lot depending on the coupon, maturity, and yield environment. Consider the zero coupon bond. The duration of a zero coupon bond is equal to the maturity; therefore duration increases with increasing maturity. Can this property be extrapolated to nonzero coupon bonds? Not all the time. For deep discount instruments there is a point at which duration actually decreases with increasing maturity, as illustrated by the 3 percent coupon bond's plot.

Interestingly, as the high and volatile interest rate environment of the late 1970s unfolded, a number of innovative researchers pointed out that, measured on a duration basis, the risk of long-term bonds was much closer to that of intermediate bonds than it had been in the past. Looking at the plot for the

Figure 9A-9. Duration vs. Maturity.

15 percent coupon bond selling to yield 15 percent, it is apparent that as yields rise the duration does not increase much with increasing maturity.

On the other hand, in examining the 15 percent coupon bond selling to yield 6 percent, it is apparent that in that environment duration does increase much more rapidly with increasing maturity. The bottom line of this discussion: duration is not always an intuitive measure and the manager has to keep his finger on what is going on.

Duration and Term Structure

Another interesting area is the relationship between the term structure of interest rates and duration. Note that term structure is not the same as yield to maturity. The brokerage industry is enamored with yield to maturity. If any trade involves increasing the yield of a bond portfolio, they believe it should be done. Instead, what is under discussion here is the structure of interest rates across the whole spectrum of maturities.

It is important to understand the structure of spot interest rates in analyzing bonds of widely differing coupons. Since coupons in recent years have ranged from as low as 3 percent to more than 17 percent, many bonds of identical maturity have widely varying cash flow patterns. Since each future coupon payment is discounted at a different spot rate, the volatility characteristics and yield to maturity of these bonds can be quite different. For a more complete discussion of this situation, see Sharpe [1985].

One of the limitations of Macaulay's duration is that all the cash flows are discounted at the same rate. That is clearly not the case in the real world except under special conditions, such as a flat yield curve where all spot rates are equal. Since each bond's cash flow stream is discounted at the bond's yield to maturity in the calculation of duration, and because the bonds in a portfolio generally have different yields to maturity, a weighted average portfolio duration measure is somewhat inaccurate and misleading. It can be concluded that, by working with the entire predicted term structure, other measures of duration can be developed that at least eliminate this bias.

The Real Controversy

The controversy over duration should not be over the measure itself, but over the way it is used. For example, if duration is used as a measure of volatility for a specific change in yield, then there is no quarrel. However if duration is recommended for use as a complete measure of risk, some serious problems may arise.

More specifically, the difficulty arises in trying to use duration in a decision-making model that takes into account all kinds of changes in the term structure of interest rates.

Figure 9A-10 is an example of how the structure of yields might change. From the hypothetical curve labeled "initial," yields could move in an additive or parallel fashion. Although this type of change does not occur that often,

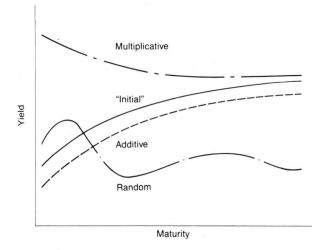

Figure 9A-10. Various Yield Curve Shifts.

especially for large shifts in yields, one of the major assumptions behind a lot of duration research is that yields change in a parallel manner.

Yields could also change in a multiplicative fashion. That is, the shift could be expressed as a factor that is multiplied by the yield, rather than added to it, similar to the shift from the initial to the top curve in Figure 9A-10. Most professionals would probably agree that the multiplicative shift comes closer to modeling how yields do, in fact, change from an upward-sloping initial position.

Interest rates could also do what they probably do most of the time: change in a random fashion that really cannot be predicted. The key is to somehow model this process in a measure of duration. Many researchers have tried. As a result a number of forms of duration exist, durations that could be called "awesome" in their complexity. Of course, there are some shifts, some ways the yield curve changes that simply cannot be satisfactorily duration-modeled.

In summary, if one can predict how yields will change, one could develop a measure of duration that would perfectly immunize his funds, which is what semiactive management is really concerned with. Of course, such predictions cannot actually be made, so the concern is *how close can one get to perfect immunization and how much of a difference does it make to get that close?* How difficult is the problem or how involved does the user need to get to solve it in a satisfactory fashion?

Reinvestment Risk Considerations

Another major point is the very serious uncertainty, with respect to managing portfolios, that is related to reinvestment risk. The manager has to be able to control that risk. Remember that it is assumed that coupon-bearing instruments are being used. Hence, the reinvestment rate (and the risk it implies) is just as important as the measure of duration that is used. Obviously, the less reinvestment risk there is, such as with low or zero coupons, the less need there is to accurately model the yield curve shift.

MECHANICS OF IMMUNIZATION

Earlier it was said that the primary motivation behind establishing an immunized portfolio is to minimize the uncertainty associated with reaching a particular level of wealth at the end of a pre-selected horizon period. Furthermore, there is a theory of immunization based on Macaulay's duration that states that, if the duration of a portfolio is equal to the time remaining until the investment horizon, then the assets are immunized. This is the basic theory and only the first step. As simplistic as it is, however, it goes a long way. That is, there are a lot of bond managers who are advertising themselves as limited risk managers who are not even matching durations, and as a result are taking incredible risks in terms of the effects of yield curve shifts on investment results.

Limiting Assumptions

There are some very limiting assumptions that surround this basic theory, but at least it is a way to begin. The assumptions are unrealistic: a flat yield curve, parallel yield curve shifts (that is, those additive shifts discussed previously), and an instantaneous change in yields.

Of the three, the last one, an instantaneous yield curve shift, is especially important. The manager who has matched durations is immunized, in a sense. This immunization is not permanent, however, because with every passing day the characteristics of any bond portfolio change. Tomorrow it is one day less to maturity and yields are either higher or lower. Any of these changes can create immunization problems. One may be immunized at one point in time but it will be difficult to remain immunized as time passes.

These are less restrictive assumptions than one might suppose. Much of the recent research in the area of immunization strategies has focused on the development of a better duration measure unfettered by the limiting assumptions accompanying the use of Macaulay's duration. To the extent that a duration measure that more accurately models future yield curve shifts can be developed, the quality of immunization improves.

One of these advances is illustrated by Khang's duration measure. Chulsoon Khang developed this measure to immunize a portfolio against a multiplicative yield curve shift. It is:

$$\ln (1 + \alpha D) = \int_{o}^{m} CF_t \ln (1 + \alpha t) \, e^{-r(0, t)t} dt$$

But while these formulas—and there are a number of them—fit into a nice mathematical model, most are unusable in practice. In Khang's formulation, for example, the exponent on the variable e, $-r(0, t)t$, is the spot rate at time t. However, it is simply not realistic to expect to get estimates of spot rates on a minute-to-minute basis. In short, many measures of duration do not work much better than Macaulay's. Thus, for practical purposes, Macaulay's duration or some modification of it tends to be used and it had been found that these are perfectly adequate measures of duration.

PRINCIPLES OF IMMUNIZATION

Consider a situation in which a client tells a manager, "I'd like to immunize for five years. Here's my money. What rate can you give me?" Once the account has been acquired, there is the question of setting a return objective. That is, a target rate of return must be established to provide both the manager and client with a benchmark for the measurement of the success of the strategy. What does the manager do? Look at the yield curve? Pick a yield to maturity? What is an appropriate benchmark?

Setting the Target Rate

Generally speaking, the best and most sensible benchmark is the yield to maturity of a zero coupon bond maturing on the horizon date. There may not actually be a zero coupon bond maturing on the horizon date, but from the term structure, the manager can get a pretty good idea of what a riskless investment would earn.

It is difficult to make a case for immunizing a coupon bond portfolio if the manager cannot at least promise to improve somewhat on the zero coupon return. The manager has introduced more (reinvestment) risk through the use of coupon bearing bonds and there has to be something on the return side as compensation. Hence, the use of a zero coupon bond yield as the benchmark. Of course, there is a little more to the story exemplified by questions such as: "What if all bonds other than U.S. Treasury issues are used? How does one get a zero coupon curve for agencies or corporates or Ginnie Maes?" The answer is that the manager has to be flexible. Generally he will augment the base zero coupon Treasury yield with some empirically observed spread over the Treasury yields.

Some managers will estimate their return to horizon by averaging the yields to maturity of their initial immunized portfolio. This should not be done. Using yield to maturity can create difficulties for a manager depending on the slope of the yield curve at various points in the future. This is considered later in the discussion of rebalancing the portfolio and practical problems with immunizing.

Measuring and Minimizing Risk

Previously, it was indicated that simple duration matching is not sufficient. The manager gets the money to manage, buys a computer system or does the work by hand, and determines that durations are matched. More is involved, however. The manager must be concerned with variability—dispersion of the future cash flows—associated with any immunized portfolio that can significantly influence returns, and that spells risk.

For example, the two portfolios represented abstractly in Figure 9A-11 both represent portfolios immunized for a four-year horizon. The portfolio durations are both equal to four years, but they are obviously different portfolios. The individual bond durations in portfolio B are tightly clustered at about year four whereas those in A are divided (in "barbell" form) between groups at one and seven years. Intuition tells one that if the manager owns portfolio B, regardless of what happens to interest rates, reinvestment risk is going to be a lot lower than if portfolio A is owned. The durations are matched in both portfolios, but they are *not* identically risky portfolios because the dispersion of the individual bonds is so different.

Macaulay's duration, or whatever measure is being used, is satisfactory as long as the yield curve changes in the manner that was predicted, but that almost never happens. With a portfolio such as A, the assets are really exposed to unexpected twists in the yield curve. Clearly, one of the objectives of creating an immunized portfolio using coupon bearing bonds is to make it look as much like a zero coupon security as possible. Not surprisingly, one way to do this is to concentrate the durations around the horizon date, that is, the target duration date.

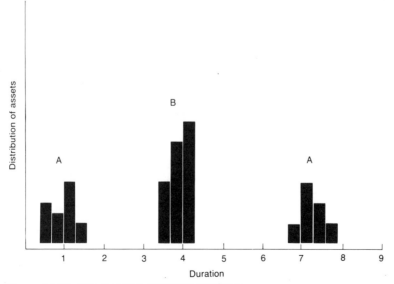

Figure 9A-11. Two Duration-Matching Portfolios.

Another approach is to calculate a *measure of variability that measures the dispersion of cash flows around the horizon date.* It is calculated more or less by squaring the differences between the time cash flows are received and the horizon date, then multiplying this result by the present value of the cash flow divided by the price of the bond, and then summing the products. The result is akin to a variance, or if the square root is taken, a standard deviation. The wider the dispersion of cash flows around the horizon, the larger this number is. Clearly, it is an important measure of the risk being assumed in the portfolio.

The importance of this risk measure cannot be emphasized strongly enough because it is a valuable control, not only when building the original immunized portfolio, but also as a means of evaluating the effect of changes the manager might make to that portfolio.

Error in Promised Return

A related problem, once the manager has been foolish enough to go on record with a guaranteed rate to the client, is estimating how much error is involved in this rate. There have been some preposterous claims about the tracking error involved in immunized portfolios that would lead one to believe that a manager can realistically come within three, four, or five basis points of the promised return. While this error is probably going to increase with the length of the horizon, numbers like 3 to 5 basis points are, with any horizon length, unrealistic. However, because it is important that the manager establish realistic client expectations when the business is sold, there must be some way to estimate tracking error with some degree of accuracy.

One of the ways of approaching this problem is historical simulation. What if this portfolio had been held in 1969 or 1974? How would it have done given the yield changes that were experienced in the past? Would the portfolio really have been immunized? The solution is to do some historical simulations. Through the use of computer simulations and a large number of historical yield curve observations, one can estimate the tracking error inherent in an immunized portfolio at any time. This estimate becomes quite important in establishing realistic client expectations and as a benchmark for performance measurement.

As an example of a situation that could, but should not occur, consider a client that pulls out the memo a manager wrote five years earlier that says there should be $4,000,633 in portfolio assets at the end of 5 years, then looks at the actual portfolio market value of $4.9 million, and wonders why. This should be prevented from happening. Clients should be continually advised to make sure their return or terminal value expectations are realistic. The zero coupon bonds are troublesome in this process because there is no confidence interval at the horizon date for those instruments, and managers constantly run the risk that coupon bond portfolios might not meet the return promised with the zeros.

A minimized-variability portfolio certainly protects against unexpected yield curve shifts, but it is not necessarily *the* optimal solution. By searching long enough, the manager may (or may not) find higher return or lower risk portfolios. Still, by minimizing horizon variability, most of the risk-minimizing benefits of a zero coupon bond portfolio can be achieved.

Selecting the Bond Universe

Once the client has specified the horizon, it is important to agree on the client's credit risk tolerance, identify key risk factors, and select a bond universe that meets these criteria, at least in general terms. The nature of the problem can be exemplified in the following question: Is a World Bank bond a federal agency bond? The answer is not obvious. If a client asked for a Treasury and agency portfolio and the manager put those World Bank bonds into it, the yield might increase significantly. That is the problem. The client discovers that the World Bank bond is not an agency issue at all. The issuer just happens to be located in Washington, D.C. and is involved with a lot of potentially troublesome loans. Although some believe that the quality of World Bank debt is conceivably superior to that of an agency, it is not generally regarded as an agency of the U.S. government. Therefore, it is important to be clear on the risk specifications for the universe that is used, because the universe more or less determines the rate that the manager is able to guarantee.

Use of Computerized Techniques

When considering the actual construction of the portfolio, it is fair to say that immunizing without the assistance of a computer is unrealistic. Once there is agreement as to issuers, quality, and degree of call protection, a computer-based immunization program is used to build the portfolio. There are a number of fine computer services to assist the manager in structuring his portfolio. The firms vary a little in their approach to creating immunized portfolios, especially their definition of duration and how they approach it, be it Macaulay's duration or a Fisher-Weil formulation incorporating current and expected term structures and beyond. Beyond that, they may go to risk models involving quantification of call and sinking fund risk or to models that assess the dynamics of spreads between corporates and governments. As a result, there is a fairly rich and complete choice.

One system involves a linear program that has an objective function involving the expected return of the portfolio, variability, duration match, and transaction costs. An immunized manager spends a great amount of time making trade-offs among these variables. What about high coupon bonds? Their variability is too high. They involve too much risk. What about the transaction costs? What about the small mismatch of duration and time-to-horizon? The manager is constantly making trade-offs. It is not as simple as telling a broker, "I want a 4.3 year duration bond with a variability of two years." That simply does not make sense. A manager who is going to contribute anything to the management of the portfolio should be able to contribute the judgment necessary to make sensible trade-offs. Is the risk taken in creating a wider confidence interval around the target return worth the additional potential return? Clearly, because high coupon bonds offer additional return possibilities and because they do not have the low yields that low coupon bonds often have (because of their potential tax benefits for taxable investors), high coupon bonds would normally be appealing to tax-free investors. However, their variability at the horizon date is much greater. So how does the manager weight each of these elements?

The initial approach to immunizing portfolios that was recommended by many computer models was to buy 8 percent coupon issues. This was in a 12 to 15 percent yield environment, which produced low variability because the cash flows, like those for portfolio B in Figure 9A-11, were concentrated near the horizon. But these bonds also had low expected returns—more so in the corporate area than in the government area—because managers were competing for them with insurance companies that preferred lower quality deep discount bonds because of their tax advantages.

The end result was that some immunized managers may have sacrificed too much expected return to give themselves some assurance of minimizing variability. It may not have been the appropriate trade-off and, while this is not something about which unambiguous judgments can be made, it is the kind of trade-off that the manager must evaluate in making decisions.

One interesting by product of immunization using Macaulay's duration (as pointed out in Gifford Fong's Chapter 9 in the main volume) is that if there is a parallel shift, the expected wealth at the horizon date will improve no matter which way interest rates go. This is illustrated in Figure 9A-12 by the curved line labelled "B" as rates either fall or rise in parallel fashion. It is an interesting phenomenon and a stimulating exercise in mathematics. Still, how useful is it, considering how often yield curves shift in parallel fashion in the real world? Even though a portfolio is not perfectly immunized with Macaulay's duration, in actuality, in this very special situation it is better than perfectly immunized because, regardless of the direction of the parallel shift, its terminal wealth will be enhanced.

Comparing Volatility

Another approach used to control the risk of a portfolio is the measure of *portfolio market value volatility or beta*. Relative to horizon date cash flow variability, it approaches risk control from a completely different point of view. Using a market value volatility measure, the volatility of the immunized coupon bond portfolio is compared to the volatility of a zero coupon bond maturing on the horizon. It is a different approach than duration matching or variability minimizing.

This approach asks: based on a simulation of how yield curves might change, how is this portfolio going to behave in a variety of interest rate

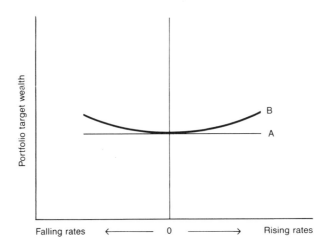

Figure 9A-12. Changes in Value of an Immunized Portfolio for Parallel Yield Curve Shifts.

scenarios relative to a zero coupon bond. Many estimates of bond betas rely heavily on empirical studies of the past few years, and the ones that are used admittedly use too little data. Nevertheless, this procedure is a check to determine whether, if durations are matched and variability is minimized, there is still a risk being taken that the manager is not cognizant of and therefore has not protected the portfolio adequately.

Rebalancing the Portfolio

Establishing an immunized portfolio is in certain respects the easy part of the whole semiactive management process. The manager starts with cash, the computer tells what to buy, and the process is in operation. The real problems arise in *rebalancing*. Clearly this is where the immunized manager earns his money, because immunized portfolios are much more complex than they were ever thought to be. Basically, the manager is constantly faced with the tradeoffs between minimizing risk and reducing return, and minimizing transaction costs.

When is the best time to rebalance? Should it be done as soon as rates shift; as soon as the durations change, that is, as soon as there is a mismatch; or as soon as variability grows? The answer, generally, is: none of the preceding. As bond seminar speaker William Nemerever put it, in answering this question, "Depending on the slope of the yield curve—don't laugh now—you should do it either just before or just after interest rates change. The unfortunate thing is that few of us are able to or, as immunized portfolio managers, are expected to forecast changes of this sort."

Consider, for example, a situation where the manager is generally shortening durations because the portfolio is approaching the horizon and thus getting close to a termination point. If a positive yield curve environment exists, shortening generally involves a give up in yield as portfolio maturities roll down the yield curve. In this situation, the manager wants to postpone rebalancing (to shorten duration) as much as possible to get the benefits of those higher yields. Of course, the point at which interest rates change is uncertain. If the yield curve becomes inverted, then it is desirable to rebalance to shorten durations as soon as possible, because yields will now increase rather than decrease by doing so. Perhaps the best approach is for the manager to begin the client meeting by saying, "I don't know where interest rates are going, therefore we want to be as immunized as we can at all times."

When and how much to rebalance is a difficult question. For example, 1982 was an exceptional year because rates changed so dramatically. All immunized managers were faced with durations that lengthened very rapidly. They had to do several extensive rebalancings. In a normal year, a manager should not have to rebalance that often, perhaps every six months, but certainly the portfolio will be experiencing enough periodic coupon inflow to require rebalancing about that frequently.

Furthermore, the manager who is not planning to rebalance for six months does not want to set the portfolio's duration equal to the current time to horizon. The manager wants to set portfolio duration so that about halfway between now and the time rebalancing is expected to be needed, it equals the time to horizon. Otherwise the portfolio will be a little more out of balance over time than it needs to be.

Generally speaking, to the extent that the manager can shade things one way or the other, he will contribute to the quality of the immunization. Doing so also introduces some risks, primarily because in choosing a duration measure, a manager makes a bet that yield curves will shift in a certain fashion. In the final analysis, there is not much that can be done to protect against an unexpected form of shift, except to constantly work toward minimized variability.

IMMUNIZATION APPLICATIONS

Moving to some applications of immunization, one institution at which immunization should be readily usable is a life insurance company. As noted previously, it was F. M. Redington who in 1952 suggested that a life insurance company with long-term liabilities would be in an ideal situation to match its duration with long-term type assets. That is because life companies know, or they *used* to know, what their liability cash flows were from a book of insurance business such as whole life or annuity business. Life insurance actuaries spend much time forecasting liability maturities and they have incredibly good mortality data with which to do so.

The life insurance situation historically, then, has been similar to the situations for which dedicated portfolios, discussed in the next section of this chapter, are designed. With dedicated portfolios, the manager knows that specific cash flows will be needed at various points in the future. For a life company, the future cash flows represent funds needed for claim settlements, the maturity of its GICs and policy surrenders or loans.

However, the life insurance industry is really not doing dedicated bond portfolio management with their book of life business. Various observers have noted that the life industry's book of business is changing. They are rapidly moving from whole life to term products or universal life, and are faced with sizable policy loans and surrenders. It would seem that the real applications of immunization in the life insurance industry are timely and topical.

GIC Investing

Generally, the guaranteed products that life companies issue, which are really just general obligations of the company, are predominantly supported by portfolios of public bonds, private placements, and mortgages. There are equity kickers offered in some GICs, but generally these three forms of debt account for 80 to 90 percent of any portfolio backing GIC contracts.

Life insurance companies are adopting immunized strategies with greater frequency. In reality, all the life company is doing—which has nothing to do with insurance per se, except for the fact that they are guaranteeing the rate —is borrowing money from pension plans and lending it to the securities market, ideally at a profitable spread. Of course, this should only be considered if the portfolio is immunized, that is, if the asset portfolio is similar to the GIC liability with respect to variability and duration, because otherwise some tremendous risks will be taken.

Generally, the approach of insurance companies to the GIC business is not to buy bonds with GIC funds and combine them with other securities in their general account, but to create a segmented account to support the GIC line of business in the group pension area. This is not a segmented account for each contract, but a pooled account designed to immunize the company against the risk of not fulfilling the guaranteed terms of the contracts.

GIC Pricing and Rate Guarantees. In some companies, the rate guarantees associated with GICs are determined by the group pension actuary who does the pricing with rates supplied by their portfolio managers. The rates may change several times a day and are pegged to the government market. They are highly market sensitive. For one company, the actuary applied a hypothetical rate equal to the after-tax yield to maturity on noncallable 5½-year duration Baa-rated bonds. "And," as seminarian Nemerever wryly put it, "those are coming to market all the time, right?" The company in question simply decided that this was a reasonably conservative way of starting to come to grips with the situation and produce answers; certainly it is not unindicative of the underlying characteristics of the portfolio. Thus, the search begins with a

5½-year duration instrument, which recently has meant a 10- or 12-year maturity noncallable Baa bond.

The life company's pricing actuary then takes the yields to maturity of these Baa bonds and adjusts them. First, the actuary adjusts them for the competitive position the company wants to take in the market, a market that is very rate sensitive. The basic sources of information in this market are GIC brokers who are similar to traditional brokers. They are just information houses. GIC brokers call a lot of insurance companies and get guaranteed rates and then pass that information on to people who want to buy GICs. This makes the whole market very efficient and competitive. One can find out, on a daily basis, the best available rate in the country. Because it is a very competitive market, companies wanting a lot of GIC business know exactly where they will have to price their product to get that business.

The pricing actuary next adjusts the estimated yield for expenses, credit risk, and *antiselection risk*. Antiselection risk is important; it is the risk the life company assumes in making a rate guarantee for some extended period of time after the sale of the contract, such as with a profit-sharing plan. Consider, for example, a company that sold a five-year GIC, and one of the features of the plan is a *contribution window* that enables employees in the company to contribute anytime in the first year and get the guaranteed rate, regardless of what has happened to interest rates. Thus, the actuary has to anticipate this risk and factor it into the contract price, just as call provisions or default risk are factored in for the underlying portfolio. The actuary knows that if rates go down, the employees are going to want to contribute more. If rates go up, they will be less inclined to contribute. This is what is called antiselection risk. Finally, the actuary builds in a profit margin.

For some life companies, an interest rate anticipation strategy will be incorporated to a modest degree either in GIC pricing or non-full immunization of the portfolio, or both. That is, the company feels confident about their forecast of the direction and level of interest rates, and accordingly, it will not completely immunize, and may even offer a more-than-competitive rate on the GIC. In so doing, the company assumes some market or interest rate risk as part of an aggressive investment and/or pricing strategy.

GIC Contract Reserves. Another factor that relates to a constraint on GIC business has to do with the fact that insurance companies are required to put up reserves on these contracts, and the reserve is generally calculated to directly reflect how far the guaranteed rate is from a designated average of market yields and the length of the guarantee period. Thus it is possible that the company may be required to set up a reserve in an amount in excess of the funds received from the sale of GIC contracts. Such excess reserves are required when guaranteed rates exceed the designated average of market yields guidelines. The excess is a charge against surplus. Among the various states, New York State has restrictive reserve requirements that essentially limit the amount of business a company can write nationally because of the effect on surplus.

How do insurance companies finally arrive at a GIC price? Generally, they evaluate the various factors and contingencies through the use of simulation models, using many observations with a Monte Carlo approach to get an idea of the magnitude of downside risk.

Monitoring GIC Portfolios. How do insurance companies monitor all of this? Most combine these bonds into a large pool and do not keep track of individual contracts that they have written on an asset-matched basis. Basically, they create a form of dedicated portfolio or multiperiod immunization and once they have checked the asset-liability duration match, they monitor the situation by matching the cash flow against the liabilities. While this is not an inappropriate way of monitoring the process, it is much less precise than one might have expected.

One of the problems insurance companies face is the difficulty of controlling the demand for a particular form of contract, although these companies may make attempts by raising or lowering their guaranteed returns. For example, five-year guarantees have been in demand recently but tomorrow the market may be for three-year, or two-year guarantees. As a result, the companies offering GICs get mismatches in their asset-liability durations. To remedy this, many companies have approached Wall Street investment bankers and asked them to seek the creation of specific debt instruments (under SEC Rule 415) designed to fill the gaps in their maturity/duration schedules.

Finally, given that most GIC contracts are bullets (single payment contracts) with maturities in the 3 to 10 year range, the insurance companies selling these contracts with compound interest (all interest reinvested by the insurance company at the guaranteed rate) are issuing the equivalent of zero coupon bonds. That is, they are saying, "You give me money now and I'll give it back to you along with accumulated interest at a specified rate in 3 to 10 years."

Use of Weak Credits. Many life insurance companies customarily buy below-average quality credits (typically Baa-BBB and Ba-BB), because of their higher yields, resulting in somewhat risky portfolios backing their GICs. Large life insurance companies, such as John Hancock Mutual Life Insurance Company, Prudential Insurance Company of America, Equitable Life Assurance Society of the United States, and Metropolitan Life Insurance Company, have large pools of assets that they can call upon should problems arise with the low grade credits in their GIC portfolios. They attempt to take advantage of the law of large numbers and diversify most of the unsystematic bond risk. As a result the guaranteed rates offered by these companies can be much higher than what smaller non-insurers can offer. The latter managers do not have enough funds under management to sufficiently diversify or otherwise absorb the added risk of low quality credits.

Separately Managed Portfolios

The other immunization application of interest is the separately managed immunized bond portfolio designed to correspond to a specific horizon selected by a pension plan sponsor or other client with a need for a predetermined rate of return. Generally, these uses involve a specific horizon, so the portfolios are single period immunization cases—single horizon, single cash flow —as distinguished from multiperiod immunization portfolios.

What the separately managed portfolio manager does, matching durations and minimizing variability, is the same as the GIC manager. The yields are typically lower than for GICs but the quality of portfolio assets is usually higher and the marketability, on a daily basis, is higher. One of the selling points of separately managed portfolio management that is not particularly comforting is that if the plan sponsor chooses to, he can get out very quickly at market value. The underlying securities are generally Treasury and agency issues. Many of the clients are quite risk averse. Even some of the agencies and their issues are of concern to these clients.

GIC quotes are generally expressed in terms of annually compounded rates. By contrast, some financial institutions' separately managed portfolios employ semiannual compounding, reflecting market conventions. At high yields this makes a tremendous difference, so if the competition is focussing on rates, it is important to ascertain the method of compounding yields in the contract.

Performance Benchmark for Active Managers

Immunization is also used as a performance benchmark for active management. Just as the zero coupon is a benchmark for an immunized manager, an immunized portfolio should be a benchmark for an active manager over reasonable periods of time. This strategy is available to almost anybody for any reasonable period of time and the onus is on the active manager to do better over time than a naive strategy like immunization. It is possible that this use of immunized portfolios will become more popular, and there will be some manifestation of it in techniques such as contingent immunization, to be discussed in the last major section of this chapter on combination active/passive strategies.

Discerning Bond Relative Values

Consider what a manager can do with immunized portfolios besides matching durations and minimizing variability. It has been said that one of the most important functions of bond managers is to discern relative values in the bond market. They spend a lot of time on the phone with brokers and other people, and use equipment, like the Telerate system, to monitor the markets. It is an over-the-counter market where the effort spent is usually rewarded. Many managers also do a lot of work in credit analysis and they know relative values.

Given a portfolio such as an immunized one, which is relatively passive as far as maturity risk or interest rate risk is concerned, the manager can continue to enhance expected portfolio return through effective arbitrage, sector judgments, and perceptive credit analysis. If done well, these activities add real value. For example, if the manager is able to discern relative value, portfolio rebalancing can be done at very low cost. In other words, look at a swap not with respect to where the portfolio is today but, rather, where the manager wants it to be in the future.

For example, a manager is considering an arbitrage swap that may involve some maturity judgment and risk, but in addition the swap moves the portfolio's duration and variability in the direction the manager wants to go. There are programs on micro-computers that can identify and evaluate these kinds of strategies, and accessibility to programs and data that produce quick answers is important. There is not time to log onto a time-sharing system; by the time that is done, the swap may be gone. Analysis and decision making must be done quickly.

Taking Sensible Risks

Finally it is important to understand—and it is often not intuitive—how different cash flows affect the portfolio. Good semi-active managers are constantly evaluating the trade-offs among duration mismatch, volatility, return, and the confidence interval about the horizon, always looking for ways to contribute an extra margin of return. An immunized manager should encourage his clients to take some sensible risks. With some intelligent assumption of risk —credit risk, arbitrage risk, or possibly modest maturity mismatching—a manager can contribute to the return of an immunized portfolio. Bonds simply should not be bought and put away.

PRACTICAL PROBLEMS WITH IMMUNIZING

Risks with Immunized Portfolios

There are some practical problems associated with immunized portfolios that should be addressed. The greatest risk is involved with rebalancing. When should it be done? What happens to make it necessary to rebalance? It was mentioned previously that arbitrage opportunities can facilitate rebalancing and reduce transaction costs if they can be done in the direction of better balance.

Misspecified Yield Curve Shifts. What are some of the risks that the manager faces once he has set up an immunized portfolio? The major risks of an immunized portfolio include, first, the misspecification of the yield curve shift to the extent that bonds other than zero coupon bonds are owned. With coupon bond portfolios, the manager is always betting on how interest rates will change; to the extent he is wrong, he will suffer.

Unbalanced Portfolios. The second risk is the risk associated with an unbalanced portfolio. What if the manager is on an extended vacation in a remote area and interest rates suddenly drop 300 basis points? Durations have changed significantly. If the manager does not return before another shock is received, a serious situation could result. Thus, to the extent that the manager is asleep at the switch, there is a risk. A manager's ability to keep abreast of any and all developments will minimize that risk. Immunization is such a new technology that having all of the bases covered all of the time, at least until considerable additional experience has been achieved, is advisable.

Transaction Costs. Transaction costs are the third risk. They are often difficult to accurately forecast. The manager makes a return estimate based on zero coupon bonds. Once this benchmark has been set, the manager pats himself on the back and counts his basis points, and all of a sudden he realizes he did not include transaction costs, generally as measured by the spread between bid and ask quotes and any market impact. Even if he does as well as the zero coupon alternative, the manager is going to lose. It is a serious drag on performance, and the manager is pressed to do what he can to minimize these costs.

Default Risk. Bonds of the U.S. government are not going to go into default but corporate issues can and some, albeit a few, do. It is a minor risk but it is still a risk; because it is not just default; it is the perceived or actual loss of relative credit strength. If the manager of an immunized portfolio is holding a bond that is downgraded by the rating agencies, or that the market perceives is a candidate for a downgrade, then spreads will widen and the cost of rebalancing the portfolio by selling or swapping such a bond will increase.

Premature Call. Finally, to the extent that callable corporate bonds are being used and the call (repurchase) option is exercised by the issuer—or even if the bonds are not actually called but get close enough to their call price so that their relative performance reflects the fact that they are callable—there is a risk. A call feature can distort return distributions.

The Need for Rebalancing

Most of these risks are not related to "plain vanilla" immunization, straightforward immunization using Treasuries and no arbitrage swapping. However, their effects do need to be considered when the portfolio's risk parameters are stretched. An immunized coupon bond portfolio simply cannot be bought and put away. As indicated previously, managers of immunized portfolios are much more active than ever thought possible.

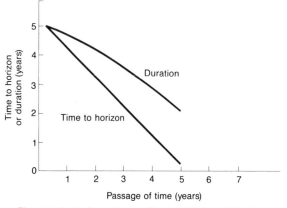

Figure 9A-13. Duration vs. Time to Horizon With the Passage of Time.

Consider the most extreme case: rates do not change. It is a constant environment. Still, even in this highly stable situation rebalancing is necessary. The example shown in Figure 9A-13 provides an explanation. Shown is a portfolio that has been immunized at five years. One of the properties of duration is that it shortens *more slowly* than the time to horizon. The starting point for Figure 9A-13 is the upper left where a five-year duration and a five-year time to horizon is depicted. As the horizon is approached, the time to horizon shortens with the passage of time on a one-for-one, or linear, basis. The duration also shortens with time but at a slower speed, that is, a less than one-for-one basis, than the time to horizon. In a sense, the vertical difference between these two lines represents the risk assumed with the passage of time. It is a gradually increasing, qualitative duration-horizon mismatch that cannot be avoided, except by buying zero coupon bonds.

Changes in interest rates can significantly affect the duration of the bond and, as a result, managers need to develop an intuitive feel for what is happening as rates change. Figure 9A-14 illustrates how the duration changes as yield is assumed to change for various maturity 12 percent coupon bonds. The illustration employs Macaulay's duration, but the conclusions are similar for other duration measures. In the latter part of 1982, yields on longer maturity bonds declined from 15 or 16 percent to 10 or 11 percent, a drop of 400-plus basis points. The effect on duration depended heavily on what maturity sector the manager was in. Not only did the durations of 30-year maturity or 10-year maturity bonds increase dramatically, but more importantly, the spread between the durations of those two different maturity bonds *widened* significantly.

It is no longer acceptable to own a long bond for the reason that it is not that much riskier than an intermediate. Long bonds are different securities in the post-1982 interest rate environment than they were before mid-1982. The durations have changed significantly. When this type of a shift occurs, the portfolio's duration and time to horizon are no longer matched and the manager must take action. At a minimum, the manager should recalculate the portfolio's duration to determine how bad the mismatch has become.

Most immunized portfolio managers did a lot of rebalancing in 1982. It was the first major instance when immunization managers were large sellers of long-maturity bonds, and active managers were large buyers of those same bonds. When the bond market is experiencing rapidly rising prices as it did the latter half of 1982, the natural intuition of a bond manager, who knows exactly where rates and prices are going and extrapolates past trends, is to hold long bonds and ride the price surge. However, as can be seen from this analysis, the immunized manager is increasing exposure to bond systematic risk by doing so. Durations on long bonds are rising fast. The mismatch eventually can become extreme and the immunizer is forced to sell long duration bonds and replace them with shorter duration issues to rebalance the portfolio. Active managers compete to buy these long bonds, with their appealing capital gain possibilities, from immunized managers, and the bond brokers benefit from the increased volume of transactions.

The reverse situation works in a similar fashion. When everybody is depressed and interest rates are rising, the durations are shortening and immunized managers are rolling out of short maturities and lengthening durations to keep their portfolios in balance. Active managers, on the other hand, will be dumping long-term issues and rushing to short-maturity investments. It is an interesting phenomenon and one of the few times when some bond managers want to sell bonds and others want to buy them.

The Value of Special Features

Where bonds with special features are being used—callable corporates, bonds with sinking funds, or Ginnie Mae pass-throughs—as interest rates change,

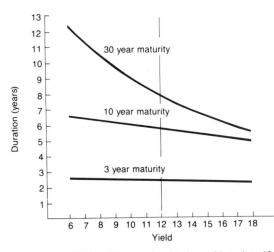

Figure 9A-14. Duration vs. Yield Change for Various Maturity 12 Percent Coupon Bonds.

the value and relative risk of these call- or prepayment-type features change. As interest rates fall, the risk of calls or prepayments increases. Many managers believe they can build in sufficient call protection by buying discount bonds. Perhaps so, but if they have underestimated how low interest rates will actually go, while there will be a lot of bonds with higher coupons that are called first, their lower coupon bonds which they bought at a discount may be called as well.

The point is that, unlike active fixed income managers, the time horizons in this environment are very long term. Semi-active managers must try to anticipate what might happen in the future, not in the next 6 to 12 months, but the next 5 to 6 years. Could rates indeed decline to as low as 6 percent, and if so, will calls and prepayments force the manager to rebalance at lower interest rates and thereby decrease the return on the portfolio? It is a risk that must be monitored.

In approaching rebalancing, the portfolio manager generally assumes no knowledge of the magnitude or timing of the next interest rate shock. Essentially he must be of the opinion that he has no idea what is going to happen next. That may be a little hard on managers, but it forces them to take less risk in terms of a duration mismatch or high variability. When there is a shock, the discipline of immunization does not permit managers to sit around thinking, "Maybe rates will go back down or go back up. Why don't we wait?" Immunized managers pay the price of increased transaction costs for the reward of greater certainty, and that is what they are paid to do. In point of fact, if Treasuries and agencies are used, the transaction costs do not appear to be a major problem, although obviously they can be a drag on returns over time.

Tracking Report Value

One of the tools that has been used to help indicate when it might make sense to rebalance is the one shown in Figure 9A-15. It is called an *Attainable Tracking Report*. The horizontal axis is the horizon, in years, of an immunized portfolio. The vertical axis is maximum shortfall of horizon wealth, which represents the percentage below a client's target wealth that might be experienced.

The lower of the two upward-sloping curves in the diagram represents, for various numbers of years to the horizon, the maximum percentage shortfall of horizon wealth that would be expected with 95 percent confidence. The function curves upward with longer horizons because, with a fixed confidence level, there will be a larger potential percentage shortfall in wealth as the horizon is extended. The lower function essentially provides trigger points, at various length horizons, when rebalancing should be done. The higher curve, a function of the lower one, represents the largest acceptable percentage shortfall for various horizons. Note how steep both functions become—how shortfall accelerates—for horizons in excess of four to five years.

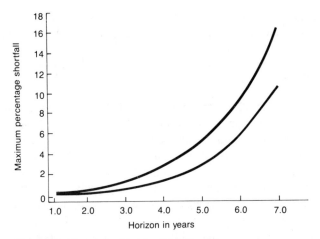

Figure 9A-15. Attainable Tracking Report.

Most organizations try to manage the maximum percentage shortfall quite closely. They do not want the portfolio to get too far out of balance. When the shortfall becomes too large, it is decided that it is time to rebalance. This is one way of measuring the risk/reward trade-off. This is not a particularly quantitative approach. As always it is a matter of judgment, but it is one approach that can be used.

Minimizing Transaction Costs

One of the ways of minimizing transaction costs, which again is a challenge, is to group bond coupon payment dates. This has more initial appeal than practical appeal. The idea is that if the portfolio receives a lot of coupons in November, the manager can do all the necessary rebalancing from this relatively large cash infusion, thereby bunching sales and paying lower transaction costs.

Another approach is to construct a portfolio that could be thought of as having the characteristics of a two-bond portfolio, one with a bond maturing on the horizon, and one with a longer bond. As the manager is forced to rebalance, he sells the longer bond position, constantly shortening portfolio duration until the desired duration is obtained.

Again, it cannot be emphasized enough that there is a continuous return/ risk trade-off. Nobody offers the pure arbitrage swap, where the purchased bond has the same coupon, same maturity, same credit rating, and so on, at a pickup in yield. It does not happen. There is always some trade-off. Therefore, the immunized manager cannot be as casual as an active manager might, moving his portfolio maturity around every six months or so. For example, the immunizer may sell mid-1986 foreign credit and buy a late 1986 foreign credit, which on its face, would seem fairly innocuous. However, that transaction may be significant in an immunized portfolio and may end up changing the duration. Thus, the manager constantly has to factor in and quantify what risks are being taken to pick up 20 basis points, 30 basis points, and so forth.

Tax Implications

There are also the tax effects to be considered. Managers are aware that the yields of high coupon bonds—although less so recently—have been much greater than yields on discount bonds because the opportunity for capital gains with their favorable tax treatment is small. As a result, there have been attractive yields for the client if that client is not taxed. However, when a manager reaches for that extra yield, the return variability problem is intensified. How far should one reach? Most managers are really not in a position to monitor this very well, especially with the proliferation of types of securities employed, including consolidated mortgage obligations, mortgage pass-through bonds, and callable bonds. For callable bonds, the additional yield may be partially or fully offset by the risk of call or prepayment.

Positive Yield Curve Effect

Another problem that was alluded to previously is rebalancing in a positive yield curve environment. As can be expected, duration is shortening with the passage of time whether or not any action has been taken, but at a slower rate than the time to horizon. Therefore, there is a need to rebalance the portfolio to reduce its duration. However, in so doing, the manager will be rolling out of longer-maturity, higher yielding securities (e.g., 30-year bonds) and into shorter-maturity lower yielding securities.

What if it is assumed a flat yield curve is appropriate and is used to make that initial estimate of horizon wealth for an immunized corporate bond portfolio? Since the Treasury-corporate yield spread is usually larger for long-maturity corporates than for intermediate-maturity corporates, selling the former and buying the latter to reduce duration will also produce a yield give-up even with a flat yield curve.

Unscheduled Contributions or Withdrawals

Another problem is unscheduled contributions or withdrawals. If a client calls and says, "I need ten million dollars from my immunized portfolio," it throws everything off. Or, likewise if a client says, "We love you. Your immunization is so great that I'm going to give you some more money." Unfortunately, they usually do that after rates have fallen.

One approach to this problem is to develop a *blended rate*. Clients constantly want a rate to monitor, and the manager does that by figuring out first where the portfolio would have been at the point the client made the contribution. This is the contribution date point on the solid curved line in Figure

9A-16. Add the amount of the contribution, accumulate that amount at the rate that is available in the market at that time, the zero coupon rate to the horizon, and a new target wealth is developed based on the contribution plus what was promised initially. At the contribution point the manager determines a blended rate that is the rate that would make the contribution plus projected wealth at the contribution date grow to the new horizon wealth. Properly handling unscheduled contributions or withdrawals is just a practical problem, but it is not trivial, because when a mistake is made, the manager will end up promising something that cannot be delivered and the manager's skills of communication will be put to the test.

Performance Measurement

Performance measurement of immunized portfolios is not at a very advanced level at present. It is a new field. One of the ways measurement is being done is shown in Figure 9A-17. The market value of the portfolio is plotted against where the portfolio should be if it constantly grows at the rate promised. As would be expected, in the immediate post-1982 market environment, the performance of immunized portfolios looked great. Interest rates had fallen and portfolio market values were way above where they were when many portfolios were immunized. Total returns exceeded the promised immunized rates. However, this is not the correct way to interpret the situation because that capital gain is being used, in a sense, to overcome the fact that managers have been and continue to be reinvesting at lower rates. In other words, the analysis is misleading. The analysis needs to be made over the proper time period. That is, *a manager should always be measured with respect to the horizon.* If a horizon has been picked, then performance should be measured to that horizon or some serious problems will arise.

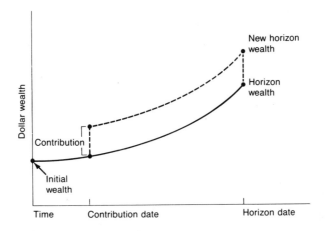

Figure 9A-16. Immunization Performance Monitoring: Multiple Contributions.

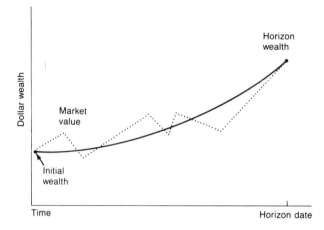

Figure 9A-17. Immunization Performance Monitoring: Single Contribution.

Table 9A-6 is an example of a key performance report that is used with clients. It shows the time to horizon, the current duration, and the estimated variability. Also indicated is where the manager is initially in terms of wealth. The key is the expected wealth, the $120 million. In other words, how much money is expected at the horizon? This is based not on what the manager promises to have, but rather, what the manager can achieve given the current market value plus the rates implicit in the market today. Tracking is done from quarter to quarter. Clearly, of greatest importance is how close the manager is to realizing what was promised. The report reflects market value changes and incorporates fees, transaction costs, and bad arbitrage judgments. Admittedly, it does not include future transaction costs, but past errors are included in the anticipated terminal market value.

Minimum and maximum future values are constructed at 95 percent confidence intervals around the expected future value. This gets to the point made previously, that initial estimates of the accuracy of an immunization strategy are probably too optimistic. The last number to the right in the table

TABLE 9A-6. Immunization: Target Monitor Report.

YEARS			Market Value ($Mil)	TARGET RANGE (AT 95% CONFIDENCE) FUTURE VALUE ($MIL)			Minimum as % of Expected Wealth
Hor	Dur	Var		Expected	Min	Max	
3.96	3.59	1.25	79.455	120.679	118.652	122.706	98.32%
Current Returns:				15.03%	14.66%	15.38%	
Annualized:				15.59%	15.20%	15.98%	
Horizon Date: 10/13/86							

SOURCE: State Street Bank and Trust Company.

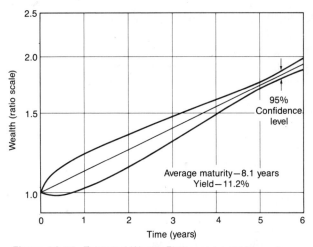

Figure 9A-18. Expected Wealth Ratios and a 95 Percent Confidence Interval Over Five Years to the Horizon Date. (SOURCE: Capital Management Sciences)

is the minimum future value as a percentage of expected future wealth, which is viewed as the worst case on the downside.

Figure 9A-18 illustrates the 95 percent confidence interval around the horizon wealth implicit in a target monitor report. The straight line in the middle plots expected future wealth on a logarithmic scale from the present to the horizon date. As would be expected, expected future wealth relative to initial wealth is projected to grow in a straight line from time zero to the horizon. This figure depicts a five-year horizon using 8-year bonds. The confidence interval, not surprisingly, is fairly broad early in the horizon period but narrows around the horizon date, because of the effect that immunization has on the portfolio. Obviously, portfolio return between now and then is going to vary. Markets will go up and down. The portfolio is not immunized for interim periods but it *is* immunized for that five-year horizon. This approach can also be used as a method for quantifying the risk involved.

Computer Software and Data Problems

Universe Shortcomings. Although there has been some improvement recently, there are still a number of problems associated with computer software and data. With respect to data shortcomings, many times the universe of securities available does not include the most recently issued Treasury and agency issues. These issues are cheap to buy, readily available in the market, and they can be bought in size (that is, in large quantities). However, since they are not in the universe, the manager has to put them in and maintain the data until, with a real lag, they appear in the data base. Also, the quality of the price quotes in a data base is poor. Even the prices used for Treasury issues tend to be inaccurate. Manual attention by the manager is critical. An optimizer, for example, recommends for purchase the cheapest bond available, which usually is the one that is mispriced. Furthermore, once that cheapest bond is identified, the programs that are available frequently try to put too much money in that bond, a real software problem. Thus, the computer actually can create problems.

Dated-Dates Problem. The "dated-dates problem" is a small but annoying problem. It is more of an issue in dedicated portfolios and is one that many computer systems just cannot accommodate. The problem occurs where, for example, the Treasury issues a bond dated in March on which equal interest payments are expected in May and November of each year. However, the bond's first interest payment in November represents accrual of interest since March. A computer program that forecasts future cash flows from the bond based on the size and timing of the first interest payment will forecast an incorrect set of cash flows. Thus, a manager cannot just say, "Run this program and buy the bonds." Each recommendation and the data supporting it have to be examined carefully. There are a number of manual adjustments required to constantly monitor and modify computer-generated immunized portfolios. Instead of improving, since William Nemerever originally wrote about this problem in 1983, the situation is actually worse.

Many of the computer systems in use do not facilitate the easy determination of the optimal trade-offs between transaction costs, turnover, variability and return. In other words, the fixed income manager must assume much of the responsibility for making these trade-off judgments.

Client Relationships

The manager's relationship with his client centers on two major concerns. The first is when to establish the initial immunized portfolio. This is actually market timing.

The second is what to do when interest rates undergo significant change after the immunized portfolio has been established. Following a general fall in rates, manager-client relationships are quite different than they are following a general rise in rates. Basically, the manager does not want rates to fall because once the client sees the great capital gains in the portfolio, he will think he made a good initial timing decision and he did not really like immunization anyway. Nemerever refers to this phenomenon as the "I want to take my money and run" game that was a real problem in the immediate post-1982 period. When rates go up it is a lot easier. There will be large market value losses, but an immunized manager can point out that if the horizon is extended, securities yielding 14 percent can be pulled into the portfolio to add to the 12 percent bonds that were immunized with originally and thereby raise the portfolio yield.

In the past, the longest duration assets available set the limits on immunization. Now, with the availability of zero coupon bonds and financial futures contracts, a manager can leverage in an almost unlimited fashion and significantly extend (or retract) the portfolio's duration. However, variability becomes a more serious factor, because confidence intervals widen as the horizon is lengthened.

Some Conclusions

Much of the preceding discussion has been devoted to mechanics and problems. However, two very important issues that must be considered are the selection of the horizon and the timing of the investment. The selection of the horizon is an asset allocation decision for two reasons. First, it gives an indication of how long there is expected to be a commitment to an immunized fixed income portfolio, as opposed to equities, for example. Second, the length of the horizon (e.g., 10 years vs. 1 year) locks the portfolio into quite different assets. Obviously, the timing of the investment is a market-timing decision. These decisions require the same skills as traditional management and they are no less critical to portfolio management performance. They overshadow considerations such as which duration measures are used, whether a minimum variance optimizer is used, or which universe of securities is chosen.

An immunized manager should expect that when the horizon is reached, if it ever is reached, a comparison will be made with alternative strategies. A client will say, "Well, how would an SEI Funds Evaluation Service median portfolio have done over the last five years?" Figure 9A-19 is a nonexhaustive example of that sort of comparison. The bars are for three- and five-year periods. The three-year period is the longer bar; the five-year is the shorter one. These are for time periods ending December 31, 1981. The little dashes indicate where immunized three- and five-year portfolios would have fallen in the performance game sweepstakes. It has been determined that the SEI universe, and perhaps other of the performance universes, includes immunized and dedicated portfolios.

Because timing is so critical and because everyone is risk averse, a strategy of *multiple horizons* probably makes sense. This strategy essentially calls for the use of different length horizons for different segments of the portfolio, although it may also call for staggering the starting (and therefore ending) times for immunization over several months. Not only is there a risk of picking rates now, but there is a risk of what the reinvestment environment will be five years from now. Because of this reinvestment rate uncertainty, one or more of a manager's major portfolios may have multiple horizons because it gives the plan sponsors a means of diversifying or spreading out the reinvestment at horizon dates. Also, although these portfolios really have very little nominal dollar risk, there is no representation that they would do anything to protect purchasing power.

In summary, the real value of immunization is not locking up 13 percent or some other high rate, but in setting a rational, sensible framework for the evaluation of risk and return choices with either active or passive manage-

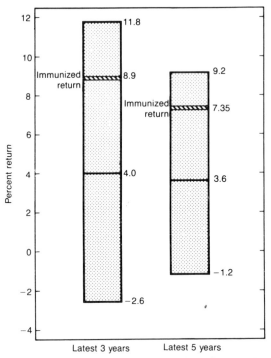

Figure 9A-19. Average Portfolio vs. Immunized Portfolio Returns for Holding Periods Ending December 31, 1981. (SOURCE: Capital Management Sciences)

ment. For the time horizon chosen, the immunized portfolio is essentially the risk-free benchmark comparison portfolio for the active manager. It is also a benchmark for the passive manager who manages portfolios with significant credit, sector, coupon, or call risks. Immunized portfolios allow for sensible means of capitalizing on what is believed to be the fixed income manager's real skills.

ANALYSTS' QUESTIONS AND ANSWERS

Question: What percentage of immunized portfolios are typically held in corporate securities?

Answer: Some of them are all corporates. One of the problems is that as the horizon shortens, the spreads between governments and corporates typically do not justify the risks. In 1983, many portfolios with long horizons were 100 percent corporates. In the post-1982 environment many managers with no previous corporate bond holdings rolled corporates in with the expectation that in a few years their holdings might be a 50-50 corporate/government split. There has been a scarcity of good quality intermediate corporates that provide decent yields.

Question: If a manager does not have zeros and does not like yield to maturity to estimate the target or benchmark return, what rate should he use?

Answer: Assuming the question is in connection with estimating the target return on an immunized corporate bond portfolio, a real zero coupon security is not needed to make that estimate. Various vendors provide daily estimations of the risk-free term structure, which are used as a basis for that judgment. Then typically, a little more yield will be added for agencies and still a little more for corporates. This is the proper benchmark to use whether or not a security actually exists.

Question: If a manager is trying to approach a zero coupon equivalent portfolio, can he take the assets he normally would select and then employ financial futures, options, or other risk modifiers to get even closer than he could by just using actual securities that are available in the marketplace? Is there a place in the daily management of these portfolios for use of futures or options, and are they typically used?

Answer: Yes, in special situations, although cash hedges are used more frequently. Typically, if a satisfactory cash hedge can be done, it will be used in preference to a futures hedge because of the uncertain costs, usually "basis risk," borne in the futures markets. Transaction costs are another factor, of course, which might favor the use of futures contracts rather than an underlying security.

Question: If the manager has a portfolio that has been around for a couple of years and there are CATS (Certificates of Accrual Treasury Securities) TIGRs (Treasury Investment Growth Receipts) and STRIPs (coupon stripped Treasury bonds) that are available for exactly the right maturity to the horizon, should he use them? Would that be an appropriate strategy?

Answer: Yes and no. Managers do use some zero coupon securities. The real problem is pricing. When zeros first came out, they were judged to be very highly priced. More recently they have been a little less expensive, so it is a more serious question. The answer is yes, if the return from that option is anywhere near competitive, there doesn't seem to be any choice. It would be imprudent not to at least put some portion of the portfolio into that type of riskless investment.

Question: Is there a reasonable explanation for why the long-term deep discount time-duration line falls beyond a certain point?

Answer: There is, but it is not short and it is not intuitive. It has to do with the fact that when the maturity on those bonds gets quite long, they all begin to look the same, and as illustrated in Figure 9A-9, in a 15 percent yield environment, the duration of the 3 percent coupon bond after a certain point gradually approaches the duration of the 15 percent coupon instrument. The coupon stream at that point tends to overwhelm the maturity payment, and an inflection point occurs where the duration of the 3 percent bond peaks and turns downward as maturity lengthens.

MANAGEMENT WITH DEDICATED PORTFOLIOS

The objective of this section will be to discuss and evaluate the various techniques for creating and managing dedicated bond portfolios. Before proceeding, however, it might be useful to state the distinction between a dedicated portfolio and an immunized portfolio. In the case of immunization, a liability must be paid in, for example, five years, and a manager will want to put aside some money to meet it, having just enough to do so in five years if more cash is neither put in nor taken out in the interim. With that cash flow profile, the total rate of return over the period is determined in advance and the performance bogey within the immunized program is the achievement of that target rate.

RATIONALE FOR DEDICATION

In contrast, the objective in a dedicated portfolio is to finance a stream of liabilities *over* time. The most common example is in financing the retired-lives liabilities in a pension fund. In that case, the liabilities typically decrease over time: $5 million might be needed for pension payments the first year, $4.8 million the second year, and so on, going out maybe 30 to 40 years. The performance objective in such a situation is to have the portfolio produce a cash flow that is just sufficient to meet *each* sequential payment as it comes due.

Over the early years of this decade there probably was a far greater volume of assets put into the dedicated form of structured bond portfolio than into the immunized form. Together, however, they accounted for billions of dollars worth of investments in 1981 and 1982. With the subsequent decline in interest rates, there has been, as one would expect, a decline in the volume of dedicated portfolios. However, most practitioners believe the concept is here to stay, and is one that will be standard consideration for the typical plan sponsor well into the future.

Not Just a Means to Reduce Contributions

Dedicated portfolios have been very popular; they have also been very controversial over the last several years. The circumstances under which they were put in place have led to a rather cynical view of what their purpose is. In an environment of poor corporate profits, many firms—perhaps most firms —that have dedicated portfolios have done so in order to reduce contributions to their pension fund.

The technical methods by which these contributions are reduced are as follows. Knowing that the assumed actuarial rate for a pension fund overall might be 7 percent, and knowing that the rate of return obtainable on the dedicated portion might be 14 percent, one approach is to increase the overall actuarial rate—say from 7 percent to 8 percent. In so doing, the present value of the overall pension liability, the total liability to the firm, will be reduced because future pension payments are now discounted at a larger rate. Therefore, the difference between the total liability of the firm (assumed to be the larger of the two numbers) and the size of the fund's assets, is reduced. Since contributions are ultimately a function of the difference between the present value of pension liabilities and assets, contributions can therefore be reduced.

Another technique is to simply value the liabilities that are being financed by the dedicated portfolio at the dedicated portfolio rate. That is, the *dedicated* rate is used to get a smaller present value of those liabilities than if a lower *actuarial* rate were used, thereby reducing the total present liability of the firm by the difference between the present value calculations.

So many firms have used dedication as an opportunity to reduce contributions that the fact that dedicated portfolios really have investment merits tends to be obscured. The view that dedication is simply a device for manipulating income is simply incorrect. It arises because the decision process for establishing dedicated portfolios is rather subtle. The decision process receives far less attention than it actually should. Because it is significant to the many investment managers who must explain it to clients or potential clients, the following discussion is divided between a discussion of dedicated portfolios, per se, and the decision process involved in dedicating.

The Dedication Objective

The general dedication objective is to choose a bond portfolio that generates sufficient cash to finance each of a sequence of liability payments as they come due. Moreover, there must be virtually no interest rate risk. There are two broad techniques for accomplishing this task. The first, which is probably the simplest, and for that matter, the one employed most frequently, is commonly called a *cash-matched portfolio*. The second technique, which is commonly believed to be a conceptual alternative but is actually a distant relative of the cash-matched portfolio, is called the *duration-matched portfolio*.

CASH-MATCHED METHODOLOGY

Determining the Liability Payments Stream

There are several simple steps to creating such a cash-matched portfolio. Assume the dedicated portfolio manager is given an annual stream of liabilities, perhaps going out 40 years. First, the manager works with the client to determine whether the liabilities will be paid monthly, quarterly, semiannually or annually, and, given a particular frequency, on which specific dates during the year they will be paid. Should the portfolio generate cash sufficient for payment of the annual liability on January 1? Since the liability is typically paid out during the year, should the money instead be available on July 1? Or should it be figured quarterly, so that four equal installments could be available on January 1, April 1, July 1, and October 1?

In working with the client, the manager needs to determine what is suitable for both investment and actuarial objectives. Commonly, the best rate and least cost is obtainable when a monthly match is done, that is, when the liabilities are broken out as finely as possible. However, there is a cost on the other side which will be described later; that is, a monthly match makes it much more difficult to do swaps during the dedication period.

Picking the Bond Universe

The next step is to pick a bond universe, again working with the client to determine what cross-section of credit (rating) levels, corporate sectors, and the like are desirable. The client might prefer nothing lower than an A rating, with an average of AA+ or better. Essentially, the manager works out investment policy guidelines with the client.

Given these guidelines, the manager selects the universe with the appropriate maturity distribution, the appropriate credit distribution—for example, some As, some AAs, and so forth—and the appropriate sector distribution. Typically, between 60 and 90 bonds are selected from a universe of 400 to 500 bonds for a dedicated portfolio of $40 million or $50 million.

Identifying the Parameters

The next step is to identify all the parameters, that is, investment policy objectives and constraints, that must be employed to do the analysis. The first is the credit risk guideline: say, A or better with an average of AA or better. In addition, there may be other constraints, such as no more than 20 percent in As or no more than 40 percent in AAs. It may also be desirable to place a constraint on the proportion in foreign bonds or other corporate sectors.

Another important parameter to pick is the reinvestment rate. This is the rate at which cash flows are *assumed* to be reinvested, from the date that they are received through the payment date of the liability being financed. If a liability is to be paid on July 1 of a particular year and the cash flows being used to finance it are accumulating throughout the first half of the year, the manager must make an explicit assumption regarding the rate of interest that those funds will be reinvested at, from when they are received until the liability is paid.

Choosing the Optimal Portfolio

Having laid out the liabilities, chosen the universe, and set the parameters, the next step is simply to price the portfolio using dealer prices and to do an optimization. In most cases, the optimization technique employed is a linear programming (LP) algorithm. The LP program typically minimizes the total cost of the portfolio, subject to the requirement that (1) all of the liabilities are met and (2) all of the constraints placed on the process are satisfied.

The resulting portfolio will be the first estimate of the optimal portfolio. It will be a portfolio that satisfies all the constraints and matches the cash flows in the following sense: in the interval between every two successive liability payments, the cash flow from principal payments and coupon receipts, plus any prior balance of accumulated excess cash, are sufficient to cover the next liability payment. The portfolio is made self-sufficient in the sense that no further trades should be required in order to continue meeting those liability payments. In practice, the manager would not want to just take the portfolio and put it on the shelf. In principle, however, if he purchased the proper set of bonds to begin with and never had any credit problems, the portfolio would just cash itself out and he would never have to do a trade.

Table 9A-7 displays a sample cash match corporate bond portfolio chosen to match a sequence of liability payments. The table includes a number of descriptive statistics of the individual securities held and the portfolio as a whole. Table 9A-8 provides an illustrative cash flow analysis of sources and applications of funds for a different cash match dedicated portfolio covering payments from May 1, 1984 to July 1, 1995. The last column in the table shows the excess funds remaining at each time period that are reinvested at the assumed 7 percent reinvestment rate supplied by the user.

Manual Portfolio Adjustments. As was indicated previously, the portfolio coming out of the computer typically will be only a first estimate, something the manager will want to modify. For example, some bonds the computer has selected will be thrown out. Why? Because the manager will be aware of special situations in the market where certain bonds have gotten more expensive and certain other bonds have gotten cheaper relative to the market since the universe was selected. The manager will want to adjust and do several iterations of the process before a portfolio that is optimal is established.

Once satisfied, the manager will normally go through another discussion phase with the client about whether or not to execute. If both believe that the estimated rate of return the portfolio will receive is acceptable, the manager will suggest that execution proceed, unless it is believed that higher rates are probable, in which case the manager may recommend delaying on the basis of interest rate timing.

TABLE 9A-7. Characteristics of a Sample Cash Match Corporate Bond Portfolio (Evaluation Date: 8-31-84).

Bond No.	Par Value	Percentage of Total	Cusip	Issuer Name	Quality	Type	Coupon	Stated Maturity Date	Effective Maturity Date	Price	YTM (Percentage)	Duration (yr.)
8	1000.	11.0	052537BH	Australia Commonwealth	AAA	0	8.250	12/ 1/84	12/ 1/84	98.125	16.14	.25
4	1000.	10.9	001688AB	AMF Inc.	BAA2	0	10.000	6/30/85	6/30/85	97.750	12.94	.80
10	1000.	11.6	173034AP	Citicorp	AA1	0	15.300	5/ 1/86	5/ 1/86	100.250	15.12	1.46
9	1000.	10.2	121897DA	Burlington Northern Inc.	AAA	0	7.375	12/ 1/86	12/ 1/86	91.000	12.06	2.07
3	1000.	10.5	5466089A	Louis. & Nash. RR CSA.	A3	4	11.000	11/15/88	11/15/88	92.000	13.54	3.33
6	1000.	7.6	035231AB	Anheuser Busch Inc.	AA	0	4.500	3/ 1/89	3/ 1/89	66.844	14.86	3.89
1	1000.	11.8	3696229A	GE Credit Corp. Loan Cert.	AA1	4	16.000	6/30/91	6/30/91	104.250	14.97	4.34
2	1000.	10.1	029990AB	American Rail Box Car CSA.	AA1	4	9.125	11/ 1/90	11/ 1/90	88.500	11.79	4.60
7	1000.	8.0	045167AB	Asian Dev. Bk.	AAA	0	7.750	4/15/96	4/15/96	69.844	12.80	6.77
5	1000.	8.4	022249AH	Aluminum Co. Amer.	A2	0	9.450	5/15/ 0	5/15/ 0	74.063	13.46	7.10

Portfolio Totals

Average Duration (Yrs)	3.251
Average Yield (%)	13.820
Duration Weighted Average Yield	13.491
Average Effective Maturity	8-31-89
Total Par Value ($000)	10000.000
Total Market Value ($000)	9102.090
Number of Issues	10

SOURCE: Gifford Fong Associates.

1985–1986 UPDATE 9A-69

TABLE 9A-8. Cash Flow Analysis of a Cash-Match Dedicated Portfolio: Reinvestment Rate—7 Percent (Evaluation Date: 3-2-84; Horizon Date: 7-1-14)

Cash Flow Date	Maturing Principal ($000) +	Coupons Paid ($000) =	Total Portfolio Payment ($000) +	Cash Inflows ($000) –	Cash Outflows ($000) =	Net Cash Flow ($000) +	Prior Cash Balance ($000) +	Interest On Inflows And Prior Balance ($000) +	Interest On Portfolio Payments ($000) =	Ending Cash Balance ($000)
5-1-84	247.	331.	578.	0.	580.	−2.	0.	0.	2.	0.
6-1-84	471.	109.	580.	0.	580.	−0.	0.	0.	0.	0.
7-1-84	375.	205.	580.	0.	580.	−0.	0.	0.	1.	0.
8-1-84	1025.	73.	1098.	0.	580.	518.	0.	0.	1.	519.
9-1-84	0.	58.	58.	0.	580.	−522.	519.	3.	0.	0.
10-1-84	822.	266.	1088.	0.	580.	508.	0.	3.	4.	512.
11-1-84	0.	65.	65.	0.	580.	−515.	512.	3.	0.	0.
12-1-84	471.	109.	580.	0.	580.	−0.	0.	0.	0.	0.
1-1-85	1404.	205.	1609.	0.	1610.	−1.	0.	0.	1.	1.
4-1-85	1212.	397.	1609.	0.	1610.	−1.	0.	0.	2.	1.
7-1-85	1230.	378.	1608.	0.	1610.	−2.	1.	0.	2.	1.
10-1-85	1250.	345.	1595.	0.	1610.	−15.	1.	0.	16.	2.

TABLE 9A-8. Cash Flow Analysis of a Cash-Match Dedicated Portfolio: Reinvestment Rate—7 Percent (Evaluation Date: 3-2-84; Horizon Date: 7-1-14)

Cash Flow Date	Maturing Principal ($000) +	Coupons Paid ($000) =	Total Portfolio Payment ($000) +	Cash Inflows ($000) -	Cash Outflows ($000) =	Net Cash Flow ($000) +	Prior Cash Balance ($000) +	Interest On Inflows And Prior Balance ($000) +	Interest On Portfolio Payments ($000) =	Ending Cash Balance ($000)
1-1-86	691.	317.	1008.	0.	1010.	-2.	2.	0.	2.	1.
4-1-86	717.	286.	1003.	0.	1010.	-7.	1.	0.	7.	1.
7-1-86	738.	268.	1006.	0.	1010.	-4.	1.	0.	4.	1.
10-1-86	759.	250.	1009.	0.	1010.	-1.	1.	0.	1.	1.
1-1-87	1492.	238.	1730.	0.	1740.	-10.	1.	0.	10.	2.
7-1-87	1252.	458.	1710.	0.	1740.	-30.	2.	0.	29.	1.
1-1-88	1072.	369.	1441.	0.	1470.	-29.	1.	0.	30.	2.
7-1-88	1843.	369.	2212.	0.	1470.	742.	2.	0.	9.	752.
1-1-89	0.	369.	369.	0.	1150.	-781.	752.	26.	5.	2.
7-1-89	765.	369.	1134.	0.	1150.	-16.	2.	0.	16.	2.
1-1-90	512.	314.	826.	0.	840.	-14.	2.	0.	14.	2.
7-1-90	837.	289.	1126.	0.	840.	286.	2.	0.	6.	295.
1-1-91	0.	244.	244.	0.	550.	-306.	295.	10.	3.	3.
7-1-91	300.	244.	544.	0.	550.	-6.	3.	0.	6.	3.
1-1-92	237.	223.	460.	0.	470.	-10.	3.	0.	10.	2.
7-1-92	1141.	204.	1345.	0.	470.	875.	2.	0.	26.	903.
1-1-93	0.	204.	204.	0.	460.	-256.	903.	32.	2.	681.
7-1-93	0.	204.	204.	0.	460.	-256.	681.	24.	2.	451.
7-1-94	0.	407.	407.	0.	900.	-493.	451.	32.	12.	3.
7-1-95	450.	407.	857.	0.	880.	-23.	3.	0.	23.	3.

SOURCE: Gifford Fong Associates.

CRITICAL DEDICATION CONSIDERATIONS

Timing of Initiation

One would think that the question of when to put the dedication into effect would be a very significant one, and it certainly is. However, as a practical matter, as soon as most clients get authorization from their pension committee or other approval body, they typically want to execute immediately. This usually occurs because the manager's most recent rate estimate is the rate used by the committee in its decision process.

If the committee has approved dedicating at this level, most of the time the client's representative will not want the manager to wait a couple of weeks just because he thinks the Treasury refunding coming up might cause the market to trade off. If a manager could have achieved the rate approved by the committee but that manager guessed wrong and the rates fell 25 basis points, no one would want to have to go back to the committee and say they had missed their chance. Therefore, most of the time, as soon as there is approval, the company pension people want to go forward without delay. Where there is latitude for waiting, the timing decision is simply an active strategy matter.

Payment Time Intervals

There are a couple of fine points about how to set up one of these portfolios that should be mentioned. It has already been discussed how critical it can be to lay out the liabilities properly in terms of monthly or quarterly time intervals. Often the client will rely on the manager to make recommendations about what timing is best. In many cases, all the client has is an annual liability from the actuary and nobody at the company has really thought about how it should be split out. A manager can add some value in this situation.

Avoiding Call Risk

Another very important factor to consider is *call risk*. In principle, the selected portfolio, if left alone, would cash itself out and pay off all of the liabilities in sequence. In this connection, since the manager does not want any bonds to be called away, he controls call risk by (1) buying noncallables and (2) buying deep discount bonds. Of course, it is a judgment call as to how deep a discount, with its attendant yield concessions, is required to get adequate protection. This is another place the manager can add value.

To develop the preceding technical fine point, there is a school of thought that says that in building a dedicated portfolio, the expected return would actually be higher if deep discounts were not bought. That is, the expected risk in question would be higher yielding, higher coupon callable bonds.

An important reason why the expected returns might be higher by using such bonds rather than discounts is that, as noted previously, discounts have certain tax advantages for taxable buyers. For that reason, they are bid up higher in price and their yield is lower than current coupon bonds of the same quality and maturity. When a pension fund buys call protection by buying discount bonds, it is also buying something it does not need, the bonds' tax advantage. The pension fund actually pays too much because, if it just bought the higher coupon callable bonds, they would have call risk but the expected return would be somewhat higher. Company pension people, although they have the option of taking the call risk and getting a higher expected return, invariably prefer the absolute risk elimination in dedicated portfolios and go for the discount bonds anyway.

Reinvestment Rate Assumption

Another important consideration is the reinvestment rate that is chosen when putting the dedicated portfolio together. Conventionally, a rather conservative rate, such as 6 or 7 percent, is used. Sometimes the rate is preassigned as being equal to the actuarial assumed rate used by the firm. As an excellent example of how important this consideration is, in late 1981, when short-term rates were 14 or 15 percent, many clients were asking the following question, "Why can't you assume 10 or 11 percent as a reinvestment rate rather than 6 or 7 percent?" The reasoning was that it was going to be quite a while before short rates went back to such low levels that a "blended" reinvestment rate as high as 10 or 11 percent would no longer be reasonable. The reasoning was that rates had been quite high for many months and that over the next five or more years they might average 10 to 11 percent as rates declined from 14 to 15 percent to 6 to 7 percent. Obviously, it did not take very much time at all for a 10 or 11 percent short-term reinvestment rate to become unreasonable. With the intervention of the Fed in the summer of 1982, short-term rates plunged to 7 percent levels in a very short period of time. So, normally, the manager wants to use a very conservative rate for his reinvestment assumption.

Another technical nuance, which is rather counterintuitive, is that the expected return would be somewhat higher overall by using a higher, less conservative reinvestment rate. With such a rate, the same required future cash flow can be produced with a smaller initial portfolio. Hence the estimated total cost of the portfolio is reduced. One could take what is saved over a lower rate, higher cost portfolio and buy long bonds with it; if rates come down such that the assumption on reinvestment rates is wrong, a manager will have made more money on the long bonds than the error in the assumed reinvestment rate cost. The point to be made is that, even in the selection of the reinvestment rate, there are little tricks that can be used when the process is understood. If the portfolio is of any size, such strategies may help a little in adding value.

Before talking about performance and how it is measured in dedicated portfolios, there is one last point to be made about the liability streams that are to be financed. Most of the liability streams that have been examined so far pertain to retired lives. They are typically diminishing-amount liability streams, although, in principle, there is no reason that an immunized or a dedicated bond portfolio cannot be built for a totally flat liability stream, or even for an increasing one.

For technical reasons, if the liability stream is either a flat stream or an increasing one that is also quite long, the portfolio begins to accumulate a lot of excess coupon income on straight coupon bonds in the early years that is assumed to be reinvested at that conservative, low rate. Frequently, that forces a manager to use zero coupon bonds and, because of the lower rates typically available on zeros, dilutes the portfolio's rate of return rather sharply. Generally, for market reasons, most managers do not find doing a dedicated portfolio with an increasing liability stream very attractive. The rate is just not as competitive as it is for other types of streams.

VALUE ADDED BY DEDICATED MANAGERS

Initial Portfolio Selection

An enormous part of the value added in the whole process of dedicated bond portfolio management is the care and effort put into the process when creating the portfolio at the outset. Significant variations exist, depending upon how carefully the universe is picked and how closely the bonds in the universe are matched to the actual liability payment dates. In addition, even counseling the client about the appropriate liability payment dates can make a considerable difference. Initial set-up of the dedicated portfolio is extremely important and deserves a great deal of time.

Credit Monitoring

Another major area of value added is the credit-monitoring function. To the extent that corporates are owned, and to the extent that the client values good credit judgment and the ability to monitor credits, a manager can add a lot of return by owning lower-rated securities in a dedicated portfolio. Ongoing monitoring of the credits is absolutely crucial, especially in an environment like the recent one where every other day there were new downgrades, not just from AA to A, but sometimes even to BB.

Swapping

Swapping is another way to add value in a dedicated portfolio, with the degree of add-on depending upon how loose the cash flow match is. There is a trade-off. At the initial set-up of a portfolio, better results—higher rates and lower total cost—generally are achieved by having a very tight match to the monthly liability stream. However, that restricts the manager substantially when engaging in swap activity, where it is desirable to sell one bond with particular maturity and cash flow characteristics, and buy another bond with similar maturity and cash flow characteristics but a higher yield, probably because it has a lower quality grade. If the new bond has to fit into a very precise monthly cash flow pattern, it is very difficult to find such exact substitutes. If there is a fairly loose match, on the other hand, it is much easier and more opportunities to add value through swapping will be generated.

Rebalancing

Probably the most important area of ongoing management, in terms of adding value, is that of general reoptimization. At a minimum of once per year, but possibly as frequently as every three to six months, it is advantageous to re-analyze the entire portfolio. The least cost portfolio to finance a particular set of liabilities at one time may not be the least cost portfolio six months later. This is because there can be very substantial changes in sector spreads and in terms on new issues, as well as in the maturing of the portfolio itself.

Cash Take-Outs. Generally, these factors can provide important opportunities for taking cash out, thereby raising return. Typically, when a reoptimization is done, the manager can take out a minimum of perhaps .25 to .50 percent of market value, and sometimes one, two or even as high as three percent, in the form of cash, because a better least-cost portfolio is available.

Eventually there will be uniform procedures for monitoring performance in dedicated accounts and all plan sponsors will understand these techniques reasonably well. The manager can anticipate that it comes down to value added from: (1) swaps, (2) the absence of credit problems, and (3) the amount of cash taken out on rebalancings. It is obviously not always the manager's fault if something cannot be taken out on a rebalancing; it may simply be that the least-cost portfolio that was put in place six months ago is still the least-cost portfolio. Nevertheless, company plan sponsors still expect a manager to go through the exercise of making sure that it continues to be the least-cost portfolio. Needless to say, they like cash take-outs!

Of course, it would be imprudent to rebalance dedicated portfolio's too frequently. Doing so would generate transactions costs that would significantly reduce cumulative cash take-outs that could be obtained if less frequent rebalancing was done. For example, if a dedicated portfolio were rebalanced every 6 to 12 months, a cash take-out of 0.5 percent might be possible, over and above the payment of transactions costs of 0.5 percent when a rebalancing occurred. On the other hand, if a portfolio were rebalanced every two to four months, a cash take-out of only 0.125 percent might be possible over and above the payment of transactions costs of 0.5 percent for each rebalancing.

The cumulative cash take-out over a year's time would likely be substantially larger for the less frequently rebalanced portfolio. Plan sponsors continue to get a better grasp of these kinds of trade-off considerations.

CASH VS. DURATION MATCHING

What are the advantages of the cash-matched, dedicated portfolio? Obviously, the virtual total elimination of reinvestment rate risk would satisfy an actuary or anyone else if the liabilities are, indeed, financed at the stipulated rate. The disadvantages of dedication can be inflexibility, detracting from the manager's ability to add value through swaps. It can increase transaction costs to the extent of forcing the manager to buy many small pieces of security issues. It can also force him to buy some bonds that may not be attractive as investments, except for their cash flow and maturity characteristics.

The foregoing has provided a brief sketch of the process of creating and maintaining dedicated portfolios of the *cash-matched* variety. There is another approach called *duration matching*.

As indicated in the discussion of immunization, bullet immunization consists of a single terminal liability. By contrast, duration-matching dedication is involved with a stream of liabilities. Take, for example, a portfolio that is established with a duration at the outset of five years, and assume that that portfolio was managed over the five-year period so that its duration always equaled the remaining time to horizon. Immunization theory demonstrates that if a manager religiously employs this technique, the target return to finance that liability will be hit with high precision. Suppose that instead of a single five-year period, the manager must fund as many as 40 liability payments. One way to approach this problem would be to set up 40 different immunized bullet portfolios. That would be one conceptual approach to doing a duration match. One may think that doing so would be foolish. Although it works for liabilities going out five to ten years, it would be extremely difficult to find the bonds necessary for doing 10-year to 40-year bullet immunizations.

Useful Duration Property

The clever thing about this duration-matching approach is that a manager does not have to worry about being able to find long-duration bonds for the following reason: if 40 different bullet portfolios were created, *the duration of the overall portfolio would equal the weighted average of the durations of the 40 individual portfolios*. That is, the aggregate duration always equals the weighted average duration of the individual portfolios. Suppose that the portfolio's duration is five. Because of the way it was set up, the duration of the liabilities would end up being five years. In other words, liabilities are simply a cash flow stream and they have a duration like anything else having a cash flow stream. A liability stream will have a duration just like a bond.

In other words, immunization theory demonstrates that a single portfolio with an overall duration of five is the financial equivalent of a group of 40 bullet immunizations whose weighted average duration is also five. The manager does not have to be able to create 40 individual bullet portfolios whose average duration is five, only one portfolio whose duration is five needs to be created. As long as the kinds of yield shifts implicit in immunization theory occur, that one portfolio will finance the liabilities as well as those 40 individual bullet portfolios would.

In all likelihood, the portfolio purchased would not have bonds maturing every year. The manager would eventually have to sell some bonds to pay off liabilities, and, most certainly, he would have to manage that portfolio over time, just as he would an individual bullet portfolio. In other words, as time passes and liabilities are paid off, the duration of the liabilities would change, specifically, it would shorten. The manager would have to stay abreast of that situation, keeping the portfolio's duration equal to the duration of the liabilities while selling off bonds to pay liabilities as they come due. Typically, the duration of the liabilities, assuming a stream of periodic outflows, will shorten at a rate faster than the duration of the assets.

That is the basic concept of the duration match. It makes use of immunization theory to finance the liability stream without going to the confining extremes of a cash match. However, it is subject to the risks of a bullet immunization. If yield curve movements are of the parallel shift variety, which allow immunization to work perfectly, then there is no risk. On the other hand, if yield curve shifts are not parallel, there is some risk of not hitting the target. The same risk that is present in a bullet immunization is present when constructing a duration-matched dedicated portfolio. There is the risk, so to speak, of those 40 individual bullets. As a consequence, some managers use techniques for choosing bonds that not only assure that the duration equals the duration of the liabilities, but also assure that the maturity distribution tends to minimize the effect of nonparallel yield curve shifts.

When evaluating the risk of a duration-matched portfolio as compared with the risk of a hypothetical set of 40 bullet portfolios, it should be realized that the shape of the liability stream will have an influence on the outcome. In particular, if the liability stream is that associated with the retired lives portion of a pension fund (that is, future payments to retirees), then the duration of the liability stream likely will remain in the four- to six-year range. Consequently, the duration-matched portfolio will always have a duration in the same four- to six-year range. Therefore, the portfolio need not suffer the effects of a steeply, positively sloped yield curve to the extent that the individual bullet portfolios would. The bullet portfolios suffer in this yield the effects of a steeply positively sloped yield curve to the extent that the passage of time requiring the sale of longer-duration, higher yielding bonds and the purchase of shorter-duration, lower yielding bonds to maintain a particular duration. Duration-matched dedicated portfolios, because of the relatively constant four- to six-year duration liability stream can avoid the most steeply sloped, short-maturity end of the yield curve environment entirely, resulting in a risk exposure substantially *less* than the set of 40 bullet portfolios.

The basic concept of the duration match then, is that the manager sets up a portfolio whose duration is equal to the duration of the liabilities being financed, and he manages that duration through time so that equality continues to exist. Unlike the cash match, it is not clear how much money should be put in at the outset for the duration match. The duration concept indicates what type of portfolio a manager should buy to match the cash flows but it does not tell him how much money to put in. The manager simply takes the immunized rate applicable for the desired duration, and computes the present value of the liabilities at that rate, in order to determine the amount of money that should be used.

Advantages of Duration Match

The advantages of using a duration-match approach rather than a cash match include the following: (1) the manager has far more flexibility in choosing bonds; he is not as limited as with cash flow matching requirements; (2) the manager has far more flexibility in swap activity and rebalancing; and (3) as a general rule, the manager has an opportunity to achieve a higher expected return (net of costs, especially transaction costs) necessary to finance the liabilities. The major disadvantage is that the duration match does not eliminate risk to the same extent as the cash match, but that disadvantage may not be as important a consideration as the advantages foregone.

As a theoretical matter, to help eliminate interest rate risk within the duration-match portfolio, the manager might want to spread the maturities out so their distribution is similar to the distribution of the liabilities. If so, the distribution of the portfolio's cash inflows will be somewhat like the distribution of its cash outflows. If that process is taken to the limit, the portfolios will end up as a cash-match portfolio, which leads to the correct conclusion that a cash-match portfolio is a very special case of duration matching. The converse, however, is not true.

DECISION FACTORS SUPPORTING DEDICATION

What are the relevant factors that lead to the decision to create a dedicated portfolio? As indicated earlier, a rather cynical view has developed that dedicated portfolios have the sole objective of reducing contributions. By coincidence, most of the firms that have undertaken this technique did so in an environment of poor corporate profits when pressures were strong to raise the pension fund's actuarial rate thereby reducing pension liabilities and contributions. There is an awareness, of course, that one of the advantages of the dedicated portfolio is that it eliminates risk in a long-term sense, so that qualitatively it is a different kind of investment than "just another bond portfolio."

However, somehow, that explicit awareness of the special risk characteristics of the dedicated portfolio is often lost when evaluating its role in the overall asset mix.

The reason this circumstance exists is that the long-run objectives of the pension fund are, of necessity, attained through time by short-run variations in the asset mix. Plan sponsors fully acknowledge that the ultimate risk in a pension plan is the mismatch between the liability stream of payments—the long-run liability stream—and the long-run earning stream of the portfolio. That fact is readily admitted, but it is extremely difficult to monitor the mismatch in terms of the short-run, day-to-day asset mix. Thus, even though a plan sponsor may be aware of the fact that a dedicated portfolio has these special and highly desirable long-run risk-control characteristics, that awareness is difficult to impound in the ongoing management of the asset mix. There is not much discussion about the role of dedicated portfolios in that context. People just invest in them without saying very much about how they are treating them internally, or about how the portfolios affect their asset mix analyses.

It is very difficult to propose an encompassing analysis that will solve this problem, but a few simple principles can be identified that underscore the theoretical role of dedicated portfolios. By linking these principles, a conceptual role for them can be illustrated.

Better Funding of Pensions

First, there is a broad tendency rising out of pension law, practice, and custom for pension funds to become increasingly better funded over time. This is just one consequence of the provisions of the Employee Retirement Income Security Act (ERISA) legislation. That is, in order to qualify as a tax-exempt entity, a pension plan has to have certain minimal funding characteristics.

Reduced Risk Tolerance

Second, as pension plans become better funded, there is an increasing awareness that unless something drastic is done, like terminating the plan, the plan sponsor may always have to put more money into it but can never take any assets out. If a pension fund is fully or overfunded, there is an asymmetrical situation where large positive returns do not help all that much but huge negative returns hurt a lot. At that point, plan sponsors tend to have a highly risk-averse view that says, "Let's keep what we've got and not try for big rewards." It is akin to the investor who has only $1,000 in total assets and bets it all on stock options. However, that same person with $10 million in assets would be unlikely to put it all in stock options. There is a tendency for the person in the latter situation not to want to get a lot richer, but to just keep what he has, since uncertainty is always present.

Attaining a Locked-Up Position

The third principle is that with increasing levels of risk aversion, corporations and other investors as well are displaying a strong tendency to go toward a locked-up position, in terms of an exact locked-up return rate. For example, any person who has a child that will be in college in 10 years, can calculate what the tuition expense will be to keep that child in college. If a parent wanted to prefund that expense and was faced with the recent relatively high rate environment, would he be more likely to put the money into the stock market or to buy zero coupon bonds, which pay off exactly at the time he is going to need the money? Most people would prefer not to gamble with their children's education. If they have the resources and like the current rate, they will buy zero coupon bonds in order to have the cash when they need it. As risk aversion increases, there is an increased tendency to go toward this type of locked-up position.

The principles just discussed need to be reiterated and linked together. First, pension plans are becoming increasingly better funded. Second, as the funding level improves—and reference here is to the true economic funding level, as opposed to certain actuarial constructs—there is an increasing risk aversion which translates into, "Let's keep what we've got and not try for big rewards." And third, as risk aversion increases, there is a tendency to move toward a locked-up position.

Resulting Role for Dedication

In considering these three points, one can see an emerging role for dedicated bond portfolios. Underscoring the discussion is the acknowledged fact that the true risk in a pension plan has to do with the mismatch in the long-run of earnings and payments streams of the portfolio. In the short-run quarterly performance situation there are three major asset categories: stocks, bonds, and cash (equivalents). In this context, cash is the risk-free asset. But in the long-run analysis, which is the one that truly matters, dedicated bonds are the risk-free asset. From a straight theoretical perspective, as funding levels go up, there is an increased tendency toward lower-risk assets and, indeed, toward a locked-up position, depending upon the relative attractiveness of rates. This tendency has become clearly evident for many clients.

These observations can be converted into a funding strategy to be used in a fairly explicit context. As a pension plan grows, and the funding level improves, the proportion of assets that are dedicated are closely monitored. Other things being equal, when short-term interest rates rise, the short-term risk-free asset becomes more attractive. When long-term interest rates rise, the long-term risk-free asset—dedicated portfolios—becomes more attractive, and more funds are put into them. As the funding level rises, more dedicated assets are warranted, and as long-term interest rates rise to make bonds more attractive relative to alternative assets, more dedicated bonds are purchased.

There is an explicit awareness that risk-free assets are to be targeted against highly predictable liabilities, namely, those that are nominally fixed, and especially those that pertain to retired lives. Assets with returns that are uncertain, such as equities or actively managed bonds, are targeted for more distant liabilities that are more difficult to predict. This ongoing process, which is internally consistent, identifies the specific role of dedicated portfolios as being the long-term risk-free asset in the context of the long-term pension funding problem.

Closing Comments

In closing, it should be emphasized that a rise in interest rates is not necessarily a sufficient justification for dedicating, increasing the actuarial rate, or reducing contributions. Any actuary will point out that an increase in interest rates and actuarial assumed rates might be only due to an increase in inflation, with the result that the salary progression rate assumption would have to be similarly increased.

In adopting a long-run perspective, plan sponsors need to carefully examine all of the liabilities to be funded and the assets that are targeted for each of those liabilities. For example, if interest rates rise due to a rise in real interest rates, thereby increasing the expected return on these assets, such that the sponsor is inclined to put more money into a long-term risk-free dedicated portfolio, the sponsor should also examine related changes in the expected returns on other assets before adjusting the actuarial rate. That is, if the increase in real interest rates that made dedicated assets more attractive results in making the sponsor's real estate assets less attractive, an increase in dedicated portfolio exposure need *not* imply that the total portfolio expected return has increased, because there may be an offsetting decline in expected return on real estate, for example.

In sum, plan sponsors, with their long-term perspective, need to carefully estimate both the liabilities that will need to be funded and the return and risk characteristics of the assets to provide that funding. To the extent that a mismatch between the cash flows needed and those generated is likely, dedication and other structured techniques need to be objectively assessed in terms of their ability to solve that mismatch problem, a problem that will increasingly complicate the future pension fund management process.

ANALYSTS' QUESTIONS AND ANSWERS

Question: With duration-matching dedication, because there is more flexibility than with cash matching, the total cost might be less. Would it not follow that a lower-cost portfolio would be possible by cash matching on a quarterly basis rather than a monthly basis?

Answer: Just the contrary—one would expect a lower cost using a monthly as opposed to a quarterly match. Consider either having one quarterly payment at the beginning of a quarter, or three monthly payments on the first day of each of the three months in that quarter. This is because the present value of $1 million at January 1, is larger than the present value of $333,000 on January 1, $334,000 on February 1, and $333,000 on March 1. In that sense, a monthly match is less expensive than a quarterly one, implying that if a manager did a quarterly instead of a monthly match, he would have to pre-fund the entire quarterly payment up front. On the other hand, if the quarterly payments were pegged to occur in the middle of the quarter, as opposed to the beginning of the quarter, a quarterly cash match would have a lower cost than a monthly cash match.

Question: It has been indicated that one of the dominant tenets that under-lies the dedicated portfolio is the known future cash outlay. Would it not be faulty to assume, even on retired lives, that pension payments would remain fixed if we were to experience something like a 40 percent annual rate of inflation?

Answer: Absolutely. It is for that reason, in fact, that it is recommended that people do not try to adhere to a very precise and exact match. Although doing something very refined may produce a lower total cost and a higher estimated rate or return at the very outset, it will inhibit swapping and re-balancing activity later. A manager really does not want that; he prefers to have swapping and rebalancing abilities, since that can add so much value. Stated differently, a manager does not want to apply a very precise model to an imprecise set of numbers. There should be a balance between them. An exact knowledge of the liabilities is normally incorrect except in cases where the pension plan is spun off and there are special circumstances.

Question: In estimating the long-term reinvestment rate, does the man-ager make a single best guess or does he use sensitivity analysis to help iden-tify the most likely rate that will minimize the chance of not achieving it due to reinvestment risk?

Answer: Normally a very low rate is selected, such that the probability of the average actual reinvestment rate falling below the rate established is extremely small. It is industry practice to pick such a conservative rate that if there are any surprises, they are happy surprises.

The use of a low rate also tends to minimize the reinvestment risk. If the manager is assuming funds will be reinvested at 6 or 7 percent when bond yields are closer to 11 or 12 percent, the computer will pick bonds that ma-ture closer to the actual liability dates, as opposed to bonds maturing very much earlier that could result in a larger amount of reinvestment risk.

This is a bit of overkill in the sense that, using a very low rate avoids risk on the face of it and, in addition, tends to minimize the exposure to reinvest-ment risk.

Question: When purveyors of dedicated portfolios first went into the mar-ket place, the actuarial profession was sharply divided on whether the practice was acceptable. At present, companies accept an ongoing role for a dedicated portfolio in the total pension management picture. Does that also imply that the actuaries have accepted this as a reasonable, rational part of a total plan activity?

Answer: There has been no recent ground swell of resistance to the notion of a dedicated portfolio, primarily because people have acknowledged that, after all, dedicated portfolios are really something they might like to own. In other words, if the profession freshly minted an actuary, did not expose that person to corporate challenges and the reality of having to make a profit, and asked him what kind of portfolio he would really like to have to take care of these liabilities, that person would say, "Give me a cash-matched portfolio."

Dedication is really near and dear to actuaries' hearts, as a matter of principle. It has become clear that much of their criticism had to do with a justified fear that the cynical view of dedicated portfolios was correct; company people were using them as a device for reducing contributions and raising the effective actuarial rate when, in fact, all factors were not being taken into account. When it was mentioned that plan sponsors should consider the factors that would imply a *reduction* in the actuarial rate, as well as those that might imply an increase, it was clear that the actuaries were simply being negative on dedicated portfolios because of their fears that it would result in only a one-sided increase in the actuarial rate without any thought of the reverse occurring. In sum, much of the resistance to dedicated portfolios was not because of a disbelief in what they could accomplish, but because of a natural, human tendency to be negative about something that they feared would be incorrectly used.

Question: Does the cash-match approach offer a good definition of what the liabilities are? How many people would have to be covered to get a good reading on the liabilities? Would using duration match be a way of minimizing liabilities within a small group?

Answer: The number of people in the pool really does not have much to do with the kind of risk that really causes concern. From statistics, it is known that the number in the sample does not have to be very large before the ability to closely predict its mean becomes fairly dependable. For example, in order to predict who is going to win the election, one only has to sample a few thousand people out of 100 million voters to closely estimate the election outcome.

An actuary does not need many people in the pool to get a very good estimate of each year's mean payment, and generally it has not been a problem, particularly with retired lives.

The real risks that plan sponsors and actuaries face are from structural changes relating to the economic realities of the business, having more to do with cost-of-living adjustments, new additions to the pool, and spin-offs where blocks of liabilities are eliminated, rather than the uncertainty of the specific mortality of the people in the pool. Those risks are largely unaffected, as can be imagined, by how many people happen to be in the pool. They are different kinds of risks.

Because a duration-match portfolio is, on the face of it, far more flexible than a cash-match, it is the portfolio that should be chosen for many purposes. If a corporation is going to make modifications in the structure of the assets—for example, if it plans to sell off a block of pension assets because a certain division was spun off—then a duration match is most definitely the type of structure that should be used.

Question: If lower-rated corporate bonds are used in the analysis and the portfolio is planned on the basis of those bonds having a certain price, how can a manager be sure he will actually be able to buy them at that price when it is time to execute?

Answer: That is one area where experience with putting these kinds of portfolios in place is helpful. If the market is going in the manager's favor, trading off or unchanged, he might wait and let people know he is interested in those bonds at a particular level. Over a couple of days, someone, somehow, will usually produce the bonds at a price the manager can live with, leaving the cash uninvested in the interim.

In other situations, if the market is moving or if it represents a substantial amount of money, it is often smart to hedge by buying Treasury notes while continuing to look for the bonds wanted.

If neither of those two options seem promising, it is advisable to continue to look for substitutes. The process of discovering that something one wants is not available is almost inevitable when one of these portfolios is put in place. Even so, assuming everything is done by a competitive offering process, 80 to 90 percent of the market value of the fund can be put in place on the day the manager begins to execute. It may take a couple of days to produce the final 10 percent. On a program of $40 to $50 million, where the manager is dealing with 60, 70, or even 80 different names, two or three substitutes—maybe as many as four or five—would ultimately be employed. If he sticks with it, he will get there in good shape.

COMBINATION ACTIVE/PASSIVE STRATEGIES

This final section discusses combination active/passive fixed income portfolio management strategies in the context of the historical bond development of risk control management techniques in the area of fixed income portfolio management.

The high level of interest rates in 1981 and 1982 and again more recently was only the spark that ignited interest in these risk control strategies. The effect of these strategies on bond portfolio management will be more fundamental and long lasting than merely providing a safe harbor during brief periods of high interest rates. They provide a clear alternative to traditional, unconstrained active management, will likely change the way fixed income investment objectives are expressed, and consequently, will change the way fixed income investment performance is evaluated.

GENESIS OF RISK CONTROL TECHNIQUES

Poor Performance of Active Management

There are two basic reasons why so much attention is now being directed at risk control procedures in the fixed income area. The first, and probably most important, is that more traditional approaches to active management in the fixed income area had not worked very well. They had produced poor absolute total rates of return, as well as relative rates of return, particularly when compared to inflation and risk-free return proxies.

The five-year period, 1977 to 1981, dramatically illustrated this point to those looking at the situation in 1982. As shown in Table 9A-9, bonds proved to be quite a surprise. For example, the median bank-managed bond portfolio, as reported by the Frank Russell Company, had a total return of 3.0 percent compounded annually during this period. This compares to −1.3 percent for the Salomon Brothers Index and 10.2 percent for 90-day Treasury bills. Inflation, as represented by the Consumer Price Index, was rolling along at 10.1 percent per year.

It should be emphasized, however, that a legitimate reason to use immunization or immunization-related types of techniques should *not* be this recent performance of active management. The investment business tends to seek out the instrument or the strategy that has performed best, and avoid the poor performers of the most recent past. The use of immunization-related strategies is just one more fatal application of that tendency.

Of more importance is the fact that most fixed income managers did, indeed, achieve their *relative* performance goals, but, at the same time, suffered poor *absolute* returns. That is, the goals that were mutually established with their clients in the mid-1970s were achieved. It was common to use a goal of one or two percentage points or more in excess of a standard of comparison such as the Salomon Brothers Index or the Shearson/Lehman Government/Corporate Bond Index. They met those objectives. Yet, there was a general dissatisfaction with the investment performance of fixed income portfolios. The reason may well be that these relative investment objectives were inconsistent with the role that bonds are expected to play, that being, to generate a stable,

TABLE 9A-9. Comparative Fixed Income Rates of Return and Inflation, 1977–81

	Compound Annual Return
Median—Frank Russell Banks	3.0%
Salomon Brothers Index	−1.3
90-Day Treasury Bills	10.2
Consumers Price Index	10.1

TABLE 9A-10. Comparative Market Rates, 1976 and 1984

	December 1976	June 1984
Yield on 90-Day Treasury Bills	4.33%	10.00%
Yield on Long Governments	7.30	13.00
Consumers Price Index	4.8	4.6
(trailing 12 months)		

relatively predictable, and competitive rate of return. That role is not consistent with a relative standard of comparison that, by its very nature, is volatile and driven by a factor over which managers have very little control, the future level of interest rates.

Ability to Lock In High Rates

A second and more important reason behind the increased interest in these new tools is the unprecedented real return that can be "locked in" with these strategies.

As shown in Table 9A-10, at year-end 1976, the differential between the yield on long-term government securities and inflation was approximately 2.5 percentage points. By the third quarter of 1984, that spread was 8.4 percentage points.

Obviously, there is a great incentive for plan sponsors, as well as investment managers, to look for alternatives that can lock in these attractive real rates of return.

The allure of these large real returns is quite strong. An immunized return of 13.0 percent compounded annually could have been locked in with an all-government portfolio at the beginning of the third quarter, 1984.

Using Table 9A-10 as a reference point, choose an inflation expectation for the next two years. It is difficult enough to estimate inflation for the next six months let alone two years. But attempt a two-year projection, choosing among the three alternatives shown in Table 9A-11. Most would agree that (in late 1984) 5 percent is (was) reasonable.

The table indicates that if a manager were to immunize a portfolio at 13.0 percent for five years, and our inflation expectation of 5 percent is accurate for the next two years, inflation would then have to accelerate to an average rate of 13 percent for the ensuing three years before a real return of less than 3 percent would be earned.

If this magnitude of inflation were to increase in straight line fashion over the entire five-year period, the rate of inflation would be a staggering 17.0 percent before the 13.0 percent immunized portfolio's return fell behind. With those types of numbers, why worry about risk-oriented fixed income management?

TABLE 9A-11. Break-Even Inflation Levels

Immunized Return: 13.00 Percent
Time Horizon: Five Years

Expected Inflation Rate For Next Two Years	REQUIRED RATE OF INFLATION TO PRODUCE FIVE-YEAR 3 PERCENT REAL RETURN	
	Average in Years 3–5	Year 5 Level
3%	14.4%	20.1%
5	13.0	17.0
7	11.5	13.8

Although yield levels as this was written in November of 1984 were lower than their third quarter 1984 peaks, real yield levels are still quite large. As long as these inflation expectation premiums are high, immunization-related management will play a major role in bond portfolio management.

THE CONTINGENT IMMUNIZATION TECHNIQUE

Having laid this groundwork, now consider risk control strategies or active/passive strategies. There are a number of them. They come in all shapes and sizes, most with strange sounding names such as *contingent immunization, enhanced-duration management, enhanced immunization,* or *active immunization,* just to name a few. Marketing staffs of investment organizations have worked overtime on creative labeling in this particular area.

Rather than briefly discussing each, this section concentrates on only one: contingent immunization. It is the best known active/passive strategy, and observations made about it are similar to those that would be made about most strategies that have a combination of active and passive components.

Investment Objectives

Consider a brief statement of investment objectives under a contingent immunization framework. Such a statement normally has three components:

1. *Immunized Base Return.* The return that can be achieved with little or no active management for a specific time horizon regardless of the future direction of interest rates. From a sponsor's standpoint, it is essentially a risk-free return.
2. *Investment Objective.* A return goal in excess of the Immunized Base Return to be achieved with active management strategies.
3. *Assured Minimum Return.* A return that can be assured with the future use of immunization if active management decisions are wrong.

TABLE 9A-12. Five-Year Investment Objectives for a Contingently Immunized Treasury Bond Portfolio in Third Quarter, 1984

Investment Objective:	14.75%
Immunized Base Return:	13.00
Assured Minimum Return:	11.25

An example of these three return objectives using third quarter 1984 yield levels is illustrated in Table 9A-12.

Monitoring Analysis

The key to the successful management of contingently immunized portfolios is the implementation of an effective monitoring analysis. An example of a monitoring analysis, as of March 2, 1985, is shown in Tables 9A-13 through 9A-15.

Table 9A-13 provides a summary description of the contingently managed portfolio and the return status of the portfolio relative to the inception date, present date, and horizon date. In the return analysis section of that table, the return to date is the return actually achieved by active management since

TABLE 9A-13. Summary Description of a Contingently Immunized Portfolio

Performance Monitoring

		Actual Asset Values ($000)	Required Asset Values ($000)
Inception Date	12-30-83	$16535.	
Present Date	3- 2-84	16852.	$16776.
Horizon Date	3- 2-89		30216.
Time to Horizon	5.00 yr.		
Actual Portfolio Duration	5.69 yr.		

Asset Value Analysis

Present Actual Asset Value	$16852.	Achievable Terminal Asset Value	$30352.
Present Required Asset Value	16776.	Required Terminal Asset Value	30216.
Present Excess Asset Value	76.	Achievable Excess Terminal Asset Value	136.

Return Analysis

Return to Date	11.25% /yr.	12-30-83 to 3- 2-84
Present Immunization Target Return	12.12% /yr.	3- 2-84 to 3- 2-89
Return Achievable with Immunization Strategy	12.09% /yr.	12-30-83 to 3- 2-89
Required Return on Assets	12.00% /yr.	12-30-83 to 3- 2-89
Achievable Excess Return (Cushion)	0.09% /yr.	12-30-83 to 3- 2-89

SOURCE: Gifford Fong Associates.

the inception date. The present immunization target return is the immunized-based return or the return that could be earned between the present and horizon dates from immunization of the portfolio only, that is, not including the active management component. The return achievable with immunization strategy is the combined return from active management between the inception and present dates and from immunization between the present and horizon dates. Finally, the required return on assets is the assured minimum return or the safety net return. The *achievable excess return* is the difference or cushion between these last two returns.

Table 9A-14 evaluates the current portfolio for interest rate change sensitivity. The various scenarios of interest rate change are shown in the bottom panel of the page. In the upper panel, under sensitivity relative to asset value analysis, the column titled "Actual Asset Value" shows the actual market value of the bond portfolio under each interest rate assumed, diminishing (from actual) with higher rates and increasing with lower rates. The column titled "Required Asset Value" provides the amounts needed (as of the present date for each interest rate assumed) that, if immunized, would result in the achievement of the safety net return. The third column in this group indicates the excess of column 1 over column 2 for each interest rate. Finally, Table 9A-15 summarizes the characteristics of the optimal portfolio.

An accurate immunization target is critical in determining not only the basis for the initial problem set-up (for example, the safety net will usually be a certain basis point difference from the target over a specified time period), but also in determining what immunization levels are available during the management horizon. A safety net too close to the initial target return makes triggering the immunization process highly likely, while too low a safety net defeats the purpose of the process since the very low satisfactory minimum return would probably never trigger immunization. Finally, without an adequate monitoring procedure, the benefits of the strategy may be lost because of the inability to know when action is appropriate.

Characteristics of Objectives

There are four characteristics of this statement of investment objectives that differentiate it substantially from more traditional active management alternatives.

Based on Known Yields. As indicated in Table 9A-12, these objectives are based on known yield levels at the time the program is set up. There is no uncertainty about the rate of return objectives.

Use of Nominal Rates. These objectives are stated in nominal rates of return and not relative standards. That is, measurement relative to the Salomon Brothers Index or the Shearson/Lehman Government/Corporate Bond Index is not done.

TABLE 9A-14. Sensitivity Analysis of a Contingently Immunized Portfolio

Performance Sensitivity Analysis

Sensitivity of Achievable Portfolio Performance to Present Interest Rates

| | ASSET VALUE ANALYSIS | | | | RETURN ANALYSIS | | | |
Interest Rate Scenario	Actual Asset Value ($000)	Required Asset Value ($000)	Excess Asset Value ($000)	Scenario Modified Return to Date (%/yr.)	Estimated Immunization Target Return* (%/yr.)	Return Achievable Immunization with Strategy (%/yr.)	Required Return (%/yr.)	Achievable Excess Return (%/yr.)
Actual	16852.	16776.	76.	11.25	12.12	12.09	12.00	0.09
2	15997.	15999.	−2.	−18.20	13.13	12.00	12.00	0.00
3	17807.	17599.	208.	47.68	11.11	12.24	12.00	0.24
4	15229.	15264.	−35.	−42.26	14.13	11.95	12.00	−0.05
5	18881.	18459.	422.	93.30	10.10	12.46	12.00	0.46
6	16885.	16809.	76.	12.47	12.08	12.09	12.00	0.09

Interest Rate Scenario	Description
2	Parallel rising rate shift, 100 B.P.
3	Parallel falling rate shift, −100 B.P.
4	Parallel rising rate shift, 200 B.P.
5	Parallel falling rate shift, −200 B.P.
6	Negative (counter-clockwise) twist in interest rates

SOURCE: Gifford Fong Associates.
* Duration weighted average yield of immunized portfolio.

TABLE 9A-15. Characteristics of an Optimal Portfolio Under Contingent Immunization

Selection Criterion: Risk Minimization

Portfolio	No. of Issues	Par Value ($000)	Market Value ($000) −	Accrued Interest ($000) =	Principal Value ($000)	YIELD TO MATURITY (%) Mkt. Val. Weighted	YIELD TO MATURITY (%) Duration Weighted	Average Coupon (%)	Average Quality Rating	Average Duration (yr.)
Current	18	18000.	16851.617	444.555	16407.	12.681	12.763	11.067	AA2	5.695
Optimal	21	26118.	16750.809	137.110	16614.	12.081	12.122	4.347	AA3	5.002
Transaction Summary										
Bought	18	22225.	13738.941	110.473	13628.	12.022	12.078	3.417	AA3	5.090
Sold	17	14107.	13839.754	417.918	13422.	12.754	12.834	11.607	AA2	5.932
Held	5	3893.	3011.867	26.637	2985.	12.347	12.342	8.590	AA1	4.604

Current Portfolio Market Value ($000)	+	Initial Cash Flows ($000)	+	Required Corrections ($000)	=	Total Initial Funds ($000)	−	Transactions Costs ($000)	=	Optimal Portfolio Market Value ($000)
16851.617	+	0.0	+	0.0	=	16851.613	−	100.805	=	16750.809

Estimated standard deviation of terminal value ($000): 150.

Estimated standard deviation of target return: 10. b.p./yr.

Estimated return at confidence level of:

90%	95%	99%
11.99%	11.96%	11.89%

Estimated portfolio value on horizon date ($000): 30171.

Internal rate of return to-portfolio payments: 12.140% (compounded semi-annually)
12.508% (compounded annually)

SOURCE: Gifford Fong Associates.

Risk-Free Rate Proxy. In addition, the immunized base return can be thought of as a risk-free return, particularly if it is constructed with a call-protected government portfolio.

Time Horizon Specified. Finally, a specific time horizon is established. Note that in this particular case, it is a five-year horizon. Time horizons now typically vary from three to eight years for a contingent immunization program.

Each of these characteristics of contingent immunization serve to differentiate it from traditional active management. Investment objectives under contingent immunization focus on current market yield levels, are expressed in nominal rates of return, and use a risk-free rate of return as a standard of comparison.

Contrast With Classical Immunization

In contrast to classical immunization, contingent immunization, as well as most active/passive combination strategies, are *primarily active* strategies. There should be no confusion about that. They are not a form of immunization strategy.

Figure 9A-20 illustrates the difference between classical immunization and contingent immunization. Classical immunization assures the holder a fixed return within a narrow range for a specific period of time regardless of the future direction of interest rates.

Contingent immunization is quite different. An investment manager accepts the risk of a compound return lower than the immunized rate arising from poor active management decision making. The right side of Figure 9A-20

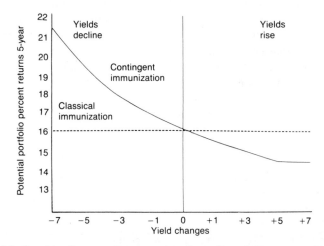

Figure 9A-20. Graphic Contrast Between the Operation of Classical and Contingent Immunization. (SOURCE: Martin Leibowitz and Alfred Weinberger, "Contingent Immunization," Salomon Brothers, Inc., Jan. 1981)

illustrates this for a holder of a 30-year bond as rates rise. In exchange, the manager can enhance the portfolio's return over and above the immunized return through good decisions. The holder of the 30-year bond happily sees his potential return improve as rates decline in Figure 9A-20, a prospect not available to the owner of an immunized portfolio.

Returns Distribution Approach. Those future return possibilities can be recast in a slightly different fashion. Specifically, they can be recast in terms of a layman's view of a normal distribution as depicted in Figure 9A-21. That is, abstract for the moment from the statistical properties and implications of a normal distribution, and instead use this figure to portray a sense of the trade-offs and alternatives available from different strategies within the fixed income sphere.

Figure 9A-21 looks forward five years from the third quarter, 1984. The distribution represents a distribution of potential fixed income mean returns from all fixed income portfolios. The immunized base return, compounded annually, represents a best estimate of the mean return for all fixed income portfolios. This is the centerpoint of the distribution.

Contingent immunization removes all possible future returns to the left of some return point of the distribution. In Figure 9A-21, that point is 11.25 percent.

In exchange for accepting the possibility of earning that worst-case return, the manager believes he can achieve 175 basis points over and above the base return. In Figure 9A-21, that return point is 14.75 percent. That is merely an estimate of what can be achieved. It could be higher, and indeed, it could be lower.

An unconstrained, actively managed portfolio can fall anywhere along the distribution, but it could very well fall painfully to the left side. In exchange for taking that risk, the manager expects to be on the right side of the distribution. Why? Because if he is not willing to make that statement, there is an alternative that can provide a more predictable rate of return, one which is contained within the restraint of contingent immunization or any other type of active/passive management strategy.

Compound annual rate of return	11.25%	13.00%	14.75%
	Minimum return	Base return	Investment objective

Figure 9A-21. Distribution of Prospective Five-Year Fixed Income Rates of Return, Third Quarter, 1984.

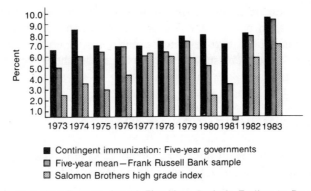

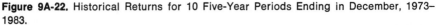

■ Contingent immunization: Five-year governments
▦ Five-year mean—Frank Russell Bank sample
▧ Salomon Brothers high grade index

Figure 9A-22. Historical Returns for 10 Five-Year Periods Ending in December, 1973–1983.

The implications of being on the left side of the distribution are serious: a major negative return surprise in the very part of the portfolio designed to provide return stability at a time when inflation and employee benefit cost pressures are increasing, a situation not unlike the recent past.

But what about the right side? It is an environment of declining interest rates, high absolute rates of return, lower pressures in terms of pension costs, and, indeed, even if the portfolio is not at the far right hand side of the distribution, the portfolio will have done quite well.

In sum, the trade-offs make a manager think carefully about whether he wants to continue with unconstrained active management when there are substantial and interesting alternatives. Note the yield levels used in the example. They are not 15 or 16 percent, but closer to 11 percent. Again, the yield level seems irrelevant, given an asset allocation decision to put at least part of the portfolio in bonds. In fact, recent history (1983-1984) suggests that initiating a contingent immunization program at relatively low levels of interest rates would have paid off fairly nicely.

Historical 5-Year Mean Returns. Figure 9A-22 illustrates the historical trailing 5-year mean returns for the period 1973 to 1983 with the underlying annual data going back to 1969. The left-most solid column for each year represents an estimate of the 5-year compound return that would have been earned by owning an immunized portfolio of government securities. The middle column for each year is the mean of the Frank Russell bank sample, and the right-most column for each year is the 5-year compound return of the Salomon Brothers High-Grade Bond Index.

In all eleven periods, an immunized portfolio would have performed in the upper half of the population of all actively managed fixed income portfolios. Why did this happen? The most important factor was simply that the environment was one of rising interest rates. The protective characteristics of this type of program worked effectively. One could even say that, if a portfolio manager had a choice between taking advantage of these protective mechanisms or not, he should prefer to do it in an environment of relatively *low* interest rates. In each of the 5-year periods when the immunized bond portfolios dominated the two benchmark portfolios, interest rates at the beginning of the period were substantially lower than where they were at the end of the period.

CONTINGENT IMMUNIZATION MECHANICS

The mechanics of contingent immunization apply to most active/passive strategies and can be used in actual decision making for a fixed income portfolio.

Setting Objectives

The set of investment objectives discussed previously is shown in Table 9A-16. To repeat some important points, they are expressed in nominal terms (third quarter 1984 yields are used in this discussion), and an arbitrary 175 basis point spread on either side of the immunized base return establishes the investment objective and minimum return.

Concept of Dollar Margin. This "return spread" between the base return and minimum return is a crucial variable in any contingent immunization program. It establishes a dollar margin of error with which the investment manager works to achieve the investment objective. The calculation of this margin is straightforward: $10,000 compounded forward at the minimum return of 11.25 percent for five years equals $17,041, but, in fact, assets can earn 13.0 percent in this example. Thus, the manager only needs $9,249, which, when compounded at 13.0 percent, will provide sufficient terminal assets to meet the minimum return objective of 11.25 percent.

The difference of $751 ($10,000 − 9,249) is the margin of error. Harshly speaking, 7.5 percent of a $10,000 portfolio could be frittered away through

TABLE 9A-16. Investment Objectives Under Contingent Immunization, Third Quarter 1984 (Time Horizon: 5 Years)

	Return Goal	Assets Required in Third Quarter 1984 to Meet Respective Dollar Targets ($000)
Investment Objective	14.75%	—
Immunized Base Return	13.00	10,000
Minimum Return	11.25	9,238

poor decisions before action would be required to protect the minimum return. Although 7.5 percent may not sound like a lot of room for error in today's markets, it is surprising just how much room it does provide.

Time Horizon Effect. There are three variables that determine how much flexibility there is in a contingently immunized approach. The first is the time horizon. Simply stated, the longer the time horizon, the more flexibility one has. That is intuitive. Mistakes can be amortized over a longer period of time.

Return Spread Effect. The second is the spread between the immunized return and the minimum return. Up to this point, a 175 basis point spread has been assumed; however, any spread could be used. The narrower the spread, the less flexibility the client is willing to give to the investment manager, or alternatively, from the perspective of the investment manager, the less flexibility he is willing to accept. At the extreme (that is, a zero spread) the manager has no management flexibility. At that point, the portfolio would be managed as an immunized portfolio.

Investment Flexibility. The final variable is the amount of investment flexibility the manager is likely to use in his active decision making. It can be expressed in terms of duration variance guidelines. That is, how long or short, in years of duration, is the manager willing to go with the portfolio relative to the duration that is required to immunize it.

One possible duration variance guideline is illustrated in Figure 9A-23 for a 5-year time horizon. The horizontal dashed lines in the vertical bars represent the duration required in successive years in a passive immunization program. The allowable spread is represented by the length of the bar in duration years (left scale) or in approximate average-maturity-equivalent years (right scale). This spread represents the fact that active decision making requires that the manager differ from the "neutral" duration position from time to time, primarily in anticipation of changing levels of interest rates.

In a properly designed contingent immunization program, the allowable range of these active duration decisions should be defined. As the range is expanded, the manager is provided more flexibility, and vice versa. It is important to note here that with a wider range of flexibility, the manager may erode his "margin of error" more quickly with an extreme portfolio duration if his rate anticipation judgment is incorrect. Table 9A-17 summarizes the cross-currents of these variables in terms of a basis point change in interest rates that would entirely use up this margin of error.

As an example, if the manager is allowed to use a spread of 175 basis points between the base return and the minimum return and a spread of four duration years around the neutral duration position, two in each direction, interest rates have to move adversely by 402 basis points before action must be taken. At that point, the margin of error would be totally eroded and the

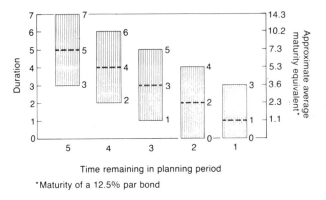

Time remaining in planning period

*Maturity of a 12.5% par bond

Figure 9A-23. Portfolio Variance Duration Guidelines Under Contingent Immunization.

portfolio would then be restructured into an immunized portfolio to protect the minimum return.

Note that this 402 basis point number is a cumulative total over the time horizon, which in this example is five years. If the portfolio loses 40 and then 60 and then 100 basis points, it has lost a cumulative total of 200 basis points. If the portfolio loses 40 and then gains 40, it is even.

Is the 402 basis point a constraining number? Probably not. With 402 basis points to work with, the manager not only has to be wrong on his interest rate forecast, he has to be wrong in the other direction by 402 basis points. A 402 basis point adverse yield change limit to force immunization should provide sufficient flexibility to an active manager under a contingent immunization framework.

TIME HORIZON AND PERFORMANCE ANALYSIS

Contingent immunization, as well as other immunization-related strategies, requires that a specific time horizon be used. It is essential to the measurement of investment performance. Unfortunately, the use of a specific time horizon exposes the portfolio to an element of reinvestment risk.

TABLE 9A-17. Adverse Yield Change to Force Immunization (Time Horizon: 5 Years)

Spread In Duration Guidelines	Immunized Base Return Less Minimum Return (Basis Point Spread)			
	200 b.p.	175 b.p.	100 b.p.	50 b.p.
±1	916	805	466	235
±2	458	402	233	118
±3	305	268	155	78

This reinvestment risk should be addressed regularly by the investment manager and plan sponsor or other client. Fortunately, performance analysis under contingent immunization addresses this reinvestment risk directly and with precision. An example might help illustrate this point.

Figure 9A-24 illustrates the progress of a portfolio relative to its immunized base return goal of 16.60 percent and a minimum return of 15.10 percent, a spread of 150 basis points. The time horizon used in this example is six years. The initial market value of the fund was approximately $17 million. The starting date was October 1, 1981. The chart covers a 13-month period of time, a period during which interest rates were generally declining. Lines 2 and 3 measure the asset values required to meet the base return and minimum return respectively. For example, $24.5 million was required on October 31, 1982 to meet the portfolio's original base return of 16.60 percent. As interest rates were falling during this period, more and more money was required to meet a fixed-dollar return goal because it was reinvested at lower and lower yield levels. Some $22.7 million was required on October 31 to meet the original minimum return goal of 15.10 percent.

The actual market value of the managed portfolio can be compared to these values to determine: (1) the contribution, either positive or negative, from active management (line 1 versus line 2) and (2) the margin of error available before the portfolio would have to be immunized to preserve the minimum return (line 1 versus line 3). The regular monitoring of a portfolio's progress against these standards will provide both the client and the manager with a series of strategy alternatives that address the continued usefulness of the original time horizon and the associated reinvestment risk.

In this example, the difference between lines 1 and 2 indicates that an excess of $1.4 million over the base return asset value has been earned from

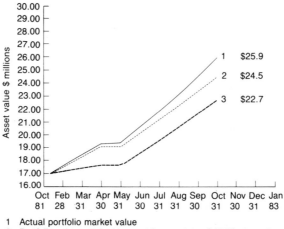

1   Actual portfolio market value
2   Portfolio value required to meet base return of 16.60 percent
3   Portfolio value required to meet minimum return of 15.10 percent

Figure 9A-24. Contingent Immunization Reporting Format, October 1, 1981 through October 31, 1982.

9A-98 MANAGING INVESTMENT PORTFOLIOS

the active management effort. Table 9A-18 presents a summary of some of the strategy alternatives that might be considered in these happy circumstances. The trade-off centers on the degree of management flexibility (risk tolerance) to be given the manager, versus a more conservative "capturing" of this premium return. Intertwined in this decision, of course, is the ever-present decision concerning an appropriate time horizon.

Alternative A

No action is taken. The initial return objective and time horizon are maintained. However, a very real decision is being made. The investment manager is provided significantly more flexibility because he has a wider margin of error. He not only has his original margin, created by the difference between the base return and the minimum return, he also has an earned premium that he can now put at risk. The plan sponsor, in effect, says he has greater confidence in his manager by placing a bigger bet on that manager. Note that the reinvestment risk at the end of the 6-year time horizon is not addressed with this alternative.

Alternative B

This alternative is fairly straightforward. The premium return of $1.4 million converts to a 6-year compound annual return improvement of 107 basis points.

TABLE 9A-18. Presentation of Fixed Income Strategy Alternatives—December 1982

Alternatives	Return Objectives		Time Period
	Base	Minimum	
A. Maintain minimum at 15.10% for original 6-year period.	17.67%	15.10%	10/1/81–9/30/87
B. Increase portfolio objectives to "lock in" premium return for original 6-year period.	17.67	16.15	10/1/81–9/30/87
C. Extend time horizon to 7 years. Link 5 year, 11 month future returns to 53.6% known portfolio return.	16.80	15.47	10/1/81–9/30/88
D. Extend time horizon to 7 years and maintain minimum return of 15.10%.	16.80	15.10	10/1/81–9/30/88

This improved return can be locked in by raising the base return and minimum return by approximately 107 basis points. When expressed in terms of Figure 9A-24, the value of the assets required to meet the base return, line 2, is increased to the market value of the actual portfolio, line 1. The minimum return portfolio value is increased by a similar amount.

Again, reinvestment risk is not addressed. Unlike alternative A, no additional flexibility is given the investment manager. This is probably the most risk averse of the alternatives presented.

Alternatives C and D

Both alternatives suggest extending the time horizon from six to seven years by linking the known total return (53.6 percent) for the past 13 months with immunized return goals for a 5-year, 11-month period of time. The only difference between alternatives C and D is the additional flexibility provided the manager in D. By keeping the minimum return at 15.10 percent in alternative D, the margin of error is expanded as it is in alternative A.

As one might imagine, a periodic review of these alternatives will focus attention on the need to progressively extend the time horizon to a more meaningful length for most institutional types of plans. In fact, quantification of investment performance and the clarity with which alternatives are presented is an important advantage of contingent immunization and other risk control strategies. Of course, the same decisions are made every day with traditional active management, but they are certainly not made with the same amount of precision.

SUMMARY

In summary, these types of approaches to fixed income management (1) provide a set of investment goals that is more useful and more consistent with the role that fixed income portfolios are intended to play in most pension, profit-sharing and endowment funds; (2) are set in nominal terms over which managers have some control, understanding, and ability to predict; (3) are particularly useful in terms of trying to make investment decisions; and (4) provide useful information in trying to analyze actual performance of fixed income portfolios.

They are certainly not superior to active management or immunization. They merely represent an alternative that sponsors and money managers should consider as they do other investment tools in the fixed income area.

ANALYSTS' QUESTIONS AND ANSWERS

Question: Is there the risk that, over a 5-year time horizon, there would always be so much market volatility that most of the time the manager would be forced to immunize and be locked into the minimum return and thereby consistently miss return opportunities?

Answer: Probably not if investment flexibility, via specific duration variance guidelines, is properly established at the outset. In fact, if a spread as large as 300 to 400 basis points is allowed and immunization is triggered, a manager probably deserves to be locked into a passive portfolio.

There is only a small probability that a manager would be forced to immunize a portfolio if he employs the investment guidelines suggested in this section of this chapter. It should be added that, once the portfolio is immunized, it is immunized for the remainder of the horizon period. The profit opportunities from active trading with a fixed duration constraint are very limited. It is unrealistic to expect a manager to add substantial value within an immunized portfolio framework.

Question: As the time horizon unfolds and duration flexibilities get more and more narrow, does the manager not have a real problem to deal with? Should the behavior of the active manager change and, if so, how? That is, should these guidelines be allowed to dramatically affect a manager's investment strategy? Or should he just actively manage and if the portfolio has to be immunized, so be it?

Answer: To some extent the guidelines must affect a manager's strategy, if the goals of contingent immunization are to be met. The problem can be addressed via a discussion of possible changes with the client. One possible change the manager might ask the client to consider is an extension of the time horizon another five or six years. In fact, that is what traditional active managers are likely to do. In these client meetings, historical performance is discussed, and the client is informed that the portfolio is to be structured with a specific duration, but no one has any real sense of the magnitude of the bet being placed under contingent immunization. That is, for each of the alternatives in Table 9A-18, the sponsor does not know how well the portfolio is going to do. With contingent immunization, however, the sponsor *is* provided with a more accurate measure of the *riskiness* of a given portfolio strategy. In this connection, the sponsor must understand that decisions affecting the time horizon are an important part of contingent immunization, perhaps as important as investment management decisions.

Question: What happens if the sponsor wants to keep the time horizon constant, for example, at four years?

Answer: That is quite different from contingent immunization, and is known as a constant duration portfolio. The most important difference is that nominal return standards cannot be used.

FURTHER READING

For an alternate treatment of many of the topics in this chapter, see Fong and Fabozzi (especially for Fong's pioneering work in active bond portfolio management) [1985], Leibowitz [1979] and Logue [1984]. For more on duration and its uses, the reader should see Bierwag, Kaufman and Toevs [1983] and [1984] and Kalotay [1985]. Immunization bond portfolio management strategies are explained in Babbel [1984], Fong and Vasichek [1983] and [1984], Leibowitz [1982], McEnally [1980] and, especially, Granito [1983]. Dedicated management is covered in Leibowitz [1985], Leibowitz, et al. [1984], and Leibowitz and Weinberger [1981]. Active management is the primary topic in Barnes, Johnson and Shannon [1984], Billingham [1983], Lane [1979], Meyer [1978], and Stock [1982]. Contingent immunization is elaborated on in Leibowitz and Weinberger [January 1981], [Fall 1981], [1982], and [1983]. Contingent insurance portfolio management strategies are discussed in Platt and Latainer [1984]. The material in this chapter is now beginning to appear in investments textbooks; one of the best treatments to date is in Reilly [1985].

BIBLIOGRAPHY

Ascher, Leonard W., "Selecting Bonds for Capital Gains," *Financial Analysts Journal,* March/April 1971.

Babbel, David F., "Real Immunization with Indexed Bonds," *Financial Analysts Journal,* November/December 1984.

Barnes, Tom, Keith Johnson and Don Shannon, "A Test of Fixed Income Strategies," *The Journal of Portfolio Management,* Winter 1984.

Bierwag, G. O., G. G. Kaufman, R. Schweitzer, and A. Toevs, "The Art of Risk Management in Bond Portfolios," *Journal of Portfolio Management,* Spring 1981.

——— and ———, "Duration Gap for Financial Institutions," *Financial Analysts Journal,* March/April 1985.

———, ———, and A. Toevs, "Duration: Its Development and Use in Bond Portfolio Management," *Financial Analysts Journal,* July/August 1984.

———, ———, and ———, eds., *Innovations in Bond Portfolio Management: Duration Analysis and Immunization,* Greenwich, Conn.: JAI Press, 1983.

———, ———, **Robert L. Schwitzer, and Alden Toevs,** "The Art of Risk Management in Bond Portfolios," *Journal of Portfolio Management,* Spring 1981.

Billingham, Carol J., "Strategies for Enhancing Bond Portfolio Returns," *Financial Analysts Journal,* May/June, 1983.

Brennan, Michael J. and Eduardo S. Schwartz, "Bond Pricing and Market Efficiency," *Financial Analysts Journal,* September/October 1982.

Dietz, P., H. R. Fogler, and A. Rivers, "Duration, Nonlinearity, and Bond Portfolio Performance," *Journal of Portfolio Management,* Spring 1981.

———, ———, **and D. Hardy,** "The Challenge of Analyzing Bond Portfolio Returns," *Journal of Portfolio Management,* Spring 1980.

Fabozzi, Frank J. and Irving M. Pollack, eds., *The Handbook of Fixed Income Securities,* Homewood, Ill.: Dow Jones-Irwin, 1983.

Fong, H. Gifford and Oldrich A. Vasicek, "A Risk Minimizing Strategy for Portfolio Immunization," *The Journal of Finance,* December 1984.

—— and ——, "The Tradeoff Between Return and Risk in Immunized Portfolios," *Financial Analysts Journal,* September/October 1983.

——, **C. Pearson, and O. Vasicek,** "Bond Performance: Analyzing Sources of Return," *Journal of Portfolio Management,* Spring 1983.

——, "Active Strategies for Managing Bond Portfolios," in D. L. Tuttle, ed., *The Revolution in Techniques for Managing Bond Portfolios,* Charlottesvillle, Va.: The Institute of Chartered Financial Analysts, 1983.

—— and **Frank J. Fabozzi,** *Fixed Income Portfolio Management,* Homewood, Ill.: Dow Jones-Irwin, 1985.

Granito, Michael R., *Bond Portfolio Immunization,* Lexington, Mass.: Lexington Books, 1984.

——, "Managing Bonds with Dedicated Portfolios," in D. L. Tuttle, ed., *The Revolution in Techniques for Managing Bond Portfolios,* Charlottesville, Va.: The Institute of Chartered Financial Analysts, 1983.

Gross, William H., "Coupon Valuation and Interest Rate Cycles," *Financial Analysts Journal,* July/August 1979.

Hawawini, Gabriel A., ed., *Bond Duration and Immunization: Early Developments and Recent Contributions,* New York: Garland Publishing, 1982.

Homer, Sidney and Martin L. Leibowitz, *Inside the Yield Book: New Tools for Bond Market Strategy,* Englewood Cliffs, N.J.: Prentice-Hall, 1972.

Hopewell, Michael H. and George C. Kaufman, "Bond Price Volatility and Term to Maturity: A Generalized Respecification," *American Economic Review,* September 1973.

Kalotay, Andrew J., "The After-tax Duration of Original Issue Discount Bonds," *Journal of Portfolio Management,* Winter 1985.

Klaffky, T., "Coupon Stripping: The Theoretical Spot Rate Curve," Salomon Brothers, Inc., October 1982.

——, "The New World of Coupon Stripping," Salomon Brothers, Inc., August 1982.

Kritzman, Mark, "Can Bond Managers Perform Consistently?" *Journal of Porfolio Management,* Summer 1983.

Lane, Morton, "Fixed Income Managers Must Time the Market!" *Journal of Portfolio Management,* Summer 1979.

Leibowitz, Martin L., "Matched-Funding Techniques: The Dedicated Bond Portfolio in Pension Funds," Salomon Brothers, Inc., February 1985.

——, "Pros and Cons of Immunization," Salomon Brothers, Inc., January 1980.

——, "Goal Oriented Bond Portfolio Management," *Journal of Portfolio Management,* Summer 1979.

——, **et al.,** "Horizon Matching: A New Approach to Dedicated Portfolios," *Journal of Portfolio Management,* Fall 1984.

—— and **Alfred Weinberger,** "Contingent Immunization-Part II: Risk Control Procedures," *Financial Analysts Journal,* January/February 1983.

—— and ——, "Contingent Immunization-Part II: Problems Areas," *Financial Analysts Journal,* November/December 1982.

—— and ——, "Risk Control Procedures Under Contingent Immunization," Salomon Brothers, Inc., February 1982.

—— and ——, "The Uses of Contingent Immunization," *Journal of Portfolio Management,* Fall 1981.

—— and ——, "Optimal Cash Flow Matching: Minimum Risk Bond Portfolios for Fulfilling Prescribed Schedules of Liabilities," Salomon Brothers, Inc., August 1981.

—— and ——, "Contingent Immunization: A New Procedure for Structured Active Management," Salomon Brothers, Inc., January 1981.

Logue, Dennis E. (ed.), *Handbook of Modern Finance.* Boston and New York: Warren, Gorham & Lamont, 1984.

Macaulay, Fredrick R., *Some Theoretical Problems Suggested by the Movement of Interest Rates, Bond Yields and Stock Prices in the United States Since 1856,* New York: National Bureau of Economic Research, 1938.

Maginn, John L. and Donald L. Tuttle, *Managing Investment Portfolios: A Dynamic Process,* Sponsored by the Institute of Chartered Financial Analysts. New York: Warren, Gorham & Lamont, Inc., 1983.

McEnally, Richard W., "How to Neutralize Reinvestment Rate Risk, *Journal of Portfolio Management,* in Berstein, P. (ed.), *Theory and Practice of Bond Portfolio Management,* 1980.

——, "Rethinking Our Thinking About Interest Rates," *Financial Analysts Journal,* March/April 1985.

—— **and Calvin M. Boardman,** "Aspects of Corporate Bond Portfolio Diversification," *The Journal of Financial Research,* Spring 1979.

Meyer, Kenneth R., "Forecasting Interest Rates: Key to Active Bond Management," *Financial Analysts Journal,* November/December 1978.

——, "Managing Bond Portfolios with Combination Active/Passive Strategies," in D. L. Tuttle, ed., *The Revolution in Techniques for Managing Bond Portfolios,* Charlottesville, Va.: The Institute of Chartered Financial Analysts, 1983.

Nemerever, William L., "Managing Bond Portfolios Through Immunization Strategies," in D. L. Tuttle (ed.), *The Revolution in Techniques for Managing Bond Portfolios,* Charlottesville, Va.: The Institute of Chartered Financial Analysts, 1983.

Pantages, Jeffrey B., " 'Active' Dedicated Portfolio Is Not Without Its Pitfalls," *Pension & Investments Age,* September 3, 1984.

Platt, Robert B. and Gary D. Latainer, "Risk-Return Tradeoffs of Contingent Insurance Strategies for Active Bond Portfolios," *Financial Analysts Journal,* May/June 1984.

Redington, F. M., "Review of the Principle of Life Office Valuations," *Journal of the Institute of Actuaries,* 78:1952.

Reilly, Frank K., *Investment Analysis and Portfolio Management,* Second Edition, Chicago: The Dryden Press, 1985.

—— **and Rupinder S. Sidhu,** "The Many Uses of Bond Duration," *Financial Analysts Journal,* July/August, 1980.

Richards, R. M., D. R. Fraser, and J. C. Groth, "The Attractions of Closed-end Bond Funds," *Journal of Portfolio Management,* Winter 1982.

Roll, Richard, "After-tax Investment Results from Long-term vs. Short-term Discount Coupon Bonds," *Financial Analysts Journal,* January/February 1984.

Sharpe, William F., *Investments,* Third Edition, Englewood Cliffs, N.J.: Prentice-Hall, 1985.

Stock, Duane, "Does Active Management of Municipal Bond Portfolios Pay?" *Journal of Portfolio Management,* Winter 1982.

Trainer, Francis H., David A. Levine, and Jonathan A. Reiss, "A Systematic Approach to Bond Management in Pension Funds," *Journal of Portfolio Management,* Spring 1984.

Tuttle, Donald L., ed., *The Revolution in Techniques for Managing Investment Portfolios,* Charlottesville, Va.: The Institute of Chartered Financial Analysts, 1983.

Van Horne, James, *Financial Market Rates and Flows,* Second Edition, Englewood Cliffs, N.J.: Prentice-Hall, 1984.

Weinstein, Mark I, "The Systematic Risk of Corporate Bonds," *Journal of Financial and Quantitative Analysis,* September 1981.

———, "Bond Systematic Risk and the Option Pricing Model," *Journal of Finance,* December 1983.

APPENDIX
The Computation of Duration

Duration is a weighted-average term to maturity-type measure where the cash flows are stated in present value terms and the weights are the numbers of the time periods when the cash flows will occur. In equation form, Macaulay's duration is

$$
\text{Duration} = \frac{\dfrac{\text{Present value of}}{\text{period 1 cash flow}} \times 1}{\dfrac{\text{Present value of}}{\text{total cash flow}}} + \frac{\dfrac{\text{Present value of}}{\text{period 2 cash flow}} \times 2}{\dfrac{\text{Present value of}}{\text{total cash flow}}}
$$

$$
+ \cdots + \frac{\dfrac{\text{Present value of}}{\text{period N cash flow}} \times N}{\dfrac{\text{Present value of}}{\text{total cash flow}}}
$$

$$
= \frac{\text{Present value of}}{\text{period 1 cash flow}} \times 1 + \frac{\text{Present value of}}{\text{period 2 cash flow}} \times 2
$$

$$
+ \cdots + \frac{\text{Present value of}}{\text{period N cash flow}} \times N \quad \frac{\text{Present value of}}{\text{total cash flow}}
$$

where the present value of the total cash flow is identical to the bond's current market price.

Assuming semiannual interest payments and no call or sinking fund features, the cash flow for a bond for periods 1 to $N - 1$ is one-half the annual coupon rate in dollars. In period N, both the semiannual coupon and the principal or face value of the bond are received. The discount rate used to calculate the present values is the bond's promised yield or yield to maturity. The resulting computation produces a duration value in half years; to obtain duration in full years, divide the half years duration value by 2.

The illustration below shows an example of a duration calculation for a 13 percent coupon bond with eight years to maturity and selling for $1168.50 to yield 9 percent. The duration for this bond is 5.57 years.

Period	Cash Flow	PV at 4.5%	Present Value Cash Flow	Present Value Cash Flow × Period
1	$60	.9569	$ 57.414	$ 57.414
2	60	.9157	54.942	109.884
3	60	.8763	52.578	157.734
4	60	.8386	50.316	201.264
5	60	.8025	48.150	240.750
6	60	.7679	46.074	276.444
7	60	.7348	44.088	308.616
8	60	.7032	42.192	337.536
9	60	.6729	40.374	363.366
10	60	.6439	38.634	386.340
11	60	.6162	36.972	406.692
12	60	.5897	35.382	424.584
13	60	.5643	33.858	440.154
14	60	.5400	32.400	453.600
15	60	.5167	31.002	465.030
16	1060	.4945	524.170	8386.720
Total			$1168.546	$13016.128

$$\text{Duration in half years} = \frac{13016.128}{1168.546} = 11.1387$$

$$\text{Duration in full years} = \frac{11.1387}{2} = 5.5694$$

Part VI

Enhancement of Portfolio Management Via Futures and Options [New]

CHAPTER 16

The Market for Futures and Options Contracts

David M. Dunford, CFA

Robert W. Kopprasch, CFA

INTRODUCTION

The growth of the financial futures and options markets has been rapid both in terms of size and liquidity. The underlying market value of bond and stock futures traded regularly exceeds the market value of actual stocks and bonds traded on a daily basis. Similar size and liquidity characteristics are observable in the options market, particularly the markets for options on individual stocks. The more recent markets for options on fixed income instruments, stock indexes, and stock market subgroups are in general displaying sustainable and growing liquidity.

The broad range of possible strategic uses of fixed income and equity futures and options in portfolio management indicates continued rapid growth over the foreseeable future. The role of options and futures as strategy tools should be viewed within the total process of portfolio management where maximum investment returns are sought within a predetermined appropriate investment risk exposure or risk pattern. Futures and options are important investment instruments that contribute to return by facilitating strategic portfolio moves and by controlling risk in a timely, cost-effective manner.

This chapter and Chapters 17 and 18 discuss the characteristics of the various futures and options contracts and review various applications of these new instruments in portfolio management. The chapter begins with a brief overview of the general strategies and techniques for maximizing portfolio return, and the role options and futures can play within the fixed income and equity portfolio management process in maximizing portfolio return. Next, a description of the various contracts available as of October 1985 is provided. Finally, the trading mechanics for each basic contract type are discussed. Chapter 17 treats the valuation techniques for the new instruments, first for futures contracts and then for option contracts.

Chapter 18 follows with a discussion of the basic uses of futures and options in modifying and controlling portfolio risk. The emphasis here is on the difference in risk modification between a future and an option in a portfolio context. The remainder of the chapter is devoted to a discussion of the uses of these new instruments in managing fixed income and equity portfolios. The section on uses starts with a detailed discussion of utilizing options and futures in asset allocation. This discussion is based on, and is an extension of, the material on asset allocation in Chapter 8 of the main volume. Next, the specific strategic uses in fixed income portfolio management are addressed. Finally, the strategic uses in equity portfolio management are reviewed.

The utilization of futures and options in portfolio management is still in its infancy. It is likely that many new contracts and strategic portfolio applications will be developed in the future. This chapter is meant to provide a framework within which new options and futures contracts may be properly analyzed and utilized in the portfolio management process.

HISTORY AND RATIONALE OF OPTIONS AND FUTURES DEVELOPMENT

Before describing either the fixed income or equity offerings of futures and options, it is useful to make some observations regarding the history and rationale of the two markets. Both futures and options evolved quite differently, with the result that there are wide differences in the contracts that are available.

Organized exchanges began trading options on equities in 1973, while exchange-traded debt options did not appear until 1982. On the other hand, fixed income futures began trading in 1975, but equity-related futures did not begin until 1982. When the nature of the markets are compared, one can immediately discern some differences that could have led to this difference in evolution. It should also be remembered that the exchanges introduce contracts that they think will be successful, and thus contract design is also a function of marketing. At this point, it would be useful to explore the reasons why and when certain of the new instruments appeared on the money and capital markets scene.

In the equity market, a relatively large proportion of the total risk of a security is unsystematic. At the same time, many equities exhibit a high degree of liquidity that (in the absence of epochal events such as takeovers) can be expected to be maintained for long periods of time—liquidity in the sense of being able to buy and sell relatively large amounts quickly without substantial price concessions. These two factors—large unsystematic risk and liquidity—

point toward the success and viability of trading equity options on individual securities.

For the contracts to have been successful, the underlying securities had to be traded "in large size" (that is, with large volume) and with price continuity so that option-related transactions would not cause more than minor disturbances in the market. In addition, the perpetual nature of common stock, an instrument with no maturity date, meant that successful options could remain on the exchanges for a potentially long time. Furthermore, over-the-counter (OTC) trading in equity options had been in existence for several decades, so the exchanges merely formalized (and certainly enhanced) a form of trading that already existed.

In the debt market, a much larger proportion of the total risk of securities is systematic—risk that cannot be eliminated by diversification within the debt market. Debt instruments are also finite life securities with limited marketability due to their small size relative to many common stocks. These factors favor, for the purpose of both portfolio hedging and speculation, the introduction of a derivative security that is based on some broader market than an individual security. When the Chicago Board of Trade (CBT) designed the Government National Mortgage Association (GNMA or Ginnie Mae) mortgage-backed bond futures contract, it recognized that there already existed a "forward" market in mortgage-backed securities, and, similar to what had been done in the equity market, the exchange simply standardized the terms to facilitate organized trading. Yet, at the same time, it would not have been wise to require delivery of only one security because of supply problems, and the GNMA contract offered a "market basket" type delivery mechanism allowing sellers of the contract to deliver a variety of eligible GNMA instruments. When Treasury bond futures contracts were introduced, they also contained a market basket delivery mechanism.

In the debt market, exchange trading of options did not begin until 1982, but options had existed in a nonseparable form for a considerable length of time. Bonds with conversion features are obvious examples. Call features on bonds represent a disguised form of option, at least from the point of view of the issuer, not separable from the underlying bond, but an option nevertheless. Mortgages represent a subset of callable bonds, because the mortgagee's right to prepay a mortgage is simply the right to call it at par. Investors were also able to purchase nonseparable options in the form of putable bonds, or bonds with a put option feature, that were issued by a number of finance companies and municipalities. These bonds allowed the investor to put the bond (that is, sell it) back to the issuer (usually at par) prior to the stated maturity date. Likewise, some Canadian bonds had extendable or retractable maturity provisions.

However, none of these options could be traded separately by the investor, and the ability to buy a debt option did not exist until December, 1980, when the Kingdom of Sweden issued a note that contained detachable warrants. These warrants (calls) allowed the investor to buy another note at par even if rates had declined. After the success of this issue, an avalanche of similar issues were sold. In addition, several large dealers in government securities also sold OTC options on Treasury issues, with the result that the market became accustomed to OTC trading in options. Thus, when exchange trading in debt options began in 1982, the exchanges once again only formalized the trading that had been taking place for several years, and the securities did not represent a totally new instrument.

The options that were introduced in the debt market included both options on actual bonds on the Chicago Board Options Exchange (CBOE) and options on futures on the CBT. The options on futures have been a resounding success, but those on actual bonds have experienced lower trading volume.

All of the options and futures mentioned thus far have an actual physical delivery required if the futures or option transaction has not been offset or reversed prior to expiration or delivery. However, when the Kansas City Board of Trade designed the futures contract on the Value Line (common stock market) Index, it provided for cash settlement instead. It would have been extremely difficult to require physical delivery of a portfolio representing the index. Cash settlement allowed the economic consequences of the trade to prevail without requiring vast restructuring of portfolios.

More important to this discussion, however, is the fact that the contract was based on an index, rather than on individual securities. It was relatively easy in the debt market to provide conversion factors to allow delivery of different Treasury bonds to satisfy that contract, because all of the eligible bonds had similar maturity and credit risk characteristics. It would be an extremely difficult if not impossible task to design a system of substitution for individual common stocks if the contract called for actual delivery of one of several stocks.

Along these same lines, by late 1984, trading in domestic CD futures contracts had dropped considerably. One problem with the CD contract is that it calls for physical delivery from a market basket of securities, but similar to the previous common stock example, the securities are not homogeneous because of potential credit risk problems with the banks on the allowable list. By contrast, the Eurodollar contract had become the most active short-term contract, largely because it requires cash settlement. Because it is a clean and direct way to determine profits and losses, it is likely that more contracts will have this settlement feature, especially if the underlying securities are not well adaptable to physical delivery. Having identified the broad groups of futures and options contracts available in the marketplace, it would be instructive to learn, in a basic sense, how these contracts are used by each of the three generic types of portfolio managers described below.

FUTURES AND OPTIONS IN THE PORTFOLIO PROCESS

There are three general techniques or strategies for maximizing the risk/return tradeoff in managing portfolios: passive, active, and semiactive. All three strategies or techniques as applied to fixed income and equity portfolio management are covered in depth in Chapter 9A of this Update and Chapter 10 of the main volume.

Another form of semiactive portfolio management that can play an important role is the various *insurance* strategies involving option contracts. The portfolio benefits of insurance arise from two sources: (1) the ability to shape return patterns of the portfolio to more precisely reflect an investor's utility function and (2) the potential to advantageously buy or sell insurance that is mispriced. Options perform this insurance function and all option activity is some variation of it. A portfolio manager buys insurance if options are purchased and sells insurance if options are sold.

Applications of option buying strategies include: (1) buying put options on securities in a portfolio and (2) buying call options with a small portion of a portfolio's funds while holding the remaining assets in cash equivalents. Applications of option selling strategies include overwriting, or selling, call options on securities held in either an actively managed portfolio or in a passive index fund.

All the strategies and techniques encompassed in these three general categories—passive, active and semiactive—have to be executed. Both observable and unobservable costs are incurred during execution. The contribution a strategy or technique makes to maximizing portfolio return must be calculated net of execution costs. Since there can be considerable loss of return depending upon the amount of activity necessary, the apparent expected returns of some portfolio moves may not be capturable because of execution costs.

A number of trading techniques have been developed that involve buying or selling large stock and bond positions at, or very near, existing market prices. Transaction costs have been minimized to a significant extent. Chapter 12 in the main volume presents an indepth discussion of the costs of execution.

A second method of executing strategic judgments and techniques involves futures contracts instead of the underlying securities. This is the important role that futures can play in a strategic sense in a portfolio. Futures offer an alternative technique to buying or selling stocks or bonds or to increase or decrease bond or stock exposure.

Both futures and options importantly contribute to the portfolio process by providing a means to manage portfolio risk while minimizing execution delay and costs. When using futures contracts and options contracts to modify portfolio risk, a distinction is made between hedging uses and speculative uses. In general, hedging uses are those uses of futures and options that serve to reduce the risk of a portfolio. By contrast, speculative uses are those where the risk of a portfolio is increased.

Although there may be some question as to whether certain portfolio uses of futures and options should be classified as hedges or speculations, most uses tend to be clearly identifiable as one or the other. Most of the portfolio applications, discussed in much greater detail in Chapter 18, are of the hedge variety.

TYPES OF NEW INSTRUMENTS

The types of new instruments covered here are severalfold and are discussed in the following order: (1) futures contracts on individual fixed income securities, (2) futures on fixed income indexes, (3) option contracts on futures on individual fixed income securities, (4) options on (actual) individual fixed income securities, (5) futures on common stock indexes, (6) options on futures on stock indexes, (7) options on stock indexes and subindexes, and (8) options on individual stocks.

FUTURES CONTRACTS ON INDIVIDUAL FIXED INCOME SECURITIES

Futures contracts have been traded on fixed income securities since 1975, yet there are only six different contracts currently trading. This is likely due to the nature of the fixed income market (high correlation of price movement or returns among securities) and the broad coverage that becomes available with only a limited range of contracts. The contracts available, summarized briefly in Table 16-1, cover short, intermediate, and long maturities in the Treasury and government-related market, with two other private credit instruments (Domestic CDs and Eurodollar Deposits) in the short-term sector.

Futures Contracts on Treasury Securities

The highest volume contract on a Treasury instrument is the Treasury bond contract traded on the Chicago Board of Trade. The high degree of liquidity provided by this contract makes it a favorite of hedgers, outright speculators, and basis traders, who try to profit from expected changes in the price difference between a futures contract and the actual underlying physical commodity (the basis), in this case the Treasury bond. Hedgers of Treasury bonds, corporates, and even mortgages use this contract because of the high correlation of its returns with returns on most long-term debt instruments. Figure 16-1 shows the volume of trading in the contract between early 1980 and mid-1984, compared with the volume in the underlying Treasury bonds in the cash market.

The bond contract is based on delivery of a nominal 8 percent Treasury bond with at least 15 years to maturity or first (earliest possible) call. Actual physical delivery is required of all short positions not closed out prior to the end of trading. Consequently, all long positions must take actual delivery if the long position is not closed out before trading in the contract ceases. The actual invoice price on delivery is based on the settlement price of the contract on the day notice to deliver is given (or on the final contract settlement price if trading has ended) multiplied by a *conversion factor* designed to adjust

TABLE 16-1. Futures Contract Specifications for Selected Debt Securities and the Municipal Bond Index

Contract	Exchange	Contract Volume 10/9/85	Contract Size	Minimum Price Fluctuation	INITIAL MARGIN	
					Hedgers	Speculators
Treasury Bond	CBT[a]	148,718	$ 100,000	1/32 = $31.25	$2,000	$2,500
Treasury Note	CBT	8,706	$ 100,000	1/32 = $31.25	$1,500	$2,000
Treasury Bill	IMM[b]	5,837	$1,000,000	.01 = $25	$1,000	$1,000
GNMA 8% CDR	CBT	131	$ 100,000	1/32 = $31.25	$2,000	$2,500
Domestic CD	IMM	8	$1,000,000	.01 = $25	$1,000	$1,000
Eurodollar Deposit	IMM	28,465	$1,000,000	.01 = $25	$1,000	$1,000
Muni Bond Index	CBT	1,890	$1,000 × Bond Buyer Muni Bond Index	1/32 = $31.25	$1,500	$2,000

CBT = Chicago Board of Trade
IMM = International Monetary Market
  CD = Certificate of Deposit
CDR = Collateralized Depositary Receipt

[a] Treasury bond futures contracts, $50,000 in size, also trade on the MidAmerica Commodity Exchange (MCE); 10/9/85 estimated volume was 900 contracts.
[b] Treasury bill futures contracts, $500,000 in size, also trade on the MCE; 10/9/85 estimated volume was 110 contracts.

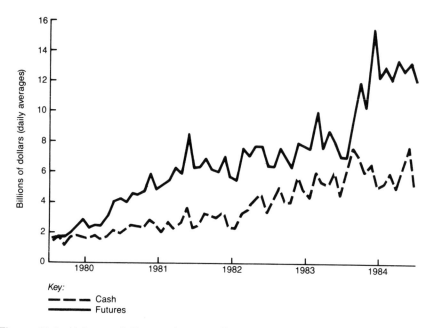

Figure 16-1. Volume of Transactions in Treasury Bonds, Mid-1979 to Mid-1984. (SOURCE: Salomon Brothers, Inc.)

for the actual coupon (versus the nominal 8 percent assumed) on the bond delivered. A table of deliverable Treasury bond conversion factors for a recent month is shown in Table 16-2. This adjustment process is explained further in the section in Chapter 17 on pricing and the *cash and carry*. As in the cash market, accrued interest must be paid by the buyer. Prices of bond futures contracts are quoted in points and 32nds, so that 72-05 represents 72 5/32, or 72.15625, or in actual dollars, $721.56.

Treasury note futures contracts, also traded on the Chicago Board of Trade, are based on the same pricing mechanism (8 percent nominal coupon rate with the application of a conversion factor at delivery) as the bond contract. The contract specifications are virtually identical except that the allowable maturity ranges from 6½ to 10 years instead of the minimum 15 years of the bond contract. Volume in the note contract is not as high as the bond contract, but is high enough that all but large hedging programs can access this market without liquidity problems.

The Treasury bill contract was, for many years, the only viable contract on a short-term instrument, and was used for *cross-hedging* (that is, approximation hedging) commercial paper, domestic CDs, and deposit liabilities such as thrift money market CDs. Because most hedgers were attempting to hedge private credit-related instruments, the appearance of the CD and Eurodollar Deposit contracts diverted some of the volume away from the bill contract. Nevertheless, the bill contract remains viable and liquid. This is demonstrated by Figure 16-2, which compares volume in the bill futures contract with volume in the cash market.

TABLE 16-2. Selected Deliverable Treasury Bond Conversion Factors as of March 1985

Coupon	Issue Date	Maturity	Sep 85	Dec 85	Mar 86	Jun 86
7-5/8	2/15/77	Feb 15 2002-07	.9660	.9665	.9666	.9670
7-7/8	11/15/77	Nov 15 2002-07	.9885	.9884	.9887	.9885
8-3/4	11/15/78	Nov 15 2003-08	1.0709	1.0702	1.0700	1.0693
9-1/8	5/15/79	May 15 2004-09	1.1077	1.1068	1.1064	1.1055
10-3/8	11/15/79	Nov 15 2004-09	1.2300	1.2284	1.2273	1.2257
11-3/4	2/15/80	Feb 15 2005-10	1.3649	1.3631	1.3608	1.3589
12-3/4	11/17/80	Nov 15 2005-10	1.4701	1.4673	1.4651	1.4623
13-7/8	5/15/81	May 15 2006-11	1.5873	1.5840	1.5814	1.5780
15-3/4	10/7/81	Nov 15 2001	1.6926	1.6867	1.6816	1.6755
14	11/16/81	Nov 15 2006-11	1.6056	1.6024	1.5998	1.5965
12	8/15/83	Aug 15 2008-13	1.4158	1.4144	1.4124	1.4110
13-1/4	5/15/84	May 15 2009-14	1.5524	1.5500	1.5482	1.5458

SOURCE: *The Financial Futures Professional,* Marketing Department, Chicago Board of Trade, November 1984, Vol. 8, No. 11.

As in the case with note and bond contracts, the bill contract calls for physical delivery (in this case, of 3-month Treasury bills) if the contracts are not closed out prior to delivery. Delivery is essentially constrained to one day in the contract month, in contrast to the note and bond contracts that allow delivery anytime during the delivery month. The price quote in the bill futures market is 100 minus the annualized discount rate. Thus, a price of 90 on a 90-day bill reflects a discount rate of 10 percent, and the delivery price could be computed as for any Treasury bill. The price discount for a Treasury bill is equal to $10,000 times the discount rate, in decimal terms, times a fraction equal to the number of days to maturity divided by 360. For the example cited, this would be $10,000 times .10 times 90/360 equals $250. Then, price equals 100 minus the price discount. In the example, $10,000 minus $250 equals $9750.

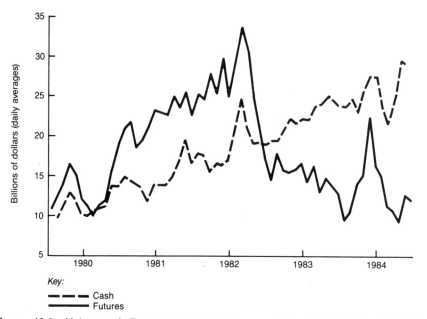

Figure 16-2. Volume of Transactions in Treasury Bills, Mid-1979 to Mid-1984. (SOURCE: Salomon Brothers, Inc.)

Futures Contracts on Government-Related Securities

The current GNMA Collateralized Deposit Receipt (CDR) contract offers a mortgage-related security that is often used for hedging in the mortgage market. The contract design does not, however, force the futures to closely follow the "current" coupon mortgage market, and this introduces problems to both hedgers and speculators. The primary reason why the contract fails to follow the current coupon market is a result of mortgage price action above a price of par. Mortgages tend to "stall" somewhat above par because they are "callable" (by the homeowner) at par. That is, the borrower has the right to prepay the mortgage in order to refinance the property or because the property was sold. Thus, the highest coupon GNMAs tend to trade "cheap," at a lower price and a higher yield than lower coupon GNMAs. They can be purchased for delivery into the futures contract for a smaller total outlay than current coupons, so the contract tends to follow the high coupon cheap market more than the current coupon market.

The GNMA contract calls for the delivery (it, too, is a physical delivery market) of sufficient collateral to provide a monthly income to the holder of $635 per month. This structure is unique in the fixed income futures market, because the potential liability of the "short" is not complete after the collateral delivery. Because the GNMAs deposited as collateral will experience some principal paydowns, the collateral will fall below the minimum necessary to generate the required cash flow. When this occurs, the short must replenish the collateral, resulting in a potentially perpetual liability. The lack of correlation with the current coupon market, among other factors, has caused a dramatic decline in the popularity of this contract. This is shown in Figure 16-3.

Futures Contracts on Private Credit Instruments

Domestic CD Contracts. Domestic CD futures contracts have been traded since 1981. The contract calls for delivery of a 75 to 105 day CD (issued by one of the banks on an approved list) during the last half of the delivery month. The contract price is quoted as 100 minus the annualized 90 day CD futures rate. Thus, a CD rate of 12 percent is shown by a quote of 88, although the delivery price (including accrued interest) for a $1,000,000 par 90 day CD would actually be determined by taking the final maturity value and dividing by 1 plus settlement yield times 90/360, where the settlement yield is the closing yield on the settlement date. The pricing mechanism provides that each .01 (that is, one basis point) change in price is worth $25 in margin flow.

Eurodollar Deposit Contracts. The Eurodollar (Time) Deposit (ED) contract, the most liquid of the short-term contracts and also one of the newest of the fixed income futures, is based on the Eurodollar deposit rate (usually very close to the London Interbank Offering Rate (LIBOR)) but is the only fixed income futures contract to feature cash settlement. Because of some liquidity problems in the domestic CD contract and the fact that the Euro-

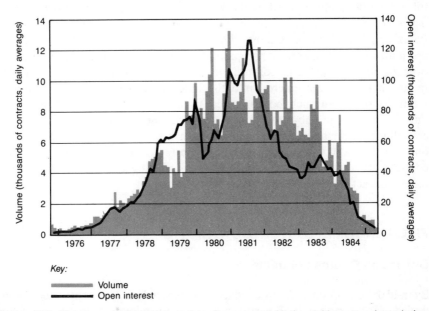

Key:
▬▬▬ Volume
━━━ Open interest

Figure 16-3. Volume and Open Interest in Government National Mortgage Association Collateralized Deposit Receipts Futures Contracts, October 1975 to March 1985. (SOURCE: Salomon Brothers, Inc.)

dollar deposit rate typically more closely mimics private funding rates than do Treasury bill rates, the contract has become enormously successful. The price mechanism is similar to the bill and CD contracts, with the price reflecting 100 minus the annualized 90-day Eurodollar futures rate. As in the bill and CD contracts, a one basis point change in price is worth $25 in margin flow.

One of the more interesting features of the ED contract is that it is traded on more than one exchange. The Singapore exchange recently began trading the ED contract with full offset capabilities against the contract traded on the IMM. Thus, an investor can open a position on either exchange and close it out on either exchange. The practical significance is that the trading day is extended well beyond the Chicago business day by the Singapore trading. Another exchange, the London International Financial Futures Exchange (LIFFE) also trades a Eurodollar Deposit contract very much like the IMM and Singapore contract, but mutual offset was not possible in mid-1985.

FUTURES CONTRACTS ON FIXED INCOME INDEXES

In mid-1985, at the time this chapter was written, there was only one futures contract on bond market indexes, the Muni Bond Index contract traded on the CBT. The early popularity of this index contract likely reflected the need for greater liquidity and hedging vehicles in the municipal bond marketplace.

There are probably several reasons for the absence of additional index contracts in the fixed income market when there are a number of successful ones in the equity market. The first is that it is difficult to construct a meaningful index that could be used as the basis for such a contract. While such indexes do exist, such as the Salomon Brothers High Grade Corporate Bond Index and the Shearson Lehman Government/Corporate Bond Index, they are not as straightforward as the more popular equity indexes because of the over-the-counter nature of corporate bond trading and the relative illiquidity in the market. Prices entered into the index calculations are often traders' estimates of where such bonds would trade if there had been trades, and thus there is some subjectivity in the indexes. Second, because of the generally high correlation in movement of securities in the fixed income market, one can view a high grade bond futures contract, such as the Treasury bond contract, as a sort of index contract, thus reducing the need for a specific index contract.

FIXED INCOME OPTION CONTRACTS

Options on Futures Contracts

By mid-1985, options on three fixed income futures contracts were being traded—Treasury bonds, Treasury notes and Eurodollar deposits—as shown in Table 16-3. However, the most popular fixed income option contract was the option on Treasury bond futures. This option has, as its name implies, Treasury bond futures contracts as the underlying security; both puts and calls are traded. If a call holder elects to exercise, he receives a long position in the underlying futures contract at the guaranteed strike or exercise price, and the call writer becomes short at that same price. Because the option contract is likely to be in-the-money (that is, the price of the underlying futures contract is greater than the call option's strike or exercise price) if exercised, the call writer must immediately pay to the exerciser what is called the *mark-to-market variation margin* or the margin required of the call writer equal to the difference in price between the strike price and the current market price of an in-the-money call option when it is exercised. A similar transaction occurs with the exercise of puts, except that the put buyer acquires a short position (by selling the futures contract to the put writer) at the strike price. In effect, at exercise, the call (put) holder buys (sells) the contract from (to) the option writer at the strike price, but, as in any futures trade, there is no "cost" except for the initial margin that must be put up on the futures contract.

Several potentially confusing elements need to be explained. First, although there are as many as eight different bond futures contracts trading at one time, options are available on only the three with the nearest delivery dates. Second, the option's stated maturity corresponds to the delivery month of the futures contract. That is, only a March option is available on the March futures contract and only a June option is available on the June futures, and so on. Finally, the options expire in the month *prior* to their stated maturity, that is, in the month preceding delivery of the contract underlying the option. Thus, the March bond futures option expires in February, the June option in May, and so forth. The reason for this is to prevent the expiring options from

TABLE 16-3. Options on Fixed Income Futures Contracts and Actuals

Fixed Income	Exchange	10/9/85 Contract Volume	Principal Value	Delivery Months
Options on Futures				
Treasury Bonds	Chicago Board of Trade (CBT)	44,690	$ 100,000	March cycle
Treasury Notes	CBT	1,185	100,000	March cycle
Eurodollar Deposits	Chicago Mercantile Exchange (CME)	3,204	1,000,000	March cycle
Options on Actuals				
Treasury Bonds	Chicago Board Options Exchange (CBOE)	206	100,000	March cycle
Treasury Notes	American Stock Exchange (AMEX)	30	100,000	February cycle

interfering with, or being affected by, the delivery process in the futures market. The prices of the options are quoted in points and 64ths. Thus a price of 1-45 represents "1 and 45/64 points" or 1.703125.

It may appear from the sound of "options on futures" that this is the ultimate leveraged instrument, but this is not the case. The option trades very similarly to how an option on an 8 percent long maturity Treasury bond would trade if one were available. In fact, if one thinks of the Treasury bond futures contract price as simply an index of the government market, the essence of the option contract is captured. The only real difference occurs as a result of exercise, something which is not possible in index options. Exercising actually increases the leverage (and the attendant downside risk potential) by converting the option position into a futures position.

Options on Actuals

Options on Treasury Bonds. As indicated in Table 16-3, options on Treasury bonds are traded on the CBOE. The options cover a $100,000 par amount of the underlying bond. As each quarterly Treasury refunding takes place, the newest bond is added to the list, and one of the older bonds will have its last option expire. The options are quoted in points and 32nds, and a price of 2-14 represents "2 and 14/32 points" or 2.4375.

Options on Treasury Notes. Options on Treasury notes are listed on the AMEX, but trading volume is so low that it is difficult to say that they are "traded" on the AMEX.

Liquidity in the Options Market

One of the major advantages of exchange-traded options is the liquidity provided by the market, so that buyers and sellers can expect to trade at prices close to the last visible trade and to get a price determined by competitive forces. Unfortunately, the options on actuals market falls somewhat short of this standard, and the AMEX options hardly trade at all. For comparative purposes, the total volume on the CBT for options on futures on October 9, 1985 was in excess of 45,000 contracts, while the CBOE options on bonds traded 206 contracts and the AMEX only 30 call contracts in notes. The conclusions are obvious: very large trades or "programs" are directed to the CBT options on futures for their greater liquidity, while smaller trades can be directed to either the CBT or CBOE. Another source of volume for the CBOE is the investor without a futures account; such an account is necessary to trade futures options because exercise will result in a futures position.

FUTURES CONTRACTS ON STOCK MARKET INDEXES

Futures contracts are currently being traded on most of the major stock market indexes. These futures contracts include contracts on the Standard & Poor's 500, the New York Stock Exchange Composite Index, the Value Line Composite Index, and the Major Market Index. While futures contracts on market subindexes are being discussed, no such contracts existed in mid-1985 (although there are subindex contracts in the options market—to be discussed later).

Specifications

The contract features and trading mechanics of these futures contracts are very similar with only minor differences in contract specifications. The owner of a stock index futures contract is obligated to deliver or accept an amount of cash equal to a specified amount—$500 for the S&P 500, Value Line, and NYSE contracts, $250 for the Major Market Maxi and $100 for the Major Market Index contract—times the difference between the initial futures transaction price and the final contract settlement price. The final settlement price may be either the price of the futures contract if sold before expiration or the index value if the contract is held until expiration.

Table 16-4 presents a summary of the important specifications for each of the stock index futures contracts being actively traded on various exchanges as of October 1985. The value of a single stock index futures contract is equal to the price of that contract times its specified dollar multiple. For example, each S&P 500 futures contract is equivalent in value to $500 times the quoted futures price. If the S&P 500 stock index futures price is 180, the S&P 500 futures contract has an equivalent value of $90,000. On the day of expiration, the final settlement value of the contract is equal to $500 times the closing price of the S&P 500 on that day.

Volume

Trading volume in stock index futures contracts has grown significantly since the initial trades in the Spring of 1982. Figure 16-4 compares the trading volume in all stock index futures contracts with the trading volume in the underlying equity markets. The white bar indicates the average daily trading volume of equities traded on the New York Stock Exchange. The black bar represents the equivalent daily volume traded on all of the stock index futures exchanges. In a brief two year time period the equivalent market value of equity exposure traded on the stock index futures exchanges became larger than that of equity traded on the NYSE.

TABLE 16-4. Stock Index Futures Contract Specifications

Index Contract	Exchange	10/9/85 Contract Volume	Contract Size	Minimum Price Fluctuation	INITIAL MARGIN	
					Hedgers	Speculators
Standard & Poor's 500	Chicago Mercantile Exchange (CME)	61,710	$500 × Price	.05 = $25	$3,000	$6,000
New York Stock Exchange Composite	New York Futures Exchange (NYFE)	9,676	500 × Price	.05 = 25	1,500	3,500
Value Line	Kansas City Board of Trade (KC)	5,060	500 × Price	.05 = 25	2,500	6,500
Major Market	Chicago Board of Trade (CBT)	4,819	100 × Price	1/8 = 12.50	500	1,750
Major Market Maxi	CBT	1.590	Price 250 ×	.05 = 12.50	1,250	3,500

Delivery Months: March, June, September, December (March cycle) for Standard and Poor's 500, New York Stock Exchange Composite, Value Line, and Nearest 3 months plus March cycle for Major Market.

Note: The CBT anticipated trading in a NASD-100 contract on an index of 100 large capitalization, actively-traded non-financial OTC stocks would begin in late 1985. Similarly, the CME anticipated trading in a S&P 250 OTC contract on an index of 250 large, actively-traded OTC industrial stocks would begin at about the same time.

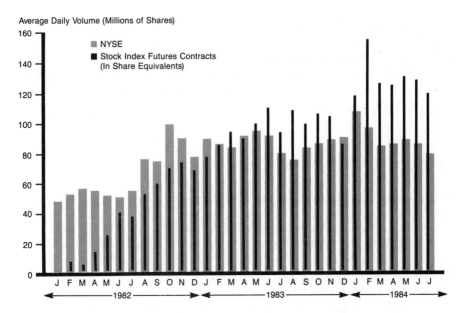

Figure 16-4. Average Daily Volume of NYSE-Listed Stocks and Equivalent Average Daily Volume of Contracts Traded on All Stock Index Futures Exchanges, January 1982–July 1984. (SOURCE: Salomon Brothers, Inc.) Note: With the S&P index at 180, an S&P futures contract represents a $90,000 position in the index. Since the average price of a stock in the S&P 500 is about $40, one futures contract is approximately equivalent to 2,250 shares of the average stock. This is the approach taken in calculating the equivalent average daily volume for the stock index futures contracts.

Price Fluctuation

The minimum price change for each of the index contracts is specified by the exchange. For all of the stock index futures contracts currently being traded the minimum price change is 0.05 (that is, five basis points) except for a ⅛ minimum for the Major Market contract. A change of .05 represents, for example, a move in the S&P 500 from 180 to 180.05. Since the S&P futures contract value is 500 times the S&P futures price, a change of .05 represents an actual change in value of $25. A 1.0 (or 100 basis points) change in the price of the futures contract means a gain or loss equivalent to the dollar multiple specified for that particular contract. For the S&P 500, a one point change would be equal to a gain or loss of $500 per contract. There are currently no limits on the daily maximum price change allowable on any of these stocks index futures contracts.

Contract Settlement

As with Eurodollar Deposit futures contracts previously discussed, an important feature of stock index futures contracts is that settlement of the contract occurs in cash. Actual delivery of a basket of equities is not required should a stock index futures contract be held until expiration. Settlement is made in the cash equivalent of the index at that point in time. For each of the index futures contracts, expiration or delivery months are March, June, September, and December with delivery in the nearest three months also available in the Major Market contract.

COMMON STOCK OPTION CONTRACTS

Options on Index Futures

Option contracts on common stocks can be divided into three groups: options on index futures contracts, options on stock market indexes and sub-indexes, and finally, options on individual common stocks. Options in mid-1985 were being traded on two stock index futures contracts, the S&P 500 and the New York Stock Exchange Composite. Table 16-5 presents a summary of the characteristics of each of these two options contracts.

Each of the two stock index futures options has a value of $500 times the price or premium of the option contract. For example, an S&P 500 call option expiring in March with a strike price of 180 had a price, or premium, of 3 and a total premium value of 3 times $500 or $1,500. As with the underlying futures contracts, the option premium has a minimum fluctuation on any trade of 0.05 points. Similar to the futures contracts, this 0.05 move indicates a minimum value fluctuation of the option of .05 times $500 or $25 per option contract. Again, like the underlying index futures contract, the futures option has no daily trading limit or maximum allowable price change set by the exchanges. Option contracts on the nearest three futures contracts in the March, June, September, December cycle will expire on the last day of trading in the underlying futures contract.

TABLE 16-5. Options on Stock Index Futures Contract Specifications

Futures Option	Exchange	Underlying Instrument	10/9/85 Contract Volume	Strike Price Interval
Standard & Poor's 500	CME	S&P 500 Futures Contract	3,217	5 points
New York Stock Exchange Composite	NYFE	NYSE Futures Contract	371	2 points

Contract Premium: $500 times premium (price) quote
Delivery months: March cycle
Minimum Premium Fluctuation: .05 ($25)

TABLE 16-6. Options on Stock Indexes and Sub-Indexes Contract Specifications

Option	Exchange	10/9/85 Contract Volume	Delivery Months	Contract Position Limits
Options on Indexes				
Standard & Poor's 500	Chicago Board Options Exchange (CBOE)	0	Nearest 4 Months	15,000
Standard & Poor's 100	(CBOE)	213,757	Nearest 4 Months	15,000
Major Market (AMEX)	American Stock Exchange (AMEX)	29,951	Nearest 3 Months	10,000
AMEX Market Value	AMEX	36	Nearest 3 Months	10,000
New York Stock Exchange Composite[a,b]	New York Stock Exchange (NYSE)	5,698	Nearest 3 Months + March cycle	$300 million
Value Line Composite	Philadelphia Exchange (PHLX)	9,065	March cycle	$300 million
National OTC	PHLX	47	March cycle	$300 million
NASDAQ-100	National Association of Securities Dealers (NASD)	4,108	Nearest 4 Months	$300 million
Options on Sub-Indexes				
Computer Technology	AMEX	37	Nearest 3 Months + January cycle	8,000
Oil	AMEX	363	Nearest 3 Months + January cycle	8,000
Transportation	AMEX	0	Nearest 3 Months	8,000
Gold & Silver	PHLX	319	Nearest 3 Months + March cycle	6,000
Technology	Pacific Exchange	90	Nearest 4 Months	15,000

Contract Premium: $100 times the price quote.
Minimum Premium Fluctuation: 1/16 ($6.25) for prices less than $3.00 and 1/8 ($12.50) for prices greater than $3.00.
Strike Price Intervals: 5 points.

Note: The CBT anticipated trading in a NASDAQ-100 contract on an index of 100 large capitalization, actively-traded non-financial OTC stocks would begin in late 1985.

[a] *"Double Index" put and call options on twice the value of the NYSE Composite Index are also traded with 10/9/85 volume of 5,129 contracts.*
[b] *Minimum premium fluctuation is 1/16 ($6.25) for all prices.*

Options on Indexes and Subindexes

The number of different options on major stock indexes and sub-indexes has grown rapidly over the last few years. Put and call options are now directly available on the S&P 100, the New York Stock Exchange Composite Index, the AMEX Major Market Index, the AMEX Market Value Index, the Value Line Composite Index, the National OTC Index, and the NASDAQ-100 Index. Options are also available on five different market subindexes. Table 16-6 presents a summary of the specifications of each of the seven index options and the five subindex options.

Options on Individual Stocks

The final group of options, and by far the largest in terms of size, volume, and impact, are options on individual common stocks. The owner of a call option on an individual common stock has the right to buy that common stock from the call option writer or seller at the specified contract price or strike price during the life of the contract. Alternatively, the owner of a put option on an individual common stock has the right to sell or put that stock to the put option writer or seller at the contract value or strike price any time during the life of that contract. The first trades on an exchange of individual common stocks occurred in 1973, and the market has exhibited substantial growth ever since that time as shown in Figure 16-5.

Option contracts on individual common stocks are traded on a number of exchanges including the Chicago Board Options Exchange (CBOE), the American Stock Exchange (AMEX), the Philadelphia Stock Exchange

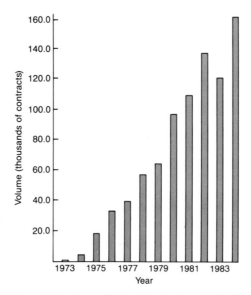

Figure 16-5. Total Contract Volume on Option Contracts on Individual Stocks on CBOE and AMEX, 1973–1984.

(PHLX), the Pacific Stock Exchange (PSE), and the New York Stock Exchange (NYSE). Delivery months, or expiration months, differ by stock and are structured for maturities in three, six, and nine month time periods for each stock. Settlement, or exercise, requires delivery of the shares of the underlying stock. Each option contract on an individual stock is equivalent to 100 shares of the underlying stock and requires delivery of 100 shares at exercise. The premium cost is $100 times the option price quote. Minimum price fluctuations are 1/16 for option quotes less than 3 and ⅛ for quotes greater than 3. There are no maximum daily price limits. Strike prices are generally set at intervals of 5 points.

TRADING MECHANICS FOR FUTURES CONTRACTS

Margin

Margin payments are required by the exchanges to avoid large, unexpected payments at futures contract settlement time and as a means to somewhat modify the highly leveraged nature of this type of instrument. These margin requirements are the initial margin, the maintenance margin, and the variation margin.

At the time of the initial transaction of the purchase or sale of a futures contract, an *initial margin* deposit is required on the part of both the buyer and the seller. This required margin deposit varies by exchange and intent of the transaction but in all cases is properly viewed as a "good faith" deposit that eventual settlement will be made. The initial margin is good faith in the sense that the deposit is still an asset of the contract buyer or seller. The buyer or seller may put up the initial margin either in cash or in interest bearing cash equivalents, usually Treasury securities, and in the latter case earn the interest on those instruments while that initial margin exists.

Variation margin, which must be made or received in cash rather than cash equivalents, is the dollar value gained or lost daily as future contracts are marked-to-market. The margin account of the buyer or seller is adjusted by the broker daily by an amount that is the difference in value between that day's closing price of the future and the prior trading day's closing price. If the price of a futures contract increases, then the margin account of the buyer, or owner of the contract, will be credited with or increased by an amount reflecting the increase. These funds can be withdrawn or invested. If the price of a futures contract declines, then the margin account of the owner of the contract will be debited or reduced by an amount reflecting the decline.

Some brokers permit adverse market moves to reduce the margin account to a level below the initial margin amount. That minimum level is called the *maintenance margin* level. Should the funds in the margin account fall below the maintenance margin level, then the contract buyer or seller is required to make a (cash) variation margin payment to the account sufficient to raise the total amount of funds held on margin back to the level initially required. As a practical matter, however, maintenance margin levels are equal to or only slightly below initial margin levels and futures traders keep little if any excess cash in their margin accounts. Hence, adverse variation margin translates into immediate cash payment requirements for most traders.

Table 16-7 illustrates a simple example of the mechanics of margin payment. Assume that an investor buys an S&P 500 futures contract on Day 1 at a price of 160. The equivalent value of that futures contract is 160 times $500 or $80,000. The investor puts up an initial margin of $6,000. Assume on Day 2 that the future increases in price from 160 to 170. The equivalent value of the future has increased from $80,000 to $85,000, or 170 times $500. The margin account of the owner of the contract is increased by the difference between the ending and beginning value of the contract, or $5,000. Assume on Day 3 that the contract falls from 170 to 165. At a price of 165 the contract has an equivalent value of $82,500. At the end of the third day the margin account is debited for or reduced by $2,500. Finally, assume on Day 4 that the contract declines further from 165 to 150. The margin account is debited for the marked-to-market loss for the day of $7,500. This debit reduces the funds held on margin to $1,000, which is below the maintenance margin level of $3,000. The owner of the contract is required to provide an additional variation margin deposit of the difference between the $6,000 initial margin and the $1,000 ending margin balance, or $5,000. This daily marking-to-market and the provision of any further required variation margin continues on all open futures positions until the positions are closed.

Trading Mechanics

The mechanics of trading futures contracts is similar at all the exchanges. An investor wishing to buy or sell a futures contract contacts a broker. These brokers are known as futures contract merchants and must be registered with the Commodity Futures Trading Commission. A futures contract merchant (FCM) may or may not be an actual member of the exchange. The FCM contacts either its own brokers on the floor of the exchanges or the brokers of member firms in order to execute the actual transaction. Trades

TABLE 16-7. S&P 500 Index Futures Margin Example

Futures Purchase Price: 160

Initial Margin: $2,500
Maintenance Margin: $2,500

Day	Closing Futures Price	Futures Value	Marked-To-Market	Margin Payments	Total Margin Funds
1	160	$80,000	—	$6,000	$ 6,000
2	170	85,000	$5,000	—	11,000
3	165	82,500	−2,500	—	8,500
4	150	75,000	−7,500	5,000	6,000

are made in an open-outcry auction system within areas on the floors of the respective exchanges. The types of orders transmitted to the floor brokers are similar to the orders transmitted to the brokers on regular stock exchanges including market orders, limit orders and stop orders. The market, limit, and stop orders together represent the largest percentage of transactions on the futures market exchanges.

Each exchange has a clearing corporation that serves as a guarantor for trades on the floor. During the trading session each trader turns over completed orders and trades to the trader's clearing firm, which is a member of the clearing corporation. The clearing corporation settles the account of each member firm at the end of each trading day and exactly matches each of the day's purchases and sales. All losses are collected and all gains are paid through this central clearing corporation.

The clearing corporation interposes itself as the buyer to every seller and the seller to every buyer. By taking this posture the clearing corporation for each exchange involving futures and options insures that each buyer and seller is subsequently free to buy and sell independently of the other. For example, a buyer who wishes to sell his futures contract need have no concern whether the original seller desires to buy it back. The buyer may sell the contract to any willing and able buyer at any point in time up to expiration. As a party involved in every trade, the clearing corporation guarantees the opposite side of the transactions while the positions remain open. The market participants, or investors, need not be concerned with the identity or reliability or credit worthiness of the opposing party to their trade because the financial integrity of the clearing corporation stands behind open futures and options positions.

Commissions

Commissions on trades of futures are fully negotiable and are based on a round trip. As an example, for institutional traders, commissions on a stock index futures contract are generally in the $20 to $30 range. If an S&P 500 futures contract is selling for 180, then $90,000 of equivalent stock exposure can be purchased and sold for approximately $25 in commissions. By comparison, buying and selling $90,000 worth of stocks where each share is priced at $40 and the commission is about 5 cents a share *each way* involves a total round trip transaction commission of about $255.

TRADING MECHANICS FOR OPTIONS ON FUTURES

There are no margin requirements for the buyer of an index futures option. The only cash outlay is the option premium value. A seller of a stock index futures option contract that is at- or in-the-money is required to put up as margin: (1) the initial margin normally required for investing in the future, (2) the option premium received, and (3) the variation margin as the underlying futures contract is marked-to-market. A seller of an out-of-the-money contract must meet these same margin requirements less part or all of the amount the contract is out-of-the-money.

The trading mechanics of options on stock are similar to those of the trading in the underlying futures contracts. The execution and order placing process are similar. The exchange clearing corporation plays a generally similar role. The major difference in the role of the clearing corporation occurs at the time of exercise of the option by the buyer. The clearing corporation randomly assigns the exercise to an option seller. The clearing corporation will then establish futures positions appropriate to the option buyer and seller at the strike price.

TRADING MECHANICS FOR INDEX OPTIONS

As with index futures contracts, settlement of options on indexes and sub-indexes at expiration occurs in cash. A standardized contract combined with the clearing corporation settlement system allows the option contracts to be transacted by any party at any point in time. Actual orders are placed and executed similar to transactions in common stocks where orders are placed with brokers and are conveyed to a floor broker who actually completes and executes the trade.

TRADING MECHANICS FOR OPTIONS
ON INDIVIDUAL ACTUALS

Unlike the other instruments discussed in this chapter, there are currently no margin requirements for trading in options on individual bonds or common stocks. Because settlement is made in the actual underlying bond or common stock instead of cash and because futures contracts are not involved, no margin is deemed to be necessary. By far, the bulk of the trading volume is in options on common stocks.

Holdings of any group of options on any one common stock are generally restricted, via position limits, to 4,000 contracts by Securities and Exchange Commission regulation. Similar to trading the options on the stock indexes and subindexes, the order placement process and execution process are like that of trading in the actual common stocks. An investor places orders with a broker who then in turn places the orders with the floor brokers and members of the exchange for execution. Again, the clearing corporation plays a similar role of matching a buyer and a seller and being the guarantor that provides the standardization and liquidity of the contract plus the financial strength and integrity of the process.

Similar to transactions in futures contracts, commissions on trades in the various option contracts are fully negotiable. For example, individual stock options for institutional traders have one-way commissions that typically range from $1 to $5 per contract.

SUMMARY

The purpose of this chapter was to provide the background and descriptions of financial futures and options contracts. The chapter reviewed the history of the contracts, particularly noting the impact the characteristics of stocks, bonds, and contract specifications played in the evolution of the markets. The role futures and options play within the portfolio management process to maximize portfolio return and control portfolio risk were noted. Finally, the range of new instruments contract specifications, and trading mechanics were discussed. The descriptive material in this chapter is extended to valuation models for futures and options in Chapter 17, which follows.

FURTHER READING

Most textbooks on investments contain definitions and descriptions of futures and options contracts including discussions of trading mechanics. Examples of such texts include Cohen, Zinbarg, and Zeikel [1982], Fischer and Jordan [1983], Khoury [1984], and Reilly [1985].

Other sources include descriptive publications by the exchanges and discussion material published by major broker-dealers. An excellent summary of the descriptive characteristics of futures and options along with principal users and basic investment strategies has been prepared by Atchison, DeMong, and Kling [1985] published by The Financial Analysts Research Foundation.

BIBLIOGRAPHY

A Guide to Financial Futures at the Chicago Board of Trade, Chicago: Chicago Board of Trade, 1984.

Atchison, Michael D., Richard F. DeMong, and John L. Kling, *New Financial Instruments: A Descriptive Guide,* Charlottesville, Va.: The Financial Analysts Research Foundation, 1985.

Chicago Board of Trade, *Interest Rate Futures for Institutional Investors,* Chicago: Chicago Board of Trade, 1985.

The Chicago Board of Trade's Municipal Bond Futures Contract, Chicago: Chicago Board of Trade, 1985.

Chicago Mercantile Exchange, *Inside S&P 500 Stock Index Futures,* Index and Option Market, Chicago: Chicago Mercantile Exchange, 1984.

Chicago Board of Trade, *Contract Specifications and Vendor Guide,* Chicago: Chicago Board of Trade, 1985.

Cohen, J., E. Zinbarg and A. Zeikel, *Investment Analysis and Portfolio Management,* Fourth Edition, Homewood, Ill.: Dow Jones-Irwin, 1982.

Cox, John C. and Mark Rubinstein, *Options Markets,* Englewood Cliffs, N.J.: Prentice-Hall, Inc., 1985.

Fabozzi, Frank J. and Gregory M. Kipnis, (eds.), *Stock Index Futures,* Homewood, Ill.: Dow Jones-Irwin, 1984.

Chicago Board of Trade, *Financial Futures: The Delivery Process in Brief,* Chicago: Chicago Board of Trade, 1982.

"The Financial Futures Professional," a monthly bulletin of the Marketing Department, Chicago Board of Trade.

Fischer, Donald E. and Ronald Jordan, *Security Analysis and Portfolio Management,* Third Edition, Englewood Cliffs, N.J.: Prentice-Hall, 1983.

Fischer, Donald E. (ed.), *Options and Futures: New Route to Risk/Return Management.* Sponsored by The Institute of Chartered Financial Analysis. Homewood, Ill.: Dow Jones-Irwin, 1984.

Futures Industry Association, *An Introduction to the Futures Markets,* New York: Futures Industry Association, 1982.

Gastineau, Gary L., *The Stock Options Manual,* Second Edition, New York: McGraw-Hill Book Company, 1979.

Gay, Gerald D. and Robert W. Kolb, *Interest Rate Futures: Concepts and Issues,* Richmond: Robert F. Dame, 1982.

Goldman Sachs & Co., *An Introduction to the Futures Markets,* New York: Goldman Sachs & Co., 1984.

Goodman, Laurie S., "New Options Markets," *Quarterly Review,* Federal Reserve Bank of New York, Autumn 1983.

Hanson, Nick, et al., "Futures Contracts on Stock Indexes," Salomon Brothers, Inc., 1982.

Hanson, Nick and Louis Marolis, "Futures Contracts on Stock Indexes—the First Year," Salomon Brothers, Inc., 1983.

Khoury, Sarkis J., *Speculative Markets,* New York: Macmillan Publishing Company, 1984.

Kolb, Robert W., *Interest Rate Futures: A Comprehensive Introduction.* Richmond: Robert F. Dame, Inc., 1982.

—— **and Gerald D. Gay,** *Interest Rate and Stock Index Futures and Options: Characteristics, Valuation and Portfolio Strategies.* Charlottesville, Va.: The Financial Analysts Research Foundation, 1985.

Kopprasch, Robert W., "Early Redemption (Put) Options on Fixed-Income Securities," Salomon Brothers, Inc., November 1981.

——, "An Introduction to Financial Futures on Treasury Securities," Salomon Brothers, Inc., December 1981.

——, "Exchange Traded Options on Fixed-Income Securities," Salomon Brothers, Inc., February 1982.

Leibowitz, Martin and Robert W. Kopprasch, "Contingent Takedown Options on Fixed-Income Securities," Salomon Brothers, Inc., January 1981.

Merrick, John and Stephan Figlewski, "An Introduction to Financial Futures," Occasional Paper No. 6, Salomon Brothers Center for the Study of Financial Institutions, New York University, 1984.

Nix, William and Susan Nix, *The Dow Jones-Irwin Guide to Stock Index Futures and Options,* Homewood, Ill.: Dow Jones-Irwin, 1984.

"Open Outcry," a monthly newsletter for members and staff of the Chicago Mercantile Exchange.

Powers, Mark J. and David J. Vogel, *Inside the Financial Futures Markets,* New York: John Wiley & Sons, 1981.

Reilly, Frank, *Investment Analysis and Portfolio Management,* Second Edition, Chicago: Dryden Press, 1985.

Rothstein, Nancy H. and James M. Little (eds.), *The Handbook of Financial Futures,* New York: McGraw-Hill Book Company, 1985.

CHAPTER **17**

Valuation of Futures and Options Contracts

_____ **Robert W. Kopprasch, CFA**

VALUATION OF FUTURES CONTRACTS

With the advent of the new instruments, futures and options contracts, and their nontraditional return patterns, it was obvious that the valuation methods applied to the underlying securities could not be applied to these derivative instruments. New valuation guidelines were developed in both the futures and options markets, and, though futures and options certainly differ from each other, each is surprisingly consistent across the equity-fixed income spectrum. Just as present value and dividend discount models are used as valuation frameworks for fixed income and equity securities, respectively, specific valuation methodologies have been developed for futures and options contracts. This chapter addresses the valuation of these new instruments and the application of the valuation methodology to the specific markets.

Futures contracts can be evaluated in a number of ways, though not all are equally valid. In the early days of financial futures, some participants priced contracts based almost solely on their expectations of future price. While such a method will generate profit if the expectations become reality, such pricing will probably also be profitable for arbitrageurs, who are only too happy to provide liquidity for the expectations trader. In exploring more satisfactory approaches to valuation, arbitrage pricing will be examined first followed by an examination of situations in which arbitrage pricing does not apply and expectations become more important.

Arbitrage and the Cost of Carry

Most forward commitments are priced on a net *cost of financing* basis. The cost of financing refers to the rate that would have to be paid to borrow funds to buy the asset, or the rate that could be earned on the proceeds if the asset were sold. Net financing adjusts this cost for any monetary benefits received as a result of holding the asset. Holders of Treasury bonds receive coupon income; holders of gold find that they can "lend" their gold (via a depositary receipt) and receive a fee, say 2 percent; and holders of stock portfolios receive dividends. In any model of pricing, these "yields" must be considered.

The term *cost of carry* (or "carry" for short) is used to refer to the net financing cost after consideration of the yield on the asset. Thus, while financing cost is always referred to as negative because it represents a cash outflow for the asset holder, carry can be either positive or negative. Positive carry implies that the yield on the asset is greater than the financing costs, while negative carry implies the opposite.

Arbitrage Pricing

The methodology for the valuation of forward commitments is explained in the following example. Consider an asset that has a market value of $100 and offers a yield of 5 percent (assumed to be earned evenly throughout the year but paid at the end of the period). If the financing rate is 8 percent (also assumed to accumulate evenly throughout the year), what should the forward price be? An investor can buy the asset for $100 (which he borrows) and knows that by the end of the year he will have accumulated an income of $5 (i.e., 5 percent times $100) and a financing cost of $8. This results in a negative net carry of minus $3 (a cost). Thus, he must receive at least $103 in order to break even. If the forward price is any higher, say $105, an arbitrageur will engage in this transaction and will, without risk, earn $2 on every unit asset in the trade. He would buy for 100 (borrowed), and sell forward at 105. At the end of the period, he would collect his "income" of $5, deliver the asset to the forward buyer at $105, and simultaneously repay his loan of $100 plus $8 interest for a $2 net profit (5 plus 105 minus 108 = $2). This is the very nature of arbitrage, the buying and selling of the same asset in different markets to take advantage of a momentary price differential. Note that the profit at the end of the period equals the excess of the forward price of $105 over the theoretical price of $103.

That example is one of negative carry, in which the theoretical forward price (103) is above the current or "spot" price (100). If the example had involved a positive carry, the theoretical forward price would have been lower than the spot price. *Note that an expectations-based future price never enters into the forward price.* The reason for this is the arbitrage process, the buying and selling pressures from which will bring the prices back into line until no further arbitrage profits are available.

In order to demonstrate this, assume that short selling is permitted and that the short seller has use of the funds raised. If bearish forward sellers drove the one-year forward price down to 101, arbitrageurs would enter the market, buy forward at 101 and sell the asset short at today's spot price of 100. They would earn 8 percent on the $100 raised and would have to pay the $5 yield to the lender of the asset. This would leave them with $103, only $101 of which is required to take delivery of the asset on the forward settlement date. The asset thus purchased is used to settle the short positions, resulting in a profit of $2, the difference between the theoretical forward price ($103) and the actual forward price ($101). As expected, when the forward price is too low, the arbitrageur buys the contract because it is too cheap.

The arbitrage pricing process can be described in terms of the following equation:

$$F_0 = S_0 + rS_0 - yS_0$$

or, in words,

$$\text{current forward price} = \text{current spot price} + \text{cost of financing} - \text{income from asset}$$

$$= \text{current spot price} + \left(\text{financing rate} \times \text{current spot price} \right) - \left(\text{yield} \times \text{current spot price} \right)$$

The forward price, as discussed and shown in the previous equation, should equal the spot price today plus the financing cost minus the yield on the asset. Note that the financing rate (r) and the yield (y) represent periodic, not annualized, rates. In the case of stock index futures, note also that yS_0 represents the dollar dividend paid at the end of the forward period.

The equation can be rearranged to read

$$F_0 = S_0 + S_0 \times (r-y)$$

or, in words,

$$\text{current forward price} = \text{current spot price} + \text{current spot price} \times \left(\text{financing rate} - \text{yield} \right)$$

$$= \text{current spot price} \pm \text{net carry adjustment}$$

When the financing rate is greater than the yield, the forward price should be above the spot price, or should *trade at a premium to cash*. When the financing rate is less than the yield, the forward price should be below the spot price, that is, it should *trade at a discount to cash.*

Several assumptions were made in the simple model just described:

1. The nature of the asset at delivery is identical to its current form. This assumption is necessary to allow the arbitrageur to use the asset purchased forward to cover his short sale, or, in the opposite transaction, to allow him to deliver the asset purchased today to satisfy his forward sale.
2. The asset price is known (the asset price is needed to derive the theoretical forward price).
3. The asset can be sold at any time.
4. The proceeds from the short sale are either available to the investor or are "invested" for him to provide a positive return.
5. The yield on the security is known and paid at the end of the forward period (or, if paid earlier, a reinvestment rate must be assumed).
6. The financing rate is known and paid at the end of the forward period. (Note that items 5 and 6 together determine carry.)
7. There are no transaction costs.

PRICING TREASURY BILL FUTURES CONTRACTS

One of the most direct applications of the arbitrage model is the pricing of a Treasury bill futures contract. For example, assume that the nearest contract is exactly three months away. That means that a six-month Treasury bill will be deliverable against the contract. The price of that six-month bill is known, and alternative investment (borrowing) rates for the next three months are also known. It is thus a straightforward task to determine the breakeven (or equilibrium) price for the forward contract for the following given situation:

91-day bill quoted discount rate =	8.00%
Price of 91-day bill =	97.97777

$$\text{CD equivalent return on bill} = \frac{100 - 97.9777}{97.9777} \times \frac{360}{91} = \quad 8.1651\%$$

182-day bill quoted discount rate =	8.60%
Price of 182-day bill =	95.65222

Using the first of the two preceding equations, the forward price of the 182-day Treasury bill, for delivery in 91 days, is determined as follows:

$$F_0 = \quad S_0 \quad + \quad\quad\quad\quad rS_0 \quad\quad\quad\quad\quad\quad - yS_0$$

$$F_0 = 95.65222 + [.081651 \times (91/360) \times 95.65222] - 0$$

$$= 97.62644$$

A forward price of 97.62644 corresponds to a quoted discount rate on the bill of 9.3899 percent. If the futures were priced at this forward price, it would be quoted at 90.61 (that is, 100 minus 9.3899, rounded to two decimal places). This price is called the *breakeven futures price.*

Normally, Treasury bill futures are priced so that the cost of financing represents the *repurchase agreement rate* (the *repo rate*) rather than the Treasury bill rate for the period. Thus, in the example above, the futures contract probably would be priced closer to 90.83, which is the solution to the equation above with 8.40 percent used as the annualized financing rate (r). This represents a reasonable repo rate when the CD-equivalent bill rate is 8.1651 because the repo rate is the collateralized short-term borrowing rate for U.S. government securities dealers in which the longer-term securities owned by the dealer are pledged as collateral under an agreement to purchase them at a later date. A differential of about 25 basis points is typical. If the futures contract is trading at the breakeven price, there is no incentive for arbitrageurs to enter the market. However, when the market price is above or below the breakeven price, there are opportunities for profit by selling or buying the contracts, respectively. It is this action that prevents the contracts from deviating too far from the "fair" price.

The Implied (or Breakeven) Repo Rate

Although the pricing method just discussed is straightforward, a slightly different form has evolved as the favorite in the fixed income market. It involves the calculation of the *implied repo rate,* also called the *breakeven repo rate* because it is the financing rate that produces a breakeven situation between the (spot) cash and futures markets, that is, a situation where there is no profit or loss. Hereafter it will be referred to simply as the *implied rate.*

Market participants essentially say that there is no need to calculate the breakeven futures price because the futures price can be found in the market. For dealers, who can represent significant arbitrage activity in the Treasury bill futures market, the implied repo rate is more important. Dealers are constantly looking at the profitability of the *cash-and-carry,* which involves the purchase of the underlying security and the sale of a futures contract. The dealer is especially concerned with his cost of financing the repo rate. Assuming that the price of the futures contract is equal to the result obtained in the preceding calculations, the calculation of the implied repo rate is demonstrated as follows:

Purchase price of six-month Treasury bill = 95.65222
Sale price of bill via futures contract = 97.6264

Return earned on 91-day investment:
$[(97.6264 - 95.65222)/95.65222] \times [360/91] = 8.165\%$

That is, the return on the six-month Treasury bill from day zero to day 91 is equal to the 91-day Treasury bill futures contract selling price minus the six-month bill purchase price divided by the bill purchase price, converted to an annualized percentage rate.

From the dealer's perspective, the cash-and-carry will earn 8.165 percent[1]

---

[1] This rate is prior to the effect of the timing of the margin flows. See the section entitled Hedging the Interest Cost or Profit on Margin.

and will be profitable *only* if the position can be financed at a repo rate of less than 8.165 percent, which explains why this figure is referred to as the implied or breakeven repo rate, or more recently, the implied rate. Note that the return earned on this investment with a futures price of 97.6264 has to equal the three-month rate of 9.3899 percent from the previous example because that is the rate used to determine the futures contract price.

PRICING TREASURY BOND FUTURES CONTRACTS

The Treasury bond futures contract is somewhat more difficult to value than the Treasury bill contract because of the income that is accruing (and possibly being paid) on the underlying security, and the fact that there are a number of different deliverable instruments that must be evaluated. In addition, the contract design allows delivery any time during the delivery month at the option of the short. This last factor is discussed when the various delivery options are reviewed.

One of the simplest ways to understand the pricing of Treasury bond futures contracts is to look at their use in creating synthetic money market instruments. While this may sound formidable, it is actually quite simple in theory and is a useful way of viewing contract pricing. It is, in fact, essentially the same as the arbitrage pricing discussion. While it is necessary to complicate the discussion with details of futures contract specifications, it might be useful to remember that understanding pricing is the goal of this section. If accrued interest, conversion factors, and the like are not totally understood, that lack of knowledge should not impede a basic understanding of the pricing relationships.

Shortened-Maturity Treasury Bonds

If an investor purchases an underlying security such as a bond instrument that is deliverable under a futures contract and then sells a contract, he has effectively shortened the maturity (and duration) of the security, thus creating a synthetic money market instrument. The new "maturity" is the delivery date, and the new "redemption value" is the price implied by the futures price quote. (When the futures are viewed simply as exchange-traded forward contracts, this maturity contraction becomes obvious.)

For example, a 20-year Treasury bond can be shortened to a two-month instrument with a known selling price. (An example of this is provided in Chapter 18.) The returns on such investments are readily calculated because all elements of return are known—the purchase price of the instrument, its selling price (via the futures contract), and the length of the holding period. Note that, in the case of a Treasury bond contract, a reinvestment rate for any coupons received during the holding period must be assumed in order to calculate the true effective return.

Just to review the procedure followed: A long-term Treasury bond (which qualifies as "deliverable") is purchased and the appropriate number of Treasury bond futures contracts are sold, locking in the sale price of the bond. Margin considerations are slightly more complicated than for Treasury bills, for example, because of the variety of deliverable bonds. An 8 percent coupon bond is assumed used in the first example, because the futures contract is based on a nominal 8 percent coupon bond and the margin effect is thereby simplified. Another deliverable bond is used in subsequent examples.

Another difference with the Treasury bond versus the Treasury bill example is that the bond return over the two-month holding period involves accrued interest at the purchase and sale dates, and may involve payment of a coupon during that period. Thus, the purchase price of the bond must include accrued interest, although the price quote does not. Similarly, the quoted delivery, or invoice, price under the futures contract does not incorporate accrued interest, but it is included in the actual transaction. Additionally, if a coupon is paid during the interim, a reinvestment rate would need to be assumed to determine the bond's full value at the delivery date. The annualized return on this investment is calculated as follows:

$$\text{return} = \left(\frac{\text{total proceeds} - \text{initial investment}}{\text{initial investment}} \right) \times \text{annualizing factor}$$

where:
initial investment = bond price quote + accrued interest
total proceeds = sale proceeds + coupon
sale proceeds = (futures price × conversion factor) + accrued interest
(if any) = compounded value of coupon at delivery

The conversion factor used in the preceding equation, as explained in Chapter 16, is the factor that adjusts the price of the actual coupon bond delivered to a nominal, 8 percent bond assumed delivered. In this example, let us assume that the 8 percent coupon bond paid a coupon three months ago (and therefore there is three months of accrued interest at time of purchase) and is selling for 60. Given that the futures contract is selling for 60 16/32, the return is calculated as shown:

initial investment = purchase price + accrued interest

$$= \quad 60 \quad + \quad \left(4 \times \frac{3}{6} \right)$$

$$= \quad 60 \quad + \quad 2$$

$$= \quad 62$$

sale proceeds = (futures price × conversion factor) + accrued interest

$$(60 \; 16/32 \quad \times \quad 1.000) \quad + \left(4 \times \frac{5}{6} \right) = 63.833$$

coupon = none

$$\text{return} = \left(\frac{63.833 - 62}{62} \right) \times \frac{12}{2} = 17.74\%$$

This return would be compared with other short-term investment alternatives to determine its attractiveness.

If the "cash" price at delivery had been 62, and if the 8 percent bond were the only deliverable bond, the futures contract would also sell at 62 because of *convergence* or the gradual coming together of the futures and spot prices as a contract approaches the delivery date.[2] The investor would receive 62, or the futures price times the conversion factor plus accrued interest. This increase of 1 16/32 (from the original futures sale price of 60 16/32) would be offset by the margin payments that would have been made during the two-month period. These would net to zero, however, because a 1 16/32 (1.5 percent) change in delivery price on $100,000 par amount of bonds equals $1,500, the margin payment for the transaction. Present value effects are small over the short two-month period.

The problem becomes slightly more complex, however, when a bond with a coupon other than 8 percent is used, as is likely to be the case. If a 1:1 position—that is, $100,000 par amount of bonds and one contract—is used, the total of the margin payments on the contract will not equal the change in delivery price of the bond because of the conversion factor. For example, if the conversion factor were 1.500, and the contract's price changed by one point over the two-month period, the delivery price would change by one point times 1.500, or 1½ points, or $1,500. The margin payment from a move of one point in the futures price would total only $1,000, calculated by multiplying the margin flow per 32nd, $31.25, by the number of 32nds in one point, namely 32. This mismatch of the change in delivery price and the amount of margin flow must be compensated for, and is easily done by multiplying the original number of contracts by the conversion factor. In this way, the dollar change in delivery price per one-point change in the contract price is matched by the dollar amount of margin flow required for the larger number of contracts (or fewer if the bond's coupon is *less* than 8 percent).

For example, assume that a 10 percent Treasury bond was selling for 80, and that the conversion factor was 1.333. Using the previous futures prices and assuming the bond had paid a coupon three months ago:

$$\text{initial investment} = \text{purchase price} + \text{accrued interest}$$
$$\quad\quad\quad\quad\quad 80 \quad + \quad 2.50 \quad\quad\quad = 82.50$$

$$\text{sale proceeds} = \left(\begin{array}{c}\text{futures}\\\text{price}\end{array} \times \begin{array}{c}\text{conversion}\\\text{factor}\end{array}\right) + \begin{array}{c}\text{accrued}\\\text{interest}\end{array}$$

$$\quad\quad = \quad (60 \tfrac{16}{32} \times 1.33) \quad + 4.1667 = 84.813$$

$$\text{return} \quad = \quad \frac{84.813 - 82.5}{82.5} \times 6 \quad\quad = 16.82\%$$

[2] In a contract that is very clean (i.e., free of complicating factors) like the Treasury bill contract, convergence occurs with a high degree of "accuracy" (that is, although the *way* in which convergence occurs is not known and the *interim* values produced by the convergence process are not predictable, the ultimate outcome is highly predictable). In the bond contract, however, because of various options that are available to the "short" in the delivery process, the convergence is less than perfect and the contract usually winds up trading at a price that appears too low. At this point in the discussion, the lack of perfect convergence will be ignored.

If the investor sold 1.333 contracts per $100,000 par amount of the 10s purchased, and the futures contract moved to 62, as previously illustrated, his extra delivery proceeds of 1 16/32 percent times 1.333 times $100,000 would be $1,999.50. At the same time, the margin payments would total:

required margin payment	=	price movement in 32nds	×	cost per 32nd	×	number of contracts
	=	48	×	31.25	×	1.333
	=	1,999.50				

Weighting the futures position by the conversion factor assures that if the bond is ultimately delivered at a different price than originally expected due to a change in the futures price, the difference will be offset by the total of the margin payments resulting from a change in the price of the futures contract. In essence, the cash and futures positions are weighted to have *equal dollar volatility*. The "extra" contracts purchased (because the conversion factor is greater than 1.0 for all bonds with coupons greater than 8 percent) are simply closed out before delivery and the bonds held are delivered against the remaining contracts.

Convergence and the Most Deliverable Bond

A short seller of the contract who holds the contract until delivery is required must purchase a bond in the market if he does not already have one, and then deliver (sell) it at the invoice price.

The invoice price of each deliverable bond can be calculated by multiplying the futures' settlement price by the relevant conversion factor. If the difference between the invoice price and the actual market price for each bond were calculated, it is unlikely that all would be equal. The bond that provides the greatest profit or smallest loss to the short on this final transaction is known as the *most deliverable* or *cheapest-to-deliver* bond.

If the futures price were converging to or moving toward the cash price from *below* (that is, the delivery prices were lower than cash prices), the most deliverable bond would be the one that provided the smallest loss to the short seller who purchased the bond in the cash market and delivered it at the lower invoice price. If the futures price were converging from *above,* the most deliverable bond would be the one that provided the greatest profit to the short as he bought the cash bond and then delivered it at the higher invoice price. As indicated previously, the direction of convergence—from above or below —is primarily a function of the shape of the yield curve.

At delivery, the most deliverable bond is easily determined—it is the one that produces the greatest dollar profit or smallest dollar loss on the delivery transaction. At some time *before* delivery, however, a different criterion applies. One can compute the return for every deliverable bond if purchased and sold by selling a futures contract. The bond providing the highest return is considered the most deliverable for that particular contract at that time. This bond is the optimal one to purchase for the money market investment, as is shown shortly.

Note that the return calculated on the most deliverable bond is also known as the implied or breakeven repo rate discussed previously. When dealers enter into this type of cash-and-carry transaction, they have to finance (carry) the purchased bonds, usually at the repurchase agreement (repo) rate. Obviously, if the return on the investment is 13 percent, the position must be financed at an average rate of 13 percent to break even. Thus, the breakeven repo rate is constantly compared to actual repo rates and the traders' expectations of future repo rates.

Changes in the Most Deliverable Bond and the "Lock In" of Return

An investor buying a bond and selling a futures contract can compute the return expected because the purchase price, sale price (conversion factor times futures price), and holding period are known. The "lock in" of return depends, as previously described, on matching the net margin flows with the changes in the delivery price that result from movements of the futures price. An earlier section explained how "weighting" the position by the conversion factor assured this match. That section ignored the possibility of price changes resulting in a change in the most deliverable bond and the fact that the futures contract converges most closely to the most deliverable bond. This section will address these issues.

Consider the possibilities regarding deliverability for an investor's position. When the bond is purchased, either it is the most deliverable or it is not. At delivery, either it is the most deliverable or it is not. The combination of two states at the outset and two at delivery implies four possible paths that the investment may follow. Each path needs to be examined further.

Assume that the investor buys the most deliverable bond when the futures transaction is initiated and that the position is properly weighted. If the bond is the most deliverable at delivery, the futures contract's converted delivery (or invoice) price will have converged to the price of the bond held by the investor. Thus, margin flows will match the change in delivery price, and the original expected return is "locked in." Because we have defined most deliverable at the initiation of the position as the bond that promised the highest cash-and-carry return, the investor will have locked in the best return available on the day he entered the market.

If the investor buys the most deliverable bond at the outset, but another bond is more deliverable at delivery, the situation is slightly more complicated. If the investor delivers the bond already held, the original return will be locked in. However, the fact that the bond is not the most deliverable at the delivery date means that the delivery transaction will produce a profit that is not as great, or a loss that is larger, than would result if he delivered the most deliverable bond.

Instead, the investor can sell the bond in the market (instead of at the delivery price) and then buy and deliver the most deliverable. The net proceeds of this transaction will be greater than the delivery price of the original bond, and the investor's return will exceed his original expectation.

If the investor originally purchased a bond that did not promise the highest cash-and-carry return, and it was the most deliverable bond at delivery, the original return would be locked in. Of course, this would not be the highest return that the investor could have locked in.

Finally, if the bond originally purchased was not the most deliverable at either the outset or delivery, the realized return, based on a swap into the most deliverable, will be higher than the rate originally expected, but the original rate would not have been the highest rate available when the investment was made.

The four possibilities are enumerated in the following summary of the effect on return of deliverability:

Deliverability When Position Is Initiated	Deliverability At Delivery	Original Return Expected	Realized Return R*
1. Most	Most	R_M	$R^* = R_M$
2. Most	Not Most	R_M	$R^* > R_M$
3. Not Most	Most	R_N	$R^* = R_N < R_M$
4. Not Most	Not Most	R_N	$R^* > R_N$

where R_M is the anticipated shortened-maturity investment return on the most deliverable bond (that is, bond M's breakeven repo rate) and R_N is the anticipated shortened-maturity investment return on the not-most deliverable bond (that is, bond N's breakeven repo rate) where bond N is one of a number of not-most deliverable bonds available in the marketplace. Situation 1 is straightforward. Because the bond is most deliverable both at the outset and at delivery, R^* equals R_M. In situation 2, the investor can swap out of the held bond at delivery, since it is not-most deliverable, and into the most deliverable, and in so doing will earn a return, R^*, in excess of the return had he not swapped, R_M. In situation 3, given a not-most deliverable bond at the outset, the best the manager can achieve is R_N by swapping into the most deliverable at delivery, but the return earned, R_N, which is also R^*, will be less than R_M. In situation 4, the investor can swap out of the not-most deliverable and into the most deliverable at delivery, thereby earning R^* which will be greater than R_N, the return earned if no swap took place. No definitive relationship to R_M can be inferred in this last case.

It should be apparent that the investor desiring to lock in a competitive money market rate over the term should purchase the most deliverable bond, if its promised return is satisfactory, because the realized return must equal or exceed this rate. For a not-most deliverable, the promised return is also the *floor* (guaranteed minimum) *return,* but the floor is lower than that of the most deliverable issue. If a bond becomes the most deliverable (also known as cheapest-to-deliver) during the delivery period, any investor who engaged in a cash-and-carry and delivered the bond would find that he had earned the originally calculated floor return. If the bond held is not the most deliverable, the investor would earn more by selling his bond in the cash market and either closing out the futures position or buying the current most deliverable bond and delivering it against the contract. This results in a return that is higher than the floor return.

Timing of Margin Flows

In the preceding sections, the anticipated return was said to be "locked in" if the change in the delivery price of the bond was matched by the net margin flow. In fact, however, margin inflows would be reinvested and would provide a greater terminal flow, and margin outflows would have to be financed, resulting in a larger total cost. This can be thought of as a *margin multiplier*, with the effect determined by the length of time until the position is unwound and the rate that is prevailing during that period. Thus the multiplier changes during the life of the position and must be compensated for by a second weighting factor that also changes as time elapses. This is discussed in the section on "Hedging the Interest Cost or Profit on Margin" elsewhere in this chapter.

Delivery Options in the Treasury Bond Futures Contract

Several options are held by the short seller of the Treasury bond futures contract. The short decides when in the delivery month delivery will take place, and determines which bond will be delivered. The design of the contract also gives the short an *afternoon put option* during the delivery month. Each of these options is discussed with reference to the effect on the futures price that the existence of the option is likely to have.

Effect of Delivery-Timing Option. The option to determine when in the delivery month actual delivery will take place would probably not have too much value in the absence of the other options. This option would generally result in delivery on the first delivery date in a negative carry environment and on the last possible date when the short was earning positive carry. In any calculations of the implied repo rate, the proper time period would have to be specified. There is no doubt that a change in the optimal delivery date would have an effect on the futures price, but as an option it is not worth very much unless this change in the optimal delivery date occurred during the cash-and-carry period.

Effect of Bond-Delivered Selection Option. In the section on the Treasury bond cash-and-carry, the most deliverable bond and the criteria for determining which bond it is were discussed. Because the short is not locked in to delivering the bond that was originally determined to be most deliverable, any changes in the most deliverable during the cash-and-carry period will represent a benefit to the short (an increase in the "floor" return) and a cost to the long.

Effect of Afternoon Put Option. An important aspect of the contract design is the afternoon put option that is created by the differences in closing times for the cash versus futures markets and by a delivery time for the short that occurs later than both closing times (all are New York times). The cash market trades until as late as 5 P.M. while futures trading ceases at 3 P.M. During the delivery month, the short has the option to deliver on any business day, but can tender notice to deliver as late as 8 P.M., at the delivery price that was set at the 3 P.M. close. This gives the short the opportunity to watch the market from 3 to 5 P.M. and decide later whether or not to deliver. The bond will be delivered unless the cash market price of the bond rises to a level that, net of transaction cost, makes it profitable to sell the bond and deliver instead the delivery *price* of the bond. An example of the potential value of this option occurs on Thursday afternoons in the delivery month, when the Fed releases the money supply statistics. Unanticipated changes often cause the bond market to rally or sell off substantially in the trading that follows. If, for example, the market trades down (that is, prices decline), the short can elect to deliver his bonds at the (higher) price set earlier when the futures market closed.

The combination of options is certainly worth something to the (potential) short, but since there is no explicit fee for the options, the short pays for the options by accepting a lower futures price. As a result, the futures price is normally lower than arbitrage or carry considerations would indicate. This becomes obvious when calculating the breakeven repo rates, which tend to be lower than the implied repo rates for similar time frame bill futures by up to several hundred basis points. To the uninitiated, futures prices may look "cheap" (too low) when in fact they are correctly priced in view of the options included. Thus, although arbitrage pricing can provide a guide to the value of Treasury bond futures, it essentially gives an upper bound to the price because of the options inherent in the contract.

Last Week in the Delivery Month Option. There is one final option available to the short. Trading in the bond futures contract ends eight business days before the end of the month, but delivery is permitted until the last day of the month. If a contract is not closed out before trading ends, delivery must be made during those final eight days at the settlement price of the contract at the end of trading. The short no longer has an option to deliver, because delivery is mandatory, but he still can select the delivery date and the bond that is delivered. If the bond that is most deliverable changes during this period, the short will find it profitable to swap in the cash market and deliver the new most deliverable bond. This feature can be valuable in a period of relatively high bond price volatility. This extended delivery period causes the contract to not converge completely by the end of trading, with 4/32 often being the difference between cash and futures at final settlement.

PRICING STOCK INDEX FUTURES CONTRACTS

When stock index futures began trading, the experience of the debt market regarding arbitrage and pricing was applied to the new market, with the result that many participants had models of "fair value" from the start. Despite the apparent differences between the underlying markets, and the fact that the equity futures were based on an index rather than an individual security, the basic methodology developed in the debt market can be applied to stock index futures. This section addresses the model and the assumptions and difficulties of applying it to the stock index futures market.

The basic arbitrage pricing equation is a logical starting point for the valuation of stock index futures. In the equity case, this equation is usually rearranged into the following form

$$F_0 = S_0 + (S_0 \times r) - D$$

or, in words,

$$\begin{matrix} \text{current} \\ \text{forward} \\ \text{price} \end{matrix} = \begin{matrix} \text{current} \\ \text{spot} \\ \text{price} \end{matrix} + \left(\begin{matrix} \text{current} \\ \text{spot} \\ \text{price} \end{matrix} \times \begin{matrix} \text{financing} \\ \text{rate} \end{matrix} \right) - \begin{matrix} \text{dollar} \\ \text{dividend} \\ \text{to be paid} \end{matrix}$$

In other words, the futures price is equal to the spot price (S_0) moved forward at the short-term rate (r, unannualized) minus the dividend that is paid at the end of the period. If the futures contract were on a single stock instead of a portfolio, the only adjustment needed to the preceding equation would be for dividends paid during (instead of at the end of) the period.

Assumptions Used in Stock Index Futures Pricing

The validity of the arbitrage pricing equation is based on the assumptions previously listed and their relationship to the actual marketplace. The assumptions are examined in the order listed in this chapter, although no ranking of importance is meant to be implied.

Nature of the Asset at Delivery. For most forward contracts, this assumption does not come into play, but for futures contracts it can be very important. Stock index futures do not have a simple asset underlying the contract, and the investor must attempt to own (or short) something that acts like the index. But the actual structure of the index may change prior to delivery (due to stock splits, mergers, or substitution of other stocks in the index population), and the portfolio may no longer represent the index.

Price of the Underlying Asset. Accurate forward pricing requires that the asset price be known, but the actual price of a portfolio meant to replicate a stock index is probably not known until all of the securities are purchased. Bids and offers may not be good for the size necessary, or the quotes may be "old" due to lack of volume in some stocks.

Short Sales of the Asset. It is obvious to market practitioners that short-ing an entire portfolio can be difficult. The "uptick" rule that prohibits short sales except on an uptick (or zero plus-tick) can compound the diffi-culty even further.

Proceeds of the Short Sale. This is not a concern to most institutional participants in the market, because the funds are available, whether the transaction is done as a *borrow versus cash, borrow versus collateral,* or *borrow versus letter of credit.* In a borrow versus cash, the lender of the securities to be shorted requires collateral, and the cash raised by the short sale is used as the collateral. But just as the short seller must pay the cash flows on the shorted security to the lender, the lender must pay a short term rate (usually 75 percent of the broker call rate) to the short seller. In the other types of borrowing, the lender has protection against credit risk, and the funds from the short sale remain with the short seller.

Retail investors will find that not only do they not receive the proceeds of the short sale, but they must put up at least another 50 percent of the value of the trade as margin.

Dividend Known and Paid at End of the Period. One of the assump-tions made in the derivation of the basic arbitrage pricing equation cited earlier was that the dividend payment date coincided with the settlement date of the contract. This assumption is not necessary and was included only for mathematical simplicity, so that D could be the actual dividend. However, the dividend can be adjusted for the time value of money between the pay-ment date and the settlement date. That is, if the dividend were to be re-ceived before settlement, it could be reinvested at the risk-free rate until settlement, in which case D would be larger than the actual dividend received. If the dividend was to be received after settlement, it should be discounted at the risk-free rate. In mathematical terms, the adjusted formula would be

$$F_0 = S_0 + rS_0 - D'$$

where r is an overnight rate and where $D' = D(1 + r)^n$ when the pay date is n days *before* settlement or, alternatively, $D' = D/(1 + r)^n$ when the pay date is n days *after* settlement and D is the actual dividend paid. However, unless n and/or r is large, the error made by assuming that D' and D are equal is negligible. For example, with a 10 percent annual risk-free rate and a divi-dend of $1.75 that is received 91 days before or after settlement, D' and D differ by only about four cents. Thus, the approximation that D' equals D can continue to be used. The reader, however, should be aware of this compound interest or discount rate effect, and check its size, particularly in the case of futures with a long time until settlement.

A much more important effect when valuing futures contracts on stock indexes is the seasonality in the dividends. Even though an index may con-tain several hundred stocks, the dividend yield until settlement may vary in a nonlinear fashion with time. This is illustrated in Figure 17-1, which depicts this nonlinearity for the Standard & Poor's (S&P) 500 for the 91-day period

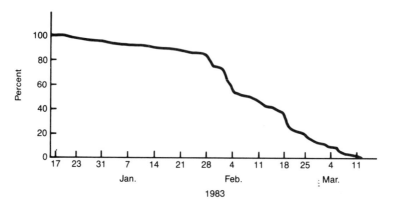

Figure 17-1. Percent of the Quarterly Dividend Remaining in the S&P 500 Stock Composite Index Stocks for the 91-day Period Ended March 17, 1983. (SOURCE: Salomon Brothers, Inc.)

ending March 17, 1983, the last day of trading of the S&P 500 March 1983 futures contract. From this figure, it is apparent that only about 15 percent of the total dollar dividends for the quarter have gone ex-dividend by about January 28. Thus, the holder of the S&P 500 over the second half of the mid-December to mid-March settlement quarter will receive about 85 percent of the quarter's dividends.[3] Naturally, this makes the effective annual dividend considerably larger, as shown in Figure 17-2. An interesting result of this is that a properly priced futures contract can sell at a discount to the index if the dividend yield until settlement exceeds the risk-free rate until settlement. This becomes immediately obvious if the original arbitrage pricing equation is rearranged so that

$$\frac{F_0 - S_0}{S_0} \quad = \quad r - y$$

or, in words,

excess of current forward price over current spot price per unit of spot price = excess of financing rate over dividend yield

or, in other words, in equilibrium,

the basis = excess of financing rate over dividend yield

where the dividend yield, y, is equal to D/S_0 or dollar dividends relative to the current spot price. If r is greater than y, then the basis, $(F_0 - S_0)/S_0$, is

---

[3] The change in the ex-dividend date of AT&T has changed this to about 75 percent. The figures reflect the statement in the text.

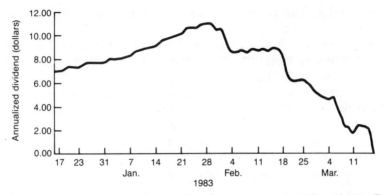

Figure 17-2. Annualized Dividend of he S&P 500 Index, January 15 to March 17, 1983. (SOURCE: Salomon Brothers, Inc.)

positive. If y is greater than r, it is negative. And, if r and y are equal, the basis is zero.

This is in contrast to other types of futures contracts, such as Treasury bond and note futures, where the underlying securities accrue coupon income evenly within each semiannual period. This results in a constant *effective semiannual coupon* that does not depend on the calculation date. If the coupon date falls before the settlement date for the futures contract, the actual/actual date arithmetic[4] used for Treasury bonds causes a slight change in the effective semiannual coupon, but the impact is small. With respect to Government National Mortgage Association (GNMA) futures, the exact cash flows associated with the underlying GNMA securities are not known (because of potential mortgage prepayments) and therefore must be estimated.

ARBITRAGE PRICING VS. EXPECTATIONS

The discussion to this point has demonstrated that Treasury bill futures can be priced quite accurately using an arbitrage model because the arbitrage is quite direct and easy to implement. Bond futures have options inherent in the contract which cause arbitrage pricing to give an upper bound to the price. Stock index futures have many features that make the underlying arbitrage somewhat difficult to perform, and thus prices tend to vary around the fair value, with periods of "cheap" prices followed by periods of "rich" prices (when evaluated as if the arbitrage could be performed). But for some contracts, the arbitrage cannot be performed at all, or at least not by many of the market participants. In such cases, arbitrage considerations may provide

---

[4] Actual/actual date arithmetic for bonds is where the actual number of days elapsed is related to the actual number of days in the semiannual coupon period, which will vary from 181 to 184 days in length depending on the particular semiannual period involved.

a guide to value, but expectations become more important in the actual marketplace.

Consider the difference between the Eurodollar futures contract and the Treasury bill futures contract with reference to the underlying security. Treasury bills are extremely liquid and can be purchased and sold short by many market participants. Eurodollar deposits, on the other hand, can be created only by banks (and only when investors deposit funds) and cannot be bought and sold or sold short by other market participants as Treasury bills can. Thus, for most investors, there is no arbitrage that can be contemplated, much less attempted. As a result, Eurodollar deposit contracts often trade with an *expectations component* embodied in their price.

HEDGING THE INTEREST COST OR PROFIT ON MARGIN FLOWS[5]

The descriptions of hedge ratio construction and of futures pricing proceeded on the assumption that the futures were actually forwards. This section addresses the difference between the two and provides an adjustment factor for hedge construction.

The major difference between a futures contract and a forward contract results from variation margin, the daily mark-to-the-market of an open futures position, that works as follows. If an investor is long a futures contract, and its settlement price on a given day is below that of the previous day, he is required to *post* the price difference in cash. If the price rises, he will *receive* the price difference, again, in cash. By contrast, with forward contracts, only *paper* profits or losses occur daily. No cash changes hands until expiration of the contracts. Thus, an investor who purchases Treasury bills and fairly valued forward contracts on the S&P 500 (such that the beta is 1.0) will realize exactly the same return as an investor who purchases the S&P 500 if the position is held until expiration of the contracts. In fact, the requirement that these two returns be identical led to the pricing equation for the forward contract, $F_0 = S_0 + rS_0 - D$.

Consider the investor who has purchased Treasury bills and futures contracts. If the futures price drops, he will have to meet the variation margin by liquidating some of his Treasury bills. He thus loses the interest on these funds. Of course, if the futures price rises, cash will flow into his account and he will gain interest by investing these funds in Treasury bills. The net effect of these daily cash flows is to alter the return on his position by the net interest gained or lost. Summarizing in mathematical terms,

    a. Treasury bills and forward contracts: $R_A = R_{S\&P\ 500}$
    b. Treasury bills and futures contracts: $R_B = R_{S\&P\ 500} + i_M$

where i_M is the net interest gained or lost from variation margin.

---

[5] This section is based on the chapter by N. Hanson and R. Kopprasch, "Pricing of Stock Index Futures," in Fabozzi and Kipnis [1984], pages 75–79.

If the overnight rate of interest, r, remains constant, there exists an adjustment to the number of futures contracts purchased that will make the term i_M equal to zero. To illustrate this, suppose that three days are left until expiration of the futures, depicted as follows:

Day	0	1	2	3
Settlement price	F_0	F_1	F_2	F_3

F_3 is the value at expiration of the futures on Day 3. Since the futures contract is marked to the index at expiration, F_3 equals I_3, where I_3 is the stock index level for day 3.

Suppose a futures contract is bought at some time during Day 0 for price F. At the close of Day 0, the dollar return is equal to $(F_0 - F)$. If F_0 is greater than F, this money can be invested at the overnight rate of interest for three days. At the end of Day 3, $(F_0 - F)(1 + r)^3$ dollars will have accumulated. If F_0 is less than F, $(F - F_0)$ Treasury bills will be liquidated, thus losing an amount of interest equal to $(F - F_0)(1 + r)^3$. This procedure is repeated each day, as illustrated in Table 17-1. The dollar total return to the holder of the *futures* contract is the sum of the terms in column 4 of Table 17-1.

$$R_{fut} = (F_0 - F)(1 + r)^3 + (F_1 - F_0)(1 + r)^2 + (F_2 - F_1)(1 + r) + (I_3 - F_2)$$

or, in words,

return on a futures contract from day zero to day 3	positive or negative variation margin flow on day zero compounded forward for 3 days	positive or negative variation margin flow on day 1 compounded forward for 2 days	positive or negative variation margin flow on day 2 compounded forward for 1 day
=	+	+	

positive or negative + variation margin flow on day 3

The ultimate return is dependent on the daily settlement prices.

The total return to the holder of a *forward* contract is given by the sum of the terms in the third column of Table 17-1.

$$R_{fwd} = (F_0 - F) + (F_1 - F_0) + (F_2 - F_1) + (I_3 - F_2) = I_3 - F$$

Thus the forward contract return depends only on the initial and final prices and is independent of the intermediate daily settlement prices.

TABLE 17-1. Settlement Price, Variation Margin and Variation Margin Plus Interest at Expiration for a Three-Day

Day	Settlement Price	Variation Margin	Variation Margin Plus Interest at Expiration
0	F_0	$F_0 - F$	$(F_0 - F)(1 + r)^3$
1	F_1	$F_1 - F_0$	$(F_1 - F_0)(1 + r)^2$
2	F_2	$F_2 - F_1$	$(F_2 - F_1)(1 + r)$
3	I_3	$I_3 - F_2$	$I_3 - F_2$

SOURCE: Fabozzi and Kipnis [1984].

Suppose that rather than holding one futures contract for the three-day period, the investor holds n_i contracts on Day i. The first equation above may then be rewritten

$$R_{fut} = n_0(F_0 - F)(1 + r)^3 + n_1(F_1 - F_0)(1 + r)^2$$
$$+ n_2(F_2 - F_1)(1 + r) + n_3(I_3 - F_2)$$

By inspection, it can be seen that if

$$n_0 = \frac{1}{(1 + r)^3}, \quad n_1 = \frac{1}{(1 + r)^2}, \quad n_2 = \frac{1}{(1 + r)}, \quad \text{and } n_3 = 1,$$

the preceding equation reduces to $R_{fut} = I_3 - F = R_{fwd}$.

Thus, the return on the futures position is identical to that on the forward position. There is no net interest gained or lost due to the variation margin. Embodied in the rewritten futures return equation is the assumption that the daily adjustment to the number of contracts, Δn, is implemented by adding to the futures position at the opening the next day at a price equal to the previous day's settlement price. Note that this procedure does not eliminate the daily cash flows. It just assures that no net interest is gained or lost due to meeting them. We have created a *forward equivalent*. In general, if there are N days left until expiration of the futures, the appropriate number of futures contracts to hold to equate to one forward contract is

$$n = \frac{1}{(1 + r)^N}$$

and

$$\text{one forward equivalent} = \frac{1}{(1 + r)^N} \text{ futures contracts.}$$

Note that as the number of days until expiration decreases, n increases and approaches unity as N approaches zero. Table 17-2 gives the number of futures contracts required to be in the equivalent position of 1,000 forward contracts, assuming an annual interest rate of 10 percent.[6]

[6] One thousand forward contracts at an S&P 500 price of 180 represents a $90 million ($500 × 180 × 1,000) position in the index.

TABLE 17-2. Number of Futures Contracts Equivalent to One Thousand Forward Contracts at Various Time Periods Remaining to Expiration Assuming a 10 Percent Annual Rate of Interest

Time until Expiration	No. of Forwards	No. of Futures
1 year	1,000	909
6 months	1,000	953
3 months	1,000	976
2 months	1,000	984
1 month	1,000	992
1 week	1,000	998
1 day	1,000	1,000

SOURCE: Fabozzi and Kipnis [1984].

Even if this position is closed out before expiration of the futures, the return is still the same as that which would be obtained with a forward. For example, suppose n_0 contracts were purchased initially during Day 0 at price F and sold later during Day 0 at price F_0. The return would be

$$n_0(F_0 - F) = \frac{F_0 - F}{(1 + r)^3}$$

Had this been a forward contract, in order to close out the position, the investor would have to sell a forward at F_0. Since no money would change hands until delivery, his return today would be the present value of the difference in the two prices, or $(F_0 - F)/(1 + r)^3$, identical to that in the above equation.

While this procedure is applicable to futures contracts on any commodity, in the real world it only allows a futures position to approximate a forward position. Varying (intraday) interest rates, correlation between spot price changes and interest-rate changes, the inability to purchase futures contracts in the morning at the previous day's settlement price, and the inability to purchase fractions of a contract introduce frictions that prevent creation of a perfect forward equivalent. Nevertheless, for stock index futures, this procedure is quite effective in reducing i_M to an essentially negligible amount.

Obviously, there is a more complex relationship for interest rate futures. The movement of interest rates during a hedge of interest rate futures (especially Treasury bill or Eurodollar futures) favors the short. If rates rise, the short will receive margin, and can invest at the higher rate. If rates fall, he will have to pay variation margin, but can finance it at the lower rate. It has been argued that this bias should be reflected in futures prices that are slightly lower than forward prices. See Cox, Ingersoll and Ross [1981].

The bottom line of this forward-futures equivalence argument is that if short-term rates are stable or reasonably so, the prices of futures contracts and forward contracts with identical delivery dates should be nearly equivalent. Note that this does not mean that futures and forwards are equivalent in terms of actual price volatility per contract. For contracts of identical size, futures are more volatile than forwards because of the immediate mark-to-market on the futures. As previously shown, the profit on a forward position is the present value of the difference in purchase and sale prices, while the profit on a futures contract is the undiscounted difference between the prices. Thus, if a strategy is conceived in terms of forwards, and then implemented with futures, the number of contracts must be adjusted to reflect the difference in volatility.[7] When futures positions and forward positions are weighted this way, there is no difference in economic profit between them.

VALUATION OF OPTION CONTRACTS

It is rare to find an institutional participant in the options market who is not concerned with the "value" of options as determined by a mathematical model. There are a number of commercially available models, many of which are variations of the original Black-Scholes model,[8] and are referred to as *riskless-hedge models*. These models will be discussed from an overall conceptual perspective first and then decomposed and studied in more detail. But before doing so, two key concepts with respect to option valuation need to be defined and discussed.

Intrinsic Value and Time Value

The value of an option contract can be separated into two components fairly easily. The first component, called intrinsic value, is the value of the option if it were exercised today,[9] or zero, if that is higher. The second component, called time value, represents the value inherent in holding the option rather than exercising, primarily because it may become more valuable in the future. If an option can be exercised immediately, arbitrage normally assures that the market value of an option is at least as great as the intrinsic value, and any excess of the market value over the intrinsic value is referred to as the time premium or time value.

The intrinsic value of a call is shown in Figure 17-3. If the price of the underlying security or index is greater than the exercise or strike price, the option will be *in-the-money* and the intrinsic value will be positive. If the

[7] One might also think of the futures contract as having the volatility of a forward contract of greater size than the futures. This greater size is simply the compounded value of the nominal amount found by multiplying the nominal amount by $(1 + r)^n$, where r and n are as previously defined. Thus, if one buys 1,000 units of the underlying instruments, one might sell futures contracts on 900 units if the 900 units have the volatility of 1,000 forward units. As this position moved through time, the futures position would be increased because $(1 + r)^n$, the volatility factor, declines as n declines.

[8] Black and Scholes [1973].

[9] So called American options can be exercised at any time until expiration, while "European" options can be exercised only at expiration.

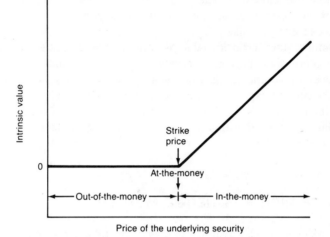

Figure 17-3. Intrinsic Value of a Call Option Contract.

price of the underlying is equal to the exercise price (*at-the-money*) or below (*out-of-the-money*), the intrinsic value is zero. The importance of the intrinsic value is that it determines the value of an option at expiration (when, of course, there is no time value), and it sets a floor on the value at any time prior to expiration.

The intrinsic value of a put is shown in Figure 17-4. Because a put is the right to *sell* a security at a set price, the put increases in intrinsic value as the price of the underlying falls *below* the strike price. The terminology for a put is similar to that of a call: If the price of the underlying security is below the strike price, the intrinsic value is positive and the option is

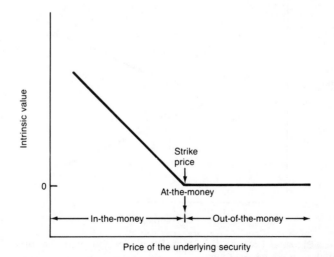

Figure 17-4. Intrinsic Value of a Put Option Contract.

said to be in-the-money. If the price of the underlying equals the strike price, it is at-the-money, and it is out-of-the-money if the price of the underlying exceeds the strike price.

Determining the intrinsic value is straightforward, but the time value estimate is more difficult. The time value for both puts and calls will depend on a number of additional factors, such as the volatility of the underlying security, the time to expiration, and the level of interest rates. The remainder of this chapter addresses the estimation of the total value of an option. It may help to think of this as estimating how much time value should be added to the intrinsic value.

BASICS OF RISKLESS HEDGE MODELS

The riskless hedge model assumes that one can take a position in an option and a weighted position in the underlying security that will result in the same wealth position at the end of the next period, regardless of whether the security goes up or down in price. Because the combined position results in the same wealth, it is said to be a riskless, or neutral, hedge position. Take one such position, using the "binomial" model, as diagrammed in Figure 17-5.

The goal is to determine the value of a call option at the first point ($t = 0$), when the underlying security is priced at 99 and the option expires one "period" later ($t = 1$). Of course, it is a simple task to value the call at expiration, because it will be worth either the security price minus the strike price (if positive), or zero. These values for the two assumed outcomes have been added to the diagram in Figure 17-6.

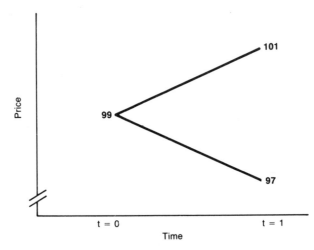

Figure 17-5. Binomial Process for Stock Prices for the Valuation of a Call Option Contract With a Strike Price of 98.

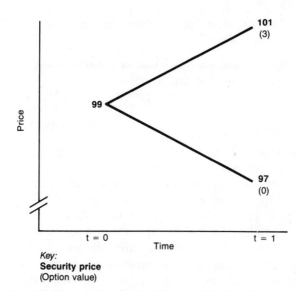

Key:
Security price
(Option value)

Figure 17-6. Binomial Process for Stock Prices and Option Values for a Call Option With a Strike Price of 98.

Given the possible outcomes of the security at 101 and the option at 3 or the security at 97 and the option worthless at 0, is there a position that can be taken when the security is 99 that will leave the investor indifferent as to the outcome that occurs? In fact, there is, and it involves holding one unit of the security and selling short 1⅓ options. (How this "hedge ratio" is determined is detailed in a later section of this chapter.) The possible outcomes of such a position are shown in Table 17-1.

TABLE 17-3. Example of a Binomial Process for Stock Prices and Option Values for a Call Option with a Strike Price of 98 to Produce a Riskless Hedge Position

Security Value at Expiration	Option Value	Short Position Option Value × 1⅓	Net Value of Position
101	3	−4	97
97	0	0	97

As shown, the position is worth 97 at expiration whether the security goes to 101 or to 97, so the position of long one unit of the security and short 1⅓ options is riskless. Because it is riskless, it should earn only the risk-free rate over the period, assumed to be one percent. Thus, an investor would only be willing to pay 97/1.01, or 96.0396, for the position. Because the position is long one unit of the security costing 99, the 1⅓ options sold short must generate the difference between 99 and the total portfolio cost of 96.0396, or 2.9604. The options must therefore sell for 2.2203 each. In summary, the steps followed are:

Number of options sold short per unit of the underlying:	1⅓
Value of hedged portfolio at expiration:	97
Value of portfolio discounted one period:	97/1.01 = 96.0396
Total value of options:	99 − 96.0396 = 2.9604
Value per option:	2.9604/1.33333 = 2.2203

Notice that what is postulated in this model is that the ratio of options to stock in the hedged position is constantly modified at no commission cost to offset gains and losses on the stock with losses and gains on the option. Because the position is theoretically riskless, the option premium at which the hedge yields a pretax return equal to the risk-free interest rate is the fair value of the option. Notice also that the option value was determined without any reference to the probability that the security would go up or down in price. This is probably the most surprising aspect of the model for most investors. Before extending the model to two periods, the way in which the parameters used in this simple case affect the value of the option should be examined.

Short-Term Rate

First, consider how the solution would have differed if the short-term rate over the period was 1.2 percent instead of 1.0 percent. None of the values in Table 17-1 would have changed, but the value of the discounted portfolio when the security was 99 would be 97/1.012, or 95.8498, and the 1⅓ call options would be worth 3.1502. Each option is therefore worth 2.3626 (versus 2.2203 when the rate was 1 percent per period). This is a general result: *Call option values are higher, other things being equal, when the short-term rate is higher*. This result has intuitive appeal, because the call option seller (who is constructing the hedge) has a higher opportunity cost for the funds invested in the security when short-term rates are high, and must be compensated in the form of a higher premium. The steps followed are:

Number of options per unit of underlying:	1⅓
Value of hedged portfolio at expiration:	97
Value of portfolio discounted one period:	97/1.012 = 95.8498
Total value of options:	99 − 95.8498 = 3.1502
Value per option:	3.1502/1.33333 = 2.3626

Strike Price

If the strike price were lower, say 96, the value of the call would be higher. This can be demonstrated by using the same approach as before. In this

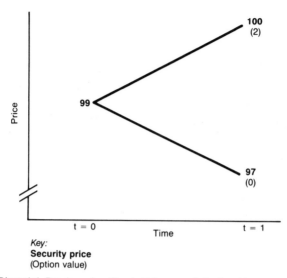

Key:
Security price
(Option value)

Figure 17-7. Binomial Process for Stock Prices and Option Values for a Call Option With a Strike Price of 98 in a Lower Volatility Environment.

case, the hedged portfolio would now consist of one unit of the security and short one call option (again, deferring temporarily how this hedge ratio is determined), and the portfolio value at expiration would be 96 (the value of the security less the value of one option). As the analytic summary below demonstrates, the value of the option would be 3.9505. Thus, *a lower strike price does indeed increase the value of a call.*

Number of options per unit of underlying:	1.0
Value of hedged portfolio at expiration:	96
Value of portfolio discounted one period:	$96/1.01 = 95.0495$
Total value of options:	$99 - 95.0495 = 3.9505$
Value per option:	$3.9505/1.0 = 3.9505$

Volatility

Although the term volatility has not been used thus far in describing the example, it is this characteristic that determines how wide the spread is among the ultimate outcomes. If the volatility was lower, the original diagram might look like Figure 17-7.

Proceeding in the same manner as previously, the call option is valued as follows with the call value lower than it was in the high volatility case. This is a general, but not universal, result: *Lower volatility leads to lower option values, and vice versa.*[10]

---

[10] Options that are very deep in-the-money or very far out-of-the-money may be insensitive to small changes in volatility.

Number of options per unit of underlying: 1.0
Value of hedged portfolio at expiration: 98
Value of portfolio discounted one period: $98/1.01 = 97.0297$
Total value of options: $99 - 97.0297 = 1.9703$
Value per option: $1.9703/1.0 = 1.9703$

Price of the Security

As long as the security price is not too far from the strike price, an increase in the current security price will increase the value of a call, and a lower current security price will lower the value. Without resorting to the model, it is easy to see that if the security was priced at 105, the option would have more value, and if the security was priced at 90, the value would be very low (probably zero) because the probability that the security would reach the strike price is negligible except for high volatility securities.

Time to Expiration

The simple model just described above can be easily extended to situations involving more than one period. Figure 17-8 shows how the example above might look if there were two periods to expiration. Note that the distribution of possible outcomes is wider (from 95 to 103 versus 97 to 101) even though the volatility *per period* is the same as in Figure 17-5.

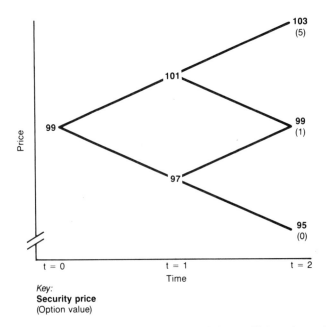

Figure 17-8. Binomial Process for Stock Prices and Option Values for a Call Option With a Strike Price of 98 in a Multiple Period Environment.

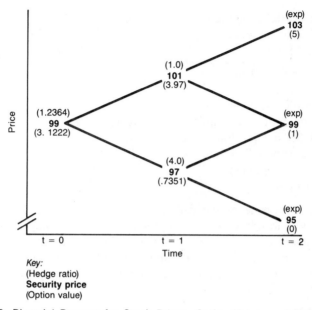

Figure 17-9. Binomial Process for Stock Prices, Option Values and Hedge Ratios for a Call Option With a Strike Price of 98 in a Multiple Period Environment.

The procedure for determining the value proceeds just as in the previous examples: Start with the known values at expiration, and solve for the value(s) one period earlier. When those values are known, solve for those one period before that, and so on, for longer-period models. The following summary demonstrates how to calculate the value of the call option when the security value is 101 and there is one period to expiration. The calculations for the other points employ the same approach, and are shown in the two summary tables that follow. The overall results are shown in Figure 17-9.

Branch of Binomial Distribution:	Upper
Security value:	101
Periods until expiration:	1
Number of options per unit of underlying:	1.0
Value of hedged portfolio at expiration:	98
Value of portfolio discounted one period:	$98/1.01 = 97.0297$
Total value of options:	$101 - 97.0297 = 3.9703$
Value per option:	$3.9703/1.0 = 3.9703$

Branch of Binomial Distribution:	Lower
Security value:	97
Periods until expiration:	1
Number of options per unit of underlying:	4.0
Value of hedged portfolio at expiration:	95

Value of portfolio discounted one period: 95/1.01 = 94.0594
Total value of options: 97 − 94.0594 = 2.9406
Value per option: 3.9406/4.0 = 0.7351

Branch of Binomial Distribution:	Initial
Security value:	99
Periods until expiration:	2
Number of options per unit of underlying:	1.2364
Value of hedged portfolio at expiration:	96.0910
Value of portfolio discounted one period:	96.0910/1.01 = 95.1397
Total value of options:	99 − 95.1397 = 3.8603
Value per option:	2.9406/4.0 = 0.7351

Note that the value of the call option is greater (3.1222 vs. 1.9703) when there is a longer time to expiration. *In general, longer options are worth more than shorter options.* However, European options on currencies (which are exercisable only at expiration) offer one example for which increasing the time to maturity may actually decrease the option value.

Using the Binomial Model

The binomial model is a good instructional tool because it is possible to see what is happening at each point in the valuation process. In addition, it offers some flexibility, because it is possible to construct the "tree" of price movement such that either volatility or the short-term rate can be modified as a function of time or of price. However, it is necessary to use many periods to obtain a fine distribution of prices. The solution procedure may even strain a computer's resources. As a result, the binomial is usually used only when its additional flexibility is necessary to reflect the modeler's view of the world or some complicated option contract specifications. A much more commonly used model, the Black-Scholes model, is discussed next.

The Black-Scholes Model

The now famous riskless-hedge model by Black and Scholes was published in 1973. This was about the same time that the Chicago Board Options Exchange (CBOE) began trading options, and the model's popularity grew with the market. The primary advantage of the model is that it is a "closed-form" solution, which means that it is in the form of an equation that can be solved directly by inputting the correct parameters, with no iteration necessary. The model is shown as follows:

Call value $= S \times N(d_1) - Ee^{-rt} \times N(d_2)$

where S = stock price
        E = exercise (strike) price

N( ) = the value of the cumulative normal distribution at the point ( )

$$d_1 = \frac{\ln(S/E) + (r + .5\sigma^2)t}{\sigma \sqrt{t}}$$

$d_2 = d_1 - \sigma \sqrt{t}$

$\ln$ = natural logarithm

r = short term riskless rate (continuously compounded)

t = time to expiration, in years

e = base of natural logarithms

σ = annual standard deviation of return (usually referred to as "volatility")

or, as Cox and Rubenstein [1985] have observed, call option value equals the present value of *receiving* the stock if, and only if, its price is greater than the strike (or exercise) price *minus* the present value of *paying* the strike price if, and only if, the stock price is above the strike price.

As an example of the use of this complex formula, consider the following case:

stock price = 48
strike price = 50
short term rate = 10% (.1)
volatility (annual standard deviation) = 30% (.30)
time to expiration = 3 months (.25 yrs.)

In order to determine the call value, C, the above parameters are inputted into the model and evaluated.

Step 1:   Solve for d_1 = $[\ln(S/E) + (r + .5\sigma^2)t]/\sigma\sqrt{t}$
= $[\ln(48/50) + (.10 + .5 \times .09) \times .25]/ .3 \times .5$
= $[- 0.04082 + .03625]/.15$
= $- .03047$
$N(d_1)$ = .4878 from a cumulative normal probability distribution table.

Step 2:   Solve for d_2 = $d_1 - \sigma\sqrt{t}$
= $- .03047 - .15$
= $- .18047$
$N(d_2)$ = .4284 from table.

Step 3:   Solve for e^{-rt} = e^{-rt}
= $e^{-.1 \times .25}$
= .9753

Step 4:   Solve for C = $S \times N(d_1) - Ee^{-rt} \times N(d_2)$
= $48 \times .4878 - 50 \times .9753 \times .4284$
= $23.4144 - 20.8909$
= 2.52

Hedge Ratio

In the examples using the binomial model, the amount of the underlying security was held constant at one unit, and the number of options to sell to maintain the riskless hedge position was determined. The accepted definition of *hedge ratio* when discussing options looks at the position from the opposite viewpoint: *how many units of the underlying security are to be paired with one option.* In the first binomial example used here, the investor had to sell 1⅓ options per unit of the underlying. Because the hedge ratio is quoted as units of the underlying security relative to units of options, the ratio would be the inverse or 1/(1⅓) or .75.

The Black-Scholes model also provides a hedge ratio for the riskless hedge. It is computed as part of the overall calculation of the call price, because the hedge ratio is simply the value for $N(d_1)$ in their model. (Actually, it is $-N(d_1)$, with the minus sign to signify that the positions in the security and the call option are opposite, long and short.) In the preceding Black-Scholes example, the hedge ratio is .4878 (technically minus .4878); that is, the investor should go long 49 shares for each (100 share-based) option contract sold short.

What Does the "Value" Mean?

It is important to understand exactly what the value from a riskless hedge implies, and what it does not. An option is fairly priced if the riskless hedge earns exactly the risk-free rate. If the option is overpriced, that is, the price is higher than the model-determined value, this simply means that the riskless hedger can earn more than the riskless rate. If the option is underpriced, the "long stock, short option" continuously hedged portfolio would earn less than the risk-free rate. The model does not suggest that simply buying underpriced options will result in a profit over any particular short or long period of time. Similarly, writing covered calls (that is, using an unchanging hedge ratio of 1.0), even if the calls are overpriced, need not result in an increase in the rate of return over the non-option writer.

The riskless hedge models value the option relative to the stock, but no claim is made that the stock is fairly priced. If a stock is clearly overpriced, a call option on that stock should not be expected to provide an above market return, even if the call option is "underpriced." For an example of this, take the example used in the binomial model section titled "Volatility". The security in that example was priced at 99, with possible outcomes of 100 and 98. If it is assumed for the moment that there is a .5 probability of the higher price occurring and .5 for the lower price, the expected return on the stock over the period is zero percent. Yet the option is priced at almost its maximum possible expiration value of 2. How can this option be fairly priced, if it has a 50 percent chance of being worth 2 and a 50 percent chance of becoming worthless?

First, one might say that it is unlikely that the probability of a price increase is only .50, because then the holder of the security will have an expected return of less than the risk-free rate. In fact, for the holder to have an expectation of only the risk-free rate, the probability of a price increase must exceed .99. If this is the market expectation, then the option buyer could expect a better than 99 percent chance of a two-point payoff on the option, and thus the 1.97 price is not unreasonable.

It is not necessary to resort to probabilities, however. Consider the potential investor in the stock, who knows that the potential values are 100 and 98 but does not know the probabilities. An alternative to paying 99 for the stock is to buy a call option for 1.9703 and put the remaining 97.0297 into a risk-free security earning one percent over the period. (A more in-depth discussion of this strategy can be found in Chapter 18 of this Supplement.) The risk-free investment would be worth 98 (= 97.0297 × 1.01) in any event and the option would be worthless if the underlying security is priced at 98 and worth 2 if that security is priced at 100. Thus, the investor would have the same wealth and return as if he had bought the security itself. Obviously, if the option sold for any less than 1.9703, the option and risk-free investment strategy would dominate the security. Thus, the option is fairly valued *relative to the security*. However, even if the call price is 1.90, an investor who simply buys the call is given no guarantee that the transaction will be profitable, even if repeated many times. (Note that in this example, one option was bought instead of one unit of the underlying because the hedge ratio was 1.0.)

Assumptions of the Black-Scholes Model

The Black-Scholes model, as formally derived, contains a number of assumptions. These include continuous trading in the security, no price "gaps," no transactions costs, no taxes, no dividends (or any cash flows) on the underlying security, and a constant short-term rate. While these assumptions look fairly restrictive, the model is fairly robust even when these restrictions are eased. It should be obvious, however, that the model's values will always be lower than the price at which a potential riskless hedger would be willing to sell the option because of transactions costs.

Another major assumption of the model is that the option is "European," which means that the option can only be exercised at expiration. "American" options can be exercised anytime until expiration. As a result, the model does not actually represent the type of options traded on the major U.S. exchanges. For nondividend paying securities, this poses no real problem for call valuation, but for calls on dividend paying securities and for puts, the values will not be correct without some modifications to the model. Included in the "dividend paying" category are most fixed income securities, with the exception of zero coupon bonds. More will be said about the early exercise of American options shortly.

Finally, the Black-Scholes model proceeds under the assumption that the security price "walks" through time in such a way that the final outcomes are distributed lognormally. This is not an unreasonable assumption for equities, but it probably is unreasonable for bonds, whose values through time must ultimately approach par or redemption value. At the same time, the assumption of a constant short-term rate makes the model useless for valuing options on Treasury bills, for example. As a result of the inapplicability of the model to a variety of real world situations, a number of modifications have been suggested, as well as many other models designed for these specific cases.

Modified Black-Scholes Models

The first modification is a model that provides correct values for securities that pay out some form of known cash flows prior to the (European) option's expiration. In this situation, the portion of the security's price that represents the cash flows to be received before expiration is subtracted from the actual price to determine the adjusted price of the security to be used in the model. This is done by subtracting the present value of the cash flows from the price, and this new adjusted price is used in the standard Black-Scholes model.

At almost the same time that the original Black-Scholes model was published, Merton[11] suggested a modification for securities paying continuous (and proportional) dividends. While this may sound like a model built for a nonexistent security, it does in fact have several applications. One can think of a currency with an established forward market based on interest rate differentials as being a security that pays a continuous and proportional dividend. This model was used for many years for over-the-counter currency options, and is now used for exchange-traded currency options.

Most options on fixed income securities are structured so that the exerciser of a call must pay accrued interest in addition to the strike price. This makes a bond resemble a continuous (though not proportional) paying security, and for options with reasonably short time to expiration, the Merton model provides a quick approximation to the value.

The Merton model is essentially identical to the Black-Scholes model with the following changes: (1) replace S in the formula with Se^{-pt}; (2) replace r in the d_1 and d_2 terms with $r - p$, where p = payout rate expressed as an annual percentage. An alternative is to simply replace S by Se^{-pt} everywhere in the model (including the d_1 and d_2 terms), and do not explicitly introduce $r - p$.

Pricing Puts

Once a value for a European call has been determined, it is possible to value a put with the same strike price and expiration date using a simple formula. This concept is based on the notion of *put-call parity* that says that there is a specific relationship that must exist between puts and calls with the same underlying security and the same terms. Consider the following: buy or go long

---

[11] Merton [1973].

the security, short or sell a call and go long a put. For simplicity, assume that the security is priced at 50 and that the strike prices on the put and call are also 50. An investor in this position has a riskless portfolio that will surely be worth 50 at the options' expiration. If the security is worth 50 at expiration, the options will be worthless and the portfolio will be worth 50. If the security is below 50, the call will be worthless but the investor will "put" the security to the put writer at 50. If the security is worth more than 50, the put will be worthless, but the holder of the call will exercise it and pay the investor 50 for the security. In either case, the portfolio will be worth 50 (the strike price) at expiration.

Given the portfolio value of 50 at expiration, one must discount that value at the riskless rate (just as in the binomial examples above) to determine its value today. Assume that that value is 49; what is the value of the put? It depends on the value of the call. If the call is worth 3, the put must cost 2 so that the portfolio costs 49. Buying the security costs 50, selling the call nets 3, so the net outflow so far is 47. Buying the put for 2 results in a portfolio that costs 49, as it should because it is riskless. If the call sells for 5, the put should sell for 4.

This simple and direct relationship between the values of puts and calls leads to some possibly counter-intuitive results. For example, during an extremely bullish period, one might expect that calls would be bid up in price but that puts would fall. In fact, if calls are suddenly bid up (with no change in the underlying price), puts will similarly increase in price. If they did not, arbitrageurs would engage in the transaction above (known as a *conversion*) and would generate riskless profits above the riskless rate. For example, if calls increased from 3 to 4, but puts remained at 2, the riskless portfolio could be assembled for only 48. Its value of 50 at expiration would result in a return well above the risk-free rate.

It is important to note that this relationship holds strictly for European options, because otherwise the possibility of early exercise—to be discussed shortly— would change the return to the investor.

Additional Models not of Black-Scholes Derivation

Many securities in the debt market have embedded options that defy the riskless hedge mechanism because no ratio other than 1:1 is possible.[12] Callable bonds represent one example, and there are many others. More complex examples include mortgages, which are essentially callable anytime during their lives, and putable bonds with multiple exercise dates. In these cases, no riskless hedge can be constructed, and another model must be employed.

For exchange-traded debt options on long-term securities that will allow a riskless hedge, a Black-Scholes variant may be used for options that expire

---

[12] Some would argue that other highly correlated securities could be used to obtain a hedge ratio other than 1:1. If such hedging were actually possible with a high degree of accuracy, this would be true. It would also make the author's job considerably easier.

in the near future. For longer options, the lognormal price distribution assumption will usually be inappropriate, and another model must be used. One approach is to model the yield, and let the yield perform the lognormal "walk." Then, yields are converted into prices and the option can be valued.

More complex models are available for debt options. A "two state" model by Brennan and Schwartz[13] attempts to model the yield curve by reference to a short and a very long rate. A distribution of yields is determined from the yield curve model, and the option is then valued. Many proprietary models have been developed by Wall Street firms for their own traders and customers, and most of these are closely guarded instead of being published in academic journals. As more and more debt securities are introduced with optional characteristics, the need to value the new options will continue to provide new valuation models for some time.

A Note on Early Exercise

Throughout the option valuation sections, it was assumed that there was no early exercise possible. Yet American options permit early exercise, and valuation models must allow for this. In this section, the factors affecting early exercise will be enumerated, and then how the models must be altered to reflect this possibility will be described.

The basic rule for determining whether early exercise makes sense is to answer the following question: Is this option worth more today based on intrinsic value than its "forward looking" value as an option? If the answer is yes, then the option should be exercised. A few examples illustrate this point.

Consider a put (on a stock) with a strike price of $50, with six months remaining until expiration. Imagine that the stock price is zero, or very close to it. Exercising the put will bring the holder $50, which is the most he can hope to reap even if he waits until expiration. Thus, it is clear that he should exercise today and start earning a return on the $50 instead of waiting and collecting a maximum of $50 at expiration. (Of course, if the stock rallied, the investor would receive even less than $50 at expiration.) If this option were European, its value today would be the *present value* of the $50 rather than the full $50 intrinsic value of the American option. This is a clear example of the value of the American (early) exercise feature for puts.

For call options, it is usually a dividend payment that will trigger early exercise. Consider a call with a strike price of $50 that will expire in two days, on an equity currently priced at $51. The value of the call would be about $1. But assume that the stock is going to go ex-dividend in one day, with the dividend at $2. On the ex-dividend date, the stock will probably drop by about $2, leaving it at $49 and the call out-of-the-money and virtually worthless with only one day remaining. It obviously is in the call holder's

---

[13] Brennan and Schwartz [1983].

interest to exercise (or sell the call to someone else who will exercise) before the dividend goes "ex."

These two examples are admittedly extreme, but they were chosen to illustrate the reasons for early exercise. Puts reach early exercise points when they are deep in the money because of two factors: the upside value of a put is limited (the maximum value of any put is the strike price, regardless of the amount of time left to expiration or the level of volatility), and second, the present value effect (the return that can be earned if the value is captured early) may outweigh any potential increase in value. Stated differently, a deep in-the-money put with a relatively long time to expiration will be exercised if its intrinsic value is larger than the present value of its maximum value as a put contract.

It is normally optimal to exercise calls early only just before dividend payments, because the value of the equity drops but the strike price does not.[14] That is, just prior to the ex-dividend date for a stock *and* near the expiration date for an in-the-money call option on that stock, the call option will be exercised to capture its value (that is, just prior to the decline in price of the underlying stock due to the ex-dividend effect).[15]

As the parameters in the examples are changed, it may not be so obvious that exercise is optimal. In the put example, if the option were 8 points in the money instead of 50, would it still be optimal to exercise? Would the call be exercised if there were three months until expiration? The basic rule still holds: If the option is worth more dead (exercised) than alive (as an option), it should be exercised.

The binomial model is especially easy to adapt for American options. At each node, one solves for value as in the earlier examples, but then checks that value against the value if exercised at that point. If the exercise value is greater, then that is the value placed at that point and used in subsequent calculations.

SUMMARY

As shown in this chapter, futures and options have introduced new measures of valuation in the fixed income and equity markets. In the fixed income sector, investors have used yield to maturity and current yield as their primary yardsticks, while equity investors have used P/E ratios, return on equity,

---

[14] Call options on debt instruments are not usually subject to early exercise because, unlike stocks, the nominal strike price is continually adjusted for accrued interest (i.e., the strike price has accrued interest included in it). When the coupon is paid and the full price of the bond drops, the strike price declines by a like amount because the accrued interest declines to zero. Thus there is no particular benefit to exercising bond call options before the cash flow.

[15] Taxable investors or arbitrageurs, who are simply attempting to extract value from the call, would probably sell the stock immediately to avoid the tax liability associated with receiving the dividend.

and others in the search for performance. In the futures market, it is the breakeven repo rate that is the measure of richness and cheapness for both equity and fixed income futures. In equity futures, the breakeven repo rate is sometimes referred to as the return to the hedged portfolio or RHP. When analyzing either debt or equity options, the implied volatility has come to be the accepted measure of value.

Thus, for all the differences in the underlying markets, the futures contracts of debt and equity are analyzed similarly, as are debt and equity options. This commonality, and the similarity of the many uses of these new instruments in each of the markets, seems to be bringing the markets closer together. It is not uncommon to hear equity managers talk about the relative attractiveness of bond futures, and many fixed income managers carefully watch stock index futures. Some of the newly available strategies, discussed in the next chapter, promise to continue this intermingling of sectors.

FURTHER READING

In contrast to the paucity of literature on the valuation of futures contracts, there is a fairly large body of literature on option valuation, most of it based on the original Black-Scholes model. An excellent summary of the literature on option valuation can be found in the Smith [1976] article. Many of the early references on option valuation are based on variations on the original Black-Scholes model and deal with traditional options. By contrast, the more recently published research involves variations on the binomial model and deal with more recently introduced options contracts.

One of the first attempts to create and synthesize a body of knowledge on the valuation of stock index futures contracts can be found in Fabozzi and Kipnis [1984].

BIBLIOGRAPHY

Black, Fisher, "The Pricing of Commodity Contracts," *Journal of Financial Economics,* January/February 1976.

————— **and M. Scholes,** "The Pricing of Options and Corporate Liabilities," *Journal of Political Economy,* May/June 1973.

Brennan, M. J. and E. S. Schwartz, "Alternative Methods of Valuing Debt Options," *Finance,* October 1983.

Cornell, Bradford and Marc Reinganum, "Forward and Futures Prices: Evidence from the Foreign Exchange Markets," *The Journal of Finance,* June 1981.

Cox, J. C., J. E. Ingersoll, and S. A. Ross, "The Relation Between Forward and Futures Prices," *Journal of Financial Economics,* September 1981.

—————, **Stephen Ross, and Mark Rubinstein,** "Option Pricing: A Simplified Approach," *Journal of Financial Economics,* 1979.

————— **and Mark Rubinstein,** *Option Markets,* Englewood Cliffs, N.J.: Prentice-Hall, Inc., 1985.

Elton, E., M. Gruber and J. Rentzler, "Intra-day Tests of the Efficiency of the Treasury Bill Futures Market," Working Paper, New York University, 1982.

Fabozzi, Frank J. (ed.), *Winning the Interest Rate Game: A Guide to Debt Options,* Chicago: Probus Publishing Company, 1985.

———— **and Gregory M. Kipnis (eds.),** *Stock Index Futures,* Homewood, Ill.: Dow Jones-Irwin, 1984.

French, K. R., *The Pricing of Futures and Forward Contracts,* Ph.D. Dissertation, University of Rochester, 1982.

————, "A Comparison of Futures and Forward Prices," Working Paper, UCLA, 1982.

Geske, Robert and H. E. Johnson, "The American Put Option Valued Analytically," *The Journal of Finance,* December 1984.

———— **and Richard Roll,** "On Valuing American Call Options with the Black-Scholes European Formula," *The Journal of Finance,* June 1984.

Jarrow, Robert A. and Andrew Rudd, *Option Pricing,* Homewood, Ill.: Richard D. Irwin, 1983.

———— **and G. S. Oldfield,** "Forward Contracts and Futures Contracts," *Journal of Financial Economics,* September 1981.

Jones, Robert A., "Conversion Factor Risk in Treasury Bond Futures: Comment," *The Journal of Futures Markets,* Spring 1985.

Kamarra, Avraham, "The Behavior of Futures Prices: A Review of Theory and Evidence," *Financial Analysts Journal,* July/August 1984.

Kawaller, Ira G. and Timothy W. Koch, "Cash-and-Carry Trading and the Pricing of Treasury Bill Futures," *The Journal of Futures Markets,* Summer 1984.

Leibowitz, Martin L., "Yield Basis for Financial Futures," *Financial Analysts Journal,* January/February 1981.

Livingston, Miles, "The Cheapest Deliverable Bond for the CBT Treasury Bond Futures Contract," *The Journal of Futures Markets,* Summer 1984.

Meisner, James F. and John W. Labuszewski, "Modifying the Black-Scholes Option Pricing Model for Alternative Underlying Instruments," *Financial Analysts Journal,* November/December 1984.

———— **and** ————, "Treasury Bond Futures Delivery Bias," *The Journal of Futures Markets,* Winter 1984.

Merton, R. C., "Theory of Rational Option Pricing," *Bell Journal of Economics and Management Science,* Spring 1973.

Modest, David M., "On the Pricing of Stock Index Futures," *The Journal of Portfolio Management,* Summer 1984.

Park, Hun Y. and Andrew H. Chen, "Differences between Futures and Forward Prices: A Further Investigation of the Marking-to-Market Effects," *The Journal of Futures Markets,* Spring 1985.

Pitts, Mark, "The Pricing of Options on Debt Securties," *The Journal of Portfolio Management,* Winter 1985.

————, "Options on Futures on Fixed Income Securties," Salomon Brothers, Inc., December 1983.

Posdena, Randall J. and Ben Iben, "Pricing Debt Instruments: The Options Approach," *Economic Review,* Federal Reserve Bank of San Francisco, Summer 1983.

Rendleman, R. J. and C. E. Carolini, "The Efficiency of the Treasury Bill Futures Market," *The Journal of Finance,* March 1979.

Richard, S. F. and M. Sundaresan, "A Continuous Time Equilibrium Model of

Forward Prices and Futures Prices in a Multigood Economy," *Journal of Financial Economics,* September 1981.

Rubinstein, Mark, "A Simple Formula for the Expected Rate of Return of an Option Over a Finite Holding Period," *The Journal of Finance,* December 1984.

Smith, C. W., "Option Pricing: A Review," *Journal of Financial Economics,* January/March 1976.

Stapleton, R. C. and M. G. Subrahmanyam, "The Valuation of Options When Asset Returns Are Generated by a Binomial Process," *The Journal of Finance,* December 1984.

Sterk, William E., "Option Pricing: Dividends and the In- and Out-of-the-Money Bias," *Financial Management,* Winter 1983.

CHAPTER **18**

Futures and Options: Return/Risk Modification Properties and Use in Portfolio Management Strategies

David M. Dunford, CFA
Robert W. Kopprasch, CFA

INTRODUCTION

The discussion in Chapter 16 showed that futures and options contracts share many similarities including trading mechanics, price limitations, and margin requirements. Futures and options are also similarly based on the same underlying investment instruments—stocks or bonds—and both types of contracts, especially in terms of large-volume regularized trading, are relatively new. Futures and options contracts, however, are fundamentally and substantially dissimilar in their impact on a portfolio of assets. Because futures and option are distinctly different, their respective strategic uses in portfolio management are different.

MODIFYING PORTFOLIO RISK

The important distinction between a futures contract and an option contract is that the futures contract is an *obligation*. When an investor purchases or sells a futures contract, the investor has an obligation to accept or deliver, respectively, the underlying commodity on the expiration date. For the bond and stock index futures contracts reviewed in this chapter, that underlying commodity is either the appropriate bond or the cash settlement equivalent to the value of the stock index. In contrast, the buyer of an option contract is not *obligated* to accept or deliver the underlying commodity but instead has the *right,* or choice, to accept or deliver the underlying commodity anytime during the life of the contract. This difference between an obligation and a right has an important effect on the *risk* faced by a futures contract buyer or seller versus an options contract buyer or seller.

Risk Modification With Futures Contracts

Futures and options modify a portfolio's risk in different ways. Buying or selling a futures contract has an impact on a portfolio's upside risk or volatility and downside risk or volatility by a similar magnitude. Some literature has referred to this as *symmetrical impact.* The price of a futures contract varies directly with the price of the underlying bond or stock index, both as the price of the bond or index moves up and when it falls.

Figure 18-1 offers a view as to how the Standard & Poor's (S&P) 500 index moved over the time period from June 1983 through November 1983 versus the price of the December S&P 500 futures contract. The figure indicates how close the prices of the two instruments have been to each other both on the upside and the downside. The shape of the two lines is virtually identical. The area between the two lines represents the difference between the absolute S&P 500 price and the price of the future. On average, it can be expected that the futures price will be a very close approximation of the price of the S&P 500 index. Owning (or shorting, if that is possible) one is essentially equivalent to owning the other.

Figure 18-2 displays the fair value price action of an S&P 500 stock index futures contract versus a given change in the S&P 500 index. The X axis of the figure represents a dollar value change in the S&P 500 index at an instantaneous point in time. The Y axis represents the dollar change that will occur in the futures contract. The diagonal 45 degree straight line on the chart indicates that there is a dollar-for-dollar relationship in the price change of the

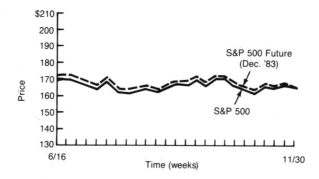

Figure 18-1. S&P 500 Future (December 1983) vs. S&P 500. (SOURCE: Travelers Investment Management Co.)

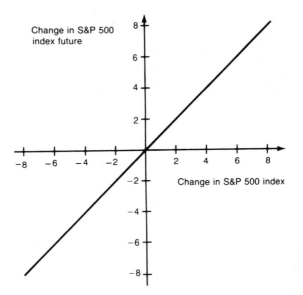

Figure 18-2. Index Futures Price Sensitivity.

S&P 500 index and the price change of the S&P 500 index future. In capital asset pricing model terms, the beta of either asset relative to the other is 1.0. This dollar-for-dollar relationship holds both on positive or upside changes in the index and negative or downside changes in the index. For example, assume that the S&P 500 index is selling at a price of 160. Also assume that the S&P 500 stock index futures contract is selling at 165. Should the S&P index rise to a level of 162, the futures contract price will increase from 165 to 167, assuming that the contract price stays at fair valuation. Since the value of a one point move in this contract is $500, the value of the contract increases by two times $500 or $1,000. Should the S&P index fall from 160 to 158, or two points, the price of the futures contract will simultaneously fall two points from 165 to 163, again, assuming the maintenance of fair value. The exception to this process would be as the futures contract nears expiration when its price converges toward the level of the index.

The risk modification impact of a futures contract on an equity portfolio is displayed in Figures 18-3, 18-4, and 18-5. Figure 18-3 is the return distribution of an equity portfolio over a one-year time period assuming that the underlying equity portfolio is the market and has a market value of $160 million. If it is assumed that the expected return on the S&P 500, $E(R_{S\&P500})$, is 16 percent over a one-year time period with a standard deviation of that return, $\sigma_{S\&P500}$, of 20 percent over that one-year horizon, then Figure 18-3 indicates the possible distribution, or dispersion, of actual returns that could occur in that portfolio. Assume also that the risk-free rate of return (R_f) for the one-year holding period is 10 percent. The probability values on the Y axis of Figures 18-3, 18-4, and 18-5 were determined by calculating the probability of the portfolio return falling within a 2 percent interval (that is, plus or

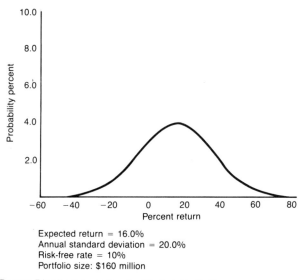

Expected return = 16.0%
Annual standard deviation = 20.0%
Risk-free rate = 10%
Portfolio size: $160 million

Figure 18-3. Return Distribution of Equity Market Portfolio.

minus one percent) around the X-axis return value. Different interval assumptions would result in different derived probability values, but the basic shape of the distribution would remain the same.

Selling or buying stock index futures contracts does not change the general "bell" shape of this return distribution. Selling or buying futures contracts contracts or expands this distribution, or the risk exposure of the portfolio, similar to increasing or decreasing cash (equivalents) in a portfolio.

Figure 18-4 displays the risk characteristics of the portfolio assuming that the manager has *sold* stock index futures contracts to reduce the overall portfolio risk. The example assumes that an amount of stock index futures equivalent to one-half the market value of the portfolio, or $80 million, has been sold. At an index value of 160, this requires the sale of 1,000 contracts. Since selling or buying a stock index futures contract is equivalent to selling or buying the same amount of stock exposure in the actual stock market, this action has the effect of selling one-half of the stock exposure of this portfolio. The sale of 1,000 futures contracts has created a portfolio equivalent to a $160 million portfolio that is 50 percent invested in stocks and 50 percent invested in risk-free cash instruments. The expected return of the resulting portfolio, $E(R_p)$, is:

$$E(R_p) = E(R_{S\&P500}) \times \text{stock weighting} + R_f \times \text{cash weighting}$$
$$= 16\% \times .5 + 10\% \times .5$$
$$= 13\%$$

The standard deviation of the resulting portfolio, (σ_p), where cash has a zero standard deviation or risk is:

$$\sigma_p = \sigma_{\text{S\&P500}} \times \text{stock weighting}$$
$$= 20\% \times .5$$
$$= 10\%$$

The resulting portfolio then has an expected return of 13 percent with a standard deviation over the one-year time period of 10 percent. Figure 18-4 displays the return distribution corresponding to this portfolio. The basic shape of the risk pattern of the portfolio has been maintained. Selling futures has narrowed the distribution, or dispersion, of possible returns, and lowered the risk level of the portfolio.

Figure 18-5 displays the opposite activity. The example assumes that stock index futures contracts have been *purchased* in an amount equivalent to one-half the market value of the portfolio or $80 million. At an index price of 160, 1,000 S&P 500 futures contracts have been purchased. The effect is *equivalent to borrowing on margin* an amount of cash equal to one-half of the value of the portfolio at the risk-free rate and reinvesting the borrowed proceeds into stock. By buying stock index futures contracts the equity portfolio has been significantly leveraged to the point where the portfolio weighting in stocks is 150 percent while cash is weighted minus 50 percent. The expected return of the portfolio of 19 percent over the one-year time period and a standard deviation or risk level of 30 percent can be derived using the previously stated formulas.

In summary, buying or selling futures contracts in a portfolio produces symmetrical effects on the risk exposure of the portfolio. Buying or selling a future is exactly equivalent to subtracting or adding cash from that portfolio.

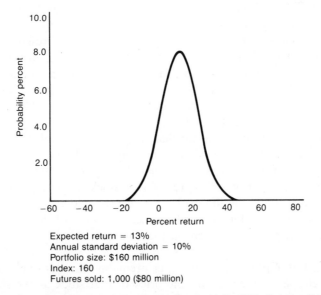

Expected return = 13%
Annual standard deviation = 10%
Portfolio size: $160 million
Index: 160
Futures sold: 1,000 ($80 million)

Figure 18-4. Return Distribution of Equity Market Portfolio With Futures Sold Equal to One Half of the Portfolio.

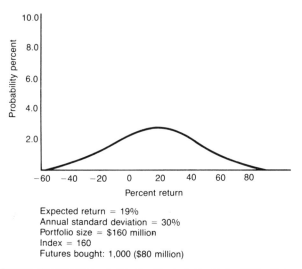

Expected return = 19%
Annual standard deviation = 30%
Portfolio size = $160 million
Index = 160
Futures bought: 1,000 ($80 million)

Figure 18-5. Return Distribution of Equity Market Portfolio With Futures Purchased Equal to One Half of the Portfolio.

In fact, cash can be "subtracted" to such an extent by buying futures that the underlying portfolio can become substantially leveraged, depending on investor risk aversion preferences and maximum margin borrowing regulations.

Risk Modification With Options Contracts

The addition of a call or put option to a portfolio does not have an impact on upside portfolio risk and downside portfolio risk to a similar magnitude. Unlike futures contracts, the impact of options on the risk profile of a portfolio of assets is not symmetrical. The distinction in risk modification of options versus futures is seen in the definition of a call option and a put option. The owner of a call option on an individual stock has the right to *buy* shares of that individual stock at the agreed upon contract price or strike price any time during the life of that contract. The owner of a call option is not faced with the risk of having to pay more for that stock. The terms of the contract state that the owner can buy stock at the agreed upon strike price and the seller of the call option must sell the stock at that strike price. In contrast, the owner of a put has the right to *sell* shares of that stock at the agreed upon strike price any time during the life of the contract. Should the actual price of the individual stock fall below the strike price, the owner of the put still may receive that strike price upon exercising the put option.

Buying Call Options. The price, or premium, of a call option on an individual stock varies directly with the price of that stock as the stock's price advances as long as the stock's price is above the option's strike price (that is, the option is in-the-money). The price of the call, however, does not vary directly with the price of the stock should the stock price be below the option's strike price (the option is out-of-the-money). The call price cannot fall below zero.

Figure 18-6 displays the price action of IBM stock and the price of the IBM call option with a strike price of 110 and expiration in July 1984. The figure covers the period March through June 1984. The price of the call option moved fairly responsively with the price of IBM stock when the option was in-the-money during the first half of the time period, but much less responsively relative to the IBM stock when the option was out-of-the-money during the second half. Unlike a futures contract, a call option contract is not an exact equivalent to owning the underlying security, in this case the individual stock of IBM. There is essentially unit elasticity between the call option and the underlying stock when the option is in-the-money but less than unit elasticity when the price relation changes such that the option becomes out-of-the-money.

Figure 18-7 displays the relationship between the price of the underlying stock and the fair price of the call option on the stock based on the Black-Scholes option pricing model. The example assumes that IBM is selling at a price of 120 and the call option is at-the-money (that is, market price is equal to the strike price) with a strike price of 120 and six months to maturity. The X axis is the price of a share of IBM stock while the Y axis is the price of the call option. Should the share price of IBM increase from 120 to 125, the price of the call option will increase from 8½ to about 11¾. The diagonal line in the upper right quadrant indicates that there is a one-to-one relationship between the price of the underlying stock and the intrinsic value of the

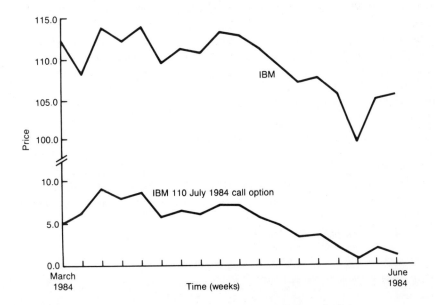

Figure 18-6. IBM 110 July 1984 Call Option Price vs. IBM Stock Price.

call as the call becomes in-the-money. Should the price of the IBM stock fall five points from 120 to 115 and become out-of-the-money, the fair price of the call would fall only 2¾ points to a price of 5¾. Should the IBM stock price fall 10 points from 120 to 110, then the call would only fall to 3⅝. Any further decline in the price of the IBM stock is reflected in only a minimal decline in the price of the call option. This is because while it is out-of-the-money and therefore has no intrinsic value, the option still has ever-diminishing time value reflecting the chances of the stock's market price to rise above the strike price in the time remaining to expiration of the option contract. The call option cannot have a value of less than zero. The price of the call option does not move symmetrically with the price of the underlying asset, in this case a share of IBM.

Owning a call option is like owning an insurance policy on the underlying stock. A premium for the insurance is paid in terms of the price of the call. Paying the premium allows the call option owner to participate in the upside down action of the stock with limited participation in any downside movement. Insurance against downside price movement is obtained.

The risk modification characteristics of an option contract can be viewed in terms of its impact on the risk profile or forecasted return distribution of the underlying portfolio. Assume that the underlying portfolio is the stock market as represented by a stock market index such as the S&P 500. Again, assume that the expected risk-free rate of return is 10 percent, and as in the previous example, the expected return on the underlying portfolio of the stock

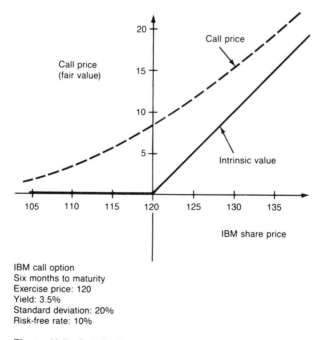

IBM call option
Six months to maturity
Exercise price: 120
Yield: 3.5%
Standard deviation: 20%
Risk-free rate: 10%

Figure 18-7. Call Option Price Sensitivity.

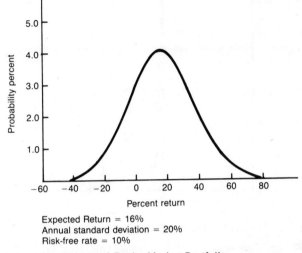

Figure 18-8. Return Distribution of Equity Market Portfolio.

market over a one-year holding period is 16 percent with an annual standard deviation of 20 percent.

Buying Calls Plus Cash Equivalents. Figure 18-8 shows the risk profile, or projected return distribution, of the underlying portfolio over a one-year time period. Figure 18-9 displays the forecasted return distribution of a portfolio that includes cash (equivalents) and call options on the market index with the portfolio having equivalent upside market value exposure as the stock market portfolio displayed in Figure 18-3. The index call options purchased are one-year at-the-money calls priced at the Black-Scholes-model-determined fair value. The model input assumptions, as discussed in Chapter 17, are an annual standard deviation of the index of 20 percent, a risk-free rate of 10 percent, and a dividend yield of 4.5 percent. The resulting fair price of the call option is $10.20. The cash plus index call options portfolio is then 89.8 percent invested in cash and 10.2 percent invested in call options.

The return distribution is truncated at a minimum loss level of approximately minus one percent. The truncation occurs at the point where the call options have fallen to a price or value of zero. The cash equivalents held in the portfolio remain and are assumed to earn the risk-free rate of return. Buying the call option has created this skewed risk profile where insurance against participation in adverse price outcomes has been obtained at a cost equal to the price of the call option.

Figure 18-9 indicates that the expected return of the cash plus call option portfolio of 13.7 percent is moderately less than the expected return of the all-stock portfolio of 16.0 percent displayed in Figure 18-8, the difference being the premium paid for the insurance protection.

Buying or selling option contracts in a portfolio of assets changes the shape

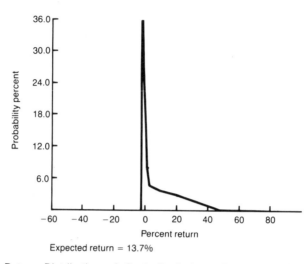

Expected return = 13.7%

Figure 18-9. Return Distribution of Cash Equivalents Plus Index Call Options of Equivalent Market Exposure.

of the return distribution and provides a significant skewness to the risk profile of the portfolio. For example, options will truncate upside price potential or downside price risk depending on whether the investor is selling a call or buying a put option within the portfolio. A few numerical examples display the impact that different option contracts have on the risk profile of the portfolios.

Figure 18-10 displays a specific example of the risk profile of the call option plus cash equivalent portfolio versus a stock only portfolio. Two strategies are compared. The first strategy is a single stock portfolio strategy where one share of stock is bought at $50 with no dividends expected. The second strategy involves buying one call on the same stock with the balance of funds not invested in the call option held in cash equivalents. It is assumed that for a six-month call at a $50 strike price or exercise price, the premium (or price) of the call is $6. Forty-four dollars is then invested in cash equivalents, such as Treasury bills, at 10 percent interest per year. For both portfolios the total assets involved are $50.

The table in the center of Figure 18-10 views the returns on each of these two portfolios given a change in the price of the underlying stock. If the stock price falls at the end of six months to $35, then there is a loss on that share of stock of $15. This results in a return on Portfolio 1, which includes just the stock, of minus 30 percent. In Porftfolio 2, where a call option and Treasury bills have been bought, the call option falls to a price of approximately zero, given a $15 decline in the stock, while the remaining $44 in Treasury bills earns 5 percent, or $2.20, for the six-month time period. Portfolio 2 then has a value of $46.20, or $50.00 minus $6 lost on the call plus $2.20 interest. The net loss in the portfolio is $3.80 for a portfolio return of minus 7.6 percent.

Should the price of the stock increase to a level of 65, the gain in Portfolio 1 is then $15 for a return of 30 percent. In Portfolio 2, the call option at the end of six months will have a value of $15, which is the difference between the price of the stock and the exercise price of the option. The total value of the portfolio at the end of the six months period will then be $50 plus the $15 value of the call option minus $6 paid for the call option plus $2.20 interest on the Treasury bills for a total portfolio value of $61.20. This represents a gain of $11.20 for a portfolio return of 22.4 percent.

The difference in the risk profile between the stock only Portfolio 1 and Portfolio 2 containing the call option is visibly displayed at the bottom of Figure 18-10. The portfolio containing the call option moves with the stock-only portfolio as the stock's price advances and lags only by the premium paid for the call option less the return on the Treasury bills. The portfolio return

Compare two strategies:
  (1) Buy stock—$50/share no dividends
  (2) Buy 1 call on same stock/balance in bills
     • $6 for 6-month call ($50 exercise price)
     • $44 in T-Bills @ 10%/yr.
       Total—$50 in assets

At the end of six months (maturity of call):

Stock Price	Gain (Loss)	Portfolio Return	Buy Call Buy Bill	Gain (Loss)	Portfolio Return
$35	$−15	−30%	$46.20	$−3.80	−7.6%
40	−10	−20	46.20	−3.80	−7.6
45	−5	−10	46.20	−3.80	−7.6
50	0	0	46.20	−3.80	−7.6
55	+5	10	51.20	+1.20	2.4
60	+10	20	56.20	+6.20	12.4
65	+15	30	61.20	+11.20	22.4

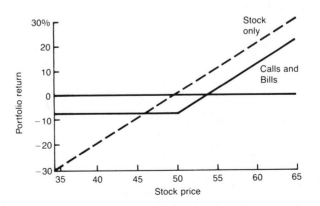

Figure 18-10. Performance of Call Option and Cash Portfolio vs. Underlying Common Stock Portfolio. (SOURCE: Travelers Investment Management Co.)

of the portfolio containing the call and Treasury bills is truncated at minus 7.6 percent, while the return of the stock only portfolio continues to fall with the decline in the stock's price. The risk profile of the calls plus bills portfolio has been truncated and is skewed to the upside. Insurance has been purchased at a cost equal to the price of the call premium.

Writing Covered Call Options. Figure 18-11 displays the return and risk modification from selling a call option on a stock held in a portfolio. The exhibit compares the portfolios containing the strategies of owning only the stock and owning the stock with a call option sold or written against that stock. Assume that the first portfolio involves buying one share of stock at a price of $50 with no dividends over the time period. Assume that the second portfolio

Compare two strategies:
    (1) Buy stock—$50/share no dividends
    (2) Buy stock—$50/share no dividends
        Sell 1 call on same stock
          • $6 for 6-month call
          • $50 exercise price
            Net asset value—$50

At the end of six months (maturity of call):

Stock Price	Gain (Loss)	Portfolio Return	Buy Stock Sell Call	Gain (Loss)	Portfolio Return
$35	$−15	−30%	$41.00	$−9.00	−18%
40	−10	−20	46.00	−4.00	−8%
45	−5	−10	51.00	1.00	2%
50	0	0	56.00	6.00	12%
55	+5	10	56.00	6.00	12%
60	+10	20	56.00	6.00	12%
65	+15	30	56.00	6.00	12%

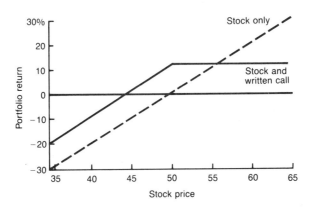

Figure 18-11. Performance of Stock with Written (Sold) Call Option Portfolio vs. Underlying Common Stock Portfolio. (SOURCE: Travelers Investment Management Co.)

involves buying one share of the stock at a price of $50 and selling one six-month at-the-money call option with an exercise price of $50 for $6. The total assets in each of the two portfolios again equals $50.

The table in the center of Figure 18-11 displays the returns generated on each of these two portfolios given different changes in the stock's price. If the stock's price falls to $35, Portfolio 1 containing just the stock has a loss of $15 for a portfolio return of minus 30 percent. In Portfolio 2, which contains the stock plus the sold call option, the stock has fallen $15 for a loss of $15, while the call option, which was originally sold for $6, falls to zero for a gain of $6. The net value of the portfolio then is $50 minus the $15 loss on the stock plus the $6 gain on the call option, or $41. The net loss is $9 for a portfolio return of minus 18 percent.

Should the stock price instead increase to $65, Portfolio 1 experiences a $15 gain over the six-month time period for a portfolio return of 30 percent. In Portfolio 2 the stock increases $15 while the call option increases to a value of $15 for a loss on the sold call option position of $9. The net gain on the portfolio is $15 minus the $9 loss on the call option, or $6, for a total portfolio value of $56. This represents a portfolio return of 12 percent, which is demonstrated in the table to be the maximum return achievable. The portfolio return distribution for Portfolio 2 is truncated on the positive return side at plus 12 percent. The return can never be any higher no matter what the price of the underlying stock does.

In summary, selling a call option on a stock portfolio has the opposite effect on the portfolio's risk profile of buying a call option plus holding cash equivalents. When a call option is sold, a portfolio's return distribution is skewed to the downside with the upside portfolio potential truncated at a specific positive percentage return. The downside portfolio returns are cushioned by the amount of the call premium received when the call option is sold. This downside cushion is achieved only at the expense of some participation on the upside. By contrast, a calls plus bills portfolio results in the portfolio's return distribution being skewed to the upside with the downside portfolio potential truncated at a specific, usually modestly negative, percentage return.

Buying Put Options. Buying or selling a put option produces a return and risk modification counterpart to buying or selling a call option. Figure 18-12 displays the fair price of a put option versus the price of the underlying stock. As in Figure 18-7, the example assumes that IBM is selling at a price of 120. The put option is at-the-money with a strike price of 120 and six months to maturity. The X axis represents the price of a share of IBM stock while the Y axis is the price of the put option. An increase in the price of the IBM from 120 to 125 results in a reduction of the put option's Black-Scholes fair price from 4⅞ to 3¼. As the price of the stock continues to rise, the price of the put option falls toward zero. On the other hand, should the

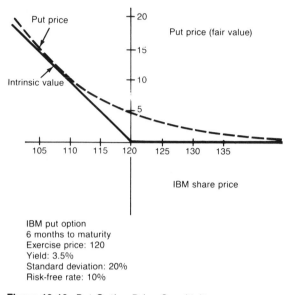

IBM put option
6 months to maturity
Exercise price: 120
Yield: 3.5%
Standard deviation: 20%
Risk-free rate: 10%

Figure 18-12. Put Option Price Sensitivity.

price of IBM fall from 120 to 115, the fair price of the put option increases from 4⅞ to 7⅛. As the price of IBM continues to fall, the price of the put option moves positively with the price decline of the stock on an approximate one-for-one basis. The diagonal solid line in the upper left quadrant indicates this relationship.

Figure 18-13 displays a numerical example that compares a stock only portfolio with a portfolio containing both the stock and a put option on the stock. Portfolio 1 includes just a share of stock, assumed to be purchased at $70 per share with a semiannual dividend of $2. Portfolio 2 includes the share of stock, having a dividend of $2, and a six-month put with a strike price of $70, purchased for $5. The table in the center of Figure 18-13 displays the returns on each of these two portfolios given changes in the price of the underlying stock. If the price of the stock falls to $55, the loss incurred in Portfolio 1 is a $15 capital loss plus a $2 dividend, or a net loss of $13, for a portfolio return of minus 18.6 percent. In Portfolio 2, which contains the stock with a put option, the value of the portfolio is $55 for the share of stock plus $15 for the value of the put option minus the cost of the put option of $5, plus the $2 dividend for a total portfolio value of $67. This represents a net loss of $3 for a portfolio return of minus 4 percent. By contrast, if the stock price increases to $85, Portfolio 1 has a total gain of $15 plus $2, or $17, for a return of 24.3 percent. Portfolio 2, which contains the stock and put option, has a total value of the stock of $85 minus the $5 cost of the put plus $2 in dividends for a total of $82. The net gain is $12 for a portfolio return of 16 percent.

The return and risk profiles of the two portfolios are displayed at the bottom of Figure 18-13. The downside risk exposure of the portfolio containing the put option is limited to minus 4 percent in this example. The put option in Portfolio 2 has modified the return/risk profile of the stock portfolio to an extent where participation in the downside is limited with some upside participation maintained.

Results of Empirical Studies. A number of simulations using historical data on portfolios containing these and other combinations of stocks and put and call options were conducted by Merton, Scholes, and Gladstein [1982]. Their results confirm the hypothesized impact that options have on modifying the return/risk profile of a portfolio.

Table 18-1 presents a brief summary of a portion of the results of the study. Historical simulation data are provided for the Dow Jones 30 Industrial

Compare two strategies:
  (1) Buy stock—$70/share
     • Dividend $2
  (2) Buy stock and 6-month put at $70:$5
     • Dividend $2

At the end of six months (maturity of put):

Stock Price	Gain (Loss)	Portfolio Return	Stock With Put Option	Gain (Loss)	Portfolio Return
$55	$−13	−18.6%	$67	$−3	−4.0%
60	−8	−11.4	67	−3	−4.0
65	−3	−4.3	67	−3	−4.0
70	+2	2.9	67	−3	−4.0
75	+7	10.0	72	+2	2.7
80	+12	17.1	77	+7	9.3
85	+17	24.3	82	+12	16.0

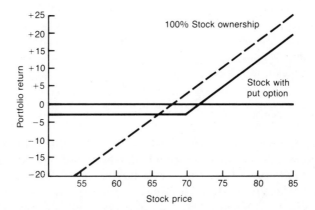

Figure 18-13. Performance of Stock with Put Option vs. Underlying Common Stock Portfolio. (SOURCE: Travelers Investment Management Co.)

Stocks portfolio and for three option strategies: selling calls on all the stocks in a portfolio, maintaining a portfolio 10 percent invested in call options and 90 percent invested in commercial paper, and buying puts on all the portfolio's stocks. The simulation period covered 28 six-month time periods from July 1, 1963 through June 30, 1977. For each strategy, the stock portfolio was assumed to be an equal-weighted portfolio of the Dow Jones 30 Industrial Stocks. The weightings were rebalanced every six months. The fair value option prices were calculated using the Black-Scholes model for calls and the Merton model for puts.

The results in Table 18-1 assume the purchase or sale of at-the-money puts and calls with six months to maturity. The options were purchased or sold at the beginning of each six-month period and held to maturity. The inputs to the option pricing model were: (1) the price of the stock at the beginning of the period, (2) the risk-free rate of return on six month prime commercial paper, (3) the stock's dividend yield, (4) the option exercise price equal to the current stock price, and (5) the stock's return variance that was assumed to be equal to the variance of the previous six month time period.

The results in Table 18-1 verify the risk modification characteristics of option strategies. The stock only portfolio containing the 30 Dow Jones Industrial Stocks exhibited a range of six-month returns from minus 16.4 to 49.1 percent. A portfolio where covered calls were written on all 30 stocks in the portfolio produced returns ranging from minus 9.2 to 16.9 percent. Upside stock price movements were truncated while the downside moves were cushioned. A portfolio containing (purchased) call options on all 30 stocks plus cash equivalents in the form of six-month commercial paper exhibited returns that ranged from minus 5.7 to 34.4 percent. Either the risk-free rate or upside stock price movement was reduced by the cost of the insurance. Finally, a portfolio containing stocks plus (purchased) put options on each of the stocks exhibited returns from minus 1.8 to 35.1 percent. The downside stock price movement was truncated at the expense of some upside movement. The historical simulations confirm the risk modification patterns for these three option strategies exhibited in Figures 18-10, 18-11, and 18-13, respectively.

The Merton, Scholes, and Gladstein studies conducted many additional simulation analyses covering different option strategies and in-the-money and out-of-the-money option alternatives.

Modifying Systematic Risk

The various futures and options contracts can be used to modify or control both the systematic and the unsystematic risk in a portfolio. Portfolio systematic risk relates to the risk or volatility of the stock or bond market as a whole. Unsystematic risk in a portfolio is the sum of the risk or volatility of market subgroups plus the risk or volatility specific to any individual security. Futures contracts on Treasury bonds and stock market indexes, options on high quality bonds and bond futures, and options on stock indexes and stock index futures

TABLE 18-1. Return and Risk Measures for Historical Simulations for Four Investment Strategies for Six-month Holding Periods from July 1963 to June 1977 Employing the 30 Dow Jones Industrial Stocks as to the Underlying Stock Portfolio

	Dow Jones 30 Industrial Stocks	Stocks Plus Fully Covered Call Writing	Call and Commercial Paper Buying	Stocks Plus Protective Put Buying
Average Rate of Return (%)	4.6	3.1	5.4	4.5
Standard Deviation (%)	13.7	6.1	10.4	7.9
Highest Return (%)	49.1	16.0	34.4	35.1
Lowest Return (%)	−16.4	−9.2	−5.7	−1.8
Average Compound Return (%)	3.7	2.9	4.9	4.2

SOURCE: Merton, Scholes, and Gladstein [1982].

all can be used to modify the systematic risk exposure of bond and stock portfolios.

Systematic risk in a fixed income portfolio can be thought of as the risk of changes in interest rates. Thus, the exposure of a fixed income portfolio to systematic risk is measured by the duration of the portfolio. Futures contracts on Treasury bonds or other Treasury securities can be used in a fixed income portfolio to increase or decrease the exposure to interest rate risk by altering the duration of the portfolio—a measure of bond price volatility explored in Chapter 9A of this volume—through buying or selling the bond futures.

Table 18-2 presents an example of modifying the systematic risk, or duration, of a fixed income portfolio by buying and selling futures contracts. The table assumes an initial portfolio of $70 million invested in Treasury bonds. The portfolio has a duration of 8.0. If the Treasury bond is assumed to sell at a price of 70, then the sale of one Treasury bond futures contract is equivalent to the sale of $70,000 of Treasury bonds. Selling 100 Treasury bond futures contracts is equivalent to selling $7 million of Treasury bonds, or one-tenth of the portfolio. Selling 100 futures contracts reduces the portfolio's duration proportionately or by 10 percent from 8.0 to 7.2. Selling 200 futures contracts reduces the duration of the portfolio to 6.4. Buying 100 futures contracts increases the systematic risk or duration of the portfolio from 8.0 to 8.8, and buying 200 futures contracts increases the duration to 9.6. Alteration of bond portfolio duration is discussed in greater detail elsewhere in this chapter.

Options on fixed income instruments can be used to modify the systematic risk exposure of the fixed income portfolio in a *nonsymmetric* manner. Table 18-3 assumes that put options are bought on the $70 million portfolio using additional funds. These put options are assumed to be six-month, at-the-money options on Treasury bond futures with a strike price of 70. The table shows the duration of the $70 million portfolio for different amounts to put protec-

TABLE 18-2. An example of Systematic Risk (Duration) Modification Using Fixed Income Futures

Portfolio: $70 million
Portfolio Duration: 8.0
Treasury Bond Price: 70
Futures Value: $70,000/contract

Treasury Bond Futures Contracts Transaction	*Portfolio Duration*
Sell 100 contracts	7.2
200	6.4
300	5.6
Buy 100 contracts	8.8
200	9.6
300	10.4

TABLE 18-3. Systematic Risk (Duration) Modification Using Put Options on Treasury Bond Futures

Portfolio: $79 million
Portfolio Duration: 8.0
Treasury Bond Price: 70
Put Option on Bond Future: Strike Price $70 with Six Months to Maturity
Risk Free Rate: 10%

Bond Price	PORTFOLIO DURATION GIVEN THE PERCENTAGE OF TOTAL PORTFOLIO ASSETS PROTECTED BY PUT OPTIONS				
	20%	*40%*	*60%*	*80%*	*100%*
80	7.9	7.8	7.8	7.7	7.6
75	7.7	7.4	7.1	6.7	6.4
70	7.2	6.5	5.7	4.9	4.1
65	6.7	5.5	4.2	2.9	1.6
60	6.5	4.9	3.4	1.8	0.3

tion and for different instantaneous changes in the price level. The variation in duration contained in the table is a direct result of the skewed impact that option contracts have on the risk profile of a portfolio. At different put protection levels, the exposure to risk in the portfolio varies substantially for any particular price change of the underlying bond. Duration changes little in response to bond price changes in a 20 percent put protected portfolio but it changes significantly in a 100 percent protected portfolio.

In an equity or common stock portfolio, the systematic risk portion of the total portfolio risk arises from the movement of the overall market and can be measured by the portfolio's beta. Stock index futures contracts may be used to alter the beta of a portfolio similar to the fixed income duration example.

Table 18-4 presents a numerical example of the use of stock index futures in altering the systematic risk exposure of stock portfolios. The initial portfolio is assumed to be $80 million in size with the S&P 500 index at a value of 160. Buying or selling one future is equivalent to buying or selling 160 times 500 or $80,000 worth of common stock. It is assumed that the beta of the $80 million portfolio, as measured against the S&P 500 Index, is 1.0. If 100 S&P 500 stock index futures contracts are sold, equity exposure is reduced by $8 million and beta is reduced from 1.0 to 0.9. If 200 contracts are sold, beta is reduced to 0.8. If 100 S&P 500 futures contracts are bought, beta is increased from 1.0 to 1.1, and if 200 contracts are bought, beta is increased to 1.2.

Buying a put option on this $80 million portfolio has a similar impact on modifying the systematic risk profile of the portfolio as just discussed.

Table 18-5 assumes that additional funds are used to purchase at-the-money put options on $80 million of the S&P 500 index with a strike price

TABLE 18-4. Systematic Risk (Beta) Modification Using Stock Index Futures

Portfolio: $80 million
Portfolio Beta: 1.0
S&P 500 Index: 160
Index Futures Value: $80,000/Contract

S&P 500 Index Futures Contracts Transaction	Portfolio Beta
Sell 100 contracts	0.9
200	0.8
300	0.7
Buy 100 contracts	1.1
200	1.2
300	1.3

of 160. The table presents the beta or systematic risk exposure of the portfolio, given different percentages of portfolio put protection and an instantaneous change in price of the underlying portfolio, which is the S&P index. For example, a portfolio that holds stocks with a beta of 1.0, and put options with the characteristics listed in Table 18-4 sufficient to put protect 60 percent of the total market value of the portfolio, exhibits a beta of .75 at an index price of 160. Should the price of the index rise to 170, the put options would move out-of-the-money (where their price is less responsive to changes in the price of the index because it has no intrinsic value) and the portfolio beta would increase to .84. Should the price of the index fall to 150, the options would move in-the-money (where the price of the put option would become more responsive to changes in the index's price) and the portfolio's beta would fall to .63. Similar to duration, beta varies as the S&P 500 index changes due to the nonsymmetrical impact that options have on the systematic risk profile of the portfolio.

Modifying Unsystematic Risk

The ability of futures and options contracts to modify unsystematic risk is more limited. In a fixed income portfolio, unsystematic risk is the sum of any sector spread volatility plus any default risk on individual issues. Yield spreads of bond market sectors against Treasury bonds have considerable variability and can produce considerable unsystematic risk. Fixed income futures and options, however, cannot be used to modify unsystematic risk because substantially all futures and options contracts are based on Treasury bonds and Treasury yields. Treasuries can only hedge the interest rate risk of Treasury securities or, alternatively, movements and changes in the shape of the Treasury yield curve. Futures and options contracts on Treasury bonds cannot modify the risk of sector yield spreads. Therefore, there is currently no contract among the new instruments that allows for modification and control of unsystematic risk in a bond portfolio. However, as indicated in Chapter 16, there is relatively little unsystematic risk for investment grade bonds as compared to common stocks, making the need for such new instruments less acute.

In an equity portfolio, unsystematic risk, or residual risk, relates to portfolio volatility not due to movement in the underlying market, represented by a stock market index. For a diversified portfolio, as much as 95 percent of the total portfolio risk may be due to systematic risk. We have indicated this systematic risk can be modified and controlled through the use of futures contracts on the stock indices. The remaining 5 percent of portfolio risk, the unsystematic risk, can only be minimally affected through the use of stock index futures or options on those futures contracts. On the other hand, options on market subgroups and options on individual stocks can be used to significantly impact the unsystematic risk of a portfolio. These options can be used to change the risk profile of a portfolio's unsystematic risk by buying or selling insurance on the portfolio's exposure to individual stocks and stock subgroups.

FUTURES AND OPTIONS IN ASSET ALLOCATION

As indicated in Chapter 8 of the main volume, the asset allocation decision— how much of a portfolio's assets should be placed in broad asset classes such as stocks, bonds, real estate, and cash equivalents—ultimately has more impact on the performance of the portfolio than any other investment decision. The active control of asset allocation, whether derived passively or as the result of

TABLE 18-5. Systematic Risk (Beta) Modification Using S&P 500 Put Options

Portfolio: $80 Million
Portfolio Beta: 1.0
S&P 500 Index: 160
S&P 500 Put Option: Strike Price: $160 with Six Months to Maturity
Yield: 4.0%
Risk-Free Rate: 10%
S&P 500 Annual Standard Deviation: 20%

| | PORTFOLIO BETA GIVEN THE PERCENTAGE OF TOTAL PORTFOLIO ASSETS PROTECTED BY PUT OPTIONS | | | | |
Index Price	20%	40%	60%	80%	100%
180	.97	.94	.91	.89	.86
170	.95	.86	.84	.79	.74
160	.91	.83	.75	.66	.58
150	.87	.75	.63	.51	.40
140	.78	.57	.37	.18	.00

an active judgment, is a key element in maximizing portfolio return/risk tradeoffs.

Futures and option contracts offer a means to control a portfolio's risk exposure in the asset allocation decision and maximize the benefits of that decision in terms of incremental returns for the level of portfolio risk chosen. The strategic use of futures and options in the control of the asset allocation of a portfolio is perhaps the most effective and fundamental utilization of these new instruments. The use of futures and options contracts in asset allocation are each discussed below.

Futures in Asset Allocation

Financial futures can play a very important role in portfolio construction by facilitating the execution of the asset allocation decision. Once it is decided how much of a portfolio's assets should be in stocks and how much should be in bonds, this decision has to be implemented, a process that is not costless. Nevertheless, the contribution that the asset allocation decision makes to portfolio return must be viewed net of execution costs. Because the potential returns from an active asset allocation judgment can be substantially diluted by execution costs, many institutional investors limit asset allocation decisions to strategic rather than tactical judgments.

The asset allocation decision may be executed in a portfolio by using futures instead of transacting in the underlying securities. Futures offer an alternative to actually buying or selling stocks and bonds in order to increase or decrease stock or bond exposure. A review of the costs incurred in executing the asset allocation decision indicates the strategic role that stock index futures and Treasury bond futures, for example, can play in portfolio management.

Asset Allocation Execution Costs. There are four costs that could be incurred during the execution phase. These costs are best illustrated by a simple example. Assume that an increase of a portfolio's exposure to common stock by $40 million is desired. This may be accomplished by either buying $40 million of common stock in the stock market or by buying $40 million of equivalent stock exposure through stock index futures. Assume that the S&P 500 index future is currently selling at 160. One futures contract is, therefore, equivalent to 160 times $500, or $80,000, of common stock exposure.

Brokerage Commissions. The first cost is commissions. If the average price per share of a common stock is assumed to be $40, a purchase of $40 million of stock under the first method involves buying one million shares of stock. At a commission rate of 5 cents a share, a rate currently lower than the average for all institutional trades in early 1985, the method would involve total commissions of $50,000. The alternative is to buy $40 million of stock exposure by purchasing futures. If each future is equivalent to $80,000, then 500 futures contracts would be needed. The commission to buy 500 contracts is one-half the round trip commission of approximately $25 per contract, or $12.50 times 500 contracts, for a total commission of $6,250. Commissions are reduced about 88 percent by utilizing futures.

Market Impact. A second cost is market impact. A stock purchase of $40 million can be expected to have an adverse impact on the price level of the shares. You may have to pay up an eighth or a quarter of a point in order to transact. The market inpact of buying 500 S&P 500 futures contracts can be expected to be less because of the greater relative liquidity currently observable in the futures markets and the commonality of that single contract, the S&P 500 future. It can be expected that the purchase of 500 contracts can occur at or near the current market price.

Transaction Time. A third execution cost is time. It can take time to buy $40 million of stock, especially if market impact is considered large, time during which strategic opportunity may erode and the portfolio may be at an investment risk level different from that targeted. Given the relatively greater liquidity of the futures market, it would take less time to purchase futures contracts than to buy the stock outright.

Disruption. The fourth important cost is perhaps the least observable of all, the cost of disruption. If the first execution method of actually buying common stock is chosen, the $40 million must come from somewhere. Perhaps the $40 million will come from a portfolio run by another manager or from part of a balanced portfolio. A large transfer from one funds source to another will cause significant overall portfolio imbalance for some time period, during which the judgments of the investment managers will not be reflected accurately. The result could be the loss of at least a portion of the incremental return expected from undertaking the asset allocation change. Execution using futures does not require the movement of funds of such magnitude. The margin deposit required for futures typically will be much less than funds involved in the purchase of actuals. Potential disruption and the loss of incremental return is accordingly minimized.

The four costs—commissions, market impact, time, and disruption—can be significant drains on portfolio performance. Futures offer an alternative for strategy execution and cost minimization.

Example of an Asset Mix Change. Table 18-6 presents an example of how futures are used to execute the asset allocation decision. Assume that the manager of a large portfolio wishes to change the stock/bond mix to reflect new investment judgments. Assume that the mix today of a $400 million portfolio or pension fund is 60 percent in stocks or $240 million and 40 percent in bonds or $160 million. Assume also that the manager's judgment calls for a lowering of stock exposure and a raising of bond exposure by 10 percent of total value or $40 million in each asset category. In order to achieve the new

TABLE 18-6. Asset Allocation Application of Treasury Bond and S&P 500 Stock Index Futures Contracts

Fund Size: $400 Million				
Asset	Actual Mix		Target Mix	Net Change
Stocks	60%	($240 Million)	50% ($200 Million)	$−40 Million
Bonds	40%	($160 Million)	50% ($200 Million)	$+40 Million

Action to be taken:
   Sell 500 S&P 500 Stock Index futures contracts
   Buy 571 Treasury bond futures contracts

target of 50 percent in stocks and 50 percent in bonds, $40 million of stocks would have to be sold and $40 million of bonds would have to be bought.

There are two ways of executing this strategy. The traditional way would be to actually sell $40 million in stocks in the market and buy $40 million in bonds. The alternative would be to use futures. A portfolio manager could sell the equivalent of $40 million of stock exposure by selling stock index futures, and buy the equivalent of $40 million of bond exposure by purchasing Treasury bond futures. If it is assumed that one stock index future is equivalent to $80,000 of stock exposure and one Treasury bond future is equivalent to $70,000 of bond exposure, this would involve the sale of 500 S&P 500 stock index futures contracts and the purchase of 571 Treasury bond futures contracts.

In addition to the advantages of lower transaction costs, quicker execution, and minimal portfolio disruption, a further advantage is that less money need be involved to alter the asset mix due to the leveraged nature of a futures contract. Assume that the manager of a $400 million fund may alter the stock/bond mix within a 10 percent range around some long-term normal mix, such as 60/40. Asset allocation changes of this degree could be accomplished using the futures approach with approximately $8 to $10 million of cash necessary for margin requirements while $80 million would be required via the buying and selling of stocks and bonds. More funds can therefore remain available to the specific security selectors to generate additional sector or individual security alpha returns.

Discussions in Chapter 8 of the main volume indicate the controversy as to whether an active asset allocation decision can add incremental return to a portfolio. Much of the skepticism on the value of this decision is based on the fact that actual incremental returns generated in portfolios over the past due to asset allocation appear small or nonexistent. This is mainly due to the inability to quickly and cheaply execute the asset allocation decision. The utilization of financial futures offers a technique to capture the maximum benefit from the asset allocation decision and to minimize its dilution.

Advantages in a Multiple-Manager Environment. The use of financial futures to execute an asset allocation decision is particularly attractive in a multiple-manager structure. A common investment structure in evidence today in medium- to large-sized pension funds involves the hiring of a number of external money managers with each specializing in either stocks or bonds. As a result, the stock/bond asset allocation of the fund commonly is the sum of the individual pieces. Often, control of the stock/bond mix on the aggregate level is not attempted due to the difficulty of controlling the actual mix. Traditionally, the only methods to control the stock/bond mix on the aggregate level have involved either redirecting the contributions flow to the appropriate managers, a very time consuming process, or reallocating funds from one set of managers to another set of managers. Reallocating funds can be both time consuming and disruptive to the managers involved.

Using financial futures to achieve the target stock/bond mix on the aggregate level in a multiple manager environment avoids this loss of time and portfolio disruption. The individual investment managers specializing in their markets or market subgroups need not even know that the futures activity is occurring. The aggregate fund can gain incremental return by benefiting both from the alpha judgments of the investment managers on individual stocks and the asset allocation decision of stocks versus bonds made at the aggregate level.

Options in Asset Allocation

Option contracts help to structure the optimum asset mix for a client and the client's portfolio. The discussions in Chapter 8 of the main volume indicated the importance of the interaction of capital market expectations, and their implications for expected returns and risk, with the risk tolerance, or utility function, of the portfolio owner or the client in determining the appropriate asset allocation. The analysis in Chapter 8 requires willingness to accept a key simplifying assumption. The assumption is that investors or portfolio owners have a utility function or risk preference function based solely on the mean or expected return and the variance (or its square root, the standard deviation) of the return distribution. The expected return is viewed as having positive utility while variance is viewed as having negative utility. A greater variance indicates more portfolio risk and, other considerations aside, diminishes utility to the investor. Restricting an investor's utility function to mean and variance underpinnings implies that insurance or the skewness of a risk profile has no value.

Skewness Preference Strategies. With the frequent introduction and the rapid growth of option contracts, it is becoming increasingly common to find fund sponsors who invest a fraction of their assets in option instruments. Incorporating option contracts into a portfolio changes the underlying return distribution of the portfolio. As has been previously demonstrated, the resulting portfolio will have a sharply changed distribution skewness or risk profile.

Writing Call Options. What are portfolio strategies where skewness preference plays a role in portfolio selection? Some fund managers prefer to write call options against the underlying stocks in their portfolios. This has the effect of modestly increasing the portfolio's return when the stock returns are flat or negative, and limiting it when the stock returns are up sharply. This strategy limits the portfolio's upside potential and is indicative of either an irrational lack of preference for positive skewness or, more likely, a strong probabilistic belief that returns will be flat or negative.

Buying Protective Put Options. A second strategy is to buy put options on the underlying stocks in a portfolio to protect the portfolio against large negative stock returns. The puts reduce return when the stock returns are flat or increasing but protect the portfolio against large losses. This is an indication of a preference for positive skewness and is compatible with rational investor risk aversion.

Buying Bills and Call Options. A third strategy, similar in effect to the protective put strategy, is to invest a large portion of the portfolio, typically 90 percent, in Treasury bills and to purchase call options with the remaining 10 percent. This strategy gives the investor upside potential if stocks perform well while sharply reducing downside exposure if stocks decline significantly. Use of this strategy is also an indication of a preference for positive skewness. The objective of this strategy is to earn the risk-free return net of the cost of the calls at a minimum while having the potential for large returns if the stock market does well, with the size of those returns being determined by such factors as the beta of the underlying stocks, whether in-, at-, or out-of-the-money calls are used, the exact percentage split of the portfolios between calls and bills, and the like.

Example of an Asset-Mix Change. Buying or selling risk insurance or modifying the risk profile of a portfolio with options has been demonstrated to be an attractive portfolio management technique. Table 18-7 and Figures 18-14 and 18-15 present a detailed example of how including stock options in a multiasset portfolio effectively alters the portfolio's asset allocation and changes the return distribution to more closely match a fund sponsor's desired risk profile.

Assume a fund sponsor must choose an optimal portfolio from the following five asset classes: U.S. equities, U.S. long-term corporate bonds, real estate equities, foreign equities, and Treasury bills. Also assume that the sponsor prefers a more positively skewed distribution than any combination of these assets allows. By adding a portfolio of 30 purchased call options to the list of asset classes, a positively skewed return distribution or risk profile can be achieved in this multiasset portfolio. The first step is to determine the fund sponsor's optimal portfolio from all combinations of the five basic asset classes.

An efficient frontier of optimal portfolios including all asset groups ex-

TABLE 18-7. Capital Market Assumptions About Five Major Asset Classes

Asset Class	Expected Return (%/year)	Upper Bound	Annual Standard Deviation
U.S. Equities	16.0%	100%	20.0%
U.S. Corporate Bonds	11.8	100	10.0
Real Estate	13.5	20	12.0
International Equities	16.5	15	21.0
Treasury bills	10.0	100	0.0

CORRELATION MATRIX

Asset Class	U.S. Equities	U.S. Corp. Bonds	Real Estate	Int'l Equities	Treasury Bills
U.S. Equities	1.0				
U.S. Corporate Bonds	0.4	1.0			
Real Estate	0.1	0.4	1.0		
International Equities	0.65	0.1	0.2	1.0	
Treasury bills	0.0	0.0	0.0	0.0	1.0

SOURCE: Nadbielny and Dunford [1984].

cept the option portfolio can be derived. Table 18-7 presents the asset class assumptions used for the purpose of this example. The top part of the table lists the annual expected return on each of the five asset classes, the upper bound of the asset class representation in the portfolio and the annual standard deviation of the expected return. The bottom half of the table presents the correlation matrix for the five asset classes.

Following the analytical techniques discussed in Chapter 8, the efficient frontier of portfolios across the risk/variance spectrum can be derived. Assume that the fund sponsor chooses the optimal portfolio at the plan's desired risk or variance level that produces a portfolio that is comprised of 42 percent U.S. equities, 23 percent U.S. corporate bonds, 20 percent real estate equities, 15 percent international equities, and zero percent cash.

Figure 18-14 displays the probability distribution of expected returns of the portfolio for a one-year holding period. The probability distribution is based on a simulation involving 1,000 trials. The return distribution for the fund sponsor's optimal portfolio is approximately symmetrical around the annual expected return of 14.6 percent with a standard deviation of 12.4 percent.

A portfolio containing 30 purchased call options can then be added to this portfolio to alter the risk profile and obtain the desired positive skewness by redirecting a portion of the portfolio's funds out of the five asset class optimal mix in proportion to their original weightings and into the calls. Assume that the calls are all at-the-money with six months to maturity and are priced at fair value. They are all equally weighted and held to maturity.

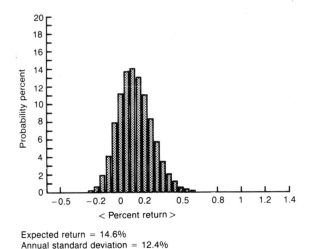

Expected return = 14.6%
Annual standard deviation = 12.4%

Figure 18-14. Probability Distribution of Returns for 100 Percent Portfolio A. (SOURCE: Nadbielny and Dunford [1984]).

Figure 18-15 displays the probability distribution or risk profile of a new portfolio comprised of 90 percent of the five asset class optimal portfolio, all with their original *relative* weightings and 10 percent invested in the purchased call option portfolio. The resulting probability distribution derived from 1,000 simulations displays a marked positive skewness. The expected return of this multiasset portfolio containing call options is 18 percent with a standard deviation of 24.1 percent. Both of these are considerably higher than the former optimal portfolio of five asset classes due to the higher risk nature of the call options. For the 1,000 simulations, however, the minimum return achieved was a loss of approximately 39 percent while the maximum return was a gain of 210 percent on the portfolio over the one year time period.

The probability distribution is no longer symmetrical around the expected return. The addition of call options to the portfolio containing multiasset classes can alter the risk profile to more closely fit the fund sponsor's desired risk tolerance measured now in three, rather than two, key dimensions.

In summary, both types of new instruments, futures and option contracts, can play an important role in asset allocation. Futures contracts offer a means to execute a portfolio asset allocation decision in a timely, cost-effective manner, and with the result that the majority of potential benefit able to be derived from the asset allocation decision can actually be achieved. Option contracts offer a means through their insurance characteristics to alter the risk profile of a multiasset portfolio to more closely reflect an enhanced and enriched definition of the desired risk patterns—as exhibited by a preference for positively skewed return distributions—of the portfolio owner or fund sponsor.

NEW INSTRUMENTS IN FIXED INCOME PORTFOLIO MANAGEMENT

There are a number of strategies where utilizing futures or options offers cost and portfolio risk control advantages and incremental portfolio returns. The following review of possible uses is separated into five categories:

1. General uses of futures and options appropriate to all portfolio management activities independent of the investment manager's style. These include: hedging the timing difference between receipt and investment of the funds, and hedging the rate to be received on floating rate securities.
2. Uses in passively managed, "buy and hold," or index fund portfolios.
3. Uses in semiactive or passive/active portfolio structures such as altering the duration of an immunized portfolio when a mismatch between duration and time to horizon develops.
4. Uses in actively managed portfolios such as in rate anticipation strategies; hedging the value of the portfolio with futures contracts; and protecting the value of the portfolio with put options.
5. Uses in the creation of synthetic securities.

The following discussion primarily focuses on the uses of futures contracts. Generally speaking, option contracts perform the same or similar functions as futures in a portfolio but with insurance skewness.

There are a few uses of the new instruments in managing a portfolio that

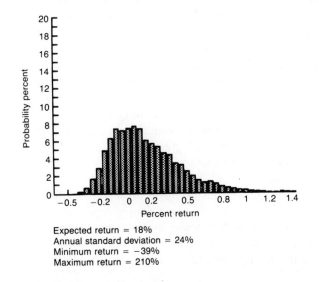

Expected return = 18%
Annual standard deviation = 24%
Minimum return = −39%
Maximum return = 210%

Figure 18-15. Probability Distribution. (SOURCE: Nadbielny and Dunford [1984].)

are very general in nature. These uses are specific to the portfolio as an entity and are independent of the manner in which the specific securities held in the portfolio are selected or for what purpose. Normal portfolio activity occurs in any group of assets brought together as a portfolio. Such activity includes deposits, withdrawals, managing the risk of the overall portfolio appropriate to the liabilities or cash flow needs of the portfolio owner, and finally, implementing strategic market judgments through trades of specific assets and groups of assets.

Hedging Assets: The "Short Hedge"

An asset hedging transaction is entered into to preserve the market or sale value of the assets in question. The decision to hedge should be made by the portfolio manager only after considering other alternatives for reducing or eliminating the cause of the potential loss in market value, which for fixed income securities is most frequently interest rate risk. For assets, the most obvious means of reducing the risk is selling the asset and, generally speaking, this is the recommended action unless there are constraints that prevent selling or lessen its attractiveness. At the same time, the manager must recognize the limitations and risks of hedging, and weigh these against other alternatives.

Constraints that Lead to Hedging. There are a variety of potential constraints that lead portfolio managers to hedge their portfolios rather than liquidate them. In some cases, the securities may not be liquid enough for selling quickly—private placements that "trade by appointment" is an example. For managers who have spent time accumulating a particular security that is appealing to them, hedging may be more attractive than selling because it may be difficult to find out and buy the securities at a later date. Some institutions (life insurance companies, for example) carry their securities on the books at cost (or amortized cost) rather than at market value. If the market value of these securities are below cost (that is, they are "under water"), the institution may be reluctant to sell them and recognize the loss. Economically, the loss has already occurred, but for regulatory purposes it has not. When the sale would cause recognition of greater losses than the institution desires, hedging may be an attractive alternative. These types of portfolios are referred to as *loss constrained*.

If a portfolio manager has decided (or been told) to liquidate a portion of the portfolio, but no decision on particular bonds has yet been made, then a *macro hedge* can be used to lower the volatility to the desired level. As the actual bonds are sold, the hedge would be lifted. Since this type of hedge is so similar to the strategy of altering duration, it is covered in the following section.

Asset hedging should be utilized primarily by active managers. Because hedging reduces the effective duration of the hedged securities to close to zero, it is inappropriate for duration-matched or immunized portfolios. It is also inappropriate for dedicated portfolios whose cash flows already match a stream of liabilities. Any losses from hedging would likely make the portfolio unable to meet all of the future cash flows. Passive buy-and-hold investors would probably not use asset hedging, but might if the "hold" strategy was dictated by book-loss constraints instead of conscious decision.

The Hedge Target: What Can Be Achieved?   Because hedging is used in place of the sale of the assets, perhaps the economic consequence of selling the assets is a guide to what is achievable. When a long bond portfolio is sold, the proceeds are normally invested in the money market until the market becomes attractive again. Thus, in three months, for example, the portfolio would be worth its current value, moved forward at some short-term rate. In an upward-sloping yield curve environment, the manager would give up some income in order to eliminate downward price potential from interest rate risk.

Another guide to the hedge target is to consider the *cash-and-carry* transaction explained in the futures pricing section of Chapter 17. In that section, it was shown that if an appropriately weighted long bond, short futures position earned more than the short-term rate, arbitrageurs would enter the market, driving down the rate until arbitrage was no longer attractive. As a result, the cash-and-carry earns approximately the short-term rate. Likewise, a hedge of a Treasury bond, being nothing more than a cash-and-carry transaction, should earn a short-term rate, *not* the rate on the long-term bonds in the portfolio.[1]

There is another method for hedging a debt portfolio not yet considered, and that involves the forward sale of the bonds. In the Treasury market, dealers are usually willing to quote a forward as well as "spot" market, and the forward sale can be used to eliminate risk for the specified time horizon. Forward pricing was described in Chapter 17 on valuation and is based on carry considerations. A forward sale nets the investor a short-term rate appropriate for the time to settlement of the sale.

These three separate (though related) approaches to eliminating risk in portfolios suggest that a hedged portfolio ought to earn the short-term rate during the hedged period. This is not surprising, because if price risk is eliminated by hedging, the portfolio should act very much like a short-term portfolio—little price risk and a rate from the short end of the yield curve. This is an important lesson for potential hedgers: *One cannot earn the long term rate*

---

[1] Arbitrage is not as straightforward in the equity market. In addition, dealers (the most active arbitrageurs) find that the net worth "haircut" required for equity arbitrage is far more onerous than for debt arbitrage. That is, the net worth requirements per dollar of investment is typically much higher for equity instruments than for debt instruments. As a result, stock index futures are often "mispriced" and cash and carry hedges may return far more than the short-term rate.

without taking price risk for short periods of time. Hedging cannot achieve the equivalent of yield curve magic.

It has become all too common for hedgers to expect to eliminate risk without giving up yield (as must be done in a positive yield curve situation) and to blame the failure of the hedge to achieve its unrealistic objective on *basis risk.* There is indeed some basis risk in futures hedging, but the predictable convergence of cash and futures is known, and contributes little risk to the hedge. Basis risk should not be a catch-all for the failure of the hedger to properly determine the target return on the portfolio.

Selection of the Hedge Vehicle. Hedging involves adding something to a portfolio that will have price movements that are opposite in direction and approximately equal in magnitude to the price changes of the target security or portfolio of securities. This does not mean that the hedger must find a security whose price movements move dollar-for-dollar with the target security. The hedge can be weighted to achieve balanced price movements. It is most important in the debt market that the yield movements of the target and hedge vehicle are related, and this is one criterion for selection of the hedge vehicle. Choosing a hedge vehicle that is close to the target security in maturity eliminates yield curve reshaping as a source of hedging error. To achieve the opposite price movement necessary for hedging, it is necessary that the hedge vehicle can be sold short, and this requirement eliminates some potential contenders. It is also necessary that the hedge vehicle have sufficient liquidity for the size of the hedge.

These criteria lead most often to the Treasury market as the source of the

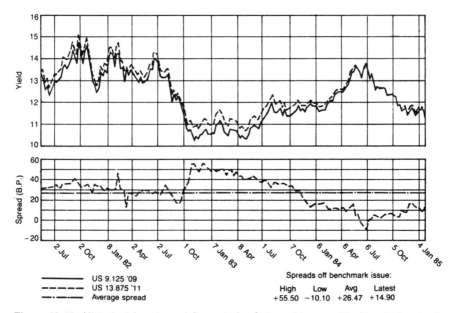

	High	Low	Avg	Latest
Spreads off benchmark issue:	+55.50	−10.10	+26.47	+14.90

——— US 9.125 '09
‒ ‒ ‒ ‒ US 13.875 '11
—·—·— Average spread

Figure 18-16. Historical Levels and Spreads for Selected Issues: Weekly closing levels from May 15, 1981 to January 25, 1985. (SOURCE: Salomon Brothers, Inc.)

hedge vehicle, either by short sale, forward sale, futures transactions, or options. Each of these is approached in the same way for setting up the hedge position, although the section on weighting concentrates on futures.

One final criterion for the hedge vehicle concerns the relative price of the hedge vehicle. If assets are being hedged, it requires a short sale. If the hedge vehicle is viewed as under-priced, it would not be attractive for a short sale because it would be unlikely to drop in price as much as the average security, thereby producing a smaller gain on the short-futures position. Instead, a relatively "rich" (overpriced) security would be attractive for a short sale.

Determining How Similar Yield Movements Are Likely to Be. The easiest method for screening a potential hedge vehicle is to look at a chart of past yield relationships, as shown in Figures 18-16 and 18-17. The top graph of each figure shows that there is a reasonable relationship between the yields of the securities, and the bottom graph shows the spread relationship through time. Spread changes are a source of risk in hedging, but if the spread is a function of the level of rates, that can be incorporated into the hedge weighting.

Measuring the Yield Relationship. If the chart depicts a reasonable relationship, the next step is to measure that relationship. One method frequently used is to perform a regression analysis to determine the yield relationship. The model usually assumed is:

$$Y = a + bX + e$$

where Y is the yield on the target security, a is a constant term, b is the regres-

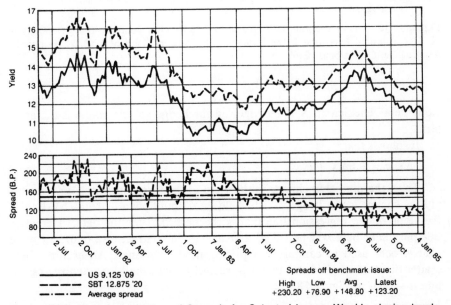

Figure 18-17. Historical Levels and Spreads for Selected Issues: Weekly closing levels from May 15, 1981 to January 25, 1985. (SOURCE: Salomon Brothers, Inc.)

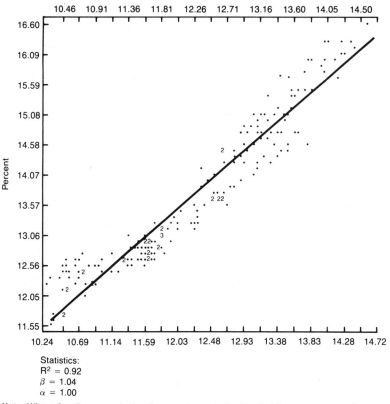

Statistics:
$R^2 = 0.92$
$\beta = 1.04$
$\alpha = 1.00$

Note: Where 2 or 3 appears in the diagram, it is an indication that there were two or three identical yield pairings in the data.

Figure 18-18. Scatter Diagram of Yields of 12 7/8 Percent Southern Bell Telephone of 10/5/20 (Vertical Axis) and 9 1/4 Percent U.S. Treasury Bond of 5/19/09 (Horizontal Axis). (SOURCE: Salomon Brothers, Inc.)

sion "beta" coefficient, X is the yield on the hedge vehicle, and e is the error term.

It follows that:

$$\Delta Y = a + b\Delta X + e.$$

Thus, the predicted change in the yield of the target security (ΔY) is simply the change in the hedge vehicle yield (ΔX) multiplied by beta (b). Beta is the slope of the regression line that is the best "fit" for the data.[2] Hereafter this particular beta will be called a *yield beta* in contrast to a return or price change beta used in capital asset pricing model parlance. An example of a scatter diagram of yields on two debt securities with the associated regression line is shown in Figure 18-18.

[2] It is important to follow proper statistical procedures for time series data, paying special attention to autocorrelation.

One of the statistics provided by most regression packages is R^2, which is between zero and one. If it is zero, there is no (linear) relationship between the variables. The closer it is to 1.00, the better the fit and the more confidence the hedger can place in the yield beta and the expected effectiveness of the hedge. Visually, R^2 is measured by the vertical scatter of the data points around the line in Figure 18-18. If R^2 equals 1.0, all of the points would lie on the line, an unusual and highly suspect occurrence.

Determining the Proper Hedge Ratio. The hedge ratio is the actual weighting of the hedge vehicle to the target security. The term *hedge ratio* has the same ultimate meaning as in options—the ratio of the amount of one security to another—but it is determined quite differently and is usually quoted as the face amount of the hedge vehicle per one unit of the security to be hedged. The hedge ratio to be used when one bond is used to hedge another, and the modification of the hedge ratio for futures, is examined as follows:

The goal of the hedge ratio is to match price changes, thus

$$\text{Hedge ratio} = \frac{\Delta P_y}{\Delta P_x}$$

This can be rewritten as:

$$\text{Hedge ratio} = \frac{\Delta P_y}{\Delta Y_y} \times \frac{\Delta Y_y}{\Delta Y_x} \times \frac{\Delta Y_x}{\Delta P_x}$$

where $\dfrac{\Delta P_y}{\Delta Y_y}$ = the price value of .01 percent or one basis point change in yield on security Y

$\dfrac{\Delta Y_y}{\Delta Y_x}$ = yield beta from the yield change regression, and

$\dfrac{\Delta Y_x}{\Delta P_x}$ = 1/(price value of .01 percent or one basis point change in yield on security X)

or, in words,

	price change for a one basis point change in yield on security Y		yield beta from the yield change regression		inverse of the price change for a one basis point change in yield on security X
Hedge ratio =		×		×	

The hedge ratio can be most easily rewritten as

$$\text{Hedge ratio} = \text{yield beta} \times \frac{\text{PVBP}_y}{\text{PVBP}_x}$$

PVBP refers to the *price value of a one basis point change in yield* and is determined by moving the yield up and down one basis point from a starting level, calculating the absolute value of the price change for each move, and averaging.

An example of a hedge ratio calculation is shown in Figure 18-19, with a scenario analysis in Figure 18-20.

The Futures Hedge Ratio. The hedge shown in Figures 18-19 and 18-20 utilizes the *most deliverable* bond as the hedge vehicle, and that is the first step in determining the hedge ratio for futures. In effect, the futures hedger is substituting a futures position for the bond position, and must substitute enough futures contracts to replicate the price movement of the bond instrument being hedged. As shown in the section on bond futures pricing that discussed the cash-and-carry, the face amount of the underlying security, multiplied by the conversion factor (CF), must be used. Thus, the futures hedge ratio is

$$\text{futures hedge ratio} = \frac{\text{yield}}{\text{beta}} \times \frac{\text{PVBP(target)}}{\text{PVBP(most deliverable)}} \times \begin{matrix}\text{conversion} \\ \text{factor for} \\ \text{the most} \\ \text{deliverable}\end{matrix}$$

Note that if the hedger was trying to hedge the most deliverable, the futures hedge ratio would equal the conversion factor because both beta and the PVBP ratio would equal unity.

A scenario analysis of the futures hedge would be virtually identical to the cash hedge results such as in Figures 18-19 and 18-20. The reverse repo rate (same concept as repo rate used in Chapter 17 except the borrowing-lending relationship of the market participants is reversed) shown in the cash hedge analysis would be missing from the futures hedge analysis because the cost of carry is already embedded in the futures price.

Investor wishes to hedge $10 million (face amount) of SBT 12 7/8 of 10/15/20, from January 30, 1985 to June 20, 1985, when the funds are needed for another purpose.

Settlement date: January 30, 1985

Target asset: SBT 12.875 of '20

    Price: 103.8800
    Yield: 12.382%

Hedge vehicle: US 7.625 of '07

    Price: 71.5603
    Yield: 11.103%

Price value per basis point (PVBP) on 6/20/85 at starting yield levels:

    SBT 12.875 of '20 = 0.08262
    US 7.625 of '07 = 0.06210

    Hedge ratio $= \dfrac{0.08262}{0.06210} = 1.330$

Figure 18-19. Example of a Hedge Ratio Calculation for a Southern Bell Telephone (SBT) Bond Using a U.S. Treasury Bond as the Hedge Vehicle.

	CORPORATE BOND YIELD SPREAD CHANGE		
Treasury Bond Yield Change	*+20 BP*	*0 BP*	*−20 BP*
+100	−2.346%	−0.939%	0.508%
0	−2.591%	−0.963%	0.715%
−100	−2.822%	−0.921%	1.041%

Example for no change case

Interest paid on US 7 5/8:	−3.9436*
Reverse repo interest received:	3.1273*
Change in US 7 5/8 price:	−0.1467*
Change in SBT 12 7/8 price:	−0.0002
	−0.9632

* Includes hedge ratio of 1.33.

Note: The loss of approximately .96 percentage points under the zero-basis-point spread change is a reflection of the yield give up necessary in a positive yield curve environment as effective maturity is shortened.

Figure 18-20. Scenario Analysis and Corporate Bond Yield Changes for Three Treasury Bond Yield Changes and Three Corporate Bond Yield Spread Changes.

Protecting Portfolio Value With Puts

As indicated previously, put options have an asymmetric payoff pattern that allows them to be used to protect portfolio value in a manner like insurance. If bond prices fall, a put increases in value, helping to offset the decline in value. If bond prices rise, the put can be ignored, and the hedger loses a maximum of the premium. The hedger can also select different "deductibles" by utilizing out-of-the-money strike prices. Because the strike price of an out-of-the-money option is below the current price of the underlying asset, the underlying is not fully protected by the put until equality of the strike and current prices is approached, because up to that point, the put's value does not move inversely to the price of the underlying on a one-for-one basis.

The primary difference between hedging with futures and hedging with puts was shown in Figure 18-13. The effect of the cost of the premium is clearly evident, because the put hedger's return (or, alternatively, value of his portfolio) is never the maximum possible. If the market rallies, the hedger participates but still loses the premium. If the market falls, the hedger is protected but the premium is still lost.

Like asset value hedges, put protection strategies are pursued primarily by active fixed income managers.

The Put Option Hedge Ratio. When hedging with puts, the puts are used as "one-sided," or skewed, surrogates for the underlying security, whether that security is a cash bond or a futures contract. If the underlying security is below the strike price at expiration, the put will be worth the excess of the strike price over the market price. Assuming an at-the-money strike price for a moment, the put buyer will thus be "paying" exactly what a short seller of the underlying would, with the additional cost of the premium. It follows, then, that the hedge ratio that was determined for a hedge using the underlying, would be appropriate for a put hedge.

When the strike price is other than at-the-money, the hedge ratio can be determined by using the PVBP values for the underlying at the strike yield and the target security at the yield level that satisfies the regression equation. The resulting hedge ratio will be almost identical to the at-the-money hedge ratio, with differing price convexity the only factor that alters it.

Altering the Duration of a Portfolio

Several types of portfolio managers may wish to alter the duration of their portfolios. Managers of immunized portfolios may wish to rebalance using futures instead of cash market transactions. These same managers may deliberately select securities with the "wrong" durations but with other desirable characteristics (yield, liquidity, protective covenants, etc.) and achieve the desired duration with futures. Macro hedgers may wish to lower the volatility of their portfolios with futures for general risk reduction or until securities are sold. Duration can be altered either up (longer) or down. As demonstrated in the discussion of Table 18-2, futures contracts (usually Treasury bond futures) can be purchased to lengthen duration, or sold short to shorten it.

Although duration is usually presented with the formula for Macaulay's duration, it is more helpful to think of duration as a measure of price volatility, as discussed in the section on the "Uses of Duration" in Chapter 9A of this volume. From the price-yield equation of a bond, it can be shown that

$$\frac{\Delta P}{P} \times 100 = \frac{-D}{[1 + (Y/f)]} \times \Delta Y$$

where P = the full price of the bond, including accrued interest
  D = Macaulay duration
  Y = the yield of the bond
  ΔY = the change in yield in absolute percentage points (that is, 100 basis points equals one percentage point)
  f = the frequency of the payments per year (that is, 2 for semiannual pay bonds, 12 for mortgages, and so on)

In words, this says that the percentage price change of a bond can be estimated by multiplying the modified duration [D/(1 + Y/f)] by the yield change in absolute percentage points. The negative sign signifies that the price change is in the opposite direction of the yield change. Another way to look at this equation is to arrange it to read

$$\Delta P = \frac{-D}{1 + (Y/f)} \times P \times \frac{\Delta Y}{100}$$

meaning, the price change equals the modified duration times the full price (including accrued) times the yield change in basis points. If ΔY equals .01 percent (one basis point), then ΔP will equal the price value of a basis point (the PVBP used in the hedge-ratio section).

Assume that a portfolio manager wants to achieve a Macaulay duration of 5.0 for a $100 million (market value) portfolio. The first step in calculating how many futures contracts to use is to determine the volatility of the desired portfolio. This is shown for an assumed yield of 12 percent as follows.

$$\Delta P = \frac{-5}{(1.06)} \times \$100,000,000 \times \frac{.0001}{100}$$
$$= -\$47,170$$

This means that the desired portfolio has a total price change per basis point yield change of over $47,000. The actual price sensitivity of the existing portfolio must also be calculated, using either weighted PVBPs of the individual securities or an overall portfolio duration measure. If it is assumed that the existing portfolio has a price sensitivity of minus $70,000 per basis point,[3] the required futures position must reduce the portfolio's volatility by $70,000 minus $47,170, to equal $22,830 per basis point.

In order to determine the required number of futures contracts, it is necessary to know the volatility (price value per basis point) of a futures contract. This can be closely approximated by

$$\frac{\text{PVBP per}}{\text{contract}} = \frac{\text{PVBP most deliverable}}{\text{conversion factor}} \times \frac{\text{face amount of contract}}{100}$$

Assuming this value is $50, the required number of futures contracts is

$$\text{number of contracts} = \frac{\text{desired volatility} - \text{actual volatility}}{\text{PVBP per futures contract}}$$
$$= \frac{\$47,170 - \$70,000}{\$50}$$
$$= -457$$

Thus, to achieve a duration of 5 for the portfolio, the manager would have to short (the minus sign signifies this) 457 contracts. To avoid concern about the sign convention in the preceding equation, simply remember that futures must be sold to reduce volatility and purchased to increase volatility.

When altering duration to a specific value as in the preceding example, and especially for an immunized portfolio, it is important to remember that a pool of liquid assets must be kept ready for variation margin purposes. This may mean that some of the portfolio must be sold for cash, and the portfolio

---

[3] Calculated by moving the aggregate yield one basis point and noting the price change, or by using the duration and market value as shown in the earlier equation.

volatility must be calculated after any liquidating transactions, because such transactions affect the volatility of the *remaining* portfolio.

Will the newly structured portfolio actually behave like a "natural" portfolio with the same duration? This depends on how the natural portfolio is defined and on the assumptions made with regard to how portfolios should behave. Because futures can be used to reduce duration significantly as well as to increase it to levels achievable only with zero coupon bonds, it may be difficult to specify an objective measure of performance. Most immunization models assume parallel shifts in the yield curve, and the futures model just used also does. However, if the duration is lengthened significantly using futures because there are no securities available with the desired duration, what portfolio becomes the comparison portfolio? In the preceding example, with the duration set at 5, is one bond with a duration of 5 the "bogey" or is it a laddered or a barbell portfolio that is to be the standard? These questions need to be answered because nonparallel shifts of the yield curve will alter the values of these portfolios differently, and none of them is necessarily a better measure.[4]

The performance of the portfolio with duration altered by futures will react to at least two points on the yield curve, and perhaps many if the portfolio contains many bonds with varying maturities. The contribution to longer or shorter duration will come from the movement of the bond(s) underlying the futures contract used, and the overall performance is thus tied to that part of the yield curve. In the preceding example, if long bonds have a downward yield move that exceeded the rest of the market, the duration-altered portfolio will perform poorly relative to many other portfolios with a duration of 5. This is because of the short position in a sector of the market that is outperforming the rest of the market. Either a laddered maturity or a barbell portfolio, with a significant amount of long maturity/duration bonds, might qualify. Similarly, the duration-altered portfolio would perform favorably if the long bond sector performed poorly.

Logically, a duration-altering strategy would be a valuable tool for semiactive bond portfolio managers. It would be very useful for immunized portfolios whose duration has become somewhat longer than the remaining time to horizon with the passage of time and without any appreciable change in the yield curve as discussed in Chapter 9A of this volume. It would be especially appealing in those mismatched situations where the mismatch is temporary and is expected to be at least self-correcting. One example is the just-cited mismatch of a long maturity/duration portfolio that naturally occurs with time elapse and that is expected to be corrected by a duration-shortening parallel upward shift in interest rates in the near future. Another is where a portfolio's relatively long duration has been somewhat shortened by a modest parallel rise in yields and will be again matched to the time to horizon with the passage of time if no further rise in rates is anticipated.

---

[4] Even parallel shifts will have slightly different effects on these portfolios because of the differing "convexity" values for each. Convexity, a complex concept, is not pursued here primarily because of the slightness of effect involved.

Hedging Timing Differences

There are several types of timing differences that can be hedged using futures: those that are of concern to active, semiactive, and even passive bond portfolio managers. Consider the case of the insurance company portfolio manager who knows that funds from a guaranteed investment contract (GIC) thrift plan will be received quarterly over the next year, and that a rate on those funds has already been set and, in fact, guaranteed. In a very real sense, the portfolio manager is mismatched and is at risk due to the timing difference between committing for a rate (now) and earning a rate following the receipt of the funds (from one to four quarters in the future). If market rates decline before the funds are received, the manager will be unable to meet the investment requirements of the committed rate. This situation is often aggravated by the fact that, if allowed, the amount of funds invested often increases above projections when rates have declined below the promised rate. Of course, if rates rise prior to receipt of the funds, the portfolio will produce a surplus above the original expectation. Yet, if the amount invested is sensitive to rate levels, it is likely that a smaller amount will be received when alternative rates have moved higher.

Another example of timing difference occurs when a portfolio manager expects a cash inflow soon (a pension fund contribution or maturity proceeds of a bond issue, for example) and wishes to lock in a rate today for the investment of the funds when they become available. Unless the portfolio has obligations on which the rate has been set, however, the manager may not be at risk in the mismatched sense. His performance may be at risk in his mind, but a change in rate does not necessarily produce a portfolio that cannot meet its obligations. In this case, the manager is actually market timing instead of simply hedging a timing difference. This is covered in the section on rate anticipation trading.

The manager who is actually hedging a timing difference has several alternatives. Securities can be bought forward, thus locking in the forward yield as of the settlement date of the forward sale, or futures can be used to accomplish the same objective. (As discussed in the hedging section, today's rate cannot be locked in by hedging.) A manager can also buy calls to put a floor on the return earned, yet at the same time this action will allow some potential for higher returns.

If the manager knows the sector of the market in which he is likely to invest, some alteration of the hedge position may be used to offset the effects of changing yield spreads that are yield level dependent.[5] The basic steps that should be followed in setting up this type of hedge are shown below:

1. Determine the amount of funds to be covered by the hedge.
2. Determine the market sector to be hedged (coupon, maturity, credit quality) and its yield spread from Treasuries.

---

[5] Level dependent spread changes are taken into account by using a *yield beta* as described in the hedge ratio determination for short hedges.

3. Using the statistical procedures outlined in the first hedging section, determine if a relative yield volatility assumption of other than 1:1 is appropriate.
4. Determine the number of futures contracts or calls to purchase.

The first step may be quite simple for contractual agreements that specify a precise sum of money to be invested, or it may involve some estimation, as in the GIC case previously described. When the amount is known, a futures hedge is appropriate; when the amount is uncertain, options may provide a better hedge because only a relatively small insurance premium is at stake.

The manager must have some idea of the market sector into which he would put the funds (if they were available today) so that the hedge can be structured to match movements in that sector as closely as possible. Unfortunately, hedging cannot usually capture the "relative cheapness" of a particular sector. This is covered in the next section.

Hedging the Spread on Corporate Bonds. There are many reasons why a manager selects a particular sector for investment. Some of the reasons have to do with the liabilities of the portfolio—term to maturity, sensitivity to interest rate changes, cash flow requirements, and so forth. Within those constraints, portfolio managers attempt to maximize return subject to certain risk constraints. This usually directs them to seek out undervalued securities, those that are "cheap" in market parlance.

The manager who is hedging a timing difference is likely to attempt to identify "cheap" market sectors and structure a hedge to capture that cheapness, but the hedge vehicles that are available normally cannot meet that objective. Cheapness is usually defined by the spread of the security's yield off of the Treasury yield curve at the same maturity point.[6] If the spread is wide historically, the bond is considered cheap, and if the spread is narrow historically, the bond is considered rich. If relative cheapness occurs, in order for a hedge to capture that cheapness, the manager would have to be able to preserve the high spread for his delayed purchase of the bond, regardless of the level of rates. At the same time, he would have to be insulated from changes in the level of rates. It is quite easy to demonstrate the difficulty in achieving this goal.

Consider an example in which a corporate bond is selling at a historically wide spread of 150 basis points to the same maturity Treasury. The manager attempts to hedge to "lock-in" the attractive spread and level of the market. Regardless of the hedge position taken in options, or Treasury forwards, the portion of the spread that is not "level dependent" cannot be hedged. Only one scenario is necessary to demonstrate this. Suppose that virtually overnight

---

[6] This is not meant to suggest that this *should* be the criteria, because of coupon spreads, the shape of the yield curve, etc. For an excellent explanation of how the shape of the yield curve affects coupon spreads, see Schaefer [1977].

the spread narrows to 100 basis points, without a change in the Treasury market. The Treasury-based hedge would produce no profit to offset the rise in value of the corporate. This would be true even if the change in spread took place over a more realistic period.

The only way to hedge the Treasury corporate spread (relative cheapness or richness) would be to use hedge vehicles that were somehow related to the corporate market directly. But there are no corporate-bond futures contracts available nor are there likely to be. Forwards on corporates would solve the problem, but New York Stock Exchange (NYSE) member firms cannot offer them because they would violate margin requirements. Buying a forward resembles a purchase with no money down, and at least 50 percent must be paid under current margin requirements.[7] At least one firm has offered options on corporates at a specified spread off Treasuries, but the options tend to be rather expensive because of the risk and the difficulty of hedging the position.

Determining the Hedge Ratio for a Long Hedge. The method of determining the hedge ratio is the same for a long hedge as for a short hedge. The PVBP of the target security and the hedge vehicle are computed for the expected hedge termination date at their respective forward yields. The *forward yield* on the corporate is usually assumed to be the sum of today's corporate-Treasury yield spread and the forward yield of the Treasury. If the corporate's price is deemed to be especially cheap (and yield is very high), and a narrowing of the corporate-Treasury spread is expected, the forward yield of the corporate for PVBP purposes can be the Treasury forward yield plus the "normal" spread for the bond. This will cause the PVBP (corporate) to be higher, and will increase the hedge ratio slightly. This will not hedge against the change in spread, but will hedge with the assumption of a change in spread.[8] With this adjusted PVBP, the hedge position will more effectively hedge as changes in the level of rates occur assuming that the spread narrows. If the spread does not revert to its "norm," this adjustment will leave the hedger in a slightly long position instead of perfectly hedged. He will thus perform slightly better in a market that improves (spread narrows with corporate's yield falling and price increasing) versus one that "backs up" (the opposite occurrence).

---

[7] Because a forward purchase allows the purchaser to "control" the securities and reap the benefits, and risks, of any price movement away from the forward price, the forward appears to be a margin trade that involves no money downpayment. Under current Federal Reserve Regulation T requirements, "no money down" trading is not permitted, and purchasers (and short sellers as well) must deposit at least 50 percent of the value of the securities, usually within five business days following the trade.

[8] Another way to view this is to recognize that a combined yield level move and yield spread change can be analytically viewed as occurring in two steps: first the yield spread change and then the market or yield level move. The hedger acknowledges that nothing can be done about the yield spread move and therefore hedges for the yield level move given that the spread move has occurred.

The hedge ratio is calculated as previously described:

$$\text{hedge ratio} = \frac{\text{PVBP(target)}}{\text{PVBP(hedge vehicle)}} \times \text{yield beta}$$

The results of a long hedge are summarized in Figure 18-21.

Hedging the (Asset) Rate on Floating Rate Securities

Floating rate notes are purchased by portfolio managers for many different reasons. Some managers view them as defensive investments, to be held until the outlook for the market improves. Some will be aggressive buyers when they think that the floating rate sector (or specific notes) are undervalued. As floaters, they tend to have price fluctuations that are not too large, and thus,

Investor wishes to purchase $10 million (face amount) of SBT 12 7/8 of 10/15/20 on June 20, 1985 when the funds become available. However he would like to hedge the June 20 purchase on January 30, using the Treasury Bond Futures Contract.

Hedge ratio

Price value per basis point (PBVP) on 6/20/85 at starting yield levels, adjusted by the futures conversion factor (yield beta assumed equal to one):

Conversion factor for the US 7 5/8's of '07 and the June CBT bond contract = 0.9660

$$\text{Hedge ratio} = \frac{0.0826}{0.0621} \times 0.9660 = 1.2851$$

Scenario analysis results: Effective yield on corporate bonds for selected changes in Treasury bond yields and corporate bond yield spreads.

Treasury Bond Yield Change	CORPORATE BOND YIELD SPREAD CHANGE		
	+20 BP	0 BP	−20 BP
+100	12.6721%	12.4967%	12.3208%
0	12.7032	12.4996	12.2961
−100	12.7326	12.4945	12.2572

Note: The hedge is essentially insensitive to the change in Treasury market (based on the zero basis point spread change column). However, changes in the corporate spread do affect the effective yield. When the spread rises, the effective yield increases, and vice versa.

Figure 18-21. Example of a Hedge Ratio Calculation and a Corporate Bond Effective Yield Scenario Analysis for Three Treasury Yield Changes and Three Corporate Bond Yield Spread Changes for Hedging a Later Corporate Bond Purchase Using Treasury Bond Futures.

do not usually fall into a category that warrants hedging. However, it is possible to purchase floaters (or enter into interest rate swaps as the fixed rate payor and floating rate receiver) and hedge the future level of floating payments. A successful hedge essentially transforms a floater into a fixed rate instrument with a known (but not constant) coupon rate.

The Target Rate. As in the case of hedging long-term instruments, it is not the current rate on an instrument that can be achieved by hedging, but the forward rate. This can be illustrated by a simple example.

Consider a floater ($1 million face amount) for which the rate is reset to the Eurodollar three-month time deposit (ED) futures rate every quarter. Assume further that the reset date corresponds to a futures delivery date. If the portfolio manager can buy a Eurodollar contract with a rate of ten percent, that is the target rate. If, when the contract expires and the rate on the floater is reset, the three-month Eurodollar futures rate is 8 percent, the coupon will be reset to 8 percent. The futures contract will provide a profit of 200 basis points, however, and the effective interest received by the portfolio will be 8 percent plus 200 b.p. to equal 10 percent. This corresponds to the target rate as determined when the hedge was initiated.

Notice that the three-month Eurodollar rate on the day the hedge was initiated was not even mentioned because it did not affect the target rate. To illustrate further, assume that on the day the hedge was initiated, the cash rate was 8 percent and the futures rate (and thus the target rate) was 10 percent, and consider the following scenarios:

    I. Three-month Eurodollar rate is 12 percent on the reset date.
    II. Three-month Eurodollar rate is 10 percent on the reset date.
    III. Three-month Eurodollar rate is 8 percent on the reset date.

Since the reset date corresponds to the futures delivery date, and the ED contract must "converge" to the time-deposit rate at delivery, the futures contract rate on the reset date must be 12 percent, 10 percent and 8 percent for scenarios I, II, and III, respectively. Thus, in scenario I, the hedge produces a 200 basis point loss (bought at 10 percent, sold at 12 percent), while cash rates have moved 400 basis points. However, the effective coupon rate of 10 percent (12 percent actual coupon less the hedge loss of 200 basis points) equals the target rate of 10 percent as shown in Figure 18-22. In scenario II, the hedge produces no profit or loss even though cash rates moved 200 basis points, but the new reset rate of 10 percent equals the target rate as indicated in Figure 18-23. In scenario III, the cash rate does not change, but the futures contract produces a gain of 200 basis points (bought at 10 percent, offset at 8 percent, as illustrated in Figure 18-24). The effective coupon rate would again be 10 percent (8 percent reset rate plus 200 basis point profit).

These examples illustrate that the futures contract need not move the same amount as the cash rate to be effective. In fact, futures can move in the opposite direction, as would have been the case if the cash rate at delivery were

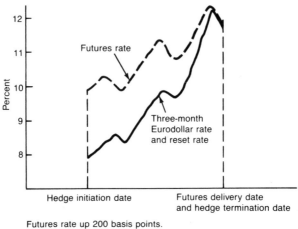

Hedge initiation date   Futures delivery date
                          and hedge termination date

Futures rate up 200 basis points.
Cash rate up 400 basis points.

Figure 18-22. Illustration of a Three-Month Eurodollar CD Hedge Where the Futures Rate Increases 200 Basis Points and the Cash Rate Increases 400 Basis Points. (SOURCE: Salomon Brothers, Inc.)

9 percent, resulting in a cash move of plus 100 basis points (from 8 percent to 9 percent) and a futures move of minus 100 basis points (from 10 percent to 9 percent).

The Hedge Ratio. The aforementioned simple example assumed that one futures contract would hedge one million dollars of the underlying asset. This is probably not correct because of a difference in the number of days covered by the quarterly reset on the floater and the assumed 90 days of the ED contract. Most LIBOR (London Interbank Offering Rate) or Eurodollar rate-based floaters pay coupons based on an "actual/360" calendar. This means that the actual coupon amount is determined by multiplying the face amount by the reset rate times the actual number of days in the quarter divided by 360. If the quarter had 91 days, slightly more than one futures contract would have been necessary.[9] The futures contract's margin flow per basis point equals:

$$\begin{array}{c}\text{futures}\\ \text{contract}\\ \text{margin}\\ \text{flow}\end{array} = \begin{array}{c}\text{face}\\ \text{amount}\end{array} \times \begin{array}{c}\text{one basis}\\ \text{point}\end{array} \times \begin{array}{c}\text{fraction}\\ \text{of year}\end{array}$$

$$= \$1,000,000 \times .0001 \times 90/360$$

$$= \$25.$$

[9] Before making the adjustments to be discussed.

However, a one basis point change away from the target on the floater would produce:

floater
margin = $1,000,000 × .0001 × 91/360
flow

= $25.28

This difference requires an increase in the hedge ratio of approximately one percent, to 1.01 contracts per million.

For semiannual floaters, the hedge normally consists of one each of two successive three-month contracts. Sometimes known as a *strip,* two successive contracts hedge a six-month rate better than a *stack,* or two (or more) of the same contract. Why? Because a strip captures yield curve effects that cannot be captured by a stack. That is, a six-month rate is sensitive to both the nearest three-month rate and the next three-month rate. A stack captures only moves of the first three-month forward rate but not the second three-month forward rate. Also, daycounts would be important to fine tune the six-month hedge, but the magnitude of the adjustment would be small.

Several other factors affect the hedge ratio and the selection of contracts used in the hedge. For example, when the reset date does not correspond to a futures delivery date, it is likely that the futures contract(s) used will not have converged with the cash rate, and hedges will not be "perfect" in achiev-

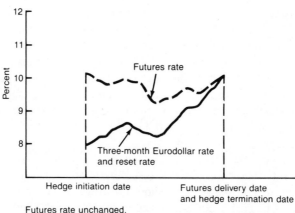

Figure 18-23. Illustration of a Three-Month Eurodollar CD Hedge Where the Futures Rate Remains Unchanged and the Cash Rate Increases 200 Basis Points. (SOURCE: Salomon Brothers, Inc.)

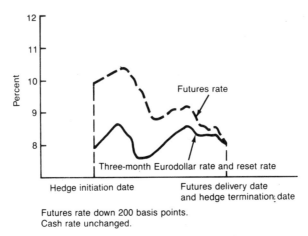

Futures rate down 200 basis points.
Cash rate unchanged.

Figure 18-24. Illustration of a Three-Month Eurodollar CD Hedge Where the Futures Rate Declines 200 Basis Points and the Cash Rate Remains Unchanged. (SOURCE: Salomon Brothers, Inc.)

ing the target rate, as shown in Figure 18-25. When this is the case, some combination of contracts can be used to minimize the error of the hedge.[10]

Another factor of the hedge ratio concerns the timing of the margin flows, of which there are two aspects. First, margin flows will probably take place during the entire life of the hedge. This is addressed in the section entitled Hedging the Interest Cost or Profit of Margin in Chapter 17. Second, the profit from the hedge (in the form of the net margin flows) will be available to the hedger on the reset date when the hedge is lifted, but the actual cash flow from the newly reset coupon will be delivered three (or six) months later. To actually achieve a target of 10 percent, for example, the total amount of the flow (coupon plus interest cost or gain on margin) should equal a 10 percent coupon on the coupon payment date. The hedges just described provided the margin contribution early (on the reset date) and thus provided too much. One only needs the present value of the nominal amount, and this can be achieved by multiplying the hedge position by a present value factor, using the target rate as the discount rate and the time between the reset and payment dates as the time.

Hedging with futures is not usually "perfect" in the sense of exactly matching the target rate, and some error is to be expected. This error can be positive or negative to the hedger, and should average out over time. When the rate that is being hedged is closely related to the rate on the hedge instrument, as in the LIBOR floater and the ED contract, these errors can be expected to

[10] See Kopprasch and Pitts [1983] and Pitts and Kopprasch [1984]. Although these papers specifically address liabilities, the methods described are equally applicable to hedging asset rates.

be small. When the rates are not directly related, as in a cross hedge, the error may well be larger, but this too should average out over time if the model of rate relationships is correct for the periods hedged. The hedger must determine, given the possible risk, whether a hedged position has less risk than an unhedged position. As portrayed in Figure 18-26, across a broad spectrum of short-term interest rates, the hedger shoots for a specific target rate with the hedge structured so as to produce a minimal error around that target.

Creating Synthetic Assets

The ability to add or subtract volatility from a portfolio by using futures contracts allows the portfolio manager to create assets that are somewhat different from those available in the market. One such example was shown in the section on altering the duration of a portfolio, in which a "synthetic" asset with a duration of 5 was created. The creation of synthetic long bonds from a portfolio of money market securities, or the creation of synthetic money market instruments from long bond portfolios is discussed in this section.

Why Create Synthetic Assets? Given that long Treasury bonds exist, why should anyone bother to create them synthetically, with the added inconvenience of variation margin? The obvious answer is price, that is, a synthetic asset can often be created with a higher yield than its "real" counterpart in the market. In a perfect world that conformed to all of the assumptions of the

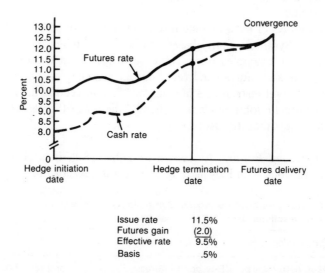

Issue rate	11.5%
Futures gain	(2.0)
Effective rate	9.5%
Basis	.5%

Figure 18-25. Example of Basis Risk Exposure When Hedge Termination Date Occurs Prior to Futures Delivery. (SOURCE: Salomon Brothers, Inc.)

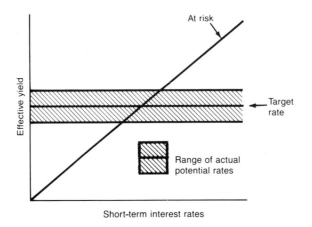

Figure 18-26. The Target Rate and Range of Actual Potential Rates for a Hedged Floating Rate Security Across a Spectrum of Short-term Interest Rates. (SOURCE: Salomon Brothers, Inc.)

previously presented pricing model, this would not be possible. However, all investors do not have the same borrowing rates, tax rates, volatility assumptions, time horizons, and so forth, and these variations lead to price variations. Futures sometimes trade "cheap" and sometimes "rich." When they are rich, they can be sold short in a portfolio of longer securities to create short-term instruments with higher yield than real short-term instruments. When they are cheap, they can be purchased for a portfolio with short-term instruments to create longer-term instruments with better yields than actual long-term instruments.

Some examples of fixed income instruments that can be created are shown in Table 18-8. Synthetic equity-based assets are discussed later.

Several of the examples from Table 18-8 have been demonstrated, such as changing a floater into a fixed rate bond in this chapter, and creating synthetic money market instruments in Chapter 17. This section demonstrates the creation of synthetic long bonds, specifically, the longest Treasury bond, normally the one most recently issued.

Synthetic Long Bonds. As shown in Table 18-8, it is possible to create a synthetic long bond by adding a long futures position to a portfolio

TABLE 18-8. Examples of Fixed Income Synthetic Assets and the Portfolio Instruments and Futures Transactions Used in Their Creation

Portfolio Holding	Futures Transaction	Synthetic Asset
Money market instruments	Buy bond futures	Long term bond
Long term bonds	Sell bond futures	Money market instrument
Floating rate note	Buy bill or ED strip futures	Fixed rate note

of money market instruments. This is demonstrated by an example using three-month Treasury bills and bond futures. The steps in constructing the portfolio are as follows (assume a $100,000,000 synthetic bond portfolio is desired):

1. Find the volatility (**PVBP1**) of entire Treasury bill position
2. Find the volatility (**PVBP2**) of the target bond position ($100,000,000 market value)
3. Find volatility (**PVBP3**) of one bond futures contract
4. Determine futures position

As in the preceding section on altering duration, the futures position is determined by:

$$\frac{\text{number of futures contracts}}{\text{to create synthetic long bond}} = \frac{\text{PVBP2} - \text{PVBP1}}{\text{PVBP3}}$$

How well does such a methodology work? Figure 18-27 demonstrates how this approach would have worked over the period first quarter 1981 through third quarter 1984. The chart shows that the actual asset outperformed the synthetic in the earlier periods, when futures were overpriced. However, they became systematically underpriced toward the end of 1982, and the figure shows that the synthetic is regaining lost ground against the bond position. Figure 18-28 shows the difference in return between the actual bond position

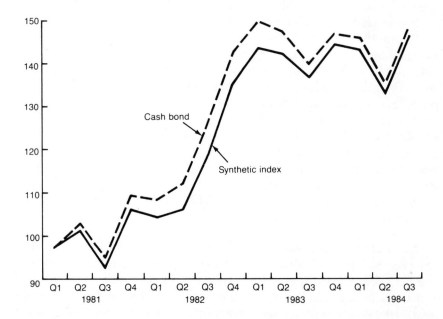

Figure 18-27. Performance of Synthetic Treasury Bond Index vs. Cash Treasury Bond, First Quarter 1981 Through Third Quarter 1984. (SOURCE: Salomon Brothers, Inc.)

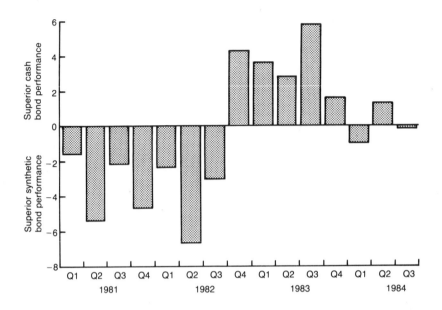

Figure 18-28. Difference in Annalized Returns Between Synthetic and Cash Bond, First Quarter 1981 Through Third Quarter 1984 (Percent). (SOURCE: Salomon Brothers, Inc.)

and the synthetic bond position. It is obvious that both overpricing and underpricing can prevail for extended periods of time.

During 1981 and 1982, investors in money market instruments could have increased their return by buying long bonds and selling overvalued bond futures to create synthetic short-term instruments. As shown, in 1983 and 1984, investors in long bonds could have improved their returns by switching their portfolios to a combination of Treasury bills and futures.

The charts shown represent a very mechanistic approach to replicating long-bond positions. All trades took place on the first day of each delivery month, and on that day the newest 91-day bill was purchased and the futures position was set up to match the newest long bond from the Treasury. No attempt was made to market time or replicate cheap Treasury bonds. It is quite likely that a manager could apply his judgment to the trading and achieve superior results.

Using Options to Create Synthetic Assets. The synthetic long bond just described had the disadvantage of tracking the long bond not only in up markets but in down markets as well. If this risk is not one that the portfolio manager wants to bear, call options could be substituted for the long futures positions. The long-term effect on the portfolio is a function of the levels of premiums paid and the ultimate direction of the market, but some generalizations can be made. In strong rallies, the portfolio would reap most of the increase in value of a long bond portfolio, lagging only because of the premiums paid. In strong down markets, the portfolio would outperform a long bond portfolio, and would lose only the value of the premiums and the difference in income between short and long instruments. These outcomes are shown in Figure 18-29. It should be noted that this figure could also represent the outcomes of a long bond portfolio protected with puts.

The availability of these new synthetic instruments makes the portfolio manager's task both easier and harder. When the synthetics can produce extra return, the portfolio manager can add incremental return to the portfolio with very little risk, probably much less than would be required to generate the incremental return through trading or some other technique. At the same time, the job is now more difficult because of the increased number of markets and combinations of securities that must be tracked. Managers prohibited from using the new instruments (by charter or board decision) will find it more difficult to perform in the top tier of managed funds.

Rate Anticipation Trading

Active portfolio managers trade in order to achieve maximum performance within the constraints imposed upon them. If no "average maturity" or duration constraint is imposed, active managers will trade the yield curve based on their expectations of interest rate levels in the future. Options and futures allow these managers to express their views, without having to dismantle their portfolios and pay large transaction costs.

At this point in this chapter, it should be obvious how these new securities can be used as speculative vehicles, independent of the rest of the portfolio.

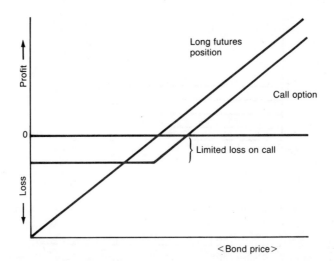

Figure 18-29. Profit-Loss Diagram for a Long Futures Position vs. a Call Option on a Bond.

Call options and long futures positions can be used to capitalize on expectations of falling rates and rising prices. Similarly, put options and short futures positions can be used profitably if market prices fall.

The choice of option versus future is dependent upon premium levels and the manager's expectations and tolerance for risk. Figure 18-29 shows the basic difference between futures and options as speculative vehicles. The diagram is essentially the same as that portrayed for stock only versus calls and bills in Figure 18-10 and stock only versus stock with puts in Figure 18-13.

Options add another dimension to the possibilities by offering a choice of strike prices, with higher strike prices resulting in lower premiums for calls. Higher strike prices require a larger price move in the underlying to become profitable, but then they can provide a dollar-for-dollar movement. After choosing options, or while still evaluating the choice between futures and options, a manager must consider this effect of the strike price on the ultimate profitability of the trade. Probably more clearly than with any other security, options provide a lesson in risk versus return that is easily recognized. Figure 18-30 depicts the profitability of call options with different strike prices and therefore different premiums. Vertical distances above the zero breakeven line represent profits and those below this line represent losses.

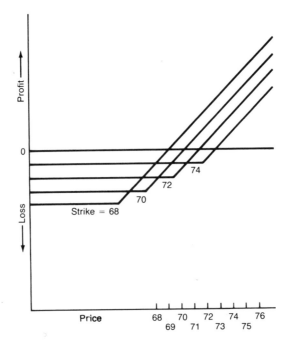

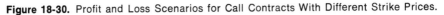

Figure 18-30. Profit and Loss Scenarios for Call Contracts With Different Strike Prices.

A short futures position or the purchase of puts can provide profits in a declining market. Once again, because the puts give the holder the *right* but not the *obligation* to sell the security, the put holder can lose no more than the premium. A schematic of profit/loss on futures versus puts is shown in Figure 18-31. Puts, like calls, offer several strike prices and patterns of return that are similar to calls except that they are reversed with respect to market direction. The profit/loss picture for puts with several different strike prices is shown in Figure 18-32.

NEW INSTRUMENTS IN EQUITY PORTFOLIO MANAGEMENT

As was true for fixed income portfolio management, there are a number of ways that futures or options can be used to control risk, minimize costs, or add incremental return in managing common stock portfolios. Some techniques, such as hedging timing differences, are generally applicable to all equity managers while others are used primarily by either passive (or index fund) or active or semiactive managers (such as completeness fund managers) discussed in Chapter 10 of the main volume.

General Portfolio Management

There are a few activities of equity portfolio managers, such as deposits and withdrawals, that are generally of concern to all managers. Deposits and with-

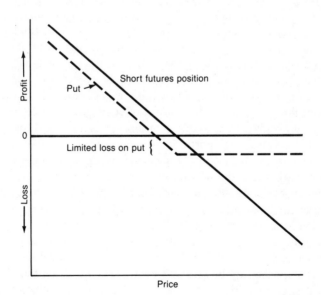

Figure 18-31. Profit-Loss Diagram for a Short Futures Position vs. a Put Option on a Bond.

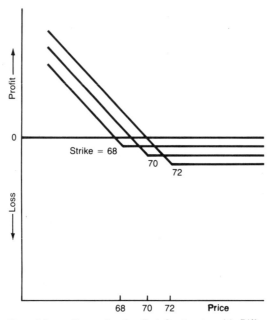

Figure 18-32. Profit and Loss Scenarios for Put Contracts with Different Strike Prices.

drawals can occur in any portfolio at any time. Futures and options can play very important roles in these primary portfolio activities. A cash contribution or a large deposit is a common occurrence in equity portfolio management. Buying additional common stock with a sudden large cash inflow may take time—time during which the portfolio is exposed to significant market moves. For example, any portfolios that were started with cash in the last quarter of 1982 or early in the first half of 1983 most likely underperformed the market, perhaps significantly, because in the rising market it took time to fully invest the cash contribution. Stock index futures offer an attractive alternative.

Table 18-9 presents an example of utilizing stock index futures to hedge a large deposit into an equity portfolio. Assume on Day 1 that there is a $50 million deposit to the portfolio. This deposit could immediately be invested in the stock market and the desired stock market exposure achieved by buying $50 million worth of futures contracts with the initial margin deposit and the balance of the $50 million above that deposit being invested in cash equivalents. If you assume that the S&P 500 is selling at 170 then one S&P 500 stock index futures contract is equivalent to 170 times $500 or $85,000 of common stock exposure. Buying $50 million worth of stock market exposure could be accomplished by buying 588 contracts. These contracts can then be sold off as desired individual issues are purchased for the portfolio.

Assume, as in Table 18-9, that such stock purchases occur evenly over a ten-day period from Day 2 through Day 11. On each of these days a portfolio

TABLE 18-9. Contributions Application of Stock Index Futures

Deposit on Day 1:	$50 million
Day 1:	Buy 588 stock index futures contracts
Days 2–11:	Buy $5 million stock Sell 59 contracts

manager buys $5 million worth of attractive stocks and sells 1/10 of the futures contract position or approximately 59 contracts. The desired stock market exposure of the portfolio is maintained at all points in time. The important point illustrated in this application is that futures offer a significant means to control the risk level of a portfolio and to reduce exposure to unintended risks and unintended investment judgments. For example, the manager's investment strategy may have been to be 95 percent invested in stocks over a certain time period. Because of the large deposit and the time it might have taken to invest it in attractive stocks, the portfolio may have actually been only 80 percent invested. An important penalty to incremental return would have been incurred that could have been avoided through using futures contracts.

Futures contracts can be used in a similar fashion to manage portfolio withdrawals although in the opposite way. Let us assume that 11 days from now a portfolio will have a large withdrawal of $50 million demanded in cash. The traditional method in portfolio management to accommodate this large cash withdrawal is to gradually sell $50 million worth of securities or stocks over the next ten days and fund the $50 million withdrawal on Day 11. If these stock sales occur evenly over the ten-day sale period then for that ten-day period the portfolio will have, on average, a $25 million cash position. This cash position may cause the portfolio's risk exposure to be significantly less than intended. In a period of a rising market the portfolio would incur a penalty to incremental return due to this unintended risk posture of the portfolio.

Table 18-10 precents a numerical example of utilizing stock index futures to hedge the risks of a large portfolio withdrawal. Assume on Day 11 that there will be a $50 million withdrawal from the portfolio. Again, assume that one S&P 500 stock index futures contract is equivalent to $85,000 of stock market exposure. Fifty million dollars in market value is then equivalent to 588 futures contracts. The desired risk or market exposure level of the port-

TABLE 18-10. Withdrawals Application of Stock Index Futures

Planned withdrawal on Day 11:	$50 million
Days 1–10:	Sell $5 millon stock Buy 59 stock index futures contracts
Day 11:	Withdraw $50 million cash Sell 588 contracts

folio can be maintained and stock disruption minimized by evenly selling $50 million in stocks over a ten-day period from Day 1 through Day 10. On each of these days, a portfolio manager sells $5 million worth of the least attractive stocks and buys one tenth of the total futures contract position or approximately 59 contracts. By the end of Day 10, $50 million in cash has been raised through the sale of stocks while the portfolio maintains $50 million of common stock exposure by owning 588 contracts. On Day 11, the withdrawal of $50 million in cash can occur and the futures contracts can immediately be sold. Portfolio risk or market exposure has been controlled at the desired level using stock index futures to facilitate the withdrawal.

An alternative method of using futures to manage a portfolio withdrawal involves selling 588 contracts on Day 1 and then selling the stock and buying back the futures on Days 2 through 11. While this method of managing withdrawals may appear attractive, the desired risk level of the portfolio is, in fact, not maintained. This approach immediately reduces portfolio risk below desired levels on Day 1 by reducing stock exposure by $50 million.

Stock index futures can be purchased when net future portfolio contributions or deposits can be accurately estimated as to timing and amount. This is known as a long hedge. A hedge where stock-index futures are gradually purchased as stocks are sold and then liquidated on the day of withdrawal could be used when future cash withdrawals are predictable.

Option contracts can also be used to hedge the portfolio risks of deposits and withdrawals. In the example of a $50 million deposit in a portfolio, a portfolio manager could buy $50 million of stock market exposure by buying call options instead of buying $50 million of equivalent market exposure with stock index futures. Assume that the S&P 500 is selling at 170 and assume that an in-the-money call option on the S&P 500 index has a strike price of 165, with a call premium of $6. Assume that this in-the-money call option will move point-for-point with the S&P 500 index. One call option at an index price of 170 will be the equivalent of 170 times $500, or $85,000, of stock market exposure. The cost of this call option is the premium of 6 times $500, or $3,000. To immediately hedge the $50 million deposit, 588 option contracts could be bought using funds from the portfolio. The cost of these contracts would be 588 times $3,000 or $1,764,000. As in the futures examples, these call option contracts could be sold, as attractive stocks are identified and actually purchased. The desired risk exposure to the market is maintained.

Passive Portfolio Management

The applications of futures contracts and options contracts in passively managed portfolios or index funds are limited because of the emphasis on full equity diversification, minimal portfolio activity, and minimal use of investment judgment or expectational inputs. Cash inflows into an equity index fund cause specific portfolio problems. Since the goal of an index fund is to match as closely as possible the return on the index over every time period, any amount of cash held in the portfolio will cause greater tracking error of the index fund versus the index.

Stock index futures can be used to minimize this risk. As cash inflows or common stock dividends are accumulated in a portfolio, an equivalent amount of stock index futures can be purchased. This process can continue until enough cash is accumulated so that the index fund can be rebalanced with minimal transaction costs. During the rebalancing, the stock index futures can be correspondingly sold. Cash inflows are a problem or risk common to the management of all index funds. Utilizing stock index futures helps to hedge this risk.

Utilizing option contracts can also be helpful when rebalancing an index fund. An index fund can move out of balance in terms of individual stock representation or subgroup representation when either a cash rebalancing is less than perfect or a deposit into an index fund is made in stock instead of cash. When an individual stock, such as IBM, or an industry or subgroup, such as the oil and gas industry, are overweighted in an index fund relative to the benchmark index, then call options on IBM stock, or on the oil and gas subgroup index, can be sold in the proper amount as an alternative to selling actual securities. The call options can then be repurchased as the underlying securities are sold. Should futures on market subgroups become available, they could similarly be used to rebalance a subgroup overweighting or under-weighting.

Stock index futures may be used to construct an enhanced index fund. These funds have the potential to have a risk level similar to the index with the potential for positive incremental return. A numerical example illustrates the construction mechanics. Table 18-11 summarizes the data of the example.

Assume that a client wishes to structure an index fund of $100 million and that the current price of the S&P 500 is 170. Each contract is, therefore, equivalent to a common stock exposure of 170 times $500, or $85,000. To gain the equivalent exposure of $100 million in common stocks, one could easily and quickly purchase 1,176 S&P 500 futures contracts, or $100 million divided by $85,000.

There are many advantages to such a portfolio construction approach. The benefits of lower transaction costs have been mentioned. The low commission rate on futures trades and the high level of liquidity in the futures market offer the potential for significant cost savings. Second, portfolio construction via futures contracts offers the advantage of actually buying the index. When

TABLE 18-11. Enhanced Index Fund Application of Stock Index Futures

Fund Size:	$100 Million
Index Price:	170.00
Contract Value:	$85,000
Contracts Purchased:	1,176

index futures are purchased, exposure to all 500 stocks, weighted by each stock's market value relative to the aggregate market value of all 500 stocks, is also purchased. Also, since buying a futures contract is equivalent to buying the index at all points in time, the portfolio is no longer exposed to changes in the names of the 500 stocks included in the index. The change in the composition of the S&P 500 due to the AT&T breakup illustrates that such changes may not be insignificant. A third significant advantage is that there are no dividends to reinvest. Periodic rebalancing of the index fund due to cash dividends is not required since the futures approach does not involve the receipt of dividends. As indicated on the comments on valuation, dividends are already priced within the futures contract. A fourth advantage is that portfolio flexibility is maintained to more creatively invest the cash equivalents to obtain a rate of return higher than Treasury bills or the equivalent.

An index fund can also be constructed with stock index futures contracts to actively take advantage of the misvaluation of futures contracts. An index fund of stocks can be actively arbitraged with an equivalent amount of stock index futures depending upon the undervaluation or overvaluation of the futures contract since the price of the future must converge to the index price at expiration. When the futures contracts are undervalued, the index fund can be constructed with cash equivalents and futures. When the futures contracts are overvalued, the cash and futures can be swapped into the underlying stock index fund. The result should be a portfolio with a risk or volatility equivalent to the S&P 500 with a return somewhat higher than the S&P 500 over time depending, of course, on the frequency and magnitude of mispricing.

In addition to the uses already discussed, option contracts may also be used in an index fund portfolio by selling call options against individual securities or groups of securities where the call option is believed to be overpriced. While some upside movement of the stock index fund could be truncated, the increased portfolio income from the sale of call options that are misvalued most likely will lead to an incremental return above the S&P 500 over the long term.

Active Portfolio Management

Actively managed equity portfolios can also benefit from strategically using futures and options contracts to hedge the risk of deposits and withdrawals. Other uses of futures and options contracts in actively managed portfolios can be split between applications that manage systematic risk and applications that impact unsystematic risk.

Control of Systematic Risk. Investment managers in general or market timers in particular can use stock index futures and options on index futures to control the beta level or systematic risk exposure level of a portfolio. For example, assume that a portfolio manager has a positive outlook for the stock market and wishes to raise the exposure of the portfolio to the market by raising the portfolio's beta.

Table 18-12 presents an example that illustrates the alternative methods of implementing the strategic systematic risk decision. Assume that the manager has a $20 million portfolio with a target beta of 1.2. Assume, also, that the beta of the present stock component is 1.1. Stocks currently represent 95 percent of the portfolio with the remaining 5 percent in cash. One way to move the portfolio to the beta target of 1.2 is to sell a number of the lower beta stocks and buy an equivalent amount of higher beta stocks. This procedure maintains the stocks at 95 percent of the portfolio but raises the stock only beta to a number such as 1.25. The result would be a portfolio with an overall beta of 1.2. Implementation by this method could be a long and costly process with significant turnover likely. The alternative approach is to raise the beta by buying an appropriate amount of stock index futures. Assuming that one S&P 500 index futures contract is equivalent to $85,000 of underlying market exposure, one need only purchase 36 futures contracts. The appropriate number of futures to purchase results from the equation:

$$\$19 \text{ million} \times (1.1) + \$85,000 \times \frac{\text{number of}}{\text{index contracts}} = \$20 \text{ million} \times (1.2)$$

The advantages of controlling beta in these circumstances by using stock index futures are the following:

1. The target beta of 1.2 could be achieved almost immediately and the portfolio would then be constructed to reflect the desired investment judgments.
2. The transaction costs would be considerably lower, particularly since turnover could be very high in trading the lower beta stocks for the higher beta stocks.
3. The optimal stock mix would be maintained.

This last advantage is extremely important. Presumably the stock component with the beta of 1.1 represents the optimal mix of stocks—the one with the highest alpha potential. By selling low beta stocks and buying high beta stocks, the portfolio manager most likely is adding stocks with lower alpha expectations to the portfolio. The manager may be reducing the expected alpha of the stock component and giving up the potential incremental return

**TABLE 18-12. Beta Control Application
of Stock Index Futures**

Portfolio Size	$20 Million
Portfolio Target Beta	1.2
Stock Only Beta	1.1
Stock/Cash	95%/5%
Contracts Purchased	36

from the stock selection judgments. This loss of incremental return is avoided by achieving the portfolio target beta through buying S&P 500 futures.

Stock index futures can also be used to completely eliminate the systematic risk of a portfolio. The example illustrated in Table 18-12 presents a $20 million portfolio that is 95 percent invested in stocks and 5 percent invested in cash. The beta of the stock component is 1.1. The beta, or systematic risk, of the portfolio could be reduced to zero by selling 246 S&P futures contracts using the same pricing assumptions. The appropriate number of contracts, X, is derived again using the formula:

$$\$19 \text{ million} \times 1.1 - \$85,000 \times \frac{\text{number of}}{\text{index contracts}} = \$20 \text{ million} \times 0$$

By selling 246 futures contracts, systematic risk has been reduced to zero. The unsystematic risk of the stock component remains untouched. The reward expected for incurring this unsystematic risk, alpha, remains intact. The resulting portfolio would then exhibit an expected return of the expected risk-free rate plus the expected alpha return on the stocks. Such a strategic application of futures contracts might be appropriate for an investment manager who wishes to emphasize the stock selection capabilities while minimizing any impact from systematic return.

Control of Unsystematic Risk. Because futures on stocks are only available currently on indexes or systematic risk proxies, option contracts are the only new instruments available that can be used to manage unsystematic risk in an actively managed equity portfolio. As discussed in Chapters 2, 3 and 10 of the main volume, unsystematic risk in a portfolio is comprised of risk due to group or industry movement plus risk due to variability of individual stocks. Investment managers who are group rotators could use market subgroup index options to hedge against or lower the risk of unexpected sector or industry movements and decrease unsystematic risk exposure. These managers could also leverage or increase exposure to an expected positive sector price movement.

Table 18-13 presents an example of this application of option contracts. Assume that an investment manager is managing a portfolio of $100 million that has an exposure in the oil and gas industry of $12 million or 12 percent

TABLE 18-13. Sub-Index Options as a Strategy Tool to Alter Portfolio Unsystematic Risk

Portfolio Size:	$100 million
Oil and gas industry holdings:	$ 12 million (12%)
Oil and gas index:	100
Oil and gas put option price:	$ 5
Oil and gas put option value:	$ 10,000

Goal: Reduce oil and gas industry exposure by $6 million

Strategy: Buy 600 put options

of the portfolio. Assume also that the investment manager likes the oil companies that are held in the portfolio on a specific company-by-company basis but does not want such a high exposure to the overall oil and gas industry in the portfolio. Assume the oil and gas subgroup in-the-money put option is selling at a price of $5 and that each option is equivalent to a market value or exposure in that subgroup of $10,000. If the investment manager's target is to reduce the portfolio oil and gas industry exposure by half, this could be accomplished by buying $6 million worth of oil and gas subgroup put options, or 600 contracts with funds from the portfolio. Using option contracts in this example offers the unique ability to maintain the portfolio's exposure to the desired specific risk of the individual oil companies while reducing and controlling the risk of the oil companies as a group.

Finally, options on individual stocks can be used to actively control a portfolio's exposure to the unsystematic risk of individual stock holdings. Table 18-14 presents an example of this application. Again assume that a portfolio manager is managing a $100 million portfolio. Assume also that the manager wants a $5 million position in an attractive $50 stock. If portfolio cash is not available to buy that stock, a $5 million position can be equivalently constructed by buying an appropriate amount of calls. Assume that the call option on stock XYZ has a strike price of $45 with a premium of $6, and assume also that the in-the-money call option will move point for point with the stock. If each call option is equivalent to 100 shares of stock, then each call option is equivalent to $5,000 of equivalent exposure in the stock of Company XYZ. In order to obtain a 5 percent or $5 million portfolio position, 1,000 calls would have to be bought. At a premium of $6 per call, this could be done for $6,000. This position could be immediately established by buying call options with portfolio funds. The call options could be sold as cash is generated in the portfolio and the shares of stock XYZ are actually purchased. This example is, as well, a form of hedging timing differences with individual stock options.

Active/Passive Portfolio Management

The applications of stock futures contracts and stock option contracts in an active/passive portfolio structure are similar to those discussed previously.

TABLE 18-14. Options on Individual Stocks as a Strategy Tool to Alter Portfolio Unsystematic Risk

Portfolio Size:	$100 million
Desired position in XYZ stock:	$ 5 million (5%)
XYZ stock price:	$ 50
XYZ call option price:	$ 6
Call option value:	$5,000

Goal: Purchase a $5 million exposure in XYZ stock

Strategy: Buy 1,000 call options on XYZ stock

Within the passive part of the portfolio of such a structure, futures may be used to hedge the risk of deposits and withdrawals. Futures may also be used either to construct an enhanced passive part of the portfolio by buying an equivalent amount of futures and creatively investing the cash or to arbitrage the misvaluation of futures by swapping the futures contracts for a portfolio of stocks that is indexed at the appropriate times.

Option contracts can be used within the active part of the portfolio structure in the manner previously discussed, to manage and control the unsystematic risk in terms of both sector representation and the representation of individual securities. Long or short positions in market subgroup option contracts or options on individual securities can be established to quickly and efficiently accumulate or decumulate positions in the nonpassive or actively managed portion of the equity portfolio.

In Chapter 10 of the main volume, the concept and construction of a semi-active completeness fund was discussed. A completeness fund is constructed by first noting and accumulating the positions of the various active stock managers. Sector and within-sector industry underweightings are observed. The completeness fund is then constructed to adjust the weightings of those sectors and/or industries that are either underweighted or overweighted in the active portfolios to their appropriate weightings in the overall market index. The situation may occur where one active investment manager specializing in one sector or industry subgroup is replaced by another manager with a different specialty. For example, if a manager with a constant overweighting in technology stocks is replaced with a manager whose universe and portfolios are dominated by utilities, the overall fund will then be exposed to a systematic underweighting in the technology area. The appropriate representation in the completeness fund to rebalance this underweighting in the technology industry could be implemented quickly and efficiently by buying the appropriate equivalent amount of technology subindex call options. The application and the mathematics are similar to the examples illustrated in Tables 18-13 and 18-14.

Creation and Use of Synthetic Equity Securities

As discussed previously with respect to fixed income securities, stock index futures and stock options may also be used in portfolios to create synthetic securities or instruments. Futures and options may be combined with equity or debt instruments in a number of ways to duplicate or to facilitate the duplication of other security types. For example, a noncallable convertible bond may be viewed as a straight bond plus a call option on the stock shares. As the price of the stock increases above conversion parity, the call option becomes in-the-money and the price of the convertible bond increases. Similar return patterns can be produced and a convertible bond can be synthetically approximated by purchasing any straight bond and an appropriate amount of call options on the bond issuers stock.

Two specific applications of stock index futures contracts highlight the portfolio creation of synthetic securities: (1) the use of futures to synthetically create cash equivalents, and (2) the use of futures to facilitate the creation of synthetic put protected portfolios through a dynamic hedging strategy.

Cash Equivalents. A cash equivalent can be synthetically produced by constructing a diversified portfolio of stocks and completely hedging away the systematic risk by selling the appropriate number of stock index futures. The resulting pretax expected return of this synthetic cash portfolio should be the expected risk-free rate of return if the futures are fairly valued when sold. For a taxable entity such as a corporation, this synthetic cash portfolio provides a superior after tax return compared to owning cash equivalents outright. Since common stock dividends are a large part of the return on this synthetic cash portfolio, and since dividends are 85 percent excluded for tax purposes, the after-tax returns on the synthetic cash portfolio are superior.

Table 18-15 presents an example of the relative returns achievable from the two cash management strategies over a one year time horizon. Assume that the expected risk-free rate of return for a one year time period is 10 percent. Portfolio 1, which includes $100 million of cash equivalents, would expect to earn 10 percent or $10 million during the year on a pretax basis. If the corporation is paying taxes at a 46 percent tax rate, then the after-tax return to the corporation is 54 percent of $10 million or $5.4 million. Portfolio 2 is a $100 million portfolio that is fully invested in an index fund or a highly diversified group of stocks and completely hedged with the sale of futures. The portfolio is assumed to have a dividend yield of 4 percent. Over the one year time period, the portfolio also is expected to generate a total return equal to the risk-free rate of return of 10 percent, or $10 million, $4 million of which is derived from dividend income with the remaining $6 million being derived from capital gains, either from the short futures positions or the stock holdings.

If we make the overly simplified but arithmetically convenient assumptions that the tax treatment of the stock capital gains and losses is similar to the treatment of futures gains or losses, and that the capital gain is long-term, then the after-tax return to the corporation of Portfolio 2 is the sum of the capital gains times one minus the capital gain tax rate plus the nontaxable dividends received plus the taxable dividends received times one minus the corporate tax rate. Since the capital gains are $6 million and the capital gains are taxed at 28 percent, the after-tax capital gain is $6 million times (1 minus .28), or $4,320,000. If 85 percent of the $4 million in dividends received are excluded from taxation, then the nontaxable dividends are $4 million times .85, or $3,400,000. If the remaining 15 percent of the $4 million in dividends is taxed at the corporate tax rate of 46 percent then the taxable dividends retained are 15 percent of $4 million times (1 minus .46), or $324,000. The total after tax expected return for Portfolio 2 is then seen to be the sum of the

TABLE 18-15. Tax-Advantaged Cash Equivalent

Portfolio:	$100 million
Expected Risk-Free Rate:	10%
Corporate Tax Rates:	46% net income
	85% dividend exclusion
	28% long-term capital gains

PORTFOLIO 1

$100 million in cash equivalents	
Pre-tax expected return:	10% ($10 million)
After tax expected return:	5.4% ($5.4 million)

PORTFOLIO 2

$100 million in S&P 500 Index fund hedged with S&P 500 futures

Yield:	4%
Pre-tax expected return:	10% ($10 million)
After tax expected return:	8.044% ($8.044 million)

three components or $8.044 million. The after-tax return to a taxable corporation of this synthetic cash instrument using stock index futures is superior.

Since tax laws are constantly being reviewed, it would be appropriate to consult the current tax laws to determine the appropriateness and viability of this strategy.

Dynamic Hedging. Stock index futures may also be used to facilitate a dynamic hedging strategy. The dynamic hedging strategy or dynamic portfolio insurance program seeks to synthetically alter the return profile of a stock portfolio to that of a stock with put option portfolio without using actual put option contracts. The return profile of a stock with put option portfolio was shown in Figure 18-13.

The discussions of Figures 18-12 and 18-13 indicate that as the aggregate price of a stock portfolio falls, a put option on that stock portfolio will become more in-the-money to the point where for every one point move in the price of the stock portfolio, the price of the put option will move one point in the opposite direction. When the put option is substantially in-the-money, the stock plus put option portfolio will, as a total, be insensitive to changes in the aggregate price of the stocks. The portfolio will effectively be out of stocks and earning the risk-free cash equivalents return. Under these circumstances, the price sensitivity hedge ratio of the stock portfolio plus put option is zero.

As the aggregate price of the stocks increases and the put option moves out-of-the-money, the opposite occurs. For every one point change in the price of the stock only positions, the price of the put will change very little. The stocks plus put option portfolio will essentially move with changes in the price of the stock holdings and will effectively be 100 percent invested in the stocks. Under these circumstances, the price sensitivity hedge ratio of the stock portfolio plus put option is 1.0.

The dynamic hedging strategy duplicates the return profile of a stock plus put option portfolio by replicating the price sensitivity hedge ratio with stocks and cash. As the aggregate price of a stocks only position falls, the synthetic put option moves in-the-money, and the ratio falls. Such an effect can be duplicated in a stock and cash portfolio by selling the appropriate proportion of stocks. As the stock component increases in price, the effect is to increase the ratio by buying more stocks. By frequently adjusting the stock and cash proportions to reflect the appropriate put option price sensitivity hedge ratio, the return profile of a stock plus put portfolio can be synthetically duplicated by a portfolio containing only stocks and cash.

A historical simulation, conducted with the Wilshire Associates' Risk Control Model, demonstrates the dynamic hedging strategy, its turnover characteristics, and comparative returns. The results of the analysis are presented in Table 18-16. The study was done over the 14-year time period: 1970–1983. The study assumed that a six-month at-the-money put option was purchased on the S&P 500 at the beginning of January and July each year through dynamic hedging replication. The put option valuation model, using the previous period's standard deviation as the S&P 500 volatility input, was used to determine target stock/cash proportions. The table indicates the resulting average proportion of the portfolio invested in the S&P 500 and the six-month turnover. For this analysis it was assumed that transactions would occur only when a portfolio shift in the S&P 500 proportion of greater than 5 percent was required. It was also assumed there were no transaction costs. The final three data columns in the table summarize the return data on Treasury bills, the S&P 500, and the dynamically hedged risk-control portfolio.

Portfolio turnover is high using this technique. The simulation showed average semiannual turnover of 115.2 percent. This number can vary significantly depending upon (1) the transaction filter assumption—the higher the filter, the less the turnover, and (2) the actual market volatility exhibited, which impacts the frequency of changes in the targeted hedge ratio. By using stock index futures to execute these portfolio shifts between stocks and cash, the costs of implementing this technique can be greatly reduced.

SUMMARY

This chapter completes the discussion of the new investment instruments. Chapter 16 began the discussion with a review of the background and descriptions of financial futures and options contracts. A summary of valuation models and methodologies followed in Chapter 17. Finally, Chapter 18 focused on the impact futures and options contracts have on portfolios of assets and on strategic uses in portfolio management.

The chapter began by emphasizing the dissimilarities of futures and options when these instruments are used in a portfolio context. Futures have a symmetrical impact on the risk profile of a portfolio while options have a nonsymmetrical impact. Examples were cited illustrating that buying or sell-

TABLE 18-16. Dynamic Hedging Simulation 1970 to 1983: Wilshire Associates Risk Control Model
Transaction Filter: 5.0%
Minimum Required Return: 0.00%

Date	Average Percent Invested	Percent Turnover	Treasury Bills	S&P 500	Risk Control Portfolio
1/70 to 6/70	14.91	107.7	3.17	−19.44	0.01
7/70 to 12/70	83.57	72.2	3.22	29.07	22.44
1/71 to 6/71	80.66	78.2	2.10	9.85	6.02
7/71 to 12/71	9.63	82.3	2.15	4.03	0.00
1/72 to 6/72	67.95	126.3	1.95	6.42	2.82
7/72 to 12/72	77.56	191.7	1.91	11.74	8.24
1/73 to 6/73	16.39	92.3	3.41	−10.35	0.00
7/73 to 12/73	43.24	200.6	3.47	−4.79	0.01
1/74 to 6/74	20.26	121.2	3.87	−10.16	0.08
7/74 to 12/74	6.15	80.4	3.97	−19.12	0.02
1/75 to 6/75	75.89	81.1	2.70	41.79	25.43
7/75 to 12/75	7.18	66.8	2.92	−3.26	0.15
1/76 to 6/76	88.95	61.6	2.49	17.82	12.20
7/76 to 12/76	29.88	160.3	2.40	5.10	0.94
1/77 to 6/77	7.01	41.1	2.37	−4.37	0.19
7/77 to 12/77	16.91	120.0	2.92	−2.95	0.01
1/78 to 6/78	6.32	84.0	3.28	3.03	0.00
7/78 to 12/78	59.81	135.6	4.00	3.32	0.08
1/79 to 6/79	81.36	79.5	4.75	10.02	7.77
7/79 to 12/79	80.31	234.1	5.23	7.70	3.14
1/80 to 6/80	36.80	97.1	5.98	8.79	0.00
7/80 to 12/80	87.36	72.9	5.45	21.68	16.17
1/81 to 6/81	46.51	212.5	7.16	−1.12	0.94
7/81 to 12/81	24.91	113.5	6.86	−4.03	0.00
1/82 to 6/82	15.66	132.9	6.10	−7.92	0.00
7/82 to 12/82	87.14	101.0	4.54	31.55	28.09
1/83 to 6/83	72.00	83.8	3.86	22.17	15.20
7/83 to 12/83	35.43	195.6	4.27	0.08	0.29
Average	45.71	115.2	7.73	8.86	10.37

SOURCE: Wilshire Associates Risk Control Model.

ing futures is equivalent to subtracting or adding cash to a portfolio. Further examples were given indicating the insurance characteristic of options including purchasing call options and cash equivalents, purchasing/holding stock and selling call options, and purchasing/holding stock and purchasing put options. Examples of modifying both portfolio systematic (beta and duration) and unsystematic risks were reviewed.

The discussion of specific strategic uses of futures and options in portfolio management began with a detailed explanation and illustration of the new instruments' role in asset allocation. The use of futures to effectively execute an asset allocation decision and the use of options to structure a portfolio's risk profile best suited to the needs of the portfolio owner were highlighted. The chapter concluded with discussions of a number of strategic uses in fixed income and equity portfolio management indicating uses and techniques appropriate to general portfolio management (deposits and withdrawals), passive, semiactive, and active management, and the creation of synthetic securities. The new instruments of futures and options contracts offer the means to structure and control portfolio risk in a timely, cost effective manner. The instruments should be viewed within the entire spectrum of investment vehicles available when creating a portfolio with maximum return/risk characteristics.

FURTHER READING

There are a number of investments textbooks that contain discussions of strategic applications of futures and option contracts in portfolio management. Examples of texts emphasizing option strategies include Jarrow and Rudd [1983], Bookstaber and Clarke [1983], and Cox and Rubinstein [1985]. Bibliographies to these texts are particularly extensive. A good summary of strategies using stock index futures can be found in Fabozzi and Kipnis [1984]. A discussion of the foundations of dynamic hedging can be found in Rubinstein and Leland [1981]. An excellent discussion of the use of futures contracts in building and maintaining immunized portfolios can be found in Yawitz and Marshall [1985].

BIBLIOGRAPHY

Belongia, Michael T., and G. J. Santoni, "Hedging Interest Rate Risk with Financial Futures: Some Basic Principles," *Review* of the Federal Reserve Bank of St. Louis, October 1984.

Black, Fischer, "Fact and Fantasy in the Use of Options," *Financial Analysts Journal*, July/August 1975.

Bookstaber, Richard M. and Roger G. Clarke, "Problems in Evaluating the Performance of Portfolios with Options," *Financial Analysts Journal*, January/February 1985.

—— and ——, "Option Portfolio Strategies: Measurement and Evaluation," *Journal of Business*, October 1984.

—— and ——, *Option Strategies for Institutional Investment Management*, Reading, Mass.: Addison-Wesley Publishing Company, 1983.

—— and ——, "Use of Options in Altering Portfolio Return Distribution," Library paper, Institute for Quantitative Research in Finance, Columbia University, 1982.

——, *Option Strategies for Institutional Investment Management*, Reading, Mass., Addison-Wesley, 1983.

——, "The Description and Evaluation of Option Portfolio Strategies," Unpublished Paper, Institute of Business Management, Brigham Young University, Provo, Utah, 1983.

Chambers, Donald R., "An Immunization Strategy for Futures Contracts on Government Securities," *The Journal of Futures Markets,* Summer 1984.

Chance, Don M., "An Immunized-Hedge Procedure for Bond Futures," *The Journal of Futures Markets,* Fall 1982.

Cox, John and Mark Rubinstein, *Option Markets,* Englewood Cliffs, N.J.: Prentice-Hall, 1985.

Dattatreya, Ravi and Mark A. Zurack, "Asset Allocation Using Futures Contracts," Stock Index Research, Goldman Sachs & Co., February 1985.

Fabozzi, Frank J. and Gregory M. Kipnis, (eds.), *Stock Index Futures,* Homewood, Ill.: Dow Jones-Irwin, 1984.

Figlewski, Stephen, "Hedging Performance and Basis Risk in Stock Index Futures," *The Journal of Finance,* July 1984.

Fisher, Donald E. (ed.), *Options and Futures: New Route to Risk/Return Management.* Sponsored by The Institute of Chartered Financial Analysts, Homewood, Ill.: Dow Jones-Irwin, 1984.

Gay, Gerald D. and Robert W. Kolb, "Interest Rate Futures as a Tool for Immunization," *The Journal of Portfolio Management,* Fall 1983.

Hegde, Shantaram P., "The Impact of Interest Rate Level and Volatility on the Performance of Interest Rate Hedges," *The Journal of Futures Markets,* Winter 1982.

Hill, Joanne M. and Thomas Schneeweis, "Reducing Volatility with Financial Futures," *Financial Analysts Journal,* November/December 1984.

———— and ————, "Risk Reduction Potential of Financial Futures for Corporate Bond Positions," in G. Gay and R. W. Kolb, (eds.) *Interest Rate Futures: A Comprehensive Anthology,* Richmond, Va.: Robert F. Dame, 1983.

————, et al. "An Analysis of the Impact of Variation Margin in Hedging Fixed Income Securities," *Review of Research in Futures Markets,* 1983.

Ibbotson, Roger and Rex Sinquefeld, *Stocks, Bonds, Bills and Inflation: The Past and the Future,* Charlottesville, Va.: The Financial Analysts Research Foundation, 1982.

Jarrow, Robert and Andrew Rudd, *Option Pricing,* Homewood, Ill.: Dow Jones-Irwin, 1983.

Kane, Alex, and Alan J. Marcus, "Conversion Factor Risk and Hedging in the Treasury-Bond Futures Market," *The Journal of Futures Markets,* Spring 1984.

Kolb, Robert W., *Understanding Futures Markets.* Glenview, Ill.: Scott, Foresman and Company, 1985.

Koppenhaver, G. D., "Bank Funding Risks, Risk Aversion, and the Choice of Futures Hedging Instrument," *The Journal of Finance,* March 1985.

Kopprasch, Robert W., "Introduction to Interest Rate Hedging," Salomon Brothers, Inc., November 1982.

————, and Mark Pitts, "Hedging Short-term Liabilities With Interest Rate Futures," Salomon Brothers, Inc., April 1983.

Kuberek, Robert C., and Norman G. Pefley, "Hedging Corporate Dept with U.S. Treasury Bond Futures," *The Journal of Futures Markets,* Winter 1983.

McCabe, George M. and Charles T. Franckle, "The Effectiveness of Rolling the Hedge Forward in the Treasury Bill Futures Market," *Financial Management,* Summer 1983.

Merton, Robert C., Myron S. Scholes, and Mathew L. Gladstein, "The Returns and Risk of Alternative Put Option Portfolio Investment Strategies," *Journal of Business,* 1982.

————, ————, and, ————, "The Returns and Risks of Alternative Call-Option Portfolio Investment Strategies," *Journal of Business,* April 1978.

Moriarity, Eugene, Susan Phillips, and Paula Tosini, "A Comparison of Options and Futures in the Management of Portfolio Risk," *Financial Analysts Journal,* January-February, 1981.

Nadbielny, Thomas and David Dunford, "Determining Optimal Asset Allocation Given a Skewness Constraint," Unpublished Paper, Travelers Investment Management Company, May 1984.

Nordhauser, Fred, "Using Stock Index Futures to Reduce Market Risk," *The Journal of Portfolio Management,* Spring 1984.

Parker, Jack W., and Robert T. Daigler, "Hedging Money Market CDs with Treasury-Bill Futures," *The Journal of Futures Markets,* Winter 1981.

Peck, A. E. (ed.), *Selected Writings on Futures Markets: Exploration in Financial Futures Markets.* Book V, Readings in Futures Markets, Chicago: Chicago Board of Trade, 1985.

Pitts, Mark, "Options on Futures on Fixed-Income Securities," Salomon Brothers, Inc., December 1983.

Pitts, Mark and Robert W. Kopprasch, "Reducing Inter-temporal Risk in Financial Futures Hedging," *The Journal of Futures Markets,* 4:1, 1984.

Rebell, Arthur L. and Gail Gordon, *Financial Futures and Investment Strategy,* Homewood, Ill.: Dow Jones-Irwin, 1984.

Rubinstein, Mark and Hayne E. Leland, "Replicating Options with Positions in Stock and Cash," *Financial Analysts Journal,* July/August 1981.

Schaefer, Steven, "The Problem with Redemption Yields," *Financial Analyst Journal,* July/August 1977.

Senchack, Andrew J. Jr., and John C. Easterwood, "Cross Hedging CDs with Treasury Bill Futures," *The Journal of Futures Markets,* Winter 1983.

Singleton, J. Clay and Robin Grieves, "Synthetic Puts and Portfolio Insurance Strategies," *The Journal of Portfolio Management,* Spring 1984.

Trainer, Francis H., Jr., "The Uses of Treasury Bond Futures in Fixed-Income Portfolio Management," *Financial Analysts Journal,* January/February 1983.

Welch, William W., *Strategies for Put and Call Option Trading,* Cambridge, Mass.: Winthrop Publishers, Inc., 1982.

Yawitz, Jess B. and William J. Marshall, "The Use of Futures in Immunized Portfolios," *The Journal of Portfolio Management,* Winter 1985.

Cumulative Index

[References are to pages in the main text and to chapter and page in the Update. References to the Update are preceded by "U."]

[References are to pages in the main text and to chapter and page in the Update. References to the Update are preceded by "U."]

[References are to pages in the main text and to chapter and page in the Update. References to the Update are preceded by "U."]

[References are to pages in the main text and to chapter and page in the Update. References to the Update are preceded by "U."]

[*References are to pages in the main text and to chapter and page in the Update. References to the Update are preceded by "U."*]

[References are to pages in the main text and to chapter and page in the Update. References to the Update are preceded by "U."]

*[References are to pages in the main text and to chapter and page in the Update.
References to the Update are preceded by "U."]*

[References are to pages in the main text and to chapter and page in the Update.
References to the Update are preceded by "U."]

[*References are to pages in the main text and to chapter and page in the Update. References to the Update are preceded by "*U*."*]

[*References are to pages in the main text and to chapter and page in the Update.
References to the Update are preceded by "U."*]

[*References are to pages in the main text and to chapter and page in the Update.*
*References to the Update are preceded by "*U.*"*]

[*References are to pages in the main text and to chapter and page in the Update. References to the Update are preceded by "U."*]

[References are to pages in the main text and to chapter and page in the Update. References to the Update are preceded by "U."]

[*References are to pages in the main text and to chapter and page in the Update. References to the Update are preceded by "U."*]

[References are to pages in the main text and to chapter and page in the Update. References to the Update are preceded by "U."]

[References are to pages in the main text and to chapter and page in the Update. References to the Update are preceded by "U."]

[References are to pages in the main text and to chapter and page in the Update.
References to the Update are preceded by "U."]

[*References are to pages in the main text and to chapter and page in the Update. References to the Update are preceded by "U."*]